"Though the U.S. annual expenditures for information technology now exceed half a trillion dollars, it is not their operating costs, but the information asset value of the data managed by computers that represent the true value of what well-managed information can do to improve the productivity of the information workforce.

Data becomes transformed into economic value only as it is converted into usable information. For that purpose, it must become a coherent and intelligently accessible collection, rather than isolated record entries. The most powerful tool for achieving this transformation is the concept of arraying data into "data warehouses" to appear as easily available displays for effective decision making.

Lou Agosta's book is a guide to a better understanding of how collections of separately collected bits of information can be organized to serve the needs of an enterprise. Agosta's book offers technical and managerial insights into how to leverage the data warehousing concept for best advantage."

—Paul A. Strassmann
Chairman and CEO, Software Testing Assurance Corporation

"A 'how-to' guide for extracting detailed pictures of individual buying behavior from millions of transactions—a must for growing relationships with customers, building a brand, or gaining stronger insights into market dynamics."

—Arno Penzias
Nobel Laureate

"A totally comprehensive resource on data warehousing. Whether you are are building a data warehouse or are stuck on a particular issue regarding data warehousing, you will find the answers in Lou Agosta's *The Essential Guide to Data Warehousing.*"

—Eric Warner
President, Greenbrier & Russel, Inc.

"Not a cookbook but a contribution of robust recipes for practitioners at all levels. Agosta's book is filled with useful insights for managers and data warehouse developers. His penetrating, solid advice covers the business and technical range of data warehousing."

—John E. Pomeranz
Chief Information Officer, TrizecHahn Office Properties

"Lou Agosta's *The Essential Guide to Data Warehousing* is exactly what its title proclaims it to be. Each chapter covers an essential and relevant topic of data warehousing.

Data warehousing used to be a competitive advantage for those firms that had one. These days, a data warehouse is a cost of doing business. While a data warehouse can have a large return on investment, it can become a money pit if it is implemented incorrectly. To implement a data warehouse successfully and within a budget, it is important to learn from history. Be sure to learn from the mistakes of the data warehousing pioneers who have journeyed ahead of you and take note of their best practices. This book is full of both.

It is an excellent book for the newcomer to data warehousing to read from cover to cover, but serves equally well as a reference guide and source of inspiration for the seasoned veteran data warehouser.

I wish I had been able to read this book before I embarked on my first data warehousing journey. Instead, I learned many of the lessons described in this book the hard way, and it was a rough journey, indeed."

—Larry Mohr
Vice President Business Intelligence Systems, Perseco

"Agosta's *The Essential Guide to Data Warehousing* affords the nontechnical manager with key tools for directing the implementation of a data warehouse. As data warehousing continues to move into the mainstream of management tools, the ability to direct and manage these assets becomes increasingly essential for corporate survival and success.

The book provides clear descriptions of a number of important technical topics for the nontechnical manager. In particular, the book provides an excellent introduction to the issues of how to position the data warehouse to complement core business processes, how to review alternative hardware architecture issues, and methods for ensuring data quality."

—Owen Shapiro
Project Manager Marketing Research, Leo J. Shapiro Associates

The
Essential
Guide to
Data Warehousing

ISBN 0-13-085087-X

90000

9 780130 850874

Essential Guide Series

THE ESSENTIAL GUIDE TO TELECOMMUNICATIONS, SECOND EDITION

Annabel Z. Dodd

THE ESSENTIAL GUIDE TO DATA WAREHOUSING

Lou Agosta

The Essential Guide to Data Warehousing

LOU AGOSTA

Prentice Hall PTR, Upper Saddle River, NJ 07458
http://www.phptr.com

Library of Congress Cataloging-in-Publication Data

Agosta, Louis
   The essential guide to data warehousing / Lou Agosta.
      p.   cm.
   Includes bibliographical references.
   ISBN 0-13-085087-X
   1, Data warehousing.   I. Title.
   QA76.9.D37A36   1999   99-40534
   658.4'038'0285574--dc21   CIP

Editorial/Production Supervisor: *Nicholas Radhuber*
Acquisitions Editor: *Mark Taub*
Editorial Assistant: *Audri Bazlen*
Manufacturing Manager: *Alexis Heydt*
Interior Series Design: *Meg VanArsdale*
Cover Design: *Anthony Gemmellaro*
Cover Design Director: *Jerry Votta*

Published by Prentice Hall PTR
Prentice-Hall, Inc.
Upper Saddle River, NJ 07458

The publisher offers discounts on this book when ordered in bulk quantities.
For more information, contact:

Corporate Sales Department
Prentice Hall PTR
One Lake Street
Upper Saddle River, NJ 07458
Phone: 800-382-3419; FAX: 201-236-7141
E-mail (Internet): corpsales@prenhall.com

Printed in the United States of America

10 9 8 7 6 5 4 3 2 1

ISBN 0-13-085087-X

Prentice-Hall International (UK) Limited, *London*
Prentice-Hall of Australia Pty. Limited, *Sydney*
Prentice-Hall Canada Inc., *Toronto*
Prentice-Hall Hispanoamericana, S.A., *Mexico*
Prentice-Hall of India Private Limited, *New Delhi*
Prentice-Hall of Japan, Inc., *Tokyo*
Prentice-Hall (Singapore) Pte. Ltd., *Singapore*
Editora Prentice-Hall do Brasil, Ltda., *Rio de Janeiro*

Table of Contents

Part 3
Operations and Transformations   *239*

Preface

Naturally, as the author, I would like to give everyone permission to read this book from cover-to-cover. But if priorities require choices in what to read first, the following suggestions will be useful. The extensive and detailed *Glossary* is a valuable resource. Although a conscientious effort is made in this book to define technical terms upon first use, if a reader wishes to skip around, then that reader is encouraged to consult the *Glossary* frequently for those terms whose introduction may have been skipped. Everyone will want to read Chapter One: *Basic Data Warehousing Distinctions*, Chapter Two: *A Short History of Data*, Chapter Five: *Business Design*, Chapter Six: *Total Data Warehouse Quality*, Chapter Twelve: *The Information Supply Chain*, Chapter Thirteen: *Metadata and Metaphor*, and Chapter Eighteen: *Breakdowns: What Can Go Wrong*. In addition, executives, business leaders, and information consumers of all kinds, will benefit most directly from the Introduction: *Data Warehousing Between Uncertainty and Knowledge*, Chapter Three: *Justifying Data Warehousing*, and Chapter Nineteen: *Prospects for the Future*; project managers, data architects, and designers should add Chapter Four: *Data Warehouse Project Management*, Chapter Five: *Business Design* (even though already mentioned), Chapter Seven: *Technical Design*, Chapter Fourteen: *Aggregation*, and Chapter Fifteen: *OLAP Technologies*; developers will be interested in Chapter Eight: *Data Warehouse Construction Technologies: SQL*, and Chapter Nine: *Transaction Management* (a word of caution—this book does not teach SQL or coding and the reader is referred to the extensive bibliography for help with that); database administrators and information managers of all kinds will be interested in Chapter Ten: *Data Warehouse Operation Technologies: Data Management* and Chapter Eleven: *Data Warehousing System Performance*; business analysts, technical specialists, and other information producers in various areas will want to consider Chapter Fifteen: *OLAP*

Technologies, Chapter Sixteen*: Data Warehousing and the Web*, and Chapter Seventeen: *Data Mining*.

The real purpose of the Preface is to give the reader insight into the origin of the book. What could the author possibly have been thinking that led him to produce this result? In comparison with the book itself, the Preface functions rather like the distinction in science between the context of *discovery* and the context of *justification*. How an idea or discovery is first formulated is often irrelevant to how it is justified. Many readers benefit and enjoy receiving background on how ideas and views originate aside from their validity. The accidental human details and feelings that occasioned the emergence of something new—or at least an original synthesis of existing ideas—add texture and motivation to the drier, more impersonal logical structure that is required to validate or justify the undertaking objectively. However, if you, dear reader, are one who is *not* interested in such a background briefing and longs to get into the details of data warehousing, then please feel free to skip immediately to Chapter One: (*Basic Data Warehousing Distinctions*), with the option of returning later. The author, whose job after all it is to serve the reader, will not be offended, and no significant loss of continuity will occur.

Now, after having tried to discourage the reluctant reader, to those still reading this Preface, let me say this book is born out of three convictions. First, amidst paradigm shifts, data warehousing is *not* another paradigm shift. Second, the essential key to producing knowledge rather than more data by means of data warehousing is the alignment between the dimensions of the data warehousing system and basic business drivers and imperatives. Third, the data warehouse system is both an information product and a method of knowledge generation. In this, it is rather like a lens on a telescope, which incorporates knowledge of the principles of optics in the service of enabling us to see (and so come to know) things at a distance that we had not previously imagined. This sometimes also requires a new kind of seeing.

This finds confirmation in places that are more relevant than they might at first seem. So, for instance, when the Renaissance scientist Galileo pointed his new fangled telescope at the moon and saw mountains (as on Earth) instead of heavenly perfection, Galileo's seeing was informed by a framework for understanding of a unified system of heavenly bodies to which the earth and sun and moon all belong. But when the learned Church scholars of the day looked through the same strange device, the patterns detected by their differently informed seeing were not mountains but rather were designs so unfamiliar as to result in what they saw being labeled the work of the devil. Do not believe that such matters are trivial, because this resulted in poor Galileo being placed under house arrest by the Inquisition. Although the data warehousing architect and data miner can realistically expect to escape such a fate, they should be careful when raising data quality issues.

The point is that the origins of this essential guide—which differs from its justification—is to be found in three dynamic terms: "paradigm," "alignment," and "knowledge." These are protean words that have at times been badly abused. The promise here as that they will be carefully explored, rigorously defined, and used selectively. (All three terms are defined in the *Glossary*.)

The case of "paradigm shift" is of interest because it was first popularized in 1962 in a controversial book on how scientific knowledge develops, Thomas Kuhn's ***The Structure of Scientific Revolution*** (1962). Amid many engaging examples from the development of scientific knowledge, Kuhn focused on the celebrated example of the shift from regarding the Earth as the center of the solar system (and universe) to regarding the sun as the center. The shift from the sun going around the Earth to the Earth going around the sun is a fundamental one. This is the very paradigm of a paradigm shift. In fact, that the Earth revolves around the sun is on the list of the great discoveries of the past thousand years. (Usually dated as 1643 with the publication of Nicolaus Copernicus's ***On the Revolution of the Heavenly Bodies***.) Many of the same facts as are contained in the older systems are accommodated by the new system, many new facts that previously resisted clarification are integrated, and additional facts are constituted ("constructed") by the framework of the new paradigm. This example underscores the point that how a discovery is made is often tangential (if not irrelevant) to how it is justified. Copernicus's paradigm shift—his new theory—was actually the result of an intricate logical speculation that was nearly as confusing and counter-intuitive as the system it was designed to supplant. For instance, Copernicus continued to reason that the path traced by the planets was a circle, not a ellipse. But much of the alleged simplification of the new candidate paradigm is lost without the use of elliptical motion. Another two centuries of step-by-step advances in physics and mathematics were required to satisfactorily justify what according to rigorous scientific criteria we now take for granted. Indeed, a significant part of that justification was the construction of a data warehouse—yes, the term must be used—of accurate, consistent, conformed observations of the planets by Tycho Brahe and his student Johannes Kepler (published in 1625 as the ***Tabulae Rudolfinae (Rudolf's Tables)*** after the local monarch, Prince Rudolf). But when thus completed by a series of sustained, incremental improvements (including the history of modern science in the works of Galileo, Kepler, and Newton), the new candidate paradigm finally begins to look like a breakthrough.

Thus we get to the essential conviction with which this book began—data warehousing is not a paradigm shift. The enticing but superficial analogy between enterprise data and the graphical user interface (GUI)—between the sun and the Earth—has its charms. But is far too limiting. There is no shift of emphasis either from the mainframe to the presentation layer or from a data-centric to a GUI-centric model (or back). Both were available at the beginning, and both continue to be essential components of a complete computing system architecture. Hearing this may disappoint some readers for whom the term "paradigm shift" has come to represent the possibility of breakthrough or solution. On the other hand, those readers fatigued by being bombarded by paradigm shifts in the trade press and marketing releases will be relieved to learn that incremental progress is still possible. In either case, we are *not* dealing with something like client-server, the relational database, the network computer, or the

Web-based Internet "revolutions." To be sure, data warehousing is a system architecture that builds on these designs and products in a variety of forms. But in every form we are dealing with the technological imperative to manage data—customer, product, market, information—as a corporate asset to be understood and applied to decision making. The injunction that the data *is* the business is one that has stood fast. It is as true today as it was in 1980 when the author first encountered it or when statistical (and other) methods were first applied to decision making in the late 1960s.

The second idea with which this book began is referred to as "alignment." One of the essential methods of producing knowledge rather than merely more data through data warehousing is the alignment between the data dimensions defining the warehouse and basic business imperatives and drivers. This idea leads in the direction of how we use language to describe the world. It turns out that everyday language is just the more general case of all kinds of systems of signs, including computing systems, used to express and constrain situations in the world.

Naturally, the uses of language are not restricted to the simple representations of factual situations in the world (here, at the risk of redundancy, "language" is a synonym for all kinds of computing system applications). Language is also both instrumental and pragmatic in its alignment with business imperatives. It leverages results through means-ends relations and the embedding of systems in the context of business processes in which coordination and communication are of the essence. Thus, "alignment" becomes a proxy for the way the computing systems—and data warehousing in particular—represents the world of business interactions between customers, products, and markets. The data warehousing system represents and—as designers like to say—"exposes" the levers and dials of the targeted markets, products, and customers. These levers and dials, in turn, are structures that literally help the builders and operators of the data warehousing system find and define the real world references of the system. For example, the forecast of the demand planner is almost completely a system artifact. It may seem like a miracle that the world (mostly) operates according to it. Nevertheless, it is not all relative—accurate features of the business situation are really expressed, and the system objectively refers to things that are happening in the environment. If this seems circular, well, it is. The system designer (and builder) is an essential part of this loop, which is a productive, not vicious, circle. This suggests why the process is inherently iterative—an alignment between data warehousing system and the context of its use is not merely discovered. It is constructed. (Of course, selected, given business practices will already always be in place in any situation. These are abstracted, captured, and sometimes transformed beyond recognition in being implemented or supported by the automated system.) The resulting system both represents the business situation as well as makes it accessible. The part of the designer's science that remains part art is to know when to stop iterating, because the essential minimal characteristics of the situation have been captured in the system architecture, and the remaining features are distractions from the business imperatives. Thus, we have a two-way alignment of three things—the system, the world, and the system designer (and builder). The result is knowledge.

This leads us to the third of the three dynamic words, "knowledge," out of which this book was born. These days, knowledge means anything from content to patented intellectual property to an inventory of PowerPoint presentations on a consulting firm Intranet. Intuitively, to say that something is "knowledge" confers on it a certain dignity, a mark of excellence, or a suggestion of high esteem. This intuition is unpacked and motivated in Chapter Six in the section entitled "The Information Product." The approach taken in this book suggests that a data warehousing system is an information product. Furthermore, the data warehouse is indeed a source of knowledge. It is an "enabler." It is a condition of possibility of knowledge. But, in itself, it is not knowledge. Rather, the knowledge in question emerges in the conversation between the staff and the data warehouse content. The knowledge is not "in the heads" of the staff who pose queries using SQL or other user interface methods. Rather, the knowledge is in the interaction between the query poser and the answer provider. The knowledge is in the relation between the question and answer. In short, the knowledge is in the coordination of information and actions that are reflected in a firm's commitment to answering questions, at least some of which haven't even been posed yet. Thus, the data warehousing system is an essential part of a business process whose outcome and results are knowledge.

The relationship between information and knowledge looks different depending on whether it is approached from a technology or a business perspective. From a technology perspective, knowledge is on a continuum with information. As the quality of the information improves, it gets closer and closer to being knowledge in the full sense. Knowledge is a point on the horizon toward which information is always improving and progressing. Information is just data that has been subjected to a defined process of improvement. If this process is sufficiently extended, then (the argument goes) knowledge is the result. From a business perspective, knowledge is qualitatively different than information. There is a yawning abyss separating information, no matter how high the quality, from knowledge. The "best available information" never results in knowledge without something special mixed in to fortify it. There is a certain something that has to be added to information in order to yield knowledge. That something is commitment. When information is made the basis for a business decision, then a commitment is implied and mobilized. Decision support questions are addressed and answered by the data warehousing system by providing instrumental and pragmatic knowledge for action. This book will especially emphasize the practical aspects of knowledge in business in knowing customers and knowing the behavior of product brands in the market. It is *not* a miracle that dirty data gets scrubbed in the information supply chain and knowledge is one of the results. But it does sometimes seem like a miracle because the commitment of those exceptional firms that make this happen is not in the headlines or on the surface. The result is instrumental knowledge in which means are applied to ends. Knowledge generates actionable results for the benefit of the business. This further entails pragmatic knowledge in which knowledge becomes the basis for commitments, in which business processes are coordinated, essential business imperatives addressed, and fundamental decision support questions answered by the data warehousing system. The latter way in which knowledge is defined (and fortified) by commitment is the singular "spin" that this work puts on our understanding of knowledge in a business context. This commitment of data warehousing to knowledge is what puts the decision back in decision support.

Acknowledgments

Numerous mentors, colleagues, and associates have reviewed and commented on the manuscript in various stages of its development. This is the place to thank them warmly for their efforts to provide the author with perspective on the big picture, as well as clarifications on the details: Ray Clodi, Howard Fosdick, Gary C. Garrett, Peter G. W. Keen, Larry Mohr, Murray Pratt, Arno Penzias, John Pomeranz, Venkat Reddy, George Rosenbaum, Owen Shapiro, Paul Strassmann, and Eric Warner—all contributed significantly to product improvement in more ways than can be listed here. Naturally, the remaining rough spots are my own responsibility.

Other individuals who have been supportive of my efforts to develop professionally as an IT professional and a business person also deserve my thanks and acknowledgment. This book would not have been possible without their many and varied contributions. These persons include: Eusibio "Bing" Alabata, Tom Angell, Chauncey Bell, John Cisek, Ramon Barquin, Margaret Couch, Joe Dolan, Vincent Dupuis, Jack Endicott, Bob Gerber, Dick Hackathorn, Dan Hancock, Andy Kaufman, Steve Liczewski, Brad Mitchell, Bill Morstadt, Craig Mullins, Phil Ravid, Bill Robb, Craig Rodkin, Ted Sofos, Vic Stein, Herman Strahan, Stephen Toulmin, Gary Whitman, Duane Wilson, and Gabrielle Wiorkowski.

I wish to thank Ron Powell and Jean Schauer, the executive and managing editors, respectively, of *DM Review*, for permission to use material first published in *DM Review* in January 1997 as "Extending the Client-Server Revolution." Special thanks to Ron and Jean for their encouragement and support.

Likewise, I wish to thank the principals at Greenbrier and Russel, Inc. (G&R) for permission to use material professionally first published as a "Technical Tip" under copyright to G&R in the *IDUG Solutions Journal* in March 1998. I learned many valuable lessons and made many friends while at G&R—special thanks to Howard Blietz, Eric Warner, and Eric Wasowicz. The executive and managing editor of the *IDUG Solutions Journal*, Sheryl Larsen, and Linda Pearlstein, also have my warmest thanks for their support throughout the years. An early version of material in Chapter Eleven was published in May 1999 in the *IDUG Solutions Journal* as "Parallel Join Processing."

Since completing this manuscript, I had the chance to share ideas from it on an informal basis with professionals at Giga Information Group (www.gigaweb.com). This is the place to thank Merv Adrian, Chip Gliedman, Gig Graham, Dan Mahoney, and Brian Testa for their feedback, professional coaching, and the opportunity to work with them.

Thanks is also due to Mark Taub, Editor-in-Chief, Nick Radhuber, Production Editor, Marti Jones, Copyeditor, and AudriAnna Bazlen, Editorial Coordinator, at Prentice Hall for their outstanding support in the development and execution of this project.

My parents, Lou and Violet Agosta, have repeatedly asked me about the title of my book, finally requiring that I write it down and send it to them. It is good to know that it will receive extensive promotion among the residents in Fort Myers, Florida.

This book is dedicated to Alex and Michelle, my wife and daughter, who have sustained me through occasional moments of doubt or grouchiness with copious cups of good-mood tea and lots of tickles. Special thanks goes to Michelle for her work on the graphic of the black-necked swan in the Introduction. Due to grown-up logic, it has proven necessary to edit out an image of a smiling sun with sunglasses from this graphic.

Lou Agosta, Ph.D.
lagosta@acm.org
Alleingang, Inc.
Chicago, IL
May 17, 1999

Introduction to Data Warehousing: Between Uncertainty and Knowledge

In this introduction…

LEARNING TO LIVE WITH UNCERTAINTY

Every age has to learn the same lessons anew—every age and every generation, and at new levels of detail. Today, we are learning to live with uncertainty. This is true in our lives and in the world of business. The compressed time horizon within which products and services are introduced, the whims of customer loyalty, and opportunistic behavior on the part of consumers—all add up to uncertainty on the part of business leaders, managers, and the staff as to what next to expect—unless it is more of the unexpected.

The truth is that virtually all business processes now have computing systems (software, databases, networks) as an essential component. Indeed, in many cases, the only product in view is digital. For example, financial products and instruments have always been highly abstract. Now, their representation in digital form is almost indistinguishable from their separate existence. Even complex manufactured products—tractors, printers, copiers, 757 airplanes, and software systems—are accompanied by a CD-ROM version of the instructions for use or product documentation. Often, a supplementary web site is referenced to provide answers to frequently asked questions. There are now two orders of magnitude more chips embedded in cars than are riding on desktops—some tens of billions over and above the hundred million desktops.

Increasingly, the framework within which buyers and sellers meet is mediated by—totally built of or at least supported by—digital artifacts, electronic channels, and software components of all kinds. The Internet may be the most dramatic instance of that, but it is by no means the only one. Not just the content, but the entire organizational and technology frameworks are shifting. The world of business and the market transactions that form it are characterized by dynamic and fluctuating interaction between buyers, sellers, and the business and technology structures and institutions within which they relate.

This introduction takes an approach to data warehousing from the 50,000-foot level. It provides positioning, motivation, and orientation, as well as insight into the genesis of this book. These are useful things. However, if the reader is eager to engage the business and technical details of data warehousing and simply cannot wait, the recommendation is to proceed at once to Chapter One: Basic Data Warehousing Distinctions. The introduction can be read any time later without loss of continuity.

BOMBARDED BY PARADIGM SHIFTS

Business managers are literally being bombarded with paradigm shifts—client-server computing, object-oriented technology, electronic data interchange, enterprise resource planning systems, intranets, the rebirth of the mainframe as the enterprise server, and the integration of legacy systems. When one cross-references the ongoing transformation of the technology infrastructure with business parameters—such as customer intimacy, just-in-time supply chain management, visibility to the up- and downstream value chains of vendors and partners, targeted marketing and promotions, product- and customer-sustaining systems, activity-based cost initiatives, and self-service everything—one has the formula for an astronomically large number of combinations of business initiatives. Which ones are the ones to be engaged first? Once again, uncertainty is the mark of what is or ought to be one's priorities in such a situation. At the risk of creating suspense that will not be resolved until Chapter Two (see Figure 2.1), we must ask, Is there something that has stood fast amidst the flux of paradigm shifts?

REDUCING UNCERTAINTY THROUGH KNOWLEDGE

A key question is how business leaders and managers can use these electronic systems, these digital artifacts, to reduce uncertainty through knowledge. To get hands on the levers and mechanisms of the business enterprise—the supply chain of product delivery and the value chain of customer service—it is useful, indeed essential, that managers and leaders have a representation of the business ready at hand. Often, solving a problem simply means representing it so as to make the solution obvious or transparent. If the problem solving could actually be organized in these terms, the issue of representation would be seen to be a central and useful approach.[2] This representation, implemented by shared databases, networks, and software applications, is a powerful and, indeed, critical method of applying knowledge to reduce uncertainty.

The metaphor of the business decision maker as a commander going into battle is limited in these times of strategic partnership and cooperation. Still, the image of simulating a battle by moving miniature tokens around on a map, a representation of the field of action, is relevant to the daily struggle for market share, product rollout, and customer care. Things may not go according to plan; but measuring adjustments, results, and exceptions against a plan is a method intuitively recognized as superior to random groping, thrashing, and dumb luck.

THE DATA WAREHOUSE PROVIDES KNOWLEDGE AS A SPECIAL KIND OF REPRESENTATION

The simple proposition of this book is that the data warehouse is such a map and representation and, as such, is a fundamental source of knowledge, not only of the business enterprise, but of the field of action within which it undertakes its campaigns of profit and growth. The basic dimensions of the product (or service) and the customer, and their interaction at a particular time and place are the foundation for building and using the data warehouse. What, then, is this knowledge provided by the data warehouse? How does it provide an antidote to uncertainty for business leaders and managers alike?

KINDS OF KNOWLEDGE

What kinds of knowledge are at stake here? An executive summary is in order. The basic working definition of *knowledge*: Knowledge is the result when a framework, a scheme of organizing concepts, is applied to experience and validated. When people think of knowledge, they often think of theoretic knowledge, the results of science. Science teaches us that both structure and data are required to transform experience into knowledge. When data is structured and organized in a coherent way, experience is made to validate or refute our statements and becomes knowledge. Frameworks of concepts without data are empty; data without frameworks are blind. Both are required to have knowledge in the full sense of the term.

That is, indeed, the stuff that makes up the performance of the hardware, the logical operations of if-then-else logic, and the biological and psychological makeup of the consumer. An understanding of theoretic principles—especially of logic and human nature—is a firm foundation and framework for getting results in the market, in the lab, and in the executive suite. From a theoretic perspective, knowledge is characterized by the process of validation and attempted refutation. The statement "All swans are white" is usually considered knowledge until one is reminded of the black-necked swan (*Cygnus melancoryphus*) native to South America (see Figure I.1 and Harré, 1970: v). Then "I know" gets turned into "Gee, I thought I knew—but I didn't." The really interesting thing here—aside from the always-limited certainty and tentative confidence—is the way in which saying "I know" implies a commitment. If a person says "I know," people may rely on what is said more than if the person merely says "I believe" or "I hope." The person who says "I know" is held accountable, held responsible as if they had made a commitment. That is because they *did* make a commitment—they said "I know." So if the person's statement turns out to be wrong, the person is required to give an explanation, an excuse, or an account of what happened. They must explain why the knowledge was incomplete or what exceptional conditions occurred this time. At the very least, the commitment requires refinement—"All swans are white, except for that one in South

Figure I.1
Cygnus melancoryphus: South America's black-necked swan

America." We are reminded once again that today's general theories are tomorrow's special cases. This is analogous with making a promise. If a person says "I promise," that creates an obligation to perform, a commitment. If the promised action does not occur, the person is subject to being held responsible for violating the commitment, even being blamed, conditional on providing excuses or extenuating circumstances. The analogy is quite exact—we still make promises and assert our knowledge, even though things happen that overturn, qualify, or refute the respective commitments. Promises still exist and bind us to perform according to our word, even though it sometimes happens that we fail to perform. Our human knowledge is finite and always subject to revision in the light of further experience (see above, on the black-necked swan) but is no less worthy of the name of *knowledge* for all that. It is this aspect of commitment that is particularly relevant to the application of knowledge to business issues. This dimension of commitment points in the direction of at least two other forms of knowledge that are just as important in business as theoretic knowledge. They now require consideration. These are what we might call *instrumental* and *pragmatic* knowledge. Let's consider each in turn.

Instrumental Knowledge

Instrumental knowledge relates means and ends. If the shipment is to reach the West Coast by Monday morning, it must leave the dock for the airport by Friday night. If you put one medium-sized pig in the top of the process, 50 cases of frankfurters come out of the bottom. If maintenance of the equipment is deferred past month's end, then likelihood of an equipment failure by mid-month following increases by 30%. Increasing the advertising budget by 30% will give us a 3% lift by year's end. If you want to attain the goal stated in the first part of the statement, use or deploy the means specified in the latter part of the statement. The if-then form is characteristic of the commitment of instrumental knowledge.

Pragmatic Knowledge

Pragmatic knowledge, on the other hand, is context-specific, subject-matter-oriented, and embodies practical behavior. Motivating, structuring incentives, highlighting trade-offs and benefits—all of these require a pragmatic grasp of human behavior. "Let's assign the tiger team to solve the problem of getting that gateway working right." "The team now understands the benefit of satisfying the customer requirement, so we'll schedule enough overtime to get the job done." "When the project is delivered on time, the entire team benefits." How to do things with words is the managerial task in its essence. It is also the marketing task. "Buy now and save" or "buy now and demonstrate your impeccable taste and style" or "buy now and solve your problem"—these are the subtexts of the three stereotypical forms of marketing. Getting people to do things and getting them to do things by means of words applies the pragmatic parts of language to performing actions.

Instrumental knowledge is a representation that connects means and end in a practical, toollike manner. Pragmatic knowledge is a representation that gets people to do things, take action, through a communication, a form of words. To be exact, it is not so much the form of words that is knowledge (because sometimes "buy now and save" is just a trick); it is rather the entire conversation, a conversation for and about actions to be taken to produce results in the business enterprise. "May I help you?" when stated by a customer service representative, expresses a commitment to mobilize significant, even vast, resources to address whatever complaint about the business commitment surfaces next. The pragmatic knowledge is the expression of the connection between the statement and the action for which it provides an incentive or motivation. To say that such statements are "knowledge" gives them a certain dignity. That is why the claim to scientific objectivity is qualified by saying that they are instrumental or pragmatic. What these forms of knowledge represent are "imperatives." What does this mean?

FUNDAMENTAL BUSINESS IMPERATIVES

An *imperative* is a command, something that must be done if you want to produce a certain result. Thus, imperatives have the form of instrumental knowledge: If you want an on-time delivery, schedule the assembly by the end of week two. They also have the form of pragmatic knowledge—conversations about what are, in point of fact, business goals and how to motivate their realization. These statements are not true in a scientific context. Yet such instrumental and pragmatic connections provide mechanisms to generate business results in the market. As we shall see, these fundamental imperatives of the business undertaking are the source of the design, the reason for being, of the data warehouse.

THE THREE IMPERATIVES

Know the customer! Build the brand! Know who is buying what! These three imperatives provide a powerful mechanism for moving the data warehouse in the direction sought by the entire enterprise. In turn, the warehouse constructed with such fundamental principles in mind becomes like a long-range forecasting tool, a sort of weather satellite for the company. The relationship is, indeed, a circular but productive one. This is the power of representing the features of the business in the database and application software.

If I am uncertain as to whether I can fill an order for 50 pumps for the Agriculture Cooperative by a particular date, I can apply instrumental knowledge of supply chain management to determine the chances of success. If the assembly line is operating at a given capacity, the parts are available, and the distribution network is functioning at a given speed, then the generated schedule shows the outcome. If I have the available means and deploy them in a timely way, the end is likewise obtained in a timely way. If we have a scorchingly hot summer, then it is reasonable to conclude that sales of iced tea, soft drinks, and other refreshing beverages will be stimulated and will increase. Likewise, with snow blowers and winters filled with storms. This kind of knowledge generating capacity is embedded in resource planning software. It is instrumental knowledge: It connects means and ends in a necessary and useful way. The making of products, including their design with the manufacturing and distribution process in mind, often entails the use and deployment of instrumental forms of knowledge.

If I am uncertain as to whether a customer will purchase a product or service by the end of the reporting period, I can apply pragmatic knowledge of consumer behavior, the delivery and understanding of messages and communication, and the mechanisms of motivation to influence the outcome or result. The paradigm of this form of knowledge is the principle of enlightened self-interest. Appeal to people's self-interest in a way that benefits both buyer and seller. "Buy now and save!" Discounts, incentives, and promotions all appeal to the consumer's desires, interests, and needs. Pragmatics is different than the instrumental approach, because we must be prepared to deal with the unintended consequences of our communication. There are plenty. Thus, the consumer buys sooner to take advantage of the discount, shifting a purchase in time but not creating a genuinely new sale; what is worse, next time the consumer will not even buy until a discount shows up. Opportunistic and gaming behavior are the order of the day—people will subscribe to the three-month trial subscription to Groovy Magazine in the summer, when they have free time to read it, then will let it lapse in the autumn when they get busy again. They might pick it up in the winter, after the first of the year, when the order entry system shows a different calendar year on the subscription application, allowing it to pass the edit that the promotion is valid only once a year. The use of promotions, advertising, and marketing strategies, with specific reference to customer and consumer behavior, often entails the use and deployment of pragmatic forms of knowledge. Likewise, the conversations expressing a commitment to customer service, brand development, or satisfying human needs and aspirations while growing the business, though less easy to express as slogans, are the authentic form in which pragmatic forms of knowledge are mobilized and where they most powerfully make a difference to the business enterprise.

THE DATA WAREHOUSE REPRESENTS THE BUSINESS

These two dimensions, customer and product, integrate backward into the supply chain by means of instrumental knowledge and forward into the marketing interface toward the customer by means of pragmatic knowledge. The complete enterprise data warehouse captures and represents these key dimensions in the software applications and database records in such a way that both the enterprise (the firm) and the market within which the company functions are available. Both are depicted and able to be engaged, manipulated, through the system. It is precisely this feature of representation that lends the data warehouse its power. The data warehouse system is designed and constructed to depict accurately the reality of the business world within which the firm is operating. This depiction is what gives the data warehouse its usefulness and influence. There are definite methods, steps, and tools that can be applied to make sure the necessary conditions of an accurate representation are satisfied. Their treatment is the main objective of the chapters on constructing the data warehouse system (in particular, Chapters Seven through Eleven).

COMPLEX ARTIFACT, SIMPLE PRINCIPLES

As a system construct, the data warehouse is one of the most complex and important software artifacts known to commercial enterprise. Yet the basic principles and practices of building and running it are so simple, elementary, and fundamental that they seem obvious and self-evident, once made explicit. In many businesses, the data warehouse is or aspires to be the jewel in the crown of the enterprise. It is the target of intense business and technology integration but often sinks back to the level of being the mere slave of the fragmented and disparate operational or legacy systems upstream from it. The data warehouse is not necessarily required to solve operational problems, but rather to represent the business in a systematic and logical way; to represent the business in the warehouse software; to represent the business in the database; and to do so in order to use this systematic representation to steer, guide, and drive the business.

In order for the data warehouse to be of use in guiding and driving the business, it must represent the business. This is a fundamental point about representation that belongs toward the start of an essential guide to data warehousing. At its simplest level, the relationship (of representing) is rather like a map. Draw a one-to-one correspondence from the points on the map to the streets in the city neighborhood. The map depicts the relations between the streets in miniature. Washington Street is to the north of Madison Avenue—that is toward the top (north) of the map. However, representation is not limited to mere one-to-one comparisons. An instruction manual, for example, is a representation of how to do something. It relates how to install a printer, providing a representation of the procedure or action to be taken. All kinds of statements made by people—asking, inquiring, suggesting, commanding, telling—represent situations we want to understand and influence. These are forms of representing in language. Finally, software itself has a relationship of representing the business events and transactions that transpire and are able to be captured within the business system that it makes possible and enables. Thus, if customer A buys 30 units of product B, certain actions are triggered: increment customer A's balance due; decrement inventory for product B by the given amount; and send a message to the scheduling system to queue up the items for delivery (etc.). All of these things represent states of affairs. Obviously, a severe penalty is incurred when the representation breaks down. The software reports that the database shows that Customer A purchased 30 items on May 10, but that is not the case, according to the customer. Things that can go wrong with particular reference to the data warehouse are the subject of the chapter on what can go wrong and the leaning cube of data (see Chapter Eighteen).

ALIGNING THE BUSINESS AND THE WAREHOUSE

Strategically, the relationship whereby the warehouse "represents" the business is called *alignment*. We say that the warehouse is aligned with the business. Therefore, the warehouse is able to be applied to directing decision making and managing uncertainty through the application of knowledge. For the warehouse to guide the business, it must have already been constructed with specific connections to the essential features of the business in mind. That, too, is alignment. Simply stated, the way to align the data warehouse with the structure of the enterprise is to let the business imperatives driving the company constrain the design, implementation, and operation of the data warehouse. What alignment looks like in more detail from the technology angle is the design and implementation of data dimensions corresponding to such structures as customer, product (or service), channel, promotion, and the like. What alignment looks like in more detail from the business angle is fourfold. First, unpacking the meaning of alignment yields visibility to the scope or extent of business structures represented by the data warehousing system. For example, the 20% of customers that provide 80% of sales are driving the acquisition of sales data for that partition. Can the firm reach all of its customers—even if all of the customers are included in the automated system, are all actively promoted? Second, alignment is the volume and depth of business experience captured. For example, to operate a forecasting system, three to five years of historical sales data are required. Third, the extent of services that can be provided to the business is a mark of overall alignment. Forecasting was mentioned as an example. Other examples include cross-selling, sales trend analysis, measuring the effectiveness of promotions, and all aspects of just-in-time logistics. As we shall see, those data warehouses that focus on the customer dimension often emphasize marketing services; whereas those that concentrate on the product dimension end up delivering services in supply chain management. Finally, the speed with which the data warehousing system can adapt to shifts in the market is also a function of alignment. The role of a flexible system architecture (as discussed in Chapter One: Basic Data Warehousing Distinctions) in achieving responsiveness must be emphasized. Such flexibility often requires many-to-many alignment as, for example, when dynamically changing customer identities in a legacy system are stabilized, systematized, and subjected to version control in the data warehousing system. This brings us full circle to technical alignment, because such many-to-many variations on alignment are able to be represented within the computing system using the tools of relational database modeling (see Chapter Five: Business Design: The Unified Representations of the Customer and Product). A basic take-away here is that alignment is the result of design and implementation effort. Alignment then shows up as the connection between data warehousing and essential features of business activity. This is a key principle to guide management thinking and acting in conceptualizing, building, and operating a data warehouse.

If one drills down on the customer dimension, one gets a warehouse effort that emphasizes customer knowledge, cross-selling, customer-sustaining activities, and customer intimacy and service based on the buying or use behavior, as captured in the warehouse. MCI's famous program of Friends and Family is an example of the power of alignment at a detailed level between the database representation of associations among friends and family and the overlapping networks of people really wanting to call one another. The complexity of tracking and billing who gets to call whom under the program would be impossible without marshalling vast database—including data warehousing—resources in the service of the "six degrees of separation" that separates everyone on the planet. (The "degrees of separation" refers to the ability to hand deliver a letter to a person in the remotest place on the planet—say a central Asian republic—by only six "hops" between persons who know one another.) Obviously, the management of such a Friends and Family program requires accurate, "clean" names and addresses. The representation of such an overlapping network of family and friends is a pragmatic and actionable form of knowledge within the business and marketing context of such a Friends and Family program. What may at first seem like a miracle—clean up the data and you get knowledge—is actually the result of aligning the way the data is represented in the database with the way people interact (over the phone) in the world. To be more precise, the "miracle" is the result of the information supply chain process that includes such alignment as its first and basic principle of design. (See Chapter Twelve: Data Warehousing Operations: The Information Supply Chain.)

On the other hand, if one drills down on the product dimension, one gets a warehouse that emphasizes the management of the product in the context of the supply chain, product-sustaining, and brand development activities. Inventory control and supply chain management are the breakthrough opportunities here. The importance of realizing smooth supply chain commitments and handoffs, coordinating deliveries, and forecasting applications is so critical at firms such as Wal-Mart that the head of logistics, H. Lee Scott,[3] is now mentioned as candidate to become the CEO. This outcome is the result of data warehousing efficiencies and successes that have literally redefined and transformed what is logistically possible. Recent industry experience shows that financial services, banks, and insurance companies are concentrating on the former; whereas retail firms and companies that must store and transport physical things emphasize the latter. Nevertheless, the complexity of the undertaking must be realistically assessed and appreciated. For example, the American Automobile Association of Michigan reportedly combined over 10 million records from at least three mainframe MVS computing systems.[4] The data sources contained membership and insurance policy information. The resulting 3.5 million customers in the combined customer dimension were stored on IBM's DB2 database and enabled significant reductions in erroneous names and addresses, and in costs associated with the simple task of getting a clean list of customers and the products and services that they use. What seemed at first glance to be a "simple task" required literally billions of comparisons between disparate, heterogeneous data sources to reduce the 10 million redundant, overlapping customers to the resulting warehouse customer dimension.

The one essential key to producing knowledge, rather than just more data, via data warehousing is the alignment between the data dimensions defining the warehouse and basic business imperatives. In its simplest form, *alignment* refers to the basic mapping of data warehousing system structures and functions to business entities, processes, and transactions. For instance, think of the elementary example of a customer buying a product: Customer C buys P. This results in a sales fact when combined with a few additional parameters or dimensions, such as store location and time of the event. This oversimplification harbors a profound insight. The way we craft our statements to represent the world—in this case, the market *is* the world—makes possible the very facts through which we come to know the world. This simple view of language is a synonym for all kinds of system-building activities, such as data warehousing, in which progressively more concrete models of the system are built, culminating in the model formed by executable code. This is readily seen in data modeling, whereby the parts of the statement reach out like feelers and exactly map to the parts of the world of interest, which, in spite of its simple approach, is nevertheless very powerful for many ideal cases. In essence, it employs the top-down, structured method. Complexity is at first hidden beneath basic, high-level distinctions that get unpacked in the course of further drill down and analysis.

Rarely is the alignment between the data warehousing system and the business situation of such a simple one-to-one picture of the modeling language capturing corresponding parts of the world. In point of fact, many-to-many alignments occur in abundance. For example, think of mapping real-world customers in several different transactional systems who use natural identities, such as names and addresses, to a unified, arbitrarily assigned system identity in a data warehouse. (This is where the power of a relational database to represent many-to-many relations can provide, if not a silver bullet, at least an approach to engaging the issue productively.)

A further penetration of the limits and content of alignment can be appreciated by a four-way dissecting of the idea itself. First, *alignment* refers to the extent of the customers, products, promotions, channels, or other hierarchical data integrated in the correspondence of the data warehousing system dimensions and the functioning enterprise. For example, does the data warehousing system capture and represent all the customers, those 20% that generate 80% of the business, or those 80% that account for the remaining 20% of the business? Can the firm reach all of its customers? Second, *alignment* refers to the time horizon within which transactional data can be summarized and massaged to address decision support questions. Third, the range of services available to the business from the data warehousing system is also a function of alignment—sales analysis, forecasting, resource planning, demand planning, cross-selling, and value chain management. All of these services and more constitute an alignment between data warehousing technology and business imperatives to build the brand and know the customer, enabling answers to fundamental queries about business direction and strategy. Finally, the speed and responsiveness of the data warehousing system to developments in the market, the enterprise, and the business environment at large is a fourth dimension of alignment. (See summary in Figure I.2: Alignment, and Keen, 1991: 180; the extension to data warehousing, however, is my own inference.) This "alignment cube" is not a multidimensional cube in the way the term is usually

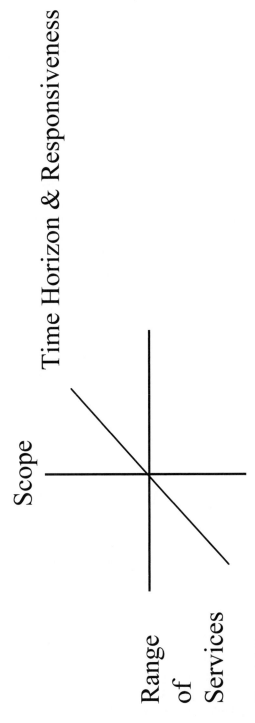

Figure 1.2
Alignment

employed in data warehousing (for those new to the subject, please refer to the Glossary entry for *cube* at this point). However, it is an example of the power of multidimensional analysis—cross-referencing, overlapping, and related terms—in both data warehousing and strategic IT thinking together.

DATA WAREHOUSE MAP OF THE BUSINESS

One of the most significant lessons to be taken away from this discussion is that the data warehouse system maps exactly and precisely to the structure of fundamental business imperatives: know the customer, know the product, and know when/where they interact. This puts substance on the imperative "know the customer." This puts substance on the imperative to know how to "build the brand." This adds meaning to the imperative to "know who is buying (using) what." When properly designed and implemented, the data warehouse system ends up being a model, not just of the business itself, but of features of the market, the customer, the distribution channel, and the transactions that occur there.

Organizational lessons, as well as technical ones, loom large. To make a fully functioning data warehouse happen in an enterprise, the cooperation and active collaboration of the owners of legacy data have to be added to the graphical user interface (GUI) expertise in the front-end tool, deployed to present the trends in the data as an array or graph. The layers of technology that have to be traversed include a transaction monitor to support scalability and fast utilities to counter a constrained batch window. That means that system integration has to happen. In this age of uncertainty, shrink-wrapped desktop tools to help slice and dice are in the foreground. Off-the-shelf applications, too, are in the foreground. Criteria for evaluating their usefulness in context—pragmatic knowledge—is part of the (Chapter Fifteen) OLAP technologies. However...

CAN'T SHRINK-WRAP KNOWLEDGE OF THE BUSINESS

What can't be shrink-wrapped is knowledge of the business—how you define and find a customer, how you roll out a new product, how you capture and transform operational data. What can't be taken off the shelf are problem-solving and fundamental system integration competencies. However, just because such knowledge can't be shrink-wrapped doesn't mean that it can't be systematized. Stated positively, transaction data can be transformed into knowledge of the business by being made the target of systematic survey, organization, indexing, and storage. In comparison with breaking open the shrink wrap, this can be the difference between chemistry and alchemy. It requires data warehouse science and management alchemy to transform the sometimes-leaden legacy of history into the gold of customer and product knowledge. (That is the subject of the Chapter Twelve: Data Warehousing Operations: The Information Supply Chain.)

A SINGLE VERSION OF THE TRUTH

Life is messier than we would wish. The world is more chaotic, less organized, filled with more uncertainty and surprises than we care to admit. Every enterprise, every business initiative, and every project is an engagement in overcoming that uncertainty and chaos. How, in general, do we go about it?

Rather than give up hope of making sense out of the seemingly irrational change of conditions and requirements of technology and business, the recommendation is to "fake it." Not to fake it in any dishonest sense of pretending to have order or rational procedures where there are none, but to fake it in the sense of "simulate." That is, in fact, the point of one of the essential documents of modern system design, "A Rational Design Process: How and Why to Fake It," by David Parnas and P. Clements. We all know what designing a software artifact, a system, is like with the benefit of 20-20 hindsight—define requirements, design, code, test, and implement. We start out intending to follow step-by-step procedures. We start out according to an orderly rational definition of a defined process. However, unexpected events break in on us—the business environment changes, the technology changes, the company gets acquired or merged, staff resign or retire, the requirements change. Does that mean we are reduced to reacting, hacking, behaving irrationally? Well, not exactly. Even if the process of system design is not rational, there is much benefit to be gained by pretending that it is rational, that it does make sense. There is much value in reconstructing the process and treating it as if it were a defined step-by-step process. The motivation for doing so—the "why" of the "how and why"—is to create order out of chaos, to provide a coherent framework where there was none. By simulating a rational design process, one is actually brought into existence. (The details of simulating a rational design process will be taken up again in Chapter Four: Data Warehousing Project Management.)

That is the value, and that is the point of a single version of the truth. Consider a simple example and a complex example. First, the dimension of time is simple, in that we all share the same calendar. However, every company has its own unique way of defining reporting periods. Does the week begin or end with Saturday or some other day? Is Founder's Day in the summer or in another season? Is Columbus Day one on which the business is open? Is Martin Luther King Day a holiday? These things are relatively easy to encode in a database structure representing the time dimension, once the facts are surfaced—easy until the firm wants to do business in an oil-rich central Asian republic that uses the eastern Orthodox calendar instead of the Gregorian.

A more complex example is the determination of profitability and costs. To build a profitability data warehouse, costs must be subtracted from sales to determine the profit. Sales of a product or service are relatively easy to determine, but costs can be another thing. Getting one's arms around them can require deploying a business approach—one might say "technology"—such as activity-based costing (ABC). What enables a product to be produced includes such activities as scheduling, moving materials, setting up and breaking down batches, designing, inspecting, training, and supporting.

Purchasing, sales, logistics, and related services all support the product. On a day-to-day basis, these may seem like fixed costs. Other than materials and direct, assembly line labor, every service in sight seems to be a fixed cost. However, if one takes even a step backward, these things start to appear amenable to scaling up or down from one month to another or from one quarter to another. They are more variable than at first appears.

With sufficient planning and perspective, many fixed costs turn out to be variable. This planning and perspective are precisely what the data warehouse is designed to deliver to management. The challenge is to boot-strap the entire firm in that direction, even if only on a case-by-case basis. Consider two products—a standard lead pencil, S, and a customized mechanical one, C. If product C is highly customized and requires frequent setups or breakdowns for small batches, along with individual sales and support, one would expect its costs to be higher than those for product S, which is produced in large batches and sells that way. Reaching an agreement on how to allocate costs is on the critical path to generating a result that is useable in determining what activities are traceable to what products, customers, or business outputs. That is common sense, but it is common sense that is often not recognized by the traditional cost accounting systems whose main purpose is to report to the tax authorities.

Agreement as to which business drivers are the source of costs is a task for a process of analysis of the business, guided by management insight and understanding of the business. Tracing these drivers to products or customers is a job that management has to engage and accomplish. There is room for variation, but it is better to be approximately correct most of the time—in the ballpark—than to be precisely wrong.

Cost can be based on actual day-to-day expenses. This creates fluctuations, which, from a statistical quality control point of view, are best ignored. If a machine requires a week's down time for quarterly maintenance, is the machine's efficiency higher in the two months when no maintenance occurs than in the month when the maintenance happens? The cost of operating the machine is the same in every time period, regardless of when the maintenance occurs. As the reporting period shrinks, the danger of distortion rises unless conscious steps are taken to normalize or standardize the cost, based on actual experience. Naturally, the actuals should inform the budgeting process, but they should not pass through on a day-to-day basis to determine overall product cost or efficiency. Costs should be based on budgeted or normalized cost driver rates agreed on by management. Without agreement at an organizational level as to how costs are or ought to be allocated—and that means both marketing and products in this case—it will be impossible to design and build a profitability warehouse. Here, the hooks into the business go very deep indeed. Dozens of activities have to be identified, defined, and represented for the cost factors to be captured and aggregated into a meaningful value posted in a profitability data warehouse. That is why a single version of the truth is both the consequence and the condition of the data warehouse. This is perhaps one reason the profitability data warehouse is usually not recommended to be the first one rolled out. Nevertheless, it is one of the most powerful and useful that a firm can envision.

Many of the same considerations apply to all the dimensions of the data warehouse. Who are the customers? If both parent corporations and their subsidiaries are customers, how are they uniquely represented hierarchically? What are our products and how are they represented? Time, store, locations, demographics, employees, patients—the list is long and varies by subject area and vertical industry. Getting agreement on the dimensions is, for all intents and purposes, aligning on single version of the truth. How do we go about that alignment?

AN INVENTORY OF KNOWLEDGE: PUTTING THE "DECISION" BACK INTO "DECISION SUPPORT"

A first step in the process of alignment is to ask, What do you need to know? Decide? Accomplish? Make an inventory of the kinds of knowledge available to the business. Toward the top of the list is knowledge of customers, their buying habits, and behavior. Knowledge of products, their attributes, and costs to manufacture and distribute is next on the list. Knowledge of the interaction of customer and products, two key dimensions, is a set of facts that are significant in detail and in depth. Finally, knowledge of the causal factors influencing the performance of the products and the behavior of the customers is on the critical path of a system design and implementation capable of representing the levers and dials that move the business forward. Because such knowledge is expected to be one of the results of the functioning data warehouse and a way of evaluating its robustness, usefulness, or success, it is quite likely that such knowledge is embedded tacitly in a combination of operational systems—order entry, for example—and even as implied dimensions in the minds and experience of the marketing department if the warehouse is still under design.

The next steps include: justifying undertaking the data warehouse project; the construction of a basic data warehouse fact; the construction of a unified view of the customer and product; the formulation of the key question—and related inquiries—to be answered and satisfied by the warehouse; the implementing of data quality in the information supply chain; the development of the architecture to get the answer—metadata; the development of the architecture to get the answer—aggregations and OLAP; the identifying and avoiding of things that can go wrong; and the exploring of future prospects for data warehousing. (This is, in fact, an outline of the remainder of this book.)

As is indicated in Chapter Two: A Short History of Data, if the warehouse had not already existed from time memorial—certainly prior to automated computing systems—it would have had to be invented. Learning to live with uncertainty means acknowledging our limitations and interests. It means distinguishing what we know from what we don't know and being open to the possibility that we don't always even know what we don't know.

The automation of everyday life has gone from being common to being ubiquitous. Automatic point-of-sale scanners in stores, ATM machines, credit and debit cards, home shopping, electronic funds transfer, local telephone calls, and long-distance records—all are opportunities to lay down electronic traces in operational systems. Mountains of data are being generated and stored every day. Back in the late 1970s, IBM (International Business Machines) had a commercial: "Not just data, reality." Corporations have been accumulating data since that time. The data warehouse is a powerful way of organizing this "information overload" to provide valuable knowledge about customers, products, and services. This knowledge enables business people to work smarter in providing customer service, product brand development, and customer- and product-sustaining activities, and in capturing the "moment of value" when the customer buys the product. To transform these isolated transactions into meaningful relations with customers and product development strategies requires the definition and deployment of a data warehouse aligned with the business.

In this book, the basic working definition of *knowledge* is that it is the result—one might say "product"—of bringing an organized framework or concept to experience, such that the experience validates the framework. (Actually, knowledge also results, even if the framework is refuted or invalidated, though in less obvious ways.) Figure I.3 shows at least two major aspects of knowledge. The first is depicted by the arrow from right to left—factual reports about the business are described, represented, and expressed by the system. The second is depicted by the arrow from left to right—the computing system prescribes, constrains, and makes access possible to the details of the business context. These details are actually constructed by the two-way alignment between the data warehousing system and business context, which is otherwise open and fluctuating. Decision support questions get answered by data warehousing feedback into the business context. This occurs in the form of instrumental and pragmatic knowledge for action. A third form of knowledge is not shown by an arrow, though, in a sense, it shows itself. That third form is the alignment between the system and the context. That alignment—which is named in both lists of correspondences—is made explicit as metadata, structures which allow the system and the context to work together (*interoperate* is the computing term).

This study especially emphasizes the practical aspects of business knowledge in knowing customers and knowing the behavior of product brands in the market. This leads to instrumental knowledge, in which means are applied to ends, and in which knowledge generates actionable results for the benefit of the business. This further entails pragmatic knowledge, in which knowledge becomes the basis for *commitments* in which business processes are coordinated, essential business imperatives addressed, and fundamental decision support questions answered by the data warehousing system. The latter way in which knowledge is defined (and fortified) by commitment is the singular "spin" that this work puts on our understanding of knowledge in a business context. In addition to all the other necessary stuff about framework and validation, knowledge implies a commitment. It stands fast, and does so even if it is subject

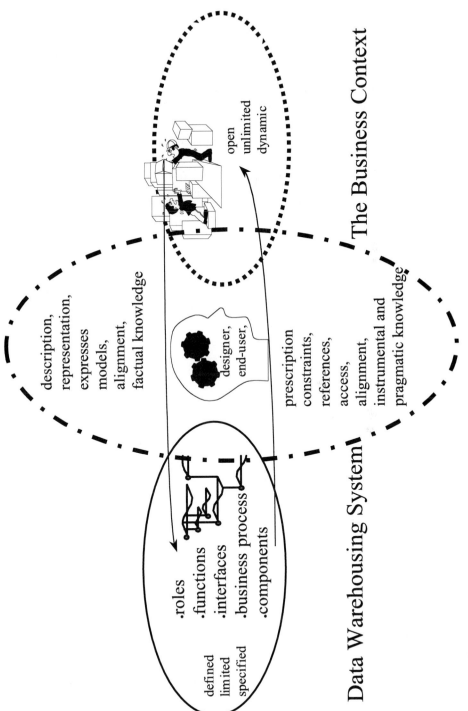

Figure 1.3
Knowledge

to revision and improvement in the light of further experiences (how this is so is explored further in Chapter Six: Total Data Warehouse Quality).

First, knowledge is operationalized in the information supply chain by being placed in continuity with quality information. To the naïve, it may seem like a miracle that dirty data is scrubbed and knowledge is the result. From the operational perspective, knowledge is a point on the horizon toward which the ever-improving quality of information progresses. Second, from the business perspective, when that same quality information is made the basis of action—a choice that puts the "decision" back in "decision support"—the notion of a commitment is surfaced and applied. That commitment brings the quality information along and gets it over the hump to being something on which we count, something on which we rely. We get to data warehousing knowledge in the full sense. This transforming of data about products and customer interactions into business knowledge is the topic to which we now turn.

[1] Personal communication.

[2] This is a close paraphrase of what is said by Herbert A. Simon in *The Sciences of the Artificial*, Cambridge, MA: MIT Press, 1969: 77.

[3] See "At Wal-Mart the Man in Line to be CEO," Emily Nelson, *Wall Street Journal*, March 12, 1999.

[4] For example, see Barbara DePompa, "Scrub your Data Clean," *Information Week*, December 16, 1996: 88. Also see the Glossary for definitions of *MVS* or *mainframe* if the reader so requires.

Part 1

Fundamental Commitments

(Chapters 1 through 4)

Basic and non-trivial definitions are provided for data warehousing distinctions. The one fundamental question of data warehousing is discussed. The significance and meaning of alignment between data warehousing technology and basic business imperatives is explicated. The essential minimal working set of data warehousing components are discussed in terms of architecture. When made the target of a fundamental inquiry, data warehousing architecture turns out to be a variation on work flow. "Work flow" is understood as a coordination of commitments, not an assembly line. Commitment is not usually regarded as a feature of architecture. But it is. Data warehousing addresses the basic business commitments to know the customer, develop the brand, and master marketing dynamics. The answer to the question "What stands fast?" is data and the imperative to manage it as a corporate resource. Data warehousing is distinct in that it is not yet another paradigm shift. It is a continuous, progressive development based on decision support. A perspective is offered on managing data as an enterprise asset with a view to linking history to the future. Data warehousing is a management tool and is justified as such. Business is the management of uncertainty, and data warehousing rests on an architecture for structuring information in ways that reduce and manage uncertainty.

1 *Basic Data Warehousing Distinctions*

In this chapter...

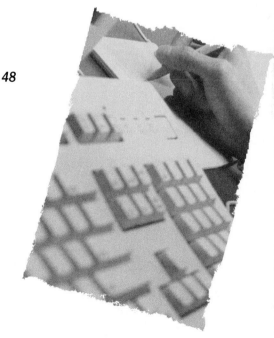

AN ARCHITECTURE, NOT A PRODUCT

The data warehouse is not a software product or application. It is a system architecture. An *architecture* is an arrangement of methods according to first principles. These principles make possible business processes through client, network, and database software. These processes, in turn, provide knowledge, addressing fundamental business imperatives. This is an important point. Given that the data warehouse market place is filled with useful and innovative software products claiming to be "solutions," taking a moment to gain perspective is a necessary step. To be sure, these products have merit and deserve attention. Check lists will be provided later in the discussion for evaluating products, though the approach of this book is not product-oriented. Likewise, many of these products imply an architecture, because "no product is an island." However, the point remains—no product in itself is an architecture.

As an architecture, the data warehouse combines a number of products, each of which has operational uses besides data warehousing. Simply stated, a data warehouse architecture is a blue print, an arrangement, or a map.[2] When implemented, the architecture provides an infrastructure that makes possible business applications that deliver certain special forms of knowledge of the customer. These will be considered in detail shortly. The data warehouse system architecture provides patterns within which applications are consistently connected with one another and integrated with hardware, operating system, database, network, and interface software, and cross-referenced with business processes.

In elementary terms, a working set of data warehousing software includes a database engine, including stored procedures containing data access and manipulation logic; an analytic application server to perform complex business processes, such as forecasting, customer profiling, or promotion evaluation; an end-user interface, typically, a graphical user interface (GUI) on the client work station or desktop; and connectivity to bind the client and server(s), possibly across a wide area network (WAN) using an intranet-based web browser. Software to provide a navigation layer and all-important metadata (the subject of an entire chapter below) is required for the long-term viability of the warehouse. Provision must also be made for "on the fly," user-defined ad hoc inquiries against the data. This list of minimal essential components of a data warehouse will be helpful when planning or shopping for products. However, the main reason for making this list is to throw it away—at least temporarily. This is done to make a point. What makes the data warehouse a warehouse is not primarily all this software, but rather the way the software represents dimensions—and so provides knowledge—of the business enterprise: the customer, product, the channel, and their interaction in time and location (and other related structures). The way that these dimensions line up, or are aligned, with the business is the origin of the promise and the power of the data warehouse as a source of knowledge to be used in driving the business forward.

It is the essential nature of architecture to stand fast. It is the nature of requirements to be in flux. Although it is beneficial in constructing systems to freeze requirements prior to implementation and during migrations of system components, this is a temporary measure. Likewise, any architecture, no matter how robust and flexible, can be extended only so far. The point is that, in comparison with a data warehouse system architecture, end-user requirements are dynamic and fluctuating. Because these requirements are constantly evolving, dynamic, and undergoing refinement, building a system based on requirements alone risks surprises. With all-too-common inevitability, unanticipated events in the business environment cause external shocks to the data warehouse planning or construction effort. If the architecture is brittle, it will be overtaken by dynamic events, be cut off from business meaning, and be obsolete, even before implementation. On the other hand, if the architecture provides a flexible platform that encompasses a myriad of possibilities in a highly coherent, loosely coupled framework, it will be able to adapt to the inevitable slings and arrows of outrageous fortune, bend without breaking, and continue to be of service in a variety of evolving contexts.

Data warehouse architecture does its work by cross-referencing the essential features of any information system with the system construction methods. In this way, the conceptual and logical vision of the architecture gets physically implemented. For example, basic architectural categories refer to data, application functionality, connectivity, presentation (user interface), events (time series data or schedule), and business drivers. Any robust architecture implies methods for its own implementation. The progression is like that of a project implementation in time. It proceeds from scope, through conceptual, logical, and physical models. At this point, the target technology implementation—the representation of the data, functions, and rules in system hardware and software—becomes a constraining and overriding factor in the construction and deployment of the system. As an illustration of a robust flexible architecture, John Zachman's legendary framework for information systems architecture is an example of itself—it is a flexible and survivable construct encompassing many possible requirements scenarios (see Figure1.1 for an adaptation to data warehousing that it inspired).[3] Although originally published prior to the impact of the client-server revolution, the addition of human interface and presentation have brought that dimension up to date. The communication network—including the WAN dimension—was always a feature of the framework. That means that it is still friendly toward network-centric, Internet computing platforms. In fact, entire books have been written on this architecture (e.g., see Spewak and Hill, 1993). It is a superset of client-server architecture, arguably the most prevalent form in which

	Data	Functions	Connectivity	Presentation	Events	Business Drivers
Scope	Relations between fundamental entities	Business intelligence	Metadata	OLAP	Time horizon of forecasting	Knowledge of the customer, market, product; brand development
Concept	Structures	Decision Support	Library science	Cubes	Time series	Decision making
Logical	Data Definition Language	Data transformation	Navigation	Canonical aggregates	Irreversibility	Coordination of commitments
Physical	Containers	Data scrubbing	Repository	"Reach through"	Scheduling	Value added business goals
Build	Consistent dimensions, relevant facts	Aggregation	Indexing and retrieval	OLAP server engine	Three to five years of data	Visibility: market share, profitability, product performance
Deploy	Star schema join	Information supply chain	Systemic inter-operability	"Invisible" interface, transparent access	Speed, accuracy of decision making	Customer service, demand planning, cross selling, warranty program, profitability

Figure 1.1
Data Warehouse Architecture

systems are currently being implemented. In the following discussion, architecture will provide a thread guiding us through layers of system components and functions—business drivers, data applications, connectivity, time series, work flow, and presentations.

Reading Figure 1.1 from left to right, a few special features are worth comment. These will be the target of detailed discussion in the remainder of the book. However, a preliminary pass will provide an overview and orientation.

Data warehousing emphasizes data structures distinguishing between dimensions such as customer product, time, place, and facts, such as quantity of product sold, delivered, or used by a customer at a particular occasion. This joining of different dimensions into a meaningful, unique fact structure provides the famous "star schema," which will be discussed in detail. Many of the functions (processes) of data warehousing require transforming data from the raw form in which it is produced in transactional systems into a form that provides decision support. This includes summarizing the data into meaningful aggregations that provide decision support perspective. It also includes scrubbing the data—purging it of inconsistencies or inaccuracies that may have occurred in traversing operational systems. The way in which data is transformed between transactional and decision support systems requires tracking and synchronizing the semantics from source to target systems. The aggregation of data requires tracing and synchronizing summary to details. When performed for dozens or hundreds of programs and systems, this requires the ability to index, store, catalog, and retrieve vast amounts of information about how these systems interoperate. The central role of a repository is akin to the coordination delivered by library science. Called *metadata*, this is one of the most challenging features of data warehousing and can crucially advance or limit the scalability, flexibility, and maintainability of the overall data warehousing architecture. In general, the way human factors show up in a data warehousing context is by "slicing and dicing" information on the desktop of the "power user." That is the realm of OLAP (on-line analytic processing). The time horizon of decision support events is significantly different than that of transactional systems. The latter is often focused on thirty-day "open inventory," whereas decision support applications such as forecasting require a time horizon of three to five years of available data. The acceleration of decision making and the making of better-informed decisions is an important deployment objective of data warehousing architecture. The business goals from which data warehousing aims to furnish architectural support are different than those basic to the day-to-day operation of the enterprise. These include strategic processes such as brand development, cross-selling based on knowledge of the customer, and a variety of supply chain and value chain (logistic and marketing) initiatives. In short, Figure 1.1 is a comprehensive overview, and much of the rest of this book may be read as a "drill down" on it.

Data warehouse architecture maps closely to the form of client-server computing. At the back-end is a data store, usually a relational database; at the front-end are desktop presentation tools to slice and dice the data cubes and aggregates returned from the data store; and in the middle is a variety of auxiliary applications—navigation, aggregation, analytic, and metadata layers—quite complex in themselves but designed to hide complexity and deliver a uniform and coherent interface to the end-user (see Figure 1.2: Client-Server Definition). In fact, the three layers described here—front-end, middle, and back-end—are not guaranteed to map neatly to the desktop work station (usually a PC), midsized NT or UNIX server in the middle, and mainframe or enterprise server at the back-end. As astute system architects have pointed out (see Loosley and Douglas, 1998), this is really a three-by-three matrix (see Figure 1.3: Alternate Client-Server Partitioning). Consider: The presentation, application, and database layers could all be implemented by computing cycles executing on a main-

Presentation Application Database

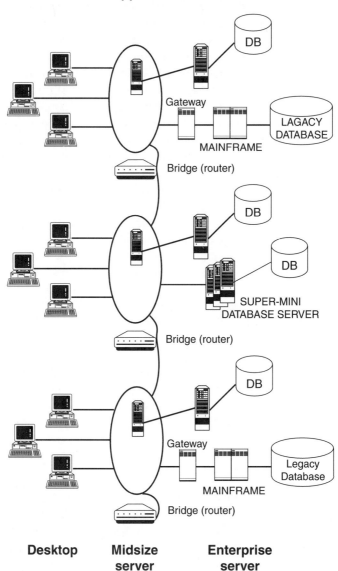

Figure 1.2
Client-Server Definition

frame, as in the days of 3270 dumb terminals. That is the bottom row of Figure 1.3, where presentation, application, and database are at the back-end, enterprise server layer. Alternatively, the presentation layer could be a process on a middle layer server, as occurs with the so-called X-Windows system (corresponding to the middle row in Figure 1.3, as indicated) or all three could be implemented on a high-powered workstation at the desktop by OLAP tools (will be treated in detail in a latter chapter). (Figure 1.3 actually shows connectivity to a database on the middle, server layer, but it is heavily front-end loaded.) Also different partitioning of the application functionality can be distributed between the fat client on the desktop, containing lots of validation and application logic and processes such as stored procedures, and triggers on the database at the back. In this scenario, client-server collapses into the two-tiered implementations, common in the early 1990s, when such tools as PowerBuilder and SQL Server made visible alternatives to mainframe data center computing.

How, then, does this apply to data warehousing? Data warehousing applications encompass the basic issues of marketing, brand (product) development, inventory or asset management, and generation of satisfaction for customers and stakeholders up and down the value chain. They provide the business analyst, demand planner, marketing manager, product development specialist, or knowledge worker in general with visibility to the behavior of fundamental quantitative features of the business processes vital to the firm. The business motivations are as multivariate as the goals of the business itself. Often, these applications are described as OLAPs to distinguish them from traditional day-to-day operations as on-line transaction processing (OLTP).[4]

To be sure, data warehousing is bound to be a data-centric architecture. That is, data-centric—having to do with databases—as opposed to computation-centric, or real-time- or operational-control-focused. Yet, if ad hoc, end-user inquiries against the data warehouse are being considered as an application, a connection with user-centric computing, previously restricted to the information center, is in view. In no way is this an add-on to or any kind of legacy system "solution," because many enterprise systems feed the data warehouse, including electronic commerce and enterprise resource planning systems. Still, the data warehouse is likely to require data extraction, scrubbing, or transformation from one or more legacy systems, along with other enterprise systems. These systems may be local or remote, that is, distributed. Thus, to accommodate data-intensive processing using even the most state-of-the art database management systems tools and techniques, the data warehouse will have to be a simple model that exploits common patterns among various business functions.

OLAP: Application on the desktop

X-Windows: Presentation from the server

Mainframe: Presentation and applications at the back-end

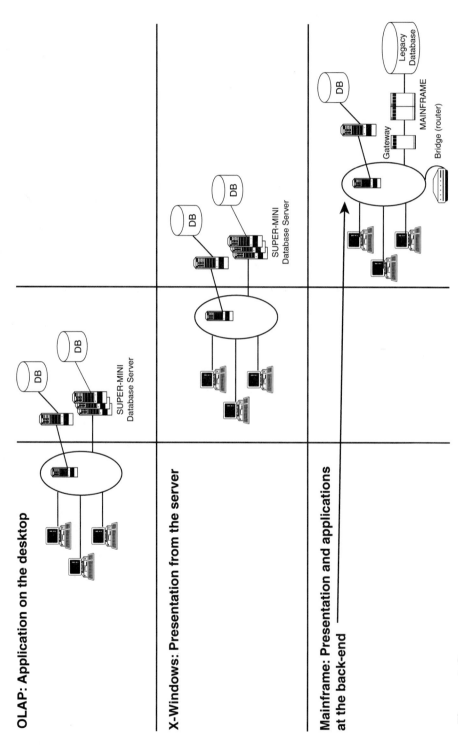

Figure 1.3
Alternate Client-Server Partitioning

Like the rest of the planet, data warehouse systems are migrating in the direction of open Internet standards and protocols. Sometimes described as "the cavalry to the rescue of the IT department" (Keen, 1997), such standards promote the cooperation of customers and suppliers, along the material and informational supply chain out across WANs. Thus, although data warehouse content tends not to be the sort of sensitive data that firms routinely share with customers or suppliers, exceptions are to be found in situations like that at Wal-Mart, where suppliers are invited (i.e., required) to access the data warehouse in order to manage their own inventory control and stock replenishment.

Issue: Is Architecture Made Obsolete by Web Development

At least one industry analyst, Richard Fichera of the Giga Information Group, makes a strong case that considerable overlap exists between allegedly competing architectures and the important benefits derived from having any architecture as opposed to the particular advantages of a certain one. How does this claim hold up in the face of the claim that the web makes obsolete (or irrelevant) the requirement for enterprise architecture planning in any case. In an article on the subject accessible on the publicly available portion of www.gigaweb.com, Mr. Fichera engages this issue. Web development often is initiated by groups outside of the IT mainstream using bottom up and opportunistic methods to get the job done. When operating on Internet time there is a severe penalty for slow results, and marketing, production, and customer care departments are strongly incented to fast track system development around the defined process of centralized IT planning and justification. Use is made of staffing and outside consulting resources that cut their teeth on Internet development independent of the mainstream of the professional IT organization. The response is threefold. The development of the digital economy *via* the web has taken everyone by surprise. So everyone is scrambling to catch up. *Gonzo* development works well for web publishing and is valid as a prototype. However, by the time mission critical 7x24 electronic commerce applications are in question, where real customer relations are at stake, the requirement returns with full force for rigorous, rapid planning, execution, backup management, version control, change control, and scheduling. The trade off remains operative between short term gratification *via* tactical solutions and long term business advantages sustainable thanks to infrastructure not purchasable by anyone (e.g., the competition) as a vendor package. There is a fire hose of data coming at the enterprise off of business activities on the web and nothing less than an enterprise approach will be sustainable. Gaining business advantage from the output of such activities requires a disciplined approach as exemplified by data warehousing. This is a natural conclusion from the experiences and insights marshaled here at the executive level.

Data warehouse information frequently deals with time series data—how sales or deliveries or prices vary from one time period to another. This data can be complex in a variety of ways. It's abstract, dealing with multiple dimensions, including time, place (geography), product, and a host of other dimensions to be considered. It is voluminous. There is a lot of it. Also it tends to involve comparisons of quantities. To manage this complexity, visual presentation is useful. For selected people, visual presentation may be an operational necessity. Complexity becomes accessible and manageable through a clear graphical presentation. The presentation of complex time series data by means of a simple linear design makes for an intuitive and pleasing elegance. These are important pointers for any designer of GUIs on the desktop. The chief idea of human interface design is to get the interface out of the way of the presentation. In other words, the best interface is invisible (easier said than done, to be sure). When widgets, buttons, and boxes are in the foreground, the meaning is not accessible, and the point is lost. The interface should be like a good waiter—there when you need him but otherwise unobtrusive.

Data warehouse architecture enables a particular variation on work flow. In terms of three-tiered client-server, this is situated in the middle layer, where an analytic application engine implements business processes relevant to decision support, such as customer profiling, forecasting, product promotion, and the like. There is a difference between work flow as coordination and as assembly line. The groups of people brought together by a data warehouse system are likely to be cooperating in a different kind of work flow than that characteristic of operational transactional systems. Rather than an information assembly line, where repetitive processes are automated and passed around in input-output stepwise progress, the data warehouse enables work flow as a coordination of interconnecting commitments—requests and satisfactions of requests. Commitments? For example, estimating product demand based on the knowledge of prior experience and promotions implies a commitment to source and deliver the product. Without the interconnection of a commitment between availability and source, the planning operation is an idle wheel. The work and the product literally do not flow. With the interconnection between source and delivery, however, real improvements are possible in supply chain hand-offs, reductions in inventory show up, and just-in-time processing works for all the stakeholders, employees, and customers. For the mechanism represented by the data warehouse system to be engaged, commitment is of the essence. That commitment shows up as a shared architecture, providing work flow as a coordination of commitments. Naturally, those commitments extend beyond the boundary of an individual enterprise. Commitment is usually not thought of as a feature of architecture, but it is. So architecture includes technology but is not limited to it. The data warehouse includes a representation of features of the market itself—customer buying behavior, deliveries, and relevant service behavior. All of these and more are made visible and captured by the system architecture.

The data warehouse architecture supports processes whose time horizon is different than that of day-to-day system operations. Here is a system whose objective is to rise above the perspective of day-to-day operations. The objective is to reduce risk of surprises and to increase control of performance and operations of the business by envisioning options and opportunities coming at us out of the future. The idea that the future will be like the past is a useful working assumption. Many data warehouses use three to five years of historical data, subjected to statistical corrections, to make inferences about the behavior of customers, products, services, and sales. The time horizon is long, transactions are long, and the business events are of interest from a decision support perspective. This doesn't mean that the future is an unknown quantity coming at us out of the void, though that is undoubtedly all too often the case. What this means is that one way of knowing the future is by bringing it forth from our actions, based on a plan of our own formulation. Data warehousing provides business with a powerful tool for doing so. Note, however, that the better thought out and flexible the plan, the more powerful and useful the data warehouse architecture is likely to be.

To encourage the use of common patterns among system technology components, a data warehouse architecture has to provide for more than a dozen essential features. These features are not unique to data warehouse systems but the data warehouse presents certain priorities in understanding and using them. The more valuable the information contained in the warehouse, the more essential is security. It must provide for defense, preferably using group authorizations, against intentional or accidental attack or damage, based on authorization control on the desktop, in the network layer, and at the back-end data stores. The whole point of an architecture is to escape from the birth and death cycle of ever-changing business requirements. Therefore, the architecture must be flexible—that is, it must be able to adapt to changing business requirements and contexts, allowing for effective modification, administration, and management. Because corporate mergers and divestitures are the order of the day, the data warehouse must be transportable. Components of the system are able to be installed in a variety of hardware/software implementations without heroic rewriting. This, in turn, implies the use of open, standards-based components with reusability and important characteristics. The design guideline of high coherence and loose coupling remains valid. The parts of the system should be tight and coherent. They should able to stand on their own behind well-defined interfaces that represent the contract by which they are able to be accessed. At the same time, they should be loosely coupled. A change in one module must not cause a bug to show up as a side effect "over there" in another module. The data should be hidden behind consistent, well-defined interfaces. However, if you know the API (application programming interface), then it must be available. Information and functionality are available by defined interfaces, paths, and connections from elsewhere in the system, including across distributed nodes. Data and transactions must work together across environments from different vendors and implementations. Complexity of implementation is hidden; simplicity of design is presented. Scalability remains one of the nontrivial and highly desirable features of any system architecture. It is particularly important in a data warehousing context where volumes of data are large. A scalable system is one where performance improves linearly or nearly linearly as system components are added to handle additional data volume, users, and processing requirements. In this context, flexibility is the inverse side of scalability. Performance in the face of evolving business context and volume deteriorates gradually without sudden loss of viability, allowing time to respond with corrective action. Those general features of a data warehouse architecture that focus on the technology aspects are summarized in Table 1.1.

Table 1.1: Features of a Data Warehouse Technical Architecture

Secure	Defensible against intentional or accident attack or damage, based on authorization control on the desktop, in the network layer, and at the back-end data stores
Robust	Able to adapt to changing business requirements and contexts, allowing for effective modification, administration, and management; gradual (not sudden) degradation under stress
Transportable	Components of the system can be installed in a variety of hardware/software implementations without heroic rewriting
Open	Implemented either in publicly available standards, independent of the power of single firm, or in the dominant technology design, representing a de facto standard; application programming interfaces are published and modified by change control
Coherent	Made of individual components with defined interfaces that are unaffected by changes in the implementation of other components
Maintainable	Useful life of the system can be prolonged, perhaps indefinitely, by routine attention to features that change or (in effect) wear out due to changes in the environment
Extensible	The system components can be extended to new, unanticipated contexts and situations
Instrumented	The system is provided with built-in sensors or data gathering devices so that if things go wrong, diagnosis is possible without heroic efforts
Reusable	Components are well defined, subjected to configuration management, and documented, so that they can be used again in different contexts
Connected	Information and functionality are available by defined interfaces, paths, and connections from elsewhere in the system, including across distributed nodes
Collaborative	Data and transactions work across environments from different vendors and implementations
Hidden [Data Hiding]	Interfaces are well defined, complexity of implementation is hidden, simplicity of design is presented
Scalable	Performance improves linearly or nearly linearly as system components are added to handle additional data volume, users, and processing requirements
Flexible	Performance in the face of evolving business context and environment deteriorates gradually without sudden loss of viability, allowing time to respond with corrective action

THE ONE FUNDAMENTAL QUESTION

This points directly to *the* one fundamental business question to be answered in the architecture and building of an enterprise data warehouse, and it does so in such a way as to define and address the constraints on constructing a data warehouse aligned with business imperatives. This is the reason why building and operating the data warehouse provides such a powerful lever—a mechanism for management in moving the enterprise in the direction of addressing critical business issues relating to brand development, customer intimacy, and the information supply chain in time. Successful data warehouses are those that accurately represent these issues and the possibility of engaging and resolving them productively in the software, capturing the necessary data, transforming it in the information supply chain, and making it accessible to business analysts and decision makers.

THE ONE QUESTION—
THE THOUSAND AND ONE ANSWERS...

This is *the* fundamental question that the data warehouse is designed and implemented to answer. The number of dimensions that can be "hung" off of a statement of this form tends to grow rapidly. However, the simple and basic idea is to identify, discover, and track who is buying what and at what specific time and place are they doing so. Thus, in its 1001 forms, the data warehouse is designed to answer the question, Who is buying what—and when and where are they doing so? Who [which customer] is buying / using / delivering / shipping / ordering / returning what [products/services] from what outlet / store / clinic / branch [location] on what occasion [when] and why [causation]? With this fundamental question in view, let us now take a step back and consider the basic distinctions on which the data warehouse will be built.

THE FIRST DISTINCTION:
TRANSACTION AND DECISION SUPPORT SYSTEMS

The first distinction is between transactional and decision support systems. This fundamental distinction is between information technology systems that drive business operations on a day-to-day basis and those that determine the outcome of decisions about strategic moves in the market relating to customers, products, suppliers, etc., and the timing of exchanges between them and the firm. This is the difference between transactional (operational) and data warehousing systems. Transactional systems address everyday operations about business events significant to individual customers, products, suppliers, and those mandated by government regulations and agencies. Transactional systems may indeed be strategic, as well as tactical, but strategic the way that a hotel chain that ties its reservation system into that of an airline reservation system is strategic. The competitive advantage of locking down one reservation at the same time that the other one is being made is a good move under any interpretation. Decision support systems, on the other hand, take a broader and more global perspective, especially in terms of a longer and more continuous time horizon over which sales, usage, and product trends are compared and contrasted. Decision support systems, likewise, can be tactical, as well as strategic, but tactical the way that having the right amount of product at the right store at the right time is tactical, even within an overall strategy of reducing inventory through better forecasting.

Much of the transactional work of operational systems concerns answering day-to-day questions about customer service inquiries, product function, delivery schedules, payment schedules, exceptions to expected outcomes, and relations with other business entities (suppliers and customers, up and down stream roles and functions).

As an illustration, transactional questions from an operational system might include:

- When did Mr. Ralph's package with tracking number 423 leave the dock?
- How much is owed on Ms. Arendt's order as of 01/15/1999?
- Has Mr. Wittgenstein's insurance coverage taken effect as of the last week in September?
- How much does Dr. Ramon charge for procedure RKO?
- How many times did Mr. Douglas see Dr. Ramon and on what dates?

These matters are mission critical to the day-to-day business transaction. *They are not data warehouse questions.* To be sure, these are important matters and significant transactions, especially to the customer. But there is a "but." From a data warehouse point of view, these transactions are logically prior to—one might say "subatomic" with respect to—a business relationship with a customer, developing a brand, or driving customer- and product-sustaining activities.

What does *subatomic* mean here? This addresses the level of granularity at which data warehouse facts are defined. For example, if an atomic fact is defined as how much of product Y customer X bought on day Z, then a transaction for product Y in the morning, at noon, and at night are subatomic. To get to the basic, atomic level, the three purchases must be added (aggregated) up to the atomic level. That is not to be taken for granted.

Instead of addressing internal operations and customer service issues, data warehouse questions tend to address marketing and sales analysis, including sales trend and sales analysis, including competitive analysis, product comparisons in a regional (space) or seasonal (time) framework, causal connections between events (advanced applications), usage (including sales) trends, and the behavior of customers as part of a group or profile. Examples of the kinds of questions that get posed:

- What is the weekly shipment for each product, along with the weekly year-to-date amounts, for the eastern region?
- What is the profit attributable to department *XYZ*?
- What are sales by responsible product line manager for September?
- What is the productivity of factory ABC by materials input, shift, and week ending date?
- What is the six-month moving average of product shipments for the last quarter of 1998?
- What are the top ten products, based on first quarter sales and sorted by product name?
- What is the cost of health care services used by employer group X for the third quarter?
- Which dinner menu of the seven optional menus generates the most sales?

These questions invite answers that are different than those required by day-to-day operations. They are both more general and more abstract—more general because they often deal with accumulations of data by brand, region, marketing manager, or extended time period; more focused on understanding and diagnosis than mere descriptions of what is so; more abstract, because quantities are often compared across time and place.

DATA WAREHOUSE SOURCES OF DATA

Data warehouses are sourced from three kinds of transactional systems. These include legacy, ERP (enterprise resource planning), and electronic commerce systems (see Figure 1.4: Data Warehouse Sources of Data.)

Legacy systems used to mean systems hosted on mainframes or midrange computers, usually developed prior to client-server computing initiatives that emerged in the early 1990s. Recently, the term has come to refer only half jokingly to any system already in production. The surprising thing about legacy systems has been their durability. People building systems in the 1970s never expected them to still be around twenty-five years later, but many of them are. It turns out that, if designed properly— a big "if"—software is basically immortal. Once the curve of discovered bugs levels off, it (the legacy system) is really more stable and robust than recent alternatives,which have not proven themselves in a variety of different situations. That is also the case with many legacy systems, which are the bread-and-butter systems for day-to-day transactions and business operations.

However, everyone agrees that the year 2000 bug does present a new situation and one that many older systems will be challenged to accommodate because of near-sighted design decisions of years gone by. This bug is really a highly dramatic special case of lack of attention to testing and accountability for design in a profession that was still struggling to find rigorous standards. It is driving the replacement of many legacy systems with ERP packages. Rather than try to disentangle the years of patches, maintenance, and enhancements under which the millennium bug lurks, replacing the entire configuration actually seems easier. At least it is easier to justify from a management perspective, because additional business requirements can be accommodated. The implementation, however, is in no way easy.

Make no mistake about it, ERP systems are transactional systems. They are run-your-business databases and applications whose data structures are highly snowflaked, normalized, and optimized for high-volume update activity. This is a performance profile at variance with the "read mostly" star schema and dimensions. The "sweet spot" for the implementation of ERP systems are those firms that are fragmented ("diversified") in form but which would benefit from centralization. Benefits include better integration and related processing efficiencies with trading partners who are also implementing ERP systems and improved vertical communications within the firm up and down the internal supply chain. Notice that business processes will have to be changed to accommodate the ERP system, not vice versa. See the discussion in the text box entitled Marriage Made in Heaven or Shot Gun Wedding?

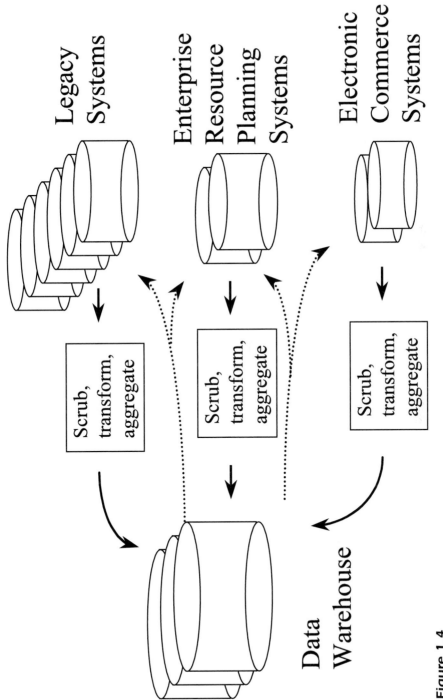

Figure 1.4
Data Warehouse Sources of Data

> ### Marriage Made in Heaven or Shot Gun Wedding?
>
> For example, the Coca-Cola Company and eleven of its major downstream supply chain partners—those are called *anchor bottlers* in the soft drink business—signed a contract with SAP[5] for a single license that covers a dozen or so separate companies. Traditionally, bottlers have a strong heritage of independent operations. As far as the details of business operations are concerned, that is changing. The mandating of a single set of business processes, dictated by the software, on all of the partners is expected to have a unifying result. Much of the value of this undertaking will be realized as Coke's North American data warehousing systems are expanded to accommodate the additional inputs. This will enable Coke and its bottlers to quickly assess the success of promotions or ads for particular brands in certain regions, down to the individual store. For example, the critical path for increasing sales lies through answering such questions as how well 2-liter bottles of Sprite or Diet Coke are moving in one market versus another, whether different sizes of containers would perform better, or whether select products on store shelves would benefit from different positioning. It is important to note that the data warehousing system is a central component, but not the only one, in a process of coordinating the sharing of information (about what's selling, where, and why) between a dozen separate firms unified by a brand, a transactional ERP product, and a data warehouse.

Upon first implementation, the direction in which the data flows is from transaction system to warehouse. This is the typical scenario as operational data is scrubbed and massaged to assist in decision support processes. However, a surprising result occurs as the unified representations of the dimensions built to support the warehouse "feedback" into the transactional system. It turns out that the representations of the customer, product, and other crucial enterprise dimensions in the data warehouse are consistent, coherent, and of a superior data quality than are those in the transactional system. This is most often the case with legacy systems that have data quality and integrity issues, but it is also the case with new ERP systems that may have different quality and integrity issues, precisely because they are getting the "kinks" worked out in the "college of hard knocks." This is depicted as the dotted line "feedback" in Figure 1.4: Data Warehouse Sources of Data. Such feedback does *not* make the data warehouse into a data hub, which is and remains a separate architecture and product space. The point of data warehousing remains decision support, but a decision is an idle wheel unless, at times, it moves relevant parts of the transactional systems, and that is what is depicted here.

For example, feedback from the data warehouse to transaction systems is a typical advanced application in data warehousing. The data warehouse actually becomes the "front-end" at one phase in the information supply chain. When the data warehouse is used for a forecasting application, orders can be generated to the transactional system. The idea of a forecast is precisely to prepare transactional systems to accommodate expected demand. This demand is invisible, as long as one remains at the level of elementary detail transactions. But when the warehouse forecasting application surfaces, a trend based on aggregations is visible, as long as one is viewing only elementary transactions detail. Orders can be generated from the warehouse to the transactional system to adjust inventory, to provide replenishment, or to take actions to allocate resources to accommodate the forecasted demand. This is sometimes called *sourcing* the forecast because that is what it does—provide a source to satisfy orders.

On the other hand, the "nightmare scenario" for those contemplating ERP implementation is the complementary situation. The firm is decentralized *and* has competitive advantages from such diversity of processes and approaches. Construction companies, investment banking firms, and technology firms whose work varies significantly from project to project fit such a profile. They benefit from local customizations and accommodations that do not necessarily scale to uniform processes at the total enterprise level. Such firms are poor candidates for standardization through ERP systems because they eliminate the differences that are the source of advantage.

A development occurring as this book goes to press—too recent for much experience to have been accumulated with the option—is the offering of data warehouse products from ERP vendors. Such an option might make sense if the only source of warehouse data is the ERP system itself. After all, no one knows an ERP system better than its own vendor. On the other hand, different competencies and methods are involved in building transactional and warehouse systems. The first are optimized for update, direct manipulation of single records, and high numbers of short transactions, the latter for "read mostly" access, browsing, and relatively smaller numbers of longer transactions. It makes sense to apply to the ERP vendor "warehouse solution" many of the distinctions and methods that will be developed in the following chapters on metadata, the information supply chain, OLAP, and aggregation. Does the product construct a cube on a special purpose server, does it have "reach through" back to underlying relational data, is it a star schema or a snowflake approach?

Finally, a third source of data for the warehouse is electronic commerce (EC) systems. Business-to-business electronic commerce systems include intra- and Internet-based systems. These build on the business imperative of electronic data interchange (EDI), cost reductions, and increased efficiencies in supply and value chain management. The business case for eliminating manual processing has always been a strong one. The coordination of commitments entailed in optimizing the distribution of products in manufacturing and retailing invites "action at a distance," the real power of commerce "over the wire." This case is augmented by pressures for just-in-time deliveries to manage and reduce inventories, for vendor-managed inventories (where the supplier has visibility to the customer's on-shelf inventory), and for disintermediation (eliminating the middleman). What the Internet does is insert a new group of "open" technologies on which to base action at a distance. It provides a sort of entry level "value-added network" (VAN) for the conduct of EC, thus lowering the bar to small and midsized companies. Business-to-business EC is what has experienced solid, low double-digit growth for years on the order of 20%.[6] However, it is consumer sales over the Internet that has generated the buzz in the trade and popular press outlets. To be sure, as the trust of the consumer grows—especially where branded products are concerned (FedEx, Amazon, Toys-R-Us, United Airlines)[7]—the bet is that the Internet as a channel will be perceived as being as reliable as the telephone. With good industrial strength security—once again, a big "if"—the Internet holds the promise of being even more reliable. Thus, TCP/IP is the new dial tone for deliveries to the busy professional. Capturing this data in useable form and forwarding it for analysis to the data warehouse, either directly or through intermediate transactional systems, is essential to have a complete picture of enterprise business systems at work. The real knowledge occurs when business managers are able to answer questions about what percentage of business is occurring in what channel—call center business, retail outlet, Internet sales—and what factors influence the mix and dynamics of each. This points in the direction of yet another advanced application—data cubes, aggregations, and dimensions based on who is clicking on what web pages and who is ordering from them.

Each of these sources of data—legacy, ERP, and EC systems—represents a different path or different channel for capturing inputs to the data warehouse. Relative to the data warehouse, they are systems functioning as information producers; the warehouse itself includes the information manager function; and the business analysts who use the warehouse, in turn, are the information consumers. The movements of data between these systems implies a work flow as a coordination of commitments. The commitments are business imperatives, such as developing customer relations, developing product brand, and optimizing the supply and value chains. The knowledge to understand and further these initiatives emerges from the interaction of enterprise systems in the crucible of invention of information technology application to the optimization of business processes.

DIMENSIONS

The one fundamental question names basic business drivers—customers, products, services, suppliers, locations, channels, periods of time within which events occur, and additional other entities significant to the business. When these business drivers are abstracted and represented in a relational database, they are called *dimensions*. Dimensions are what give meaning to facts and make them unique. As you can see, dimensions are really very close to what data modelers and database administrators call *entities*. Normal people would call them whatever we designate by means of the nouns in our language. They are the basic states of affairs—persons, places, things—of which the real world is composed, that is, the real world of business being represented in the database. Database professionals sometimes have strong feelings—bordering on religious intensity—about how many structures (tables and relations) are required to represent accurately the real world of the business without redundancy or risk of inconsistencies during update processing. The "right answer" is generally described as "normalized data," and when compromises are intentionally made to improve performance, that is "denormalization." However, it should be clear from the business drivers that, if one has a reasonable approximation to the structure, relations, and components of the business, one can practically and pragmatically use them to

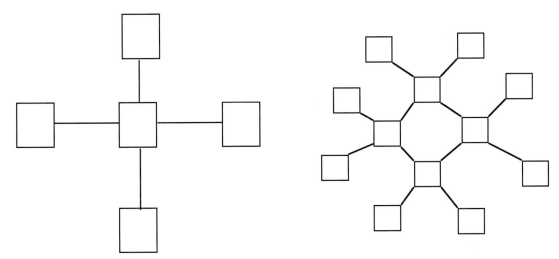

Figure 1.5
The Star Schema and the Snowflake

guide the decision-making activities of that business. Keep in mind throughout this discussion that agreement in detail on these fundamental business drivers—the dimensions—will go a long way toward avoiding misunderstanding. Such agreement is not to be taken for granted and often must be attained as a result of a struggle between professionals of good will willing to compromise with reality and one another.

Some information technology (IT) professionals—database administrators, in particular—are concerned about building a consistent and extendible model of their data. They do this (among many reasons) to validate that the system is logically coherent and workable, prior to incurring the effort and expense of implementing it in hardware, software, and applications. At a high level, this model consists of things—products, customers, locations (stores), and time periods)—and relations between them—customers "buy" or "take delivery of" or "use" products, etc. Naturally, based on these two basic components, the model is called an *entity-relationship* diagram (ER diagram). Of course, there is a lot more to an ER diagram than this, but as soon as one introduces the term *dimension*, a controversy occurs.

It is now a matter of controversy in the data warehousing industry whether a different kind of model, method of analysis, or even principles of thinking are required to deal with dimensional data, as opposed to classical ER diagrams. It is true that, as a visual presentation, the resulting diagram of a data warehouse data model has a significantly different visual appearance than does that presented by the ER diagram of a transactional system. In short, the resulting data models certainly appear to be different. The one looks a bit like a snowflake, elegant and complex. The other looks more like a star, a simple central body surrounded by multiple structures (see Figure 1.5: The Star Schema and the Snowflake).

The essential claim of this guide is that the methods and principles of relational model are valid and sound when applied to data warehouses. This may not be completely clear to the reader until the chapter on data warehouse technical design, but the executive summary must be attempted. Whether the data modeling exercise is called *dimensional* or *ER*, the rules are the same: Atomic data satisfies first normal form. Each attribute is dependent on a primary key. Each attribute depends on the key, the entire key, and nothing but the key. Deciding between multiple candidate keys requires appreciation of data semantics and functional dependencies. Independent attributes, whether constrained by particular business rules, should be broken out into separate tables to eliminate redundancy and to update anomalies. The same method yields different results because the purposes of transactional and decision support systems are different. So, the degree of abstraction and perspective on the analysis are different. This results in different boundaries to the entities that have been identified. Both entities and dimensions are abstractions of business objects that we encounter in the world of commerce and trade. The one is abstracted and refined to speed concise update processing. The other is abstracted and refined to speed access and inquiries. Nevertheless, considerable overlap exists. The fact table, as an entity, satisfies third normal form, but it is rather like an abstract data type (ADT), in that it represents a point in time where a customer interacts with (buys, takes delivery of, uses, etc.) a product. The supporting dimension structures, such as product, customer, calendar, promotion, or channel, are consciously denormalized into long, attribute-filled structures to improve performance. In particular, browsing performance is optimized in this way. Notice, however, that this denormalization is a defined and proven method of solving certain problems within the ER diagram and relational model under any interpretation. It is quite consistent with the ER method.

Issue: Dimensional Versus Entity-Relational Diagramming

Reasonable persons might disagree about whether it (dimensional data modeling) is useful in one context or another, but that disagreement occurs within the framework of the classic ER approach to data analysis and definition. In fact, if one looked at other kinds of systems, one might easily come up with other figures besides a snowflake and a star. Systems that store images of documents ("imaging" systems) tend to have a bulky back-end, due to the collection of binary large objects—the BLOBs. They resemble a hippopotamus. Others are shaped more like a giant squid, with tentacles in every direction. The shape is interesting but accidental. It is a useful mnemonic device but otherwise without significance. Mark down the imagined requirement for a different method of data analysis from relational modeling for data warehouses as one of the great nonissues of data warehouse development. The rigors of data modeling cannot be escaped that easily. If you already understand ER diagramming, don't sign up for yet another course in dimensional data modeling. The course will tell you when to break the rules of ER diagramming. But it will not really provide any fundamental new rules. Rather, study the questions, parameters, and concepts of your business and how they appear in the business of decision support.

Finally, dimensions provide the paths along which basic aggregation, roll up, or drill down of the data occur. This path lies along a hierarchy. Thus, customers are often grouped into geographic hierarchies—individual customer, section, district, region, or area (for example). Customer purchases or uses of relevant products at selected places and times are summarized into sections, then into districts, then into regions, and, finally, into areas. A high-level customer aggregate—say, at the region or area level in the hierarchy—summarizes a lot of information about the behavior of customers. Products often fall into the hierarchies with which we are familiar as consumers—universal product code (UPC), item, product, brand, or category. Alternative hierarchies can coexist and result in different "segmentations" of the market or ways of using the product. Products in the insurance, finance, or subscription services industries have their own characteristic groupings, highly customized by industry. The basic point being made here is to note that the paths along which "drilling" or "aggregation" occurs is laid out in advance by the contents of the dimensions.

THE DATA WAREHOUSE FACT

A customer buys a product at a certain location at a certain time. When the intersection of these four dimensions occurs, a sale is made. The point at which these dimensions intersect, providing an answer to the fundamental question, is a basic business event—a transaction. That sale is describable as amount of dollars received, number of items sold, weight of goods to be shipped, etc.—a quantity that is a continuous value that can be added to other sales similar in definition. A meaningful and *measurable* event of significance to the business occurs at the intersection point of these dimensions. The intersection of these dimensions—it is hard to visualize more than three at a time—provides us with a fundamental feature. We have now defined a *fact*.

A *fact* is a measurement captured from an event in the marketplace. It is the moment of value when the customer intersects with the product at a particular space and time. It is the raw material for knowledge—observations. This is a significant result. (See Figure 1.6: What Is a Data Warehouse Fact?)

A data warehouse *fact* is defined as an intersection of the dimensions constituting the basic entities of the business transaction. Naturally, a *transaction* is not yet a business relationship. Brand development, customer intimacy, sales trend analysis, and product trends are of the essence. These are what provide a breakthrough for the business. However, we at least have a start in understanding how the structures are designed and built that will provide the subsequent breakthrough.

At this juncture, the number of dimensions that can be drawn through the point of intersection is easily and usefully multiplied—store (location), vendor, promotion, ship-to location, sales personnel, and department. The dimensions tend to define the boundaries of the vertical industry segment. The dimensions are a catalog of entities and attributes of significance to the vertical market and industry in question. If you are

What is a Data Warehouse FACT?

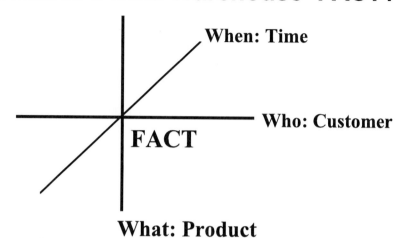

What: Product
[FACT: For Performance: Numeric, Continuous,
Additive; and an Intersection of Dimensions:]

Figure 1.6
What Is a Data Warehouse Fact?

selling seats in an airplane, frequent flier number is an important dimension. If you are selling rooms in a hotel, room type, service, and classification are important. If you are a managed care health maintenance organization (HMO), the diagnosis, procedure code, physician, lab tests, etc. are significant. The thing to keep in mind is that the logic and principles are fundamentally the same as those that apply to product and customer.

Describing a data warehouse fact occurs in terms of the key term, *granularity*. Granularity, as the label suggests, expresses how much detail is captured in the elementary fact. Are we dealing with a line item on an invoice? Or are we dealing with all customer purchases of a given product for a given day? Or week? How much detail is required to make decisions about business practices, strategies, and initiatives? Operational systems contain the most detailed data available, because that is where it is originally generated—think of the lines on the invoice. However, they usually do not attempt to store and manipulate three to five years of this data. The work-in-progress data stores of transactional systems usually encompass two to three months—a fiscal quarter. The rest gets archived to inexpensive media, such as sequential tape. Thus, the determination of the level of granularity—how elementary or composite are the facts—is an important consideration throughout the data warehouse life cycle. It is a critical performance factor, but it is a factor driven by the business questions that we want to answer, not by the technology. To be more precise, it is a factor driven by the business and constrained by the technology. Too large a granularity, and specific details are lost and much processing time is wasted trying to decompose aggregates;

too small a granularity, and the trees obscure the forest. Much valuable processing time is wasted building aggregates.

Along these lines, an issue of the first importance arises when a dimension gets restated due to corporate reorganization, change in business process required to support marketing or product design, or merger and acquisition. For example, *restating geography* means that the customers belonging to region *A* and *B* are now defined as belonging to regions *X* and *Y*. Indeed, there is some volatility in the geographic dimension, due the benefit of periodically realigning customers with marketing talent and distribution of service resources. In these days of the "virtual corporation," it is easier to rearrange hierarchies conceptually to accommodate business processes to which geography may be irrelevant. Because the dimensions are what make the aggregations of facts meaningful and unique, the redefinition of a geographic dimension implies that the aggregate has to be rebuilt. This is possible only if the data available is sufficiently granular. If the details have been "thrown away," once the aggregate has been built, the meaning of the aggregate has been irretrievably lost because the dimension is redefined. Customer "Lou" used to belong to region *A*, but now belongs to region *X*. It is no longer possible to compare an aggregate containing (using) region *A* at a point in time *prior* to the redefinition with one containing region *A* at a point in time *after* the redefinition. This is because they mean something different—region *A* used to contain data relating to customer Lou, but now does not. One must be able to break down all of the related and relevant aggregates into their respective details and add them up again to restate the meaning of the aggregate in *consistent* dimensional terms. It is sufficient to note the trade-off here between the work of carrying the granular, detailed data and the flexibility of being able to rebuild aggregates and facts if the definitions of dimensions are restated. This is indeed an advanced case—discussion of it is resumed in the section on reinterpreting the past in the chapter on data warehouse data quality.

The basic distinctions between dimensions and facts is now available. Therefore, it is appropriate to turn to design, admittedly at a high level, as befits a chapter on basic distinctions.

THE DATA WAREHOUSE MODEL OF THE BUSINESS: ALIGNMENT

The data model resulting from building a central fact structure with the smaller, supporting dimensional structures placed around the periphery resembles a star. The intersection of different dimensions to form a structure off of which, in effect, a fact table is "hung" actually looks like a star. The fact table in the center and the various dimensions are the many points of the star. Hence, the name given to this form of joining together the various dimensions is the "star schema." When a customer id, a product id, and a time period are used to determine which rows are selected from the fact table, this way of collecting the data is called the *star schema join* (see Figure 1.7: The Star Schema). In many ways, this is another name for the entire dimensional model. The really important and interesting thing to note is that the model includes and represents aspects of the market and the product supply chain, as well as the transactions driving the business. This is not an entirely new feature because, to be useful, any minimal data model requires a working representation of the customer, but it is a new emphasis. Rather than modeling only those features internal to the integrated firm, other relevant and useful aspects of the business environment are brought onto the radar, so to speak—up- and downstream suppliers, vendors, partners, channels, and customer- and product-sustaining activities of all kinds. Thus, the alignment of the structure of the data warehouse and fundamental aspects of the business are so logical, precise, and exact that one might suspect a preestablished harmony (see Figure 1.8: The Data Warehouse Model of the Business).

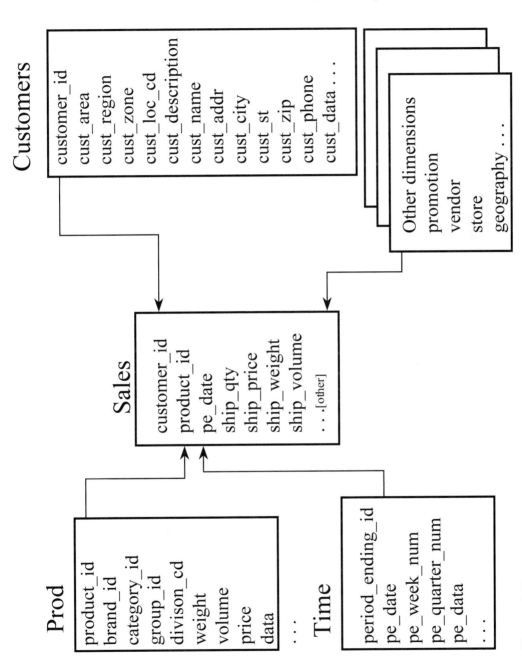

Figure 1.7
The Star Schema

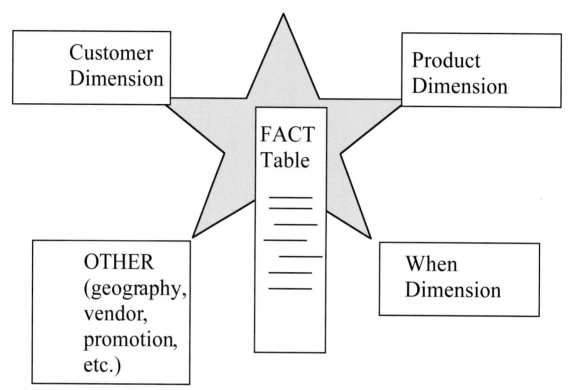

Figure 1.8
The Data Warehouse Model of the Business

THE DATA CUBE

First among these is the data cube. The *cube* is defined as the available aggregation by
basic business drivers, depicted as completed data structures suitable for inquiry by
SQL or an other interface. The cube is the intersection of dimensions to provide a
structure of facts of interest to the business. The classic cube is customer by product
by time or place (see Figure 1.9: The Data Cube). If a customer, Lou, buys a Tasty
brand granola bar on April 2, 1999 for one dollar, that transaction is given meaning as
the intersection of customer, product (item), and date. The most important quantities
associated with the transaction are the sale price (one dollar) and the item sold. These
quantities form the granularity of the cube. The granularity of the cube is a function
of the intersecting of the dimensions. Granularity is the specific level of detail that
results when dimensions intersect—usually, a quantitative, continuous, value, able to
be added. If an individual customer intersects with an individual product, the result is
an elementary granularity or atomic transaction. Cubes are listed toward the top of the
list of available *metadata*. Although not limited to cubes, metadata are defined as the
available aggregations by basic business drivers, usually defined and maintained in a
repository built on a relational catalog. Thus, cubes end up being a subset of metadata,

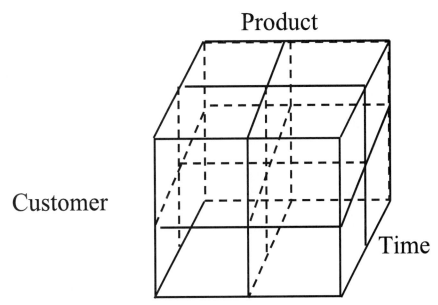

Figure 1.9
The Data Cube

which, however, is a more encompassing category to which a chapter in this book is devoted (see Chapter Thirteen on metadata and metaphor).

What is not easy to depict visually in Figures 1.7 and 1.9 by means of the star schema and the data cube is the trade-off between the two approaches. In general, the star schema join is a method and a result of using a relational database to represent the data by means of associations between multiple dimensions and facts. In general, cubes are contrasted with the star schema in comparing the methods and results of OLAP engines with relational databases. However, this is an inaccurate oversimplification, because cubes can be translated into star schemas, and vice versa. The real issue is trade-offs involving performance and efficiency. High-level aggregations are more efficiently stored as cubes, having been precalculated; alternative roll-ups across changing dimensions are more efficiently and flexibly performed by star schemas, based on available details. (Further details on the strengths and limitations of OLAP will be addressed in Chapter Fifteen.)

AGGREGATION

Having defined data cubes, we can define aggregates in terms of them. Aggregates are cubes that accumulate (summarize) basic transaction data, based on a meaningful intersection of nonelementary levels in the dimensional hierarchy. Customers are grouped into regions. Brands contain products. A single sale occurs as a customer buys a product. A region does not buy a brand. There (obviously) is no such elementary transaction, but a group of customers in a region buy a set of products contained in a brand. This abstraction—sales of brand X to customers in the southwest region—generates an entirely new level of emerging insight, a knowledge of the behavior of a brand and customers. An aggregate reports on the accumulation of brand by region. Here, the granularity is not an atomic (or basic or elementary) transaction, but rather an aggregation. As indicated, an aggregation is an accumulation or summing of additive values, based on a meaningful intersection of dimensions. The dimensions in questions are typically nonindividual and themselves describe a group, as in the cited example. The variety, number, and uses of aggregations are functions of the groupings of customers, products, and other dimensions into hierarchies. One can arbitrarily start combining customer by product, customer by subbrand, customer by brand, customer by product category, and region by product, region by subbrand, region by brand, region by product category, etc., up and down the available hierarchies. Next, cross-reference these and similar aggregates by time period—customer by product by week, customer by product by month, customer by product by quarter, region by brand by week, region by brand by month, region by brand by quarter, etc. This is useful only as an intellectual exercise to appreciate the multiplying diversity of aggregates. Other methods—to be examined in Chapter 14 on aggregation—will be required to proceed efficiently into this area.

DATA WAREHOUSE PROFESSIONAL ROLES

Roles are divided into three kinds. Roles include information producers, information consumers, and information managers. The administrator who collects information from a customer who is opening an account at a bank is a producer. A bank automatic teller machine (ATM) is an information producer. The thousands of detailed transactions are captured in data stores, logs, and electronic media of all kinds. Likewise, a point of sale terminal—a cash register—at a retail discount store is a data collector and information source. As shoppers and buyers of merchandise and services, we are all information producers. We leave literally hundreds of electronic traces per day on operational systems every time a credit or debit card is swiped at a gas pump or lunch counter. These transactions, in turn, trigger others—interbank transfers of money or names and addresses added to mailing and direct marketing phone lists. Automated data processing systems are an entire class of information producers. Once the data is captured, processes up and down the information supply chain are triggered to manipulate, transform, and report on the relevance and results of the processing. Every time we pick up the phone or other communication device, we leave traces for telephone billing systems to charge back to us or to telemarketers to try their latest promotion. This yields a vibrant image of the modern digital economy. In truth, insofar as these transactions find their way into warehouse data structures, we are all caught up in the data warehousing initiative, whether we know it or not. Thus, in the data warehouse world, other systems—legacy, ERP, and EC systems, the detailed transactions of the day-to-day operations—are the information producers. They are the source of data to be extracted, scrubbed, transformed and aggregated, and loaded into the data warehouse structures.

Information consumers include marketing specialists working on positioning or selling products and services. The users of automated systems are in the role of consumers of the information that the system is designed to deliver. Customer-focused firms contain legions of staff devoted to consuming all kinds of information about the customers to whom they are dedicated. Product performance staffs are consumers of data about the behavior of their products. Because of handoffs from one phase in the information supply chain to another, one person's information producer is another's information consumer. However, in general, in the data warehouse world business analysts, marketing and product specialists, and knowledge workers of all kinds are the main consumers of the data warehouse content. The thousand and one questions they pose about who is buying what and where and when are what the data warehouse is designed and constructed to answer. Answers to our questions, especially when they enable timely and useful business initiatives, are good examples of the benefits of knowledge.

The information managers—caretakers or custodians—are charged with lining up the questions posed by the knowledge workers and the information consumers, with the data captured in the data warehouse from the information producers. It is this lining up—this "alignment"—that presents the challenge faced by the traditional information technology roles. This alignment is what makes answering the questions and what makes the data warehouse an information product—a form of knowledge—in itself.

To be sure, the traditional IT roles—designer, developer, network administrator, security administrator, storage administrator, and data and database administrator—are still valid. For example, the distinction between data administration and database administration is captured by assigning tasks emphasizing logic, design, and modeling to the data administrator; whereas, the database administrator is responsible for physical implementation, backup, and maintenance of the database proper. However, both roles are now informed by the requirement not only to do software engineering and integration but to applying these skills to knowledge management and integration.

From the designer's point of view, this means that requirements are not complete until the questions are answered. What would we like to know about the behavior of the customer (or product, service, etc.) and how can we use the available data to address the answer? Here, *knowledge engineering* means constructing an answer that traces the data forming the answer back to the question and doing so in context.

From the development perspective, *knowledge engineering* means using desktop tools, database-stored procedures, and application code to represent the answer to the question in such a way that it is understandable, meaningful, and actionable in a timely way.

The more accurate and useful the content stored in the data warehouse, the more important that it be secured against unauthorized access, whether accidental or malicious. The security administrator is charged with leading the effort to secure the enterprise's resources. It is important that the knowledge be made accessible to those who need it, regardless of time or place. Here is the case for distributed and WANs. The network administrator provides the leadership.

From the DBA's (database administrator) perspective, data quality is critical path. If the data possesses the features that mark it as a quality product—if it is accurate, unambiguous, credible, and has other attributes, to be discussed in the Chapter Six on data warehouse data quality—it deserves the respect and dignity that we accord to information when we call it *knowledge*. Another way of saying the same thing, with a significant difference in emphasis, is that the DBA is the "lightning rod" for data integrity, the first mark of data quality, even if the end-user is the ultimate owner of the data and ultimate arbiter of its validity. In any real world situation, as soon as the DBA team provides "access to data" (makes it available within the framework of a basically sound warehouse design), the phone is likely to ring with an opportunity to improve data quality. Something is incomplete, and a "bootstrap" operation is initiated, within which data quality is pursued as an iterative goal.

THE DATA WAREHOUSE PROCESS MODEL

The data warehouse process model can now be defined. It is defined as that which transforms operational into decision support data. This includes the processes of data scrubbing, denormalization, aggregation, partitioning, parallel access, and asking business questions grounded in the data to generate the business intelligence (knowledge) that makes a difference in reaching a firm's business objectives and delivering competitive advantage. This process will be the subject of Chapter Twelve: Data Warehouse Operations: The Information Supply Chain.

The information supply chain makes data warehousing seem like a miracle in many ways. The input is dirty data and, after a serious amount of data scrubbing, out comes what we call *knowledge*. Although an oversimplification, that is what happens in the information supply chain. The data warehouse itself is an information product of the highest degree, which, when used to answer questions about the business, generates knowledge in the full sense of the term.

SUMMARY . . . .

Data warehousing is a system architecture, not a software product or application. Architecture refers to first principles of representation, design, and information technology processing results. The essential minimal working set of data warehousing components includes the database engine, application (analytic) server, connectivity, and presentation layer. When made the target of a fundamental inquiry, data warehousing architecture turns out to be a variation on work flow. Here "work flow" is understood as a coordination of commitments, not an assembly line. Commitment is not usually regarded as a feature of architecture. But it is. Commitment to the business imperative to know the customer, build (develop) the brand, know who is buying what.

Data warehousing addresses *the* one fundamental question: Who is buying (using) what product (service) and when and where are they doing so? This immediately implies the first distinction between transactional and decision support systems. Data warehousing sources of data are itemized as transactional (legacy) systems, ERP systems, and e-commerce systems. Basic business drivers get represented in the data warehousing database as structures such as customers, products, services, suppliers, locations, calendars, etc. The point at which dimensions intersect – a customer buys a product at a certain store on a certain day (say) – is a quantitative, measurable event (transaction) that can be captured as a data warehouse fact. The definition of a fact and its granularity is a significant result. Other basic distinctions are defined including, the data cube, aggregations, the star schema (the data warehousing model of the business), data warehousing professional roles, and the data warehousing process model.

[1] Brown, G. Spencer. *The Laws of Form*, New York, NY: The Julian Press, Inc. 1972, p. 1.

[2] The word *architecture* contains the ancient Greek roots *arche,* meaning "ruling principle" or "first principle," and *techne,* meaning "method," from which we get *technology.* Thus, *archeology* is the study of first (or old) things, and *archetype* is another word for first patterns or basic designs.

[3] A graphic of the full-blown Zachman framework document is available for noncommercial use as a free download in TIF format off of Zachman's web page at www.ZIFA.com, courtesy of the Zachman Institute for Framework Analysis.

[4] The reader will note the challenge to the author (and so to the reader) of defining many interrelated terms at once. For those instances where a subsequent chapter is devoted to a term or subject or when the reader finds that the terms come too fast, an extensive glossary is provided. Please make good use of it.

[5] As reported by Bob Violino in Extended Enterprise, *Information Week*, March 22, 1999. SAP stands for Systems Applications & Products in Data Processing. See www.sap.com.

[6] The relevant technologies will be detailed below. Here, the emphasis is on understanding interacting enterprise business systems. In my opinion, the best concise introduction to the subject of EC is Peter G. W. Keen and Craigg Ballance, *On-Line Profits: A Manager's Guide to Electronic Commerce*, 1997, which cuts through the hype of growth doubling every year and documents good, solid year-to-year gains. (See also www.PeterKeen.com.)

[7] Another work by P. Keen, T. Terragrossa, and W. Mougayar makes an important distinction between brands born on the web—Amazon, Virtual Vineyards, Auto-by-Tel—and brands successfully extended to the web—FedEx, UAL, Cisco Systems—see *The Business Internet and Intranets* (Harvard Business School Press, 1998).

2   *A Short History of Data*

In this chapter...

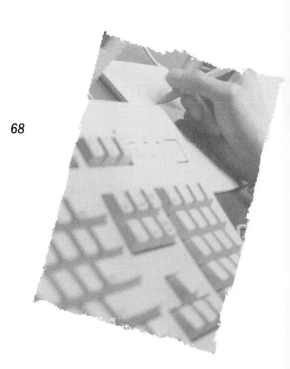

IN THE BEGINNING . . .

This chapter has a historical title and perspective. Indeed, history is the form in which the technology dynamics are presented. However, this history also implies an approach to the development and transformation of technology, so the last section of this chapter addresses a model of technology dynamics.

One of the earliest records we have of anyone building a data warehouse occurs toward the beginning of the Gospel according to Saint Matthew. Paraphrasing the biblical narrative: The word went out from the Emperor Caesar that an accounting and a census for tax purposes was to occur; and the people were to be counted in the towns of their birth. Now it happened that Mary, being about to give birth, and there being no room at the inn, sought shelter in a stable. Thus, the first databases were accumulations of records mandated to govern an empire. The first data cube was probably a summarization of revenue with the dimensions of locality, tax collecting agent, and time period. An even earlier but perhaps less well-known example occurs as Moses and Aaron were leading the people of Israel out of bondage to Egypt. All people twenty years old or above are numbered and "ransomed"—that is, taxed—a half a shekel apiece to support centralized "service of the congregation" (see Exodus 30:11–16). The same idea of a census and tax to support administrative expenses of the community is operative. Naturally, these records were stored, not on electronic media, but on parchment. They were, however, true databases, consisting of information and methods to access the data. Insofar as this revenue was put to productive uses building roads, harbors, libraries, and bastions against barbarian invasion, it is not an exaggeration to assert such infrastructure formed the foundation of Western civilization.

FAST FORWARD TO MODERN TIMES

Fast forward to modern times. In this case, *modern* means 1905 because in the period following that year, records at the legendary DuPont Corporation indicate that a true data warehouse function was in operation. A frenzy of data gathering, organizing, and aggregating was underway in an attempt to bring order to the emerging vertically integrated, multifunction corporation. Not only was data on sales orders, invoices, and shipping orders accumulated—aggregated—into daily sales reports, but the dollar quantity of product sold by each branch office was captured. This, in turn, was used to provide insight, that is, knowledge, into market trends and pricing behavior, with a time delay of five days. By the end of the five days, the vice president had reports on his desk. In addition, the numbers were aggregated by branch and the data was entered on punched cards, using end-of-the-century (nineteenth century, that is) technology.[2] Thus was born the first data cube by sales, branch, and date. Make no mistake, this was true data warehousing. Functionally the leaders at DuPont were working with (and, indeed, inventing) the distinction between the knowledge required for decision support of the firm and that provided periodically for summary financial statements. The system was designed to encourage salesmen to consider both price and volume in their marketing activities. Also because such consideration was precisely what was required to line up the salesperson's incentives with the overall interest of the firm, this knowledge tended to maximize profit for both the company and the sales force. Today, this would be called *alignment*. It forms the nucleus of the distinction between decision support and financial transaction (operational) information.

THE VERY IDEA OF DECISION SUPPORT

As Figure 2.1 indicates, as soon as a firm starts collecting and summarizing transactional data, as DuPont did in 1905, there is an immediate idea of using it to guide, support, and direct management decisions of all kinds. The number of systems required to achieve decisions support, in addition to basic operations, is not immediately or intuitively obvious. To attain unity of purpose and consistency of results, analysts and system designers might reasonably conclude that one system is the answer.

This was probably the case in 1970 at Management Decision Systems (MDS) in Waltham, Massachusetts, just up the road from the Massachusetts Institute of Technology (MIT), where John Little and Glen Urban were applying ideas on statistics and decision trees to making business judgments (see Keen, 1978; Raiffa, 1968; Strassmann and Hespos, 1957). MDS had two consulting practices in which they were attempting to model markets and financial results. The focus was on modeling, not data, because the data capture function was not sufficiently rationalized, and computer systems simply didn't have the horse power to crunch it. Although it was just a speck on the horizon then, there was also a product called *Express*, used on a time-sharing basis in the

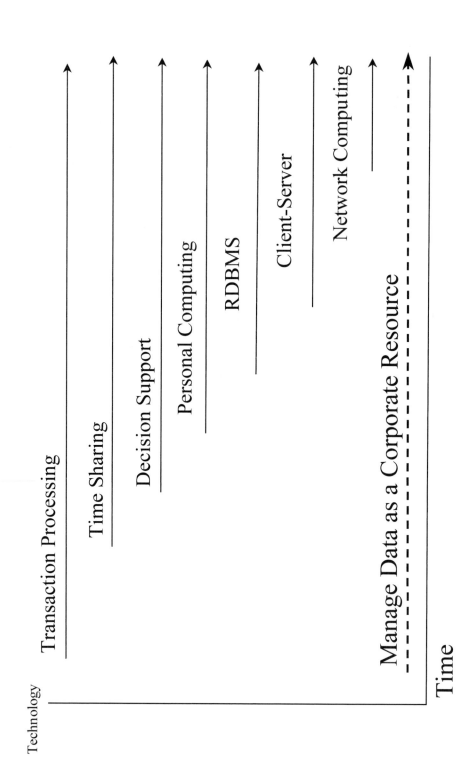

Figure 2.1
A Short History of Data: Managing Data as a Corporate Resource

marketing, sales analysis, and financial modeling projects. First, the MDS consultants would gather requirements from the client financial staff. Next, they would gather requirements from the marketing staff (or vice versa); then they would try to reconcile them in a single-system deliverable. Of course, this often resulted in a processing loop, from which no timely exit could be found. This was due to differences in scope, scale, and time horizon of the financial and marketing decision support processes. The bottom line results at MDS as an ongoing business concern apparently reflected these frustrations, and Information Resources, Inc. (IRI) acquired MDS, with the Express product eventually going to Oracle. Oracle, in turn, after several rewrites, promoted it as a central part of its OLAP and data warehousing tool chest. Naturally, one way to identify the pioneers is by the arrows in their backs. By the end of the 1970s, pioneers on the decision support trail had both progress and causalities to report.

In an unrelated initiative, several of the designers of the prototype personal computer, the Xerox Star Workstation from the Xerox Palo Alto Research Center (PARC), founded a company named *Metaphor*. In 1982, Dave Liddle and Don Massaro left Xerox to found Metaphor, accompanied by Yogen Dalal, Charles Irby, and Ralph Kimball. Due to the limited performance capabilities of the hardware at the time, dedicated file server hardware was required to execute decision support applications. The Metaphor computer system, basically a server with database-like capabilities plus hardware, was launched in 1983. It prompted many new features, such as a client-server architecture and the application of multidimensional cubes to relational data that would eventually form the essence of dimensional data warehousing. The fact that separate hardware was required forced the decision support system to be separate from the transactional system. So, between 1983 and 1988, about 400 data warehousing systems were installed.[3] By then, the economics of special purpose hardware had crossed the line of the emergence of the relational database and the personal computer. Liddle was responsible for IBM acquiring Metaphor in 1988, after which he founded a research and development center called *Interval*.[4] Dr. Kimball went on to found Red Brick, which he left long before its acquisition by Informix. However, the validity of making the decisions support system a separate one for reasons of scope, scale, and performance had its proof of concept many times over.

Personal Vignette

It is an act of complete immodesty on the part of the author even to mention his name in the same section as some of these giants of modern business and computing. Nevertheless, I can recall starting an assignment at a market research client to build a consumer product analysis database using client-server tools and DB2 in about 1992 and witnessing various workstations being packed away for removal in boxes labeled *Metaphor*. Even earlier, when the author was a recent university graduate, he was hired as an employee by Blue Cross of Illinois in 1980. Shortly thereafter, he attended a Warnier/Orr design class. The lesson in understanding and reengineering any system was to work backward from system results to necessary inputs. This had the effect of mapping output from reports, screens, and interfaces onto input supplied by upstream information producers. Whatever else was left over had to be derived from rules for manipulating the data. The lesson—remember, this was in 1980—was to manage data as a corporate resource. That meant unified definitions of data elements, a data dictionary from which the inconsistencies and anomalies had been expelled, and a view of the system as regarded by the end-user, the information consumer. It would be fair to say that this was a "best practice" in its day and is still one today.

As the text box entitled *Personal* Vignette testifies, the imperative to manage data across the enterprise as a corporate-wide asset has been taught in the industry for nearly 20 years. As these words are being written, after the client-server revolution has come and given way to network-centric computing, after object-oriented computing has been transformed and validated as component technology, after the death and rebirth of the mainframe as the enterprise server—managing data as a corporate resource is still the guiding goal and sometimes elusive vision for business leaders, system architects, infrastructure builders, and technology specialists at every level. Professionals of all kinds in companies small, medium, and large acknowledge the result is incomplete in spite of application of the best available business practices, talent, and technology. Why has this proven to be so difficult to accomplish? Why are things going to be different this time?

FROM MAINFRAMES TO PCs

Once real business computers became available—that would, among others, be the IBM 360 in 1964—data center operations were defined and driven by time-sharing. These were fast machines sharing computing cycles between slow streams of input data. The image of data was that of a sequential stream of card images, to which relatively expensive and scarce computing cycles were applied. The idea of random access to a central repository or shared database was a breakthrough. In point of fact, the deployment of individual, hierarchical files on a process-by-process or application-by-application basis presented a "good enough" solution and a dominant design.[5] It allowed incremental, step-by-step development without the big bang required by migrating to, loading, and turning on a centralized database. Two or three related hierarchical files could give most of the functionality, concurrency, recoverability, and data integrity of a genuine database without the expensive licensing and database staffing requirements.

However, for large systems requiring high performance and high standards of centralized backup, recovery, storage management, and data integrity, the centralized database provided powerful and, indeed, indispensable mechanisms for data management. The hierarchical and network databases, furnished by IMS and IDMS from IBM and Cullinet (the latter purchased by Computer Associates), dominated the market for large-scale databases in the mid-1980s. Both the costs and the results were impressive by any measure. However, large, centralized staffs of database administrators were required to provide access to the data in a way that came to seem like a secret rite of initiation. The limitations of the paradigm percolated ever closer to the surface, especially in contexts where astute business analysts wanted to manipulate summary data for decision making.

Then the personal computer revolution hit in the mid-1980s. Data was decentralized and distributed to the information center, a hot bed of end-user computing. There, people who understood the business were able to slice and dice on their desktops, using that breakthrough technology, the spreadsheet. However, the PC, for all its power and pizzazz, was an interface without depth. Connectivity to corporate data had to wait. That connectivity promised to be really significant, but it had to wait another few years until the 1990s. Meanwhile, simultaneously and in another context, in the late 1980s, the relational database (and the English-like interface to it) were emerging as a candidate dominant database design for processing transactions that, within a few years, would end up assimilating and replacing the hierarchical and network database models.

THE PROMISE OF THE RELATIONAL DATABASE

The relational database management system (RDBMS) is an implementation of a simple yet sophisticated view of data that represents collections of business events or other objects of interest to the enterprise as tables. The relational database has proven to be a popular and effective approach to database design, attaining the status of a "dominant design" in the market. That is a solution of useable hardware, software, and business procedures that the market regards as defining the terms of competition. This loyalty is demonstrated as customers vote with their dollars. Any seller who wants to be a participant in such a market has to adhere to the conventions, standards, and design features of the dominant design.

The reasons for this outcome—the success of the RDBMS—are many. They are commercially available with a variety of options. Money and interest are behind the approach. They are intuitive. Business people feel comfortable with the form of a table, which is a glorified spreadsheet (and more). They are fundamental—they appeal to thinking in rows and columns—that is, groupings of entities and attributes. In hiding complexity behind a simple approach, tables satisfy an inclination to effortless accomplishment. Finally, relational technology is an implementation of a simple yet powerful branch of mathematics called *set theory*. Basically, tables are sets, which, in turn, are collections of members or elements, with a relationship that defines their membership.

As an illustration, all customers are identified as belonging to the collection of customers by means of a uniquely identifying social security number (for example). Other defining characteristics—address, city, state, and zip—are grouped together with the individual customer to form an entity (a person, place, or thing of interest to the business). Likewise, products have a unique product identifier. A small number of basic operations—union, intersection, difference—act on tables to produce other tables. As an instance of a relationship, consider that when a customer *buys* a product, the association between the two is stored, along with the date and time and amount of sale or other defining attributes, in yet another table. This third table might be called the *sales* table, because it captures that relationship. You start with tables, apply basic operations, and end up with other tables. The system is complete, closed, practical and efficient from a processing point of view. In practice, systems get considerably more complex. However, simple and elegant defining principles means that getting started is easy. The basics are within reach. Advanced principles build on them. To be sure, the details of such theory are abstract and complex, but they are also pervasive because, like the idea of number, they form part of the very structure of the way we describe business and its operations.

These tables—rather like individual spreadsheets, where each row is guaranteed to be unique by the presence of a primary key—are connected to one another and to events in the real world of business. These connections may be very concrete—sales order to the line items, type of, inclusion of part to whole—or abstract—one-to-one, one-to-many, many-to-many. Indeed, the more general version of the connection is abstracted and placed in the relational database model to cover the multiplicity of business cases that arise. Examples of two of the more common cases are the order and line items contained within and the header and detail of the retail order. When these transactional structures are transformed into data warehousing ones, the header information about customer order and general product attributes become data dimensions, and the detail information about line items are cross-referenced and captured in the fact structure(s). When the connections defining business entities—customers *buying* products—are represented completely within the information system, they are captured as relationships in the precise sense indicated above. However, when the connections are between the data warehousing system representing this relationship and the world of business in which this activity is occurring, the connection is harder to capture precisely. The uses of data modeling and semantics discussed in Chapters Seven (section on data normalization) and Thirteen (section on semantics) will be useful to better understand the nature of this connection. The connection between the data warehouse and the world of business it represents is this feature of alignment between the business and the technology implementing it. Much that is exact can and will be said about this alignment but, ultimately, it is something that just shows itself.

As indicated, the reasons for the success of the relational model were many. Ultimately, it was the user interface—something first called *Structured English-like Query Language* or *SEQUEL*—that really resulted in the early enthusiasm for and "take-off" of the relational approach. The interface to the technology is intuitive and powerful. The same form of language—structured query language (SQL)—is used to add and update data as is used to inquire against it. SQL is a well defined standard. It has been implemented by a wide range of database vendors. Thus, applications based on SQL are relatively easy to port from one environment to another (as long as one avoids vendor-specific extensions). SQL is also the language used to inquire against the relational catalog, a central repository ("database about the database") that provides information on the basic constituents of the database—e.g., the columns contained in tables, the data types of the elements making up the tables, the relations between indexes and columns, and the like. So, as a general rule, the application programmer uses the same language interface as the database administrator, thus promoting a kind of data democracy.

DATA EVERY WHICH WAY

The promise of the RDBMS, according to Ralph Kimball, is delivery of data "every which way" (Kimball, 1995: 23).[6] This is a fundamental insight into the history of data. Whereas other databases require a redefinition of the database schema (the record layout) to represent, store, and access data differently, the relational database allows any arbitrary column to be selected and concatenated with any arbitrary column from any other table. Such concatenation is not free. Computing cycles are required, and the operation may become cost-inefficient. Nevertheless, the transformations are feasible and defined within the implementation. New possibilities are opened and defined. Thus, the relational database is the natural platform for the data warehouse. In terms of the relational model, the essential data warehouse is the intersection of three relations: the customer, the product (or service), and the event of their intersection (purchase, use, delivery). Thus, the fundamental question of data warehousing is, Who is buying (using) what and when? Naturally, the question has a thousand and one variations: Substitute services for products and delivery, use, and other actions for purchases.

The tables collect features, characteristics, or attributes related to the basic entities being represented. For example, customers have such features as age, income, address. For purposes of data processing, a unique way of identifying the customer is essential. When this identifier is unique and makes sense, it is said to functionally determine (that is, define) the basic entity represented. In data warehousing terms, these relations are called *dimensions* if they map to concrete business entities, *facts* if they are quantities that are made unique by the dimensions.

FROM CLIENT-SERVER TO THIN CLIENT COMPUTING

The most visible part of client-server systems is the GUI—a way of presenting data using buttons, boxes, and iconic widgets of all kinds in the fashion of the familiar windowing format. The relational database, along with the GUI, made possible client-server computing. Above all, the promise of client-server was to provide the user of the computer with access to data. GUI at the front-end, RDBMS at the back-end, and a connectivity layer in between, typically, a piece of software called a *gateway* for translating PC to mainframe encoding—that is the basic architecture that made possible client-server computing. Such client-server architecture is inherently data-warehouse-friendly. It conveniently facilitates the mapping of data extraction and transformation tools to the back-end database. It locates data analysis tools at the front-end to perform OLAP. Finally, metadata is situated as the middle layer, binding both front- and back-ends together in a flexible and intelligible way. An entire chapter will be devoted to metadata (Chapter Thirteen)—but in the meantime, a good working definition is that metadata is basically the principles by which transactional and data warehousing systems interoperate or work with one another.

What client-server computing did not sufficiently count on was the complexity of maintaining a consistent image of hundreds or thousands of different desktops across an entire enterprise. Of course, the issue that client-server brought to a new level of intensity was that between the flexible response to individual needs and corporate efficiencies of centralized control. After coming up in the liberty and unstructured freedom of the PC world, end-users were less than enthusiastic about surrendering control to the centralized data center over what versions of personal software and utilities they could keep on their personal computer hard drives. Yet, central oversight had its advantages. This is because inconsistent software or worse (i.e., viruses) could prevent them from accessing the shared resources to which they were entitled and depended on by virtue of the very definition of client-server architecture. Security, version, and change control of software, system development, and evolution invite centralized management.

Client-server, as it emerged historically, is built on leveraging distributed computing cycles to the desktop. Hence, client-server contained within itself the seeds of its own limitations and even downfall. The client on the desktop became fatter and fatter. *Bloatware* is the descriptive term that surfaced to describe the approach of including all software components and applications—database, browser, utilities—as part of the operating system.[7] The desktop is at risk of collapsing under its own weight. Alternatives start to look attractive, and they get a foothold in the market. The number of desktops within a given enterprise continues to grow to the thousands. The total cost of ownership escalates dramatically; and the impracticality of upgrading so many personal computers one by one becomes evident. Automated software distribution seems like a requirement but it continues to be frustrated by simple things like PC users who routinely turn off their work stations at the end of the day. What better case could be made for the attractiveness of network computing? Thus, the allure of the "thin client," whereby a piece of software called a *browser* is able to read and download applications ("applets") from the network server without anything having to be stored on the local storage (hard drive) of the computer.

All these vicissitudes hastened the emergence in 1995 of Internet computing based on open standards, and the intranet, in which the sun sets on the "fat client"—the PC—and client-server computing is reborn by replacing the end-user interface with the universal client, the web browser. Here a small set of enabling technologies—HTML, Java, TCP/IP, HTTP, the web browser, the router—makes possible the distribution of data on what is literally a planet-wide basis.[8] The power of action-at-a-distance is realized by the Internet. The "webification" of the planet—and of the corporation by means of the Intranet—raises the stakes of data "every which way" to data "every which way any time any place."

WHY WILL THINGS BE DIFFERENT THIS TIME?

The dilemma deepens as business enterprises continue to thrash from both too much and too little data. Raw transactions on an elementary level about basic business events are vast in scope and depth. Think about what gets archived in application transaction logs and how difficult it can be to extract any significant information from such sources. The marketing staff is frustrated by the length of time and amount of effort required to produce intelligence on the purchasing behavior of key customers. They are even frustrated at trying to identify the candidates for key customers. The paradox of knowledge hunger amidst plenty of raw data is characteristic of the misalignment of software systems with the underlying business processes (and vice versa). After almost 20 years of effort, the lesson of managing data as a corporate asset or enterprise-wide resource is still a real challenge. This challenge is actively being engaged, explored, and pursued. The outcome is not to be taken for granted (see Figure 2.1: A Short History of Data: Managing Data as a Corporate Resource). The result of this short history so far is that, amidst all the paradigm shifts, what stands fast is data. However, why will things really be different this time?

Survey Answers, Not the Answer

The claim has been made in academic contexts that the data warehouse is required to improve data quality.[9] Logically, this is to mistake the cause and effect, though in practice the data warehouse can become a lightning rod for concentrating all manner of data quality issues. Data quality is logically established prior to a successful data warehouse initiative. Data quality is a presupposition of a successful data warehouse installation. The statement "the warehouse is required to improve data quality" sounds like the answer to a survey question. Surveys often surface the rationalization for doing something rather than the actual motivation or incentive. As J.P. Morgan pointed out, there is the reason people give and then there is the real reason. In fact, without quality data, the data warehouse is just another data garage sale, a collection of possibly useful but throw-away stuff, mostly copied from the transactional and operational systems. The data warehouse is a lens that brings quality into focus. At the risk of mixing the metaphor, this is rather like the tail that wags the dog. The warehouse—at the back-end—has got the upstream enterprise systems moving back and forth to provide the data quality, without which the warehouse has no point. Quality may indeed be free but that's because quality is priceless, not effortless (see Chapter Six on total data warehouse quality).

THE MORE THINGS CHANGE, THE MORE THEY STAY THE SAME

What, then, is the answer to the question? Why, after 20 years of trying to manage data as a corporate resource across the enterprise, will things be different this time? What are the prospects of finally getting it right?

There's the one-word answer, the paradoxical answer, and the answer that is really a drill down on the one-word answer. The one-word answer is *alignment*. Line up the business questions and the technology used to represent the answer to the questions. What that means will become evident shortly.

The paradoxical answer is that the more things change, the more they stay the same. We are still trying to manage data as a corporate resource, because it's difficult to reconcile local differences with global definitions. While trying to reconcile the local parts and the global whole, the meaning of *data* changed. In 1980, it referred to the data in transactional and operational systems. By 1990, it also referred to the data in decision support systems. For better or worse, operational systems work well enough. The heroics required to keep the transactions flowing have been made routine. Schedulers in the data center set off the beepers, scrambling the staff needed to put out the fires and deliver the reports on the transactional data on time. However, it seems as if we are fighting the same battle again but over different questions—decision support issues and queries—and directed at different data.

The business and technology are aligned in the warehouse by accurately representing those dimensions of the business that define, implement, and sustain such activities as customer service, brand development, market penetration, supply and value chain operations, and the like. This alignment is the critical path for successful construction, deployment, and use of the data warehouse. Things are going to be different this time, because the pragmatic knowledge made possible by the warehouse enables a bootstrap operation that is self-reinforcing and self-perpetuating. Those organizations that don't succeed in locking onto the cycle of positive feedback will not be around, at least not in their current form, to know—or tell—the difference. True, management must still use the available talent and technology to survive the day-to-day struggles. If we knew what technology could protect us against our own mistakes, everyone would agree to get more of that. The proper profile of such a technology is one by which risk is reduced and insight enhanced.

The phrase "manage data as a corporate resource" now means constraining and even torturing the data to answer questions that drive decisions about both day-to-day operations (tactics) and business direction (strategy and decisions support). That is another way of expressing the function of the data warehouse. Thus, the pendulum of business and technology alignment swings back in the direction of centralization and the server. As Peter Keen has stated, the server is the strategy (Keen, 1997), but with a difference. Data warehousing as a business solution and a system artifact is reaching take-off speed, due to the convergence of several dominant designs of technology. These dominant designs include relational databases, increased computing power of commodity hardware platforms, decreased prices of electronic storage, commercially workable solutions to such grand challenge computing problems as parallel processing, computing industry open standards such as SQL, and the availability of sufficiently robust desktop tools to slice and dice data. The relational database catalog has always been regarded as a great idea, as well as a teasing taste of something more and better. The idea of a repository to keep track of business intelligence and rules, data dictionary information, and knowledge specific to a given enterprise has been around since at least as long as the first client-server systems. This technology initiative has regrouped under the influence of data warehousing as the requirement for metadata. Once the questions to be answered by the data warehouse start multiplying and the forms of knowledge start to include scheduling and tracing source to target data definitions and systems, a metadata repository becomes an operational necessity (see Figure 2.2: Data Warehousing Take-Off Technologies). As a business integration technology, data warehousing has quietly reached take-off speed and is now more than ever a business imperative for corporate America. This is a quiet transformation, in comparison, for example, with the press coverage—much of it well deserved, to be sure—surrounding the Java language and network computing. It is a transformation, nonetheless.[10] Amidst all the paradigm shifts, what has remained firm is the imperative to manage data as a corporate resource. However, as an isolated technology, the data warehouse can no more do that than can any other technology in isolation, but as a method of aligning business imperatives and their representation in the system, data warehousing can, indeed, make a crucial difference. This short history of data, culminating in the emergence of the data warehouse, implies an underlying model of technology development. To that model we now turn.

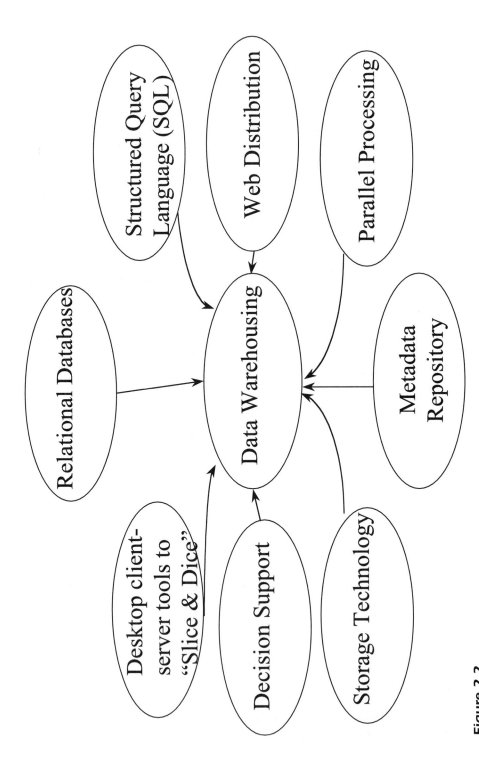

Figure 2.2
Data Warehousing Take-Off Technologies

MODEL OF TECHNOLOGY DYNAMICS

The purpose of this model of technology is to make sense of the questions, Why data warehousing? and Why now?

The dynamics of technology change are often pictured as a series of waves. This is a compelling image but one that is little understood. Why waves? Why not a fountain or the unfolding of a caterpillar into a butterfly (for example)? Actually, any picture of discontinuous change would work. The waves are discontinuous. If you, i.e., your firm, miss catching a ride on the one, you will be becalmed and behind the pack until the next wave arrives. (The idea of catching the wave is attributed to Fumio Kodama, 1991.)

Each wave represents a candidate for successful innovation, a technology that makes a difference. Each wave represents a system on which the market has voted with its dollars. It is a de facto standard, a dominant design, something on which a firm supplying technology must align and address itself if it is to have any hope of attaining market share or success with prospective customers. Likewise, the dominant design is that which customers, firms using technology, regard as the standard satisfying the majority of requirements for functionality and enabling mutually beneficial and orderly operations and communication within an industry segment.

Time after time, in the history of technology, one technology is displaced by another that has apparently arrived out of left field. These include both large innovations and small ones. They apply to hardware as well as to software and they apply to computing technologies as well as to noncomputing technologies. This applies to transistors, electronic calculators, integrated circuits, Winchester disk drives, and supercomputers, as well as steam shovels, typewriters, refrigeration, steel mills, and retailing. Thus, the typewriter manufacturers—Smith Corona, Remington, and Underwood—were among the last in the world to realize that the computer was really the ultimate word processor. The ease with which typographical errors could be corrected—no messy correction fluid—presented a compelling case, in spite of the initially more complex infrastructure and user interface (more complex until voice recognition software is generalized). In a completely different context, the leading traditional retail chains, such as Montgomery Ward, Wiebolts, R. H. Macy, and Bloomingdale, were driven into the ground by the emergence of discount chains. Only those such as S.S. Kresge and Dayton Hudson, which reinvented themselves as K-Mart and the Target chain, weathered the storm. Each of these technologies—discount retailing, the word processor, the hydraulic excavator, the minimill—represents a dominant design.[11]

In its own day, the mainframe computer represented a dominant design. So did the IBM 360 Operating System. Whatever one may say about today's mainframe option, OS/390, it is a direct descendent. It presents continuous, incremental change, no matter that orders of magnitude more computing power, usability, and robustness are deployed.

While the mainframe vendor was interested only in jobs budgeted at the high end of the market in the multimillion-dollar range, the client-server upstarts were able to get a foothold at the bottom end of the market. The risks were minimal in buying a couple of copies of SQL Server and a point-and-click GUI builder for a few thousand dollars. It offered a radical and discontinuous computing option. In many ways, it was a less powerful computing option, because client-server configurations actually had fewer machine instructions available, though arguably at a more favorable price point. From the perspective of mainframe computing, these client-server upstarts were disruptive of the status quo. The customers they attracted were a side show.

From the perspective of a multibillion-dollar mainframe market, these customers were not really surmounting the corporate hurdle. They were not really worth bothering about. This was an entirely rational judgment from one perspective. If you are a 50 billion-dollar company, the price point is a $5 million-dollar (or so) sale, not a $50,000 one. They were not a significant percentage of anyone's current business—unless you happened to be a small and hungry client-server upstart. The big players would rather fight it out in a crowded market than risk entry into an unproved market of unknown and possibly limited extent. These were customers in small- and medium-sized firms for whom mainframe computing was an expensive and not altogether satisfactory solution. Then all of a sudden it turned out that even the larger corporations were composed of literally thousands of departments that fit the description of this computing profile. The resulting march up market of the client-server option transformed the very definition of the mainframe itself. The march up market meant not only increasing client-server market share but the application of this technology to vertical market niches where mid-range servers or small mainframes were used previously.

In fact, client-server presents dominant designs within a dominant design. With Windows on the desktop and a relational database at the back-end, client-server is composed of dominant designs from at least two different computing models.

It is in this context that data warehousing represents the transition from transaction-based, operational systems to decision-support processes. In both the mainframe, client-server, and network computing options, the relational database management system has presented a dominant design in handling enterprise data.

Now one might think that the universal database (UDB) presents the next wave. But, in many ways, the UDB is completely continuous with relational database systems and presents step-by-step progress with them based on "accessing data every which way" in a rule-governed form according to Codd's twelve principles. (On E.F. Codd, see Codd, 1972, and Chapter Eight, the section entitled "Twelve Principles.") However, saying that the UDB is pure incremental progress is a misleading oversimplification. True, it is a sustaining technology in the best sense of the word, building on the relational foundation. In so many ways, the variety of data types that can be handled—text, image, web-based documents, video, etc.—promises new applications about which previously we could not even dream (text mining, web harvesting, or warehouse-enabled workflow come to mind). Thus, the UDB promises to be a source of discontinuous change; but it is really a matter of emphasis as to what the conclusion is because it is the application, not the underlying technology, that is the source of the discontinuous change. Despite the significance of the technology, the jury is still out as to the overall effect and evaluation of the result.

As transactional systems were made the core of routine and standardized solutions, they were encapsulated in off-the-shelf yet complex and customizable packages called ERP systems. The decision support challenge—data warehousing—moved to center stage. It is not that enterprise-wide transaction systems require less effort. Rather, the effort required is more standardized and has fewer points of tangency. Data warehousing systems are necessarily more closely coupled to the particulars of specific businesses, and, as such, they are systems where original design, integration, and construction skills are still at a premium.

As a solution to data management, the data warehouse is made possible by the convergence of several dominant technologies. The technologies that make it possible also make it increasingly attractive. These are nicely summarized in Figure 2.2 (Data Warehousing Take-Off Technologies) and include: the RDBMS, incremental advances in storage technology, especially RAID (Redundant Arrays of Independent Disks) for data recoverability without lengthy backup, slicing and dicing data functions on the desktop, the relentless march of computing power, parallel computing using commodity processors, understanding of the decision support by IT, the idea of a repository of business rules (and subsequently metadata), and the way in which software has become a part of every business process. (Each of the bubbles in Figure 2.2 will receive treatment in an entire chapter or substantial sections of following chapters.)

As an answer to decision support issues, the data warehouse, in turn, makes possible process breakthroughs in such customer and product-sustaining domains as cross-selling, brand development, supply chain management, forecasting, value chain enhancements (marketing), profitability analysis, and others. In a basic perspective, the availability of consistent, scrubbed, meaningful data aligned with basic business drivers becomes the target for slicing and dicing on the work station that reveals business trends, customer segments, and comparisons between them that were not previously visible. In an advanced perspective, the "zero latency enterprise" is enabled—one whose information architecture allows it to be informed without delay of supply chain events and to adjust automatically. The availability of warehouse data makes possible entirely new sets of applications, not previously imaged, in data mining, undirected and directed knowledge discovery, hypothesis validation, and the coordination of business commitments in the information supply chain. (These will be addressed in chapters on justifying the data warehouse from a business perspective (Chapter Three), the information supply chain (Chapter Twelve), OLAP (Chapter Fifteen), and data mining (Chapter Seventeen).)

The focus on this chapter has been a short history of data. The idea—a number of separate technologies and trends in business—has reached a critical mass. Thus, "take-off" of the enterprise data warehousing initiative occurs. This is distinct from a history of data warehousing as such. However, in conclusion, a couple of important footnotes from the history of data warehousing are worth mentioning. The roots of data warehousing lie in the domain of decision support. No sooner did business managers confront operational data than the requirement immediately surfaced to summarize, aggregate, and use it to get visibility to management's planning, controlling, and guiding roles. Decision support is the common matrix out of which both OLAP and relational data warehousing emerged.[12] An OLAP tool from the early 1970s was named *Express* and became *Oracle Express* when acquired (and reengineered) by the latter company. The defining data warehousing terms *fact* and *dimension* were used in the context of consumer goods retailing at Nielsen Marketing Research and General Mills in the late 1960s where, according to Ralph Kimball (see Kimball et al., 1998: 27), he first encountered them. Kimball was also involved, starting in 1984, with the Metaphor company and product. This was an early relational approach to facts and dimensions. Because of the limited computing power of the PCs and servers of the time, Metaphor made use of proprietary hardware and software, inspired by the usability and user friendliness of the Mac. Although a success with companies such as Nielsen, the "Metaphor machine" did not make the transition to the general, wider market, and the company was eventually acquired by IBM. Meanwhile, when managers with enough rank and clout realized that they had the influence needed to command an intuitive, easy-to-use interface, decision support became executive information systems (EIS). As an example, an early EIS product from the mid-1980s was Pilot's Command Center. The emphasis was on a simplified executive interface suitable for mouse or touch screen. Although no longer available, many of these concepts were incorporated into follow-up products from the same company. Also worthy of note are Lotus's multidimensional spreadsheet Improv and Microsoft's answer, Excel pivot tables. Naturally, one issue here is that mentioning any product name will invite a chorus of "me too" from other worthy vendors, many of whom have valid claims on being the first with a valuable and useful function or feature. That is why this chapter began as it did. If you start tracing back all the useful data warehousing features, you ultimately arrive at a singular insight—the symbol of which is a star in the winter night sky toward which wise men are converging. That insight can be expressed in several related ways – that amid all the paradigm shifts, data is what stands fast; that aligning business imperatives with the structures of the software system representing the business yields a data warehouse map of the enterprise; that the data warehouse makes possible transforming that data into knowledge. These things are fundamental. One might think that they require no further justification but, given the nature of business, everything has to be questioned and justified. Thus, it is to the matter of justifying the data warehousing initiative that we now turn.

SUMMARY . . . .

Highlights of a short history of data include early references to data warehousing in the bible and DuPont's 1905 invention of the distinction between financial reporting of day-to-day operations and summarizations for managerial control (decision support). Anecdotes from the history of data are engaged to show the vicissitudes of managing decision support data amidst paradigm shifts such as time-sharing, client-server, and thin client computing. The answer to the question "What stands fast?" is data and the imperative to manage it as a corporate asset. The suggestion is that data warehousing is distinct in that it is not another paradigm shift. It is a continuous, progressive development based on decision support. Things will be different (i.e., better) this time because key enabling technologies (needed to manage data as a corporate asset) have reached critical mass. They are detailed. In turn, this implies a model of technology development which is discussed in its relevance to data warehousing and the business imperatives data warehousing addresses.

[1] Anonymous French proverb.

[2] For further details of this fascinating chapter in the history of the modern corporation, see Johnson and Kaplan, 1988: Chapter 4, especially pp. 76, 161. The connection with data warehousing is my inference, and the authors would not necessarily agree.

[3] Ralph Kimball (personal communication). Dr. Kimball is now www.rkimball.com.

[4] Funded by Paul Allen, see www.Interval.com.

[5] A "dominant design" is explained in the last section of this chapter, "Model of Technology Dynamics." The glossary contains a working definition of the term for those who do not wish to await that section. Those wishing a thorough treatment of the subject in greater detail than can be undertaken here should consult the outstanding works of Clayton Christensen and James M. Utterback in the bibliography.

[6] Although Ralph Kimball deserves to be credited with defining the validation of dimensional data, he denies inventing it, saying the terms were used at such companies as General Mills, Kraft, and Nielsen Market Research as early as the 1960s. We stand on the shoulders of giants—or at least really knowledgeable individuals—who have come before us.

[7] I first heard the term *bloatware* at a talk by Arno Penzias in Toronto in November 1998. However, he denies having invented the term, crediting Bill Joy at a talk in Aspen the previous autumn.

[8] See Agosta, 1997: 38 for a useful glossary of Internet terms and technology.

[9] See Watson and Haley, 1998: 34 for the results of an engaging survey.

[10] The Meta Group estimates the data warehouse market already at $2.8 billion in 1996 may have reached $8 billion in 1998 (see **Knowledge Management World**, August 1998, volume 7, issue 9).

[11] For further details and additional fascinating case histories, see Utterback, 1995: 23ff and Christensen, 1998.

[12] This history and many additional fascinating details are to be found in a white paper by Nigel Pendse at www.olapreport.com. See www.olapreport/origins.htm.

3 *Justifying Data Warehousing*

In this chapter...

*Design software components to
represent basic business processes . . . .
All visions degenerate into budgets.*
Paul Strassmann[1]

COMPETITION FOR LIMITED RESOURCES

$\mathbf{B}$uilding and operating a data warehouse must compete with other business initiatives for scarce resources. For instance, one of the biggest competitors is the software maintenance budget itself. Using resources, funds, and staff to design and build a data warehouse is one way of applying the capital available to an ongoing business concern. Every dollar spent on new systems is estimated to require five to ten additional dollars in maintenance over the life of the system. That leaves stiff competition for the remaining resources, according to which new development has to be supported out of 20–40% of the overall budget. (That percentage drops further if one includes Y2K follow-up and Euro currency conversion.)

The warehouse initiative has to be compared and has to compete with ones in EC, replacing fat clients with network-centric thin ones and installing enterprise resource planning systems. Given scarce information technology staff and limited competencies in these areas, even if the funds were available, tough prioritization has to occur. This calls for strategic thinking.

Strategy distinguishes purpose from constraints. If the managerial function of a firm is at loose ends about its strategy, a data warehouse, in itself, will not provide one. However, there are many business strategies to which a data warehouse can significantly contribute. Data warehouse systems fit nicely with a variety of bread-and-butter business initiatives. These include inward-facing strategies, such as inventory reduction, more speedy inventory turns, and related operational enhancements to the logistics and supply chain; customer-facing strategies, such as brand development and improved positioning of product category development in the value and marketing chain; and innovation and breakthrough strategies, such as new and existing product quality improvement through a total quality management (TQM) initiative. Constraints describe what challenges an organization must address, handle, or overcome to move ahead. For example, access to legacy system data is not the purpose of the data warehouse but a constraint that must be addressed; likewise, with the coordination of work flow between the data warehouse and ERP and EC system. The good news is that hard, quantifiable opportunities—cost savings, market improvements, and product developments—are within reach from business initiatives, at the center of which lie data warehouse systems. These quantifiable opportunities provide a firm grounding for the step of justifying the cost of developing and operating data warehousing systems.

AN INTEGRATED BUSINESS AND TECHNOLOGY SOLUTION

The key is to organize a business-driven approach that lines up with a data warehouse technology architecture representing the business. For example, a multibillion-dollar consumer-oriented retail organization successfully implemented a pilot warehouse, subsequently rolled out company-wide, to reduce inventories by 20%. Although this was already one of the best-run companies in the world, with high levels of project management competence and *esprit de corps*, not all of the fat had been removed from the supply chain. Double-digit savings, never easy to obtain, were within the cross hairs and, at latest report, being realized by the production system.

The data warehouse played a central role in this business initiative, but it was part of an integrated solution and not the stand-alone answer. The important thing to realize is that business benefits flowed from management and coordination of people, processes, and knowledge—not from the most advanced technology. In one example, three years of transactional data from the sales system were summarized on a periodic basis by product and customer. This was used to inform and drive a forecasting subsystem. The forecast of demand itself was a major result of a complex and subtle aggregation model in which year-to-year smoothing of variables produced an estimate of future demand. The forecast was then used to provide a reality check on the performance of the analyst planning the operational logistics designed to satisfy that demand. This was not merely an inquiry function. The planning staff was further able to update the forecast, based on local intelligence—promotions, advertising, and seasonal variations due to weather and exact holiday schedules. Because accountability is usually an important part of an integrated business solution, it should be noted that the forecast, as adjusted by local business intelligence, was the one to which the staff was held accountable. In other words, it was the automated function, as subsequently refined, tweaked, and improved by the business analyst that made a difference to more accurate inventory forecasting and inventory reduction. The consequence of this integrated approach to attaining a 20% savings on nearly a billion dollars of inventory is that such savings can be captured to help defray the cost of much technology and system integration expertise.

ECONOMIC VALUE, NOT BUSINESS BENEFITS

The lesson to be gained here is that the realized savings—in this case, measurably reduced inventory—is economic value added to the business, not merely an information technology benefit. The data warehouse formed an integrated part of generating (making possible) this economic value. However, that happened when the data warehouse was used in connection with new business roles, logistic planning analysis, local business intelligence, and management coordination. The devil is indeed in the details. A management process of analysis and negotiation, based on real pragmatic dimensions of the business milieu, was required to determine the contribution of the data warehouse system to the delivery of this economic value added. Although not solely responsible for the real savings, the data warehouse provided infrastructure and applications, without which the improved planning process would be unimaginable. Furthermore, the costs associated with implementing the data warehousing system can be calculated fully and assigned to it unambiguously. The project would not be feasible without the data warehouse and would not be considered without it. Therefore, it remains only to ensure that the management champions, suitably place in the firm's hierarchy, can commit to the process of change and adequately calculate the impact.[2] In short, it is reduced carrying costs that are responsible for the savings, selling, and shipping of products that produces revenue, not the data warehouse system. However, with a data warehouse designed, implemented, accurately aligned, and representing the business drivers of the firm, a technology framework is provided to accomplish the business goals in a timely and cost-effective way. When management effectively evaluates the accomplishments completed with the cooperation of computer-empowered information workers who understand, deploy, and apply the knowledge made possible by the warehouse, the economic value of the data warehouse comes into focus.

Enhanced customer service, superior supply chain management, reduced costs from defects and rework, increased visibility to profitable products and customers—all of these translate into economic value only if they generate a cash flow that exceeds the amount of capital used to produce these benefits. It is beyond the scope of this book to elaborate the complete theory of economic value added (EVA); but the idea is that the only real basis of value is cash. The operating profit (sales minus taxes, expenses, deductions) minus the cost of all the capital used to generate that profit is the free cash flow. As every mom and pop shopkeeper knows, it's the amount of cash in the cigar box behind the counter at the end of the day that counts, not how much money changed hands. Earnings on paper often look a lot better than they really are. This underscores a simple truth: Lower earnings can increase value.[3] How, then, does this apply to data warehouse systems?

Data warehouse systems are components of business processes that should be considered assets. Data warehouse systems participate in business processes that directly generate value. These include marketing, manufacturing, and pricing, for example. Data warehouse systems participate in processes that provide advantages in

Table 3.1

Cost (dollars)	No. of instances	Total cost (dollars)
2500	100	250,000
90000	3	270,000
750,000	1	750,000
Hardware/software Total		1,270,000
Integration, development, and BPR Total		5,180,000
Integration + (hardware/software) Total		6,350,000

dealing with uncertainty and change, including planning and forecasting systems. Finally, data warehouses participate in processes that are required to keep up with the competition. As newer technologies inevitably slide into being commodities, customer- and product-sustaining activities become a cost of doing business. In all of these areas, the data warehouse is a mechanism for providing insight and knowledge into the levers and controls for driving the business.

At this point, an example of how to justify the cost of building the data warehouse is useful. A word of caution is also proper. The following is a simulation of the cash flow analysis for an imaginary data warehouse project. The total cost of the project is estimated as follows (see Table 3.1):

- additional software licenses for a relational database, metadata tool, disk storage, and scheduling resources on the enterprise server of choice are estimated at $750,000
- three additional middleware gateways at $90,000 each, including software licenses, for a total of $270,000
- front-end (desktop) OLAP tools at $2,500 a seat, up to 100 seats, for a total of $250,000
- system integration, development, definition of new business roles, and business process engineering (BPR) costs at five times the cost of the software and hardware—in other words, software and hardware are 20% of the cost of the project; resulting in a total cost of $6.530 million (see Table 3.1).

The cost savings realizable by the project are estimated in terms of inventory carrying costs, coordination costs, and supply chain management costs. A working assumption is that inventory costs 7% of its value to carry and manage. If the enterprise total of $2 billion in inventory could be reduced by 20% through better forecasting and

Table 3.2

Total inventory (dollars)	2,000,000,000
20% of total inventory value (dollars)	200,000,000
Cost of inventory (dollars)	14,000,000
Cost of inventory as %	0.07

Table 3.3

Incremental savings (dollars)	Total savings (dollars)	Year	Rollout
0	0	1	0
4,662,000	4,662,000	2	0.333
4,662,000	9,324,000	3	0.333
4,662,000	13,986,000	4	0.333
14,000	14,000,000	5	0.001

supply chain management using a data warehouse, a $200 million reduction is within reach. Now, 7% of that is $14 million (see Table 3.2). For the sake of discussion, let's say that savings is realizable in 33% increments, starting at the end of year one for a period of three years thereafter (see Table 3.3). It is worth noting that, although 20% inventory reduction was chosen, a number such as 25% is feasible. So, if one wishes to "raise the bar" by undertaking further costly engineering of the related business processes toward the "zero latency enterprise," there is room to grow on the savings side, too. This estimate is, thus, conservative, in that, at this point, it uses numbers less favorable than those that might be marshaled in favor of the project.

The project is estimated over a period of five years, under the assumption that, at the end of five years, the technical, business, and market environment will have changed significantly enough to warrant a basic reappraisal. (Actually, that will be required on a yearly basis.) The hardware budget will be an incurred cost at the end of the first year ($1.25 million), though a depreciation schedule might ameliorate that, and the development and integration costs will be estimated to be used at a rate of $1 million a year on a yearly basis.

The savings will be engaged at the end of year one at a rate of 33% of the inventory carrying and coordination costs. They are expected to level off at the end of year five. Note that the value of reduced inventory continues to accrue on a yearly basis thereafter, in perpetuity. However, the table shows the costs leveling off at that time (after five years), under the assumption that the environment will have shifted enough in that time to render a reappraisal necessary.

An initial investment will be required to build the system, enabling enhanced inventory management through the data warehouse. Thus, the net cash flow for the first year will be negative. Let's estimate the rate of return at a negative 25% if there is an available above-average project that represents a lost opportunity cost. Thereafter, the rate of return improves significantly. The second year, a total of $3.81 million has been spent, and a savings of net $852,000 is realized. That's a 22% return. The third year, total savings start pulling ahead of costs significantly. About $5 million are spent and over $4.2 million are saved, for a return of 84%. However, due to starting out "in the hole," the average rate of return over the five years is about 49% (Table 3.4). This allows for a substantial risk premium on the economic value added. Another thing is usefully emphasized here. Data warehouse integration, development, and coordination costs can be substantial in both absolute and relative terms, and they (the information system development costs) are not the only required investments. Significant coordination costs are implied with the emergence of a new staffing role, the product demand analyst, and the managerial direction and follow-through to get line and staff people to act (or not act), based on the informed and updated forecast. (These costs are depicted in Table 3.1 as 5,180K and are why the integration costs dwarf the hardware/software ones.) In any dynamic industry and market, understanding of the business is incomplete. It is like trying to hit a moving target. This is because much of what is defined as understanding is a snapshot that requires resynchronizing and alignment with reality on a periodic basis. The data warehouse is a tool to implement that alignment. Now, let's take a step back and consider some specific uses of the data warehouse to implement the alignment between business imperatives and the technology.

The Data Warehouse, a Good-Enough Technology

One of the most successful data warehousing projects known to the author provides a further lesson here. No complicated or multimillion-dollar desktop tools were deployed in the initial rollout of the above-cited forecasting system simulation. Indeed, the basis for the success was what the Nobel laureate and technology guru Herbert Simon called a *good-enough technology* (see Simon, 1969: 64). In this case, that meant a back-leveled (old) version of IBM's DB2 database software at the back-end, Microsoft's Visual Basic plus a shrink-wrapped time-series data VB control for the desktop, and the hoary MDI/Sybase gateway connecting the two. Do not let the hyperbole in the trade press about large storage volume numbers render one blind to the importance of ruthlessly prioritizing business imperatives. The target size for the warehouse was on the order of 50 gigabytes.

Table 3.4

Annualized rate of return [avg]	Difference [net cash flow (dollars)]	Total cost (dollars)	Cost incremental (dollars)	Savings incremental (dollars)	Total savings (dollars)	Year	Rollout
-0.25	(2,540,000)	2,540,000	2,540,000	0	0	0	0
0.22	852,000	3,810,000	1,270,000	4,662,000	4,662,000	1	0.333
0.84	4,244,000	5,080,000	1,270,000	4,662,000	9,324,000	2	0.333
1.2	7,636,000	6,350,000	1,270,000	4,662,000	13,986,000	3	0.333
0.83	6,380,000	7,620,000	1,270,000	14,000	14,000,000	4	0.333
[0.494]						5	0.001

SELLING THE DATA WAREHOUSE

In addition to objectively justifying the data warehouse proper, building support for the undertaking also requires persuasive communication. How many worthy projects have succumbed to other priorities simply because those charged with executing them lacked marketing savvy and a perspective on "building the bigger team"? These days, almost any project worth doing requires forging mutually beneficial alliances with other departments and functions for the greater good of the firm as a whole. These other departments and groups are likely to be swamped with work so that they have to appreciate the value of the data warehousing undertaking to make room for the extra effort required to contribute to yet another mission-critical project initiative. Getting other groups to show the same urgency and commitment as the "home team" requires leadership—sometimes also called *selling*—as well as management. Therefore, ideas on selling the data warehouse are reviewed here, not necessarily in any particular order.

First, if people are living in a situation of abundant data but scarce knowledge, the data warehouse, properly designed and implemented, can feed that hunger. Simply delivering more data will not do the job. Delivering knowledge that can be used to make decisions that are of value to the business unit and customer will make a difference.

Second, if a careful description and analysis of the current situation discloses specific unhappiness with which people are living, that can be a powerful lever to move in the direction of data warehousing. If it takes (for example) ten hours to generate fairly basic reports on revenue per customer, stock outages per product per period, supply chain throughput, margin per product, etc., data warehousing can realistically provide relief. In general, change is easier when there is unhappiness with the current situation. In fact, many of these considerations, when quantified with reasonable estimates of deliverables, feed back into the above-cited metrics for justifying the data warehouse.

Third, deliver results early and often. That means partnering with a needy end-user to generate a prototype data warehousing system. The advantages of being able actually to see and touch the solution to one important issue or requirement cannot be overestimated. If carefully crafted, an actual functioning prototype can create a miracle by showing the accuracy (or lack of it) in the data reporting of existing legacy decision support systems. It may sound cynical, but there are many data quality problems "out there" that people are simply blindly accepting. Responding to data problems that have suddenly been made visible in production legacy decision support systems requires the cooperation and commitment of all the key groups. If it turns out that the warehouse information is more accurate, useable, timely, or of a better quality than that delivered by the existing transactional systems, that can create an overwhelming demand among the end-users that even skeptical executives and budget committee are hard-pressed to ignore. This becomes an opportunity for the data warehouse team to provide a solution and everyone else's committed participation as the way to assure the result is attained.

Finally, on the basis of initial small-scale data warehousing success, a vision of the knowledge-based firm can be articulated. In a situation where everyone is already working hard, the prospect of getting the tools to work smarter is an inviting one. The data warehouse is a structure which, when aligned with basic business imperatives, delivers knowledge that can be used to make decisions about running the business. The prospect of having a resource to provide answers to questions we don't even know yet builds confidence and professionalism at many levels in the firm. The alternative is having to build a data warehouse after it is too late to glean competitive advantages and as a mere cost of doing business—just because everyone else has one and knows how to use it. That point may be closer than anyone realizes.

In the remainder of this chapter, the focus shifts from justifying and selling in a narrow perspective to describing the benefits and uses of different types of data warehousing initiatives. Examples of types of data warehousing systems and case vignettes from the companies that use them contribute to the justification of the data warehouse initiative.

THE REPORTING DATA WAREHOUSE: RUNNING FEWER ERRANDS

When designed and implemented properly—big "ifs" under any interpretation—shared data warehousing technology can provide alternatives to support and fund the very job displacement it causes. "Today, millions of well-dressed, desk-bound humans still earn a living by 'running errands' between [computing] machines . . . just to keep the information moving" (Penzias, 1995: 50). The squeeze on middle-management continues as the information required to support decision making becomes available to lower-level staff in productive, line-of-business roles without necessarily having to be massaged and analyzed by layers of middle managers. The role of "knowledge worker" has been around at least since 1973, when Peter Drucker gave it currency in the context of management practices and principles. Now, after over two decades of automation, IT systems are starting to deliver on the promise of providing these information consumers with content worthy of their role.

As an illustration, a data warehouse was built to provide decision support reports and guidance in a large health insurance company. Transactional reports to satisfy regulatory requirements, day-to-day operations, and formal financial closings were left where they were properly defined as belonging, on the transactional system. However, the data warehouse team had done its job in providing scrubbed, consistent, quality data. When the number of quality features and metrics attributable to the data warehouse data begins to get extensive enough, it starts to possess the dignity of "knowledge." All of a sudden, the warehouse data looked superior in quality and, thus, in usability. Would it be possible to use the warehouse data for these other purposes? This presents one of those problems that is also really an opportunity.

If a data warehouse implementation is successful, a reasonable expectation is that the supply of quality information that answers basic business questions will bring forth additional demand. This is good and to be welcomed. The best approach is to incorporate other uses of the warehouse into the planning cycle and ruthlessly prioritize the allocation of business development and technology resources in addressing the requirements. The next best approach is a working partnership between the business and IT experts to reprioritize requirements in the light of new opportunities. For example, decision support reporting cycles are driven by business strategy and initiative, not by regulatory requirements or traditional financial or accounting closing cycles. Therefore, issues of timing abound. Even if these can be resolved, accommodation must be made for additional capacity for end-users, load on the system, and throughput. Despite specific challenges and tasks, this presents the "low-hanging fruit" from the IT perspective. They will yield results based on the usual amount of hard work. All of these accommodations can be generated by the core competencies of accomplished IT teams.

THE SUPPLY CHAIN WAREHOUSE

A significant slice of the time of business managers is devoted to trying to figure out what the demand for the firm's products will be and how best to satisfy that demand. The supply chain data warehouse is an effective tool in addressing quantity and price variation in situations of competitive uncertainty and limited information. By gathering observations of transactions on who is buying what, when, and where, a repository of valuable business intelligence, or actionable knowledge, can be accumulated and made the object of forecasting, replenishment, sourcing, and delivery systems built on the information in the data warehouse.

Along the same lines, a dramatic example is provided on a weekly basis with the case of Wal-Mart, the giant U.S. retailer. Apparently, the competitive advantage to putting out the story in the trade press as a matter of strategy is to let any competition that might still be left standing know what happens when Goliath learns how to use a sling shot. Wal-Mart designed its business process around a data warehouse, which, in turn, became a key to corporate strategy. Wal-Mart initially led the way with investments in point-of-sale systems. These are operational, not decision support, systems. Yet, they have in view knowing exactly which products sold and when and where. Thus, Wal-Mart collected sales data at its nearly 2,800 stores, supercenters, and wholesale clubs, and maintained this data in its warehouse, now estimated at 24 terabytes, (TB, a trillion bytes).

Redesign of the dominant business processes in the entire retail industry is implied as Wal-mart's 4,000 suppliers were given ("required to have") access to the warehouse. In turn, they were held jointly responsible for managing Wal-Mart's inventory and shelf stock—down to the individual store level. Thus was "vendor managed inventory" (VMI) invented. This made the data warehouse the fulcrum of a lever that would end up moving an entire industry in the direction of just-in-time replenishment and quick response. Those companies that didn't invest in this way—Kresge, Dayton Hudson, or smaller discounters top the list—soon found themselves out-flanked, out-maneuvered, and sometimes out of business as Wal-Mart became hyperresponsive to dynamic market conditions. As Henry Ford is supposed to have said, they found themselves forced to incur the costs without getting the benefit. Indeed, evidence is available that the data warehouse revolution, until recently, was a relatively quiet one—in the shadow of the hoopla (largely justified, for once) about the prospects for the web-ification of the planet. With 80% of organizations now claiming to have a data ware-house—admittedly, according to a very large number of definitions—the warehouse may be approaching being a pure-and-simple cost of doing business.[4]

THE CROSS-SELLING WAREHOUSE

The next example turns from the product dimension to that of the customer. As early as 1991, a large Midwestern-headquartered insurance company selling everything from life and casualty insurance to group health insurance and annuities contracted with one of the then big eight firms to build a client repository to drive cross-selling of products between customers. On what was then over a billion-dollar market, com-pany-wide sales growing by a relatively conservative 7% covered the cost of the project and a double-digit return on the investment.

Seven years later, the competition are still trying to catch up. The trade press reports that in 1998, Prudential Insurance was building an enterprise-wide data ware-house to support its business units cross-selling to customers. The CIO (Chief Information Officer) states that the goal is to enhance Prudential's "knowledge" of cus-tomers, especially how the company interacts with them across its five business units: insurance, investments, securities, health care, and diversified. The objective is to iden-tify and determine which products customers of one line of business would buy from another group. The opportunities are great. The company estimates that 70% of its 50 million customers use only one of its products. The value proposition is that shared data will make possible more profitable customer relationships. "A customer who has a low-value product in terms of margin for us might have a very valuable relationship if you look across the entire enterprise," says the CIO, "so we're building an information warehousing capability that allows us to recognize those relationships."[5]

THE TOTAL QUALITY MANAGEMENT DATA WAREHOUSE

The slogan that "quality is free" came at the beginning of our awareness of the importance of quality as an integral part of all manufacturing (and now all business) processes more than ten years ago. The effort and cost that went into correcting defects and rework could be better devoted to avoiding mistakes in the first place. By "doing it right the first time," the extra effort to keep quality on target could be recouped at the back-end of the assembly line, where significantly less rework was required. Now, at the end of ten or more years of incremental progress in plucking so-called low-hanging fruit, quality remains as great a challenge and imperative as ever. However, the meaning of "quality is free" has changed. It means that it is priceless, not effortless. When quality is indistinguishable from the product or service itself, quality is truly a most important product.

One of the many lessons of the Japanese firm's Kaizen ("gradual, unending improvement") was that cost, quality, and time are inseparable. Defects can be reduced by working slower or using more costly inspections. But is that really improvement? All three dimensions have to be attacked simultaneously to make a difference. Otherwise, one is shifting, rather than reducing costs. Thus, we have another fundamental cube—cost, quality (defect rate), and time—different from the delivery of products to customers. This cube, in effect, moves backward into the vertically integrated corporation and upstream into the production line.

Although the manufacturing assembly line is the primary arena in which such TQM cubes have been applied, they are applicable wherever a repetitive process or operation takes place. Many service organizations have repetitive processes. Banks, health care facilities, insurance companies, and government offices perform standard procedures and tests—some already highly automated, some not—which are good prospects for data warehousing. In those business processes that are already automated, the capture, extraction, and transformation of the data are relatively straightforward next steps in the deployment of product and service improvement programs.

In one fascinating study, metrics on the costs of machine downtime, throughput, and scrap (nonfinancial numbers) were supplemented with reports on spending for such indirect stuffs as supplies, tools, scrap, overhead expenses, and support enabled the area manager to construct a pseudo-profit statement at the work group level with which to attack quality improvement opportunities. The TQM data warehouse was one essential leg of the approach to quality improvement in the context of teamwork, performance management, and statistical quality control. The construction of a daily income statement resulted in such dramatic improvements in quality that the team set new records for throughput and quality. This basic data cube relating to income, product, and time was so effective in generating quality improvements that other unexpected, negative results showed up downstream. A downstream process—several steps later—failed.

Chemical trace elements required for a later chemical reaction had been carried by impurities in intermediate products. However, all known impurities had been eliminated as a result of the quality breakthrough "enabled" by the TQM data warehouse. Naturally, further fine-tuning allowed the urgent request to be accommodated to permit some impurities to be allowed back into the process.[6] This case provides a wonderful example of how rigorous work and precise definitions, combined with understanding and aligning the business and technology components, can furnish breakthrough results for business leaders, managers, and staff alike. (A more detailed treatment of data quality issues occurs below in Chapter Seven: Data Warehouse Data Quality.)

A necessary word of caution is proper here. Just as quality is not a limited attribute of a product or service, neither is it the responsibility of a single department among other departments. It is the responsibility of all staff in relation to specific tasks, a feature described as "worker empowerment." The people who do the work know best the areas for improvement and the challenges faced in undertaking such progress. When Florida Power and Light, winner of the Malcolm Baldrige award for quality in the U.S., abolished its 85-person quality department, customer service actually improved (Keen, 1996: 190). But this seemingly counter-intuitive result is due to making every individual responsible for performing tasks so as to produce quality results, regardless of job title, instead of the impossibility of making bureaucrats responsible for everyone else's quality.

From the perspective of continuous improvement, taking the long-term view and staff empowerment, "no problem" is a problem. This is because such a reactive attitude is likely to overlook opportunities for incremental gain. For example, Federal Express (FedEx) managers are responsible for quantitative and objective quality measures. One of these is the number of packages damaged in shipment (Keen, 1996: 186). The one damaged shipment may have been the only one out of tens of thousands. Yet, if you are the recipient, it is a 100% failure of quality.

To manage by means of quantitative facts, one must have numbers over periods of time long enough to track the 5%, 10%, or 15% improvements, not the big 50% advance, that add up to dramatic progress. The warehouse is a powerful method of recording, tracking, managing, and measuring the results of actions. Paradoxically, "quality" is not primarily qualitative. Quality requires exact quantitative metrics—number of repairs per 1,000 units, on-time delivery performance, reports on customer ratings, warranty costs, etc. By tracking the details of operational measures of quality over time, a TQM warehouse enables business leaders to manage by fact, and a fact that answers our question constitutes knowledge in the full sense of the word.

THE PROFITABILITY WAREHOUSE

Sales are just great! Are we making any money? This answer is less obvious than you might think, but it is completely in agreement with what every small mom-and-pop shopkeeper knows. It is how much is left in the cigar box behind the counter when the day is over that counts.

The determination of that "how much" gets more challenging with the increase in the number of activities in which an enterprise engages. The cost of goods sold is a straightforward calculation only so long as the only two inputs are material and labor. Additional factors that are now essential parts of doing business can easily dwarf the latter costs. These include the costs of distribution, promotions, advertising, marketing staff time allocation, general and administrative expenses, and the cost of money itself. A data warehouse to track profit or loss goes to the heart of the enterprise. It cannot possibly provide accurate results without mapping the alignment between business cost drivers and the database and application components that represent these drivers. Consider further.

Traditional cost systems rely on unit-level cost drivers, such as hourly labor, cost of materials, machine hours, or units produced. For all but the most elementary production functions, these traditional systems distort the true expense involved in serving and developing individual products and customers. Compare facilities that produce newly introduced products and mature ones, high-volume batches and low-volume ones, complex and simple setups. Compare a sales staff that serves high-volume standard products with one that serves customers who order small volumes, odd-sized lot volumes, or who require pre- and postsales technical support.

The economics of complex and multiproduct marketing efforts require the sophisticated business insight available in an activity-based costing (ABC) system. The cost object—a product, service, customer, or process—makes a demand on a resource. These, in turn, can be traced by cause-and-effect relationship to the service and activity that supports them. If business analysis can determine a reasonably good approximation of costs in accordance with the 80-20 rule, a profitability data warehouse becomes a real possibility. Compromise or even disagreement among reasonable people about the allocation of costs is not a problem. The rational allocation of costs according to a business-based procedure is of the essence. The one thing that doesn't work in allocating costs is an *arbitrary* allocation. That is likely to produce misleading information. The firm may think it knows product X is the more profitable, whereas the more Xs are sold, the larger the losses will be (due, for example to the costs of warranty repairs, follow-up services, or even environmental cleanup). If no agreement on cost allocations is attained, the data warehouse will be burdened with what is a knotty business dilemma. If this is so, the profitability component of the data warehouse is best deferred until such a consensus can be constructed.

In fact, the imperative to build the data warehouse can be used as a kind of lever for change to force the firm to come to grips with arbitrary and outdated cost systems. This must be done with eyes open, not accidentally. However, the finance department,

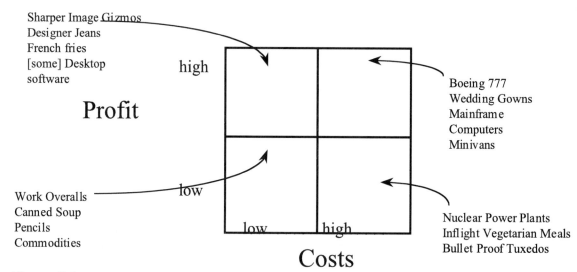

Figure 3.1
The Product Profit Matrix

not the data warehouse team, is the proper leader of a project to determine costs. The data warehouse team is properly a user of this information. Its incorporation into a cost dimension within the warehouse would make a difference. It would be a distraction and expensive digression to charge IT with such an undertaking. However, with agreement on cost allocation and its representation in appropriate database structures, such as the product and customer dimensions, powerful business knowledge emerges.

The data warehouse then makes possible the distinction between profitable and less profitable products. This is using knowledge, in the best sense of the word, to guide strategy. With a shift of focus from design and assembly to marketing and service conditions, the same determination can be made about customers. The idea of the two-by-two matrix (see Figure 3.1) to compare low- and high-cost products with low- and high-profit products is a compelling one. The goal is to go straight north, according to this picture. That is, the upper left quadrant with low cost and high profit is where you want to be. Going northeast is also good, because high profits and high costs are winning, though more complex, options. You can get there a couple of ways. If the price that the market will pay is such as to allow a profit margin large enough to launch the product into the upper left corner, regardless of relatively modest unit sales, that generates the result. Examples of high-profit/low-cost items include designer blue jeans and certain desktop software. Once reasonably well debugged, the markup on the latter is very favorable indeed. The northeast quadrant is also favorable, though more expertise is required there. Here belong complex assemblies that command high margins. These days, both Boeing 777s and ERP software systems are on the list. In addition, if enough volume of the product is sold so that it generates a large profit by aggregating many smaller increments, that, too, produces the north-most result. Just as an illustration, french fries are a high-profit/low-cost item, due to the sheer volume sold. A diesel loco-motive might be a high-cost/low-profit product, due to the railroad industry being both a regulated and a depressed market. The recommendation is to raise prices or exit the business. Finally, a low-cost/low-profit product might be lead pencils or any other prod-uct that behaves like a commodity. Naturally, one wants more of the north-most quad-rant and to reduce exposure in the lower right quadrant, whether by exiting the market or raising the margin, if competition will allow it. The data warehouse provides the knowledge to make these distinctions and options.

As usual, matters are more complicated than they at first seem. This is because profit on a product is actually a function of both the cost of designing, assembling, and disposing of the product and the cost of selling and supporting the product. It costs more to sell 1,000 pencils to 1,000 customers than to sell 1,000 pencils to one customer. It costs more to sell 1,000 pencils of different colors to one customer than to sell 1,000 black pencils to one customer. We have high- and low-cost products combined with high- and low-cost customers. Once again, as an illustration, remember that because the product is complex (and costly) and the customers are demanding (major U.S. and international air carriers) does not mean that the industry is unprofitable. Selling air-planes to demanding customers is frequently more profitable than operating the planes once they are in service. So we actually have a cube—product cost by customer cost by profit on transaction (see Figure 3.2: The Profit Matrix Cube). Another representation of this data is available in Table 3.5, which makes clear all the logical possibilities. It should be noted that the data warehouse makes possible the substitution of specific numbers, or rankings, where Table 3.5 shows only "low" or "high."

As a final illustration, the profit and loss data warehouse made possible identi-fying and rehabilitating two customers. These two customers were both the most unprofitable ones and also in the top five of sales volume. It is perhaps shocking to realize that large customers can generate large losses. But when you think about it, small customers are too limited in scope and impact to do so. The causes? Large num-bers of small orders? Large numbers of orders of small volumes of specialty or unstocked items? Having visibility to these comparisons enables the firm to lay its cards on the table with its customers, professionally and candidly. In one case, it turned out that the customer had switched to just-in-time (JIT) manufacturing and appreciated the possibility of submitting its small orders directly into the vendor's sys-tem by means of a remote terminal provided to the customer, instead of by the usual manual process. In the other case, the customer was provided with pricing incentives to order according to a more normalized profile, with the option to order specialty items at a premium price that actually covered the costs of the business. This was less of a problem than one might imagine. No customer wants its supplier to go under. But systematic information and hard data—in short, knowledge, are required to build a compelling case. Based on the knowledge provided by the profitability data ware-house, a win-win situation for both customer and supplier is created.

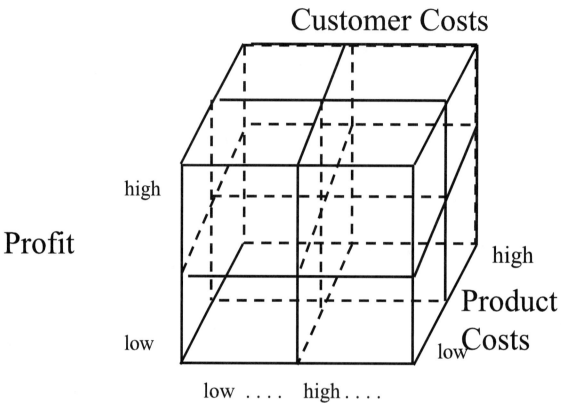

Figure 3.2
The Profit Matrix Cube

DATA WAREHOUSING CASE VIGNETTES IN THE PRESS

The following accounts taken from the trade press are meant to give a sense of the scope and diversity of firms implementing data warehousing systems. The cases are anecdotal and impressionistic. One of the reasons for this is that many companies are not bragging about their data warehousing systems, they are using them quietly to drive strategy as an integrated part of the firm's business. Although Wal-Mart has gained advantages from "bragging" in the trade press, many other firms have quietly gone about trouncing the competition, using the knowledge gained from their data warehousing systems. You do not read much about them, except when a vendor announces the sale of a front-end data warehousing reporting tool—implying, of course, that back-end data warehousing systems are being integrated as part of the information supply chain. (In the following vignettes, the reader is encouraged to use the Glossary for terms such as *Extranet, Web,* or *OLAP* that either have not yet been defined or require review.[7])

Table 3.5   Product / Customer / Profit Cube

	Customer Cost	Product Cost	Profit	
	1. high	high	high	
	2. high	low	high	
	3. low	high	high	
	4. low	low	high	
	5. high	high	low	
Grow	6. high	low	low	
this	7. low	high	low	Exit market
segment	8. low	low	low	or raise margin

One way of describing CCC Information Services (CCCIS) is that it makes lemonade out of lemons by leveraging information about automobile crashes. It provides automobile claims information about the value of vehicles "totaled" in accidents based on surveys of the sticker prices of used cars of similar make, model, and history. The resulting "Total Loss" data warehouse cross-references vehicle, insurance, and salvage firm information. Collision repair shops and auto insurance agencies are the main customers. An interesting spin on the Total Loss product occurred when it was made available to insurance sales representatives over the Internet, providing web-based data analysis.[8] Being able to view and evaluate vehicle data while the sales reps were out in the field had significant impact. However, this capability to exert "action at a distance" was not a simple add-on but the result of a dedicated system development effort, including critical system architecture that can be used in future information product development efforts. CCCIS, with under $100 million in assets (though publicly traded), is a beautiful example of how data warehousing is not for just the "big guys," multibillion-dollar enterprises. Size is not the determining variable—information density is. Many of CCCIS's services are actually compact (and densely packed) information products.

Alltel Corporation, a $9 billion-dollar telecommunications company, recently acquired a reporting data warehouse when it acquired 360° Communications, the latter being the second largest wireless company in the U.S. The data warehouse reportedly provides time-series analysis of sales trends combining rate plan, markets, and aggregates of customer call detail.[9]

Land O'Lakes built a traditional retail data warehousing system to provide managers and brokers with timely feedback on product and marketing trends. Thanks to having key elements of an information architecture already in place, it was then able to migrate the information and make it accessible over an Extranet to provide the customers of the data warehouse with information literally "at their fingertips," independent of location or time.[10] Despite the glowing press reports of the in-house effort at

Land O'Lakes, the coordination costs of mounting this effort were such that a letter of intent to partner was signed with A.C. Nielsen in March 1999 (according to the Nielsen press release) as the firm's "New Business Insights Provider," in effect outsourcing the acquisition of data warehouse content to one of the inventors of market research. Still, the delivery of such syndicated data and competitive analyses to the field sales force and food brokers necessitates the operation of a sophisticated information supply chain (see Chapter Twelve: Data Warehousing and the Information Supply Chain).

Chase Manhattan bank, now the second largest bank in the U.S., is the largest financier of auto loans and the fourth largest issuer of credit cards. Chase has constructed a cross-selling data warehouse. This supports direct marketing, enabling Chase business analysts to assess their direct marketing results and using targeted weekly mailing campaigns.[11] The power and value of being able to assemble a clean, accurate list of prospects rapidly should not be underestimated.

It is a fair statement that FedEx *knows* logistics, with nearly $16 billion in sales and logistical operations that delivers 3 million packages *a day* to 200 countries. FedEx is such a master of logistics that it is entering the outsourcing business of managing the supply chains of other companies.[12] Data warehousing aggregates are provided to answer classic questions such as percentage of on-time deliveries, longest delivery time, mean and average delivery times, as well as how these performance metrics track against revenue and costs by geography, time period, and client.

Sears is the number two U.S. retailer (after Wal-Mart), with $41 billion in sales. Data warehousing is helping them to try harder to integrate information[13] from more than 830 mall-based department stores, 2,700 specialty stores (Sears Auto Centers, National Tire and Battery), as well as such home services as the repair and installation of appliances. Marketing to the aspiring middle class, Sears is also in the credit and debt management businesses in a big way, helping their customers to afford to buy the products and services that Sears sells. In addition to answering the one fundamental question, questions about product reliability, customer account, and staff performance are targets for data warehousing analysis.

Many of Minnesota Mining and Manufacturing's (3M's) 50,000 products dominate their markets. These include such notable brands as Post-It Notes, Scotch Tape, Scotchguard, as well as Life Sciences products and industrial chemicals. With $15 billion in sales, a centralized multiterabyte data warehouse enables 3M's global end-users to support the firm's move toward a business strategy of "One Face, One Voice."[14] The highly distributed and diversified form of the organization is an invitation to two things. The first is the distribution of the data warehousing information by means of Web technologies. This gets worldwide end-users into the loop. Second, what is unglamorously but usefully called the *tail-wags-the-dog* approach. With more than half of sales from overseas, an enterprise approach to data warehousing can be used as a mechanism to drive a unification strategy, in addition to cross-selling, supply chain management, and sales tracking.

MasterCard International, Inc. presents an example of a successful large project. Closing in on two terabytes of data, the data warehouse delivers consumer purchasing reports to the desktops of credit card company member banks and internal knowledge worker staff. One of the applications, MasterTaggers, permits member banks to cross-reference their customer data with the MasterCard data warehouse and run queries on the combination. A key lesson? The front-end is significant and sexy, with lots of pizzazz, but the architecture back-end is critical for capturing transactional data in a timely way. Standardized data definitions at the operation data source systems and business rule tables to cleanse data at the transaction level using automated processes and exception handling is the key to timely information at the front-end.[15]

The Coca-Cola Company (Coke) has one of the best-known brands on the planet. (It also owns other well-known brands, such as Minute Maid.) Because they are a globally distributed firm, they also have one of the more diverse supply chains imaginable. They buy raw materials such as corn syrup, sugar, and aluminum from such firms as Archer Daniels Midland, Cargill, and Reynolds Metals. Coke then services major downstream bottlers, as well as other distributors, such as Burger King, McDonald's and Wal-Mart. Coke's data warehousing systems combine sales data with information such as consumer confidence in the more than 200 countries worldwide in which sales occur. Internally and externally generated demographic research and reports on business conditions are added to inform the marketing staff, for example, that 45% of teenage males in Indonesia consider Coke Classic their soft drink of choice or what is the best-selling package of Sprite in Amsterdam. Estimating market demand for new products is also a function of the warehouse. Naturally, there is little initial sales history available for a new brand, such as the firm's first domestic bottled-water brand (Dasani), launched in February 1999. However, data on the sales of competing products, consumer confidence, and preference research can be merged intelligently to generate an assessment of when to launch and a statement of prospects of success, against which to track and manage exceptions.[16] These are obviously advanced applications of the technology, but they are completely in the spirit of the one fundamental question as to who is buying (or will be buying) and what, when, and where are they doing so.

SUMMARY . . . .

Quantifiable economic value can be traced to business initiatives at the center of which lie data warehousing systems. However, it is important to remember that both economic value and business benefits flow from the management and coordination of people, processes, and knowledge, not mere technology. Superior customer service, cross-selling, enhanced supply chain logistics, reduced costs due to defects and rework – all of these management commitments are coordinated and leveraged through data warehousing systems. A simulated cash flow analysis is provided based on a business case whereby the data warehouse enables reduced inventory costs thanks to improved forecasting. Next, the distinction is made between justifying the data warehouse and selling it. Although there is overlap with the task of quantitative justification, persuasive selling points include satisfying the hunger for knowledge amidst data; correcting inadequacies with the timeliness of decision support reporting; resolving data quality problems. The uses of data warehousing are considered in decision support reporting, supply chain management, customer cross-selling, total quality management, and profitability analysis. Examples of data warehousing case vignettes are cited from the trade press.

[1] *The Squandered Computer*, New Canaan, CT: The Information Economics Press, 1997, pp. 397, 401.

[2] In my opinion, the trade press, especially those magazines with the word "information" or "data" in them, do not sufficiently appreciate the degree to which IT enables business benefits without such benefit being directly attributable to IT. This complex interaction of the business and the IT function is addressed in a truly eye-opening discussion by Paul Strassmann (*The Squandered Computer,* 1997: 107). Strassmann presents a strong case that IT spending on the computing resource, the Gartner Group to the contrary, tracks (correlates with) the number of desktops and the bureaucratic features of a firm, not its revenue profile. (See also www.Strassmann.com.)

[3] See Keen (1997: 68–69) for a nice summary and Stewart, 1988 for the complete treatment.

[4] These numbers and other interesting ones are cited in Watson and Haley, 1998: 37.

[5] For example, see *Information Week* (7/20/1998).

[6] See Kaplan and Cooper, 1998: 62, 68.

[7] Some of the sales figures about the companies profiled in this section are taken from the *Wall Street Journal,* on-line Interactive Edition, which contains useful briefing books, including references to publicly available figures from the Securities and Exchange Commission. Naturally, all the usual disclaimers apply. See www.wsj.com, whose interactive edition also furnishes an interesting example of a "business intelligence portal" (see the section with that title in Chapter Sixteen: Data Warehousing and the Web).

[8] "Adding Value with Web-Based Analysis," *Internet Week*, August 24, 1998.

[9] "360° Communications," *DM Review*, July/August 1998.

[10] "Extranets Get Simpler," *Information Week*, December 8, 1997. However, see http://acnielsen.com press announcement following.

[11] "With Prospect DB in Place, Chase is Betting on Big Returns," *DM News*, November 24, 1997.

[12] "FedEx? Try LogistEx?" *Information Week*, October 27, 1997.

[13] "Decision Suite's Flexibility Critical to OLAP Strategy at Sears," *DM Review*, October 1997.

[14] "Open Door Policy: 3M's Data Warehouse Rolls Out the Welcome Mat," *PC Week*, May 25, 1998.

[15] "Where are They Now? Strategic Systems Revisited," *CIO Magazine*, May 15, 1998.

[16] "Extended Enterprise," *Information Week,* March 22, 1999.

4 Data Warehousing Project Management

In this chapter…

To establish a rational design process,
fake it.
D. Parnas and C. Clements[1]

SIMULATING A RATIONAL DESIGN PROCESS

The title of this section is inspired by one of the classics of the software system design literature. The classic article by David Parnas and P. Clements, "A Rational Design Process: How and Why to Fake It," presents the dilemma of developing any system and proposes a novel solution. Ideally, we want to bring science—knowledge and rigor—to the process of developing systems. That is the process in which we gather requirements, design, code, test (and test and test). Maybe the process is like a waterfall, sequential and irreversible. Maybe it is a spiral in which these rational steps are iterated and reiterated. However, the process conforms to a definition of rationality in that it is logical, traces requirements to their representation in functioning system parts, and IT professionals would agree that the procedures make sense.

The problem is that the world does not conform to this definition of rationality or, just as challenging, the world presents periods of consistency, order, and stability that are intermixed with periods of dynamic flux. Business markets, system requirements, and the intended technologies change faster than the system solution can be designed and implemented. The behavior of customers is subject to change without notice. The efforts that must be devoted to creating loyalty imply what a rare commodity it really is. Sometimes insight is available into customer motives, sometimes not. Where our enlightened self-interest really lies is neither obvious nor a guaranteed outcome according to any imaginable rules of rationality. The details of developing any system are subject to the unexpected whims of staffing, budget, schedule, and a wide variety of economic and technical risks. Even more so, there is a creative dimension to system design that may not be captured by rational steps in any case. The "Aha!" experience comes to mind, where a solution to a tricky problem emerges after a lot of hard work. In short, the world is not rational. At the minimum, a strong case can be made that rationality is more scarce than system development professionals might wish. What do we do about this predicament?

The recommendation is to fake it and to do so because that is a method of creating a rational process. A fancy way of saying the same thing would be to "simulate" a rational process by following the series of steps of a well-defined process. In this way, order and rationality show up out of the professional activities and intentions of the comprehensive development effort. These are the practical and pragmatic imperatives stressed earlier in the Introduction. A powerful way of reducing uncertainty is to create the future out of our actions and intentions. Above all, this is the imperative for management. Admittedly, it is a boot-strap operation. To attain rationality, behave "as if" the process were already rational. In this case, the process being "faked" is a solution to comprehensive data management, a solution called *data warehousing*.

MANAGING PROJECT REQUIREMENTS

Reducing uncertainty through knowledge is the opportunity offered by data warehousing. Answering questions about the business not visible at the level of day-to-day operations is the reason for the existence of the data warehouse. The questions about the business to which end-users require answers to build customer relationships, development the brand, segment the market in productive ways, and manage the supply and value chain are the first version of the data warehouse requirements.

Often, these questions will already be the subject of detailed procedures. Some of these procedures may provide answers to vital questions but do so in seemingly inelegant, clumsy, or even insane ways. However, remember one thing here. The more clumsy, awkward, ad hoc, frustrating, time-consuming, or off-the-wall these methods and procedures are, the greater is the value that can be added by a data warehousing approach.

In one instance, two weeks of effort were required to produce a clean list of customers from the transactional system for a direct mailing campaign. An equal effort was required to determine the result of the campaign. In another instance, extensive customized coding of SQL, usually involving heroic work by IT staff and end-users over the weekends, was required to answer questions based on data from the transactional system about client usage of services on a quarter-to-quarter basis. Seemingly inevitably, the quality of the data would be discovered to be a problem when the results of the query were returned. The answers to the questions did not make sense. The question was well formulated and the query was technically sound; but the data had spaces where there should be nulls or zeroes where one would expect a valid date. The process started in data available in mainframe transaction systems. The entire process involved multiple requests to the IT department and ended up in files that were presented in someone's spreadsheet. When the answer finally showed up in time, the company often gained new or additional business as a result. However, that "in-time" part did not happen regularly enough. Many standard data warehouse business requirements are to be found here—requirements to answer questions such as, Which customers might be interested in a particular special offer? Which customers were using which services during this period? Which promotions were causing shifts in the market and which were not? These are all problems addressable by a systematic extraction, storage, and retrieval process from transactional data.

Another way of surfacing data warehousing requirements is to get your best business analysts, domain experts, super-users, and responsible managers in *separate* rooms and ask them to identify the key questions about the business that they need to get answered at all, need to get answered more quickly, and need to get answered more accurately. Then consider the union and intersection of these answers. The union of the answers will provide the working version of the complete wish list. With any luck, the intersection of the answers will provide a starting point for ruthlessly prioritizing what to do first. Because the list may be long, each requirement should be marked with a judgment as to its estimated importance and added value. Here, the customer (end-user) has the primary input. In addition, each requirement should be marked with a judgment as to its estimated complexity and ease of implementation by the IT design-er. This should not require a lot of system analysis, although it may well require expert knowledge of the existing legacy systems. The proverbial "low-hanging fruit" is any requirements with high value-added and low complexity. These are easy to deliver and should percolate to the top of the list of implementation priorities.

The possibility exists that some of the questions and related issues that emerge here will have to be referred to operational system services. For example, if the question surfaced by this process is what has to happen to get the help desk to return your calls, the data warehousing project may not be the top priority. However, note that a useful purpose would have been served in any case.

The expected outcome is a requirements document. This is a working document to which both IT staff and customers can affix their authorized signatures. Because requirements can change, a method of defining how to change them—by mutual agreement on both changes and costs—should be a defined part of the document. Thus, this becomes a living document. It is, in effect, a contract between those who will be using the system and the system developers. That implies responsibilities on both sides. As such, it should have built into it provisions for being revisited and reviewed on a formal basis, both quarterly (or other default period) and upon the accomplishment of a significant project milestone.

Those multiunit organizations that are most successful in managing the require-ments process have mutual respect for one another, an ability to compromise, a healthy willingness to define and manage risks, and an ability to put a stake in the ground by agreeing on a requirements document and going forward on that basis.

MANAGING THE DEVELOPMENT OF ARCHITECTURE

The purpose of this section is not to tell you what the data warehouse architecture is (for that review, see Chapter One and Figure 1.1, in particular), but rather to provide an account of how to manage its creation. The architecture itself might be client-server, network-centric, or distributed; it might use remote procedure calls, message-oriented middleware, or common object request brokers; it might be mainframe, enterprise server, or LAN- and desktop-based. Typically, the standards and implementation technologies will be drawn from a variety of these domains, but the architecture itself is an abiding artifact that goes beyond each of them. If successful, the architecture will make possible the integration and implementation of the fluctuating data warehousing requirements first defined in the requirements document.

As a role, the architect on the data warehouse project is equal in importance to that of the project manager. The architect has to have a vision broad enough to encompass the business dimensions. This person has to have a depth of experience needed to distinguish between trivial annoyances and small omissions that can turn into large project risks. This person has to be pragmatic enough to compromise about what is feasible in the available technology and persistent enough to see things through to completion. As an individual, this person may be the senior developer on the team—the one with the professional polish and charisma to provide the leadership, communication, and focus required to get the job done and to have a good time doing it. This should be someone with whom people find it is fun to work.

A major responsibility of the data warehouse architect is to provide for an alignment between the software components that are the warehouse system and the questions about the business that usefully need to be answered. Notice that we did not say alignment with the requirements, as such. This is because the architecture should provide for an alignment with what amounts to a super-set of the questions to be answered. A robust flexible architecture has a real prospect of being able to provide the means of answering questions that have not yet even been imagined.

Naturally, in a data warehousing system, the approach is data-centric. Therefore, the conceptualization of the domain of business entities and their behavior is a key result. In particular, the architect has to manage the identification, definition, and refinement of the data dimensions, the level of detail of granularity of the facts, and integrity of the representation of these components. This must be managed by a remorseless comparison and driving out of the inconsistencies of the candidate entities. Therefore, a strong background in data modeling, semantic analysis, and a willingness to be immersed in the details of the business domain are essential characteristics of the architect.

A majority of the architect's time in the data warehouse universe can be expected to be devoted to identifying, defining, and refining the essential minimal set of dimensions required to drill down into the data. Consistent and unified representations of each of these dimensions serve as a constraining function, forcing the project in the right direction—customer, product, time, location, supplier, service, provider, diagnosis, channel—depending on the industry in question. This is the heart of the exercise in aligning the business imperatives and the systematic representation of the business in the technology. As a point of practical system building, the recommendation is to identify and define the dimensions first. Whenever feasible, preparation should be undertaken to populate (load) the dimensional structures with as complete a set of customers, products, etc. as is available. Relative to the amount of data contained in fact structures, dimensions are always relatively small, sometimes trivially so. Then, even if the judicious use of the 80/20 rule results in facts being captured for (for example) only those 20% of customers responsible for 80% of the business, a path will be implied for further releases (namely, capturing facts for the additional 80% in phased approach). Then, when the managers, analysts, or business leaders responsible for the as yet unimplemented facts for the 80% of the remaining customers are interviewed about their plans for using the data warehouse and they ask whether their customers are in the warehouse, the answer will be "yes." The provisioning of the data warehouse with facts for the relevant remaining subsets of the dimensions will, indeed, seem like the next logical step, easy to attain. Thus, an implementation approach will grow naturally out of the nature of the dimensions—get the dimensions right, then work on the facts.

Equally important with the definition of the dimensions is the level of granularity represented by and at the intersection of these dimensions. A customer buys a product at a particular location at a given time—this is an elementary transaction. If the customer does exactly this same thing three times in a week, this is an aggregation to a weekly time period. What it is that is being captured, tracked, and presented is highly significant for the level of detail of the answers to the business questions. The operational details of the system are also significantly affected. Provision must be made for capturing and maintaining this information in the data warehouse metadata system component or repository.

This is a feature that distinguishes the data warehouse architect from other architects—the importance of focusing on metadata. Metadata begin in the identification, documentation, and analysis of the sources of data in ERP, legacy, and EC transactions systems. The fact is that the visionary architect and the domain expert of the legacy system are not likely to be joined in the same individual. Therefore, interviewing skills and an ability to draw out the best in other persons are also required skills. The metadata begin by lining up the source and target data. Typically, this will result in tracking a path from the data warehouse back to the transactional systems in which the data is sourced, captured, or originated. This produces a high-level conceptualization of the applications that will be needed to extract and convert transaction to decision support data. Some of these may need to be scheduled as a part of regular production.

The Principle of High Cohesion, Loose Coupling

One of the basic ideas of software engineering with which the data warehouse architect will be familiar is the principle of "high cohesion, loose coupling." Software components ought to be highly cohesive—that is, self-contained and able to function on their own. At the same time, they should be loosely coupled with other components. Modules communicate with one another by passing parameters (or messages) from behind defined interfaces. This will assure that a change to module A will not cause a bug to show up in module B. So, for example, the presentation of time-series data invites tabular and graphical presentation modes. The clarity and crispness with which data is presented adds to its value and is a mark of its quality. The ability to drill down and across dimensions is the essential minimal set of functions required to perform analysis on the data. Since it is the dimensions that define the drill paths along which aggregation and drill down will occur, the definition of the dimensional hierarchies is seen to be critical path once again. The architect has to manage how tightly or loosely the presentation will be coupled with the underlying data. Relational implementations tend to decouple these layers. This accords with the design recommendation to aim for tight coherence, loose coupling. However, it has the consequence that each application reinvents its own access methods or interface. This fragmentation frustrates the advantages of reusability. Therefore, whether or not inheritance is available as a mechanism in the programming or scripting language, it is useful to embed the data behind shared, general modules that perform I/O (input/output). This preserves a unified approach to data access and behavior, even in the context of data-centric architecture.

MANAGING PROJECT SCHEDULE

The critical path of the data warehouse project lies in the identification and refinement of the data dimensions and granularity of the facts; the extraction, scrubbing, aggregation, and distribution of the transactional (ERP, legacy, EC) system data; and the presentations of the data to the end-user. Here *critical path* means that path that, if delayed, causes the entire schedule to slip. Another way of saying this is to point to the step-by-step refinement of the architecture design.

Nothing makes clearer to the end-user what their requirement really was than the delivery of a system or part thereof. That is to say, regardless of what the requirement says, it is a rule of system development that the end-user will have a breakthrough in understanding of it when they see a functioning product. This is a strong statement in favor of prototyping.

In one case known to the author, a prototype of the data warehouse made clear to the firm the power and importance of the questions that could be answered by the warehouse system. Although the prototype was clunky and exhibited mediocre performance, it clarified what the technology could do for the business. It presented a strong business case. As a result, significant additional resources were forthcoming. Additional refinement of the architecture addressed the performance problems in a cost-effective but not low-cost way. The organization made a major commitment of resources to the system with an aggressive but achievable rollout schedule. In another case, the prototype made clear that the firm was not yet ready for the undertaking—

not ready organizationally and technically. It showed where work had to be performed to align departmental incentives with the interests of the whole firm. Although expensive, the prototype was still less costly than a larger waterfall project with a planned big bang integration would have been—especially in view of the latter's demonstrated high probability of failure.

The data warehouse schedule should be the successive refinement of the system architecture, rather than a single big bang implementation followed by heroic efforts at completion. This is realistic and possible by a sensible segmentation of the implementation by partitioning according to customer and product dimension. As indicated above, identify and define the essential minimal list of data dimensions first. If at all possible, steps should be taken to populate (load) the dimensional structures with as complete a set of customers, products, etc. as is available. The intelligent use of the 80/20 rule shows the way. If you can identify those 20% of customer–product combinations that generate a majority of the facts of interest, that is what to implement first. Analogous segmentations of the business then follow in priority sequence. Such a partitioning is a royal road to implementation.

MANAGING PROJECT QUALITY

You know that you have a quality project if the job gets done on time and on budget, and the team has a good time producing the result. Usually, no one has a good time unless the budget and schedule are reasonably close to being accommodated. Therefore, the question remains, What is quality and how do you produce it in a data warehouse project? The details of data quality will be treated in a separate chapter (see Chapter Six: Data Warehouse Data Quality). The definition of quality borrowed from the universal commercial code (UCC) says that it is a "fitness for use." A quality hammer is good at driving nails. A quality screw driver does something similar with screws. When applied to systems composed of software, a variety of factors comes into play. These are outlined in Table 4.1: Attributes of System Quality. The point is that quality is not some additional attribute, such as color or antilock brakes, that can be added to the list of product attributes. It is the harmonious fitting together of all the components of the complete assembly in the context of its use.

If the development process is to rise above the level of hacking, data warehouse project quality means laying down a defined and repeatable process capable of being controlled and optimized (see Table 4.2: Attributes of Project Quality). In Table 4.2, each succeeding level is a super-set of the previous one and contains and consolidates the previous stages. Not shown off the top of the chart is what you might call a *level zero*: hacking, trial and error, working every weekend, and heroics on an ongoing basis—an all-too-familiar situation. On the other hand, repeatable defined project management quality means things such as the staff getting the necessary training they need to do their jobs. Deliverables are tracked, reviewed, and implemented. Colleague

Table 4.1:   Attributes of System Quality

Attribute	Definition
Correctness	The system satisfies its specifications and attains its users' objective
Reliability	The systems performs its functions within the specified level of exceptions
Efficiency	Ratio of resources consumed to results produced is defined and attained
Integrity	Results are consistent, meaningful, and under control
Usability	The resources required to operate and interpret the behavior of the system are defined and met
Maintainability	Capacity to adapt to new requirements or to improve the fit of existing requirements or other quality attributes
Testability	System is instrumented to show whether it satisfies its defined specifications or function
Security	Access to the system by unauthorized individuals or processes is either prevented or monitored, reported, and controlled
Portability	System can be moved to different hardware/software environments
Reusability	Components of the system can be combined in useful, new or novel ways to accommodate new requirements or conditions
Interoperability	System is able to communicate with or be coupled with other systems.

Adapted from David N. Card and Robert L. Glass,
Measuring Software Design Quality. *Englewood Cliffs, NJ: Prentice Hall, 1990.*

peer group reviews are the norm. Metrics are gathered, and opportunities for process improvements are identified, prioritized, and pursued. In general, the professional maturity of an entire organization is measured in terms of the scope of these project management qualities. Are one or two departments conducting peer reviews, gathering metrics on defects, and attacking project risks and issues with prototypes, while the rest of the organization is hacking, overcommitting, and getting the job done through heroics? This is a start. Let the leaders be acknowledged and provide the example for the rest. Is there an enterprise-wide commitment to the maturation of the system development process? There is no guarantee that the teams operating at less mature levels will aspire to the highest standard, rather than drift in the direction of the lowest common denominator. Indeed, day-to-day pressures seem to exert forces in the direction of disorder, rather than improving maturity. That is where leadership, commitment, and initiative make a difference in deciding the direction of progress or regression. Once again, quality comes down to commitment. This is one of those moments when management rises to the level of leadership.

The take-away here is that the successful data warehouse project—on time, on budget, and having a good time doing it—requires an advanced level of organizational maturity. That means attaining at least level two in the capability maturity model in Table 4.2—procedures are defined—where intergroup cooperation and cross-functional teams start to show up and make a difference. Because the data warehouse is one of the more complicated system artifacts that an organization is likely to build, those companies where turf wars seem to result will require a high degree of risk management and executive commitment of time and energy. Perspective on organizational goals and visibility to the bigger team is a critical success factor in producing and sustaining project management quality.

MANAGING PROJECT RISKS

Experience shows that proactively managing project risks and issues is one of the most effective available methods of controlling costs and maintaining a close approximation to the data warehouse project schedule. Maintaining a list of risks and deploying resources to work them is a major responsibility for project management. Issues often end up on the risk list, too. This is because every issue implies a decision point. Every decision point, once engaged in a committed way, in turn, implies an elimination of uncertainty. Elimination of uncertainty tends to reduce risk of surprises. Therefore, working and resolving the issues helps to manage and reduce risk.

Data warehouse risks include risks to data quality. This is so significant that an entire chapter is devoted to it (see Chapter Six: Data Warehouse Data Quality). Other potential trouble spots include risks of sloppy or late integration with transactional systems; connectivity problems in a system on a distributed network; errors in estimating the amount of storage that will be required to handle combinatorial explosion; errors in estimating which aggregations can be determined interactively and which must be aggregated off-line in advance; and insufficient depth of understanding, preparation, or maintenance of metadata.

The truth is, if we don't know that we don't know something, there is a good chance that we will find out the hard way. That used to be called the *college of hard knocks*. However, in every case, whether technical or organizational, consciousness-raising is not enough. The risk must be engaged and resolved by deploying resources to drive the risk to the surface, engage it, and implement a resolution. Sometimes that will show up as a functioning prototype. Sometimes that will be a spreadsheet that demonstrates a solution. Sometimes that will be an agreement between the project executive sponsor and the intended end-user organization to freeze requirements until the end-of-quarter release. Whenever the project calls for a network gateway to be traversed between heterogeneous platforms, that is a good candidate for a prototype. Whenever a new technology, i.e., new to the organization, is being incorporated, a pro-

Table 4.2:   Attributes of Project Quality

Project Maturity Level	Attributes
Level 1: Data warehouse project procedures are repeatable	1. Planning and management is based on experience with similar data warehousing projects 2. Data warehouse requirements, architecture, schedule, risk, and deliverables are baselined, tracked, audited, and reviewed 3. Estimates of work are negotiated with the end-user and planned, establishing mutual commitments 4. Version control is applied 5. End-users have visibility to the data warehouse product at defined occasions via the review and acceptance of major project deliverables
Level 2: Data warehouse project procedures are defined	1. Cross-functional coordination of teams are defined across the enterprise. For example, cooperation between the data warehouse team and the 'owner' of legacy system data 2. Data warehouse deliverables are reviewed by the developer's peers to identify defects and areas where improvements are required 3. Management obtains clear and frequent status reports with insight into technical issues and opportunities 4. Change control is added to version control 5. A central library of database of data warehouse life cycle documents, artifacts, and deliverables is established with version control, with dedicated staff and support if the volume of products warrants it
Level 3: Data warehouse project measures (metrics) are collected and used to take action	1. Metrics of system quality, as defined in Table 5.1, are collected and used as the basis for defect correction 2. Information collected is to be used to further the professional development of the team, staff, and the firm, not to reward or punish
Level 4: Data warehouse project processes are made the target of continuous improvement (optimization) activities	1. The analysis of defects is used to prevent their reoccurrence in the future 2. Data warehouse change management is undertaken on a systematic, enterprise-wide basis to improve development on a continuous and ongoing basis 3. New and evolving technologies are evaluated proactively and incorporated effectively into the data warehouse system and the enterprise as a whole 4. The data warehouse becomes a laboratory for innovation and effective ("best") development practices

Adapted to data warehousing from **The Capability Maturity Model: Guidelines for Improving the Software Process**, *edited by Mark C. Paulk, Charles V. Weber, Bill Curtis, Mary Beth Chrissis. Reading, MA: Addison-Wesley, 1994.*

totype is essential to avoid schedule slippage. These things are bound to contain a few surprises or lessons that need to be worked out.

This list of risks is not— indeed, cannot be—complete. The data warehouse is itself subject to the uncertainties of business, technology, and the market that it is supposed to help us address by improving our systematic treatment of knowledge. That is always the way it is with a boot-strap operation. However, having issued this basic disclaimer, there is one risk particular to the data warehouse system. Consider.

Although one can perhaps get started without metadata, the long-term viability and maintenance of the warehouse depends on coherent and useable access and update of metadata. Failure to appreciate the importance of metadata is the Achilles heal of many data warehouse projects. This is truly the "don't know what you don't know" feature of data warehousing. This is because the concept itself is relatively new. The industry is still young enough to have limited experience with how metadata increase more than proportionately with the complexity of warehouse operations. Provision must be made for its definition, storage, maintenance, and engagement with the levers and dials of data warehouse operations. This is all the more challenging because of a relatively weak Metadata Council (as will be discussed in the Chapter Thirteen, on metadata and metaphor). The metadata tools industry are badly fragmented and seemingly immature. The project might learn from and by studying existing metadata tools. However, given the relative fragmentation of the metadata tools industry, the payoff is less rapid and substantial than for other types of products. All of this tends to increase risk, so it is an area where additional resources should be budgeted. This is even an area where, as a well-known industry research group might say, there is a 0.33 probability that the data warehouse business initiative and industry will stall, due to a lack of scalable metadata tools, methods, and standards.[2]

Therefore, in developing an industrial-strength data warehouse, risks are always with us. They cannot be eliminated, but they can be managed. Concentration on developing a robust flexible data warehouse architecture tends to bring to the surface the risks in the development process sooner rather than later. They can then be made the target of active problem solving.

Every data warehousing project is a little bit like building the transcontinental RR road over the Rocky Mountains. The larger the expedition, the more persons and materials that have to be moved. The more persons and materials that have to relayed up the mountain pass, the longer you are in the avalanche danger zone. The longer in the danger zone, the greater the chance that something bad is going to happen. Therefore, travel light. Get in and get out quickly. Wherever feasible, launch a prototype to plant the flag atop the main peak; build the bypass through the neighboring valley. Never be afraid to follow the line of least resistance to getting the job done, because handling risk is ultimately a business decision. Define and implement the essential minimal list of dimensions, populate them completely, and use them to implement the most important fact structures dependent on them. Whether one wants to call that a data warehouse or a data mart, it is an approach that will scale up. However, never forget that tightening up on any one of the big three—schedule (cost), quality, or deliverables—will cause one of the other factors to pop, or to go critical. Shortening the schedule in isolation will just cause quality or functionality to slip. Tightening up on quality will risk schedule slippage as more testing is performed. All of these project attributes must be managed in relation to one another (and simultaneously) to have true risk management.

MANAGING PROJECT DOCUMENTATION

The essential minimal set of documents for a data warehouse project should include the following. The requirements document must specify the questions about the business that, to answer systematically, the data warehouse will be designed and implemented. The architecture document must include the consistent and unique representations of the data warehouse dimensions, the granularity of the facts created by the intersecting dimensions, and the method of presenting the answers to the business questions envisioned in the requirements. Design documents are appropriate for the individual applications required to extract, transform, aggregate, and present the data. Test plans are reasonably made a part of design documents. Complexities of the interface presented to the customer or end-user should be addressed in a user manual. Issue logs and resolutions, problem reports and solutions, and risk reports and action memos to address and manage them round out the required working documents.

MANAGING THE PROJECT DEVELOPMENT TEAM

The responsibility of the data warehousing project manager and chief architect include providing cover for the other members of the team so that they can do the job of designing and implementing the data warehouse system. This includes keeping them out of meaningless meetings, focusing them on activities that ruthlessly drive toward the project's goals, and allowing them time to lead a balanced life. Chronic overtime, whether compensated or not, is a sure sign of project mismanagement and what Grady Booch designates as *managerial malpractice* (Booch, 1995: p. 235).[3]

An important responsibility of the project manager is to calibrate the productivity of the individual members of the team. This is best done on a preliminary, short project, where rapid turnaround can be used to get an estimate of the individual's professional development and skills. Make no mistake about it. Years of service are not necessarily a good way to determine anything. As an illustration, Barry Boehm cites an instance where the most productive and least productive software developers on a team each had eleven years of service (see Boehm, 1981). There are no easy answers here. Develop the available talent. Look beyond the interests of individual departments to the interest of the firm as a whole, and strive to build the bigger team.

MANAGING PROJECT MANAGEMENT

The list of skills required by the data warehouse project manager continues to grow—communicator, educator, technology enthusiast, pragmatic realist, diplomat, calculator, tactician, strategist, loyal servant, charismatic leader, father confessor, mother courage, and unabashed flag waver. Experience in theatrical improvisation, *commedia del arte*, or stand-up comedy is also highly desirable. Because the required combination of competencies is unlikely to be joined in a single individual, flexibility and an ability to learn rapidly from one's own mistakes are key. Regardless of the mixture of attributes, the one essential guiding quality is self-knowledge. The ancient philosopher Socrates was considered the wisest person who ever lived because he said that he knew that he didn't know the answer. The translation into modern terms for this attitude is that the project manager should maintain a healthy skepticism about the limits of his or her knowledge and abilities. The role and the challenge is to make things happen through the knowledge and abilities of others. Knowledge of one's own strengths and limitations is gained in day-to-day experience and in taking a step back and looking at the big picture. Another word for that kind of self-knowledge is *integrity*. The analogy with database warehouse integrity is not far off the mark—consistency, keeping one's word, and working with defined boundaries to the logical unit of work (no marching and counter-marching).

Finally, what the project manager really needs is a project management data cube consisting of an intersecting network of persons, competencies, schedules, and priorities that converge in the factual grain of the project deliverable. Without a breakthrough in project management software, this is likely to remain more of an idea than a particular software product, from a project management perspective. However, even as an idea, it may have its uses. The data warehouse as an idea, and a mechanism for organizing experiences may apply to the project manager as a professional. What about building a personal data warehouse of project experiences? The suggestion is that any project manager ends up doing this implicitly, whether he or she knows it or not. Why not make this activity explicit as an approach to professional self-assessment and development? As the title of this section self-reflexively states, "managing project management" suggests that, as a tool, data warehousing be turned on itself. There could be an opportunity for an innovative approach to project management software to map out such a data cube of overlapping project commitments and dimensions.

SUMMARY . . . .

The approach to data warehousing project management undertaken in this chapter is inspired by the celebrated article by Parnas and Clement on "A Rational Design Process: How and Why to Fake It." The idea is that data warehousing system development is intrinsically complex, messy, and subject to the dynamics of changing requirements, technology, staff, and budget. However, given a ruthless focus on designing and constructing an architecture of consistent, unified dimensions (e.g., customer product, location, etc.) order can be brought out of chaos. The critical path of the data warehousing project lies through the identification and refinement of the data dimensions and granularity of the facts. Next, data warehousing project quality means laying down a defined and repeatable development process capable of being controlled and optimized. A data warehousing system is a complex artifact; and a quality (i.e., successful) data warehouse project requires a suitably advanced level of organizational maturity. Data warehousing projects are exposed to special risks in the areas of data quality, cross-functional team cooperation and coordination; and metadata definition and implementation. Many of these risks can be reduced and managed by ruthlessly focusing on consistently defining and implementing an essential minimal set of data dimensions. Naturally, project documentation and team development are discussed. Finally, what it means to manage project management is considered.

---

[1] Paraphrase of the key idea from Parnas, D. and Clements, P. "A Rational Design Process: How and Why to Fake It," *IEEE Transactions on Software Engineering*, Vol. SE-12(2), 1986.

[2] "Might say," but to the best of my knowledge, have not said anything like this. As this goes to press, there is evidence of industry alignment on the Open Information Model (OIM), which Microsoft has given to MDIS. Although a candidate de facto standard exists in OIM, metadata remains a grand challenge under any interpretation.

[3] The savvy reader will appreciate just how much of the material in this chapter is indebted to Grady Booch's approach to project management (see Booch, 1995). However, applications to data warehousing architecture, metadata, and data quality are the author's own contribution and (one might say) "spin."

Part 2

Design and Construction

(Chapters 5 through 9)

The critical path of the design and construction of the data warehousing system is identified. It is described as lying through the alignment of unified representations of the customer and product (service) data structures with fundamental business imperatives. Build consistent data structures (dimensions) corresponding to basic business drivers and align detailed transactions (facts) of appropriate granularity at the intersection points of the dimensions. Total data warehouse quality regards the data warehousing system as an information product by analogy with physical goods. Design time is the best time to provide for total data warehousing quality. Metrics are laid out and discussed. Placing knowledge on a continuum with ever improving information quality operationalizes knowledge and makes it definable in terms of the categories of information quality. Next, data warehousing technical design is engaged and data normalization is explained. The step-by-step refinement of the use case scenarios leads to the development of a logical data model. A nontrivial exercise in denormalization is performed to provide insight into mastering the problem of combinatorial explosion. Separate check lists for engaging logical design and physical design are provided by way of recommended practices. The relational database as a dominant design is discussed. The rules defining the relational database management system, the heart of the data warehouse, are reviewed and clarified.

5   *Business Design: The Unified Representations of the Customer and Product*

In this chapter...

". . . [IT successes] are conceptually undramatic initiatives that relate to the core business drivers of the firm and its industry and to the . . . rule of changing the limits of the possible in the structure of everyday life."
Peter G. W. Keen[1]

THE CRITICAL PATH: ALIGNMENT

The critical path of business advantage through data warehousing lies in the definition, design, and construction of unified views of the customer and product dimensions. Arguably, the first imperative of business is to get to know the customer. Get to know the customer's behavior and, on that basis, develop opportunities for customer intimacy and cross-selling. A unified representation of the customer in the data warehouse provides a mechanism for doing this. The next imperative of the business is to know the product, its behavior in the market and, on that basis, the building of the brand. A unified representation of the product (or service) in the data warehouse provides a method for accomplishing this. Finally, an additional imperative of the business is to get to know the moment of value where the customer and product interact and, on that basis, build the relationship between the customer and the company. The data warehouse provides a means for doing this by pointing toward the fundamental question of who is buying what and the fact structure that provides the answer. At stake are the integrity, coherence, usability, and return on the effort invested. Simply stated, the critical path lies through the definition and implementation of the data dimensions. Get the dimensions right, and the fact structures will mostly tend to take care of themselves. The result is alignment of the data warehousing technology with the business. What does this mean?

As the motto from Peter Keen implies, alignment is central to defining the scope of what is possible. As a design task, alignment has at least four aspects. First, *alignment* simply means "set inclusion." If the firm has four divisions and customers from three of the divisions are available to the data warehouse, cross-selling to the fourth division is not possible. Keeping to the present example, what is the extent of customers that can be accommodated in our unified customer dimension? Does the firm even know all of its customers? A potentially embarrassing question, but one that requires confronting if customer science and intimacy are to replace alchemy. If several legacy systems are the source of differing or even overlapping lists of customers, a preliminary and entry-level data mining task is required. A basic inventory of what is at hand needs to be compiled prior to the detailed data scrubbing to be considered in the next section. The decisions about scope—are a set of customers in or out?—is not mainly a technology decision but a business one. If a sense of urgency can be created that the "the [data warehousing] train is leaving," divisions or departments may be "incented" to "get on board," so as not to be informationally disadvantaged at a later date.

Secondly, *alignment* refers to the time horizon of experiences to be captured in the systematic representation of the business. Many businesses display cyclic patterns that emerge over the course of a year. To track year-to-year trends in those patterns already requires several years of data. Although summarizing and aggregating the data can help to manage data growth, the extensive time horizon is why data warehousing systems tend to get larger than transactional ones. (For instance, transactional systems are often satisfied with a thirty-day work-in-progress data store.) Note also that more is sometimes less. In a world where business practices and markets can change beyond recognition in five years, what is the value in tracking patterns that no longer belong to the structure of everyday life? (The family pattern of the father who works and the mother who stays home and raises 2.8 children who live within walking distance of school comes to mind.) Just maybe (let's say) three years of data, instead of five, is good enough, regardless of statistical standards, and especially when customers move on average every three years.

Thirdly, *alignment* refers to the range of services available through the data warehouse to the processes representing the imperatives driving the business. At the foundation, this entails access to the information answering the fundamental question as to who is buying what and when and where they are doing so. A variety of other services are immediately implied—the JIT delivery of what is bought through superior sales forecasting or sourcing in the context of improved supply chain management; the creation of additional sales opportunities through cross-selling of products and services; targeted direct marketing campaign or profitability data as informed by detailed demographics; or production line quality assurance through managing by the facts. Indeed, each of the implemented and available services tends to map to a fact table (or tables) in the data warehousing system. Thus, forecasting requires shipment facts, cross-selling requires sales facts, direct marketing requires user responses to promotions facts, and managing package deliveries requires facts about on-time deliveries, exceptions, and reasons for variances, and so on.

Finally, *alignment* means responsiveness of the data warehousing system to business priorities and imperatives. This is another aspect of time—not just the horizon, but the speed with which a response can be formulated and delivered. This has immediate implications for customer service, where instant service is now the norm in the mind of the customer (whether or not it needs to be) as a result of an entire nation being conditioned by fast-food franchises. It also has obvious implications that interactive systems—those that are actually able to perform—have advantages over batch ones when responding to time-critical inquiries. So, technology choices and options still make a difference. This also has significance for the rapidity with which the entire data warehousing architecture can be adapted dynamically to changing customer profiles, product mixes, and markets at large. Even here, there is some "low-hanging fruit." Experience shows that those data warehouse projects that define data dimensions first and up front—such as the ones to be detailed in this chapter—and then proceed to align fact structures with them are more likely to generate a successful outcome than those that ignore this rule of thumb. As for the fruits of design effort that lie further up on the branches of the tree of knowledge, there is no substitute for simulating a rational design process, as described in Chapter Four (Data Warehousing Project Management) and the ideas detailed in the remainder of this chapter.

A UNIFIED REPRESENTATION OF THE CUSTOMER

The challenge of building a unified representation of the customer is particularly clear in the financial services industries—banking, insurance, securities. For example, a customer may have a cash management account with her or his broker, an IRA with the same firm, and yet a third account, in which still other real estate, derivative financial products or hard assets are managed. A business rule, which, in this case, may be a reflection of the vicissitudes of financial deregulation, is required to determine who "owns" that customer. Making such a rule explicit is not a trivial matter. The data warehouse is affected by such an issue without the warehouse team alone being able to resolve it. Let's say that a commitment to best practices results in one account representative being a "single point of contact" and responsible for all of the business with a single customer. Now, align the data warehousing technology with that rule. What does that look like? Does the broker have on her desktop a unified representation of the customer through software presented on her work station? Does the unified window exist only in her head or on a paper-based synthesis that has to be laboriously constructed by cutting and pasting? Does this mapping to a unified view exist in the system, as presented on the desktop, or in someone's head only? This implies a task—if the unified representation does not exist, construct it. This task has at least two parts, including a design and an implementation phase. As usual, immediately upon engaging in the task, a firm tends to encounter inconsistent customer data. Legacy systems and modern ERP systems are "misaligned" with one another and with the prospective data warehousing system. The challenge is intensified due to the name and address data that has been captured and stored over the years being "dirty." That means inaccurate or incomplete or inconsistent data. Are "Jim Baker," "James Baker," and "James R. Baker, Jr." the same or different persons? The solution in both cases is easy to state but not so easy to implement. If you want clean data, the implementation approach is "data scrubbing."

DATA SCRUBBING

Data scrubbing has come to be a technical term for the process of comparing and rendering consistent the data extracted and transferred into the data warehouse from different sources of data in a firm. The goals are eliminating duplicates, imposing consistency according to defined business rules, flagging errors for correction, and aligning the data with the actual facts about customers in the market. As a "simple" example, using the above-cited names, the data scrubbing program—which could be custom coded in a procedural language or bought or generated as part of a package application—would compare other associated data to determine whether the Bakers in question are the same person. As usual, the devil is in the details. If they have the same address, it is a reasonable inference that they are the same person. Naturally, this pushes the problem down a level—what is the difference between "2105 W. Lawrence Ave." and "2105 West Lawrence Avenue"? In this case, the process would proceed bottom up. First, correct city, state, zip, and address data, using information available from the post office. Then attack names, parsing them into prefixes, suffixes, titles, and abbreviations. This can get computationally intensive—lots of machine cycles needed to perform all these comparisons for a million customers. Even then, a small fraction of the data may be too dirty to make sense out of and may require inspection by a human being.

Data scrubbing is on the critical path to a successful data warehouse implementation. Given the quality of data of many operational, legacy systems, this is a fair generalization. However, a word of caution is in order. Data scrubbing is not building the data warehouse. It is a necessary condition but not a sufficient one. What counts as the target definition of *good-enough data* may vary from one industry to another. If it is a governmental taxing authority determining who is to be audited, a lot less room is available for error than if it is a newspaper generating customer direct-mail promotion lists. The important point is "avoid obsessive washing." Data scrubbing is not an end in itself. It is a means to driving out inconsistencies, errors, and defects from the data. It is a means to producing data that is fit for use for the purposes of knowing the customer and building the brand. It is important for management to appreciate that a point comes when you have to get off of the data scrubbing subproject and onto completing the data warehouse.

For example, a Midwestern newspaper was searching for a better method of generating subscription lists for telephone sales, direct-mail soliciting, advertising campaigns, and related business intelligence about customer segmentation. A highly normalized operational system required about a two-week effort on the part of the marketing specialist to yield a clean list of subscription prospects. Requirements included filtering out existing subscribers, so that call center sales representatives would not seem dumb by trying to sell to people who already had subscriptions. It was considered so unacceptable to market new offers to existing customers that a conscious decision was made to err on the side of being conservative and risk filtering out legitimate prospects. If a person bought a subscription for his mother, it would still make sense to try to sell him a subscription for himself. However, a legacy system from which the extract occurred represented the distinction between the payor and the recipient of the subscription in such a way as to leave it an open question as to whether the number of individuals and the number of addresses corresponded. An additional requirement existed to tie in with the transactional system that tracked actual subscription additions, renewals, and attrition. This was because knowing the retention rate, along with response rate for a promotion, is essential to evaluating the effectiveness of the campaign. A scrubbed customer prospect database—including many-to-many associations between individuals, roles, and addresses—was determined to be a good platform on which to base a cross-selling data warehouse. Given that people change their addresses, on average, once every five years in the standard multistate metropolitan statistical area in question, data accuracy of 99% was considered a possible stretch target. However, no sooner was the design commenced than the firm realized the operational data was inherently ambiguous. Agreement on basic business definitions and rules—who is a customer, a subscriber, a prospect, a payee—was deceptively easy to state but hard to implement. As indicated, if a person buys a subscription for a home-bound mother, she is the subscriber and the one purchasing the subscription is the payor. Or is the one paying best understood as the subscriber and the person receiving the newspaper the recipient? Provided that one does so consistently and coherently, one could build a transactional business system using either set of definitions. The problem occurs when the transactional system and data warehousing one cannot reach an agreement. Of course, the transactional system has a certain priority, because it got there first but the data warehousing system is not required to implement the incompleteness of a legacy system when a properly designed many-to-many association can accommodate a wide variety of scenarios, including future ones that have not even been envisioned. Naturally, it would be that way: Order entry and cross-selling and -marketing are driven by different business priorities. The solution—really a pragmatic workaround—required the development of two applications—one to translate forward, the other backward, into terms understandable by each system. To be sure, this was not a grand challenge in computing. Nevertheless, time and effort were required to produce a result that both presented pragmatic and actionable knowledge and maintained the integrity and data quality of the operational system.

THE CROSS-FUNCTIONAL TEAM

The definition of a unified representation of the customer is a design task, not a given. In turn, this has implications about the makeup of the cross-functional team to be assembled to deliver the results. The time and effort of marketing and product managers and staff can be expected to be engaged.

Tough decisions about the scope of the project are at hand here. For example, insurance and finance companies may have multiple data stores, each representing separate lines of business. These may contain the same customers, families, or target client businesses, simply because the marketing channel is diversified by completely different marketing teams. Thus, the life insurance team in Chicago sells life insurance to everyone in the Midwest; the automobile insurance team, a completely different group of people, does the same. They each maintain their own highly sensitive, valuable, and closely guarded list (i.e., file) of customers and prospects. Similar things might be said about marketing individual banking accounts versus small business services. Representatives from the business units involved can expect demands to be made on their time and resources. One of the responsibilities of the executive function, which cannot really be delegated, is to furnish a framework for dialog, disagreement, and consensus building.

This is why the earlier statement was made—you can't shrink-wrap knowledge of the business. You can't shrink-wrap the leadership required to implement the data warehouse, either. The benefit of cross-selling is a powerful one; the expanding horizon of a growing market is likely to be many a marketing person's dream come true. Nevertheless, the fear of having another marketing person at the same company "steal" one's customers is great in a profession that sometimes quotes "all is fair in love and war" as its ethical mantra. This is where technology can make a difference.

For Once, a Technology Bullet

One of the prime features of the relational database system is data independence.[2] That means that the representation of the data is uncoupled from the underlying physical file implementation. The way that the data is presented to the end-user is relatively independent of its layout as records or segments in the database. An important aspect of that independence is the ability to define and implement a structure called a *view*. A view is a virtual table that represents a subset of the underlying physical structure. Simple and elegant, the different marketing teams can each be given their own views of the underlying unified customer structure. Information that can reasonably be expected to be shared will be visible to both. For example, the life insurance staff should know that Mr. Nietzshe has automobile insurance, but they should not necessarily know the details of his driving record, insofar as that has entered into his customer dimension record.

HIERARCHICAL STRUCTURE

Hierarchy is a proven method for managing complexity. Systems of all kinds—biological, physical, economic, and informational—use hierarchies to arrange, order, and access parts within parts (and so on). Thus, hierarchy is one of the fundamental data structures for organizing distinctions of all kinds. Entire databases are based on hierarchical structuring. For certain applications, such as bill of materials, the hierarchy is a natural fit. However, hierarchical structures are not always as flexible as one might wish in terms of arbitrary rearrangements of relations. The vision of data every which way—as long as it's hierarchical—is susceptible to improvement. So hierarchical databases have given way to ones that permit the use of associations—logical products as well as hierarchies—without being restricted to just that latter form. Nevertheless, the hierarchy is basic to understanding the power of the data warehouse alignment with the business, the market, and the technology, so it is to it that we now turn.

People spend a lot of their time thinking about groups of things. When those groups are arranged into inclusive and interlocking collections, a hierarchy is created. We think of time in terms of hours, days, weeks, months, quarters, and years. This is a hierarchy (see Figure 5.1). We think of firms as departments, units, divisions, and even companies. Alternative corporate hierarchies may exist, overlapping the same domain, as when tasks, projects, portfolios, and strategic units cover the same domain, as do corporate departments and divisions. So, for example, the country is divided into geographic areas; areas, in turn, contain districts or units; districts contain routes; routes contain stops (or a similar pattern). Alternative hierarchies may exist simultaneously, as when the traditional country, state, county, city, and zip, are added to the above-cited hierarchy. Overlapping hierarchies was a fact of life in large firms even before the mergers, acquisitions, and spin-offs that continue to occur. It is a judgment call, based on knowledge of the business, as to what extent they can be eliminated or actually provide useful perspectives on aspects of the product, market, or firm itself. Logically, they are acceptable, though when combined with other hierarchies and facts, they will produce logically distinct aggregations and perspectives (see Figure 5.2: Overlapping Hierarchies). Data dimensions will usually take the form of a hierarchical arrangement of overlapping or nested categories.

Those companies that "know their customer portfolios" are able to leverage their relations for increased profitability. A measurable connection exists between growth and customer relationship value, but it is not a necessary connection. What are the important levels in the customer dimension hierarchy for your business—the market, the group, or the individual? If you are producer of a commodity product, not highly differentiated, then the entire market may suffice as the target of the selling effort. If there are no economically distinguishable groups, then most customer relations are of roughly equal value. In a world where the value of every individual customer is forcefully proclaimed from every trade journal and every rooftop, it is useful to lean into the wind a bit. If the mean value of the customer relationship is low relative to the cost of acquiring and applying customer-specific knowledge, then it may not pay to man-

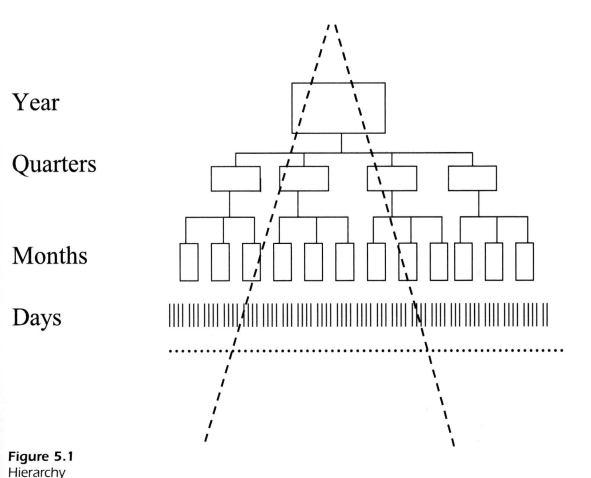

Year

Quarters

Months

Days

Figure 5.1
Hierarchy

age customer relationships at an individual level (for a detailed discussion, see Wayland and Cole, 1997: 138). The data warehouse enables one to quantify the amount of business done with the market, significant groups (segments) within the market, and the individual customer. For example, Coke tries to reach all consumers with one recipe. On the other hand, Harley-Davidson strayed from the path when it tried to do the same. It tried to broaden its market into casual, recreational lightweight cycling instead of the heavy-duty "road Hog" that represents its best standard group. There really is a distinction in the motorcycle market between lightweight and heavy-duty cycling. Meanwhile, American Express and credit card companies, in general, are very much compelled to market to individuals. A data warehouse whose customer and product dimensions contain a hierarchy similar to this—individual, group, market and item, brand, category—enables an organization to evaluate and shift between these three different strategies for reaching customers, moving up or down the market as business opportunities present themselves.

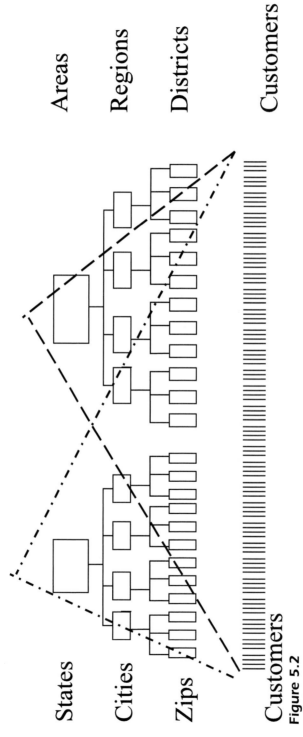

Figure 5.2
Overlapping Hierarchies—All Individual Customers Belong to Each Hierarchy

CUSTOMER DEMOGRAPHICS

In transactional systems supporting day-to-day operations and designed for frequent and fast update activity, it is typical to break the customer dimension into multiple tables. For example, a customer may have multiple addresses—ship to address, payment address, returns address. The customer id might usefully be "snowflaked" into multiple subordinate structures. However, because the data warehouse is mostly an inquiry and not an update structure, the recommendation here is not to snowflake. Do not decompose or otherwise normalize the customer dimension. It is one of the fundamental dimensions of any data warehouse data model. Chasing through a series of structures for customer demographic characteristics will cost far more in terms of I/O and response time, given the current boundaries of commercial applications, than the cost of disk storage for data redundancy. Unless you are the phone company, where, as Ralph Kimball so aptly characterizes it, the customer dimensions get really *big* and special handling is required, do not try to decompose this dimension into further structures. In those cases, the best approach is to be to normalize data into individual customer structure and a demographic structure that groups relevant demographic attributes into bands (e.g., monthly use is <30, 31–59, 60–99, 100–200, >201, etc.). These predefined bands are called *demographic minidimensions*.

A UNIFIED REPRESENTATION OF THE PRODUCT

Analogous considerations apply to the product and temporal dimensions of the enterprise data warehouse, though the details differ. Here, the business imperative is to develop a unified product structure based on business brands. The apparent exception is provided by the insurance and certain financial service industries, where products tend to become increasingly customized lines of business. Insurance companies tend to have heterogeneous products. Unlike cans on a grocery store shelf, insurance products are highly customized. Indeed, if the client is big enough, a product will be developed solely for it. What to do about such a situation is to compromise. Normalize the data on a selective basis into a generic and product-line-specific structure. This is an exception to the overall rule to have a unified product hierarchy. If the employer group to be insured is big enough, almost every product tends to be specifically customized to accommodate the requirements of the group.

In that case, the recommendation is to group those product attributes that are represented in all lines of business into a primary product structure and to break out alternative abstractions of other various product features into more generic attributes and features that can be represented in a second structure. The structure of products tends to resemble that of customers, in that it is hierarchical. Individual products are contained by brands; which, in turn, are contained by categories; which, in turn, are contained by lines of business. (Naturally, the breakout will vary by industry and by company.)

There are distinct disadvantages to breaking products into separate structures (tables) based on product type, category, and line of business, etc. Although these may be logically separate entities, from a mercilessly physical point of view, there is only one entity here, and that is the product—the can of peas, the tractor that rolls off of the assembly line, or the CD-ROM of music or software—the physical thing. The amount of space in the database that will be saved by normalizing product will be trivial in comparison with the amount of space required by product, customer, and date combinations in fact tables; and the process of data access will be slowed by chasing from one data structure to another to assemble the attributes that make up the product.

Internal Resistance

An account of how much internal company-wide resistance there is to building a unified view of the customer (or product) is an index or measure of how parts of the firm are actually competing with one another. This is not always bad in itself, because today's hot product is tomorrow's clearance item. To be sure, genuine issues of privacy and confidentiality can also be addressed by separating perspectives in a bullet-proof way, using relational database views. However, when it is a function of perception, politics, or paranoia, then it is a source of unnecessary friction. The subproject of using information technology to construct a unified perspective on the customer (or product) can actually be used as a lever to surface and drive out misunderstandings with the result that the business benefits as a whole. In a world of departmental thinking, an enterprise perspective provides a powerful lever for coordinating commitments to enact fundamental business imperatives to customer intimacy and brand development in building the bigger team.

DATA MARTS: BETWEEN PROTOTYPE AND RETROTYPE

Yet another valuable result of this approach is how to distinguish an enterprise data warehouse from a departmental data mart. The latter may have fragmented, inconsistent, or incomplete representations of customer, product, and their relationship. The definition, design, and construction of the basic warehouse dimensions is where the distinction between data mart and warehouse is determined. If a unified definition of the customer and product have been constructed with an enterprise-wide perspective, we are on the road to a data warehouse. If the definition has only local, departmental validity, we are on the path of a data mart. If the definition is inconsistent with that in other departments, we are on the way to what Doug Hackney has aptly labeled the *legamart*—a data mart as a legacy system (Hackney, 1997: 402). This is not really a step in the right direction, it is retrograde, backward movement,—to coin a term, a *retrotype*. If the definition, though perhaps acknowledged to be incomplete, is consistent with that of customers and products in other divisions, we are on our way to a prototype data warehouse. This latter is what both George Zagelow and Doug Hackney usually refer to as a data mart—an initial, local, incremental accomplishment from which the data anomalies have been driven out, expelled, and banished, with the expectation of additional step-by-step rollout in phases.

The balancing act is between time-to-implement and consistency-and-complete-ness. Advocates of the data mart favor the former; whereas exponents of the data ware-house emphasize the latter. The data mart advocates are always careful to say something such as "drive out the inconsistencies." Of course, this implies designing a data ware-house. The data warehouse advocates are always careful to say something such as "build credibility with the end-user (customer) by implementing subject area prototypes, based on conforming dimensions." In other words, design a data warehouse—get the dimen-sions right first—where *right* means "aligned with the business"—then add the fact structures thereafter. Subsequent discussion in this book will refer to *data warehouses*, not *marts,* with the understanding this is consistent with step-by-step implementation of consistent dimensions conforming to cross-functional, enterprise level design.

The value of an iterative, prototyping approach is almost beyond calculation. From a practical point of view, it is easier to assemble and justify the cost of a step-by-process rather than to do so for a big bang project. From the end-user perspective, gratification (like justice) delayed is gratification denied. The ability to plan ahead and stay the course is increasingly limited by the cruelties of beggar-thy-neighbor compe-tition, marching and counter marching as mergers and spin-offs proliferate, and sim-ple lack of understanding of complex software constructs and business processes.

No matter how savvy and how much of a super-user the end-user turns out to be, one fundamental principle continues to rule. The implementation of any new system (includ-ing implementation into production) changes the end-user's perception and understanding of what was desired, contracted for, or believed to be possible in any case.[3] Therefore, a prototype is a powerful tool in reducing the chances of a big surprise and project meltdown and, because problems are likely to occur, a useful weapon in engaging and solving them.

The difference between a throw-away prototype and an iterative prototype is the consistency, integrity, and ability to carry forward the definitions of the basic dimen-sions of the data warehouse. If these turn out not to scale across the enterprise because, for example, the Dusseldorf Division has an anomalous, secret definition of customer that is known only to the Central European staff and generates substantial revenue, then it is back to the drawing board.

In at least one example known to the author, the claim that all the inconsistencies from the definition of the customer had been driven out turned out to be significantly inac-curate. This company was serving so many customers that a significant category was below radar. Therefore, instead of a first implementation of a prototype data warehouse (one might also have said *data mart*), the firm realized that it had actually implemented a legacy data mart. After additional expense, reengineering, and hard knocks, the represen-tation in the technology and the operation of the business were successfully aligned.

Nevertheless, the point remains valid. The unified representation of the customer and product are the basic first principles on which the business design of the data warehouse is founded. It may seem paradoxical that you have to think and represent each of these as a unity to appreciate the manifold aspects of the hierarchy. However, upon reflection, you realize that is the meaning of unity—the knitting together according to principle of something with parts. You arrive at a basic principle of marketing—customer segmentation—through a unified representation of the manifold of different customer tiers. You arrive at a basic principle of product development—differentiation—through a unified representation of what gets differentiated. That is the meaning of alignment of the business and the technology—the representations of the parts and whole maps in the customer and product hierarchies to those practical and pragmatic distinctions operative in the business.

SUMMARY . . . .

The critical path of the business design of data warehousing lies in the definition, design, and implementation of unified views of the customer and product (service) dimensions. The business imperatives of knowing the customer and building the brand line up exactly with these data dimensions. This lining up – alignment – is central to the delimitation of the scope of what is possible. The four aspects of this alignment are detailed Building a unified representation of the customer is most challenging in the financial service industries where individuals may have multiple accounts in stove pipe systems, separately defined by product line – checking, savings, IRA, etc. This leads to the necessity for data scrubbing to identify actual business entities – a customer with whom one can do business. Ultimately, a cross-functional team may be required to manage the complexity of defining who is the customer in adequate enterprise terms. Hierarchy is also a proven method of managing complexity. Although out of fashion today, hierarchy is central to architecture, commitment, and the unified representation of the customer. Similar considerations apply to the unified representation of the product. Finally, the terms of the debate are laid out between the advocates of data warehousing and data marts. The trade-offs are considered, including the data warehouse project that last forever (until its canceled) and the data mart as a legacy system. One compromise that is pragmatically encountered is to design the data warehouse dimensions and implement the data mart facts based on them.

---

[1] See Keen, Peter G.W., *Shaping the Future: Business Design through Information Technology*, Boston, MA: Harvard Business School Press, 1991: 227. The author also wishes to acknowledge the value of Keen's ideas on alignment, some of which are adapted and extended to data warehousing in the discussion in this chapter (see, in particular, Keen, 1991, "Aligning Business and Technology," pp. 211–237).

[2] Details on what makes a relational database management system what it is will be addressed below in Chapter Eight: Data Warehouse Construction Technologies: SQL.

[3] Grady Booch has a nice discussion of this from an informed project management perspective quite independent of any considerations of object-oriented technology see *Object Solutions*, p. 131.

6 *Total Data Warehouse Quality*

In this chapter...

*"Quality—it's not just
for data anymore."*
Larry Mohr[1]

THE INFORMATION PRODUCT

Over the past ten years, the manufacture of physical goods has been transformed by the total quality management movement. As noted above, a TQM data warehouse forms an important part of tracking, measuring, and enabling management by facts, so central to the quality movement. This chapter will apply the same TQM methods used in the manipulation of physical goods to the information supply chain, one of the intermediate products of which is the data warehouse itself. The analogy is quite exact, though allowances must be made for the high degree of abstraction of information products. The information supply chain (to be further detailed in Chapter Twelve) connects information producers and consumers. It bridges the gap between transactional and decision support systems. This puts the "decision" back in "decision support." When this is made the basis for action, it transforms the raw operational data into information and information into knowledge.

Conventional wisdom places data, information, and knowledge on the same continuum. This makes it seem like a miracle that dirty data is scrubbed, and the result is knowledge. At one end of the line is raw data. The quality of the data is improved by subjecting it to a defined, rigorous quality improvement process, and the result is information. The quality of the information is further improved, and the result is knowledge. This conventional wisdom will not be disputed here (though one specific insight will be added).

One possible point of interpretation deserves attention, regardless of any controversy. One way of reading the conventional wisdom is that it holds the view that knowledge is information that satisfies enough of the quality attributes identified in a defined quality process so that it (the information product) is fit for use.[2] In this reading, *knowledge* is explained as—reduced to—quality information. In short, when information accumulates sufficient quality attributes, it receives the "honor and dignity" of being designated as *knowledge*. From the perspective of quality improvement technology, knowledge remains a point on the horizon of quality, toward which information progresses without ever quite getting there. By definition, we always strive to improve quality without ever quite completing the job. ("There is always room for improvement.") Yet our intuition tells us that, at least from time to time, we do, in fact, have knowledge.

This honor and dignity, however, places knowledge off of the data-information continuum. From where does the "dignity" of knowledge come? Knowledge retains a special dignity, because, unlike true information (and belief), knowledge implies a commitment. Consider. If a person says "I *believe* the customer bought 1,000 widgets yesterday," that implies no commitment. The person merely believes it. If he or she turns out to be wrong—well, they only said they "believed." On the other hand, if the person says "I *know* the customer bought 1,000 widgets yesterday," a commitment is implied. In the latter case, in effect, the person puts their integrity on the line—you can count on them. "You can bank on it. I give my word—I say I *know*."

Decision Support or Business Intelligence?

The technology of information improvement reduces knowledge to quality information. The practice of decision making in business requires that knowledge be the basis for a commitment in action. Reasonable people may agree to disagree about the direction and ultimate terms of explanation here. As Herbert Simon pointed out, "In the face of complexity, an in-principle reductionism may be at the same time a pragmatic holist" (Simon, 1969: 86). In practice, knowledge is not reducible to quality information but, technologically considered, it is part of the same whole complex of making knowledge operational in the service of customers, brands, and the like. The practice of making business decisions feeds back into quality information and adds the requirement of being able to ground a decision on it. This requires knowledge, that is, commitment. This is the one respect in which the older and less elegant term *decision support* is still perhaps superior to the caché of *business intelligence*. The echo of a commitment can still be heard in the "decision" of "decision support." Meanwhile, aside from business practices, the technology of knowledge management is based on making such a reduction to quality information in the service of operationalizing knowledge. *Operational* means the knowledge is grounded in the quality attributes and implied metrics and mechanisms to be detailed in this chapter. Although the theoretically inclined may find many problems with this approach, the result is a practical success. Operationalizing knowledge unpacks it into pragmatic, useful, instrumental terms; that is, indeed, an important and valuable result. If you want to understand the step-by-step process of transforming data or information into knowledge, then work out the attributes of information quality in a step-by-step way.

Ultimately the determining difference between knowledge and information is that knowledge entails (or implies) a commitment. If someone says "I know," then that implies responsibility and commitment to a decision. If it turns out that the person is wrong, then others are allowed to demand an explanation and hold the person responsible for the error. Making knowledge continuous with true (objective) information is an idea whose validity is limited by commitment. However, within that limit, it is validated by practice and in operations.

DATA QUALITY AS DATA INTEGRITY

Data warehouse quality is, first of all, a matter of overall data quality. If anything is wrong with the data, it is said to lack integrity. In the world of the data administrator (DA) *data integrity* covers a multiplicity of quality metrics. The way the DA, database administrator (DBA), and end-user use the word, *integrity* allows for numerous quality distinctions. The data in the information system is internally consistent within itself. An "orphan" line item on an order without a header is an example of internal inconsistency. This is also described as *referential integrity* where the *reference* indicates internal correspondences between entities that must line up. The data represented in the information system is consistent with states of affairs in the real world. The system indicates that 1,000 widgets were ordered by customer 999, and they really were so ordered. The system "lines up with reality." It has objective validity. Thus, *data integrity,* as the term is customarily used, captures both aspects of representational consistency and intrinsic objectivity.

Intrinsic Qualities

Aspects of information quality first include the intrinsic quality of the data. The distinction between "accuracy" and "objectivity" is at the top of the list. Accuracy is a feature of how well the system expresses the data distinctions that it contains; whereas objectivity is how well the system lines up with the reality of business processes in the world. Is the information accurate? If the data warehouse says 1,000 measures of cheese were sold to the ten customers in region five in the third quarter, the named quantity is really what the information system reports, regardless of the amount of product sold during that time period. The information is accurate if that is what the information system really reports. The system is accurately reporting what it contains.

A further issue is raised when we ask whether the report lines up with reality. Does the data in the system "correspond" to the world of business? Another way of saying this is that the "correspondence" of the system and the world makes it "objective." This objectivity is a mark of quality.

Objectivity is the intrinsic feature that makes us want to declare information to be knowledge, not just data. However, it is hard to keep fixed, even given modern computing systems. In many instances, the passage of time and the conflicting interests of persons causes the objectivity of the data to degrade. Was the package delivered? If the customer says no, and there is no receipt to show otherwise, what recourse is available? Indeed, who can remember what happened two days ago—much less two months ago? What does it mean to say that the computer "shows" the package was delivered? Maybe it is just as confused as the person who performed the data entry.

Data could be accurate but not objective if it corresponded to what someone believed, and what that person believed was not really the case. If someone believes that sun spots cause dandruff, it is accurate to say the person believes that absurd idea, but it does not correspond to any state of affairs in the world. It is not free of error. It is not objective. It could, however, help the sales of shampoo during certain times of the year. Now consider even a simple real world example. Are we losing sales in region R because the competition is discounting, their new product has a differentiation perceived as value-adding by the consumer, industrial espionage has compromised our sales strategy, or something is occurring outside the box that we haven't thought of yet? Although objectivity ought to be enough, it is not. Additional information features are marshalled to support or qualify the quality of the information. These include other intrinsic qualities relating to the representation of information, as well as to secondary information qualities that depend on context and reputation.

For a powerful, real-world example where compelling business reasons required subordinating objectivity to accuracy, see the section below, "Reinterpreting the Past."

Ambiguity

Another mark of warehouse information quality is that the meaning of the data is unambiguous. Lack of ambiguity is the mark of quality here. "Customer" designates one and only one individual. Customer "1234" designates "James Baker," not "James Baker" in the morning and "James Quaker" in the evening. In other words, the data element has one and only one meaning—e.g., customer description describes someone who has made a purchase in the past six months, not someone to whom we sent marketing literature and hope makes a purchase or someone who has made a purchase. That is the description of a prospective customer and should not be mixed with current customers. (See Figure 6.1: Ambiguous Representation.)

The meaning of the data is precise—not vague or fuzzy. "Ship Date" means the date the item left the dock, not the proposed date of shipment, plus or minus two days. The boundary for the data element is crisp and well defined. (see Figure 6.2: Imprecise Representation.)

I.T. System   Reality

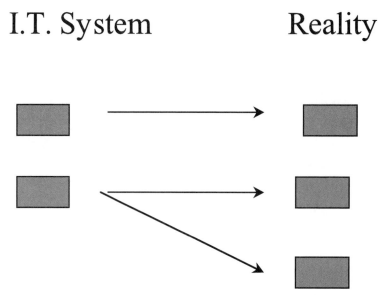

Figure 6.1
Ambiguous Representation

Timeliness and Consistency in Time

Timeliness is one of the most important aspects of information quality for any attempt to operationalize information into knowledge. Information delayed is knowledge denied (and vice versa). Under any interpretation, saying that the information is timely makes sense. If the daily snapshot contains data that is two weeks old, it may be accurate, consistent, and objective, but it lacks timeliness. For example, Thomas Davenport reports (Davenport, 1997: 7) that it took the Treasurer at IBM two months to get basic information on outstanding warranties of IBM products. A product-oriented warehouse would have helped. The CFO was unable to find out how much foreign exchange rates had affected profit margins at IBM Europe or IBM Australia. It is easy to see that a data warehouse would have helped.

Consistency in time adds a slightly different "spin" to being timely. Consistency in time is an important measure of quality. If my customer data is from the second quarter and my product data is from the third quarter, problems will arise in cross-referencing them. There may be gaps where the data doesn't overlap. Discrepancies are bound to occur based on mismatches in the point in time at which the data is frozen by being stored in the database. If you think about it, you will realize that none of the information will be more accurate than the least accurate of the data with which it is compared. This is particularly important in the context of the data warehouse. If three operational systems are feeding the warehouse and one of them is down, a mechanism is needed to show the end-

I.T. System   Reality

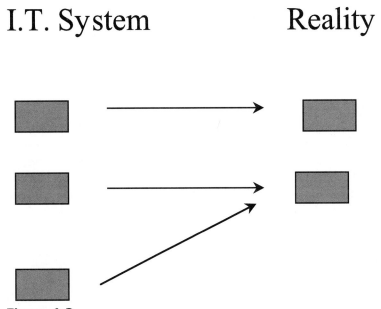

Figure 6.2
Imprecise Representation

user that the third operational system is indeed functioning but not reporting today. Issues of scheduling will be further discussed in Chapter Thirteen on metadata.

Although there is no logical reason for it, occasionally, a period of time is required for data to stabilize. This is a phenomenon characteristic of the frantic activity that occurs in periodically "closing" accounting cycles—monthly, quarterly, and annually. For example, a miskeying of a receipt may not be noticed until monthly summaries are generated and reviewed. An item may be missing or miscategorized, throwing off an overall balance. True, this is a good reason to avoid manual entry of data and to capture everything in automated fashion at the point-of-sale cash register. However, even there, cashiers have been known to reverse the key pad item to be pressed. The mere passage of time is insufficient to transform problems with data. However, what does happen is that the passage of time allows inaccurate and objective errors to percolate up or be checked for reasonableness by accountable staff and reviewers. So it seems that the data is finally stabilized when someone finally has a chance to inspect it.

SECURITY

One of the essential jobs of the data warehouse database is to protect data against unauthorized access and modification. Information quality is greatly at risk unless it is secured against unauthorized update or use. That is the reason this discussion of security is embedded in a chapter on data quality.

In other words, managing authorities and privileges—providing for security—is also one of the basic jobs of a DBMS. Working out an approach to security that prevents accidental or malicious damage and allows developers, end-users, and customers to perform their jobs efficiently and without obstacles is a challenging task that requires a skillful balancing act on the part of security administrators, DAs, and managers alike. In general, enterprise databases do a good job of locking down access to the data they contain through group authorizations and default denials of permission: "What is not allowed is forbidden." The problem is that these gates of iron are sometimes flanked by walls of paper maché. Those bent on committing mischief or malicious activities attack the strongest point only through error, accident, or incompetence. Thus, almost every act compromising information security relates to network access by means of a removable disk (Strassmann, 1997: 366), the weakest link in the defenses.

It would be hard to find a better or more compelling case for the networked or thin client desktop. However, because that is not likely to be the case in our Windows-centric world any time soon, we must define and implement tight rules, including technical ones, on how and when to store and access individual data. The allocation of a partition of disk on the server dedicated to the individual should be the only place where private data can be stored. It should be password protected and, if necessary, encrypted. Upon leaving employment, information assets can be checked in, along with keys, access cards, and photo id. This approach aligns with a policy that recognizes how personal computers make it easy for employees to use corporate computing resources for personal business—resumes, self-study, and professional correspondence. Why try to stop what it is impossible to prevent anyway? Rather, regulate it in a reasonable and professional way that enlists and recruits cooperation from the staff in a spirit of fair play.

Due Diligence or Irreparable Damage?

The thought, "It can't happen here or to me" is understandable but naïve. Ultimately, it is a bad bet. Anyone who picks up a newspaper must be aware of the variety of threats. To be sure, accident and human error belong toward the top of the list, but information terrorism, computer crime, and even information warfare now belong on the list, too.

The fact that globally managed crime earns $750 billion a year (mostly from drug traffic) (see Strassmann, 1997: 364) means that ample funds are available to recruit insiders with network access. The lesson for management here is loud and clear. Security, like so many aspects of information quality, is not just a technical problem. It is a policy and procedural imperative. This implies the requirement for coordinated security and access methods and organizational practices—including everything from security officer sign-off and accountability to the deletion of system ids and passwords of employees leaving the firm. Technology alone does not provide security. It is technology guided by management insight and responsibility that make the difference. As this goes to press, the daily news is filled with material on the U.S. Special House Committee Cox Report about the transfer of missile, nuclear bomb, and delivery system technology to a foreign power. We now get to read chilling reports on the theft of design data on the miniature M-88 warhead from the Lawrence Livermore Lab, not due to 007 espionage but rather due to leaving sensitive documents on insecure computers or insufficiently secured networks. Some of the materials were apparently accessible to students, visitors, and low-level employees. May we speak with whoever is in charge here? (See Helene Cooper and John J. Fialka, "Report on Chinese Spying Tales Big Toll," *Wall Street Journal,* May 26, 1999.)

The more valuable the business intelligence contained in the data warehouse, the more of a target it can be expected to be. Just because you are supplying macaroni and cheese—not cruise missiles—to the armed forces does not mean you are not a target of information warfare or terrorism. Without wishing to trivialize or make light of the threat, what better way to demoralize, disorganize, or defeat an enemy than through its logistics and supply function? Defective bolts in an airplane's wings or engines— or, more likely, counterfeit and inferior spare parts—would also be a grave act of industrial sabotage. Within this context, quality assurance takes on new meaning and importance as a security function. In fact, since the nature of modern terrorism is to attack at random and destroy the innocent bystander, along with the symbols of authority, no one is immune from random acts of destruction or violence. It is precisely the random nature that puts the terror into terrorism.

Because the threat is random—and that includes the threat of natural disasters, accidents due to clumsiness, and that infinite source of mischief, human error—the response must be systematic and well organized. It is both a bottom up and top down undertaking. Whenever designing new systems, security must be built in from the start. Whenever retrofitting existing systems, the framework of policies and procedures must be elaborated and extended to compensate for and balance against openings in the technical infrastructures.

Secondary Qualities

These, then, are the intrinsic metrics of information quality—accuracy, objectivity, nonambiguity, precision, consistency, timeliness, and security. These aspects of quality are most closely associated with what we describe as intrinsic features of information quality. It is also possible to detail secondary qualities. These tend to be derivative on the intrinsic quality features or a close function of context or use. The data is credible, has a good reputation for reliability, and is available (accessible). These secondary qualities often show up when a breakdown occurs.

Credibility

The worst things that can happen to a new, functioning data warehouse system—or any system, for that matter—is when the believability of the data—its credibility—comes into question. If this happens due to human error—the wrong tape is loaded—that can perhaps be quickly acknowledged and corrected. The last thing in world a data warehouse manager wants is end-users calling up and asking, "Is the data OK?" If that happens too often, which is a very small number indeed, the likelihood is that the warehouse effort will have produced shelf-ware. It will sit unused on the shelf.

QUALITY DATA, QUALITY REPORTS

Access to quality information is a treasure hard to attain. The prospect of it will attract customers from across the enterprise, and across the globe, for that matter. Warehouse data that has been extracted, scrubbed, and subjected to processes of validation can be a source of excellence in reporting across multiple business areas. Insurance companies, banks, and finance companies prefer to use it, rather than the transactional data, for regulatory reporting. Manufacturing companies prefer to use it to manage relations with up- and downstream suppliers and customers. Time and again, firms note that end-users seem to prefer access to warehouse data over problematic transactional legacy systems. Of course, this is a mixed blessing. What started out as a decision support function is on the slippery slope to transactional status and an implied 7x24 operational requirement. This, too, is a situation that requires deft managerial skill to balance competing demands on limited resources.

Metadata should include indicators as to the status and availability of the warehouse data—dates and markers that indicate when upstream computing systems have completed and the satisfactory outcome of those feeder inputs. (A mechanism for delivering this result is discussed in the Chapter Thirteen: Metadata, in the section on aggregate navigation.)

For example, in the data extraction for a data warehouse for a multibillion-dollar global insurance firm on the east coast, a strikingly high number of broken elbows are observed as having been coded in the diagnosis field. They all seem to be reported in claims stemming from one particular branch office in an outlying suburb. An instance of fraud? Conspiracy? Collusion? Not quite. The field was required in order to advance to the next stage in processing the claim; when the answer was not known, the department established the convention of entering a diagnosis code that happened to coincide with the way the diagnosis of broken elbow was coded in the legacy system. One cannot help but wonder how reliable the rest of the data was—which is precisely the problem. Contamination of reliability occurs, undermining the prospect of getting answers from the data. It may be no surprise that this same firm has a bucket in one of its systems called a "no insurance recoverable." This remarkable quantity tracks the recovery and return of those payments made to people or organizations that were paid even though they did not have coverage, that is, insurance, with the firm. The recovery is then regarded as an accomplishment, offsetting losses. It is little bit like making a blunder, then giving yourself credit for correcting it. In general, this is a good thing to do—correct errors—but why design a system around correcting the symptom of lack of data quality (the original error), rather than eliminating the cause of the error (a cause precisely describable in terms of data quality)? When an expert outside consultant pointed this out, his tenure was significantly shortened, and he was replaced with six big six staff members, who, in this case, were perceived as being better at following instructions and not making too many fundamental inquiries. Data quality was a separate project, it seems, and different than data analysis.

INFORMATION QUALITY, SYSTEM QUALITY

Not all aspects of data warehouse quality are captured by information quality alone. For example, performance, availability, scalability, functionality, maintainability, and ease of presentation belong at the top of the list. These are aspects of quality belonging to the system or the software by which the data warehouse is implemented.

The point of the TQM movement is that quality is a total commitment to continuous simultaneous improvement along all dimensions of cost, efficiency, and timelines. Quality is not some separate additional attribute of a product or service (distinguishing a washing machine from a quality washing machine, for example).

As a rule, the customer will not acknowledge or accept a product or service that misses the target of function or performance. If the product or service is deficient— lacking in quality, no matter how slightly—it will be rejected as if it were totally defective. In general, the customer will *not* acknowledge quality short of the agreed-upon target. Let's say the target is no defects 99% of the time. This is as close to perfection (let's say) as humanly possible. If we are 98% defect free, that last 1% defect is, by definition, not perfection. At the margin, quality is the difference between "good enough" and "meets the target." When that 1% is remedied or satisfactorily addressed, then and only then is the transaction truly complete in the eyes of the customer. This includes the possibility that payment is made based on less than quality as the line of least resistance to getting on with life prior to taking the customer's business elsewhere. TQM strives to reduce variability around a target standard and reduces the range of deviation in a process of continuous improvement. Thus, when the goal is hit, the bar is raised incrementally.

PERFORMANCE

A data warehouse that doesn't provide sufficiently prompt answers will not be saved by the on-target quality of the data presented, once it does show up (possibly after hours or days of waiting). A short course on performance and tuning examines, estimates, and designs for business factors, data structures, and hardware and software environments. Performance has to balance throughput, response time, and work load. As we will see, performance is meaningful in terms of a service-level agreement. It is a critical mark of system quality, and an entire chapter will be devoted to it (Chapter Eleven: Data Warehousing Performance).

AVAILABILITY

Quality data that is not available is like the tree that falls in the forest when no one is there to hear it. It might as well not have happened. Availability is a function of extracting and loading the data in the batch window. Though large systems (in particular, IBM's DB2/MVS) now have on-line data reorganization and concurrent copy, there is still no way to make data available until it has been loaded. Here, management skill in negotiating a service level agreement that represents a realistic compromise between an end-user asking for 7x24x366 data warehouse availability and finite system resources is the critical path to success.

SCALABILITY

Scalability is an essential feature for databases, systems, and other human artifacts to possess. To motivate the idea of scalability by means of an everyday example, think of selecting all of the red cards from a deck of cards. If one person does that job alone, the person will have to go through all of the cards sequentially, look at each one, and choose those that are red. Now, suppose that three other friends are available to help. With four people working at the job, it will require one quarter of the amount of time. Right? Well, not quite. One person has to act as a coordinator, thumb quickly through the cards, and divide them into four parts, one for each of the people helping. Only then can the sequential inspection begin, now performed in parallel, concluding with the coordinator collecting the red cards from each of the other three helpers as well as his own. So the amount of time required to complete the job will be more than simply dividing the amount of work to be performed by the number of workers. Coordinating the workers adds work to the sum total of work to be accomplished. This results in "diminishing returns" to the effort expended. The limiting case occurs as 52 workers are assembled to check a deck of 52 cards. The job of distributing 52 cards to 52 workers already requires scanning the 52-card deck of cards. The initial work distributing the cards is already sufficient to accomplish the task, requiring as it does traversing the complete deck. Now, however, imagine that 104 decks of cards were to be checked for red cards. The coordination effort is back down to a fraction of the total effort required to select all of the red cards, so we are back on the path of gaining economies of scale.

Thus, *to scale* means a number of things. At the top of the list, *scalability* means that a system is well behaved as the number of worker processes applied to the data grows. So, for example, if a single scan of a 100-million-row table is able to be processed in 10 minutes by a single processor, a perfectly scaled multiprocessor of 10 CPUs should be able to handle the load in 1 minute, as each processor handles 10 million rows each. Of course, the real world is far from perfect. Certain activities, such as sorting, guaranteeing update consistency across multiple users, and assigning a commit point, are either impossible or hard to perform in parallel. In addition, as the number of parallel tasks grows, a cost is incurred for coordinating the processors, even if they do not share memory but rely on a communication grid. Overhead is basically the cost of coordinating the various activities, whether in parallel or in sequence, and overhead limits salability.

To scale also means that as the amount of data goes up, the time to process it goes up in a well-behaved, linear fashion. So, for example, if one processor can handle 100 million rows in 10 minutes, a perfectly scalable system can handle 200 million rows in 20 minutes. If handling the extra rows requires 30 minutes, the scalabilty of the system is "less than proportional." It scales suboptimally. There is a bottleneck in the system, which may represent a design limitation or an accidental feature that can be corrected by tuning. All human artifacts—and business systems are complex artifacts—"hit the wall" eventually. Determining that point is a useful and important exercise of the data warehouse performance and tuning team. Finally, scalable systems display a consistent and graceful degradation in their useful behavior in such measures as response time, mean-time-to-failure, and efficiency as the amount of data grows, or scales upward.

The scalability of the data warehouse effort can be managed by the sensible selection of filtering criteria. Judicious use of the 80/20 rule can go a long way toward taming the problem of unmanageable amounts of data. What are the 20% of customers that generate 80% of business? If even an approximate answer is available (you either have to talk to the marketing reps or build the data warehouse to get the answer), those groups are prime candidates for a first implementation.

FUNCTIONALITY

Functionality is the power of the data warehouse to answer business questions about the subject areas being accumulated and warehoused, and the power to do so with a minimal amount of setup, preparation, rework, or assembly. Functionality is determined by the interaction of the available data stores, aggregations, and the slice-and-dice capabilities of the desktop tools.

MAINTAINABILITY

With corporate mergers, acquisitions, and spin-offs occurring with unrelenting frequency, maintainability is the requirement to be able to add products, customers, and dimensions to the data warehouse in operationally conforming ways. Because there is no way to guarantee in advance that the definition of *customer* at one company or division matches that in another, the necessity of defining many-to-many associations and designing and writing conversion functions must be accepted as a chore to be engaged. A table to associate and translate between the different meanings could be expected to be a key component of such a task. This is a basic information technology effort, not trivial or to be taken for granted, but solvable by means of the usual amount of hard work.

REINTERPRETING THE PAST

Still, this can lead to tough management decisions. For example, a large, integrated, diversified food processor had defined one customer hierarchy—national, area, region, market, individual—but, due to an acquisition, redefined which individual customers were in which areas, regions, and markets. In short, they had the same categories, but these categories now had different meanings and content. For example, customer A had been in the Northeast market but was now in the Southeast. There were many such examples. If the new hierarchy were simply substituted for the old, what meaning would comparisons have before versus after the date of substitution? Consistency would be lost completely, and accuracy, objectivity, and credibility could not be far behind. If both definitions of the customer hierarchy were tracked—for example, by means of a time stamp or sequence number, the amount of data to be manipulated would be increased more than proportionately, because possible combinations in a relational database grow by multiplication, not addition. It was not clear that comparisons would be any clearer, nor that it would be possible, without building and maintaining separate parallel systems, to compare the new and old histories, each containing or aggregating on identically named dimensions with different meanings. A third option was to recalculate history, based on the new hierarchy. This was a feasible and practical solution to the dramatically—not slowly—changing evolution of the market because the warehouse was under 50 gigabytes. (Had it been the 24 terabytes of data of legendary Wal-Mart fame, such an approach would not have been feasible.) This would allow for meaningful comparisons on a go-forward basis. Naturally, any incentive or staff bonuses (demand analysts and planners) would be grandfathered, so that people would be properly reviewed and credited. However, henceforth, history would, in effect, have been rewritten, once individual details of facts were rolled up into aggregates and summaries for purposes of comparisons. This is an interesting example for a variety of reasons. Here, data accuracy and consistency were deemed to be more important the objectivity. It also shows how the dimensions are what give meaning to the facts and make them unique. When the very definition of the customer geography dimension changes, as it did in this case, those aggregates, summaries, and histories using that dimension have to be rebuilt for comparisons between the present and past to be consistent and meaningful.

An issue closely related to placement of individuals with a changing hierarchy is a changing individual customer or product. Here, it is not the categorization of individuals within geographic or brand groupings that is changing. It is the customer or product itself. As examples, think of the marital status of a customer, the amount of salt in a packet of quick-frozen corn, or a book store with a coffee bar. Each of these attributes is a fundamental change in the characterization of the individual entity. This becomes important when you want to compare a subscriber at the time of an insurance claim in the past with today or to compare sales the way they are today at the coffee bar with the way they were previously, prior (for example) to the availability of espresso to inspire impulse buys. These are sometimes described as "slowly changing dimensions" because the entire hierarchy is evolving, so to speak, based on its constituent elements. In general, there are three ways of handling this. First, the new row can overlay the old one. That, of course, means history is gone. The second way is to add a modified form of the individual record and increment a version number. This allows any relevant fact structures to be constrained by the individual version or grouped by all the versions. This is probably the most common solution. Finally, an attribute can be added to the row itself, so that a new dimensional row is not created, preserving the state in which there continues to be only one individual row. The trade-off in both of these cases is additional complexity in the statements used to handle inquiries, versus objectivity in the representation of actual history and comparisons between the present and past.

SUMMARY . . . .

Total data warehouse quality regards the data warehousing system as an information product by analogy with physical goods. The methods that were successful in the total quality management of physical goods can be adapted to the information supply chain. The distinctions between data, information, and knowledge are engaged. Conventional wisdom places data, information, and knowledge on the same continuum. This makes it seem like a miracle that dirty data is scrubbed and the result is knowledge. At one end of the continuum is raw data. The quality of the data is improved by subjecting it to a defined, rigorous quality improvement process and the result is information. The quality of the information is further improved, and the result is knowledge. The specific insight that is added by Chapter Six to this conventional wisdom is that knowledge adds the dignity and stability of a commitment to information. At the same time, placing knowledge on a continuum with ever-improving information quality operationalizes knowledge and makes it definable in terms of the categories of information quality. These categories of information quality include intrinsic qualities such as accuracy, objectivity, nonambiguity, precision, timeliness, consistency, and security. Secondary information qualities include credibility and accessibility, the absence of which often show up as a breakdown in service. In addition, aspects of quality are features of the data warehousing system, not merely the data contained by it. For example, these include: performance, availability, scalability, functionality, maintainability, and ease of presentation. These are aspects of quality belonging to the system or the software by which the data in the data warehouse is delivered. Finally, preserving data consistency over time as entities in the world gradually change is a special problem addressed under reinterpreting the past.

¹ *Personal communication.*

² Much of this chapter is inspired by the work of Richard Wang and his colleagues, Kuan-Tsae Huang and Yang Lee. See *Quality Information and Knowledge*, Huang, K.T., Lee, Y.W., and Wang, R.Y., Upper Saddle River, NJ: Prentice Hall PTR, 1999. A further bit of nitpicking: Nowhere do the authors say, "OK, here is our definition of knowledge." Instead, several useful working definitions are provided: knowledge as quality information, knowledge as competency, knowledge as a "hardened," systematic product. The authors distinguish between "know-how," "know-what," and "know-why" knowledge (see p. 62). This is a useful classification between factual, instrumental, and explanatory kinds of knowledge. Note, however, that each presumes an implicit definition of knowledge. Please note that in what follows, I give my own "spin" to many of their distinctions, further complicating matters. However, they deserve much credit for the sensible things I succeed in saying about information quality. The reader may wish to review the fundamental distinction between information and knowledge made above in Chapter One in the section entitled "The Information Supply Chain."

7

Data Warehousing Technical Design

In this chapter…

"We are in danger of letting the relational database revolution pass by without making good on the original promise of delivering data that can be accessed every which way."
Ralph Kimball[1]

USE CASE SCENARIOS

The idea of a use case scenario is a simple and elegant one. It is one of those ideas that transcend boundaries and stereotypes. The object-oriented software engineering movement popularized it (see Jacobson, 1992: 154ff.). It contains a strong flavor of functionalism, decomposing systems into hierarchically related functions and procedures—unmistakably the language of traditional structured systems analysis and design (see Olle, 1991: 26 for details). If anything, that should suggest to us that use case scenarios are a practical approach, regardless of the formal methods, labels, or notations invoked.

The approach of use case analysis is to answer the question, How do people use (or plan to use) the system? This focuses the analysis on the use of the system *in context*. It constrains the analyst to talk about the business factors implicated in the design effort. The task is to describe how things work. Roles, functions, interfaces, and groupings of business processes and components are to be found in the answer. This, in turn, informs the system development process in which the software product transforms the context, by means of its staged introduction into the business (see Figure 7.1: Use Case Scenario). Also shown explicitly in Figure 7.1 is the system designer and builder, who actually needs to be a part of the loop—say, in the middle—and *not* an entity hovering above the process. This suggests why the process is inherently iterative—an alignment between data warehousing system and the context of its use is constructed, as much as discovered. The resulting system both represents the situation as well as makes it accessible. (It is no accident that Figure 7.1 closely resembles in form Figure I.3, cited above in the Introduction. It is precisely the alignment surfaced in the use cases that is "setting up" the possibilities of knowledge that are "built into" the data warehousing process by the design and development effort.) The part of the designer's science that remains part art is to know when to stop iterating, because the essential minimal characteristics of the situation have been captured in the system architecture, and the remaining features are distractions from the business imperatives.

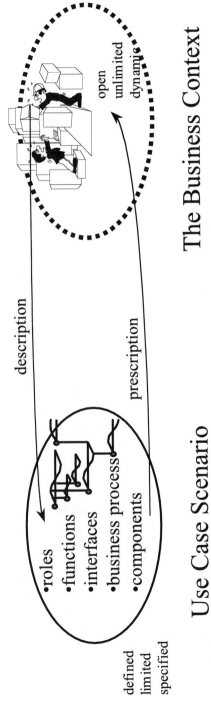

Figure 7.1
Use Case Scenario

The first arrow depicts how the use case captures essential features of the situation from right to left. Factual reports about the business are expressed, represented, and described by the use case. The second arrow depicts how the use case system prescribes and envisions constructing and makes access possible to the details of the business context from left to right. These details are actually constructed by the two-way alignment in the computing system that will be built on the basis of the use case(s) and business context, which is otherwise open and fluctuating. These are the kinds of decision support questions that get answered by data warehousing feedback into the business context as instrumental and pragmatic knowledge for action. A third form of knowledge is not shown by an arrow, although, in a sense, it shows itself. That third form is the alignment between the use cases and the context. That alignment—which is named in both lists of correspondences—is made explicit as metadata, structures that allow the system and the context to work together (*interoperate* is the computing term). The alignment of the use case and the business context leads to instrumental knowledge, in which means are applied to ends, and in which knowledge generates actionable results for the benefit of the business. This further entails pragmatic knowledge, where knowledge becomes the basis for *commitments* in which business processes are coordinated, essential business imperatives addressed, and fundamental decision support questions answered by the data warehousing system. The latter way in which knowledge is defined (and fortified) by commitment is what puts the "decision" back into "decision support" in data warehousing.

Use case analysis focuses on meaning in use. What is the proposed use of the system? Is the use of the system for sales analysis, planning, forecasting, market analysis, product or customer profitability, or promotion? If the use of the system for promotion results (examples of questions might include, What were the outcomes of sales of brand X in the Southeast region following the promotion rollout during the last two weeks of the quarter? How did this compare with sales during the previous year, during which there was no promotion)? The people who are affected by the answers to these questions include those whose role is to manage the brand. Also impacted are the roles of developing customer relations, designing and scheduling the related promotion, and evaluating and driving the initiative to increase market share. Let's say that the overall business process is brand management and development. The business components, whether called *dimensions* or *entities*, include customers and product hierarchies, sales facts, and history. The functions include aggregating product sales to the brand level, aggregating customers in the Southeast region to the regional level, and maintaining history as time-series data so that year-to-year comparisons are possible. Even the presentation of the information is sketched in the use case because, without presentation, it is incomplete. The use case might show (for instance) that it would be useful to be able to see the current weekly periods in comparison with those of a year ago on the same screen layout or page. Surfacing and exposing the commitments of staff, existing processes, business imperatives, and opportunities to attain them is the key to use case analysis.

ABSTRACT DATA TYPES AND CONCRETE DATA DIMENSIONS

The step-by-step refinement of use case scenarios leads to the development of a logical data model. The logical data model, in turn, may incorporate compromises, based on the particular environment, including denormalization for performance, and may be implemented as a physical data model using the data definition language of a particular relational database. You can make a reasonable start at picking out the entities from the use case scenarios by identifying and abstracting the nouns—the persons, places, and things. This is quite consistent with ER modeling. The basic definition of ER modeling describes it as a design method for treating data components and relationships in such a way as to eliminate redundancy and permit consistent updating of the data, usually with reference to transactional systems (see Chen, 1977). An entity is a "thing that can be distinctly identified." An entity corresponds to a person, place, or thing—a noun—in language. It has sufficient persistence and constancy that it can support attributes, associations, and subtypes. Attributes describe entities. Associations relate entities to one another. Subtypes establish a hierarchy and relations of inclusion between entities. These latter are useful in grouping products into brands, brands into categories, and categories into whatever larger aggregations of products would be helpful. Likewise, customers are segmented into geographic, demographic, delivery channel, or service level groupings (see Table 7.1: Basic Entity Relationship Concepts).

However, data warehouses are usually populated with "read-only" or "read-mostly" structures. In addition, when laid out as a pattern on paper, they often have a different, simpler geometric shape and visual appearance than do traditional ER diagrams. Therefore, the question arises whether a different method of data modeling is required for decision support systems, including warehouses and transactional systems. Ralph Kimball, one of the inventors and the deepest exponent of the discipline, has presented persuasive evidence that dimensional modeling actually preceded ER diagrams (see Kimball, 1998: 144 for the idea). He traces the vocabulary of "facts" and "dimensions," to General Mills in the 1960s and Nielsen Marketing Research in the 1970s. His proposal for reconciling the two approaches is that a single ER diagram breaks down into many fact-dimension diagrams. This would work something like a set of possibilities, classes, or options implemented and made actual by an instance or example. Consistent and actionable results can be generated with this approach. The depth of vertical industry expertise marshalled is so formidable as to make the reader suspect that an entirely new method is at hand. Almost everything said is so fundamental as to qualify as metadata in the best sense of the word. Abandoning some of the technical details of the classic ER approach also goes a long way toward explaining why end-users find dimensional models easier to understand. They incorporate useful simplifications. However, we are just climbing up and down the ladder of abstraction. We may be pardoned if we do so fast enough that we get a little dizzy.

Table 7.1:   Basic Entity Relationship (E-R)

Relational Concept	Definition	Example
Entity	an object distinctly identifiable and persisting	a customer, product, sale, shipment, location, diagnosis, date, service
Attribute	a property or quality that describes an entity	customer name, product weight, amount of sale, address of store, vendor fee
Association	an intersection of entities so that their combination is structured as one to-one, one-to-many (many-to-one), many-to-many	all customers buy brand X, some - customers take delivery of some products, customers A,B,C each buy products U, V, and W
Subtype	entity type X is a subtype of entity Y if and only if every X is a subset of Y—that is, every X is a Y	Ultra Clorox 2 Bleach is a subtype belonging to the brand Clorox; Clorox and Tide are both subtypes of the category "cleaning agents"
Primary Key	an attribute that uniquely identifies the entity	Customer identifier uniquely identifies the customer; social security number uniquely identifies the payer of social security taxes

Adapted from C.J. Date, **An Introduction to Database Systems**, *Reading, MA: Addison-Wesley, 1986.*

The suggested resolution of the controversy (class and class instance) has real potential for educating the professional audience of designers and architects without actually providing a definitive answer. Fact tables answering the question, Who bought what at what store? are perfectly consistent representations of ER diagrams. This is usually called *third-normal form* (see the exact definition below). The intersecting dimensions delimiting the fact table are indeed denormalized for performance. Undertaking such a denormalization is an operation entirely within the definitions and limits of the approach of ER diagramming. What is often overlooked is that the fact structures are more abstract than the usual persons, places, and things of the classic ER approach. Rather than an order or a line item on an order, we have a transaction at the point of intersection of a sale of an item to a customer on this date and at this store. The representation of the fact as an intersection of dimensions is more abstract than the average operational (transaction) entity. The information content is arguably denser, too, because the fact contains information from both the invoice header and detail. However, entities, dimensions, and fact structures all line up on the continuum of abstraction.

At about the same time that ER diagramming was hitting its stride in the mid-1980s, the idea of an ADT was taking off in a completely different context. An ADT is a collection of data with structure—an array, a list, a stack—surrounded by computing operations performed on that data—search, push the stack, pop up an item, add, or remove (etc.). The combination of these two components—data and operation—provides the tools needed to specify functioning software procedures, the building blocks of programming and system development (see Liskov and Guttag, 1986, for further details). When this notion is compared with that of a fact table and a dimension, they appear rather similar. The only difference is that, instead of an abstraction, such as a list, array, or stack, we are dealing with a concrete data component, such as a customer, product, channel, or time period. When these concrete data dimensions intersect to provide facts, they do indeed tend to become more abstract. However, both dimensions and facts are types of entities. The dimensions tend to be more concrete than operational entities. The intersection of dimensions tends to be more abstract than operational entities. From a data modeling point of view, it is useful to learn how to do this. In either case—dimensional modeling or ER diagramming—we are climbing up and down the ladder of abstraction.

DATA NORMALIZATION: RELEVANCE AND LIMITATIONS

To say that something is "normalized" means that it is put in a form that can be compared across different contexts and situations. Comparison across different contexts is a kind of reuse in context. The imperative is to make sense out of what is happening—in this case, in a business and technology context. The advantage of data normalization is superior performance and the ability to adapt to changing situations, priorities, and events. The "making sense" part requires applying tools and methods, including logical and formal ones, to the wealth and diversity of data distinctions with which we are confronted. These data modeling and analysis methods and tools have the kind of validity and rational justification characteristic of logic and mathematics. What they don't have is visibility to the details and idiosyncrasies of your business environment. Therefore, a word of caution: When applied to data, the process can be painful—it's like body building for your data. To develop tone, shape, and overall conditioning, you've got to break a sweat. Although it may seem silly to say it, most data needs to get well beyond the "couch potato" phase without going all the way to becoming a "Terminator" look-alike. Extreme normalization, like extreme sports, is perhaps an enlightening spiritual exercise if you are already in shape and have the time. However, it is not an easily maintainable business practice on an everyday basis.

Data normalization is, indeed, a technical task. It is as technical as one can get. However, it is not a particular vendor technology or programming language. It is a technology similar to formal logic. At the risk of oversimplification, data is normalized to make it easier to work with. That means several things. The data should not take up more space than is really required. Wasting storage space is bad, as a general rule, unless wasting a little space can significantly improve other performance features, such as speed and throughput. The data should be able to be implemented and maintained in a consistent and orderly way. The database administrator's motto applies here: Data integrity is our most important product. (Both database and data administrators will agree on this point, regardless of the occasionally differing emphasis in their roles, the former being concerned with physical implementation and the latter with data modeling.) The data should be easy to understand—it should be able to be surveyed and, if at all possible, manipulated mentally without too much mental pain. Actually, all three of these goals are nontrivial in any real-world, industrial-strength system. Make no mistake, compromises and data engineering trade-offs are required from the start.

In general, data warehouses suffer from data bloat more than from update inconsistencies (*update anomalies* is the term that will be used henceforth). This can be easily appreciated by considering that combining 1,000 customers by 1,000 products by 1,000 time periods results in a billion combinations; whereas, for the most part, warehouses are not updated by transaction data hitting them as if they were an airline reservation system (in real time, for example). The dimensional structures of the data warehouse tend to be the target of occasional individual updates; the fact tables tend to be updated on a partition-by-partition basis or made the target of "long transactions," such as loading of large amounts of data (or even total refresh actions). Updating cannot be ignored though it invites a different approach than in transactional systems.

Indeed, the concept of an update anomaly is so basic and fundamental to all relational, dimensional, and database thinking that it requires treatment. Even though data warehouses are mostly read-only database structures, they are still bound by the requirements of data integrity, consistency, and ease of understanding. Furthermore, it is the "mostly" that is the rub here. Understanding how to avoid update anomalies is a basic lesson in data integrity that fulfills the meaning of normalization by working across contexts. Table 7.2: Update Anomaly, shows the dilemma and a solution. Each row in the shipment table carries a customer address with it. If customer number 999 gets a new address, all of the occurrences of that address must be updated. In the example, one of them is overlooked. That is not supposed to happen. But how often does "not supposed to happen" actually occur? Too often. This causes an obvious service breakdown, because sometimes products are unaccountably delivered to the old address at 2105 Lawrence Street instead of to the new address at 5801 N. Ellis Drive. The solution is to apply one of the rules of normalization. The entire key of the shipment table consists of Customer_id, Product_id, and Date. The Customer_address is dependent on only part of the key, namely, Customer_id. It is unrelated to Product_id or Date. Therefore, put Customer_address in a separate Customer table, where the complete unique key is Customer_id. Although saving space is not the main advantage here, that, too, is a beneficial result. Redundancy is reduced. Customer_address occurs once and only once; it is easy to understand, find, and update in one and only one place.

Table 7.2: Update Anomaly: Example of Update Anomaly and Solution

Shipment Table (Before Normalization)

Customer_id	Product_id	Date	Qty_Delivered	Customer_address
999	123	09-01-1999	5	2105 Lawrence
908	301	09-02-1999	8	636 Belden
999	256	09-03-1999	2	2105 Lawrence

(1)

Shipment Table (Before Normalization)

Customer_id	Product_id	Date	Qty_Delivered	Customer_address
999	123	09-01-1999	5	2105 Lawrence St.
908	301	09-02-1999	8	636 Belden Blvd.
999	256	09-03-1999	2	5801 N. Ellis Drive

(2)

Shipment Table (After Normalization)

Customer_id	Product_id	Date	Qty_Delivered
999	123	09-01-1999	5
908	301	09-02-1999	8
999	256	09-03-1999	2

Customer Table

Customer_id	Customer_address
999	636 Belden Blvd.
908	5801 N. Ellis Drive

(3)

A complete list of normal forms of data representation is provided in Table 7.3: The Forms of Data Normalization, as a reference. To emphasize that metadata are all about meaning, further examples of data normalization are considered in the context of semantics and metadata (Chapter Thirteen), and exemplified in Tables 13.1–13.3. The works by Chris Date and Peter Chen will provide additional details for those who need to drill down and become apprentice data modelers (see Chen, 1981 and Date, 1991 for further examples and details).

Another word of caution: As in any essential guide, the difference between the apprentice and the advanced student (the professional) must be appreciated. The apprentice will often apply a rule in every instance and refine his or her understanding in the college of hard knocks. Trial and error can be instructive but painful. The professional is not always immune from mistakes either, but usually will be able to identify exceptions, qualifications, and, above all, trade-offs in advance.

The discipline of data normalization is required to bring a measure of science to the accidental accumulation of data. Understanding the meaning of data in context and validating its use in its natural ecological business environment is essential to producing knowledge from the data. To get answers to our questions from the data, we must make the most of the available order and structure, including laying down useful rules where at first glance there are apparently none. The limitations of normalization are the limitations of our technology. Even expanding horizons of high technology must be cautious about scanning, aggregating, or manipulating 100-million-row data structures. Storage capacity is by definition finite, and data will generally grow to fill the available capacity. The limitations of normalization are also the limitations of our organizations. We think we understand how things work; we embed that understanding in our data warehouse systems and software used to access them. Then we find out that our understanding requires refinement. Well, then so do our systems. Ultimately, the limits of normalization are those of semantics. Normalization promotes reuse of data across contexts. Semantics ties us to the particulars of a specific context. We build data warehouses between the horns of this dilemma.

Table 7.3: Forms of Data Normalization

Form	Definition	Example
1st	Data is atomic, elementary	One value is stored in each attribute or column; for example, first-normal form (FNF) is violated by embedding an array of discount prices or other schedule in an attribute or table column
2nd	Every attribute not in the key depends completely on the primary key	For example, customer address is completely dependent of customer id and belongs in the customer table; it is a violation of second-normal form (2NF) to embed customer address in the shipment table where the complete key is customer, product, date; alignment with 2NF is restored by breaking customer address (and all related attributes) off into their own separate structure
3rd	The primary key completely determines every attribute and does so in a non-transitive way; every attribute depends on "the key, the whole key, and nothing but the key"	The "transitive" part is the tricky thing here—try adding Customer_Order _Status to example 8.2. The product and date would determine the customer and the customer, in turn, would determine the status. The status for a given customer order status table would be required separate from the customer table and separate form the shipment table.
Boyce/ Codd	If multiple unique third-normal form keys exist, they overlap, are composite, and uniquely determine the attributes	The need for transitivity is overcome here. For example, a table represents sales based on a unique key customer, employee, product, promotion, but some of the customers are really employees, so they are not eligible for the promotion. The solution is to break this down into customer, employee, as one table, and customer, product, promotion, sales (or employee, product, promotion, sales), as the other table.
4th	Multivalued relations belong in separate tables	Certain kinds of ambiguities can be eliminated by this rule. Customer's can speak multiple languages and drive multiple automobiles. According to this rule, these belong in separate structures to avoid redundant entries. This is where most data warehouse experts argue that the limited space savings is not worth the fragmentation and proliferation of data structures.
5th	Multivalued relations must satisfy all the defined unique candidate keys	Similar to above with the addition of further business rules or business constraints. The recommendation is the same. This is the navel into the unknown.

DIMENSIONS AND FACTS

We have said that knowledge, in the full sense of the word, requires bringing experience to a framework and validating that framework against the experience. The framework provides structure and organizes the experience, which is otherwise chaotic raw data. Simply stated, from a knowledge engineering perspective, the data warehouse dimensions provide the framework and the transaction data provides the experience out of the context of particular business processes. Together, they provide the factual knowledge required to commit to providing an answer to fundamental business imperatives about customer relations, brand development, and the parameters of the business that make a difference. Put another way, the dimensions—customer, product, time, channel, location, etc.—are the means of representation, or the architecture, that structure and provide the persisting and enduring patterns that organize and make sense out of the facts. Facts and dimensions are the structures in which knowledge is systematized, made to stand fast, and rendered reusable.

The point of the example in Figure 7.2, taken from the health insurance industry, is to see the diversity of dimensions that intersect in a fact table. One rule of thumb in identifying a fact table is that it is a many-to-many association of dimensions. The dimensions represent the system architecture. They are what stand fast amidst the flux of facts. Getting a stable architectural framework is not a trivial undertaking. For instance, providers include doctors, hospitals, clinics, nursing homes, licensed practical nurses who visit the home-bound, ambulance services, and a host of other practitioners. Getting a unified representation of these suppliers to consumers of health care services (patients) is as important an imperative as anything facing the drive to know the retail customer.

In the health care industry, where managing physicians and hospitals were fundamentally different business processes (consider the historical *distinction* between Blue Shield and Blue Cross) the breakthrough furnished by letting the architecture guide design is the construction of the unified representation of the provider dimension. The alignment of the real-world providers with the dimensions represented in the data warehouse is an important result.

As the health care industry has evolved from business processes of fee for service to diagnostically related groups (DRGs) to payment per HMO member and case of illness, the role of diagnosis has evolved, too. It may sound incredible to a lay person, but from a system perspective, these days, the diagnosis dimension is behaving like a degenerate dimension—an invoice number. You have to back into the diagnosis. It is the procedure—the treatment mechanism or lab test—that is the expense and implies a diagnosis. However, diagnosis is useful as an example of how many-to-many relations may be required, because a sick person may require multiple diagnoses. That would require the introduction of a diagnosis group assigned to a patient. That is now called a *case,* which is the dimension shown in the Figure 7.2 example.

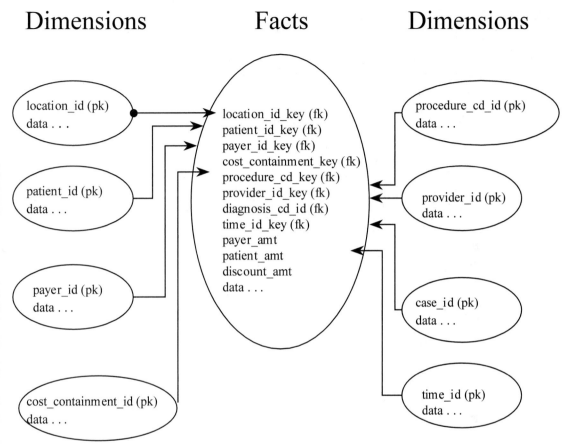

Figure 7.2
Dimensions and Facts

Each of the dimensions makes possible the answering of an entire host of questions. Given a patient identifier, questions can be answered about how much that patient has cost per period of time. Given that the patient is insured on the basis of a member belonging to an employer group health plan, the hierarchy can be traversed to yield answers about how much different groups used various services. For all the patients in a given group, what is their rate of utilization and cost? Do you think groups of relatively young adults use or require fewer health care services? That's obvious—everyone knows that, right? That's the tricky thing about knowledge. A single fact outweighs a mass of chaotic data. Think again—sports injuries are the latest epidemic. This is neither good nor bad in itself—except to the person whose knee is injured—but the cost must be factored in at the proper level. Similar logic applies to the providers, locations, and procedures. Each is a potential wealth of knowledge about the behavior of different groupings and segments of the industry.

PRIMARY AND FOREIGN KEYS

The primary key of a dimension consists of a data element that uniquely identifies an individual row in the structure (table). Thus, customer id uniquely identifies an individual customer as a set of attributes. Provider id uniquely identifies a set of attributes delivering medical services. The target of the primary key is an individual—Western Soft Drink Company or Albert Jones. This "uniqueness" is an important property of a primary key. Duplicates are not allowed and, if allowed, would create a lot of mischief. They would create a situation where a particular business object would not exist, a case of mistaken identity results, auditing would be impossible, and tracing responsibility would be problematic. Implementing the primary key depends on an underlying index that guarantees uniqueness. An attempt to insert a duplicate is flagged as an error condition by the RDBMS and is not allowed to proceed.

The foreign key of a fact table identifies an individual row, usually located in another table, in this case, a dimension table. The classic instance is that of a line item on an order. The line item tables contains several rows, each of which references the order table by means of an order number. In the health service industry example, the health care fact table has many foreign key references corresponding to each of the dimensions. None of them constitutes a unique fact in itself, but together, they make up a unique primary key.

Thus, the primary key of the fact table ends up being a composite key, composed of the multiple foreign keys of the dimensions intersecting in the fact structure (see Figure 7.3: Composite Primary Key of Fact Table). There is no requirement that the foreign key refer to a composite primary key, but that is the case when dealing with data warehouse structures. It is a consequence of the architecture whereby relatively stable dimensions intersect to provide the logical hooks off of which get hung transaction-level facts and their aggregates. Otherwise, one can easily think of an instance where the foreign key references a single primary key. For instance, a foreign key in an employee table contains a reference to the employee's department, which is a single (noncomposite) primary key in a separate department table. A variation on this theme can also be circular references, as when an employee is also a manager, so the manager's employee id occurs as both a manager and as an employee.

Among relational database experts, it is customary to debate the trade-offs between using natural keys—social security number or name—and artificial keys—a random and arbitrary concatenation or hash of digits. The intelligibility of the former must be weighed against the efficiency of the latter. That is less of a problem in a data warehousing context, because a strong case supports the use of an arbitrary key. The importance of decoupling the warehouse from the random effects of key changes, redefinitions, occasional data quality issues, and evolution in legacy production transaction systems necessitates the use of arbitrary and artificial keys. Additional benefits also exist because such artificial keys are usually smaller and more efficiently manipulated by the database engine.

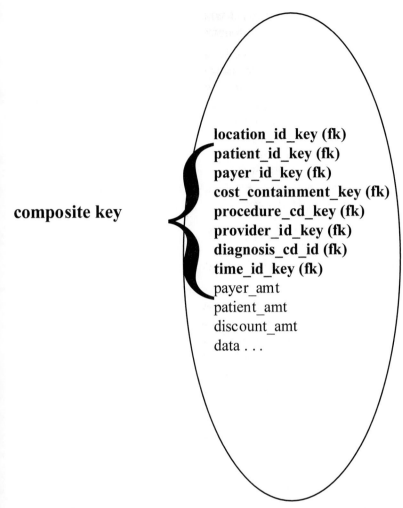

composite key

location_id_key (fk)
patient_id_key (fk)
payer_id_key (fk)
cost_containment_key (fk)
procedure_cd_key (fk)
provider_id_key (fk)
diagnosis_cd_id (fk)
time_id_key (fk)
payer_amt
patient_amt
discount_amt
data . . .

Figure 7.3
Composite Primary Key of Fact Table (Composed of Foreign Key References to Dimensions)

Logical Design Check List

The following check list will serve as a reminder to the major points of logical data design:

1. Develop use case scenarios, describing the inquiry behavior of business end-users, interfaces, and system components.
2. Validate lists of questions to be answered against and as a representation of the business requirements in context of use case scenario(s).
3. Determine preliminary roles, dimensions, and transactions from use case scenario(s).
4. Identify, name, define, and document the data dimensions.
5. Identify, name, define, and document the business process transactions to be represented.
6. Identify, name, define, and document the granularity of the fact data structures in the transactions.
7. Cross-reference and cross-validate dimensions and facts. Add any missed dimensions to the architecture; use intersections of dimensions as clues to complete universe of processes. Add any required but overlooked processes to the list of factual structures.
8. Identify, name, determine, and document primary keys for dimensions.
9. Identify, name, determine, and document primary keys for the fact structures.
10. Identify, name, determine, and document foreign keys, referencing dimensions from fact structures.
11. Determine, validate, and apply naming standards, conventions, abbreviations.
12. Surface, identify, define, and document additional attributes to dimensions.
13. Surface, identify, define, and document additional attributes to factual structures.
14. Assign attributes to domains—determine allowable values (meaning, uniqueness, nullable, default) that satisfy the attribute.
15. Assign data types to key and nonkey attributes. This will yield an exact size of the row.
16. Trace attributes in data warehouse dimensions and fact structures to their source—legacy or ERP or other systems, data entry, or applications designed to generate them. Make provisions to develop the required applications, interfaces, or connectivity to source the data attributes. If an Extract, tranform, and load (ETL) tool is used to move the data, then it should be able to automate the capture of metadata.
17. Validate that fact structures are in third normal form and that dimension structures are a single denormalized representation of the entity aligned with the business.
18. Determine sparcity factor (actual occurrence of product-customer-date combinations) based on survey of business operations.
19. Determine preliminary estimated size and number of rows per structure, based on realistic sparcity factors from the business.
20. Review and validate preliminary list of useful aggregates, based on use case scenarios, available dimensions, and intended target environment.
21. Document and update metadata repository, if available, with results so far or make provision for such future update by preparing electronic copy of materials.

DESIGN FOR PERFORMANCE: TECHNICAL INTERLUDE

Logical design drives inevitably in the direction of the physical. Logical groupings of data elements into dimensions and facts are made based on primary keys, entirely independently of the maximum number of allowable data elements (called "columns") on a row or on the maximum size of underlying operating system data sets. Those factors and many others like them are the ultimate determinants of system performance. Decisions made about logical layerings of system components at variance with physical constraints and limitations are logically impossible to correct by mere physical means. Conventional wisdom advises—denormalization to improve on-line response time at the cost of additional storage. However, data warehouse systems represent a limiting case that fundamentally violates the conventional wisdom. If properly handled, this counterintuitive result can provide a win-win situation, where both performance and improved space use occur. In any event, whatever the decision about denormalization, proceeding with eyes open and in full possession of the facts has the benefit of managing trade-offs proactively.

The question of denormalizing the dimension tables is properly answered in the affirmative. Because the amount of storage used in the dimensions is modest in comparison with the storage requirements of the fact tables, the conventional wisdom holds. That is not the issue here. Rather, what is at stake is the issue of denormalizing the fact table. The best thing to do is to proceed by means of an example.[2]

As an illustration, let's consider a data warehouse fact table row consisting of a unique primary key of product by customer by time—let's say a 14-character product identifier by an integer customer id by a date (4 bytes of storage). That's 22 bytes, to which must be added a couple of bytes overhead for space management. Corresponding to this long key is one lonely fact—how much money the customer paid for the product this time. That additive, transitive, numeric quantity (money, pounds, inventory, etc.) can be contained in an integer. Thus, we have a 22-byte key, to which corresponds a 4-byte fact column. The 26-byte row is mostly index. This will have consequences.

Now consider an elaboration of this hypothetical scenario. This is a simplification. As we shall see, even a simple example can provide insight into complex details. Suppose we have 1,000 products that can be purchased by 1,000 customers within 1,000 time periods. Even with these modest numbers—and real applications have many more customers—1000x1000x1000 is a billion-row table. At this point, working with a spreadsheet is useful. (See Table 7.4: Comparison of Normalized and Denormalized Fact Data.) Mapping rows to 4-K pages or extents for the physical data containers (sometimes called *tablespace* and *indexspace*) and then to disk devices (this example assumes a specific disk track geometry for the sake of discussion[3]) can be easily calculated. Decisions about where rounding and overhead ratios are made. However, the result delivers a meaningful comparison if consistently applied. Without

Table 7.4:   Comparison of Normalized and Denormalized Fact Data

	Count
Customer	1000
Products	1000
Periods	1000
Counter Size	4
Row Size Normalized	26
Row Size Denormalized	4022
Rows per Page Normal [max rows per page or storage extent: 137]	156
Rows per Page (or extent) Denormalized	1
Sparcity Factor: ProdxCustxTime	0.990
Sparcity Factor: ProdxCust	0.010
Rows Relevant Normalized	990,000,000
Rows Relevant Denormalized	10,000
Index Size	22
DB2 Pages Tablespace Denormalized	9,931
DB2 Pages Tablespace Normalized	7,226,277
Index Entry Size	22

(Continued)

Table 7.4: Continued

	Count
Subpage Size	4
Pages [4k] in Index	5,558,785
Total Pages Denormalized	5,568,716
Total Pages Normalized	12,785,063
Total Track Denormalized	506,247
Total Track Normalized	1,162,278.43
Total Cylinders Denormalized	33,749.80
Total Cylinders Normal	77,485.23
Model 3390-3 Disk Denormalized	10.13
Model 3390-3 Disk Normalized	23.26
Percent Difference (based on cylinders)	43.56%

compression, this example will require 24.5 model 3390-3 disks to store the combinations (both table and index).

Now consider an exercise in denormalizing the fact table on the time dimension. In other words, for every customer-product combination, provide 1,000 columns (or less, if the particular database supports a lesser number) to store the fact element corresponding to each time period. This is easy to visualize as the difference between Figure 7.4: Short, Skinny Rows: Long Structures and Figure 7.5: Long Fact Rows: Shorter Structures. In effect, first normal form is violated and an array of facts is created, one for each time period. The starting time period must be separately tracked as a single item in an independent control table. Instead of many skinny rows with one lonely fact, we have fewer fat rows with many facts on each. Of course, denormalization presents trade-offs—transforming columns into rows has a cost. First, relational built-in functions—average, sum, etc.—cannot be used on an array. Likewise, an application must be built to cascade one bucket to another as time marches onward on a periodic basis. However, assuming project management, system development, and cross-functional competencies (by no means a trivial assumption), the costs may not be as great as one might think. Consider.

Having thus denormalized, are we exposed to the penalties of denormalization—update anomalies and redundancies? The data warehouse is a "read-mostly" and inquiry structure. Updating occurs as global refresh or load. The dimensional hierarchies receive a modest amount of update activity. Therefore, update anomalies are a lot less of a problem than with a transactional system. Each fact is still represented in only one place. It is true that redundancy is introduced, in that some facts that, strictly speaking, are not needed still end up being provided with storage space. Empty buckets are stored by the denormalized row; whereas they would not occur in the normalized table. This is because in the normalized example the absence of a transaction at a given time results in the disappearance of the customer by product combination. There is simply no row. In the denormalized model, there is an empty bucket in that date column. Nevertheless, storage space is still saved. Why?

First, space is saved by denormalizing because as each bucket is added to the growing fat row, the number of combinations is reduced multiplicatively (geometrically). A kind of reverse combinatorial explosion sets in, favoring the denormalized option. The denormalized row is growing by addition, in contrast with the normalized space, which is shrinking by division.

Second, this is happening in both the index and the tablespace. Remember: The data warehouse row is mostly index, a long key with one dangling, lonely fact. Thus, the denormalized space has a dramatically reduced index size, by the removal of the explicit time dimension from the fact table itself. Also, because the index is a large proportion of the entire space requirement, the result in our example is dramatic space savings of over 55%. Finally, note that this is in addition to the response time benefit obtained by having fewer rows and all relevant facts together on the same page.

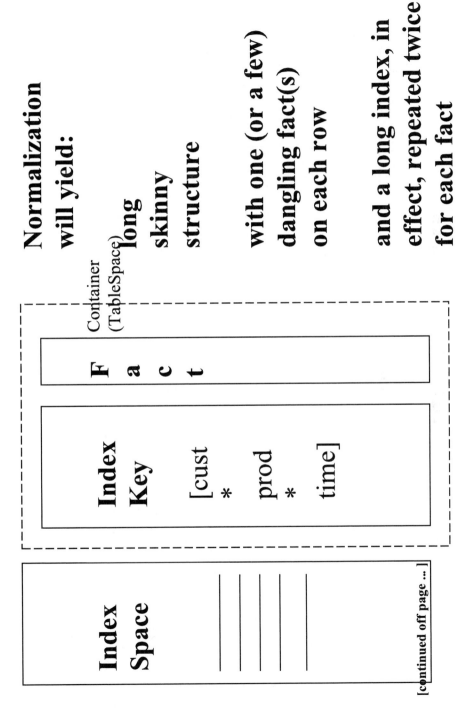

Figure 7.4
Short, Skinny Rows: Long Structures

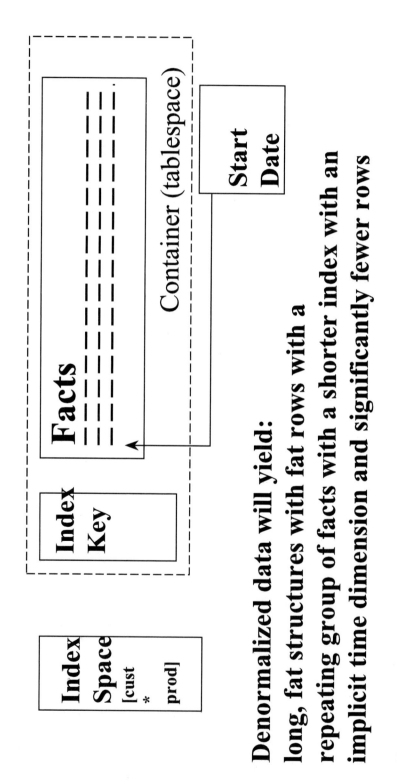

Denormalized data will yield:

long, fat structures with fat rows with a
repeating group of facts with a shorter index with an
implicit time dimension and significantly fewer rows

Figure 7.5
Long Fact Rows Shorter Structures

Logically, addition and multiplication allow no exception. However, the real world is not so simple. In the real world, customers buy only some products, sometimes. Some customers never buy a given product, anytime. This is called *sparcity*. A limiting case is where each customer buys all products one time, each product at a different time, and never again. That would require a row for every product by customer combination, with only one nonzero date fact. The denormalized model will be overwhelmed by maintaining 999 empty buckets, in addition to the one actual fact. In our example, the advantage is to the denormalized model between a sparcity factor of 1.0, where all customers buy all products all the time and a factor of 0.12, where only 12% of the possible combinations occur. Of course, a workaround would be possible to bring the limiting case within the normal range by aggregating customers and products into groups (aggregates) whose sparcity is closer to 1.0.

So much for the conventional wisdom. For a large range of customer and product transactions, denormalizing for performance actually saves space. An additional benefit is available in grouping all customer-product facts on one physical extent or page in the database. All related rows are returned together to the application. This improves response time. It also simplifies estimates of response time, thus increasing the transparency and ease of understanding of system operations. This is fortunate. Given the combinatorial explosion that occurs as customers, products, and time periods are multiplied, denormalization is often an operational and practical necessity in installations operating within constraints of gigabytes of data. For those organizations that deploy the project management, program development, and cross-functional design skills, denormalizing on the fact dimension is a powerful method for both boosting response time and saving on disk space.

Physical Design Check List

The following check list will serve as a reminder to the major points of physical data design:

1. Determine unit of I/O (page or extent) size, storage disk geometry, and map row size to storage and I/O media. Refine row size to accommodate physical media—especially if a major mismatch occurs (for example, a row just over one-half page, so that only one row per page fits).

2. Resequence column attributes to make optimal use of storage—variable characters at end of row.

3. Determine physical sequence of rows in data structure (also called *clustering sequence*) and prepare to sort data to be loaded in that order.

4. Using sparcity factor, defined level of granularity, and intersecting dimensions; determine the amount of storage required for data structures and index structures.

5. Develop partitioning strategy for large data structures—how many partitions, partitioning index, distribution of data—considering tradeoffs of partitioning by time period versus such alternatives as by-product for efficient time-series comparisons.

6. Evaluate hash keys to ensure a useful distribution of data across partitions or an effective method of round--robin rotation between partitions.

7. Evaluate size and performance profile for operational realism, and consider denormalization along the time dimension to address combinatorial explosion.

8. Analyze trade-offs in denormalizing fact structures, including the design, implementation and operation of applications to support such an approach, in relation to the organization's project management competencies.

9. Assign tables to containers (tablespace) and databases for purposes of backup, recovery, and concurrency.

10. Estimate the number of physical I/Os (input/output operations) required to answer the questions stated in the requirements and the resulting response time, based on the working assumption that, for data warehousing, 80% (or so) of the response time is spent in the database engine.

11. Consider, define, and implement additional alternate indexes to optimize question answering queries.

12. Evaluate, define, and implement or plan to implement alternate index strategies, bitmap indexing, and star-join indexing to optimize results of set retrieval.

13. Validate the resulting estimated response time against a reasonable expectation of a service-level agree-ment. (For example if the response time is 15 seconds to 2 minutes, Okay; whereas, if it is 2 hours to 20 hours, perform a reality check against expectations. Identify issues. Fit to the intended target environment.

14. Define and refine physical issues and consider alternative solutions—aggregate answers in advance, function ship into a "big batch process," more powerful processing environment, data partitioning, combination of these, etc.

15. Document and update metadata repository, if available, with results so far or make provisions for such future update by preparing electronic copy documenting physically relevant materials.

SUMMARY . . . .

Use case scenarios are a simple and powerful mechanism for analyzing the use of proposed data warehouse in context. Here meaning is use. The step-by-step refinement of use case scenarios leads to the development of a logical data model. The resolution of the controversy of whether logical data modeling using entity relationship diagrams is fundamentally different than dimensional modeling has the potential for educating the community of practice without actually producing a definitive answer. In either case—dimensional modeling or entity relationship diagramming—we are climbing up and down the ladder of abstraction with dimensions representing rather concrete entities and fact structures capturing the results of business processes. These results tend to be more abstract (but no less crucial) than the usual simple persons, places, and things of the classic E-R approach. Next, the technology of data normalization, and what that means, is engaged in detail. Basics about primary and foreign keys in the context of data warehousing facts and dimensions are covered. A nontrivial exercise in denormalization is performed to provide insight into mastering the problem of combinatorial explosion. (The conventional wisdom requires updating in this case.) Checklists for engaging logical design and physical design are provided by way of recommended practices.

[1] See Kimball, Ralph, *The Data Warehouse Toolkit: Practical Techniques for Building Dimensional Data Warehouses*, 1995, p. xxiii.

[2] An earlier version of this example was published under the title of a "Technical Tip" in *IDUG Solutions Journal*, March 1997. This is a good place to acknowledge the technical editor, Sheryl Larsen, for her support and encouragement with this work.

[3] The IBM disk device 3390-3 has a geometry that allows about 720 K bytes of useable space per cylinder and about 3,333 cylinders per device.

8 Data Warehouse Construction Technologies: SQL

*"We construct for ourselves
representations of facts."*
Ludwig Wittgenstein[1]

THE RELATIONAL DATABASE: A DOMINANT DESIGN

The relational database is a dominant design. That means several things. First, it means that customers building data warehouses using relational technology have a wide variety of target implementations from which to choose. In spite of differences in details, feature behavior, and performance, each of the vendor solutions has large areas of overlapping functionality and structure. Naturally, this is because the relational database products are all implementations of an internationally recognized standard, SQL. Even though a book-length treatment of differences exists,[2] these differences are variations on a theme. Make no mistake—this is *not* plug and play. It is more in the nature of family resemblances between siblings and cousins. The similarities are visible and palpable but not substituable without remainder.

Second, the dominant design of the relational database means that vendors wanting to succeed in the market are constrained by the relational model. This tends to be self-perpetuating with a period of dynamic innovation, such as occurred during the debates about SQL in the mid- to late-1980s. This is because marketing specialists would rather venture into a crowded market with an above-average product than into an undefined or small market with a brilliantly innovative product.

Third, this does *not* mean that the dominant design is technologically the best solution. It means that it is a "good-enough" solution over a large area of customer requirements. It is more like a Ford station wagon than either a Formula 500 race car or the two-cylinder Yugo seen in traffic in third-world capitals. The emergence of the dominant design depends on social and organizational factors, as well as technological ones. Hierarchical databases such as IBM's IMS are actually a technically superior solution for bill of materials applications. However, no new systems are being developed using hierarchical or network models, because staff members do want to work with them and because vendors are ambiguous about the prospects for the continuing evolution of the product. Although it is a matter for debate, the UDB, which has a wide variety of new and user defined data types, is a significant incremental improvement on the relational model, not a dramatic change of direction. (It does, however, enable dramatically new applications in text mining, imaging, and multimedia.)

Finally, accident and coincidence play a role in the emergence and ascendance of the dominant design. Client-server experiments were occurring in the early 1990s; and at the same time, relational databases were being implemented on a variety of platforms—small, medium, and large. A selling point was found in the ease of use of SQL and the bundling of a desktop version of an RDBMS with the latest point-and-click windowing tool. An entire industry was trained in this way. Companies that were otherwise archrivals started telling the same story about the definition, need for, and uses of relational technology and SQL as a flexible back-end to flexible point-and-click GUIs. When that happens, as occurred with relational technology, that is a strong sign of the solidification of a dominant design (see Table 8.1).

Therefore, when the task is to manage large amounts of data, as in a data warehouse, the relational database is a strong candidate. When the task is to slice and dice that data in a wide variety of ways, not all of which can even be anticipated in advance, relational technology is an obvious choice. When connectivity to a variety of front-end tools across complex architectures and networks is required, relational technology constitutes a short list of one.

Table 8.1: Rules Defining a Relational Database System (RDBMS)

Relational Rule	Definition
Data is atomic	The basic data element is the intersection of row and column; this basic data element does not contain an array or further substructure (e.g., in COBOL that would be a group level item)
Data is accessible	The data can be retrieved or referenced by specifying table name and column name; no index is required
Nulls are treated systematically	*Null* means "unknown," regardless of data type. "Unknown" is undefined as to true or false. It is not a third truth value, there remain only two. In real-world implementations, different data types handle nulls differently.
Active on-line catalog	Data is visible to an active on-line catalog; the catalog "knows" about the application tables—definitions and contents—and the catalog is itself made up of tables
Comprehensive data sublanguage	Structured Query Language (SQL) consists of a data definition language (DDL) to define and create tables, views, and related structures; a data manipulation language (DML) for transaction processing (select, update, insert, delete); and a data control language (DCL) to manage authorizations, permissions, and security
View update	A View is a virtual table—implemented by DML, not DDL. Many RDBMSs do not support comprehensive View updating. Views that ought to be updateable are not, in fact, updateable. Views that contain built-in functions such as average or sum are not updateable in any case, because the breaking down of the average into its constituents is not possible.

(Continued)

Table 8.1:   Continued

Relational Rule	Definition
High-level set or operations	SQL operates on an entire group of rows (a table) at a time. SQL does not read or write a row at a time; rather, all rows that satisfy a condition (WHERE ZIP_CODE = 60606) are treated as a set. Such operations are described as DECLARATIVE rather than PROCEDURAL: The SQL command says what to do all at once, as in a declaration rather than a step-by-step looping operation.
Physical data independence	Applications are not affected by changes in the way data is physically stored. Rows are physically stored in a table in any arbitrary order, and the ORDER BY command must be used to sort them. The ALTER command allows columns to be added to tables without converting the table. Views are independent of physical placement. Indexes are not named in the SQL/DML statement and are used only by the Optimizer to make navigation decisions.
Logical data Independence	SQL is able to return columns of data to an application in any arbitrary order. No application program or script changes are required when indexes are added or removed from tables. Navigation is automatic, based on a centralized database component, the Optimizer, which uses catalog statistics to determine optimal access path.
Distribution independence	Application programs do not have to change due to changes in the geographic location of the data. Data distributed across multiple server sites appears to the application as a "seamless" whole. This rule has not yet been attained, though vendors are working on it.
Integrity	The main function of a database is to maintain data integrity. "Data integrity is our most important product." Clients should always have a consistent presentation of the data: Support for referential integrity is declarative—primary and foreign key relations are defined and enforced by the RDBMS. For example, a order cannot be deleted if it has open line items.
Nonsubversion	There are no secret paths into the database. All access is defined by using SQL. In fact, most vendors provide "service aids," which open up a back door into the database for the expert administrator. These should be used with caution.

TWELVE PRINCIPLES

Here we take a step back and provide essential background required to understand the target implementation platform. The twelve-part definition of a relational database management system (RDBMS) is multipart and multifaceted (see Codd, 1972 for the original version). This is the heart of the data warehouse.

1. The relation is the basic constituent of the RDBMS. A relation is the mapping, representing, or juxtaposing of the basic data element as the intersection of row and column. This basic data element does not contain an array or further substructure (e.g., in COBOL, that would be a group level item). An interesting variation considered by the so-called universal database is the embedding of an array or grouplike structure in a column. The purity of the definition of relational is sacrificed for the apparent utility of the result. For example, a product price structure or customer discount schedule could be embedded in this way. Naturally, the array is immediately up against a size limitation of a finite data structure unless, of course, the definition of table is extended to allow a true table to be embedded in a column.

2. There are no links—either hierarchical or pointer—between the basic elements in the relational structure. The information is accessible and complete without such artifacts. In principle, the data can be retrieved or referenced by specifying table name and column name; no index is required, although such an auxiliary structure may be useful from a performance perspective.

3. The completeness of the information implies that you know what you know and you know what you don't know. The latter is called *null data*. *Null* means "unknown," undefined as to its objective value. A future date is a good example of a null value. If the customer cancels his subscription, effective at the end of the month, *null* becomes a definite value. The relational model calls for nulls to be treated in a systematic way. However, in real world implementations, different data types handle nulls differently.

4. Data is visible to and through an active on-line catalog. A central data store ("repository"), itself relational, is available, which registers the basic form and content of the data in the application tables. The names of tables, spaces, and databases, as well as the number of rows and occurrences of significant values in columns, are explicitly listed. The catalog "knows" about the application tables—definitions and contents—and the catalog is, itself, made up of tables. This is the beginning of metadata. However, data warehousing requires more than the relational catalog. (See Chapter Thirteen: Metadata and Metaphor.)

5. Structured query language consists of a data definition language (DDL) to define and create tables, Views, and related structures; a data manipulation language (DML) for transaction processing (select, update, insert, delete); and a data control language (DCL) to manage authorizations, permissions, and security. In general terms, this is the API to the data warehouse. When SQL was invented in the late 1970s, the idea was to create an English-like form and syntax instead of the complexities of most programming languages. However, although a noticeable improvement, except for really basic queries, even SQL turns out to be too complicated for many business professionals not really interested in coding. Therefore, a wealth of desktop and front-end tools have sprung up to generate and build SQL "under the covers" by pointing and clicking.

6. In addition, SQL is used to inquire into the system catalog, directory, and other processing management structures. There are no secret paths into the database. This is called *nonsubversion*, because the common interface cannot be circumvented or subverted. In fact, however, most vendors provide "service aids," which open up a back door into the database for the expert database administrator. These should be used with caution.

7. A View is a virtual table, implemented by DML, not DDL. This is one of the features that makes relational technology so powerful and attractive. It provides for data independence from the underlying physical implementation. This is an architectural attribute of flexibility, whereby changing requirements can be accommodated without having to convert the physical data structures. If an end-user frequently requires a combination of columns from both the customer and sales tables, a View can be prepared that combines that data. The View is really a piece of SQL that is either executed in real time as if it were just a data manipulation statement or materialized and stored in temporary storage. Updating Views is less of an issue in data warehousing, because transactions do not occur on a minute-by-minute basis, as in operational systems. Nevertheless, a complete briefing on this point requires mentioning that many RDBMSs do *not* support comprehensive View updating. Views that ought to be updateable, according to the relational model, are not, in fact, updateable. In contrast, Views that contain built-in functions such as average or sum are *not* updateable in any case, *not* updateable by definition, even according to the relational model, because the breaking down of the average into its constituents is not possible.

8. In addition to physical data independence as provided by Views, SQL is able to return columns of data to an application in any arbitrary order. This, too, is a kind of data independence. It is the logical independence of the data from the particular tables to which they are assigned. Logical data independence is also available because no application program or script changes are required when indexes are added or removed from tables. Navigation through the database and access to data is automatic. The programmer does not write any code other than the SQL, which names only tables, columns, and the action to be taken against them (insert, update, etc.). Navigation is based on a centralized database component called the *Optimizer*, which uses catalog statistics to determine an optimal access path.

9. SQL functions by means of high-level set operations, manipulating a set of data at a time rather than a single record. An entire group of rows (a table) at a time is manipulated. SQL does not read or write a row at a time; rather, all rows that satisfy a condition (WHERE ZIP_CODE = 60606) are treated as a set. Such operations are described as "declarative" rather than "procedural". The SQL command says what to do all at once, as in a declaration, rather than as a step-by-step looping operation.

10. The Optimizer is an important enough component to be capitalized. It represents a dramatic innovation in the approach taken by relational technology, and it (the Optimizer) has received steady incremental improvements since its introduction. It is finally getting close to realizing its true promise. The idea is that a centralized software inference engine, which has global visibility to content and statistics through the relational catalog, can make better choices than the average developer about efficient data access and navigation by a piece of SQL. However, the problem turned out to be that no one has yet met the average developer. Therefore, in all situations except the most elementary and basic, be prepared for discussion about why the Optimizer makes the choices it makes. A good rule of thumb is "don't try to fool the Optimizer" because, ultimately, you are only fooling yourself. An above-average developer will know how to get the Optimizer on her (or his) side by proper use of much of the same information available to the Optimizer (and the developer) in the system catalog. The action of the Optimizer is determining the access path of a SQL statement in the "bind process," and the SQL is thus said to be "bound" to the database.

11. Physical and logical data independence are not enough. They require supplementing by the data's distribution independence. Ideally, applications do not require modification simply because the data is located at a different site or location. Data distributed across multiple servers must appear to the application as a "seamless" totality. In fact, although this part of the relational model is now approaching full realization—often through the support of additional software licenses and products—the technology of multisite heterogeneous joins or updates is so complex as to be far from "seamless."

12. Support for referential integrity is declarative—primary and foreign key relations are defined and enforced by the RDBMS. For example, an order cannot be deleted if it has open line items. Declarative support for this

means that a rule is created by use of DDL, specifying an association of foreign and primary keys in tables and the action to be invoked upon—for example, on delete restrict. In other words, if a child row exists and the parent row is requested to be deleted, then restrict the delete—do not allow it and return an error message. This is in contrast to an approach using application logic or database triggers. The main function of a database is to maintain data integrity. " Data integrity is our most important product."[3]

Of course, any statement of principle is like a stake in the ground—a solid point from which to measure forward progress but also a point that is immediately left behind. The advent of data structures characteristic of the dimensional warehouse—the intersection of customer, product, and time in the star schema—has added a wrinkle to the work of the Optimizer. Whereas the Optimizer was supposed to be a completely general inference engine, the star schema presented what was, in effect, a new test case that had not been envisioned.

In the data warehouse, a join operation (the star schema join, in particular) calls for combining together several small tables (customer, product, time, etc.) and a large table (sales facts). The question for the Optimizer is how to minimize the expense of chasing all of this data, where most of the "expense" is performing I/O operations to get the rows. It turns out that limiting the expense of data access is best accomplished by strictly limiting the access to the large structure. You don't want to combine 10 customers with 1 million facts then turn around and again combine 10 products with a million facts; because you will have (in effect) accessed the largest structure twice (resulting in 2 million accesses). Rather, it is preferable to combine the two smaller tables first, then take the 100 customer-product combinations and access the 1 million-row fact table one time only. The problem was that the classic version of the Optimizer, developed for transactional systems, tended to favor the first scenario, not the more efficient second one. This was because, in this example, the customer and product structures do not share any column on which they can be joined, whereas they both share a column with the fact table. Of course, the number of rows of the two smaller structures is likely to be significantly less than that of the larger fact structure. So, once again, this left the poor developer (and you and I, in this case) in the position of trying to fool the Optimizer—or at least to figure out what it is trying to do. (At this point, without further facts, the discussion goes into a loop.) Recently, database vendors have addressed this problem and are marketing solutions that claim their Optimizers are "star schema aware," or words to that effect. The end-user is strongly advised to use the available database tool—often called the access *Explain utility*—to validate this claim against the actual behavior of the Optimizer.

THINKING IN SETS: DECLARATIVE AND PROCEDURAL APPROACHES

This last example, in which several tables are combined ("joined"), provides an example of "thinking in sets." Another word for *set* in this context is *table*. Basic operations, such as Select, are applied to tables, and the result is yet another table. The resulting table is also called a *results set*, which may also consist of one or even zero rows (records). Consider the example in Figure 8.1. Facts are being selected from the Sales table for all products belonging to the second most popular brand, Brand X. This is a condition—also called a *predicate* or a *constraint*—applied to the entire table with which the data element is associated. In the example, the association occurs by means of the abbreviation (or correlation variable) following the table name. Thus, the PRODUCT table is abbreviated as *P*, and product id is a column in that table named by P.PROD_ID. They are being selected for those customers in the Southwest region.

The SQL statement is declarative, not procedural. That is, it declares the result to be generated, not the step-by-step procedure used in obtaining the result. All of the products in Brand X are treated as a collection, a set, a table. All of the customers in the southwest region are treated as a collection, a set, a table. Conditions are named that restrict the list of rows to be returned. These conditions, also called *predicates*, are used to constrain the fact table SALES, and the result is returned all at once, as a set, to the end-user at the work station interface or on a report. It may be true that, at a micro level, the database engine is applying the predicates to one row at a time as they are returned into the processor's I/O buffer. (Of course, that may also not be true, depending on the number of processors and the partitioning of the data.) However, in every case, the appearance to the application and to the end-user is of a complete set being processed.

data elements:

SELECT P.PROD_ID
       , C.CUST_ID
       ,S.AMT
       ,S.QTY

tables and
abbreviation:

FROM PRODUCT P
     , CUSTOMER C
     , SALES S
     ,TIME T

conditions

WHERE P.BRAND = 'BRAND X'
      AND C.REGION = 'SW'
      AND T.TIME = '3Q'
ORDER BY CUST_ID

Figure 8.1
Select Facts from Sales Table

DATA DEFINITION LANGUAGE

Data definition language (DDL) is used to create and update the structures that contain and organize the data. Table 8.2 shows the basic data types that can be combined to define a row in a relational table. Although details differ from vendor to vendor, one typical approach is presented in Figure 8.2. As indicated, first a database is created. In systems on UNIX and NT platforms, the database is the outer boundary of the entire installation, whereas in mainframe environments, many separate databases may be grouped into an operational subsystem. However, in any case, the database is a logical grouping of related containers, tables, and indexes. The database has disk storage associated with it. These may be listed disk by disk. Alternatively, separate software may be installed to manage a pool or farm of disk storage devices, the allocation of which occurs according to rules called a *storage policy*. The database is represented by a dotted line because, in itself, the database is a logical grouping, not a physical construct. Within the database, a container, a physical construct for manipulating stor-

Table 8.2:   Basic SQL Data Types

Data Type	Definition
BLOB	Binary large object—may contain the operating system name of an operating system file containing the data
CHAR(n)	Fixed-length string of alphanumeric characters—*n* equal to the number of characters
DATE	Consists of year (including century), month, and day—different forms available depending on parameter. Compare 1999-04-15 and 04/15/1999
DECIMAL(p,s)	Decimal number, popular in COBOL environments. p is the total number of digits, the precision; s is the number of decimal point positions.
DOUBLE	A double-word, 64 bit, floating point number
INTEGER	A full-word, 32-bit integer
REAL	A single-word, 32-bit, floating-point number
SMALLINT	A half-word, 16-bit, integer
TIME	A representation of hour, minute, second using different separator value depending on system parameter: hh:mm:ss or hh.mm.ss
TIMESTAMP	Includes both DATE and TIME plus microsecond. For example: 1999-04-15-12.00.00.123456
VARCHAR(n)	Variable length string—n equals the maximum physical page, generally 4000 bytes.
User-defined	Arbitrarily defined data types based on the basic data types specified above

age, is to be found intermediately between the database and table. There are several reasons it is essential to have available this container structure implemented as a physical construct. First, if many small tables—such as code tables—are to be grouped together, they can all be stuffed into a single container for operational convenience. If the container (also sometimes called a *tablespace*) is the unit of backup and recovery, they will get copied or restored together. Second, the commitment of the relational approach includes the logical and physical independence of the data, but databases still reside in a material world. Therefore, a mechanism is needed to separate the logical and the physical. The container is the physical counterpart of the table, which bears the dignity of being the first-level logical construct. This is depicted in Figure 8.3, showing the database, container, and table layout. The table names are what get referenced in SQL, in the application, and in the application programming interface. Even indexes, which are essential especially for satisfactory performance in interactive scenarios, are not named in the code, but they make a significant difference; it is to them we now turn.

```
CREATE DATABASE DBWH01
IN STORAGE GROUP SGWH01 . . .

CREATE TABLESPACE TSWH01
IN DATABASE SGWH01
PRIMARY QTY 1,000,000
SECONDARY QTY 32,000
LOCKSIZE PAGE . . .

CREATE TABLE TBCUST01
CUST_ID          INTEGER NOT NULL WITH DEFAULT,
REGION_ID        CHAR(2) NOT NULL WITH DEFAULT,
AREA_ID          CHAR(4) NOT NULL WITH DEFAULT
. . .
PRIMARY KEY IS CUST_ID
IN DBWH01.TSWH01

CREATE INDEX IXCUST01
(CUST_ID) ON TABLE TBCUST01
```

Figure 8.2:
Create Data Components

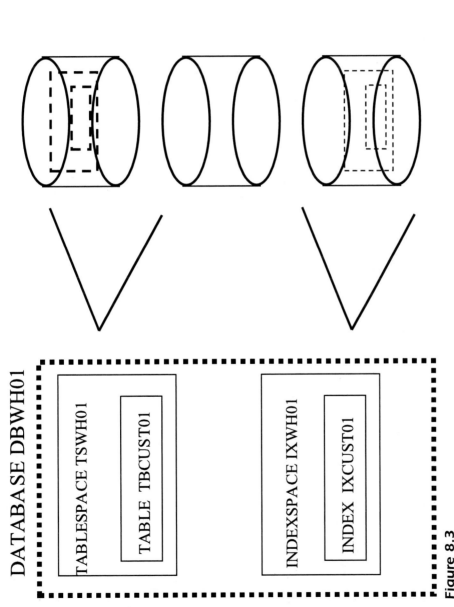

Figure 8.3
Database, Container, Table Layout

INDEXING: B-TREE

The *B-Tree index* stands for *balanced-tree index*. It remains the work horse of indexes, both in terms of use and importance in all environments, including data warehousing and transactional systems. Of course, the "tree" in question is an upside-down, inverted tree. This has led some people to say that database designers should get out more often. Still, the central benefit of the B-Tree is that the path length to retrieving the index entry remains constant (see Figure 8.4: B-Tree Index). Figure 8.4 shows the way index entries are stored on chunks of disk storage called *pages*. This is a logical property of building a tree out of a sequentially ordered list by filling a page of the index with entries, then splitting it into two halves. The two halves are, themselves, ordered sequentially. As entries are added, they will tend to be evenly distributed between halves. If one of them fills up, it is, in turn, divided in half. The data pages contain the actual data values. Leaf pages contain entries that refer to the sequential page number—the physical media on which the data is stored—and the relative row number on the physical page. That is called the *record identifier,* or RID. As indicated in Figure 8.4, the hierarchy of nonleaf pages that rises above the leaf pages grows in an orderly and symmetrical manner. Even if items are added sequentially at the very end of the index, in the worst-case scenario, space will be wasted rather than unbalance the tree. Local imbalances due to the available distribution of physical space or large numbers of insertions at a "hot spot" can be corrected by rebuilding the index, an operation that makes it temporarily unavailable in most cases. ("In most cases" is the term here because new technology in large systems now makes it possible to rebuild a shadow copy of an index while customers are using the original copy, thus greatly enhancing availability.) A constant path length, thus, implies a consistent and nearly constant response time. Unless response time is very bad indeed, in which case that is all that matters, consistency of response is what is most visible and significant to the end-user of the system.

The very definition of a B-tree index means that the index entries are always in order. The relational principle of data independence (discussed in "Twelve Principles," above) means that the actual data need not be stored in that order. In theory, it can be stored in any arbitrary order. For purposes of direct access by means of the index, the order is irrelevant. Just as many Get (access I/O) operations are required by the database engine to get a row at the start of the table as in the middle or at the very end. The root page must be retrieved if it is not already in the processor buffer. The nonleaf and leaf pages must be accessed to determine the RID. Then the RID must be chased to the exact page and record number on the page. These four Gets have to happen in any case for a single random access. However, what if the question being answered by the SQL query is a high-level aggregation requiring retrieving, in order, 15% or 20% of all the records? What happens then? It is much more efficient to return the records in order than it is to bounce around in the set of records, now retrieving one record, now chasing back up the hierarchy and down again to a record physically stored out

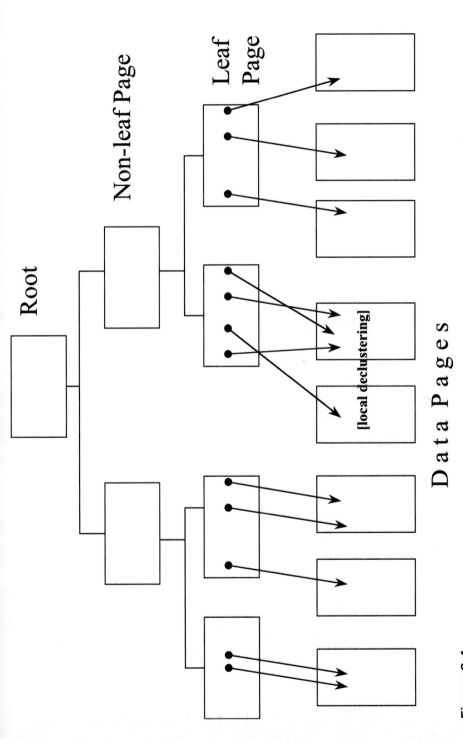

Figure 8.4
B-Tree Index

of its exact sequential order. An example of this is shown in Figure 8.4 (B-Tree Index), where what we might call *local declustering* occurs. Here and there, data pages get out of clustering order. When an index is "clustered," that means the data entries are physically stored in exactly the same order as the index entries. That is, they are in sequential order. As more and more entries are displaced from this exact physical order, the index is progressively less—99%, 95%, 80%—clustered. The advantages of clustering are significant. This is especially so for performing batch processing (as opposed to on-line), where large numbers of rows are retrieved to build a high-level data warehousing aggregate, for example. Because only one physical sequencing is possible, only one index can be the clustering one. However, the benefits of sequentially processing a large percentage of the rows is so significant that the Optimizer may actually prefer to incur the cost of a sort operation if the rows are not already clustered. Naturally, that would be performed in a temporary work space without affecting the actual physical order of the data as otherwise stored. The cost of such a sort approximates the cost of not having the exact clustering index already available and may include I/O to external storage media to hold intermediate sorting results. For a large number of records, such a cost can be significant.

The Revenge of the Librarians: A Personal Anecdote

In graduate school, there were a group of fellow students who were looked down upon. This was not fair. Even the philosophy majors held this group in a certain disdainful disregard. Those were the students of library science. How wrong we all were. In fact, if you fast-forward a couple of decades, we are all in position to appreciate anew the value of methods for indexing, storing, and retrieving information. This is little bit similar to the idea of the title of the movie *The Revenge of the Nerds*. Only this time, library science turns out to be a core competency for managing the fire hose of information coming at the business enterprise. Note well that this is not just the Dewey Decimal System. It is also the comprehensive schema for organizing information such as that provided by the Association for Computing Machinery's Computing Classification System (see www.acm.org/class/) as well as the ACM Digital Library (www.acm.org/dl/), which constitutes a significant on-line resource. It is also such work-in-progress initiatives as industry-specific Extensible Markup Language (XML) encoding of entities and attributes. An alternative view is provided by Jorge Luis Borges's prescient short story, "The Library of Babel" (1964). In this story, the universe is represented as a seemingly infinite, DNA-like, spiral staircase with shelves of books whose content forms all the arbitrary combinations of the letters of the alphabet taken in completely random concatenation. Naturally, the inhabitants of this universe spend much of their time searching for the mythical "the catalog of catalogs."

An important variation on the B-Tree index is the partitioning index based on key value. More exactly, the partitioning index is a special kind of B-Tree index, in which the table (and underlying physical container) is divided into parts (partitions), based on a range of key values. So, if 32 months of factual data warehousing data were available, each of 32 partitions might contain a month's data. Based on specific partitioning scheme, this makes deleting the content of the oldest partition and reusing the space in "round-robin" fashion a feasible alternative. This can be convenient for purposes of operations and maintenance. Partitioning by time is a common approach, but it is by no means the only one. Often, data warehouse data requires time-series comparisons—for example, tracking the sales results for a product from one month to the next. In that case, the query would have to scan multiple partitions, which is not likely to be a high-performance approach. Under such circumstances, it might make sense to partition by product, where all time periods for a given product (or brand) were grouped together on the same partition. Then the query would be limited to a single partition, that containing the time-series data for the product in question. Even when the determination is made that partitioning by time is the best approach, the desire to reuse the space in a round-robin fashion may make it useful to map dates to an arbitrarily assigned partitioning number also contained in an auxiliary or support table. Then, rather than rebuild the entire structure based on a new range of partitioning keys, the auxiliary support table is updated. The trade-off here is that such ease of use is purchased at the cost of building an application that checks such a partitioning history table and correctly assigns the partitioning number (1, 2, 3, . . ., 36), which is what is actually a part of the partitioning index key of the table (see Figure 8.5: Partitioning of Fact_Table). Thus, note in the example of Figure 8.5 that it is assumed that, when the table is created, it is partitioned into 36 parts, and the partitioning index begins with column whose data type is an integer (for example), supporting the numbering of 1 through 36. This is not the only approach to partitioning, and another one will be addressed in the next section. Unfortunately, only one partitioning index is possible per table, because, by definition, partitioning is a unique physical grouping. Therefore, trade-offs sometimes have to be analyzed and made. (Further particulars on partitioning for performance will be discussed in Chapter Eleven: Data Warehouse Performance.)

Indexes are taken for granted by both developers and database administrators. Their importance, however, cannot be underestimated. Further discussion of indexing for performance will be detailed in a later chapter on that subject. Getting at information and doing so efficiently is a large measure of what people mean when they say they know something, have "knowledge." Few of us would have thought 10 years ago that a form of library science—indexing, storing, and retrieving information—would end up constituting one of the core competencies for managing the enterprise. Nevertheless, that is the case.

In a data warehousing environment, the sizing and storage of indexes is a critical success factor in database administration. As the reader may recall from Figure 7.4, data warehouse structures tend to be vertically long and skinny, rather than broad and fat in appearance. Because a few slender factual data elements are hung off of a rela-

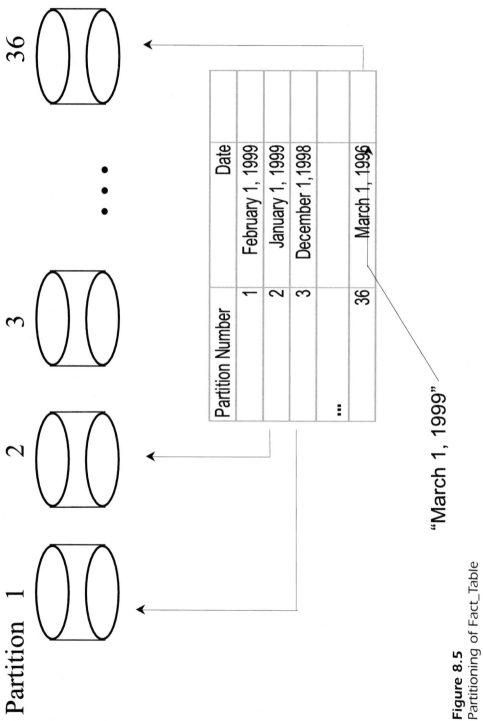

Figure 8.5
Partitioning of Fact_Table

tively large composite index (key), the data warehouse index, in effect, occurs twice. It occurs once as the data elements are stored in the table where they originally reside, and it occurs again in the index as the data elements are stored there, too. Indeed, this is always the case, regardless of the kind of system, but it is much more visible and obvious in the instance of data warehouse structures (indexes and tables). The result is that the amount of storage required for the central star schema fact table tends to approach twice the size of the table(s) alone. The approach of denormalizing on the time dimensions (as discussed earlier in Figure 7.5) does, indeed, have the advantage of producing dramatic savings in storage due to the characteristic shape of the data warehouse fact structure. However, this useful tactic tends to become less critical as the price/performance numbers of storage technologies continue to improve. The essential thing, the point here, is the recognition of the trade-offs.

INDEXING: HASHING

In general, a hashing index does not have an internal structure different than a B-Tree index. The reason it gets its own name is because it solves a knotty dilemma separate from balancing path length to the data entries. The problem is a function of a combination of size and imbalances in the distribution of data. Attaining and maintaining the uniform and even distribution of data is not a trivial problem. As data sets get larger, they become more difficult to manage, including keeping the amount of data evenly distributed. Planning for the orderly growth of the data structures gets challenging for a variety of reasons. Limitations of size occur. Because of the way computer file systems have grown up, many vanilla operating system data sets are limited to 2 billion bytes (or 2 gigabytes) of data. To be sure, that's nothing to sneeze at. But if you've got a thousand customers buying a thousand products over a thousand time periods, that is already a billion combinations, and many firms have significantly larger numbers than that. Database management systems are designed to make use of many underlying physical files for any given table. They do this without the end-user or even the developer of SQL needing to know anything about it. Even so, physical limits are encountered. For example, IBM had to go to the trouble of expanding the RID from 4 to 5 bytes (digits) to increase the maximum size of a single relational table to the trillion-byte (terabyte) range. Regardless of RID size, data partitioning is a proven method of accommodating large data structures. Mapping multiple physical data sets to a single table to expand the horizons of size is done by partitioning. A partition maps to an underlying physical structure defined at the level of the underlying container. The table remains a single name, say, SALES table, but under the cover, it is really 256 physical data sets, each of which can be 4 gigabytes. Given that, now the problem is not so much size as how to assign data to the partition to which it belongs and to do so in a balanced and uniform way. An error in the partitioning method might have all the data going to parts 32 through 34, but what about the other 253 parts?

One solution is a hashing algorithm. At risk of oversimplification, the hashing index consists of applying an elementary arithmetic operation—long division and capturing the remainder—to the key values to assign them to buckets. Those buckets are then round-robined to the available partitions, assuring an even distribution to them (see Figure 8.6: Hashing Index). This can be a particularly powerful alternative to a calendar date-based method of distributing data (discussed in the previous section). Often, sales will vary significantly with the season. As is well known, many retail firms do more than half of their business in the month prior to Christmas. Under those circumstances, it can make a lot more sense to assign partitions based on a hash of a numeric customer or product identifier than on a date.

INDEXING: BITMAP

B-Tree type indexes work well when the column being indexed contains unique or nearly unique values. Each customer or product has a unique identifier. For a million-row structure, this is a large number of distinct values. However, suppose that each customer is a person (not a company) who has one of two gender values, male or female. The count of possible values is called the *cardinality*, meaning literally the numbering of values. GENDER is a column with a low number of distinct values (two). It has a low cardinality. B-Tree indexes do not work well at all with data distinctions that have a low cardinality, a number of values significantly less than the number of rows. Why? The index represents the data in such a way that it is hard to retrieve. Little information is conveyed by the low cardinality distinction. In this example, there are only two index entries—male and female—and the million customer records would have to be associated with either of these two values by a clumsy nonrelational mechanism such as a chain or linked list. The real work of the index would then consist of chasing through this list. This is a lot less efficient than navigating through a B-Tree itself, especially for those entries toward the end of the list or chain. The power of the B-Tree—consistent path length to retrieval—is subverted and rendered irrelevant.

The bitmap index presents an alternative mechanism that resolves this dilemma in most cases. As the name implies, a bitmap index is a group of bits 0 and 1. Each distinct possible value in the column has a bitmap. Every record in the table gets assigned a relative position into the bitmap and a value (0 or 1) indicating whether the distinct value occurs for the record in question. So, for the customer corresponding to record 10, the bitmap for (M) is set to 1 because he is male; whereas the bitmap for (F) is set to 0 for this individual. A related B-Tree index orders the entries in the bitmap and relates them to the customers, in this case. Such bitmaps can be especially powerful and efficient in generating a results set by using logical AND-ing or OR-ing. (See Figure 8.7: Bitmap Indexing.) The work of the bitmap index is performed in building it in the

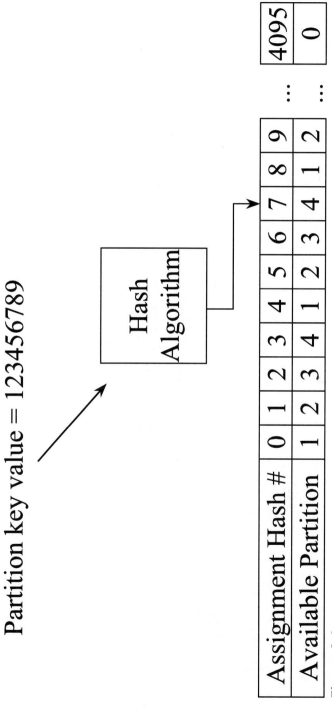

Figure 8.6
Hashing Index

Column: Gender

Number of Record: 1 Million

(M: 100010001110011010100001111. . . 00110001111)

(F: 011101110001100101011110000. . . 11001110000)

Figure 8.7
Bitmap Indexing

first place. Therefore, it is a poor choice if the column is subject to any kind of update activity. However, for read-only applications with low cardinality, it is the method of choice. An additional benefit is that the storage requirements are low to modest because each record is represented by a bit times the number of low distinct values.

INDEXING RULES OF THUMB

Here is a check list of indexing rules of thumb. This list includes items not discussed in the previous sections.

1. Primary keys are required to have an index on them; foreign keys are not required to have an index but ought to have one, unless the table is small (say, five pages of data or less).

2. Those columns named in the WHERE clause of an SQL statement are candidates for indexing. So, for example, in Figure 8.1, above, REGION and BRAND are candidates for an index. The question to be answered is whether the cardinality is high enough to be worth using a single-column index. The problem occurs if the cardinality is in the "it depends" range— not too low but far from unique. Thus, for 1,000 products, a company might have 100 brands. That makes for a long B-Tree duplicate chain but can be readily handled by a bitmap. But what about 5,000 entries? In such instances, it might be useful to perform some testing of actual behavior of the system. A composite B-Tree index is yet another option (for example, PRODUCT, BRAND, CATEGORY but see the next item).

3. In the case of a composite index (PRODUCT, BRAND, CATEGORY) the high-level columns must be available to the query in the index (not the table) that must be scanned. Therefore, the high-level columns should also be the most information-rich and have the highest cardinality. Scanning the entire index is not as bad as scanning the entire table in a single operation but sometimes scanning the index is actually the less efficient operation because, after the scan, the job is still not done. The process must then continue and further chase and fetch the data from the data pages of the table. In Figure 8.1, one possible access path is for the data manager to use BRAND to pick off the dozen (or so) PRODUCTs in the BRAND (and likewise for REGION and CUSTOMER). The high-level columns—CUSTOMER, PRODUCT, DATE—will then all be available in accessing the SALES fact table. Thus, even if these columns are not explicitly named in the query, they are available for processing.

4. Multiple indexes on the same set of columns are possible and useful in context. As an illustration, the PRODUCT table could have an index on BRAND and separate composite indexes on PRODUCT, BRAND, CATEGORY, and CATEGORY, BRAND, PRODUCT. In a read-only (or lightly updated) structure, the overhead of updating all of these separate structures is less burdensome. Many relational databases now support the use of multiple index access paths. It is an exercise for the developers, including DBA support, to use the Explain utility to gain insight, based on data counts approximating production volumes, into which indexes the Optimizer prefers. Because dropping an index and rebinding is relatively easy, such an option is a possible action during the next maintenance window.

5. Relational databases provide built-in functions to perform operations on columns. When built-in functions—Sum, Max, Substring, etc.—are applied to columns in the SQL Where clause, the data manager cannot use the index, and the process has to be passed to another component of the database engine for row-by-row handling.

6. Consider using bitmap indexes for low-cardinality columns on which searches have to occur.

7. The choice of a partitioning index for a partitioned structure should be made the subject of careful analysis. Partitions are an abstraction between a single table visible to an application and an operating system that, by definition, has constraints on the size of underlying physical storage. Choosing whether to use a data scheme, a hashing method, or yet another application method to round-robin through the data sets requires an understanding of the requirements for availability, data size, and growth profile. Any solution is likely to have operational implications for scheduling and managing the storage.

8. The database Optimizer chooses which index to use, based on statistics stored in the relational catalog. Metrics on how many rows, size of rows, number of pages or extents, clustering percent, and similar values for particular columns are gathered and stored by a statistics-gathering function. Naturally, the use of the available indexes by the database Optimizer is only as good as the Optimizer's visibility to the statistics about the index. That visibility is dependent on accurate and timely updating of the index statistics in the relational catalog. Therefore, execute the statistics utility to update the execution time statistics. The operation of binding the application to the database is what gives the Optimizer a chance to decide how the application can most efficiently access the data. Therefore, performing this operation after updating catalog statistics is an essential one. Many database administrators generally recommend the following approach: get the numbers right, bind (or rebind), and *leave it alone* until a significant change or exception occurs.

DATA MANIPULATION LANGUAGE

The simplicity and power of SQL can be appreciated, in that we can review the totality of its DML in a single section. To be sure, this review will be at 30,000 feet; to become proficient at SQL, much more study and experience are required than can be provided in one section. However, the point is that getting started is relatively easy. Even if one can "drill down" for years on the subject of SQL without quite reaching bottom, the order and coherence of the SQL DML expresses its roots in logic and a sound theoretic underpinning.

The basic idea is to take a group of operations, apply them to a table, and get a table. The operations include those belonging to classic set theory—intersection, union, Cartesian product, logical difference—as depicted in Figure 8.8. In addition, operations tailored to the relational context are introduced. These include selecting rows, selecting columns (also called *projection*), joining two or more tables or table-like structures, such as Views, and forming the complement of a table (part of the outer join operation). Let's review these operations in turn.

SELECT: Choose a row from a table based on an attribute (column) describing the scope of the retrieval of rows by a qualifying condition. This results in the operation being described as "Restrict" [see Figure 8.8(a)].

PROJECT: Select attributes (columns) from a table based on naming the attribute in the SELECT operation [see Figure 8.8(b)].

DIFFERENCE: Forms a table (results set) contained in the one but not in the other of the indicated relations—also called the *complement*. Here, the order of the operation makes a difference. The complement of (A,B,C) and (C,D,E) is (A,B). The complement of (C,D,E) and (A,B,C) is (D,E) [see Figure 8.8(c)].

INTERSECTION: Forms a table (results set) from all the rows selected in common from all of the two or more tables. The sets (A, B, C) and (C,D,E) intersect at (C) [see Figure 8.8(d)].

UNION: Forms a table (results set) from all the rows selected in both or either of the two or more tables. The union of (A,B,C) and (C, D, E) is (A,B,C,C,D,E) [see Figure 8.8(e)].

JOIN: Also called a *natural join*, this forms a table (results set) from all of the rows selected in common from all of the tables named based on a qualification contained in an expression stating the scope of the retrieval condition [see Figure 8.8(f)].

OUTER JOIN: Forms a table (results set) as above for JOIN, including the DIFFERENCE, or complement, of the one table or the other. Note further that the calculation of the difference has three variations. See Figure 8.8, where the left rectangle contains the complement of the right one—everything non-right. Reverse this and you get everything non-left. These present the "left" and "right outer joins," respectively.

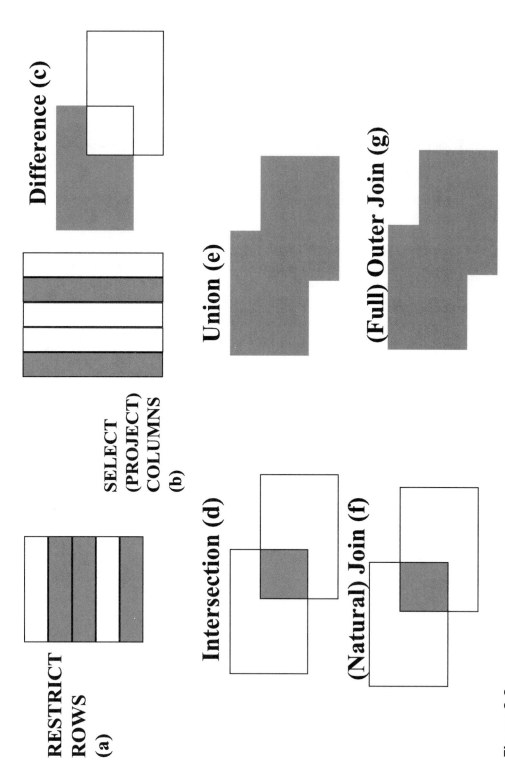

Figure 8.8
Data Manipulation Language (DML)

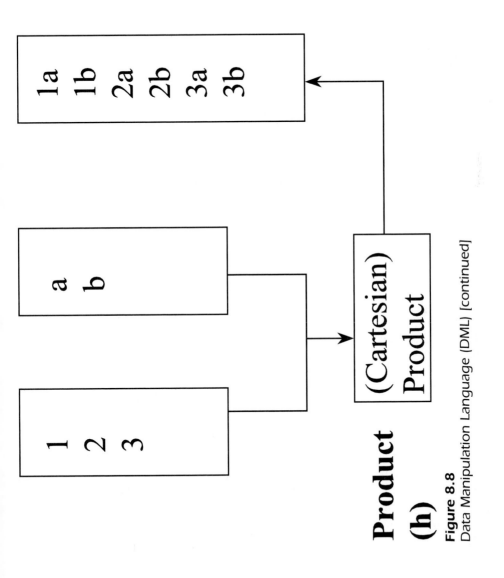

Figure 8.8
Data Manipulation Language (DML) [continued]

When all are combined together—the join, the left outer join, and the right outer join—the "full outer join" is the result [see Figure 8.8(g)].

PRODUCT: Forms a table (results set) from all the concatenated selections of rows, one from each of the indicated tables. The product of (A,B) and (C,D) is (AC,AD,BC,BD) [see Figure 8.8(g)].

The latter is a particularly useful operation. Which customers purchased no products or products that were purchased by no customers are questions that cannot be answered by the vanilla natural join. When you want to know which customers purchased no products or which products were purchased by no customers, the complementary operations, resulting in the left or right outer joins, are essential.

The complete implementation of SQL requires operations to Insert, Update, and Delete rows, based on a Where clause describing the scope of affected rows by a qualifying expression.

Because a table is another name for a relation—a grouping of attributes into individuals, based on a unique and defining attribute—these operations yield a "relational algebra." That is the name E.F. Codd gave to these operations in his famous 1971 paper (see bibliography) on database languages. Do not be intimidated by the fancy terminology, which you may use to impress colleagues and co-workers. Here, *algebra* means a "symbol system" or "notation." We should not be intimidated by the language but rather take delight in the elegance and power provided by the few simple operations.

Codd was particularly proud of the result of the property of closure—that operations on tables yield tables. This makes possible the embedding of relational expressions in other expressions. An operation selects data from a table. That Select can then be made the target of another Select. What is more, this can be done in one and the same SQL statement, which is where the real declarative power lies. The result is that a Select picks off rows from the result produced by a Select, which, in turn, picks off rows from a table. So, for example, instead of naming a table as the object of a Select statement, another piece of SQL performing a Select can be cited (see Figure 8.9 for an example). Here, an inner and an embedded Select are presented. The outermost Select chooses rows from the CUSTOMER and SALES tables and from a piece of SQL (which, itself, stands for a results set). The piece of SQL, which does duty as a table, refers to the PRODUCT table and restricts the scope of the statement to products (PROD_IDs) between 1 and 99. Because the product identifier is referenced twice—once inside the parentheses and once outside it—these are actually logically different tables, though there is only one underlying set of products in the PRODUCT table. Thus, the AS marker is needed to distinguish between the nested occurrences of the same table by means of an abbreviation called a *correlation identifier*. This is an important point and accounts for the power of SQL. Because not all vendors' implementations of SQL support this feature or all aspects of it, check the vendor's documentation to be sure this is available.

SELECT C.CUST_ID, P.PROD_ID, S.QTY
FROM CUSTOMER AS C,
    (SELECT PROD_ID FROM FROM PRODUCT AS P1
        WHERE P BETWEEN 1 AND 99)
        AS P2,
        SALES AS S
WHERE S.CUST_ID = C.CUST_ID AND
        S.PROD_ID = P2.PROD_ID

Figure 8.9
Nested Table Expression

DATA CONTROL LANGUAGE

Database security is an important part of a total approach to security. It works best as part of a solution that includes security policies and procedures that make security a responsibility for which management is accountable, both as a matter of technology and as a matter of governance. Thus, management is required to have visibility into and responsibility for the authority of the staff, including a manger's signature on authorizing documents. That means that management has visibility into the process of granting and revoking authorizations. Given the complexity of large firms and the coming and going of staff and consultants, the importance of a flexible approach to security administration is in the foreground.

The key to flexible database security administration is group or secondary authorizations. What does this mean? This means that the path to database access lies through a software security tool that acts as gate keeper. This security tool is able is to keep track of which users have which privileges and to keep track of privileges by means of a profile that groups privileges into meaningful collections.

In the example in Figure 8.10: Secondary Authorization, the security administration tool—a package such as Top Secret, ACF, or RACF—contains an assignment of table privileges to a label. One label designates a developer security profile, able to access and update a specific test database. Another label designates a clerical security profile, able to access a specific production database. A third label designates an expert user, able to access multiple production databases and to update tables or columns relative to their department. Finally, a database administrator security profile has privileges to manipulate multiple test and production databases, because the DBAs must perform implementation, maintenance, and other operations on the database structures. In setting up and maintaining these profiles, the label *DEVxx* is the target of the database privilege. For example, the DCL might specify: GRANT SELECT, UPDATE ON TEST_TABLE_1, TEST_TABLE_2 . . . TO DEVxx. Different test profiles may be crafted and implemented, corresponding to unit test, system test, and acceptance test. Note, however, that the number of profiles will be significantly less than the number of individual staff members. Up to this point, the creation of profiles has not yet caused any single individual to acquire database privileges. Now, individuals—Mark, Lou, Ralph, Larry, Diane—can be added to the proper profile, based on their roles and managerial approval. Note that the profile itself does not require updating. Only the association between an individual and a profile is updated. So, instead of GRANTing access to 500 tables each to Lou, Mark, and Larry, only four operations are issued, in which DEVxx is associated with Mark, USRyy is associated with Lou, and DBAxx is associated with Ralph. Then, if one of these individuals resigns or is dismissed, only one association requires deleting, not the revoking of access to 500 tables. The advantages of this approach in avoiding excuses and all-too-human errors in maintenance are clear. The relative ease of administration means that policies will be followed and accountability recognized.

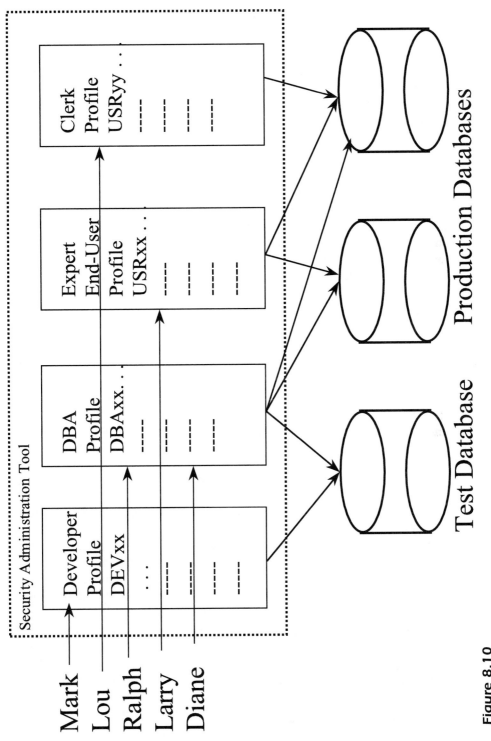

Figure 8.10
Secondary Authorization

STORED PROCEDURES

The stored procedure (SP) is an application that resides within the boundaries of the database itself. It contains database access and application "if - then" logic. This distinguishes it from a stand-alone piece of SQL, which, of course, also gets executed on the database. Stored procedures were a significant improvement when they were introduced in the early 1990s by Sybase SQL Sever. They were one of the enabling technologies of the client-server revolution and, for several years, gave the vendor that popularized them a certain advantage. Today, all major database vendors offer SPs, and IBM has even introduced them on the mainframe. Until that time, mainframe application architects had to "simulate" the behavior of the SP by embedding SQL in a host language program (e.g., COBOL) on a transaction monitor such as Customer Information Control System (CICS). This had the unintended but happy consequence of going immediately to a three-tier architecture by placing application logic on a centralized location (not the client and not the database server), the transaction processing monitor.

The four advantages of the stored procedure include the following. First, they reduce network traffic. If application logic is sited on the client, rows have to be passed from the database server to the client to apply processing logic. An application may take a position against a row in the database structure and advance through it or through a subset of it, applying a further condition to the rows accessed. Instead of passing data between the client and the server, the stored procedure allows this conditional logic to be executed on the server. The smaller results set can then be forwarded to the client for presentation to the end-user. Second, SPs allow the centralized development and maintenance of application logic on the database. This immediately makes possible two-tiered client-server. However it is also consistent with the interposition of a third layer of application logic at a later stage. Third, the centralized location lends itself to the centralized administration of access security. The client work station is notoriously hard to secure. To someone who knows what to do, SQL is relatively easy to modify but not if access is lacking to the central database and the SPs executed there. Finally, performance advantages are available in statically binding (compiling) the stored procedure to the database. Most client-server front-end tools necessarily use dynamic SQL. The access path has to be recalculated (optimized) on every separate occasion that the SQL is forwarded from the client to the server. With a permanent residency on the database embedded in an SP, database access code can be statically compiled once and for all. The SP and its input and output parameters are registered with the database. It has visibility to the statistics in the relational catalog, and the catalog has visibility to it for purposes of centralized management. Thus, the SP can be the target of a dedicated tuning process—using the database Explain utility—to determine whether it is performing as designed. This results in a predictable, consistent level of performance across multiple accesses or, if exceptions occur, the likelihood of a controlled investigation and experiment to diagnose and remedy the situation. (See Figure 8.11: Stored Procedure Example.)

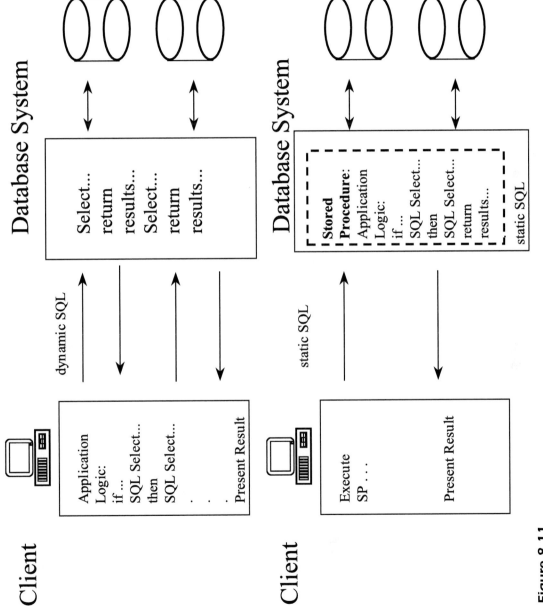

Figure 8.11
Stored Procedure Example

Under the title of trade-offs, disadvantages to stored procedures include the following. Because the process executes on the server machine, debugging can be challenging without special-purpose tools. The process is launched from the client. It goes off to the server where, for some reason, it fails. How to tell why? A trace or debug file must be written, with hooks in the SP, to write output diagnostics for later review. Also, coding and testing an SP is an activity that is neither within the realm of the database administrator nor within that of the traditional application developer. It requires skills from each domain and is really a new role that must be defined organizationally. This requires managerial attention and cross-functional coordination and sensibilities.

The development of the SP on a release-to-release basis has focused on making the approach more "open." Here, *open* means conforming to the results of published standards committees. It means independence from vendors' particular protocols and proprietary hooks. It means aligned with what was described above as a dominant design, those technology features to which all participants in a market have to address themselves to be contenders. Procedural language was required to embed "if - then" or "case" logic in the SP. This meant that a scripting language was required. Starting in the early 1990s, each database vendor had its own approach to procedural scripting. Naturally, this has restricted convertibility, portability, and database interoperability. Many commentators suggested that was the whole idea—to create barriers to switching to another database. However, by the end of the decade, larger corporations, company standards notwithstanding, have accumulated a couple of instances of each kind of vendor database. Meanwhile, more than one vendor had the idea of using standard host languages (C, COBOL, a version of BASIC, or Java) as the scripting language. These insights of IBM and Oracle was a contribution to openness and shows how relative latecomers can leap-frog the competition by addressing unresolved end-user requirements. At this point, the Java programming language is being added to the list of host languages and is a strong candidate for convergence by multiple database vendors.

The 60–80% of data warehouse queries that are predictable or part of a standard business process belong in SPs or centralized application servers. This enables them to be given the attention they deserve as mission-critical components of the data warehouse knowledge delivery process. Maintenance, security, and performance—all of these considerations and more—dictate the use of stored procedures.

USER-DEFINED FUNCTIONS

The basic operations provided with SQL can perform functions on columns and individual scalar values. For example, the column function Sum, as used in:

SELECT SUM(QTY) FROM SALES S, CALENDAR C WHERE S.CUST = '123'
AND S.PROD = 'X' AND C.QDATE = '3/01/1998' AND C.DAY = S.DAY

will provide the accumulation (SUM) of quantity sold (QTY) for the given customer, product, date range combination. Database vendors started out by providing a basic set of built-in column functions—SUM, AVERAGE, MIN, MAX. The list grows, release by release, as user groups lobby for ever-increasing functionality. However, no general solution can envision all options, nor can all the particulars of individual cases ever be imagined.

As an illustration, one area where data warehouse calculations find standard SQL to be wanting is in the calculation of time period and moving averages. The average daily account balance for the month in a person's checking account is the sum of the daily balance divided by the number of days. However, the SQL Average function (AVG) will divide by the number of rows selected from the table in the query, not the number of days. One solution is to dispense with the AVG built-in function. Rather, take this calculation into an application—perhaps a stored procedure—which accepts as input parameters the dates required to figure out the number of days and return the result. Another solution is to identify, evaluate, and buy a proprietary class library providing a set of SQL extensions.[4] This is a cost-effective approach for firms that are willing to incur up-front expenses and are able to execute rapidly to gain the three- to five-year advantage that this technology could provide. However, there is nothing to prevent a firm's competition from purchasing in short order such a solution also if there really does turn out to be a measurable advantage.

Meanwhile, the other database vendors, in addition to practicing that sincerest form of flattery, imitation, are providing tools required to design and implement your own built-in functions. These are user-defined functions. (Please note that the "user" in question is the expert application developer, DBA, or other IT professional defining the function, not the customer or the business analyst.) Strictly speaking, user-defined functions were available prior to UDBs, but they have become a basic characteristic of the UDB formula, especially if they are required to support user-defined data types, which are what give the "universality" to UDBs.

A user-defined function results in a function label that can be applied to a column, just like a built-in function. It is written in a standard host language (C, JAVA, etc.) or other proprietary scripting language and employs conventions specific to the database to intercept column data from the row being returned, store data in scratch pad area to perform accumulations, and return output to the results set prior to delivery to the application. The function has to be registered with the database by means of a CREATE FUNCTION command, compiled, and made available at execution time through proper location of the object code in a path visible to the database engine. The sequence of operations here is significant, because SQL, which references and employs such user-defined functions, will need to be subjected to version control if such a function is updated after the initial operation binding the SQL to the database. That is to say, system development discipline and procedures are required, as in any application development situation. Designing and developing user-defined functions in-house is a demanding project for those firms capable of sustaining the drill. However, such development can confer competitive advantages that cannot be purchased off of the shelf by any competitor. Finally, management should keep its radar scanners out for the emergence of a kind of cottage industry of user-defined SQL extensions that can be purchased at reasonable, "shrink-wrapped" prices. This would be in imitation of what has happened with Microsoft's Visual Basic, where a variety of "VB Controls" (windowing components) have been made available by small and innovative vendors for purchase at shrink-wrapped rates. Data warehousing functions are an attractive target for such entrepreneurial activity.

SUMMARY . . . .

The relational database is explained as a dominant design. The twelve rules defining the relational database management system (RDBMS), the heart of the data warehouse, are reviewed and clarified. The issue of the visibility of the database optimizer to the star schema is engaged and explained. A recommendation is provided. The distinction is made between declarative and procedural approaches to information processing. What is meant by "thinking in sets" is addressed. Structured Query Language (SQL) has several parts, and they are considered in this chapter. An overview of Data Definition Language (DDL) is provided. Different approaches to indexing—B-tree, hashing, bitmap—are considered. How to handle indexing—rules of thumb—are furnished. The aspects of SQL Data Manipulation Language are laid out in a dense section, supplemented by an information rich diagram. The relational approach to security—SQL's Data Control Language (DCL)—is engaged and discussed. The advantages of database stored procedures are detailed and user-defined functions explored to complete the discussion of data warehousing SQL construction technologies.

[1] See Wittgenstein, Ludwig, ***Tractatus Logico-Philosophicus***, translated by D.F. Pears and B.F. McGuinness, New York, NY: Humanities Press, 1961 (originally published 1921), proposition 2.1, p. 15.

[2] For example, see ***IBM's Formal Register of Existing Differences in SQL,*** detailed in the bibliography.

[3] For a summary of these 12 principles of the relational model, see Table 8.1: Rules Defining a Relational DBMS.

[4] As an example, the vendor Red Brick, now a part of Informix, Inc. provides SQL extensions called RISQL, which include functions for time period moving sums and averages, rankings, ratios, and related innovative operations. However, as of this date, these functions are limited to those installations that have implemented the underlying proprietary Red Brick database.

9

Data Warehouse Construction Technologies: Transaction Management

In this chapter...

THE CASE FOR TRANSACTION MANAGEMENT: THE ACID TEST

The working definition of a *transaction* is a business event as represented in the computing system. This is easy to see with the help of an example. A customer, Dominick, exchanges a case of Coke for one of 7-Up. The complete business event is an exchange. It is not a complete transaction to just decrement the Coke inventory bucket. In fact, it is an out-and-out error just to increment the Coke case counter but not decrement the 7-Up counter, too. Both of these atomic events are part of a larger business transaction. The exchange is what gives the atomic events meaning. The point is that the transaction defines a boundary, containing some things and excluding others, and encompassing the whole experience, as the quote from David Liddle implies. A further analysis of this microtransaction using a data warehouse might indicate something significant for brand management. Are people becoming more health conscious? More interested in avoiding caffeine? Or was it a cents-off coupon that made the difference? Did the exchange occur in the consumer's mind prior to any purchase at all? Often, the complete definition of the boundary of the transaction is the result of a collaborative effort between business analysts, systems architects, and technology implementers. The representation of this in the computing system is a microevent, in comparison with the work that must occur to derive knowledge of the product or consumer from it. Nevertheless, because technology in the service of knowledge of the business still requires mastery, much of this chapter will be devoted to technical distinctions.

Do not be deceived by the description of the data warehouse as a "read-mostly system." This remains true, but it is the "mostly" that requires attention. Forecasting systems often start out reporting on history and deriving an automated forecast, from history. However, a requirement soon surfaces to "tweak"—that is, update—the forecast, based on the latest promotional or business intelligence data. Given the goal of managing the supply chain, this is a reasonable request. It is true that the data warehouse should not display the kind of "twinkling," constant updating of the hundred-and-one snowflakes. The point-by-point updates of the operational systems that support airline reservations or cash machines are not required. However, selective updates to dimensional tables and updates to perform corrections and maintenance are necessary to effective operations. Then there is the example of the forecasting and estimating warehouses. Once planned or estimated data is posted to the warehouse for comparison with historical "actuals," the genie is out of the bottle. These are updateable structures. The discipline of transaction management must be engaged and mastered.

Furthermore, even inquiry-only access requires careful definition of the boundary of the transaction. To understand what a "long transaction" is, an understanding of *transaction* is required. An example of a long transaction—one that spans multiple scheduled jobs in the computing system—is the loading of the customer and product structures, such that they provide a consistent representation of the information in time. If the product structure is current as of Friday, and the customer structure is current as of the following Monday, a transaction attempting to access both to answer a question is at risk of returning incomplete or inconsistent information. What is worse, without a basic working definition of a transaction, the reasons for the anomalies and inconsistencies are not obvious. The credibility of the warehouse data requires understanding and synchronizing of such data manipulations. The important thing to note is that the consistency in time in this instance is, indeed, represented in the system; but it is not entirely understandable in system terms. That is, it is a functional business decision to aggregate sales (for example) as of week ending Friday and to ignore any products added over the weekend. The place to store such a rule is in a metadata repository.

A complete transaction then satisfies the "ACID" test. What does that mean? The transaction is atomic. If the database is changed, all the changes occur together or not at all. The transaction is consistent. The data is left in a logically coherent state. The example above—where two related dimensions are refreshed on different days—is an example of inconsistency in time. Transactions are isolated. In a dynamic environment with many concurrent changes occurring simultaneously, different processes do not overlap with one another. The one completes before the other is allowed to begin. Transactions are durable. Once a change is made, the system does not revert to a previous copy, due to an unrelated system failure. Committed means committed. (See Table 9.1: The ACID Test, for a summary of this.)

Table 9.1:   The ACID Test

Transaction Property	Definition
Atomic	All the related events are treated as if they were a single basic unit, an atom.
Consistent	Database integrity is maintained. Consistency is our most important product.
Isolated	Dynamic, multiple, different concurrent processes do not overlap. Processing is serialized.
Durable	Once committed to the database, changes do not get undone. They are persistent.

THE LOGICAL UNIT OF WORK

The logical unit of work (LUW) is the totality of events determined by the precise technical boundary of the transaction between its beginning and its "commit." It (LUW) is often used synonymously with *transaction* by technical staff. Such use is proper. By default, the commit point occurs when the application executing ends or when an explicit Commit command is issued. If the end of the application is abnormal and due to failure, the end point is really an undo (or rollback), which reverses any incomplete work in progress.

Even in the context of a read-only transaction, the LUW is significant. Why? Because database and system resources are limited—often more limited than anyone would like. At the commit point, resources are released so that system processes, database buffers in main memory, read engines, disk controllers and channels, bandwidth reservations, or even presentation cycles can be shared in an orderly way with other users of the system.

The commit is a significant event in the life of a LUW. It is the end point. If multiple events are being grouped (say for distribution across a network as part of a replication server process) the commit indicates that all is in good order. The database is in a consistent state. However, if one of the multiple related events fails to complete for whatever reason, the others must be "rolled back." It is an "all-or-none" proposition. If one fails, the other work in progress or, as the saying goes "work in flight," must be undone—rolled back.

The complete definition of the commit protocol requires a discussion of the "two-phase commit." This is the only truly "bullet-proof" method of assuring data resource integrity, whether within a single host or across multiple distributed systems. Even within a single host multiple transaction, events may be made the object of logging and data integrity activity. For example, an update to a customer database table may need to be coordinated with writing to a sequential data structure in a related flat file system. This requires a two-phased commit to assure that if what is not supposed to happen does, work is completed or rolled back in a synchronized way. As an illustration, consider the updating of three related resources, as in Figure 9:1: Two-Phase Commit Protocol. The resource that initiates the transaction will typically act as the coordinator of the update. The coordinator sends the message to the participants to "prepare to commit." The participants respond with an acknowledgment, "prepared." The coordinator then enters the second phase by issuing "commit." The participants respond with a message back to the coordinator, to the effect of "job done." The two-phase commit issues a rollback to the participants if, at any phase, the participants respond that the requested action has failed or do not respond after the system time out duration elapses. Naturally, there is always a catch. If the coordinating node fails, for example, due to interruption of electrical power, after receiving the acknowledgment "prepared," how do the participating nodes clean up the mess? This is the one instance—when the failure occurs during an "in-doubt" period—when the database administrator will have to issue a manual commit or rollback upon restart of the failing system. The advantage of this protocol, as it is called, is that it is an ironclad guarantee against loss of data integrity. Even if the power grid fails in the middle, upon resumption of electricity, the phases will be resumed and completed. The disadvantage is that these systems are tied up for a relatively long time while all of these resources are being synchronized. If the time out period is not properly set or if the number of points to be coordinated is large, the appearance may be of a system that "hangs." If one of the nodes is not available for whatever reason, the work really cannot be completed. The abort and rollback are inevitable.

Tripping Over a Transaction Boundary

A friend recently ran afoul of the boundary of a technical transaction and then of the limits of a business relationship. As a pioneering Internet consumer he was looking to explore new technology and save a couple of dollars in the bargain: He was in the process of making an airplane reservation over the Web. The next thing he knew, the session failed. Poof! Gone. Session terminated with extreme prejudice. Whether the server timed out due to a slow network or the client experienced a problem was not clear. Nor was it clear whether the transaction had completed and the reservation existed or not. What was clear that he had an important trip to make and on short notice. What to do? He called the airline's 1-800 telephone number. Up to this point, my friend had a experienced a technical problem. Next, he experienced a problem with the business relationship. He was told that the customer service representative did not have visibility to reservations made over the Web. There were separate paths into the reservation system from the Web and the call center reservation system. What happened at this point does not allow being quoted in print. The result was that an agreement was reached to make another reservation and clean up any duplication, if there was any, when the credit card bill arrived. The lesson? A unified view of the customer and the channels the customer uses to relate to the firm providing the product or service is a function of technology, coordination of communication channels, and business relationship.

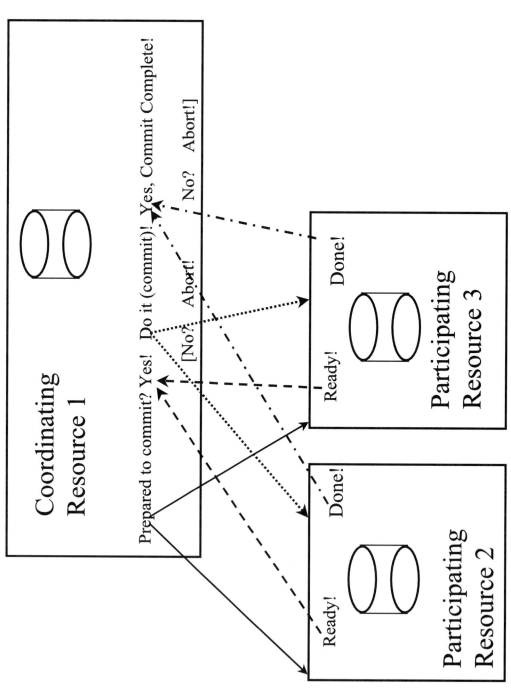

Figure 9.1:
Two-Phase Commit Protocol

The transaction processing monitor (TPM), to be considered in further detail immediately below, is what drives the commit. It determines when the commit point has been reached and, in effect, tells the database, "okay, commit" or, in the event of an exception condition or problem on the client, "not okay—roll back the work." Of course, if there is no TPM, the database, itself, performs the role of determining a commit or roll back. The database manager functions as a so-called lightweight transaction manager—lightweight because it focuses on data integrity and provides fewer queuing and messaging services. Its primary job is to manage data integrity; there are the two operations for capturing that in the database log—commit and rollback. In general, the commit occurs when the client application completes normally; otherwise, rollback processing is appropriate. This fundamental capacity to perform transaction management is what leads people to talk about "TP lite"—the ability of the database, alone and without a full-blown TPM, to manage data integrity.

TWO-TIER AND THREE-TIER ARCHITECTURES

Now that a basic business event has been defined as a transaction, the next step is to map that onto a computing system architecture. As usual, the key is to understand trade-offs.

Directly connecting clients to the data warehousing database is relatively quick and easy from a technical point of view. This direct method of connection performs well for small and medium numbers of connections. Because clients initiate requests according to a random schedule, this method is asking the database server to manage the multiple requests as they hit the server. The work must be accommodated, prioritized, and satisfied. If the request for large amounts of data or "if - then" logic in a stored procedure is invoked, database computing cycles have to be shared between the database threads corresponding to the client requests. This switching back and forth between tasks while waiting for I/O is one of the functions for which operating systems were created. Note that the database is now doing it. Indeed, database engines have been designed so they can do it, too, but it is not their specialty. Too many connections and reconnections—and soon, the database is spending as much time switching back and forth (multiprocessing) as it is performing data lookup and qualification logic (which, after all, is its main mission). The database then experiences a kind of attention deficit and hyperactivity—also called *thrashing*. If the database asks the underlying operating system to handle the thread creation and management, the coordination costs between these two major software components escalate rapidly and the handoffs become a bottleneck as volumes increase. In addition, some kinds of database operations simply cannot be performed satisfactorily using direct client-to-database connections. Accessing multiple databases directly from one client in this manner is difficult; updating them is well nigh impossible. If a large or highly variable number of clients is connecting, direct connectivity presents performance problems and limited scalability. Neither the database nor the operating system server can readily handle this variability in the work load. If the client application fails, for whatever reason, what is the status of the work "in flight" on the database? If the disposition depends on defaults set on the client, database resources may be "left hanging." Finally, if the application logic is complex or volatile, the simple two-tiered direct connectivity approach is at risk of requiring frequent changes of software on all the desktops. Thus, the amount of code on the desktop also tends to keep growing. It eventually goes beyond the description of the "fat" client—we are now dealing with the "bloated" client. In short, the two-tier client-server architecture of client-to-database connectivity reaches its limit for performance, manageability, and operational reasons. One method of addressing this dilemma is the insertion of another layer of software between the client and the database.

The interposition of another layer of software—the TPM—does, indeed, add overall complexity to the system environment, but it does so on a system-wide basis, not on every client's desktop. The TPM provides an extra mechanism for balancing the work load by sharing connections, processes, computer main memory, and underlying processes that must be created and managed. If a large or variable number of users is requesting database connections, the TPM provides the ability to queue and multitask requests between the client and database server. Requests are routed by the TPM to available database resources in an optimal way, and database resources are able to be reused. High costs of database thread startup and deletion and startup again are minimized by the sharing of pooled resources.

This is also called managing the *conversation* between the client and the server. The conversation is a connection-oriented exchange between two processes, such as a client and an application or an application and a database. The TPM is responsible for tracking the transaction from end to end. The TPM is equipped with a temporary storage or scratch-pad facility to allow it to store state information about the status of the conversation. Thus, the client can even connect, disconnect, and reconnect to complete a transaction in multiple phases. This improves the reuse of scarce database resources such as threads, allowing more work to be done due to improved scheduling. This is called *pseudo-conversational processing*, because it appears (hence the "pseudo") to be a continuous conversation with the client. However, it is actually completed in phases, based on tracking the state of the process by maintaining context information in a behind-the-scenes storage area.

The simplifying effect of introducing a third tier into the architecture is depicted in Figure 9.2 (Two-Tier and Three-Tier Connectivity). The "simplification" is from the perspective of the use and management of system resources. The underlying logic may actually be more complicated, but it is the presentation of simplicity that makes all the difference. The third tier is able to track the transaction from end to end. If one part of the sequence—for example, the client—fails, the TPM is responsible for seeing that commands to abort and undo (rollback) any in-flight database work get executed to completion. The number of failure conditions that TPM are able to accommodate is large. The world of computing being what it is, investment of resources in

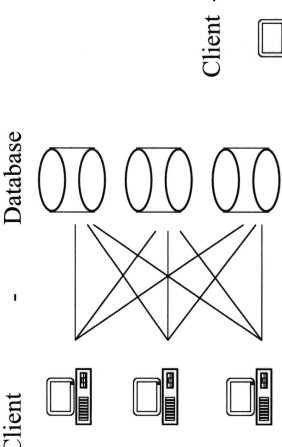

Figure 9.2
Two-Tier and Three-Tier Connectivity

robust error handling is never gold plating but always useful and important functionality. In addition, application logic can be *centrally* managed on the server. Code is installed and maintained in one or a limited number of locations, not on every desktop. Finally, the access to multiple, heterogeneous databases can be managed in a defined server interface, rather than in clumsy client code. Such a complex join operation across products from different vendors is now possible. This is another testimony to the interoperability of different implementations of the relational model. However, it (the heterogeneous join) often requires special-purpose software or an extra product license. Therefore, it is not the kind of operation that can or should be launched from a client work station.

In short, the TPM, the middle layer of a three-tier architecture, has often been compared with a "mini operating system." That is because it provides the same kind of services to its application clients—multitasking of limited and shared resources, load balancing, and integrity and coordination—as the operating system provides for basic computing processes. What often happens is that the two-tier implementation is the prototype and proof of concept; whereas the three-tier is the enterprise edition. Problem arise when this is not understood and seen with eyes open at the start of development. The insertion of that additional "tier" is a fundamental design shift and not something undertaken casually.

A gateway—such as the legendary MDI gateway now from Sybase—is an entry-level three-tier architecture. It has the extra network hop without the benefit of the centralized functionality or skinny client. All of the application work is still done on the client or the database layer, but processing has to funnel through a gateway server to complete the mainframe-to-PC encoding (EBCIDIC to ASCII) translation. The rule is without exception. If mainframe-to-PC data format translation and connectivity are required, a gateway function—not always the same thing as a gateway product—is still an indispensable component. In many ways, the amazing thing, of which we never even dreamed a few years ago, is that such connectivity can be accomplished at all. This provides a point-to-point solution, but one no less useful for all that.

In data warehousing, the middle-tier of the three-tiered architecture has come to perform three separate functions. First, it provides for scalability, work load balancing, and many-to-many connections between clients and the data stores satisfying their requests as described in this section. Second, the middle tier is where generic OLAP servers and services build and operate on data cubes and aggregates, using special purpose, proprietary databases called multidimensional databases (MDDBs). This may allow for "reach-through" from the desktop "slice-and-dice" tool through the data cube to the back-end RDBMS. This is an important enough function to require a separate treatment as part of Chapter Fifteen on OLAP technologies. Finally, the middle tier is the locus of analytic engines that operate on an application server. These provide business functions relevant to data warehousing, such as time series logic, risk analysis, and industry-specific decision support calculations. These analytic applications may be too specialized to put into a stored procedure on the database. They invite treatment by means of network-aware applications (such as those coded in Java) that are best executed on a server of their own. There is the prospect of an entire cottage industry of analytic application vendors springing up for the purpose of building and marketing business libraries of high-level components that can be configured and dropped onto the server.

DISTRIBUTED ARCHITECTURE

Today's business enterprises are geographically distributed. Mergers, acquisitions, and divestitures are reshuffling the deck of corporate boundaries. This will continue apace. Indeed, this trend is progressing in the direction of delivering services and products globally. Now, take a three-tier architecture and distribute it across the wide area network (WAN). A WAN is any communication medium connecting geographically distributed locations. Typically, the WAN employs a telecommunications backbone or Internet-like infrastructure (TCP/IP). When the communication messages are routed through the public Internet but encrypted on the path out and decrypted on the inbound path, the term *virtual private network* (VPN) is used to describe the connectivity. This is depicted in Figure 9.3 (Distributed Processing). Three different geographic locations are presented—headquarters and two other distributed sites—for example, Chicago, Los Angeles, and London.

We shall defer recommendations on the wisdom of trying to build and operate a distributed data warehouse and, instead, first lay down the basic understanding of the technologies enabling us to assess the feasibility of such an undertaking. As usual, *understanding* means understanding the trade-offs involved in distributed processing. This will be discussed in the remainder of this section and the next two on middleware.

The first approach to connecting all of these distributed components is to define them as local and remote resources to one another. From the perspective of headquarters (HQ), data at HQ is local. That data at sites one and two are remote. From the perspective of site one, HQ and site two are remote, and so on. (See Figure 9.4: Local and Remote Resources.)

Large systems—including mainframe ones—led the way in the mutually interdependent definitions of local and remote resources. Front-end processors (FEPs) running IBM's System Network Architecture (SNA) as implemented in the Virtual Telecommunications Access Method (VTAM) made transaction management resources visible on other hosts by means of entries in system telecommunications tables and SEND - RECEIVE commands coded in LU6.2 protocols (Logical Unit—the number 6.2 was based on a succession to previous types of hardware/software configurations for such communication devices as printers and terminals). Although such a proprietary solution has been available since the 1980s, it requires custom programming in the application to bring the data back by means of SQL, massage it in code,

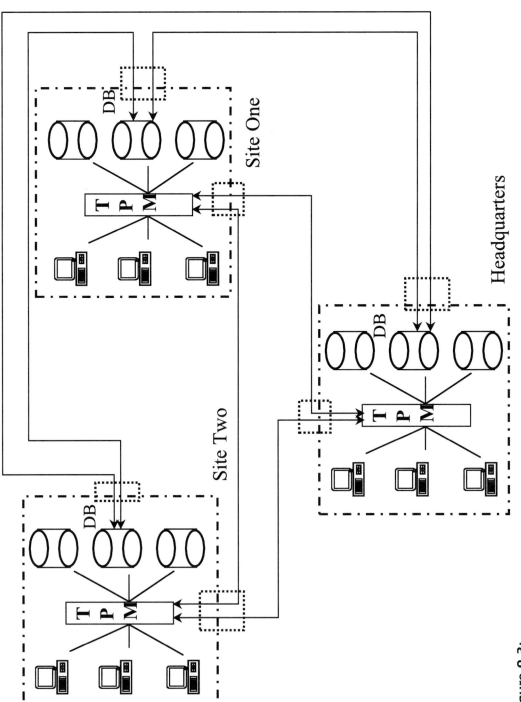

Figure 9.3:
Distributed Processing

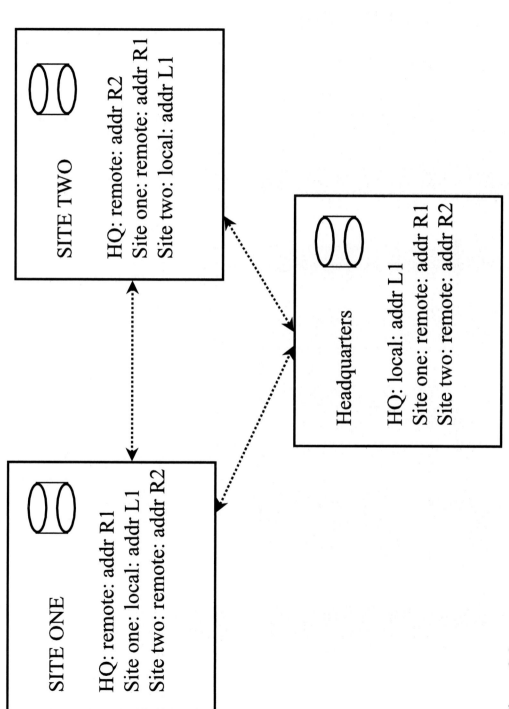

Figure 9.4:
Local and Remote Resources

and further deploy it. What used to be a proprietary front-end processor (FEP) is still called that but has, in fact, been reborn as a router.

As client-server systems distributed computing cycles across the network, the requirement became to put back together what was divided and to navigate bet the pieces. One response was a candidate standard called Distributed Rela Database Architecture (DRDA), to which vendors were invited to respond by IL Basically, database-to-database interoperability is defined by distinguishing ch requests from an application requester (AR) to an application server (AS). The fc levels of database transaction are summarized in Table 9.2. The idea is to distinguis the following:

1. single access of a client of a database
2. multiple accesses, including update of a single database
3. distributed update of multiple sites
4. distributed access, including multisite join.

Table 9.2:   DRDA Transaction Levels

DRDA Transaction Level	Definition
1. Remote Request	A single piece of SQL requesting access to a single database
2. Remote Unit of Work	Multiple commands (SQL statements) against a single database—the typical client-server scenario in a two-tier application.
3. Distributed Unit of Work	Update of data at multiple locations in a single transaction
4. Distributed Request	A single piece of SQL requesting multisite services. For example, a join spanning several databases.

The work involved, including any updates, occurs within the discipline of the two-phase commit protocol. This is a logically coherent solution—and successful implementations exist—but delays at any one point in the distributed network tend to entangle (get propagated to) the other DBMSs. That means that synchronization requirements and delays are imposed on what are otherwise mostly independent systems. This can literally be a show stopper. The end-user perceives system symptoms as the work station "hangs" while awaiting a reply. After this happens a few times, the search for alternative middleware solutions receives new impetus.

MIDDLEWARE: REMOTE PROCEDURE CALL MODEL

The idea of a remote procedure call (RPC) is to hide network complexity. A standard API is defined and the messy details of chasing up and down communication stacks is hidden behind the API. Therefore, the idea of an RPC is attractive. It embodies the object-oriented principle of encapsulation and information hiding—place the implementation details behind an interface. As an idea, the RPC will survive—and may actually outlive—the specific implementation that first popularized it, the Open Software Foundation (OSF)'s Distributed Computing Environment.[3] For example, Microsoft has incorporated a version of this RPC as its Windows NT operating system and is using it in DCOM/OLE. Although it is perhaps a stretch, stored procedures on a database have been compared with an RPC back-end when invoked from the client. The goal in all cases is the same—to make the complex appear to be simple. Specifically, it is to make a complex distributed network appear to the application as a single seamless system (see Figure 9.5: Remote Procedure Call). This is a desirable result, but, as usual, trade-offs exist.

First, the path length of the RPC is long. The client and server both require a stub to make diverse interfaces appear to be uniform. RPC execution time modules are needed for processing, and the actual network stack and transport layer still have to be traversed.

Second, because of the complexity of the network environment, "some assembly is required." Multiple hops are required. The security server must be checked and arrangements must have been made in advance for authentication and encryption. If dynamic binding is invoked between client request and servicing function, a directory or naming service must be queried to validate the address and location of the server.

Finally, this method of communication is synchronous. That means that both client and server must be available together, along with the above-cited list of supporting services, during the same real-time period. As might be expected, the illusion of a seamless, single system has its costs.

In its original conception, RPCs were limited to a uniform interface to network transport on top of directory and security services. There was no provision for trans-

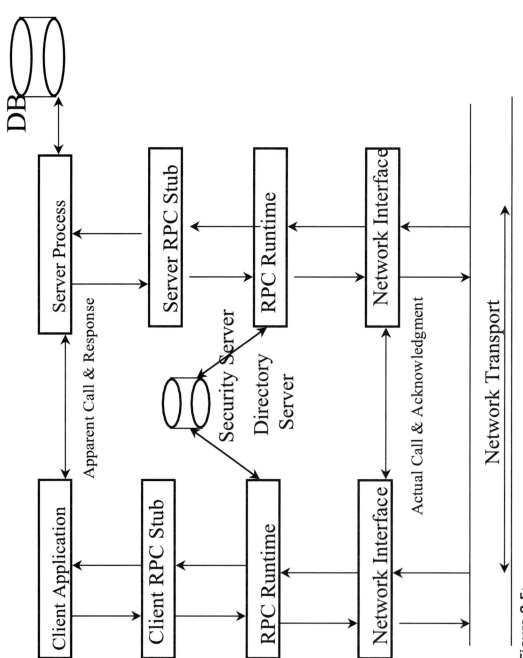

Figure 9.5:
Remote Procedure Call

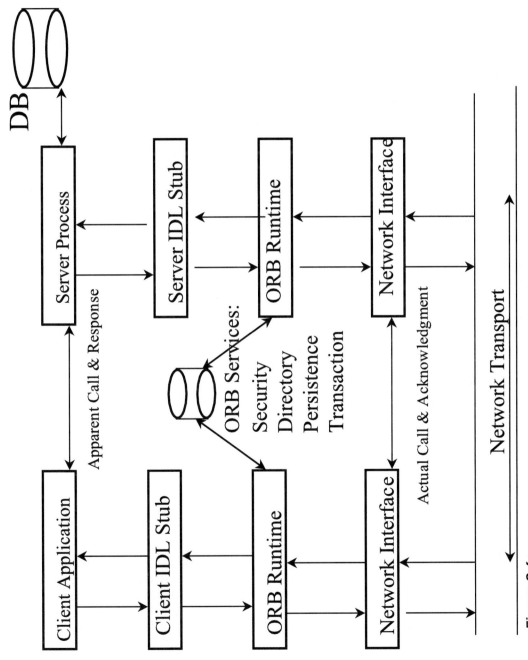

Figure 9.6:
Common Object Request Broker

action management and a host of other useful services. That is why the idea of an object request broker (ORB) had to be invented.

In 1989, a consortium of object technology vendors founded the Object Management Group (OMG) to specify a standard architecture for the interoperability of their independent languages, tools, and platforms. The overall layout and pattern depicting a common object request broker architecture (CORBA) closely parallels that of the RPC mechanism (see Figure 9.6: CORBA)—but with a catch. Once again, an architecture is not a product. Different vendors—Iona, IBM, DEC—write products that are CORBA-compliant, implementing the standard. In every case, an essential feature is an interface definition language (IDL) providing a mapping from the data types of one language to another, say C to COBOL or Java. The resulting interoperability parameters and dynamic binding are stored in a distributed repository that the ORB is responsible for, updating and maintaining in a consistent state. Recently, the addition of an Internet Inter Orb Protocol (IIOP) has sparked the vision and interest in sending ORBs out across the Internet. The bottom line is that there is nothing "lite" or lightweight about an ORB. The resulting mechanism is synchronous.

MIDDLEWARE: MESSAGE-ORIENTED MIDDLEWARE

The truth is that the chain of synchronously connected, distributed sites—like any chain—is no stronger than its weakest link. At the risk of a mixed metaphor, this is what leads Chris Loosley to describe the "single synchronous transaction paradigm" as the "Achilles heel of interdependent system."[4] The point is well taken. All of these technologies—RPCs, ORBs, and gateways—are powerful, useful, and industrial strength in the proper context. However, they are limited in their ability to support high-performance, mission-critical applications. They are limited in their scalability. Most dramatically, they are limited in that a single point of failure makes completing the transaction impossible. As the volumes of work increase across the distributed system, the effort of coordinating transactions using the two-phase commit protocol limits performance by requiring the synchronization of resources across all of the participants. While this synchronization is occurring, processing waits. Delays in one system—for example, due to database locks—get propagated to other systems in this way.

The response? A bold statement of the obvious: If synchronous transactions are a problem, try asynchronous ones. This requires breaking down the synchronous LUW into several parts, each of which has guaranteed data integrity in its own right. What does this mean? Let's trace the path from the client to the server. First, the client takes the events collected into a complete transaction and writes them to a data store one hop away ("upstream") from the client. This data store is typically called a *queue*, because it functions like one. Records are inserted in the top and, based on a first-come, first-serve basis, they are stored and forwarded to their destination. This is the queue on the so-called messaging middleware that services the source of the data, the client. The messaging middleware is then alerted; it takes over the management of the integrity of the transaction. A "message" is now defined as the transmission of all the related records (events) in a transaction from one site to another. The *message*, as the transaction is now called, is then written from the source queue to the target queue. This is a recoverable transaction. If something goes wrong, the incomplete message can be backed out, requeued, and tried again. If the server is temporarily unavailable, the message can be allowed to await the resumption of service. The job is incomplete, to be sure, but if the outage is short, the client can continue the process of pumping transactions into the top of the queue process without "hanging," waiting for a response from the server. If it (the outage) is not of short duration, the installation has more serious problems than can be solved by MQ ("message-queuing") software, which, unlike synchronous processes, would at least buy time at the front-end to fight the fire. Finally, when notified of the availability of the target database, the target queue writes the message, completing the loop with an acknowledgment back to the client by way of the same path. If, for whatever reason, the client is temporarily unavailable, the server can continue processing messages, awaiting its attention. Similar considerations of maintaining data integrity apply up- and downstream. (See Figure 9.7: Message Queuing Middleware.)

Message-queuing or message-oriented middleware (MOM) presents one of the clearest examples of trade-offs in analysis. First, if instantaneous and unexceptional update of separate sites is required, MQ software is not the answer. The asynchronous distribution of the data is indeed guaranteed as to its data integrity. It might even occur with remarkable speed under most circumstances. However, it is nondeterministic in terms of duration. It is guaranteed to be asynchronous, not completed in real time while you wait. However, when you think about it, very few systems have the synchronization requirements of an airline reservation system, an ATM cash machine, a call center help desk, or a stock market ticker tape.

Perhaps the bullet-proof, near-instantaneous service provided by the mainframe has spoiled the industry. Perhaps it has spoiled the entire customer community, too. We expect to be served instantaneously. But think about it-Real-world business transactions allow for human-scale time for reflection in terms of minutes. The "just-in-time" movements of physical goods from a loading dock to an assembly area allow for actions by workers in a factory requiring tens of minutes or an hour. The lead time for the redistribution of goods through a supply chain requires hours or even days. For all of these situations, MQing is a strong option. It is yet another example of a good-enough technology that avoids the weaknesses of a so-called superior solution.

With MOM, client and server do not have to wait for one another if they are unavailable, either for scheduled maintenance or due to unscheduled system events. The work load is balanced by enabling servers to request work from a single "first-come, first-serve" queue. This promotes scalability as the amount of transaction work escalates. Although each queue is, in effect, an integrity-protected data store—and might even be implemented by a relational table—the processing occurs in the background, asynchronously. The fallacy of the child's game of telephone—where the

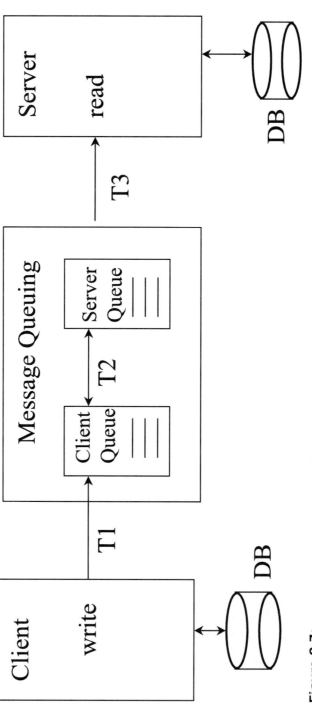

Figure 9.7:
Message Queuing Middleware

message going in the front is changed beyond recognition by the time it comes out the back—does *not* apply here. Why not? Because the MQ software is in effect eavesdropping on each hop; it intervenes in case of an incomplete or erroneous transmission. A little bit of extra time is traded for the ability to fire off a single message and get back to the work at hand, knowing that the message is in the hands of a resource that can be trusted to close the loop.

This is, indeed, yet another "divide-and-conquer" strategy. An end-to-end synchronous transaction, containing several interdependent events, is decomposed into multiple hops, which are treated separately. From a data integrity point of view, each "hop" is an LUW. (T1, T2, and T3 in Figure 9.7 are "hops.") That is, it is recoverable and bounded by the equivalent of a database commit or rollback. Each one is secured, so the independence is only relative. The power of such a store and forward mechanism is robustness in the face of interruptions and distractions.

THE LONG TRANSACTION

This shows us what a long transaction is. As an illustration, we have considered forwarding an update, for example, customer information from HQ to two remote sites. Messages are stored and forwarded in a multistep process using outbound and inbound messaging queues with hop-to-hop commitment to integrity. This transaction is "long," in that it may reasonably require an amount of time compatible with human think time—minutes. Even more importantly, it is "long," in that it is actually an amalgamation of a series of related LUWs. It is not just an assembly line, though it is perhaps like that, too. From a business perspective, it is a coordination of commitments. Each hop through the network is literally that—a commitment to the business goal supported by the information integrity of the data being transferred. Now, scale that up. Instead of just a couple of customer records, consider all of the customers in the Northwest region or all of the products in a brand. The business transaction is really a driver, such as "synchronize the customer information to coordinate a product promotion to a point in time (for example, first business day of the week, Monday) across the three separate sites." Note that the MQ software has no visibility to such a driver, and, in that sense, you still can't completely automate knowledge of the business. Management must still decide what schedule will work. However, once the boundaries of the technology are aligned with those of the business drivers, the system is capable of supporting such an objective with the supervision of an automated scheduler.

Given the complexities of synchronously connected, distributed sites, the idea of a distributed, multisite, local-to-remote database join operation is logically valid but practically perilous. For example, imagine a scenario in which the firm is geographically distributed, such that the fact table is stored at HQ, the customer dimension is stored at site one, and the product dimensions is stored at site two. A join across these sites is theoretically feasible. The technology exists to perform such a join at any one of the three sites, but such a design is asking for trouble. Issues of availability, differences in time between the different sites, network performance, multiple points of failure, data maintenance, and staffing coordination end up on the critical path. From the perspective of what is operationally feasible and practical, it is far better to copy the relatively small customer and product structures to the site with the fact table on an asynchronous basis. Then perform the join with the data all locally referenced at the same site. The point is that getting all the data at the right place at the right time is precisely a long transaction. A similar consideration applies to refreshing, maintaining, or updating the data. Given the amount and variety of data that data warehouses must manipulate, it makes sense to consider the loading or rebuilding of a table or a significant portion of a table as a complete transaction. The data from the third quarter is now available, for example. Therefore, let's append it to the previous two quarters. These activities are also long transactions against the data in the database. This large-scale management of the database is the providence of the DBA, and it is to such considerations that we now turn.

SUMMARY . . . .

The working definition of a transaction as a business event is provided. The transaction defines a boundary, marking the inclusion and exclusion of certain defined events and things. That the data warehouse is a "read-mostly" system means that the discipline of transaction management must be engaged and mastered. A complete transaction satisfies the ACID test—it is atomic, consistent, isolated, and durable. This leads to the logical unit of work (LUW), which is the totality of events determined by the precise technical boundary of the transaction between its beginning and its commit point. The "commit point" and the "two-phased commit" protocol are defined and discussed. Directly connecting clients to databases is the quick and easy approach of two-tiered applications. The interposition of another layer of software—the transaction processing monitor—provides an extra mechanism for balancing the work load, furnishes scalability, and manages the conversation between client and server. Although more complicated "under the covers," this is actually a simplification from the point of view of application management. Two-tiered and three-tiered architectures are discussed. The three purposes of the middle tier are noted. Now take the transaction and distribute it across the local and remote nodes of a wide area network. The synchronization required by the RPC model and delays imposed on what are otherwise independent systems motivates the search for alternative middleware solutions to those presented by the options of point-to-point solutions, SNA, and even sophisticated DRDA. The approach of remote procedure calls (RPCs) gives way to message oriented middleware (MOM). Finally, the long transaction is discussed. Instead of "twinkling" updates of individual rows or items, the complete load of a customer dimension, product dimension, or both is what counts as a transaction in the context of data warehousing.

[1] Liddle, David, "Design of the Conceptual Model." In ***Bringing Design to Software***, edited by Terry Winograd, New York, NY: Addison-Wesley Publishing (ACM Press), 1996, p. 30. Although originally said about the user interface, this comment applies remarkably well to defining a transaction boundary.

[2] IBM's implementation of the standard is called Distributed Database Connectivity Services (DDCS), a gateway enabling cross-platform connectivity and remote and distributed units of work for those databases that provide such support.

[3] The Open Group resulted from the merger in 1996 of OSF and the X/OPEN Consortium. The latter was the recipient of the X Windows standard for "open"—i.e., UNIX—systems, as well as a version of the SQL Common Application Environment (CAE). As regards the former, when, in the later 1980s, AT&T's Bell Labs (the owner of the UNIX standard at that time) bought 20% of Sun, IBM, HP, and DEC formed the Open Software Foundation (OSF). The joke at that time was "OSF" meant "oppose Sun forever." Since that time, the UNIX standard has gone to the stewardship (not ownership) of Novell, AT&T has bought and subsequently spun off NCR, the World Wide Web was invented, the government has sued Microsoft, and SUN has been reborn as the champion of the Java initiative in netcentric computing. These are indeed interesting times.

[4] See Loosely and Douglas, 1998: p. 526.

Part 3

Operations and Transformations

(Chapters 10 through 14)

Data warehousing operations are built on data management, performance, and the information supply chain. The vicissitudes of database backup, recovery, and storage management are narrated in detail. Key data warehousing system performance parameters are discussed. These include workload, throughput, and response time. The data warehousing information supply chain is traversed. The miracle of the information supply chain is that the data is cleaned up, scrubbed, transformed, and the result is knowledge. The secret to this miracle—and why it is not really a miracle but just good business system design—is the alignment of the information supply chain with the fundamental business imperatives directing customer and product development. The data warehousing information supply chain is a work flow coordinating commitments. The coordination entails a framework constituting knowledge, including such parameters as data quality, scrubbing, and aggregation. The path of the information supply chain from the transactional system(s) to the data warehousing one is described as an aggregation model. Aggregations are a key component of the success of any data warehousing system, and their maintenance and management is a significant success factor. The metadata captured at the time the extract, transform, and load (ETL) process is defined and executed is a crucial source of system integration. The interdependency of data extraction and setup with data presentation and analysis (OLAP) is discussed.

10 Data Warehouse Operation Technologies: Data Management

In this chapter...

DATABASE ADMINISTRATION

If the DBA's mission statement had to be summarized in one sentence, it would read like this. Data integrity is the DBA's most important product[2] but, truth be told, although the DBA has a leadership role, she or he is not the only one responsible for data integrity. As soon as the end-user is provided with access to the data, the DBA's phone is likely to ring with an "opportunity" to improve or complete data integrity in a step-by-step, give-and-take way between information producers, consumers, and managers. In many ways, "integrity" is a proxy for all manner of quality metrics and attributes. Business analysts, managers, application developers, and other information producers and managers have specific responsibilities for data integrity. If a merger or acquisition results in overlapping product or customer categories, it is insufficient for management simply to "mandate" their merger or for the end-user just to demand their reconciliation. Cross-functional resources are required to figure out the semantics and the implementation options. Here, the commitment to data integrity is virtually indistinguishable from the commitment to customer service or brand development—that is to say, to the business itself. The representation of consistent data in automated systems is the easy part, once triage has been applied to the definition and reworking of the overlapping business distinctions. This is what makes the difference between a marginally operational data store with duplicate rows—no coherent business entity— and a data warehouse, a powerful platform and repository for the acquisition of rigorous knowledge of customers and product behavior in the market.

BACKING UP THE DATA
(IN THE EVER-NARROWING BACKUP WINDOW)

At a database user's group conference a few years ago, in a question-and-answer session, one of the speakers was asked how long it took to back up her firm's data warehouse. Now, this was a large credit-reporting firm with terabytes of data. The speaker, a knowledgeable professional, said that her team had estimated it would require 18 days to back up all of it. The implication—a complete backup—not feasible. It turns out that a "workaround" was required. Namely, each day's or period's differences were archived and a restore executed a custom process to rebuild any data structures, rather than to try to restore it from scratch. That required planning, design, and an element of library science to track and index all the parts of the complete structure. In this example, what is at stake is the *availability* of the data and the answers it provides. Simply stated, backing up the data is being proactive about the possibility that things will happen that will impact availability.

Backup Proactive Space Management

To develop a backup and restore strategy for the data warehouse, someone—usually, the DBA, DA, IT manager, or someone charged with developing overall data strategy—has to interview application development management and the business experts to determine the answers to the following questions:

- How essential is the data warehouse to daily, weekly, monthly business operations?
- How frequently does the data change—every second, hour, day, week or month, etc.?
- How frequently do changes require capture?
- How up to date does the data have to be—this instant, yesterday at 6 PM, last Sunday?

Regardless of the answers to these questions, the DBA must also determine or estimate:

- How much space must be allocated for the data warehouse initially?
- How fast is the data growing?
- How much space—and what kind of space—will be required for backups and archived logs?
- What are the availability requirements for the data warehouse ("batch window" size)?
- What jobs or processes feed or are fed by the data warehouse?
- What scheduled transactional systems depend on the warehouse, and vice versa?
- What sorts of problems can be anticipated, and what provision can be made proactively to prepare for contingencies?

In general, the profile of the backup requirements of a data warehouse is less rigorous than that of a transaction system, but that is no reason to be casual about the matter. Instead of 7x24 requirements, one may have 6x16 requirements. That is a mixed blessing if one has to back up ten or a hundred times the amount of data warehousing data, in comparison with the amount of transactional data. Therefore, a word to the wise: Any successful data warehouse will tend to migrate in the direction of operational rigor for backup and restore handling. This is what is meant by the subtitle of this section about the "ever-narrowing backup window."

This point is worth discussing. The data warehouse starts out with a time window mirroring the decision support activities of key business analysts, planners, or marketing teams. That starts out being for example, 9:00 to 5:00 Central Standard Time. When teams on both coasts require access, the on-line window grows by four hours—for example, from 7 AM to 7 PM. No problem. Then further time constraints arrive from a different direction. As the loading and maintenance of the data are "operationalized," processes that hook to and feed other transactional systems (and vice versa) are put on the automated schedule. For example, if the data warehouse is supporting a forecasting function, it must be available when other transactional jobs execute. Otherwise, the forecast doesn't move any other part of the supply chain mechanism, most of which lies outside the boundary of decision support, as such. The data warehouse is not a transactional system, such as order entry or inventory control. It is now an operational system, in the same sense that transactional systems are operational—they require regularly scheduled jobs or processes to feed them and they support hooks and links to other scheduled jobs.[3] The data warehouse is operational. Its processes or jobs are a part of data center operations. If one of the jobs in an automated schedule fails for any reason, the dominoes start falling. This is the pressure to perform according to any operational schedule. The DBA role and the activities and technologies relating to data integrity and storage are the source of initiative and the first line of defense in operationalizing the data warehouse.

In addition, an understanding of the volatility of the data warehouse—its rate of growth and change—is a critical success factor. Dimensions tend to change more frequently than do fact tables—unless the fact tables also include metrics about planned or estimated quantities (for example, sales or deliveries), in which case the volatility profile is reversed. The point is: Simply saying that the data warehouse is "read mostly" is really a trap, and it is to be avoided. If that is unclear at the start, there is a risk to be managed here. Are these the kinds of decision support processes that might require "as if" planning? If so, managing the risk implies erring on the conservative side and preparing for a moderate amount of update activity. That is work, because it implies design for restore and recovery. These things are hard to retrofit when it turns out that "read only" means "read and write just a little bit now and then." Given the severe penalty for loss of data integrity, from a professional perspective, the task is unavoidable.

Therefore, a strong statement: A DBA without a backup is useless. The imperative to back up your data is a cross between carrying a spare tire in the trunk of the car and obtaining an auto club membership on the vehicle. The smallest problem, like a little puncture, can dramatically halt your forward motion, so it's good to have a quick fix available. Larger problems require larger remedies. At the risk of overextending the metaphor, it is easier to find replacement transportation than to replace the computing function and—even if you are driving a Rolls—probably cheaper, too. Let's face it—transportation is now a commodity, whereas the data to run and understand your business is not. Preparing, planning, and practicing recovering from a total disaster such as a flood or fire is a full-time occupation for a team of dedicated professionals, including managers. Best practices require such a disaster recovery plan, including off-site storage of the tapes required to recreate the computing environment, provision for obtaining the hardware and software to rebuild the environment, as well as the physical site to conduct operations. It is also useful to verify, on a sampling basis, that the backup operations were successful and the tapes (or media) contain readable, accessible data. The description of such a "disaster recovery" task is beyond the scope of this book, but the backup of the data is surely an essential part of such a plan. Here, we will focus on specific issues with data backup.

How Many DBAs Does it Take to Change a Light Bulb?

Let's hope you never have to ask this question or get it asked of you. In one installation known all too well to a friend of the author's, the DBA team was literally losing a lot of sleep over physical input-output (I/O) errors occurring on the tapes used to backup the data warehousing databases. A little background is in order here. One of the main functions of the DBA team is to make sure that data warehousing database backups get completed successfully on time. Usually the tables were backed up to tape in multistep processes that stacked many tables (data sets) on the same tape. Although ordinarily a trivial matter, due to stacking of data sets, when the job failed for whatever reason, it usually required the intervention of a DBA to get it restarted. Now as a physical media, tapes are subject to what are called I/O errors. The physical media is dirty, damaged, or not readable. This is not supposed to happen often. However, for unknown reasons, it started happening frequently. This team got into a situation where they were getting two or three I/O errors a night. That often meant that the "on-call" DBA was awakened at 2 AM, 3 AM, and 4 AM. This was burning up the entire seven-person team at a rapid rate. Meanwhile, because the installation was "outsourced" to a hardware utility, the installation was earning real cash rebates for every job failure. Although ultimately a false economy, this must have looked good to somebody. It looked to the lead DBA like this was being milked as a cash cow, a savvy guess that was never proven, at the expense of everyone's sanity and daily productivity. Therefore, the DBA in question tried applying humor. A memo was drafted urging that the tape drives be cleaned again (and again) and the old batch of tapes, probably bought at discount, be thrown away and new one acquired, regardless of the modest extra expense. The concluding question: How many DBAs does it take to change a light bulb? The answer? None, its a hardware problem! Just like the tape I/O errors. Amid general denials of responsibility and knowledge of what was happening at 3 AM, the problem simply went away. The I/O errors stopped. Problem solved. As for the lead DBA? This person had an engaging new data warehousing assignment (elsewhere) within six months. That's life in the corporate jungle.

These problems include damage or interruption to the functioning of the physical media on which the data structures are stored—the disk drive crashes, the electric power goes out, an operator varies the media off-line, etc.; incorrect update to the data in the table, for whatever reason (erroneous application process, human error, malicious activity); the requirement to restore data to a previous historical point in time to investigate a business issue or opportunity—the equivalent of a data audit or stand-alone data mining task; or system conversions, implementations, or portings of data between systems or platforms. Note that only the first two items are out-and-out system failures where something breaks. The other two are analytic activities that address business issues. All of them affect the availability of the data and of the knowledge needed both to run the business on a day-to-day basis and to engage the challenges needed to grow it.

Because the problems are multifaceted, so must the solution be multifaceted. If a piece of "in-flight" work fails and cannot be completed, the backup literally requires rolling it back from the information stored on-line in the database log. The log is an on-line backup, usually on disk, immediately available to the database. In fact, the before and after images of the changes to the data structures may actually be in main memory of the processor prior to being written to the log on disk—though from the point of view of the users of the database, no difference, other than speed of response, is visible. Thus, the database log is the first line of defense.

Note that, periodically, the logs themselves fill up and have to be backed up. This is called a log *archive*. Typically, the direct access storage device (DASD) is backed up to tape, a sequential medium. Theoretically, the entirety of database changes can be restored from the backup residing in the database log. In actual fact, this turns out to be impractical because the intermixing of images of different transactions means significant quantities of irrelevant data are mixed together. Disentangling all of these transactions requires too much processing time. In addition, structural changes to the database—the adding and deleting of entire structures—is not an event that is meaningfully captured in the log. For example, there is no Undo command for a DROP TABLE. Therefore, the log is really a log of transactions against the structures.

Therefore, it is useful to back up each database structure separately. It used to be the case in client-server databases that the unit of backup was the database itself. Naturally, that has a heavy impact on availability if a restore has to occur because of one broken, but essential, little code table in an otherwise multigigabyte database. However, recent versions of database design have introduced containers—rather like tablespaces corresponding to underlying physical files on the mainframe—as a more granular unit of backup and recovery. This enhances availability and elapsed time to complete a recovery in an essential and useful way.

Usually, backups of individual data structures are made using tapes. The tape is then labeled, possibly using a bar code schema, and placed on a shelf. When the backup is needed, it must be plucked from the shelf and popped into the tape device to be read sequentially. The tape is said to be "off line" during the period that it is on the shelf.

Recently, two innovations have occurred, due to the requirements to manage large amounts of data, including that stored in proliferating data warehouses. First, the tape can be kept and managed by what amounts to a library system equipped with a robot arm capable of tracking, plucking, and mounting the tape as needed. The report from the trenches—though robot arms are expensive (see above about the Rolls)—they do work. (Of course, so does a guy on a pair of roller blades, skating back and forth between the system console and the shelves holding the tape cartridges. The problem occurs only if you require a backup during his lunch or when the CFO considers the price of such hidden costs as liability insurance [or how roller blades got into the budget].) Although any moving part is subject to failure, experience shows they do not. What happens is cartridges and platters occasionally get jammed in the drives. All in all, this gives rise to the notion of enhancing "off-line" storage with "near-line" storage. It is important to note that tape is not the only form of "near-line" storage. Those organizations that manage large numbers of documents use optical platters as part of a library equipped with a robot arm. This tends to be of less relevance to data warehousing. However, as text documents become the target of data analysis and mining, the near-line archives, including optical, will start to make more sense and, in many instances, will already be available in this form.

The reader may have noted that we have now constructed a storage hierarchy. At the top of the pyramid is main memory—fastest access and most expensive. (See Figure 10.1: Storage Hierarchy.) As we move down the hierarchy, we encounter slower and generally less expensive media—direct access disk, near-line storage and off-line storage. Large volume backups are at the bottom of the hierarchy, where they belong for reasons of cost. However, as the price of storage media continues to fall, other alternatives are emerging. One of them, redundant arrays of independent (or inexpensive) disks (RAID), will receive treatment in a section of its own, below.

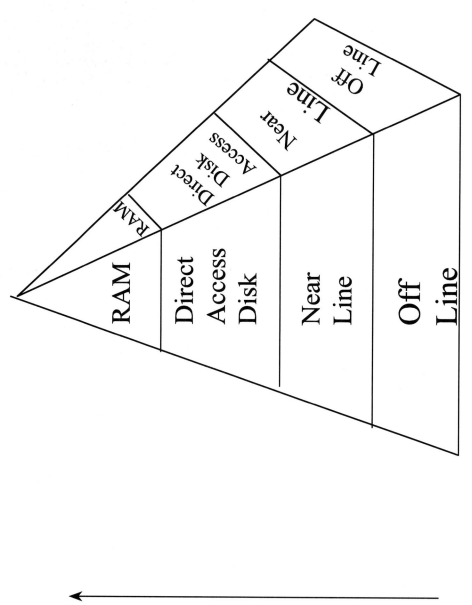

Increasing Cost & Speed of Access

**Figure 10.1:
Storage Hierarchy**

RECOVERING THE DATABASE: CRASH RECOVERY

A "crash" is the interruption of an LUW before all the changes are committed to the database. The data structure becomes inconsistent and, therefore, unusable. Crash recovery is the restoration of the data to a consistent and useable condition.[4]

As indicated above, the database log is the first line of defense against a crash. The question arises as to whether a data warehouse "read-only" database requires logging. If it is truly "read only," there is nothing to log after the initial load and backup. Periodic refresh activity, as well as incremental loading of tables or partitions, requires backup to guard against media failure. However, read-only data warehouses occur much less frequently than is generally imagined. If estimates or planned volume, usage, or sales are tracked against actuals, "read only" quickly becomes "read and write." Many kinds of "what-if" analyses result in "update scenarios." We might wish we didn't have to do the work, but as soon as any in-flight work is in process, the risk of a crash must be addressed. Even if the fact tables are read only, the dimensions (customers, products, channels, etc.) may be subject to single-point update, correction, or enhancement. Obviously, in a typical three-way join, the loss of one of the dimensions is a show stopper. Therefore, because the show must go on, provision must be made for crash recovery.

Many client-server databases support what is called *circular logging*. A fixed number of files are allocated for logging. When they are filled, including secondary allocations, they wrap around to the beginning and overwrite the logs. The space is reused. This is a kind of eternal return of the same—the same log, that is. This might seem to be a good use of disk space. It is perhaps permissible in a test environment, but it is not suitable for production. It is really a false economy. Perhaps it has its uses in getting up and running quickly in a test or prototype environment, where the penalties for failure are wasting the time of developers (as opposed to the entire firm being out of business). It may work in a pinch, but it is not industrial strength. First, you should never have an LUW larger than all the (circular) logs, right? It should not happen, but it does. Then all that work is incomplete and has to be thrown away. Next, logging has to be disabled or circumvented. The redistribution of the data has to be tried again from the beginning. Second, rolling forward to a concurrent point is not even a defined option. Finally, it creates an unprofessional atmosphere to have the DBAs truncate the log to allow processing to continue. Log truncation is exactly like burning your bridges behind you. (See above, about the value of a DBA without a backup.) In this day of best practices, it is at the top of the list of *bad* practices. In production environments, the better alternative is to define and enable the approach to archival (log retention) logging to be discussed below, which will allow archiving and recovery out of the logs themselves.

RECOVERING THE DATABASE: VERSION (POINT-IN-TIME) RECOVERY

The most common scenario from a day in the life of the DBA is performing a point-in-time recovery to fix a damaged database structure. Here, a single data structure or a small number of related structures gets "broken" and has to be restored from backup to a known point in time prior to an error. For example, overnight, a rogue application executes and damages the data in a critical order entry table, due to an application bug. How do we get the data back to a point in time—for example, 9 PM, prior to the execution of the defective process? Typically, a DBA will receive the help desk problem ticket. It may be necessary to briefly interview the end-user, application developer, or relevant managers to hone in on the problem. With any luck, a backup occurred toward the end of the day and before the application was launched. If that was not the case, see the next following section on roll-forward recovery. However, let's suppose that we are fortunate. A backup was taken immediately before the execution of the rogue application. A word of caution, in any event: The request to restore a data structure using a backup of the data from a previous point in time will apply whatever data in proper format is contained on the tape file submitted to the restore process or job. That includes data that is prior to (older than) the most recent backup. Therefore, it behooves the DBA to know what is what and to request the proper backup.

Fortunately, the relational database itself has library management resources to keep track of backup history. In any industrial-strength relational database, as backups are made, they are registered with the database catalog. The catalog is updated. The database "knows" about them. Typically, they are stored in a relational table available to the DBA (or anyone) using SQL. In addition, significant system events related to backup and recovery—such as a restore or load or quiesce (commit all work and flush buffers)—are also registered and made available in such a table. Backup performed using a copy utility supplied by the database vendor usually comes in two forms. The first is a complete backup. All of the data in the table or underlying container is taken to a sequential medium, such as tape, and that data set is registered with the database as a complete copy. For those instances where the number of changes to the table is small—for example, less than 15%—a backup of the differences between the latest backup and the current time can be obtained. This is called an *incremental backup*. This may be performed repeatedly. It takes advantage of the situation that copying 15% of the data is faster than copying 100% of it. The trade-off is that, to be used as input to a restore, the backup must be merged with other incremental copies and the last complete backup to form a complete restore. This is more complex, but it provides operational flexibility, because the merge can be done "off line," using purely sequential media, without impacting the table itself. The table may immediately be returned to service without condition or qualification. It is back in service as the target of access by users and even update activity.

What about backups not known to the database? That is, what about the execution of a copy tool or nondatabase utility that takes an image of the underlying physical media or operating system file without the database being active or aware of the operation? This can get tricky. If a record is being updated concurrently with the execution of the unauthorized backup tool, the result may be unpredictable. That is, that record may or may not be on the backup, depending on the arbitrary disposition of in-flight work in the buffer. If it is not in the backup, data integrity has just been compromised—not to mention the integrity of relations with the customer whose record was just deleted. Therefore, the relational database vendors make statements like "do not use such methods"; or, if you do, do so only after thorough testing, and make sure all activity in the database is quiesced. Such global backups of entire disk devices can be important to disaster recovery planning. Therefore, advanced database vendors have recently begun offering methods to register backups made with third-party tools. The database doesn't know about the utility as such, which it isn't authorized by the vendor, but the resulting backup gets posted to the catalog anyway. In that way, the DBA can track the knowledge of its existence and use the copy if the situation warrants it.

If the backup is performed during a period of time when no end-users are allowed to interact with the system, an off-line backup is the result. The advantage of the off-line backup is that it contains a complete image of the data structure and can be used as a complete source for restore processing. If the backup has to be executed while end-users are interacting with the system and may be issuing updates, an on-line backup must be executed. That requires application of roll-forward recovery to complete a restore from the back up. This is because the user interaction may include updates that are not captured by the backup, due to failure to be externalized—written—from the database buffer. So, when the restore occurs, the process has to be completed from the log by rolling forward through the log to the current point in time, that is, the latest commit point. It is to this roll-forward restore process that we now turn.

RECOVERING THE DATABASE:
ROLL-FORWARD RECOVERY

The essence of the roll-forward recovery scenario is applying log records to restore changes that occurred to the data after the backup was completed. This restore can occur either to a point in time or up to the very last unit of work that was committed. This differs from crash recovery, in that it cannot be done using circular logging. The log must contain the complete archival history of the database and the event activity performed against it. There is no requirement that all of those archives must have been saved—unless one wants to use them. The requirement is that all of those archives must have been created. Why is this so? Basically, it is to avoid scenarios where logs "wrap" in the middle of LUWs. It also differs from point-in-time recovery, in that it uses records from the log, not just a sequential backup (though that may be included, too) to restore the integrity of the compromised data structure.

The key to roll-forward recovery is log archiving. Just as the log provides a global backup mechanism, the log archive is a backup of the log itself. Several files are allocated to provide the on-line log. As the first of these fills up, the database automatically switches to writing change activity to the next active log in the sequence. Meanwhile, a backup, called an *archive*, of the filled log occurs. The log is written to tape or to a near-line storage pool. The archiving activity, in effect, empties that log and puts it back in rotation to receive changes. The reason for having multiple logs in sequence is to allow multiple logs to fill up, based on variability in how busy the system is. However, if, for whatever reason, the last available log fills up before the first one has completed being archived, the entire system waits for the archive to complete. Therefore, be generous in the estimation and allocation of space for logs (but not too generous). There is an advantage to capturing the change activity on a periodic basis— for example, every couple of hours or so. That way, if a physical disk device on which a log is situated fails, the amount of data at risk is not too large. The log captures changes to data in every system in the entire installation. Therefore, it is a potential point of failure with serious consequences. That is why many vendors support dual logging (Figure 10.2 shows double files as a disk icons) for each log. Naturally, each physical log file should be placed on a different physical disk device to sustain the loss of a single disk. No sense exists in dual logging if both log files are placed on the same disk and that disk fails. In addition, each physical log file should be placed behind a different control unit. (A control unit is, in effect, the "power strip" into which multiple disks are plugged or connected to the CPU.) In that way, if a control unit breaks, one of the dual logs will still be available to the database. Logs are also candidates, to which to apply fault-tolerant RAID technology, explained in detail at the end of this chapter.

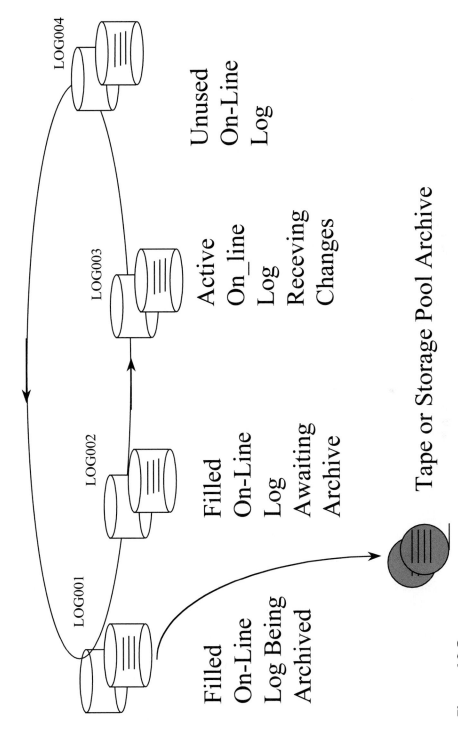

LOG004

Unused
On-Line
Log

LOG003

Active
On_line
Log
Receving
Changes

LOG002

Filled
On-Line
Log
Awaiting
Archive

LOG001

Filled
On-Line
Log Being
Archived

Tape or Storage Pool Archive

Figure 10.2
Active and Archival Logs

MANAGING LOTS OF DATA: ACRES OF DISK

Placement of data structures on disk still does make a difference. Data structures are things that have meaning in terms of business distinctions. Thus, you cannot really make a difference unless a significant understanding of the business is captured and deployed in the disk farm. For example, consider joining a sales fact table with two different customer and product dimensions. If these tables are all on the same physical disk, device contention or data collisions can occur in retrieving the data. If they are placed on separate disks, the chance of collisions is reduced.

It is a dirty little secret, commonly known among DBAs, that in your average commercial business application, processing is I/O-bound. The amount of time spent chasing data down the wire to the controller, to the I/O subsystem, and back is on the order dictated by the 80/20 rule. The greater proportion of your response time—ballpark 80% on the upper end—will be spent performing access to data on disk. This is because disk access is still orders of magnitude slower than CPU processing speed. Processors have been speeding up and disks have, indeed, been getting bigger—2, 3, 9, 18 gigabytes—but not generally faster. It still takes about 10 milliseconds—that is, 10 of 1,000 parts per second—to perform a Get Extent or Get Page off of disk. Contrast that with access to main memory, which requires 10 microseconds—10 of 1 million parts per second. That is three orders of magnitude difference.

Consider a simplified but realistic example. If a data warehouse aggregation has to be assembled out of (for example) 10,000 records, we are looking at spending human-scale time in the database—about ten seconds performing I/O alone and maybe another two seconds for all other processing. This can grow dramatically—double or triple—if both a fact and a related dimension table are placed at opposite ends of the same 9-gigabyte disk device. That amounts to a lot of bouncing back and forth movement between the fact and the dimension data. Exactly the same consideration applies in placing a fact (or dimension) table and its related index if they are placed at opposite ends of the same disk device. Whatever efficiencies might be gained through index access are lost in the clumsy file placement.

Nor is it enough simply to place indexes and their related tables on separate disks. If both of these structures are behind the same control unit, that is almost the same thing as putting them on the same disk. In Figure 10.3, the control unit is indicated by the little box off of which the cluster of disk drives is hung. (The control unit is a dedicated processor whose sole purpose is slavishly to perform execute channel program commands for the main processor.) It is the so-called I/O subsystem. In many instances, it can even be assigned its own cache memory, which presents opportunities for optimizing frequently reused records or asynchronous update activity. However, it is also a potential bottleneck. If a long-running batch process is going after data behind a controller and a business analyst requires low-level aggregations from the same data, the analyst will experience slow response time. Therefore, placement is required, not only at the disk level, but also in terms of an understanding of the layout

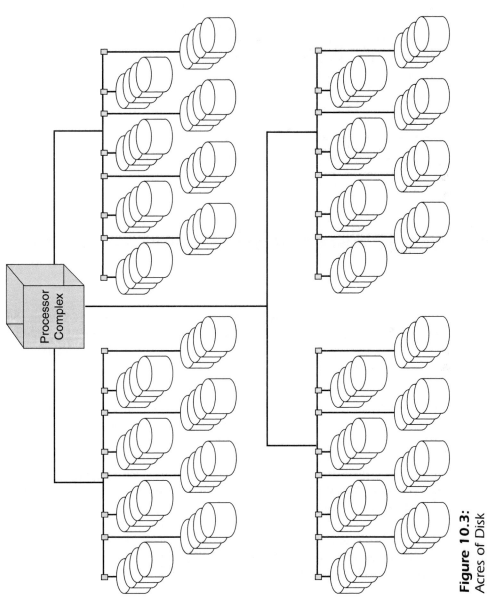

Figure 10.3:
Acres of Disk

of controllers. However, because the number of control units is necessarily less than the number of disks, one must be practical. Only those one or two of ten tables that are heavy hitters—including system logs—deserve isolation behind their own control units.

The Importance of Data Placement

DBAs are usually expected to manage data set placement onto disk, using expert judgment. The top physical data set placement rules include:

1. No fact tables on the same device as their corresponding related dimensions.
2. No indexes on the same device as their corresponding related tables.
3. No tables hit by heavy batch processing on the same device as those needed for direct on-line access.
4. Isolate very busy structures (whether tables or indexes) behind their own control unit.
5. Do not mix test and production data sets.
6. Do not mix transactional and decision support data structures on the same disk.
7. Do not mix temporary work space and sort work space used by the database with application data.
8. Keep in mind the storage hierarchy and size run-time database system buffer pools, so that selected indexes and data dimensions can be kept in the buffer pool, eliminating access to external media.

Because the profile of what is busy and what is not changes with the business and with the time of day and time of year, monitor and tune (and adjust) placement periodically, based on lessons learned, practical compromises, and feasibility.

In Figure 10.3, a central processor, consisting of less than ten CPUs, is managing 32 (8x4) control units. If each of the disk icons were a 9-gigabyte disk drive, over a terabyte of storage would be depicted. Now, make this ten-way processor a part of a ten-way complex supported by global memory or a high-speed interconnect. That yields the title of this section—acres of disk. Considerations of physical access might dictate a smaller size disk—for example, 3 gigabytes. By minimizing back-and-forth arm movement, a 3-gigabyte disk would have performance advantages in situations where random access predominates. (In random access, the access mechanism necessarily bounces around a lot.) Also, considerations of physical plant—floor space and air conditioning—require management. Not all of this hardware will fit in a broom closet. All of a sudden, it turns out that client-server operations are actually in the real estate business. The number of channel control units depicted—32—is a low to medium number of channels. Small systems have as few as eight, and larger mainframe complexes support hundreds, though practical limits of how much work the processor can support start to become more important than the sheer number of channels. Applying the above-cited eight simple rules of disk and data set placement is a reasonable thing to perform by hand for a dozen or even a hundred data sets. However, when the number of data sets exceeds a thousand, what is the DBA team to do? This can easily be the case if there are 300 tables, each of which, on average, has three indexes. Being reactive and managing by exception is good in a pinch, but a thousand "exceptions" is too many. Such an approach is likely to result in unpleasant surprises over the long run.

Wouldn't it be nice if there were a way of specifying a few simple rules and structures to the system to manage the distribution of data structures among the disk farm? This is an exciting prospect, supported by a type of software called *system-managed* or *system-controlled storage*.[5]

MANAGING LOTS OF DATA: SYSTEM-CONTROLLED STORAGE

The idea of system-controlled storage (SCS) is to specify a few basic policies and constructs and let the SCS software do most of the work. A few special situations or problems can then be managed "by hand" on an exception basis. The two key ideas are those of a storage pool and a rule or set of rules for associating and assigning paths, data sets, or the operating system files to the pool. Thus, keeping in mind the eight rules cited above, there might be separate storage pools for fact and dimension tables, separate test and production pools, and separate production index and production table pools. If one or two large and troublesome data structures exist in an installation, they might reasonably be made the subject of their own pool. The underlying paths or data structures would be assigned to their respective proper pools, based on a naming convention. For example, indexes might have "X" in them, tables might have "S" in them (for "tableSpace"). Fact table names might include an "F," dimension table names might include a "D," and so on. As long as the convention was consistently formulated and followed, that is the important thing. The SCS software is responsible for determining placement, based on rules encoded by the storage administrator into the SCS rule repository. These rules, also called *storage policies*, are referenced at the time the data structures are created, and placement occurs according to their direction.

The consequences are to free the time of legions of DBAs and storage administrators who are spending time hand coding and placing individual data structures—legions who have never been hired, resulting in the life of the rest of the one or two DBAs being like the inside of a Dilbert cartoon.

Occasionally, data center staff or even management will be stuck in a time warp. They will still be living in a time when disk was a rare and expensive item. Each production system got one disk device, and all of the test teams shared a disk. This was generous. The trade-off was that the DBAs and storage management staff spent a lot of time moving data around. Although there is no excuse for wasting any resource—surely, hardware is not free—the professionalism and responsibilities for planning and integration have grown to a point where a ruthless prioritization of values must occur. As the market value of disks have fallen, so has the business imperative to manage them, as opposed to turning over such a function to storage management software designed for that purpose. Working smarter means building a system to purge transaction data according to meaningful business criteria, rather than fretting about data bloat. Initially, when the DBA informs the CIO and CFO how much storage is required to support both the transaction and data warehouse systems, a kind of sticker shock will occur. The answer typically is, "do more with less," and that is a worthy goal. However, when the DBA informs the CIO and CFO, "If we run out of disk, we are out of business," being professionals, the CIO and CFO will properly push the job back on the DBA with, "Okay, tell me how much is needed." At this point, the DBA must have his or her spreadsheet at the ready with assumed growth rates on a quarter-by-quarter basis and clear statements of portfolio assumptions on a system-by-system and project-by-project basis (just in case the portfolio changes).

MANAGING LOTS OF DATA: AUTOMATED TAPE ROBOTS

When the time comes to execute backups of this data, the number and distribution of tape drives become a critical success factor. As an illustration, if one tape drive can back up, on average, 3 gigabytes per hour, and there are 3,000 gigabytes of data, 1,000 hours would be required. That's about 42 days, executing around the clock. Of course, that is absurd. However, notice that if there were 100 tape drives, the task is down to about 10 hours. Even though not all the data requires backup every day and not all the data requires backing up every week, the point is worth making. Provision must be made for acquiring blank tapes, using them, archiving them, and expiring them when no longer needed. It may not even be humanly possible to keep track of all these items using methods of hand labeling and shelving. If you have acres of disk, oceans of tape cartridges cannot be far behind.

Therefore, a self-contained robot tape library may be a solution. This is a hardware unit that contains blank tapes in slots, a robot pick arm, and a mechanism to track and mount on request tapes that have data stored on them. Because it is hardware, it is a depreciable capital asset. Of course, so is a pair of roller blades—but, in this instance, that would be false economy. A check list follows of questions that should be covered with the automated tape hardware vendor, in addition to the usual basics about hardware and operating system compatibility.

1. Meantime to failure absolutely and in comparison with other units on the market?
2. Kinds of problems that can occur—even if the robot arm is robust, do tapes get stuck in the drives?

3. Storage capacity of the units under various scenarios, including that not all of the tape will be filled by the backups written there, and stacking data structures on tapes may (or may not) be part of the plan?

4. How easy or hard is the management of expiring, inserting and replacing tapes, coordinating between the operating system catalog, the relational database catalog, and the tape system library?

5. Experiences of other purchasers and users of the robot solution?

6. Capacity, cost, physical robustness, and availability of the tapes themselves?

7. Maintenance schedules, scenarios, and cost of contracts (if such an option is available and relevant)?

8. Given the installation's current and anticipated growth in backup volume and the current backup and recycling schedule, will the unit's capacity be acceptable and durable?

Tape robots are *not* new technology. They have been available in the large data center operations for long enough for a body of experience to have been accumulated. Scaled-down versions are now showing up in client-server environments, as well. Like any technology, they can provide valuable support for the business when approached with an understanding of trade-offs, strengths, and weaknesses. The study and management of these issues, risks, and solutions is properly the role of a team of dedicated storage technology professionals.

RAID CONFIGURATIONS

RAID is an approach to storage technology designed to increase availability in the face of disk failure. Although significant improvements continue to be made in miniaturization and fault tolerance, including the use of solid-state technology, occasional failures have proven to be the case with storage technology. The loss of a disk can be a show stopper. The problem is not really with any single disk drive. When combining dozens of disks into disk farms, the laws of large numbers start to work against you. If each individual disk has a mean time between failures (MTFB) of about 30 years, it's easy to imagine that you are in great shape. Think again. The probability of failure as disks are linked together in series is multiplicative, not additive. By the time that 100 disks have been linked, you are looking at a failure once every four and a half months. The engineering solution was to develop a method for including redundant information in the array of disk. Because the failure could not be prevented, the goal was to make it invisible—or at least easy to overcome. The data being written to the disk was encoded and written to more than one disk. If a disk failed, the data on it could be accessed from the redundant data placed elsewhere. Therefore, RAID was invented to provide an additional tool in the battle for around-the-clock system availability.

A review of basic definitions is in order.

RAID Level 0 stripes the data sequentially across the full set of disks. No redundancy is provided here. The advantage is that the space is used up in an orderly and uniform manner. This makes for consistent response time and performance.

RAID Level 1 is disk mirroring on a one-for-one basis with a group of disks. Data is written in duplicate. That slows down the write operation. However, data can be read simultaneously from more than one spot, so a kind of hardware level parallelism occurs. This results in a read-write asymmetry. It is faster to get the data out than to put it in. This makes RAID 1 popular with data warehousing installations, because response time is affected much more visibly by read access that write duration in "read mostly" data warehouses. In the event of disk failure, the performance is comparable to that before the failure, so there are performance advantages. However, it is the most costly RAID option, because it doubles the amount of storage required. This is the kind of option one might consider for a few really critical components in a system—the database logs, the operating system software, and database engine software.

RAID Level 3 introduces the notion of parity. Parity is an encoding of the redundant information to a parallel striped array. It works by applying an exclusive-or (XOR) operation to the data being duplicated, which is reversible and allows its recreation. In the event of a disk failure, parity allows the rebuilding and regenerating of the lost or damaged disk. The parity stripes protect the remaining stripes on the corresponding disks by being written to one of the set of disks. Therefore, the parity disk becomes a bottleneck. Everyone must write to it. The disks must operate in lock step. This affects the performance in a transaction environment adversely, but decision support is, necessarily, less affected.

RAID Level 4 is similar to Level 3, except that the disks are separately accessible. It operates at the block level instead of the bit level (as does Level 3). This introduces additional calculations in rewriting the data. So, while read operations are faster than Level 3, rewrite operations are slower. However, the dedicated parity disk is still a bottleneck. This is addressed by furnishing the disk array with cache to be used in rewriting updates.

RAID Level 5 breaks the bottleneck by writing the parity data to multiple disks in the array. This provides faster write access than Level 3, but slower read access than Level 1. It is a compromise with very good price/performance characteristics. It is the most popular version of RAID in the market today, though data warehousing installations tend to be unhappy about the relatively slower read access.

RAID Level 10 is really RAID 0 plus RAID 1. In other words, it employs both striping and mirroring. No calculation of parity is involved. The redundant storage of large files is sometimes used.

In the interest of completeness, there is also a RAID Level 2. This uses an error correction and checking (ECC) technique characteristic of the management of main memory. The data is distributed at a bit level on multiple disks. If a disk fails, the redundancy scheme restores the data in real time. System operation is not interrupted. This encoding scheme is not as efficient as parity bit calculations. As a result, it is not used much in commercial applications of RAID.

In addition, an important feature, not necessarily dependent on which version of RAID is chosen, is: What happens in the event of failure? In the case of Level 1, the hiccup in performance may be hardly noticeable, due to the complete redundancy. Does a red light on the disk array go on, indicating a device failure? Is there anyone in the disk closet around to see it? Is an alert sent to the system administrator console or to an e-mail or beeper alert queued up and fired off? In the case of the other RAID Levels, although the system will continue to operate, a drop-off in performance should be noticeable. The parity calculation will be used to rebuild the data, possibly in real time as the requests for data continue to drop in. The deterioration in system performance will set off alarms in the end-users who, in turn, will cause bells of their own to start ringing. Finally, having identified the failed disk, is it "hot swappable"? That is, can it be removed and replaced without causing all users to log off the system, shut it down, and bring it back up? Even better, is a "hot standby" allowed? In the event of a failure, will the data from the failed disk be recreated onto the hot standby disk? [6]

Prior to the availability of RAID on certain platforms, the only way to protect against loss of a relational database log was dual logging. This is such an important data structure that some vendors actually mandate dual logging. The vendor does not ever, ever, ever want to hear a customer say, "I lost my log and can't get it back. Help me." (Because there is no help if the log is really gone.) These vendors make it a product specification that dual logging cannot be disabled. (Why would you want both to throw away the spare tire and to cancel the auto club membership?) In addition, selected vendors make use of asynchronous write engines within the bounds of strict data integrity to externalize the data from the log buffers at convenient times. This reduces waits to client applications, so the write level performance is surprisingly efficient. In any case, if dual logging is put on top of RAID, we have the situation like the man who wears both suspenders and a belt. As usual, the trade-offs require consideration. The dual logging makes the DBAs happy. The trade-off is between availability, which RAID promotes, and response time, which incurs a cost in RAID's asymmetric write performance. RAID satisfies the storage technology staff. As discussed above, RAID is accompanied by a performance cost when data is being written (encoded) multiple times. If dual logging is available through software, RAID is not only redundant, it is not needed. Therefore, if dual logging is available, depending on the database software and vendor, dispense with the placement of high-activity database logs on RAID devices. [7]

SUMMARY . . . .

Data integrity is the database administrator's (and data administrator's) most important product. Data integrity is a proxy for all kinds of data quality metrics and attributes. A DBA without a backup of the data is useless. The questions that have to be answered to develop a backup and restore strategy for the data warehouse are detailed. Examples of the kinds of problems that can cause an interruption in the availability of data are listed. Because the problems are multifaceted, so must the solution be. This includes the logging of transactions to enable crash recovery, version (point-in-time) recovery, and roll-forward recovery. Active and archival logs are distinguished. Naturally, data warehousing systems capture, generate, aggregate, and store lots of data. This requires acres of disk storage. It is not practical to manage such storage one file at a time. The idea of system controlled storage (SCS) is to specify a few basic policies and constructs and let the SCS software do most of the work of managing the data files. A few special situations or problems can then be managed "by hand" on an exception basis. A similar consideration applies to robot tape libraries, which are used to store the output of backup operations. Hierarchical storage management (HSM) is discussed. Meanwhile, Redundant Arrays of Independent (or Inexpensive) Disks or RAID is an approach to storage technology designed to increase availability of systems and their data in the face of disk failure. The loss of a disk can be a show stopper. When combining dozens of disks into disk farms, the laws of large numbers start to work against you. The probability of failure as disks are linked together in series is multiplicative, not additive. By the time 100 disks have been linked, you are looking at a failure once every four and a half months. The engineering solution was to develop a method for including redundant information in the array of disk. Because the failure could not be prevented, the goal was to make it invisible—or at least easy to overcome. Therefore, RAID was invented to provide an additional tool in the battle for around-the-clock system availability. The different kinds of RAID storage are discussed.

[1] *Personal communication.*

[2] At least one reader of an early version of this manuscript protested that the roles of the data administrator (DA) and DBA are being confused in the discussion and that responsibilities belonging to the DA are being attributed to the DBA. There is some truth to this complaint. Although boundaries differ from one firm to another, the DA is usually charged with logical tasks and issues, whereas the DBA has physical or implementational ones. This distinction is an oversimplification, of course, and an ideal gloss on the problem would be to designate the role of data strategist to oversee the continuity between the logical and physical aspects of the data management process. Depending on where the reader is employed, it is permissible to substitute one or the other of these where the text contains "DBA."

[3] The terms *transactional system* and *operational system* are often used as synonyms. They are contrasted with decision support systems. A slight ambiguity exists here. One of the purposes of a data warehouse system is to make decision support a part of "operations." To "operationalize" the work means to automate it, put it on a regular schedule, and apply data center utilities to its backup and maintenance. This distinction will be clear from the context.

[4] It should be noted that, originally, crash referred to the crashing of the disk head into the surface of the disk. A crash occurred if the underlying physical medium, the disk, becomes unusable. The read-write head of the disk device itself floats a microscopic distance above the surface of the electronic storage media and, if that head hits a microscopic piece of disk, it can fail catastrophically. It is said to have crashed. The disk is broken. The data structure on it becomes unreadable and, therefore, unusable. Unlike the kind of crash we are discussing here, a disk crash must be restored from a complete point-in-time copy of the data, not from the database log.

[5] Because *SMS* specifically refers to two unrelated products from IBM and Microsoft, let us employ SCS storage to refer generically to software used to manage storage and data set placement.

[6] Note that even disk mirroring does not guarantee complete fault tolerance. This is because there are so many points of failure. Are duplicate controller units available, duplicate cables, and duplicate CPUs? Even if they are, do they all plug into the same electrical socket in the wall or power grid? The case for uninterrupted power supply (UPS) is a compelling one.

[7] For example, Yazdani, Sima and Wong, Shirley S. *Data Warehousing with Oracle*, Upper Saddle River, NJ: Prentice Hall PTR, 1998, p. 138, for how this applies to one particular product: "Avoid the I/O performance hit of RAID disks on redo log groups by storing Oracle level mirroring and placing them on non-RAID disks."

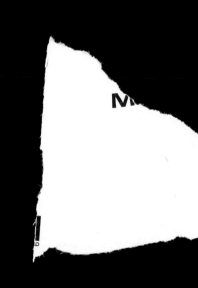

11 *Data Warehousing Performance*

In this chapter...

PERFORMANCE PARAMETERS

Three key data warehousing system performance parameters are work load, throughput, and response time. These will be examined in turn. Before doing so, however, providing a context for engaging the distinction of "good or bad" performance is required. As will be discussed in the Chapter Fourteen on aggregation, in the section entitled, "A Management Challenge," good and bad performances are relative terms—relative to a service-level agreement (SLA).[2] If the SLA specifies that interactive queries can be performed on-line in under 15 seconds when they are at or lower than the brand, district, or week levels of aggregation, an objective measure of performance expectation is laid down. A query of this description that returns a result after two minutes does not conform. Problem solving is required. If there is no SLA, then nothing as good or bad performance is possible. Common sense, corporate culture, or 20 years of on-line experience might indicate that 30 minutes is too long to wait at an interactive work station for a response. However, given inadequate, overburdened computing resources, maybe the expectation is out of line, not the response time. The point is that no suitable means is available to tell the difference without an SLA. Without an SLA, it is the squeaky wheel that gets the oil. Those end-users who are most vocal get the most attention. This is not a problem in itself—except that no way is at hand to prioritize the complaints, other than the amount of unpleasantness generated. At best, such methods line up with business priorities only by accident. At that point, management is in reaction. Therefore, to be meaningful, the following discussion of performance parameters must be understood in the context of an SLA.

Simply defined, *throughput* is the amount of work completed, divided by the amount of elapsed time. In turn, *work* is defined as the number and size of batch or interactive processes, jobs, or transactions. From a data warehouse perspective, throughput translates into how much time is available in the batch window in the evening or on the weekend in which to perform loads of large data structures, build indexes, and maintain applications accessing the data. The is supposed to be less of a problem with data warehouses than with transactional systems. The latter, like an ATM, are required to be available 24 hours a day, 7 days a week (7x24). However, this advantage is fading rapidly. With data warehouse data being made available to business decision makers in international corporations across WANs and VPNs, spanning multiple time zones and even continental date lines, this perceived convenience is in reality a vanishing factor. What time is left must be used to plan and prepare for ever-increasing data warehouse availability requirements.

In general, throughput can be optimized by grouping jobs (processes) with similar profiles together and rigorously separating and isolating jobs that hit up against the same data structures. There are scheduling tools that encode this kind of knowledge in a custom database and will allow jobs to be submitted only if the permitted circumstances occur. However, the intelligence itself must be worked out based on an understanding of the way the processes and applications actually work. Naturally, a long-running browse should not be executed while there are short, twinkling updates against one and the same structure (unless you are feeling very lucky). This is a formula for log-jammed transactions, entangled and overlapping processes, and beeper alerts. Throughput is reduced as users of system resources queue up to get access to them, further tying up resources and reducing throughput.

Throughput is a function of computing resource availability and bottlenecks. A short list of resources includes computing power proper and main memory, disk storage and the I/O subsystem (access), network bandwidth and availability, and system software, such as the operating system, database engine, transaction manager, and end-user applications. The amount of work that gets completed is a function of just how much can be pushed through these hardware and software components. Any one of these resources can become a bottleneck, reducing throughput (and occasioning other negative symptoms). The term *latency* is an idea essential to identifying and eliminating bottlenecks. *Latency* refers to the delay that occurs when resources operate at difference speeds. For example, the central processing unit (CPU) operates at speeds in billionths of a second (0.000000001). An external disk device operates at speeds measured in thousandths of a second (0.001). The difference between the two speeds is latency. Much of modern computing is designed to find something useful for the CPU to do instead of waiting and to reduce the amount of time spent waiting. Much of performance and tuning is made possible by capturing data at each of the potential bottlenecks, evaluating measures, and taking steps to eliminate or circumvent obstacles to efficient resource usage.

The second performance parameter is work load. Work load is the amount and kind of work to be performed. That forms an eight-way matrix: two-by-two-by-two: batch and on-line; predefined (static SQL) and on the fly (ad hoc) requests; inquiry and update. Although data warehouses are supposed to be "read-mostly" structures, if updates are allowed—for example, to support a forecasting function, estimating "what-if," or changing dimensions—the inquiry and update must also be distinguished. (See Figure 11.1: Work Load Matrix.)

The work load mix is of the essence. Although there is no single mix that is specifically prohibited, some combinations work better than others. The big issues are how these types of processes perform against one another—batch versus on-line, update versus inquiry, and dynamic versus static SQL. Strictly speaking, the number of end-users that a system will support is different than work load. However, in actu-

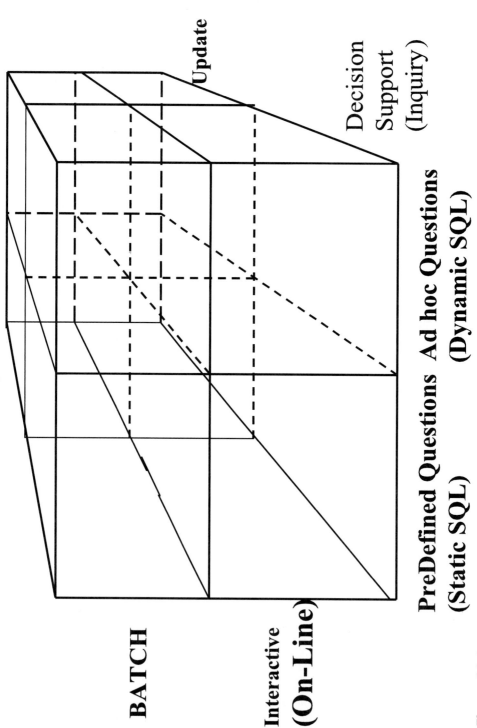

Figure 11.1:
Work Load Matrix

al practice, each end-user requires a small percentage of the available system resources to get started and remain on the system. Each end-user is submitting work constituting the work load to the system, so the number of end-users turns out to be a good proxy for making inferences about the work load. This is even more the case if one can get visibility to the kind of work they are performing, either with absolute certainty by using a system monitoring tool (which is itself a potentially heavy user of the system), or by careful interviewing of the individuals about their work profile.

By definition, a batch process will tie up a data structure or data resource for a longer period of time than a short, interactive process. Database and server vendors often promote the view that their products allow batch and on-line processes to execute simultaneously, due to dynamic resource management. Experience shows that scenarios in which resource contention occurs between batch and on-line processes are much more frequent than anyone might wish. This can be managed by requiring the batch process to issue frequent commit points, where *frequent* means every one to three records. This should be the case, even with a "read-only" process. A read-only process can lock up a data structure and lock out other critical users for the life of the process. So if a DBA needs to modify a data structure's space allocation or lock size parameter, or needs to change the buffer pool assigned to the data structure, it is in use and not available. Note, however, that a commit point cannot be issued in the middle of a piece of SQL. The SQL must be allowed to finish. A mix of batch and on-line processes becomes an impossibility if one of the processes (usually the batch process) must load the data structure, rebuild an index, or perform an application-based refresh of a large number of records. Even a single on-line inquiry can prevent an update from completing if it is against the same unit of locking (record or page or even table). Such a performance scenario results in the appearance that at least one of the processes "hangs." It is waiting on the release of the resource—in this case, the data structure— held by the other process.

The difficulty of executing updates against data structures being accessed by inquiries is a special case of the reason for the entire data warehouse initiative. One reason a data warehouse has to be built is because decision support queries are locked out by transactional updates (and vice versa). The difficulty of executing production transactional updates at the same time as significant volumes of decision support queries are processing is precisely the reason the data warehouse is designed and built as a *separate* system from an operational one. It's rather like stocking the shelves in the supermarket while shoppers are browsing for goods. Theoretically, you can do it; practically, you can do it if the store is not too busy. However, neither constituency will be well served; both will be annoyed. Understanding database locking behavior will explain why this is so.

A mixture of update and inquiry activity against the same data or index structures puts database locking in the foreground. It is on the critical path, and database locking behavior is a crucial performance factor. It is often a function of work load mix. The behavior of a "share lock" is sufficient to exclude—to lock out—an "update" action in many situations. With the introduction of an uncommitted or so-called dirty read, this problem of collisions between readers and updates is relieved. However, the cost is a slight loss of data integrity, because work in flight might be interpreted as already committed by a reader. In general, that will not be a problem when aggregating many detailed level items, but it would not be a good idea in an airline reservation or ATM cash machine type of system.

Finally, the issue of dynamic SQL versus static SQL can be a thorny one. It is sure to continue to generate discussion. *Dynamic SQL* is not predefined and is "bound" to the database on the occasion that it is first created and submitted to the system. (For a review of the action of the relational Optimizer, see above Chapter Eight, section "Twelve Principles," in particular, Principle 10.) If you are dealing with a front-end tool that generates SQL "on the fly," predefined or statically bound SQL is *not* an option. This saves developers the time of crafting, debugging, and refining the SQL statement, but it can leave people wondering what it is that is being executed. If performance is unacceptable, under any interpretation, the developer is left trying to intercept the generated SQL, make inferences about how the tool decides to do what it does, and try to "tweak" the tool to influence the outcome. Then see if the performance improves, assuming other factors can be controlled and held constant.

Because no one can anticipate all possible queries, the requirement to support ad hoc, dynamic SQL will always be with us, to one degree or another. The question is to what degree. Even if the 80/20 rule does not apply exactly, the odds are that a relatively well-defined set of SQL statements contains many of the required queries. One should be more than a little skeptical if the claim queries cannot be defined in advance. Also, if they can be captured in advance, they can be statically bound against the database or embedded in a stored procedure—that is, treated as a component of a defined, improvable business process. Many business questions—trend analysis, forecasting, and supply chain management—fall into patterns. The discipline and professionalism of mapping out these patterns and capturing them is rewarded with incrementally improving performance as a baseline execution is established, against which to iterate and on which to build enhancements.

However, what to do with those 80% of queries that are needed to answer 20% of our questions? We might get lucky—these will be short-running, returning small results sets, requiring little sorting or other system resources. But what are the chances of that? More likely, these will be the type of queries that involve low-cardinality data elements—male or female, adult or child, employed or unemployed, in stock or out of stock. These tend to set off scans of all the data stored in a given table or structure. Even when an index is available, this actually can cause more mischief, because large proportions of both the entire index and the data structures end up being scanned. Although unavoidable at times, ad hoc queries tend to degrade in the direction of scanning everything in sight. They tend to slide inexorably toward the worst-case scenario of system resource usage. Sometimes that is necessary, but generally not as frequently as it, in fact, occurs. The end result is that the end-user leaves for the weekend while the query is still cranking away hour after hour; and a DBA is left to clean up the mess at 2 AM, when a backup job or maintenance activity that requires exclusive control collides with the errant query, which just happens to be holding a share lock.

One way of managing this dilemma of ad hoc queries is to confront reality. Realize that every end-user submitting ad hoc queries has the potential, as a realistic result, to require between two and ten times more system resources to discharge work than an end-user submitting predefined queries. If the end-users have more training, are more experienced, and have better understanding of their tools, the multiplier tends to be toward the low end (two). Otherwise, the order of magnitude difference (ten) is the realistic factor. So, as an illustration, if the system can support 100 users submitting predefined queries, it can support only ten users of the former kind submitting ad hoc queries. This approach acknowledges that creating a separate system for ad hoc users separate from those performing predefined work simply may not be a realistic option. It took a while for installations to realize that performing decision support queries against operational data does not work very well. This is similar to performing ad hoc decision support against what we might call operational data warehouses. It does not work as well as expected because the work load must account for an order of magnitude more resource utilization per end-user than the average end-user profile working with predefined queries. It is as simple (and as complex) as that.

The issue of profiling kinds of work and isolating them has another aspect. Despite what is theoretically best, batch jobs sometimes must execute against on-line. For example, the amount of data being backed up simply will not fit in the batch window. Backups must execute while the data structures are being accessed by end-users or applications. The requirement is to perform backups of data warehouse data using technology able to execute against on-line queries. It is an easy thing to say while sitting on the sidelines, but if the database does not support on-line backup—backups performed while the data is available to the end-users—it might be the wrong database. On the other hand, because loading data and building indexes locks out other processing by definition, the IT function must build a team and technical environment with advanced scheduling capabilities and a high degree of professionalism to get work done during off hours and on weekends. That requires a realistic and humane flex time policy, not one that reads like it is written by certain government bureaucracies charged with collecting revenue.

The third performance parameter is response time. Response time is the performance metric most visible to the end-user. In the case of batch processing, that would be turnaround time, which is also rightly regarded as an important measure. Let's follow a query through the system, noting along the way the major system interfaces, components, and potential points at which processing performance can encounter a bottleneck. Although the following steps are indeed an oversimplification, many details are included to give the reader a sense of all the work being performed by the system in the instant between clicking and receiving a response:

1. A request to start an application is initiated at a work station as the end-user keys in identifying data and clicks or hits enter.

2. The work station operating system creates a thread or equivalent process, allocates resources, and hands off control to the application, which executes CPU cycles to perform the application logic. It makes a difference whether the application is stored at the work station disk itself or out on a network file server.

3. If the application is distributed across a WAN, network I/O must already have been completed, including time to download any "network-aware" (Java or Active-X) code. The ease of centrally maintaining an application off of a shared server includes the trade-off that additional network I/O is incurred at start of day in downloading the application. If memory (cache) is available on the work station, that penalty can be avoided upon subsequent uses of the application.

4. For the sake of discussion, let's suppose this is a "fat client," where the complied code is already stored at the work station. The request for data is then formulated by the application and sent out over the network. Communication protocols (also called *stacks,* due to the many layers that must be traversed in translating a logical command into an electronic impulse on a network medium) are invoked on both the sending client and the receiving database server. If the network is a local area network (LAN), the throughput is measured by bandwidth, such as 4, 10, or 16 megabits per second (mbps). "Heavy-duty" LANs of 100 mbps are now available, too. That is the size of the pipeline, which is a shared resource used by all the customers on the network at that time. If the network includes communication over a WAN, the bandwidth is typically measured as 1.4, 6.74, or 44 mbps (corresponding to T1, T2, T3 telecommunication lines). In such a Tx context, the number of users is larger, the cost of the resource is larger, or both. If public pathways are used, encryption of data is necessary. That will consume CPU cycles and elapsed time to scramble and descramble the data according to an encryption algorithm. Regardless of the physical distance, in the case of a WAN, the path is likely to lie through a special-purpose computer called a *router.* That is a device that supports delivering messages within the global address space defined by the networking communication protocol. It does so using software to look up addresses that are part of domains in software tables, which themselves are maintained by special-purpose databases called *domain name servers.* Such a mechanism is very flexible, adaptable, and robust—including the ability to reroute messages through alternative paths when the preferred path is unavailable for any reason.[3]

5. If the request is made from a work station to a mainframe environment, the path will lie through a "gateway." That is a server with software

responsible for translating between the data encoding used by smaller-platform computers and mainframe computers ("enterprise servers"). It entails software table lookup and translations, and can be computationally intense. All these lookups require time and take up resources. Therefore, the network is often described as the slowest part of the end-to-end path through the system.

6. Finally, we end up at the server with the SQL request. The communication protocol is translated back into a logical command from an electronic impulse off of the network.

7. Because it is a request for work to be performed by the database, a way of allocating, tracking, and managing that work is allocated. It is called a *database thread*. It is either created by the database engine from scratch (sometimes with the help of the server operating system) or allocated out of an available pool of threads that already completed work earlier and are waiting to be reused.

8. That thread represents the request for work and associated other resources needed to get the job done, which can be "hung" off of it.

9. If there is an SP named in the request, that SP will be put to work on its behalf.

10. If the request is a piece of dynamic SQL, the database engine will marshal resources to determine the access path through the database by means of the database bind and optimization process.

11. Whatever the details of the request, it will first look in the database buffers in main memory on the server to see whether the index data or detail data can be found there without incurring further work to retrieve the data from physical disk. This is a major opportunity to improve response time. Depending on the quality of processor buffer, a lookup in memory requires between billionths and millionths of a second; whereas, if the request has to go out to a physical disk device, thousandths of a second will be required. Three orders of magnitude difference in speed adds up (and shows up) rapidly.

12. In any case, the data is marked as being in use in the buffer (possibly after having been read there in the first place). SQL predicates are applied to it; it is subjected to additional address passing and manipulation by the relational database system.

13. If necessary, the data may be sorted; if there is more data than can be fit into cache memory, an external disk may have to be used. Insert the immediately preceding comment about three orders of magnitude, even if we are now dealing with disks dedicated to sorting.

14. This entire process can also be put on hold at this step if the data being requested by this thread is unavailable, for any one of a list of reasons. If

someone else is updating it and this request is asking for a high level of data integrity, the requester goes onto the chain of those awaiting service. (This is the reason why "dirty read" keeps the work flowing smoothly and is recommended if the lower level of data integrity is acceptable to the business requirements.) Such an outcome—a wait—can quickly become visible to the end-user as a "hung up" process or system.

15. Finally, once the SQL request is satisfied, the path through the network—routers, gateways, inbound and outbound communication stacks—is traversed in reverse to deliver the data to the requesting client work station.

The important thing to note is that this description is an oversimplification, though a useful one. With that in mind, we may be amazed that response time is as good as it is. Note that knowledge of system internals was necessary to even provide this high-level description. To tune such a system, one must also have instruments (software to count events and write to files) deployed at crucial points to gather data about what is hitting and happening in the system—how many users, transactions, I/O events, threads allocated or released, buffers in use or available, CPU time cycles, elapsed time duration—and to capture these numbers as applicable at the front-end work stations, at intermediate gateways and network hops, and in the database. Having adequate visibility to what is going on can be more than half the battle in arriving at a diagnosis or recommended solution. If the CPU really is 100% busy, congratulations! For a commercial, business application, you have discovered the holy grail. The most expensive computing resource, other than people, is being completely utilized—assuming that an application is *not* looping. Of course, this may imply the beginning of a hardware acquisition cycle.

The short course in performance improvement is: Identify the bottleneck and remove it. In reality, what happens is that it (the bottleneck) gets moved up- or downstream. When the performance team sees that happening, that is good news. It implies that the actions being taken actually engage the levers and mechanisms of system operation. That counts as progress, especially when, ultimately, it can be squeezed out of the system entirely. However, it is an exercise that is likely to require repetition every time a major system upgrade, new application, database, or server is installed. (It's rather like the need to recalibrate engine timing after changing spark plugs in the family car.)

Lack of Bandwidth or Lack of Imagination?

The power of action at a distance is resulting in business applications being launched out onto the WAN and, in particular, the Internet. What used to be custom-built networks, crafted with individual care and employing proprietary mission-critical protocols, such as SNA, are now outsourced to commodity providers—AT&T, IBM, MCI, Sprint—using the Internet. Firms are constructing VPNs that encrypt data, send it out over the Internet, and decrypt it upon arrival at the destination. The fiber optical backbones of the Internet ensure plenty of bandwidth on the information superhighway, but the matter of performance is more complicated than lack of bandwidth. If the lack of bandwidth were really the case, purchasing more bandwidth has to be considered a real candidate for a solution (along with reducing the outbound traffic). However, what if it is the on- and off-ramps to the information highway, the junctions, and the so-called last mile of the telecommunications loop—the boundary routers, number of hops between end points—that cause congestion and slow down response time? Naturally, the dilemma is exacerbated if the processing is data warehousing, where the amounts of data in a query are liable to be substantial. In another context, Nicholas Negroponte, founding director of MIT's multimedia lab, has said that lack of bandwidth is not the problem. It is lack of imagination. He has gone so far as to say that twisted pair is a good enough technology. Performance and tuning is one of the activities that requires imagination. We will examine solutions to this dilemma in the immediately following sections.

We have defined and examined response time, throughput, and work load. Much of this data—in particular, response time—is time-series data. The data cubes that naturally suggest themselves to the performance analyst include response time per critical transaction by time of day by number of transactions per second. Additional dimensions likely to be useful include amount of I/O per unit of work (transaction), the internal CPU time consumed (as opposed to elapsed time), and the data structures against which that work is being performed. In a batch environment, substitute process or job for transaction. The truth is that the performance and tuning team doesn't think of these metrics as data warehousing dimensions, but they are. Whether they know it or not, the truth is that many professionals in the data center are engaging in quiet data warehousing activities—especially those that are operating data centers as computing utilities. They are building their own performance cubes, aggregations, and performance data warehouses using the available tools—spreadsheets, client-server databases, SAS or SPSS or Focus programs, and flat files. Problems about granularity, additivity, and aggregations are being solved every day by performance teams without explicitly thinking about the tools that data warehousing analysis might have to offer. These teams in the data center may want to look at learning from the best practices of data warehousing, and vice versa. Data warehouse teams may want to interview the tuning and performance staff about how they work their cubes and dimensions to discover and attack performance bottlenecks, and vice versa. Because this activity has remained below the threshold of consciousness until now, both teams can benefit from cross-functional consciousness raising.

DENORMALIZATION FOR PERFORMANCE

This is the classic approach to getting more data into the application process per I/O operation. It requires design work and stands as important evidence that attaining performance is a fundamental design activity. If I am planning to perform a six-way join of customer information where different aspects of her or his behavior are presented in separate entities, these separate I/O operations have to be completed against different structures. Finding the given customer identification in each of the six separate structures and putting them all together to deliver one customer profile can generate more work than a single set of lookup against one and the same structure. There are coordination costs in a join. This is because each of the structures has an index to be traversed to find the identifying key. So, all of a sudden, we are working with twelve structures—six index and six data components. How much simpler from a processing point of view to stuff all of this information into a single structure—denormalize the data—and waste ("trade-off") storage with redundant place holders, where attributes recur or depend on partial keys. Another factor which can greatly increase resource usage in joining separate structures occurs when, for whatever reason, a good join index is simply *not* available. In that case, the database may have to perform a nested loop or merge scan join on a large number of rows. In the case of nested loop processing, the first row is selected from the first structure and compared with every row in the second structure to see whether there is a match. The second row is selected from the first structure and compared with every row in the second structure to see whether there is a match. And so on. This is computationally intense. If the data sets are large enough, the database engine may simply sort the two tables in the same order, depending on a useable sort key, and run through each of them only once. Note, however, that the cost of the sort is already substantial.

The critical performance factor in joining is not the number of tables being joined. Rather, it is really the number of rows that have to be qualified (tested) and the end size of the result set. Strictly speaking, this is more important than the number of tables being joined. So a large number of tables qualifying a few rows with indexing that tightly qualifies processing is a much more efficient process than a Cartesian product between two large structures.

Therefore, having made the case for being sensible about join processing, the number of dimensions that intersect to form a fact structure in most data warehouse processes is significant enough to denormalize the dimensional structures as such. The amount of space thus consumed is trivial in comparison with the space required by the fact structures, and performance will benefit, especially in those situations where a large proportion of the entire structure is being scanned. The trade-offs to be considered in denormalizing fact structures, were considered in Chapter Seven on data warehouse technical design to emphasize the point that the foundation for superior performance is laid in design, not after the system is in production. All of these operations speed up if the data can be cached in buffers.

Before concluding this section, it should be noted that hardware devices also make use of caching. The terminology generally distinguishes between *buffers*, which are a form of caching implemented by software, and *cache* in the narrow sense of the term, which is hardware-specific. Thus, a hardware component such as a disk controller can be furnished with cache. The actual disk speed is unchanged, but the availability of the cache enables the end-user of the data to enjoy "look-aside" hits, in the case of access, or more speedy return of control to the requesting function, in the case of write operations. A look-aside hit is precisely finding the data in the cache rather than having to seek it on external disk. The improved write performance—also sometimes called *lazy writing*—occurs because the data being put to disk is placed in the cache and marked as update pending. This frees the requesting application immediately, then the data is externalized to disk asynchronously at a convenient moment.[4]

AGGREGATION FOR PERFORMANCE

Several methods are available to provide symptom relief when the source of the bottleneck is the network.

Aggregation for performance is the first and most obvious method. Ship the aggregate through the network, rather than all the detail data. If a single row aggregate at the brand-area-quarter summarizes a hundred times a thousand times a hundred detailed rows, that aggregation has just provided seven orders of magnitude reduction in the amount of data to be transmitted through the network. Of course, if the application moved the data around the network, rather than summarizing it in a stored procedure on the database, it was perhaps badly designed to start with. Let's raise the bar and now suppose we are moving around a 10-million row, high-level aggregate. We are still "jammed," waiting for a response at our work station. What do we do?

Think outside the box. Take a step back from the model of real-time synchronous response. Here, *synchronous* means that the response to our request is synchronized (in step with) our request as part of the same LUW. For example, a phone call is synchronous when a real person answers it. E-mail or voice mail are asynchronous. Often, asynchronous is good enough—"pick up a loaf of bread on the way home." It gets the job done, relying on the principle that many important things are not urgent. Therefore, the aggregate data is distributed asynchronously across the network, using replication to local data stores, from which the warehouse queries are subsequently addressed. Or, alternatively, the requests are queued for later response using MOM (as discussed in Chapter Nine: Data Warehouse Construction Technologies: Transaction Management). The network is, in effect, taken off the critical path of performance by abandoning the illusion that immediate real-time response is required.

BUFFERING FOR PERFORMANCE

If network access I/O is the slowest path through the system, the close runner-up is disk storage I/O. The degree of latency—degree of difference in access time—can be appreciated when one compares the billionths of seconds at which CPUs operate with the thousandths of seconds at which disks access their storage. To an extent, this difference is managed by means of multiprocessing. That allows the CPU to service other work while waiting for I/O to complete for a given task. Naturally, this results in the overhead of the CPU managing multiple tasks and switching them from active to wait, based on available service. However, it is still the best approach, absent order of magnitude breakthroughs in I/O rate. Today, such multiprocessing is a standard feature in virtually all operating systems, so it is fully discounted. That is, the performance bar, the standard of perceived performance, has already been raised to account for its availability.

In short, latency has always been a fact of life in computing systems. One important technique for speeding up the effective access time of slower devices is caching data in buffers. In general, this method gains effectiveness—works—by means of data reuse. At first access, the data is fetched from the external storage disk at the usual relatively slow rate. It is then placed in a specially designated subsection of the processor's main memory. This is called a *buffer cache* or simply *buffering*. If this data is needed again by the database engine, it looks in the buffer first. If it is there, it is available much more quickly than chasing it to external disk. This is called a "look-aside" hit. Instead of going to disk, access occurs at processor speeds; we have just seen that these are orders of magnitude faster than seek times to external media. Access to the data from external disk is replaced by access to the buffer. Thus, I/O access is speeded up by being eliminated. You really can't get any faster than that.

If the database allows buffer pool sectioning, cross-referencing the assignment of different buffer pools with different work profiles makes sense. For example, one set of buffers can be assigned to handle indexes; one to the data extents of tables; one to structures involved in long-executing browses; and one to structures mostly hit by short on-line queries. In particular, separating index and data buffers is a good practice, because the index component is more self-contained than the data component and presents a better opportunity for reuse as different applications seek the same index. This groups work with similar profiles together. So a long-running browse, which is scanning through most of the data in a table, will be isolated to its own relatively less efficient universe of buffers. It will not flush out the index entries that might benefit from look-aside hits.

The Database Buffer Shuffle

The critical skill here is estimating how much main memory on the database server may be dedicated to buffering operations. To do that you must determine the total main memory available on the processor.

- Subtract how much is required to run the operating system.
- Subtract how much is required to run the database engine.
- Subtract how much is required for each SP.
- Subtract how much is required for each additional application (if any) executing on the server.
- Subtract how much is required for communication software, stacks, and protocols.
- Subtract how much is required for each additional end-user connected to the database.
- Subtract how much is required for each open file, temp work storage, and sort work heap or space.
- Subtract how much is required to account for storage fragmentation that the above do not line up.

Whatever is left over is available for unrestricted database buffer operations.

Notice that if your estimate is high and you allocate more buffers than are available in main memory, the database will still work, but you will get I/O to disk as main memory itself is "swapped out" to external media by means of dynamic address translation. This swapping to external disk is called being *paged out* or simply *paging*. It defeats the purpose of buffering, because it only substitutes one type of I/O for another. However, it still may be useful to aim high if paging on a local processor can be traded for I/O to a remote processor, because network I/O to remote disk is even less efficient than I/O to local disk.

In addition, ample database buffers are useful in enabling read-ahead fetching. Selected database engines will fetch a large number of data pages or extents at one time in an operation called *read-ahead processing* or *sequential prefetch*. Thus, instead of one data extent at a time, 16 or 32 or 64 pages will be returned to the thread evaluating the SQL simultaneously into available buffers. This can generate dramatic reductions in the elapsed time to respond to a query as processing approaches handling a thousand data extents a second. This is moving some data. Such an operation, once engaged, could easily reduce the ten seconds of I/O cited above to return 10,000 side-by-side rows in about one second. For data warehousing processes, which often fit the description of moving lots of data, this is a useful and powerful feature. Building high-level aggregates interactively is readily facilitated by capabilities like this.

PARTITIONING FOR PERFORMANCE

Partitioning, as used here can be understood in several ways.

The first is the partitioning of system functioning. The pure example of this is client-server computing. Here, work is allocated between a GUI on a client work station at the front-end; a database server at the back-end; and, at times, an application server with business logic in the middle. This is the classic partitioning of system functions—presentation, application, and database manipulation. It maps well to data warehousing functions. Of course, this also distributes computing cycles across multiple CPUs, so an area of overlap exists with the next sense of partitioning—parallel CPU processing.

Thus, the second sense of partitioning is CPU parallelism. Multiple CPUs can be connected in a variety of ways. This is considered a significant tool in dealing with the large amounts of processing that must be deployed to get answers from data warehousing systems. Further discussion of these will be deferred until subsequent sections in this chapter look at parallel processing in detail.

The third is data partitioning. To the application accessing the data, the partitioned table has a single name, so it is a single unified structure. However, it is managed as several pieces "under the covers" by the database engine and DBA. This is the most common use of the word *partitioning* in database discussions. It is a proven method for managing the large amounts of data characteristic of data warehousing.

We now consider client-server and data partitioning, in turn.

When examining data warehousing systems, client-server partitioning makes sense. It is hard to say which is the chicken and which is the egg, because both kinds of systems have been around in one form or another for a long time. This partitioning puts the "heavy lifting" of data at the back-end on the database engine, where it belongs. If business logic can be defined, isolated, and implemented on a middle layer, it can be made manageable, maintainable, and scalable. In the middle layer, connectivity services are also provided. The slicing and dicing of data is allocated to the front-end, where a variety of graphical work station controls are available to take advantage of enhanced presentation and manipulation of information by the business analyst. This allocation of resources lines up with the idea of specialization of function and enables principles of encapsulation to be applied to system development.

Understanding performance means understanding trade-offs, and client-server presents many. Indeed, because client-server computing is now mainstream, keep in mind that it is okay to knock it. That is not really the intention here, but fallout of that kind may occur.

In Chapter One in the section on architecture, we considered how the three functions of presentation, business logic, and data access could be mapped to the three kinds of hardware platforms available, work stations, midsize servers, and enterprise servers (see Figure 1.2: Client-Server Definition). We observed then how so-called three-tier logic is really a three-by-three matrix (see Figure 1.3: Alternate Client-Server Partitioning).

The performance challenge occurs when the allocation of functions is out of line with the allocation of hardware and software capabilities. For example, a standard approach to verifying the quality of data is to store validation rules in tables on the database. This is a sensible thing to do. Thus, whenever the end-user at the work station clicks on the next data field, a lookup occurs against the database. This back-and-forth message traffic is no problem on a departmental LAN in Chicago, but when the server is in Chicago and the client workstation in Madrid, the amount of message traffic puts us in the situation discussed above under network I/O in performance parameters. Even given ample nominal bandwidth, it becomes the bottleneck, due to the number of hops, because even one problem arising in traversing a distance with many points of failure is one problem too many. Throwing hardware and network resources at such a challenge is on the slope of diminishing returns. A solution such as replicating the data in Madrid is redesigning the application, not tuning or tweaking it. Still, that may be the only viable approach.

Similar considerations apply to performing aggregations in data warehousing situations. The amount of traffic generated across the network can get large. Attempting to move data to a work station to perform an aggregation function on that work station will stress resources much more than moving the function to a stored procedure or an application server, performing the work there, and shipping only the smaller results set to the work station.

Another way of describing this performance challenge is as "scalability." We would say that verifying data accuracy at the back-end "does not scale" to the level of enterprise client-server computing. Each function—database, application, desktop logic—performs well enough on its own. However, when they are connected together, the overall configuration presents problems not visible in the parts because the problem does not lie in the parts. It lies in the connections between them.

The solution is easier said than done—planning, design, scalability. In this case, planning for scalability means that the data and the functions applied to them must have locality of reference. They must be located in physical proximity. With the benefit of 20-20 hindsight, this is a bold statement of the obvious. However, if one has a successful departmental application, for example, a local data mart that requires porting to the enterprise level, be prepared to manage expectations or be prepared for trouble.

This is admittedly not an entirely satisfactory solution from a technical point of view. Nevertheless, it has the advantage of pointing out that performance is also a management challenge. Because computing resources will always be limited, the responsibility of management includes understanding the design options and tuning not only the software but the SLA to correspond to feasible and attainable expectations. (See above, Chapter Fourteen: Aggregation.)

We now turn to data partitioning for performance. This form of partitioning was born because of the mismatch between of the limited physical size of operating system files underlying database tables, relative to the amount of space required by the latter. Even without such limitations, which are now mainly of historic significance, it makes sense to "divide and conquer" large data structures by sectioning them into manageable pieces. (The reader may wish to review the basics of data partitioning as discussed in Chapter Eight: Data Warehouse Construction Technologies: SQL.)

As an illustration of partitioning for performance, by partitioning a terabyte structure (that's a trillion bytes) into, for example, 255 structures of 4 gigabytes each, several advantages are gained. First, the expectation is that the partitions will be spread across multiple disks, channels, and control units. Because as many I/O streams are available as there are disk controllers and channels, parallelism at the hardware level is available to different processes, jobs, or end-users invoking different requests against the data. This will tend to reduce response time. Second, database utilities or programs can be executed against separate partitions by processes or jobs running concurrently. This will also reduce response time. In addition, work can be scheduled in more convenient ways. Instead of attempting to back up all the day in one night—it may not even fit in the available batch window—50 pieces a night for 5 nights could be backed up. A similar consideration applies to loading such a structure. Perhaps each partition corresponds to the data for a single working month, week, or day. Such partitioning would map to a manageable schedule (whereas having the entire structure unavailable for several days to load it would *not* be manageable). In short, partitioning provides options. It provides options for scheduling, maintenance, and data center operations. This adds up to improved data availability. Data partitioning is a powerful and proven method of managing large amounts of data. (Because each vendor implements partitioning using slightly different methods, consulting product-specific documentation is necessary to get the details.)

Now, availability is not a performance metric in the narrow sense of the term, as is response time. However, it is a condition of the possibility of all such factors as throughput and work load. Therefore, it is highly relevant to performance, and anything that can be done to enhance it and its manageability will support and improve overall system performance. Finally, data partitioning is also a condition for CPU parallelism. It is part of the setup for applying a separate CPU process or task to each partition in parallel. It is to that strategy that we now turn.

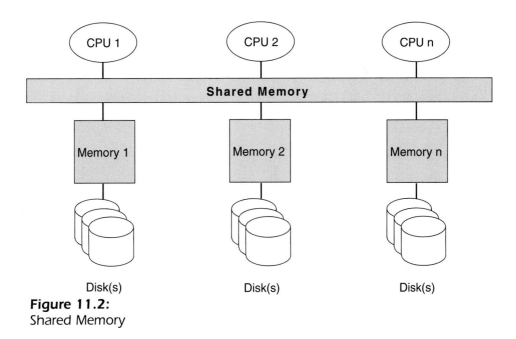

Figure 11.2:
Shared Memory

PARALLEL PROCESSING: SHARED MEMORY

Given the amount of work to be done in data warehousing processes, the strategy in improving performance here and in the following sections is to apply more workers. In this case, the workers are CPUs.

The issue is how best to coordinate the activities of the workers. Each CPU has an operating system whose activities must be closely interrelated with those of the other CPUs in the four-, eight-, or ten-CPU configuration. The operating systems all have access to the same shared memory and, in turn, through memory to the same shared external disk storage. Each image of the operating system can address the memory of all the others. Each image of the operating system has visibility to all the disk devices. The coupling is many-to-many. This is the model that is employed by mainframe computers. Because of the symmetrical access to one another's memories, this approach is called *symmetric multiprocessing* (SMP) (see Figure 11.2: Shared Memory). To the application or end-user, the appearance is only a single image of the operating system that is in control and calling the shots. However, the cost of coordinating access to shared memory escalates more than proportionately to the number of processors. Performance improvement does not keep pace with the number of processors. Doubling the number of processors, for example, from four to eight, does not double the number of coordination interfaces—it increases the number of interfaces exponentially—not the difference between 16 and 32, but the difference between 16 and 256. The point of diminishing returns of SMP is at about ten processors. At that

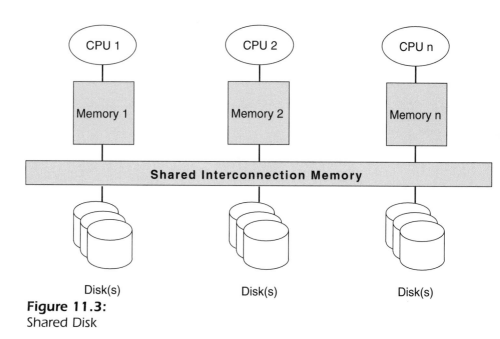

Figure 11.3:
Shared Disk

point, the cost of managing the interfaces uses up the performance benefit of supplying the additional machine cycles.

The tight coupling of processors through shared memory requires special-purpose software and hardware. Even then, given processing power available in early 1999, SMP hits a maximum at about 500 million instructions per second (MIPS). Many useful and important data warehousing systems can be built on that measure of CPU capacity. However, as of this writing in early 1999, the really large ones that get mind share and the buzz in the trade press require 10–20 times that quantity of MIPS. Therefore, the search continues for a technology that will avoid the performance bottleneck of global, shared memory. Instead of special-purpose hardware and software, an ideal solution would be to find a method of combining what are essentially commodity processors with off-the-shelf operating and database software.

PARALLEL PROCESSING: SHARED DISK

A first attempt in doing just that consists of connecting separate CPUs, each of which contains its own nonshared memory. What is shared from all the separate processors is visibility to the same disk array (see Figure 11.3: Shared Disk).

The central memory bottleneck is indeed eliminated by this architecture, but a problem that is just as knotty is introduced, namely, how to connect all processors to all disks in a many-to-many interconnection. What is even worse, the problem surfaces of how to synchronize updates and logs without the use of shared memory. The truth is that this really can't be done without shared memory, and that is what is provided in the solution. A layer of global shared memory is built on top of the interconnect that makes the disk array visible and available. A transaction management challenge similar to that in SMP remains. Global locking activities and log synchronization limit the scalability of performance improvements as CPUs and disks are added.

PARALLEL PROCESSING: SHARED NOTHING

The idea of assembling a powerful computer out of what are lightweight, commodity processors is an approach that has attracted technology enthusiasts for years. As indicated, the computing architecture represented by large mainframe systems starts to incur debilitating coordination costs at about ten tightly coupled processors. It is these costs of synchronizing updates in global memory, shared logging, and cache management through a single image of the operating system that represents the point of diminishing returns. As we have just seen, solutions that allow multiple independent, loosely connected processors to share a disk farm also hit the wall as soon as any kind of global cache or memory gets introduced. The next alternative—usually called a *shared nothing* architecture—gets its name from there being no shared cache or memory, no shared operating system image, and no shared disk. Disks are, in effect, hidden "behind" each processor that controls access. Each separate processor has its own single operating system, its own memory, and its own disk. Processors are distributed across what is best described as a network, each processor occupying a node. If a processor at node C wants data from processors at nodes A, B, D, or Z, it must send a message to them across what amounts to a high-speed interconnect, a network interface. In effect, a network is required and created to support the interconnection framework. What is not a commodity is the high-speed interconnect—the switch—used to connect all those processors. The network may use TCP/IP with an Ethernet protocol, asynchronous transfer mode, or other high-speed proprietary communication protocol to manage the back-and-forth interplay of messages between nodes. Data and computing processors are distributed across a network. This distribution causes an interesting situation. (See Figure 11.4: Shared Nothing.)

A processor can access only data on its set of disks. In effect, the processor has ownership of a partition of data. Each processor has visibility to and is responsible for accessing the data partition assigned to it by the partitioning index. Thus, it does not require a shared or global lock manager. Benefits are available within an overall approach that attempts to minimize communications between processors, because CPUs map to nodes in a network. As indicated, if processor A over here wants data belonging to processor B over there, two choices are available. Either B can send the data to A, or A can send the piece of SQL to B with the request to apply it to B's data and ship back

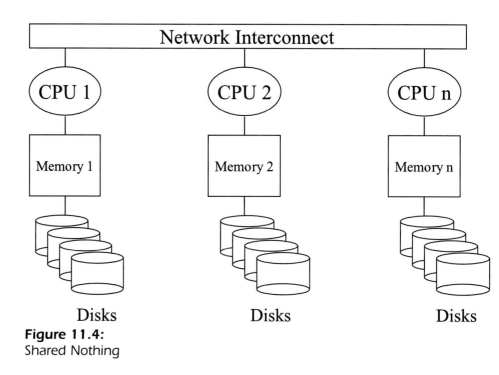

Figure 11.4:
Shared Nothing

the results set. The latter is, therefore, called *function shipping*. It moves significantly less data through the network. It is the method of choice for resolving queries.

If you are an end-user sitting at one of the nodes, entering a piece of SQL, there is nothing inherently parallel about that. If you are executing on a node that contains all of the data you require, execution is on only that node. There is nothing parallel about that, either. If you are executing on a node that contains none of the data required, and the data is on that node over there, the request is shipped over there. Here, too, it (the request) is distributed but not necessarily parallel. If the data is on multiple nodes, it is distributed *and* parallel. This is because multiple CPUs can now participate in the execution of the piece of SQL, which is otherwise no different in appearance or syntax than standard, vanilla SQL.

Such a configuration has been shown to scale almost linearly. It is available in the range of several hundred commodity processors. As an illustration, if a 10 million-row structure required 32 minutes to be scanned by a single processor, and if it were partitioned uniformly across a 32-node processor, it could be scanned in about a minute. The coordinating node sends the piece of SQL to each node. Each processor scans its portion of the data and returns a small results set to the coordinating node. The point here is that, even with a high-speed switch, the path through the network is still the critical one. Therefore, significant performance benefits are available in using function shipping rather than moving data to accommodate requests. Thus, if the data to satisfy a request can be identified as mapping to the data partition corresponding to a par-

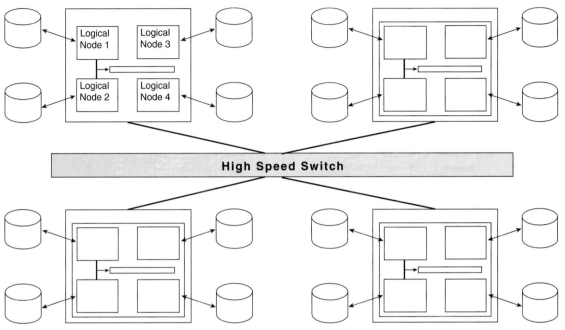

Figure 11.5:
Nonuniform Memory

ticular node, function shipping can be used. Naturally, the database catalog knows what partition and range of partitioning keys corresponds to what node. This information has to be determined and stored on the coordinating node—the point from which the requests are submitted—when the data is loaded or redistributed. Statistics must be gathered from all of the nodes to determine what is located where. Thus, database operations are performed on the nodes where the data is stored. Indeed, the function shipping approach is thus described as synonymous with the shared nothing environment. As indicated, function shipping minimizes network traffic. Once the node level result set is identified—that is to say, the SQL is applied to the data at each applicable node—the data is passed back to the coordinator node for final processing. The last step of sorting activity is performed by the coordinator node, because it is not an operation that can be performed in parallel. The entire process works like the remote procedure call (RPC) approach to distributed processing. The SQL is the standard, uniform interface; and the messy details of inbound and outbound network stacks are handled under the covers. Further details on how this works will be examined in the next section on data placement.[5]

Finally, an interesting combination of SMP with shared nothing has been developed as nonuniform memory architecture (or NUMA). Basically, the innovation is to take SMP processors and further configure them into a shared-nothing form, connecting them by the high-speed switch. (See Figure 11.5: Nonuniform Memory.) Each node is a powerful multiprocessor in itself. Within the shared-nothing configuration, each processor appears to have its own local memory, invisible to the other processors, which communicate by passing messages and function shipping requests. Within the SMP configuration, each processor has global memory, visible to the other processors within that SMP unit. This global memory, however, is relative to the local SMP node and not visible to other nodes. So it is a kind of "pushed-down" global memory with the local node. The memory is thus described as nonuniform because these two levels of memory processing are available.

DATA PLACEMENT: COLOCATED JOIN

Once the data and the computing functions are distributed, one of them has got to move to overcome the separation and complete processing. As we indicated, this can be done in basically two ways—move the data or move the computing function. In fact, a third option combines the two and does some of each, but this is a hybrid, not really a separate option.

In a parallel environment, there is no difference in the way that SQL DML appears in an application or front-end tool than in other SQL contexts on other platforms. The underlying processes are made parallel ("parallelized") by the database engine at the direction of the Optimizer. The developer gets extra command and control statements and syntax to support aspects of the parallel environment that are unique to the parallel environment (and which make no sense in an SMP context). For example, a special register is available that specifies what is the CURRENT NODE when an application is connected to a particular coordinating node of the parallel processing database. This is particular to the parallel environment.

A significant difference can show up in the SQL DDL. Syntax and a command are required to associate what amount to storage groups with the underlying hardware nodes. In turn, the actual disk is "behind" the hardware nodes. The number of physical nodes in the symbolic node group will determine the number of partitions to which a table is "hashed," based on the partitioning key supplied with the Create Table statement. Because two technologies—data partitioning and parallel processing—are converging here, thanks to "hashing" data to processing nodes, the reader may find it useful at this point to review "hashing index" by inspecting Figure 8.6: Hashing Index, before proceeding.

The simplicity of these statements belie their importance. In general, the physical implementation should not be visible in the application, which rides on top of the hardware. Nor is that the case here. However, it bears emphasis, because the partitioning is grounded in separate physical structures and it sets up—makes possible—new kinds of join operations.

SQL differs from procedural languages in performing "set-level" processing. So, too, does the parallel processing of SQL contribute (add) an additional level of abstraction. This can be described as the "parallelization"—the making parallel—of determining results sets. Consider: SQL already employs set-level processing. A Select or Update statement is "declarative," not "procedural," in that it applies a predicate in a Where clause to all the entries in a table—one might say, members in a set—that satisfy the condition. As SQL, it does this all at once in a single statement, unlike procedural code, where a looping condition has to occur in which a record at a time is returned to the application. Even when SQL is embedded in a C or COBOL procedural program, the SQL statement is declared, executed in total, and a record at a time is fetched into the program. This is entirely due to the limitations of procedural code, not due to any limitation of SQL. With a parallel database, the structures and predicates are examined to see if they can be processed in parallel—parallelized—with any chance of gaining an advantage over serial processing. Naturally, this is likely to be the case when a large percentage of a structure has to be scanned or a join of elements of tables requires large amounts of processing. Not all pieces of SQL will use the enormous capabilities of a parallel processor to their advantage, though they will work just fine in any case. The parallelization of the process is another level of abstraction, the appreciation of which can be advantageous.

In standard SQL processing, the developer is not supposed to try to trick, outwit, or improve on the Optimizer. Generally, you are fooling only yourself if you try to do so—yet everyone knows and acknowledges that it is occasionally useful or even essential to tweak the SQL to perform better in context. No matter how smart the Optimizer—and it is getting very smart indeed—it is always hard to know the details of the environment and context as well as a true domain expert with her or his sleeves rolled up. Likewise, in the case of parallel processing, one or two insights are essential to getting SQL on your side. Basically, these insights correspond to what is required for three new kinds of join operations particular to the parallel edition environment.

Recall the insight with which this section opened—in a distributed computing environment, when data and computing function are separated, one or the other has to move. Now, the shared-nothing architecture of parallel processing creates, in effect, a high-speed network, where processors share no global memory and are interconnected by a high-speed switch. So if processor C, the coordinating node, requires data from behind processors A, B, and D, either the data or the computing function has got to move. Which do you think has less overhead? Naturally, it would be ideal if all that had to happen was for processor C to send a message containing the piece of SQL or relevant partition thereof to the other three processors, rather than have them move all that data around. A high-speed network is, after all, still a network, and bandwidth should not be allowed to become a constraint. In the case of a parallel database, this solution—moving the computing function—has a name. It is called *function shipping*.

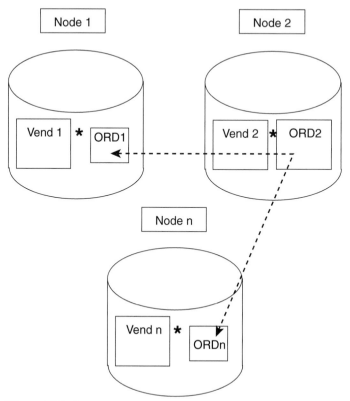

Figure 11.6:
Colocated Join: Function Ship SQL, assemble results set at coordinating node

This leads to the best-case scenario. All that has to happen is that a piece of SQL is sent across the network. Each processor at each respective node applies the predicates to the data at the node in question. The result set is determined; it alone is moved across the high-speed interconnect to the coordinating node. The latter assembles the completed results set and reports back to the application with the answer to the query. This is called a *colocated join,* and it is ideally represented by the example in Figure 11.6: Colocated Join. The vendor table is partitioned across nodes (called a *node group*) corresponding to all of the nodes in the parallel hardware configuration (with the exception, say, of node one, which contains the relational catalog and is usefully isolated). The purchase orders for each vendor likewise are stored on the same node as the vendors to which they apply. This is guaranteed by indexing the vendor table on vendor_id and the purchase order table on vendor_id, po_id. That will cause the hashing function to "colocate" the entries on the same node, which, in turn, contains the range of values on the vendor and purchase order tables. So when the piece of SQL arrives (SELECT . . . FROM VENDOR_TAB, PO_TAB WHERE DATE BETWEEN A AND Z), each processor is able to perform its own data access in parallel and in iso-

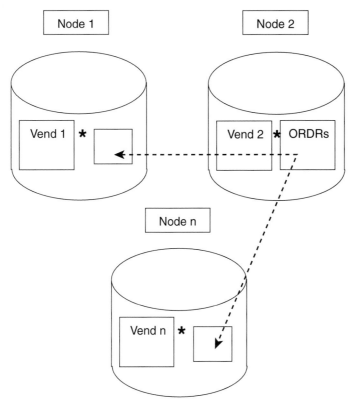

Figure 11.7:
Broadcast Join: Table at Node 2, broadcast to all other nodes

lation from the other processor(s). With the exception of assembling the results set at the coordinating node, this provides a nearly linear scalability. (Note also that because dates are usually returned in sequence, the sequential part of the sort would still have to be performed at the coordinating node. However, it would be at only the results set, not the complete tables, and that is less data than prior to qualification by the predicates.) Although rarely possible in all cases, the goal is place on each node the relevant range of values of a significant data cube—for example, vendor by order by date or other relevant dimensions—so that a colocated join is possible.

However, what if the vendors are on one node and the related purchase orders are spread across all of the other nodes? Then something has to give. In this case, data has to move and do so prior to the application of the SQL. This is called a *broadcast join*, and that is exactly what it is. The entries in one node are, in effect, broadcasted to all of the other nodes. In the case of a join between a large and a small table, you would want the broadcast table to be the small one (see Figure 11.7: Broadcast Join). Naturally, the Optimizer will try to produce that result, based on the how the row counts in the catalog line up. However, if both tables are of the same size, and that size

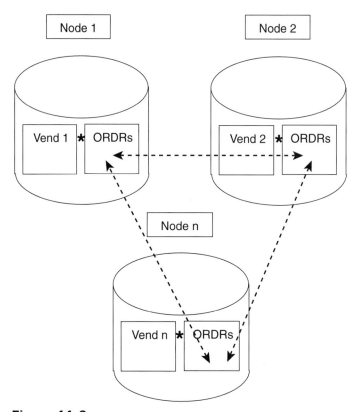

Figure 11.8:
Directed Join: Many-to-many data transfer, repartition "on the fly," and
assemble results set at coordinating node

is large, relative inefficiencies are inevitable. Such a situation can result if a table
grows unexpectedly, behaves in a way that is contrary to plan, or if there was inadequate planning. In this case, planning means providing for placement of the data in a
physical configuration corresponding to nodes that anticipates, in at least some cases,
the kinds of queries that are to be satisfied.

Next, consider the case where the vendor table is partitioned across all of the nodes
on vendor_id and the purchase order tables are partitioned across all of the nodes on
po_id. A colocated join cannot be performed because purchase orders for a particular
vendor_id could be located on any and all nodes. Data has got to move from one node
to another to satisfy the query. The Optimizer recognizes this from the partitioning information in the catalog and is likely to implement a strategy called the *directed join*.

In this case, selected purchase orders are hashed to the appropriate rows using
the vendor_id key attribute. These rows are then *directed* to the proper vendor nodes.
Data transfer is indeed necessary and may be on a many-to-many basis (see Figure

11.8: Directed Join). However, the cost of the join is limited to partitions at each node. Finally, a variation of the directed join occurs when both tables are, in effect, repartitioned and rows from each table are moved. This is followed by what is, in effect, a colocated join. To an extent, this most efficient of access methods makes up for all of the extra work that had to occur in performing an "on-the-fly" repartitioning.

The lesson here is that attention to the physical placement of data remains as important as ever. Just as in a high-performance operational environment, you would not place an index and the corresponding table on the same disk device. Likewise, setting up a highly efficient colocated join in a parallel decision support environment requires forethought and planning.[6]

Lessons In Performance

The following check list of ideas and approaches to performance will serve as an overview of lessons in performance:

1. System performance takes on meaning—is good or bad—relative to an SLA between managers of business units and those supplying them with comput-ing resources. The crafting, definition, and implementation of an SLA is almost as important as building the data warehousing system itself. (Many managers will attest that it requires almost as much work.) Management con-tributes to, gains visibility to, and influences system performance direct-ly and unavoidably through the SLA. At the same time, the SLA is a framework for understanding, communicat-ing about, delivering, and trouble-shooting per-formance. Like any useful business contract, it is the "meeting of the minds," the understanding, that counts, not the piece of paper. Therefore...see (2) through (12).

2. Systems require instrumentation to gather performance data. Many tools are available for mainframe systems. This is also true to a lesser extent for enterprise server databases. Tools are also available for enterprise networks, but they tend to be expensive to acquire and complex to operate. Therefore, application code may need to be developed to diagnose problems in work stations, gateways, and application servers. Such instrumentation is *not* gold plating and will reward the investment.

3. Measuring the performance of a system increases the work load of the system. Therefore, turning on a detailed-level database trace in the middle of a performance crisis may not have the intended result. Rather, regular sam-pling, trend analysis, and "hot-spot" analysis is likely to be more rewarding in terms of establishing a benchmark against which to diagnose exceptions and crises.

4. Gathering metrics on response time, work load, and throughput into data cubes and aggregations for trend anal-ysis, identification of hot spots, work load balancing, and understanding trade-offs is a powerful and useful method of apply-ing data warehousing expertise to performance itself.

5. Consider doing the same—building data cubes—for other performance dimensions, such as activity against disk devices; segregate (isolate) those structures (indexes or data, facts or dimensions) that are causing contention or collisions.

6. Manage the tuning of response time, work load, and throughput together. Response time can be improved by reducing ("stopping down") throughput or work load—but is that what is desired?

7. As a general rule, each ad hoc end-user submitting ad hoc SQL queries will require between two and ten times the resources required by someone using predefined, tuned SQL queries.

8. Just as you would not try to execute data warehouse work against the same transactional production data struc-tures, do not (in general) execute batch data warehouse work against the same data structures concurrently serv-ing on-line or ad hoc against predefined work.

9. Attack communication network bottlenecks by reducing the number of messages sent; if that is not feasible, consider design-signing the application to allow for replication of the data to the proximate physical locality where it is needed and referenced.

10. Attack disk bottlenecks by providing additional buffers, making judicious use of the 80/20 rule to isolate and cache that 20% of indexes most likely to be reused (accessed again and again) 80% of the time.

11. Reduce both communication network traffic and disk I/O by building aggregates using data warehousing dimensions in which end-users are most interested.

12. Use data partitioning to increase data availability to reduce response time by partitioning across different disk control units (to enable hardware parallelism), and to set up CPU parallelism.

13. Consider special hardware and database architectures—shared nothing—as dedicated platforms enabling par-allel processing and new kinds of join processing for data warehousing decision support systems.

SUMMARY . . . .

Three key data warehousing system performance parameters are work load, throughput, and response time. The particulars of these parameters are examined in turn. A Service Level Agreement (SLA) is required to define good or bad performance, and the discussion of performance parameters in this chapter must be understood in the context of an SLA. The short course in performance improvement is: Identify the bottleneck and remove it. What happens is that the bottleneck gets moved up- or downstream in the system. When the performance team sees this happening, that is good news. It implies that the actions being taken to attempt to tune the system actually engage the levers and mechanisms of system operation. That counts as progress, especially when ultimately bottlenecks can be squeezed out of the system entirely. Several strategies and tactics can be employed to influence and enhance data warehousing performance. These are reviewed in turn. Denormalization of data for performance is the classic approach for getting more data into the application per I/O, and it is a strategy that requires design work. The key here is that the number of rows to be qualified and returned by the database engine is more important than the number of tables being joined. Aggregation of detailed transactions into summary structures is a defined method for improving performance, especially where network bandwidth represents a constraining factor. Buffering for performance eliminates one of the slowest activities in the computing system, accessing external disk, by placing data in specially designated sections of the processor's main memory, buffers, entirely eliminating subsequent I/O against that data as long as it remains cached there. Next, the many meanings and uses of partitioning are engaged. These include partitioning of system functioning, CPU partitioning (parallelism), and data partitioning. Data partitioning presents I/O and operational advantages. CPU parallelism, which implies a form of partitioning, includes shared-memory, shared-disk, and shared-nothing system architectures. A sustained drill down on shared-nothing systems provides examples of parallel relational database technology. This provides new kinds of join processing including, colocated, directed, and broadcast joins. Lessons in performance are summarized as essential guidelines to take away from the discussion.

[1] See Loosley, Chris and Douglas, Frank, *High Performance Client/Server: A Guide to Building and Managing Robust Distributed Systems*, New York: John Wiley, 1998, p. 65.

[2] The performance parameters discussed here are elements of such an agreement. They require examination and understanding between the parties to the agreement. Further reading and particulars are to be found in Loosley and Douglas (1998) and Inmon, Rudin, Buss, and Sousa (1999).

[3] The Internet-based technologies implied here will be discussed in more detail in the chapter on the warehouse and the Web.

[4] Such disks with cache are often furnished with their own self-contained power supplies to allow pending updates to be externalized to disk if the electric power grid should fail.

[5] Special thanks to my colleague, Dan Hancock, for sharing many experiences relating to parallel database processing while we both worked for the same client. For further reading about shared-nothing hardware and database architecture, see the entire edition of the *IBM System Journal* devoted to the topic. In particular, T. Agerwala, et al. "SP2 System Architecture," in *IBM Systems Journal*, pp. 152ff, Vol. 34, No. 2, 1995 and C.K. Baru, et al. "DB2 Parallel Edition," in *IBM Systems Journal*, pp. 292ff, Vol. 34, No. 2, 1995. The operational reality of the "shared-nothing" approach is also exemplified by NCR's Teradata system, the earliest versions of which used the Intel 8086 processor.

[6] An earlier version of some of the material in this section was published in the *IDUG Solutions Journal*, March 1999, as "DB2 Parallel Edition Join Strategies," copyright Alleingang, Inc., Lou Agosta. My thanks goes to Sheryl Larsen, executive editor, and Linda Pearlstein, managing editor, at the *Solutions Journal* and the tremendous professionals at IDUG for the years-long interest in and encouragement of this work. The spelling of "colocation" has proven to be a point of controversy. It is spelled with two Ls in the above-cited *IBM Systems Journal,* "collocation". However, since 1995 the convention has changed, and it is now spelled most places, including this chapter, with one.

12 Data Warehousing Operations: The Information Supply Chain

In this chapter…

"Production is stranger than fiction."
Venkat Reddy[1]

A PROCESS, NOT AN APPLICATION

Data warehousing contains many applications. It contains desktop applications, which slice and dice data for the end-user's analytic inquiries. It contains database applications, which extract, scrub, aggregate, load and back up data. It contains middleware applications, which provide gateway services, communication protocols, and aggregate navigation. However, data warehousing is not reducible to its applications. It is a process. This process is synonymous with the information supply chain. From a distance, the information supply chain may seem like a miracle. You just clean up the dirty transactional data—extract, scrub, transform, and load—and all of a sudden it becomes knowledge. The secret to this miracle—and why it is not really a miracle but just good business system design—is the alignment of the information supply chain with the fundamental business imperatives directing customer and product development.

The data warehousing information supply chain is the description of this process. It is a description of how elementary operational events—dollar sales, unit item quantity sold, inventory on hand—get molded into business events and how these business events, in turn, get formed into knowledge that literally informs—gives inner form to—relationships with customers, brands, and even competitors. The information supply chain transforms elementary transactions into knowledge, addressing the decisions required by business imperatives—increased market share, reduced inventory, improved coordination of product handoffs. These are employed, in turn, to build customer relations, develop a brand, and drive the enterprise forward in time. Data capture, validation, aggregation, transformation, structuring, delivery, and presentation are the technical methods on the critical path of the information supply chain—summarized at a high level in Figure 12.1. This chapter will review each of these steps at a high level. Some oversimplification is employed with the purpose of covering the essentials before drilling down into further detail. For example, getting the information supply chain to function smoothly implies coordinating handoffs that have been designed for performance. At least brief reference to and discussion of some of these performance mechanisms is unavoidable. Because the information supply chain, among other things, is necessarily a process in time, transformations of data in the temporal dimension will be on the critical path. Those topics deserving further attention will be the subject of the following chapters in their own right. (In particular, chapters on aggregation, metadata, and OLAP will delve into details.)

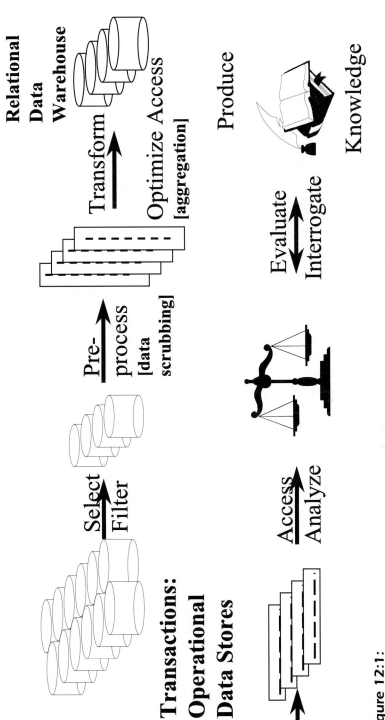

Figure 12:1:
Data Warehouse Information Supply Chain

THE GREAT CHAIN OF DATA

The end of one chain is the beginning of another. In many ways, the start of the data warehouse information supply chain is to be found in the data stores—the files, tapes, and storage dumps—that make up the back-end of the day-to-day transactional systems. Often, these are legacy, ERP, or even EC systems that make up the lifeline sustaining the business as an ongoing concern. However, this is where all the clichés about "drowning in data" occur. How do we know where to start in determining what data to extract and warehouse for decision support purposes?

The answer is remarkably easy and straightforward. The one fundamental question that the data warehouse enables us to answer is, Who is buying what, and when and where are they doing so? Therefore, the extraction operation is determined by the customer and product dimensions.

The determination of these key data dimensions is itself the back-end of a boot-strap operation, in which these essential minimal features of the business are captured in the unified and stable representations of the customer and product. If this sounds circular, well, it is, but not in a vicious sense. The entry point into the circle is the identification, definition, and populating of the dimensions. Because it is the dimensions that give meaning and furnish uniqueness to the fact structures, they (the dimensions) are on the "critical path" to the extraction of the data that populates the latter. The circle occurs because, in a sense, the data dimensions are themselves an extract from the transactional system(s); ultimately, all data originates in the line-of-business operational systems. However, the extract in question is more like a one-time or periodic (quarterly) refresh, rather than a recurring daily or weekly "pull" of transactional data. Therefore, the circle is like a boot-strap operation or even a spiral returning to the same coordinate but at a different level.

This also implies that the process entailed in the information supply chain is *not* a sequential assembly line. The language of "work flow" still makes sense here, but it is work flow as a process of coordination. Here, "coordination" has at least three aspects. First, at the technical level, coordination implies system interoperability. The transaction and the decision support system interoperate, work together, because relations between the two systems have been mapped and constrained in terms of one another. Second, at the representational level, coordination is organizing details of transactions according to a framework constituting knowledge, including such parameters as data quality, scrubbing, and aggregation. Finally, at the business level, the coordination is of commitments to satisfy the basic business imperatives at stake in instrumenting the business by means of a data warehouse—to know the customer, build the brand, and gain visibility to market dynamics.

Thus, the selection criteria and filtering rules for determining what data gets forwarded—extracted and, if necessary, scrubbed—to the warehouse are definable, first of all, in terms of applicable subsets of the relevant customer and product dimensions.

Of course, this is an oversimplification, because other dimensions are required, too. However, it has a purpose. The purpose is to demonstrate a method for defining and measuring incremental progress in the populating and maintaining of the data warehouse. Many other dimensions may be relevant or have a higher priority, in which case, the reader may substitute her or his "dimensions of choice" for the ones cited here.

PARTITIONING: DIVIDE AND CONQUER

Here, the term *partitioning* is used as an implementation strategy.[2] In this scenario, the customer dimension becomes a mechanism for a step-by-step implementation of the data warehouse. A path of incremental progress and growth is definable—provided that one has done the necessary homework to obtain a unified representation of the customer from an enterprise perspective and populated it to completion. For example, depending on the industry, the customer dimension may be grouped by geographic location, zip code, or other category. It may be grouped by telephone area code. It may be grouped by employee group, as in group insurance. It may be grouped by an arbitrarily invented key, which, nevertheless, has a random distribution of customers between the arbitrary sequences. Which grouping contains a manageable amount of the business? Is there a region with 20% of the customers that accounts for 80% of the business? Let's say that a first implementation includes only facts about those customers in the Northeast region. The subsequent phases of the rollout can be managed and implemented in the same way, extending step-by-step to facts about the Northwest, Southeast, and Midwest in each succeeding quarter. Thus, the availability of a unified representation of the customer has important implications for the scalability and rollout of the warehouse. No "big bang"—the Achilles heel of any large technology project—is required.

Alternatively, the availability of a unified perspective of the product enables a similar partitioning of the data, a stepwise rollout, and scalability of a phased implementation. For example, the first implementation might be of facts about snacks, an entire food category, to be followed by diary products, beverages, and, finally, food delivery or catering services.

As indicated above, this is one place to confront the data quality issue. Is the operational data in need of scrubbing? Is it "dirty" data? How does one know when multiple accounts correspond to the same customer—notoriously difficult in the finance, insurance, and banking business? Is "Dr. Werner von Braun" the same individual as "Werhner von Braun"? Ditto for addresses and related demographic attributes. Data scrubbing is different than building a data warehouse, but dirty data produces inaccurate results. So, depending on the accuracy of data, scrubbing may be required. Once gain, this is a separately partitionable subproject.

After taking a hard line in this regard, it is still worth acknowledging that additional editing, validation, error reporting and feedback is a proper and useful preprocess step in the warehouse information supply chain as the data is extracted from the transactional environment and pulled into the data warehouse.

In addition to validation against clean, accurate, and up-to-date versions of customer, product, vendor, store, promotion, and time dimensions, a further major preprocess step is needed. That step is aggregation.

Detailed transactional data is available in the operational environment for much less time and a shorter duration than data warehouse data. After a quarter or, at most, a year, much transactional data rolls out of the operational environment to archive or off-line storage, whereas warehouse data is just becoming useful for comparison across a three- to five-year horizon. By "detailed data," what is meant is data down to line items on an invoice or order and the granularity of such transactions.

The Weakest Link in the Chain

For those organizations with so many data quality issues—that is, low data quality—that the functioning of transactional systems are impaired or require constant balancing, patching, and maintenance, the recommendation is to fix the problem where it resides—in the operational milieu, not in the context of a new, data warehouse system. Because organizations are made of imperfect, error-prone, and sometimes opportunistic human beings, including managers, the temptation may be to displace the problem of data quality in the direction of a data warehouse project. The result is likely to be more quality issues in multiple places and a solution in none.

Make no mistake about it, the soap box is out on this one. Saying that data quality is *only* a concern of the data warehouse or of the transactional systems is misguided. This is like saying quality is the responsibility of the quality assurance (QA) department. Well, okay, it can provide leadership and training in methods, but quality belongs to the line of business processes, decisions support processes, and all of the systems that support them as such. See the example cited above in Chapter Six on data warehouse data quality where, in one firm, the QA department was abolished and quality improved. This succeeded because accountability for the QA function was successfully distributed to those doing the work. Thus, the line of least resistance suggests implementing quality improvements at the points where data is entered, captured in electronic form, or transformed. These are potential points of failure where investing in extra safeguards is well rewarded.

DETERMINING TEMPORAL GRANULARITY

Here, the discussion emphasizes granularity from the perspective of the information supply chain. Because the information supply chain occurs in time, transformations of data along the temporal dimension are on the critical path. Naturally, there are times when one wants to have data be as granular as possible, so that the analyst can drill down to it or roll up from it. What determines the level of granularity is the transaction that gets defined at the intersection of the basic dimensions—customer, product, and time period. Because customer and product are now well defined (as the result of significant system design and implementation effort), the determining factor of granularity is time. The point is similar to that made about abstract data dimensions (see Chapter Eight: Data Warehouse Construction Technologies), where the level of abstraction makes a difference. The trade-off is between having a mountain of detail available and knowing that a higher level of aggregation will perform best. Many credit card and telephone companies have the goal of marketing to the individual. The time-stamp on every transaction event may be relevant. Certainly, it is relevant to fraud or loss detection. (Perhaps less so to a promotion to get subscribers to buy theater tickets or refer friends and family to participate in a frequent user program.) They are, thus, dealing with what might be called "Wal-Mart scale" mountains of detail. On the other hand, many retailers, manufacturers, and service firms sell to demographic subgroups or even to entire markets. The aggregate use of health care services by an employee group on a weekly basis may be just the right level of abstraction for managed care purposes. Likewise, for supply chain management and marketing, where the lead time for moving products through the supply chain is two weeks for example, knowing who took delivery of what during which week is the critical level of granularity (not individual visits to the store). The detail always remains in the transaction system where it drives day-to-day processing for a relatively brief time horizon of a month or quarter. Meanwhile, the data warehouse extraction and transformation processing performs a "boot-strap" operation.

The process of coordinating the transactional and decision support systems requires "aggregating into the warehouse." Note here that "aggregation" is along the time dimension. That is, all of those unique and elementary customer-product (item) combinations for the week have to be added up from the daily invoices to weekly summary to generate the fact to be saved in the atomic (lowest level of granularity) data warehouse bucket, which is weekly, in this example. Because the aggregation is from elementary customer and product details, and merely summarizes data across an extended time period (weekly, in this case), the issue would not occur of rebuilding aggregates as when the geography or product hierarchies get redefined. Of course, that issue of rebuilding would reemerge if the time hierarchy had to be redefined—but a reorganization of the calendar is less likely than a reorganization of the marketing department.

AGGREGATE UP TO THE DATA WAREHOUSE

This is a subtle point, but it is a source of misunderstanding, so getting clear on it is useful. Under this scenario, detailed data warehouse data is still available, although the process of an aggregation to a weekly quantity has occurred to populate the warehouse as part of the information supply chain. One can drill down to individual customer-product combinations from higher-level aggregates of customer group/product brand. However, one can no longer get back to daily invoices, because the dimension of time used in determining the granularity of the fact structure(s) has been defined as weekly. The operation is irreversible, once aggregation to the weekly level has occurred. Likewise, the expectation is that such daily data would not be available or even interesting from the decision support perspective and would roll out of the operational environment of the transactional system long before the three- to five-year time frame in which the data warehouse was using it. From this data warehouse perspective, the transactional data—the line items on the invoice—are actually subatomic.

Thus, this part of the path of the information supply chain from the transactional system to the data warehouse is often described as an "aggregation model." Although the matter is the subject of controversy among the experts, most warehouse practitioners are inclined to assert that data extraction from the transactional system includes consistency checking and correction (scrubbing), and aggregation. A first-level aggregation is implied, even in populating a data warehouse with low-level data. Low-level data is that which is close to the elementary transaction captured by the transactional system. However, it is not necessarily identical to the level of detail in the transactional system. This is called *aggregating up* to the data warehouse.

For example, if during the week ending 01/01/1999, our imaginary firm, Commodity Chocolate Basics, makes three separately invoiced deliveries to a customer of 100 pounds of powdered cocoa on Monday, Wednesday, and Friday, a data warehouse data model that contains weekly data would require aggregating (summing) the three deliveries by customer, product, and date into one weekly date bucket. Thus, atomic transaction data must be aggregated to get to the level of atomic warehouse data.

There is nothing inherently superior about working with a weekly aggregation as opposed to daily elementary data quantities. The weekly aggregation might smooth over rough spots—static or white noise, so to speak—in the data, whereas the daily count would show additional granularity if there were a variation within the week that was of interest or the target of a promotion. However, the same issue can be expected to reemerge at the daily level if there were several transactions a day—for example, uses of a credit card on a shopping expedition. To get a picture of how much is charged a day, several elementary items on a daily line item have to be summed. This is the sort of process that is performed by the SQL interface to databases. For large amounts of data, the recommendation is to unload the data to a sequential, so-called flat file—flat because no hierarchy, relations, or indexing are represented—and apply a sort utility outside the database engine. Modern sort utilities will perform such aggregations on control breaks—groupings of products, customers, dates, and related types with equal values—with an efficiency that is superior to that of the database engine.

Data Warehousing Without Writing Procedural Code

The advantage of buying and deploying an extract, transform, and load (ETL) tool as opposed to writing procedural code in COBOL or C is that the tool can automate the capture and maintenance of metadata. In any significantly complicated system the mapping of transactional source to data warehousing target fields and the actions to edit, validate, and transform the data takes on a decidedly non-trivial scope and effort. Writing code is not a sustainable long term solution in the face of changes occurring as additional transactional systems are integrated into the data warehouse. This is especially significant because up to 80% of the work consists in capturing, modifying, and loading transactional data into the data warehouse. Indeed the vision being articulated by Pieter Mimno (pmimno@cove.com), an individual who is truly the expert's expert and who appears frequently in the DCI Data Warehousing World Conference circuit, is to build, populate, and operate the data warehouse "without writing a single line of procedural code." This is feasible thanks to the proliferation of ETL tools. The exception sometimes occurs if one has an unconventional data source of legacy system data that requires special handling for whatever reason. However, even here there are options. Thus, given a large number of legacy system sources of data, including ones on mainframe systems, it may be necessary to employ tools that generate procedural code. These require compiling and source code management. However, the more modern, second generation extraction tools generate executable binary code directly. This is generally an improvement. (The number of ETL tools is so large and subject to merger and acquisition processes, leaving aside marketing spin, that the reader is well-advised to find a suitable research expert or guru. Although it may seem self-serving, anything said here is likely to be obsolete before the ink on the text is dry.) The selection of a tool is an important decision—actually a highrisk decision—whose risk must be managed in a rigorous and professional manner. Why so? In comparison to switching from one relational database to another, switching ETL tools is an order of magnitude more challenging. There are no standards at all. None. In particular, forms of data representation and transformation rules cannot be moved from one tool to another. They are all proprietary. They must be rebuilt from scratch. This is a point where risk control, management support, and software acquisition due diligence are of the essence.

We have now completed traversing the information supply chain through an initial extract, scrubbing, and aggregation to the level of granularity we want in our data warehouse. At this point, loading the data is a straightforward matter. The high-level descriptors of customers (groups or regions), products (brands or categories), and dates are registered in the metadata control structure. The basic relational data has been laid down in the data warehouse.

AGGREGATES IN THE DATA WAREHOUSE

The initial aggregation up to the warehouse is distinct from building aggregates for performance. As will be treated in further detail below, *metadata* refers to many things, including how warehouse data elements map to transactional system ones, their data type, and meaning. In addition, the available aggregates are defined and registered in the metadata repository as metadata.[3] Finally, the next transformation step may include specific denormalization for performance, usually along the time dimension.

There is no controversy about the importance and value of building aggregations and tracking them as metadata. This is the case from a performance-enhancing point of view, as well as a practical and useful perspective. Once created, however, aggregations must be dated, registered, and kept current. This is part of the cost of using them. As part of the process of the information supply chain, aggregation is so important that nearly an entire chapter will be devoted to it.

THE DEBATE ABOUT THE DATA WAREHOUSE DATA MODEL

The debate about the star schema data model of the data warehouse versus the transactional data model is misguided. The fact table, with the composite key of customer id, product id, and time period, is in perfect third-normal form. It satisfies the definition completely with a small set of quantitative data element wholly dependent on the key, the whole key, and nothing but the key. Once this is realized, any debate gets shifted to the dimensional tables—customer, product, channel, time, etc.—which may, indeed, be denormalized for performance. However, the denormalization is performed in accordance with the principles of data normalization and denormalization. The method remains strictly within the approach of relational modeling. In most cases, compelling evidence is available that exploding these structures into many highly normalized ones ("snow flaking," as it is sometimes called) will only degrade browsing and other batch-like processes. It would do the same thing within the confines of a transactional environment, too, but in the latter case, the imperative to return control quickly to the end-user after a short update outweighs the cost of slow browsing activity.

The basic prototype data warehouse data model fact design satisfies third-normal form. It contains a fact structure of a long, skinny row—a single or small number of quantitative, additive facts dependent on ("hung off of") a composite key consisting of all of the dimensions. In this case, the minimal set of dimensions is customer, product, and time. This result is a table that is mostly access key (index). The key is in the table, and the key is also in the index. This results in inefficiencies in both processing and storage. Because space is being used up multiplicatively (product x customer x time), a kind of combinatorial explosion can set in. The result is the multiterabyte databases one reads about in the trade journals, where special proprietary solutions (and special licensing costs) are required. True, with organizations such as Wal-Mart, there's just a lot of data, whatever one does. Nevertheless, management may reasonably be skeptical about size for its own sake. Sometimes, more data means more technology, more integration challenges, and more staff, not more knowledge.[4]

In those organizations with superior project management, design, and integration skills, management may consider a design and implementation that denormalizes from the third-normal form of the classic fact table. The next coordination required in the information supply chain also applies a maneuver in the time dimension. All of the quantity amount buckets in the classic fact table are keyed off of the product-customer combination. Time becomes an implicit dimension. This greatly reduces the amount of storage required. Because space is being reduced by the inverse of multiplication, a kind of reverse combinatorial explosion—reduction—sets in. The result is a reasonably sized database of gigabyte, not terabyte, extent and improved response time. This is a counter-intuitive result—but, I submit—one that stands up to scrutiny. With a single customer-product "get row," all related quantity buckets are returned to the application. That is very powerful from a performance point of view. Of course, ancillary applications must be built to maintain the buckets in sequence, adding and rolling them from bucket to bucket. The trade-offs are evident. That is definitely a cost—both a construction cost and a cost in terms of a more complex operational data warehouse environment. That is why the topic sentence of this paragraph refers to firms with superior management and implementation competencies. The intention is not so much to come down on one side or the other as to highlight the distinction and to note the development possibilities. Naturally, such a subtle design is not to be undertaken lightly. However, with the proper preparation, coordination, and information technology talent, the results are impressive.

Much of the work of satisfactory data access and response time is set up in the transformation step. Once again, the 80/20 rule is significant. What are the 20% of my queries that will answer 80% of the key business questions. Design them as predefined, static SQL. No substitute is available for human judgment. Provide it with a framework for knowledge, and it is unstoppable. Much of the available knowledge has already been set up and captured in building the back-end database—much, but not all. The presentation layer where the data is finally made accessible to the knowledge worker is now in view at last.

THE PRESENTATION LAYER

The power of the presentation layer and of desktop tools to slice and dice data is significant and continues to grow. Having scrubbed and consistent data in a relational form is a definite advantage in deploying any of the variety of OLAP capabilities featured in these tools (and considered in detail in Chapter Fifteen: OLAP Technologies). Special built-in functions, such as rolling average, ranking, and percentages, are available in many OLAP tools. These are not part of basic SQL, which requires extension by these special functions. What is happening in many instances is that the OLAP engine is benefitting from the scrubbing and transformation work performed in the information supply chain up to this point. The input to the OLAP tool must line up "just right" to complete building aggregations (cubes) on the desktop, based on the underlying data. In this instance, the data is in relational format but that need not always be the case. With selected OLAP engines, flat files are the method of choice. So an additional data preparation step is implied—unload the data from the data warehouse and handle these extracts as flat files. However, more and more, end-users are generating market pressure to build and maintain "links" connecting the OLAP engine and the underlying relational data. Finally, the OLAP engine applies a wealth of built-in functions to slice and dice the data and present the results in visually interesting and provocative ways. If further detail is needed, the "best and brightest" OLAP tools can reach back down—drill down—into the underlying database to percolate up and present the detailed data represented in the aggregation and summary. For example, the OLAP tool might display sales for brand X by all customers in region Y for the second quarter of the year. Now, suppose I know that an individual customer, C, has taken delivery of large amounts of a product, P, during the period. The analyst can ask to see the particular customer by production by period combination, and the OLAP engine will "drill down" and present that level of detail. As indicated, in selected cases, the OLAP engine may require the data to be in a different form than that contained in the relational database. It may have to be dumped, unloaded, and massaged into a predefined proprietary format prior to being "grabbed" by the OLAP engine. Though the trend in the industry is definitely toward the de facto "open" standard of the RDBMS, those who evaluate and acquire tools for a firm should be sure this question of backward integration and drill-through is on the check list.

From one perspective, advantages are definitely available in manipulating the cube on the analyst's desktop, rather than doing the work at the back-end and typing up the communication network moving around large amounts of data. However, one should not overlook or forget that a lot of work—extraction, scrubbing, transformation—has been expended to get to the point where the OLAP tool itself can perform an analogous function of extraction (no scrubbing because the data is supposed to be clean by now!), aggregation, and presentation. Indeed, multidimensional databases (MDD), which were so proud of their functional efficiencies, flexibility, and proprietary formats, are now converging on the RDBMS database standard, boasting about their hooks into the back-end.

INTEGRATED DECISION SUPPORT PROCESSES

The number of "hops" is large between the point of data capture and that of information presentation to the analyst in support of decision making. A formidable number of layers of software need to be traversed. An executive engaging profitability results or brand management choices is downstream from the reconciliation of different types of data, methods of analysis, business models, and frameworks for measurement. The quality of the information produced by these processes will make the difference between such an executive being described as "knowledgeable" and as a "victim of circumstances." Tools that are able to integrate disparate data types from heterogeneous databases and provide the functionality to perform complex business processes such as forecasting and customer profiling can ease the integration of the database and presentation layers. For instance, the business function being implemented may be too complex to be accommodated by database SPs or it may require the integration of more data sources than can readily be accommodated by the proprietary back-end of an OLAP engine. In data warehousing and decision support environments, such architectural features function as analytic engines. Typically, such an analytic application server is required to support scalability, performance, and the distribution of functionality on an enterprise-wide basis. The acquisition and implementation of such an application layer should not be mistaken for an easy answer to anything. It is an approach to making good use of the data that has been painstakingly aggregated in the data warehouse that continues to put a premium on good design, project management, and system integration skills.[5]

At a conference on software engineering, a speaker expressed the view that what is really required is a tool to reverse-engineer the legacy system in such a way that the knowledge encapsulated in it is understandable and surveyable by a human of above-average intelligence and experience. But in my opinion, treating the legacy system as a pure black box is not even on the horizon of feasibility, though it is imaginable as a kind of grand challenge in computing. A "grand challenge," as we shall see in the discussion of metadata, is a major problem, such as super-computing, chess-playing programs, or parallel processing, for which significant research or coalition funding (including governmental) is available. What is worth noting is that a significant amount of effort is required to set up the operation of the data extraction, scrubbing, or transformation tool in the targeted implementation context. Naturally, tools have generic hooks, features, and handles, by which they can be inserted into context. However, there really is no substitute for understanding the environment, what fits where, and why.

Check List for Data Extraction Tool Evaluation

Tools can ease the task of building and managing the information supply chain, but no tool can make it completely transparent. No tool can make it as easy as the marketing presentation might claim. Our wishful thinking must be checked and balanced by rigorous questions about functionality and specifications. This must, in turn, be based on an organization's self-knowledge about its competencies, limitations, and strengths and addressed to the wishful thinking that managers are harboring. The following is a short check list for data extraction tool evaluation of a minimum essential set of functions and questions relating to data scrubbing, extraction, and transformation tools.[6]

- How does the tool map source data to target data? Can a person input both a procedural language (COBOL, C, Java?) record (or file copybook or layout) and a relational (or tabular) structure in the top; have the tool present both, preferably in a point and click GUI format; and enable an analyst to drag connections between them?

- Will the tool propose semantic mappings on its own, based on fuzzy name matching—is access to multiple, heterogeneous sources of data not only efficient but also transparent?

- Does the tool have preferences, "lock in," or special capabilities as to whether the target of the data extraction is a star schema or snow flake layout?

- Does the tool provide for a heads-up, easy-to-use format for the entry of procedural business rules and table-driven mapping of codes and values?

- How are exceptions reported and managed? Are automated substitution, action based on triggerlike conditions, and mix-and-match options available for reporting, deletion, or transformation in combination or individually?

- Does the tool generate procedural code to perform the extracting and scrubbing, based on the input formats, rules, and codes? Or does the tool directly generate an executable?

- What is the support for nontraditional data types—texts, blobs, and multimedia data? This is a new and emerging area and may require a tool specialized for alternative data types.

- What is the support for legacy system data access, interfaces to ERP systems, etc.?

- Operationally, what is the amount of data on which the tool has operated, the speed with which it has produced results (in elapsed time and CPU by processor); and what is its ability to *scale* from smaller to ever-growing amounts of data?

- How does the tool define metadata? How does it use it? What are the available interfaces to metadata structures and parameters, and issues of interoperability?

- Does the tool automate the capture and maintenance of metadata as data is mapped from target to source? Is this metadata easily accessible to other tools and vendors downstream? (This is critical path.)

- What are all the usual parameters about hardware requirements and operating system environment and software compatibility, and are they covered? What are the defined constraints, limitations, and tuning parameters, and how do these compare with the target implementation environment?

- How does the tool describe itself, and where is it located in the general matrix of client-server architecture—front-end presentation, back-end data transformation, middleware navigation (or coordination)?

- What are the in-depth, down-and-dirty reports of two or three other customers ("reference sites") who are similar in profile to the target firm and who actually have the tool in production and have been using it for a while?

SUMMARY . . . .

Data warehousing is not reducible to its applications. It is a process. This process is the information supply chain. From a distance, the information supply chain may seem like a miracle. You just clean up the dirty transactional data—extract, scrub, transform, and load—and all of a sudden it becomes knowledge. The secret to this miracle—and why it is not really a miracle but just good business system design—is the alignment of the information supply chain with the fundamental business imperatives directing customer and product development. The process required by data warehousing in the information supply chain is *not* a sequential assembly line. The language of "work flow" applies here. This is a work flow as a process of coordination. First, at the technical level, coordination implies system interoperability. The transaction and the decision support system interoperate, work together, because relations between the two systems have been mapped and constrained in terms of one another. Second, at the representational level, the coordination occurring is about organizing details of transactions according to a framework constituting knowledge, including such parameters as data quality, scrubbing, and aggregation. Finally, at the business level, the coordination is of commitments to satisfy the basic business imperatives at stake in instrumenting the business by means of a data warehouse—to know the customer, build the brand, and gain visibility to market dynamics. Next, partitioning as a useful method to divide and conquer and to transition from implementation to operations is considered. The path of the information supply chain from the transactional system(s) to the data warehousing one is often described as an aggregation model. The traversal of the information supply chain through initial extraction, scrubbing, and aggregation to the level of granularity required in the data warehouse is traced. The metadata captured at the time the extract, transform, and load (ETL) process is built and executed in a crucial source of system integration for up- and down-stream processes, which are constrained by the requirement to interact with this information. The interdependency of data extraction and setup with data presentation and analysis (OLAP) is emphasized.

[1] *Personal communication.*

[2] See Chapter Eleven: "Data Warehousing Performance" where *data partitioning* corresponds most closely to the technology mechanism underlying the implementation strategy under discussion here. In this later chapter, all three additional definitions of partitioning are defined and analyzed in their relevance to data warehouse performance. Partitioning is such a fundamental method of problem solving as to be synonymous with thinking itself. Hence, the reference to "divide and conquer."

[3] The automation of this process of registering available aggregates in a metadata repository is discussed in Chapter Fourteen in the section on aggregate navigation.

[4] At this point, the reader may wish to review Figures 7.4 and 7.5, along with Table 7.4 from Chapter Seven: "Data Warehousing Technical Design." For further reading, also see Agosta, 1998: 34 for the technical details.

[5] A convincing case is made for such an extension of an application server in the context of decision support by John Rymer, Upstream Consulting, in a white paper presented at www.whitelight.com. See also www.vit.com and www.mineshare.com for competing suites of products positioned in the same general area.

[6] A checklist on OLAP tools is provided in Chapter Fifteen: OLAP Technologies.

13 *Metadata and Metaphor*

In this chapter...

METAPHORS ALTER OUR PERCEPTIONS

A metaphor, as the reader may recall from high school literature, is an equating—really, a mapping one to another—of two things, meanings, or situations that are apparently different. What is really interesting is how successful metaphors often alter our perception and understanding. By equating the meanings of words that seemed to be different in scope or context, metaphors change our way of looking at things. By giving us that "Aha!" moment of insight, metaphors are useful in giving us new ways of looking at what was in front of our eyes all along. They are useful in disclosing meaning where we thought there was none. Metaphor is the royal road to meaning, and, in the context of data warehousing, so is metadata. Metadata have a remarkably similar role to play in the data warehouse. As we shall see, the way in which metadata are intrinsically metaphorical is the background to the significance and role of metadata. By equating legacy sources of data to target data elements in the data warehouse, metadata enhance our understanding of and insight into the meanings and mechanisms that move the information supply chain in the direction of the data warehouse. Let's take a step back and explore the implications for the technology of metaphor.

A NEW TECHNOLOGY, A NEW METAPHOR

The way we describe things in language influences our perceptions and constrains our understanding of them. Among the most famous of modern metaphors is the electronic desktop, where the metaphorical comparison is between electronic files marked by folderlike icons and opening physical folders on our physical desktop. Windows was a computing metaphor before it became a trademark of Microsoft Corporation. Add scheduling, mail, and messaging tools to complete the equation of the electronic desktop with the material reality of the physical desk. Work flow and imaging technology extend the metaphor to the electronic file cabinet and the electronic in and out baskets. The Internet and HTML (Hypertext Mark Up Language) extend the idea of a text (words on a page) using the metaphor of hypertext—electronic "hot links" between texts at different levels of discourse and generality. The network-aware language Java invents the metaphor of the "sandbox" as an approach to security and authentication.

A Java applet is restricted to the sandbox, within which it can "play" without access to the local hard drive or operating system, so no viruses or other mischief can be introduced. At an entirely different level, the metaphor of the information utility is a powerful one and can guide many large-scale applications of the data warehouse resource. The vision of computing cycles as available as a dial tone or electrical outlet is a compelling one—although information products themselves are likely to remain highly customized and the most valuable of them unlike commodities. The descriptions of managing data by data warehousing or mining are themselves intrinsically metaphorical. Thus, the point: a new technology, a new metaphor.

The Data Warehouse Metaphor

The expression "data warehouse" is itself a metaphor. If one goes to a business and technology conference and asks for a show of hands as to who is building or operating a data warehouse, 80% of the hands go up. Perhaps this just shows peer group pressure, because an IDC (International Data Corporation) survey in early 1999 put this same number at 40%. Just as likely, it means that the data warehouse is now a pervasive feature of the business and technology landscape. Even those who don't have one implicitly acknowledge the validity of the goal. In data warehousing, the metaphor is in the surface structure of the technology. The warehouse is the central location for the collection and disbursement of a company's goods or services. The data warehouse is where information producers store, inventory, and organize stuff—in this case, data—prior to distribution to customers, end-users, and all manner of downstream data consumers. The response to the one fundamental question, which the data warehouse is designed to engage and answer, depends on the structure of the data warehouse system mapping to the structure of business imperatives about customer, product, channel, and market knowledge. This mapping is a "carrying across" of business meaning into the technical representation of the business process. It is itself metaphorical. Therefore, the essential role of metadata in the data warehouse system is based on the way metaphors motivate and guide our understanding of the meaning of data.

METADATA ARE METAPHORICAL

Metadata trace the meanings of data from transactional to data warehouse systems. They track source to target, through various extraction, transformation, and loading (ETL) operations and, thus, make possible the interoperation, the working together, of these heterogeneous systems. Thus, metadata are metaphors equating things—mapping source to target—that are apparently different between transactional and warehouse systems, which, when examined in detail, give us new ways of perceiving and understanding what we all along had in front of our eyes. Metaphor identifies things, including abstractions, with identical (or similar) features that are not at first glance perceived to be the same. The metaphor is a formula for identifying them. Because that is also the function of metadata, in that sense, metadata are metaphorical. Like metaphors, the stuff communicated by metadata inform and sometimes alter our perceptions and understanding of the mapping of data warehouse data to legacy system (and other enterprise) inputs, the meaning of the structures that have been carried across to the warehouse, and the status, uses, and outcomes of procedures applied to the data itself.

At the limit, metadata may be the relational database catalog itself. This is entry level, zero level, metadata. More is needed than a mere technical repository. What is required is information about sources of data, mapping from legacy systems and nonrelational data stores to the target data warehouse structures, business rules, and even information about the disposition of the warehouse data, its availability and point-in-time relevance, and the aggregations available in the warehouse by basic business drivers. What is required is a detailed operational description of the extraction, transformation, loading, meaning, and scheduling of the information supply chain (as outlined in Chapter Twelve). It is true that meaning is in the mind of the end-user; still, the suggestion is that sometimes you need a bit more than that to track and disentangle the myriad of semantic interconnections among the data. Given its many forms, metadata are as much an encyclopedia as a dictionary.[2] When the idea of metadata is properly "scaled up" to the enterprise, one realizes that an entire library may be required

This is the case in both elementary and complex way. For example, the customer, Worldwide Widgets, has one address and customer number for invoicing and a different one for shipments and returns. If international names and addresses are involved, the layout of the information, including type fonts and character uses, can be challenging. All of these are mapped by metadata to the one arbitrarily assigned canonical data warehouse customer number. This number tracks the aggregation of sales and returns of various products by time period. This information is abstracted, registered, and maintained (managed) in the metadata repository structure.

Because elementary transactions—the equivalent of line items on invoices—tell us little about the brand, the business relationship, or customer intimacy, decision makers end up climbing the hierarchy laid out in the defining dimensions to gain a more global perspective and statement of fact. Aggregation is the result. For example, customer D orders 1,000 class A widgets in July, 1,500 class B in August, and 500 class C in September. This tells us about their business and our relationship with them. What is our total business with them in the third quarter? What is the trend month to month and quarter to quarter? If that is an aggregate that would tell us something useful for managing inventory, promotion, discount, or account management purposes, then our firm ends up making that a canonical aggregate—one that is built, stored, and tracked. That, too, is metadata.

SEMANTICS

Often, *semantics* means something trivial or insignificant. However, semantics is of the essence in defining and determining the meaning of data. It is semantics that determines that an order may have multiple lines on it, but a line may not belong to multiple orders. It is semantics that says something is wrong when multiple lines lack an order header—they are orphans, lacking a parent. What sense does an order without line items make? None. They (headers and lines) are semantically connected. They give one another meaning by being part of one and the same distinction, rather like two sides of an interface. A good working definition of *semantics* is that it is the relation of representing or modeling between the world and the (computing) system. This relation of representing is complex and difficult to capture completely and entirely using data structures and logic, though data modelers are bound to try. So, *semantics* also designates whatever meaning is leftover after logical data models and structures have been applied to a domain of objects in the business world. What is "leftover" are the nitty-gritty details of entities in the model and how they represent the real world distinctions that the model lets us grasp. Product weight, product volume, shipment quantity—all of these are numeric values. No doubt about that. But these are different kinds of values. That difference is semantics. Product weight and shipment quantity *mean* something different. They cannot be meaningfully compared or equated or added, but they can be multiplied to generate the product-shipment weight. How does your company distinguish a current customer from a future prospect? Which one is someone who hasn't purchased or used your service in, say, 14 months? In every case, the devil is in the details. That's semantics.

Semantics is the true path to metadata. This starts from basic elementary skills, such as mapping input to output. It extends to advanced design mechanisms, such as normalizing and denormalizing data for performance, summarizing, aggregating, navigating, scheduling, and managing. Aggregation will receive a chapter of its own (see Chapter Fourteen: Aggregation); navigating and scheduling are functions best discussed in the context of metadata tools (end of this chapter); and data normalization is treated immediately following.)

Much of designing a data warehouse system using relational database technology is about semantics. What do the tables, relations, and the database structures really mean in a consistent and precise way? How do they map to the world of business distinctions that we are trying to represent in the delivered system? For example, if one is building a forecasting system, with tightly constrained response time and batch window parameters, further semantic refining, called *denormalization* of the fact table, even prior to special aggregations and summaries, is useful or even necessary. How and why requires a basic understanding of semantics—data normalization and denormalization. Data normalization does not exhaust formal semantics, but it is an important part of it. The discipline—one might say "technology"—of data normalization has the added benefit of being so central and fundamental for the understanding of the use and operation of relational database systems as to be indispensable to a high-level understanding of relational technology. The significance of undertaking a concise exploration of the semantics of data normalization in the chapter of metadata is worth noting. It aims to reinforce the assertion that metadata are all about meaning—establishing it and moving it around in our systems. Therefore, that is undertaken here.

FORMS OF DATA NORMALIZATION
AND DENORMALIZATION[3]

First-normal form states that relational data is atomic. To satisfy first-normal form, the column in a relational table should not, itself, contain an array or table. So, for example, a data element, a single column in a relational database table, which contained a set, or array, of different discount prices for a given product would fail first-normal form (depending on month). To satisfy first-normal form, each price would be broken out as a row by itself. Another way of saying the same thing is that price is *functionally dependent* on product id and date (month); that is, product id and date *determine* the price. This "functional dependency" is what creates "meaning," that is, the semantic aspect of data normalization, which, in turn, makes possible the comparison of data across different contexts, situations, and applications. (See Table 13.1: First-Normal Form.)

Note in this example that the assumption is that different prices apply in different months. If that were not the case and one wanted to refer to different prices on different occasions for whatever reason, a simple sequence number could be substituted for the date. That would satisfy the requirement that the row have a unique identifier. Note further that this solves a problem of data normalization, not necessarily a problem of that of a perspicuous presentation of the data warehouse data. Unlike transactional systems, where the price has to be presented to a call center order clerk, there is really no separate requirement for the warehouse to track the list price. What must be captured and tracked is the amount invoiced. So, if 10 items are shipped for $100, the *implied* price is $10 per item. That avoids the problem of introducing price-sensitive date information (or date-sensitive price information) into either the fact or the product structures.

Second-normal form states that relational data is dependent on (relates in a meaningful way to) the access key used to uniquely define the row in the table (the

Table 13.1: First-Normal Form (Assigns Elements of an Array to Separate Atomic Data Elements)

Product Id	Date	Price Column
999888777	1999-01-20	19.95; 20.95; 29.95

Product Id	Date	Price
999888777	1999-01-20	19.95
999888777	1999-02-20	20.95
999888777	1999-03-20	29.95

member in the set). So, if the product's price were stored on a row whose key was customer id, product id, and effective date, price would depend only on the product id. To get up to second-normal form, price should be broken out into a separate table of its own, keyed exclusively by product id (or product id and effective date). (See Table 13.2: Second-Normal Form.)

To satisfy third-normal form, the complete key must be expressed, so that every column in the table is dependent on the key, the whole key, and nothing but the key. So, if one, in effect, hangs multiple sales amounts for a series of days (or a periodic duration of time) by customer and product off of a single product-customer combination, one has stepped back from third-normal form and created an array within the entire row (not the column). One has the key and nothing but the key, but not the complete key. To get to the complete key, you have to make explicit that each column corresponds to an implied date. Thus, each sales quantity bucket would be keyed on product id, customer id, and period ending date (day, week, month, etc.). (See Table 13.3: Third-Normal Form.)

The fourth- and fifth-normal forms deal with multivalued relations. The fourth states the if two or more multivalued relations depend on the same unique key, they really belong in their own separate structures. Certain kinds of ambiguities can be eliminated by this rule. Customers can speak multiple languages and drive multiple automobiles. According to this rule, these belong in separate structures to avoid redundant entries. This is where most data warehouse experts argue that the limited space savings is not worth the fragmentation and proliferation of data structures, especially with reference to dimension structures. A consideration similar to this applies to fifth-normal form, which applies additional business rules or constraints to the representation of the data, constraining the decomposition of the structures into fully normalized forms. The recommendation is the same—the negative impact on performance caused by the fragmentation and proliferation of dimensional data structures is not rewarded

Table 13.2:   Second-Normal Form
(Assigns Element Otherwise Dependent on Part of the Key to a Separate Structure)

Product ID	Customer ID	Date	Price	Other Data
999888777	111222333	1999-01-20	19.95	
666555444	222333444	1999-01-20	20.50	

depends on

Product Id	Price
999888777	19.95
666555444	20.50

by the modest savings of storage space. (See Figure 7.3: The Forms of Data Normalization, for a complete definition of the six basic normal forms.)[4]

METADATA ARCHITECTURE

If semantics is the path to metadata, knowledge is the payoff. Metadata encompass many kinds of knowledge in the strict sense of the word. For example, it is structural knowledge of the most important kind to know that a selected aggregate is sourced from such-and-such a legacy system, because if the legacy system changes, so must the downstream definition of the dependent aggregate. This is not just "data about data," because "data about data" is still just data. Data about data really doesn't make a difference. Rather, the short working definition of metadata is an architecture—principles coordinating of commitments—for knowledge of the interoperability between (otherwise isolated) systems and subsystems.

The architecture of metadata is the architecture of knowledge. Let's take a step back to consider what this means. All of our knowledge begins with experience, and without experience, we would not have any knowledge whatsoever. However, although, knowledge all begins with experience, it does not follow that it all arises out of experience.[5] There are other sources of knowledge. One of the most important of these is metadata. A short inventory is in order.

Table 13.3:   Third-Normal Form

Product Id	Customer Id	Amount One	Amount Two	Amount Three
999888777	111222333	70.00	60.00	50.00
666555444	222333444	20.00	30.00	40.00
333222111	444555666	90.00	80.00	70.00

Dates are implied ⬆ ⬆ ⬆

Product Id	Customer Id	Time Id	Amount
999888777	111222333	01-20-1999	70.00
999888777	111222333	02-20-1999	60.00
999888777	111222333	03-20-1999	50.00
666555444	222333444	01-20-1999	20.00
666555444	222333444	02-20-1999	30.00
666555444	222333444	03-20-1999	40.00
333222111	444555666	01-20-1999	90.00
333222111	444555666	02-20-1999	80.00
333222111	444555666	03-20-1999	70.00

First, we have entry-level metadata of the kind to be found in the relational catalog. This includes DDL structures of dimensions and facts, definitions of data elements and data types, and lists of queries, packages, and declarative referential integrity. Group this kind of information under "knowing what's what."

In a truly adequate metadata repository, the history of the changes that have occurred to the data structures making up the application tables and indexes is also tracked. If a table is dropped and redefined to change the data types of certain columns, the relational catalog shows only the latest table, not the earlier one. The implications of such a change for the forward and backward compatibility of backup copies, extracts, loads, and application level connections are significant. Especially if the name of the table remains the same, much knowledge is lost from the relational catalog. Here's the table name, but its format is different. What happened? When did it happen? Does anyone remember? An image of the before-and-after DDL format of the table is essential to understanding the change history.

There are many forms of knowing what the structure and history of the data are. They lie on a continuum between theory and practice. At the theoretical end are forms of knowledge that resemble data models, lists of data elements, and data dictionary entries. One step in the direction of more practical engagement with the knowledge is the cross-referencing of the structure of the data with the applications, programs, and processes that use them. Step by step, the metadata become operationally more relevant. The idea of "operationalizing" metadata is fundamental. It refers to the process of engaging the software "levers and dials" that drive the automated functioning of the system. For example, the metadata should also show what aggregates (cubes) are available, whether they are up to date, and how they are defined. The user of such aggregate metadata is not really the business analyst but the data warehouse system software itself, in the form of an aggregate navigator. The latter would make use of this knowledge to access the already available aggregate instead of summarizing it interactively from the detailed rows. In this way, the metadata knowledge gets operationalized in practice.

As the data warehouse gets operationalized, connections are built between the data warehouse and up- and downstream transactional systems. An extract process or job feeds the warehouse, based on filtering defined by the data dimensions in the warehouse itself. A warehouse planning process, in turn, is used to determine the sourcing of inventory in the supply chain. These connections between the warehouse and transactional systems are often automated in a job-scheduling tool, once they have been designed and implemented. The database of such a tool (usually a proprietary and nonrelational database) contains much "if-then" logic, about which jobs are triggered or put on hold on the basis of which jobs in the schedule have completed. This, too, is metadata.

Complex coordination issues can arise, for example, if an extract goes "over the wall" from the data center to a departmental decision support process. Does the scheduling tool have visibility to such downstream processing and, if not, how can accountability to the customer and job dependencies be managed? The answer is a design task. Build a work flow, such that the commitments between the up- and downstream processes are coordinated. If the customer's request for decision support information can be accommodated, that indicates that the coordination is working. It is likely that automated tools will be indispensable in managing such a work flow. However, in principle, it should be workable with no other technology than a flat stretch of sand and a stick (pencil and paper will also work). Likewise, this is metadata, and it includes pragmatic "how to get things done (with metadata)" types of knowledge.

Thus, a second major category of metadata knowledge includes "know-how." Given data in a transactional system, how does it get transformed from its source to its target format in the data warehouse? This implies a mapping from source to target by way of an IDL. Let's say that data type COMPUTATIONAL in the source language corresponds to data type INTEGER in the target (for example) or that there is no matching data type, whether due to computing language or business constraints, in which case, a true transformation rule must be invoked. Program-specified conditional logic or a lookup table must be consulted to cause the new form of the data to come into being.

Code generators have been available literally for decades. This is the kind of knowledge that lines up source and target data elements in the legacy and warehouse systems, respectively, and produces 3GL programs to extract, consolidate, and transform data in a canonical form. What should be noted is that coding is about 20% of any system development effort. Defining the requirements, designing, and testing are easily the other 80%. Therefore, the amount of automation that is occurring here, though important and useful, is less than one might at first imagine upon seeing the marketing presentation. Similar considerations apply to data scrubbing—correcting legacy system data that lacks accuracy, consistency, or other identifiable quality features. This is where tools that perform pattern matching, statistical analysis, and lexical checking can be used to give real backbone to the cleanup effort. Certain kinds of data defects resist detection through rule-based analysis, and automated "smart" technologies can identify and correct such data contamination.

Metadata encompass so many different kinds and varieties of knowledge and for so many purposes that it is, indeed, a challenge of unappreciated proportions to get one's arms around them. What is required is a measure of library science. This is usually understood as the science of indexing knowledge, storing it, and retrieving it back efficiently and easily. Traditionally, the containers for this knowledge have been books. However, in our case, the data has included such matters as data structures, specific aggregations, systems interconnections and components, and even job schedules. The containers include such things as the relational catalog, proprietary job-scheduling tool databases, special-purpose data stores, and even flat files. A more unified and general container would be helpful. It is to that and related requirements that we now turn.

METADATA REPOSITORY

With metadata, the question of whether we are documenting, processing, or driving it arises. Are we able to advance from practical knowledge to pragmatic knowledge, in which our commitments are operationalized? For example, if a new aggregate is added to data warehouse system, is that new aggregate captured by the metadata dictionary and are applications able to take advantage of it automatically, with a simple rebind of an aggregate-aware optimizer or does application program script or code have to be modified? Likewise, if a job does not execute successfully to update the data warehouse, is the end-user able to determine this for himself by inquiring into a kind of metadata scheduler, which reports on the currency and consistency of dimensions and facts? This third kind of knowledge includes pragmatic "knowing how to do things (with metadata)" in such a way that interoperability and mutual communications and commitments between systems are documented and enforced. This is the kind of information that gets stored in a metadata repository, also at times called an *information catalog* or *metadata manager* (summarized in Figure 13.1: Metadata Repository). Such repositories often still represent hard-wired, point-to-point pathways, not general solutions. Still, despite limitations, they are a start.

In being "operationalized," metadata advance from documentation—a useful artifact in any system—to engagement. They (the metadata) are no longer idle, but a mechanism that drives processing. The schematic in Figure 13.2 (Metadata Operations) is a composite of features of many systems, no single one of which has every aspect depicted. One can "jump" into the circle at any point, but a logical place to start is business imperatives. Each business imperative maps to a basic dimensional hierarchy—product, customer, channel, etc.—the data definitions that are in the repository. These inform the data extraction and scrubbing rules and processes that transform the transactional into the data warehouse facts. These are back-end, batch processes. In turn, the availability of the data is reported as a committed result to the end-user through the metadata-scheduling function. This is the source of desktop analysis—slicing and dicing according to hierarchical dimensions—to answer questions and generate actionable knowledge. These are front-end, interactive processes. Finally, an interface is required to access and manage the data—that is metadata administration, including interaction with other systems.

MODELS AND METAMODELS

Model building is a part of our search for meaning. We go around building models of things to make sense out of them; to understand them; in short, to get to know them. Once we start building models, we find that we require a guide to direct our model-building activity. That guide is a metamodel, a model of the model-building activity. For example, a metamodel is provided by the Zachman framework for architecture analysis. In Chapter One, we discussed how to apply many of these distinctions to data warehouse architecture. Peter Keen's three-way "cubing" of the business-technology platform in terms of reach, range, and responsiveness is a compelling conceptual image that qualifies as a metamodel. Ralph Kimball's data warehouse "bus architecture" is a metamodel based on the physical metaphor of the computer's bus—that component to which all other input/output devices are connected and which moves the data around internally. Grady Booch distinguishes between the Marco and the Micro processes in designing and deploying components for object-oriented systems, thus providing an overall model for building models. These are not models of any particular businesses, but they are conditions of possibility of many business models. One can sketch arbitrarily many business models according to them. Each is a powerful framework for analysis, but without engaging the details of a particular firm's business processes and components, each is an empty shell. As a general rule, it is the metamodel that knits together the high-level processes of a firm—finance, manufacturing, distri-

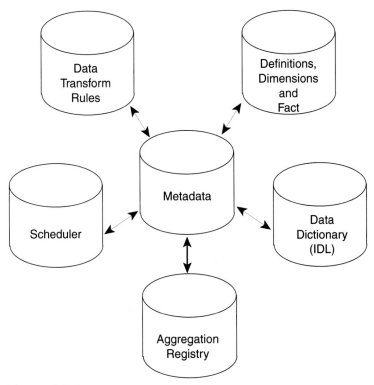

Figure 13:1:
Metadata Repository

bution, customer service, human resources with the interface to markets, competitors, suppliers, and customers. In short, you end up with the position of a firm in context, rather than in isolation. This forms the basis for business metadata.

Two other metamodels worthy of reference form the basis for technical metadata. The first of these is Microsoft's Open Information Model (OIM). In December 1998, Microsoft turned over ownership and administration of OIM to the Meta Data Coalition, which is integrating it with the below-cited MDIS. OIM is a de facto standard that defines a model for storing and managing objects in the Microsoft Repository. Meanwhile, Oracle and IBM are pursing separate strategies based on the OLAP Council's Meta Data API (MDAPI 2.0), which in turn is based on CORBA. The anecdotal evidence is that Microsoft is out in front in terms of enlisting vendors to produce software solutions that interact with its version of the repository (see www.microsoft.com/data/oledb/olap/indsupp.htm). Meanwhile, CA/Platinum is porting Microsoft's Repository from NT to the UNIX environment. Thus, a defined measure of industry openness is visible on the horizon.

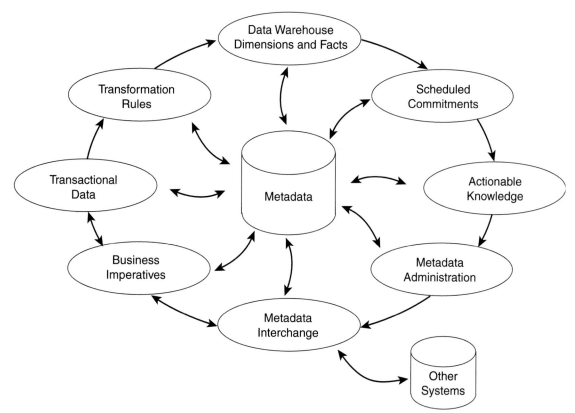

Figure 13:2:
Metadata Operations

METADATA INTERCHANGE SPECIFICATION (MDIS)

Because many vendors are offering metadata repositories, tools, and products, the idea is to create a forum in which they can work together for the overall improvement of the interoperability of tools and systems. The idea is that one vendor will export data from its repository in a common format as defined by the MDIS that allows it to be imported by an other vendor. *Voila!* Interoperability. Commerce, trade, and the market thus benefit as a rising tide elevates all the players' boats together.

We have discussed the difference between metadata as documentation and as a mechanism that drives data warehouse processes. The latter requires contractual interfaces and committed methods of interaction between different products. These include not just specific vendor metadata products, but also existing databases, scheduling tools, and other data warehousing tools, such as extract builders or desktop controls (and so on). A proper role for an industry coalition would include the definition and specification of interoperability methods. This would amount to a kind of IDL for metadata. We have also discussed the parallel between organizing different types of data warehouse metadata and library science. The key to knowledge is to be able to index it, store it, and retrieve it as the need arises. A proper role for an industry coalition would include the identification, definition, categorization, and design of an indexing mechanism for these different kinds of metadata. So far as I know, there is no general agreement as to the kinds of metadata, their relative priority or value, or even their definition. Ralph Kimball has provided what is probably the most comprehensive list of categories of metadata.[6] However, at this point, he is something of voice crying in the wilderness. One can only hope that the industry listens to him.

The Meta Data Coalition has over a hundred members, now including Microsoft. The Metadata Interchange Specification has been available since June of 1996. It provides a public API to support the batch loading of a metadata tool with various object types, including databases, schemas, files, and relationships, as well as user-defined, tool-specific metadata. (The latest version of the 90-page specification is available at www.mdis.com.) Originally criticized as a "lowest common denominator" approach—which, in truth, it is—it has recently acquired the caché of the moral high ground. The need is so great that there is almost nowhere else to turn. Meanwhile, just to make life interesting, Oracle, IBM, and Unisys has jointly submitted a request for proposal to the Object Management Group (www.omg.org) to define a metadata interchange standard based on Oracle's current proprietary Common Warehouse Metadata, as enhanced by a best-of-breed acquisition of a company called One Meaning (see www.onemeaning.com). Naturally, this leaves end-users in the classic situation with standards: The standards are good; the problem is that there are so many of them.

What is going on here? The challenge is so great, and the results are so far so limited (and limiting), that one may be suspicious and a bit skeptical that the true extent of the problem has been comprehended. Foundational thinking is in order about the limits and scope of that with which we are confronted by metadata and their uses. We now turn to that.

METADATA: A COMPUTING GRAND CHALLENGE

A "grand challenge" is a problem, the solution to which redefines what is possible both with technology and with human behavior itself. For example, putting a man on the moon and getting back required a redefinition of what was humanly possible because previously, man had only dreamed of such behavior in science fiction. Note also that the technical challenges were formidable. In computing, grand challenges have included getting a computer to play chess, a game whose sophistication belied its relatively small number of rules and finite tokens. Other grand challenges include using computers to perform such things as predicting the weather, performing machine-based three-dimensional vision, controlling nuclear fusion (without setting off an atomic bomb), and mapping the human brain (as a prelude to machine-based "thinking").[7]

It may seem a surprise to rank metadata as a grand challenge. However, if you look at the behavior of the market—recognition of the importance of metadata and frustration at the definition and redefinition of the problem(s)—it starts to dawn on us that we are dealing with a problem bigger than any of us might like to admit. And one in the face of which individual efforts are likely to be of limited use. Let's take a step back and consider.

First, metadata is like the data warehouse itself. It is an architecture that encompasses many specific purposes and requirements, not a specific product. As such, it is a concatenation of services and products, more or less coherently integrated into a functioning solution to a problem. Here, "more or less" is the operable phrase. That is because the problem that it promises to solve is the *interoperability* of data interchange between the decision support and transaction systems (and decision support systems in themselves).

Thus, metadata address a special case of the challenge of modern commercial computing at large—to get disparate, heterogeneous, mutually incompatible systems to work together in the service of the end-user (us humans). I submit the realization dawns on us that the term *metadata* is actually the name for what amounts to a "grand challenge" in computing. This should temper our expectations for a quick fix or single-point solution, but it should also encourage our efforts, because grand challenges tend to call forth significant resources and commitments. Like any really tough problem, the solution will require both step-by-step progress in increments, as well as breakthroughs, redefining the limits of the possible.

One deceptively simple question to ask about metadata is: "If we have a metadata repository for the ETL tool, for the data cube server, and for the relational data warehouse, do we really have integration?" Is the interoperation of these repositories a clumsy export-import process? Is it possible at all?

Metadata make the difference between data warehousing as a science and as ad hoc hacking. *Hacking* is applied here as another word for trial and error—activities that have their uses but are really expressions of our limitations and lack of understanding. *Science*, of course, is another word for knowledge itself—an organized body of experience, arranged and structured according to principles and rules. As we have seen, the science of metadata lies in its architecture, its basic first principles. That includes as many questions as answers. Whether metadata will end up being the Achilles heel of data warehousing or the jewel in the crown, only time will tell.

Metadata Tool Evaluation Check List

For the time being, a check list of questions with which to cross-examine vendors about their metadata products will go proxy for a complete solution to the metadata grand challenge. Here is a check list of considerations to raise in evaluating metadata tools:

- How does the tool define metadata—do not be satisfied with the trivial "data about data" definition[8]—but press the vendor for organizing principles. Does the tool have a complete list of the types of metadata handled: DDL, source schemas, copybook specs, spreadsheets, uniform resource locators (URLs), proprietary file formats from third-party tools, scheduling information?

- Does the tool track and retain the history of the data structures? Does it allow versioning and time stamping of the DDL making up the database tables, views, and related structures?

- What mechanisms are available for scanning job control language (JCL) or legacy system source code (COBOL, PL/I, C) and deriving self-describing files or components? Is XML support available?

- How does the tool perform tracking the results of extraction and transformation jobs in detail (time, outcome, disposition), rather like a job-scheduling system, integrated with the source and target environments?

- How does the tool handle data source and target logs, audits, or catalogs — where did the data come from and where is it going; aggregate definitions and modification status and time?

- What are the extent and mechanisms for managing data dictionary type information, including index and key assignments, cross-referencing surrogate keys with production legacy source; valid limits on the contents and values with which data elements can be populated?

- What are the availability and extent of relational database catalog type information—database and table schemas, user security authorization and profiles, index, partitioning, and view definitions, stored in such a way as to be integrated with the scheduling (run-time) and other pragmatic hooks into the implementation environment?

- How does the tool, index, store and retrieve data from its information catalog or repository? Is the information visible, available, by means of a web browser?

- Operationally, what is the amount of data on which the tool has operated, the speed with which it has produced results (in elapsed time and CPU), including its ability to scale from smaller to ever-growing amounts of data?

- What are all the usual parameters about hardware requirements and operating system environment and software compatibility, and are they covered? What are the defined constraints, limitations, and tuning parameters, and how do these compare with the target implementation environment?

- How does the tool describe itself, and where is it located in the general matrix of client-server architecture—front-end presentation, back-end data transformation, middleware navigation (or coordination)?

- What are the in-depth, "down-and-dirty" reports of two or three other customers ("reference sites") who are similar in profile to the target firm and who actually have the tool in production and have been using it for a while?

- What does the tool really mean by "compliance" with standards such as MDIS or MDAPI? What specific tools and versions can interoperate and what are the reference sites performing those operations?

SUMMARY . . . .

In general, metadata map the meanings of data from transactional to data warehouse systems. They trace source to target, through various extraction, transformation, and loading (ETL) operations. Thus metadata make possible the interoperation, the working together, of the heterogeneous systems. In a sense, metadata are metaphors equating things—mapping source to target—that are apparently different between transactional and warehouse systems. When examined in detail, the metadata metaphors give us new ways of perceiving and understanding what we all along had in front of our eyes. The point is made that the way people describe things in language influences our perceptions and constrains our understanding of them. Several famous digital metaphors are examined with a view to understanding how a new technology spawns a new metaphor. The metaphor of data warehousing belongs on this list. Next, semantics is described as the true path to metadata. This includes basic elementary skills like mapping input to output. It extends to advanced design mechanisms such as normalizing and denormalizing data for performance, summarizing and aggregating, navigating, scheduling, managing. If semantics is the path to metadata, then knowledge is the pay-off. Generically metadata encompasses many kinds of knowledge in the strict sense of the word. For example, it is structural knowledge of the most important kind to know that a selected aggregate is sourced from such-and-such a legacy system, since if the legacy system changes, so must the down stream definition of the dependent aggregate. The short working definition of metadata is provided: metadata is an architecture—principles coordinating commitments—or knowledge of the interoperability between (otherwise isolated) systems and subsystems. In being "operationalized" metadata advances from documentation—a useful artifact in any system—to engagement. It is a mechanism that drives processing, and it is useful to define and implement a repository to coordinate the commitments represented by metadata. Metadata standards are discussed, and a generic metadata (vendor) tool checklist is provided. Finally, the metadata "grand challenge" is discussed. The consequences for data warehousing of the metadata grand challenge are considered.

¹ *Personal communication.*

[2] This insight is based on a presentation by Vincent Dupuis, 1997.

[3] A friendly note to the casual reader at this point. If you are not interested in the details of the technology of data normalization and are willing to accept that semantics are the essence in metadata, skipping this section will not interfere with the continuity of the presentation.

[4] For one of the best short discussions of relational data normalization, including fourth- and fifth-normal forms, see Wiorkowski, 1990: Chapter 2. See also www.Gabrielledb2.com for a wealth of additional insights.

[5] Apologies to I. Kant, 1781, from which these two sentences are closely paraphrased. Since Kant would have viewed this distinction as the difference between *a priori* and *a posteriori* knowledge, I may be forgiven for not pursuing it here.

[6] See Ralph Kimball, "Meta Meta Data Data," **DBMS Magazine**, March 1998: 18ff. In my opinion, his approach and that of his few close colleagues is so rich, varied, and useful in practical terms to the consultant that most of it deserves the label *metadata*. See www.rkimball.com.

[7] The Advanced Computing Laboratory (see www.ACL.LANL.GOV) site contains explanations in everyday English of the details and work in progress of these grand challenges—one of the more intriguing things our tax dollars are supporting.

[8] The reader will note that this definition has been rigorously avoided as trivially true and so misleading. It misleads us into thinking that we know what we are talking about when we do not. "Data about data" is still just data. It doesn't make a difference; whereas metadata is an architecture—organizing principles—for knowledge of the interoperability of data between otherwise isolated systems.

14 *Aggregation*

In this chapter...

*"On-line aggregation
results in real-time aggravation."*
Steve Liszewski[1]

ON-LINE AGGREGATION, REAL-TIME AGGRAVATION

Given a thousand products in a large product category times 10 thousand customers over 10 time periods, we are easily in the range of 10 million rows required to satisfy a query with that description. Thinking about this problem resulted in Steve Liszewski's rule of thumb: "On-line aggregation results in real time aggravation." Leaving aside unproductive hair splitting about grammar, whether to send such a query off to a batch process or tie up the work station terminal is a judgment call. It really does seem to invite a batch process, unless one wants an excuse for a large number of coffee breaks. Surely, anything larger than such an elapsed time belongs in batch.

THE MANAGER'S RULE OF THUMB

Thus, the managerial rule of thumb is: Low-level aggregates should receive a response from the data warehousing system in 15 seconds or under; medium-level aggregates in under 2 minutes; more complicated aggregates in under 15 minutes, with the option to wait for an interactive response; anything requiring more elapsed time than that has to go off to a "big batch process" designed to handle it. With that in mind, designing and preparing prebuilt aggregations can be one of the most powerful methods available for improving the end-user's perception of response time.

That is, the query has to go off to a big batch process unless such a batch process has already been executed, registered with the metadata repository, and stored as a permanent summary structure. In this case, reset the stopwatch. The summary is an answer already available. It merely has to be fetched, not accessed and calculated. It is likely to fit in the five-second window. Note, however, that the amount of work to the system to produce the initial aggregate is the same, but it is distributed differently. The work is performed and the result stored prior to the end-user's request, not at the time of it. Thus, the convenience to the end-user is significantly enhanced.

Another item on the "to do" list is designing or purchasing a mechanism to track, register aggregates, and direct the access of the application to the available aggregate. Naturally, if the decision is made to purchase and integrate such a product, the real cost is in evaluating, buying, and integrating the metadata repository or equivalent function. Software must be deployed to track and manage the generation, referencing, and deployment of the set of summaries defined by the firm as belonging to the canon of required aggregates. How does one know what aggregates are required or useful?

A Basic Principle of Computing Is Tested

A basic principle of computing is that nothing should be stored that can be *easily* calculated on the fly. This is and remains a sound principle. Data warehousing tests the "*easily*." The soundness is demonstrated in realizing that a report on sales of all products for all customers for the past three years is a very big calculation—that is, aggregation—and is unlikely to be returned in a timely way to an interactive query with an end-user sitting and waiting at her or his work station. It is the obvious case for preparing a prebuilt aggregation. The issues and controversies arise because many cases are not as clear-cut as is this really large aggregate. The thorny issues arise with all the cases in between the really large aggregate and the individual product-customer-date combination.

A MANAGEMENT CHALLENGE

The solution to the problem of on-line aggregation causing real-time aggravation is actually a management challenge. It is called a SLA. The experiences of working with operational systems of the past 20 years influence the expectations of end-users, regardless of their technical sophistication. Any really thoughtful and useful SLA includes both compromises and stretch goals. The SLA is management's contribution, first line of defense, and method of gaining visibility to the performance of the data warehouse. The SLA will make the difference between being at the mercy of every problem that comes along and being proactive. In turn, the design, implementation, and use of aggregations will be one of management's critical success factors in attaining conformance with the agreed-upon goals. Make no mistake. One does not negotiate with the customer about aggregations. Rather, one uses aggregations "under the covers" as part of a flexible and robust data warehouse architecture to formulate, propose, and live up to service-level commitments made with the customer about using the data warehouse. The efforts required to build, register, and update aggregates define the limits and costs of the technically and operationally feasible. If management knows that, that is knowledge in abundance.

Good or bad performance are relative terms—relative to an SLA. If the SLA specifies that interactive queries can be performed on-line in under 20 seconds 90% of the time when they are at or lower than the brand, region, month level of aggregation, an objective measure of data warehouse performance is laid down. A query of this description that regularly returns a result after two minutes does not conform. Problem solving is required. If there is no SLA, no such thing as good or bad performance can be defined. Of course, common sense or 20 years of on-line experience might dictate that half an hour is too long to wait at a work station for a response. But suppose that the environment is a new application on the Internet using decade-old, overburdened computing resources. Maybe it is the expectation that the application is out of line, not the response time. There is simply no way to tell the difference between poor performance and a misguided expectation without an SLA. Without an SLA, it is the squeaky wheel that gets the oil. Those end-users who are most troublesome—one ought not to say "obnoxious"—get the most attention and do so regardless of business priorities. The result is unintentionally rewarding bad or at least unprofessional behavior—not the right message, in any event. The point for management is that the negotiation and determination of an SLA can be the difference between being proactive and reactive.

A formal SLA must contain information on a host of factors. It often reads like a formal contract. Who are the parties to the agreement—their roles and organizations? What are the relevant assumptions, time periods, and respective duties and obligations? The details of the services to be provided should include language intelligible to the end-user—response time as measured by the end-user at the work station, delivery or availability time of reports or job results. Some way must be found to translate distinctions meaningful to the end-user into those operationally measurable on the computer. As an illustration, see the discussion below about low-level combinations and queries that climb up the dimensional hierarchy. A single product-customer-day query translates into fewer system resources than does a brand-region-month aggregation. The amount of I/O and number of queries, jobs, CPU cycles, processors, servers, and hours of availability can be estimated on a ballpark basis. This list is not complete. Additional complications occur as provisions are made for chargeback, compensation, incentives, or discounts based on exceptions.[2]

A method of monitoring system response and resource usage will also be essential. Tools in client-server environments tend to be less well developed than those for the mainframe, but accommodations can be reached, especially if the database and server functions are well instrumented. Indeed, instrumentation and "hooks" should be a design feature of all applications and packages built or purchased for this very reason. Such tools should be evaluated in terms of their own use of system resources, because they will add work to the system. (You can't observe something without modifying it to a degree.) A mechanism for reporting exceptions—such as opening a ticket at the help desk—should be documented; and a mechanism for resolving disputes—typically, escalation to the responsible executive—should be stated. Conditions under which renegotiating the SLA will occur, termination, and escape clauses should also receive consideration.

The truth is that the computing function is not as simple as a public utility—a dial tone or turn on the switch, and, *voila*, light. The kinds of complex information products delivered by the information technology function are bound to be more varied, intricate, and customized than can be expressed by a single point interface, such as an electrical outlet or a phone jack. Nevertheless, the metaphor of the information utility is a powerful one and can guide many large-scale applications of the data warehouse resource.

The following discussion is intended to give the flavor of what a ballpark calculation preceding a proposed SLA might look like. To do this right, the risk of misunderstanding or disappointing results must be managed by means of a more detailed analysis of hardware, software, capacity, load, and application functionality. (The reader may wish to review the details on throughput, work load, and response time, the determination of which must be part of the SLA, already covered in Chapter Eleven: Data Warehousing Performance.)

Elementary, low-level combinations of simple customer, product, and date data ought to be accessed and returned in about five seconds or less. This allows time for spending a full second in the gateway connecting host and client-server work station, as well as time for the relational database engine and transaction monitor to get a running start if it is the beginning of the work day. Such an SLA concedes that the path through the gateway plus an elapsed time of a second or two in the database, transaction monitor, and network can require a couple of seconds. Aggregates one level up— low- to medium-level aggregates consisting of one product by a group of customers or one customer by a brand (a group of products)—ought to be calculated in about 15 seconds or less.

The next step up is to calculate a group of products by a group of customers— for example, a moderately sized brand of 10 products by a region of 1,000 customers for 12 weeks (a quarter). In terms of rows, that might easily amount to 120,000 (10 x 1,000 x 12). At one millisecond per row—a conservative duration—it could require 120 seconds of I/O alone to answer the query. This is still about two minutes—a reasonable amount of time, in one opinion, because office workers are known to leave voice mail messages of that duration. It's about the maximum amount of time that people feel comfortable waiting for an answer at a work station.

If an estimated two-minute aggregate were required to be returned in under 15 seconds, it would be a good candidate for an aggregate. If a prebuilt aggregate were available, it could be returned much more quickly. The cost—one well worth consideration—is in designing and implementing the infrastructure required to support aggregate navigation, application awareness, and maintenance of the aggregates.

AGGREGATE NAVIGATION

Navigation refers to a method of finding one's way. For even a simple cube with three dimensions, each of which has three levels in its hierarchy, the number of possible combinations grows rapidly (see Table 14.1) and shows all possible combinations of product, customer, and time period, assuming three levels in each hierarchy—27 to be exact. All except the very last item in the list—product, customer, day—requires aggregation of detailed rows. Any row with brand or category aggregates in the product dimension involves aggregation, because brands contain multiple products, and categories contain multiple brands. Any row with region or area aggregates in the customer dimension involves aggregation because, under this interpretation, regions contain multiple customers, and areas contain multiple regions. Any row with week or month contains an aggregation in the time dimension and involves aggregation, because weeks contain multiple days, and months contain multiple weeks.

Now, it is easy to imagine the difficulty of tracking this information manually. Let's suppose that any combination with an elementary product, customer, or day in it would be low enough level to be calculated interactively within a reasonable expectation of getting an answer, either within two minutes or at least by the end of a short coffee break. That leaves the other eight combinations as good candidates for the calculation of aggregates in advance. Further, suppose that experience showed that only four of those were ever really used or needed. That leaves only four aggregates to track. This is not many. Still, many things can go wrong. Many points of failure exist. Is the aggregate on the list of those to be calculated in advance? The end-user has requested category-area-month, but brand-area-week is the one for which they submit SQL. Do we give them both? Do we swap one in for the other? Should such an action be visible to them (the end-user) or require a change in their behavior and interaction with the system? Is the aggregate ready, based on a refresh of the latest detailed data or is the aggregate still being calculated, based on the latest detailed data, which is available? In other words, do the detail and the aggregation "line up"?

All of these questions can become issues, whether the number of combinations is 27, 2,700, or 27,000. If we really had to do so, a sufficiently well-organized human might track and resolve these questions for 27 combinations. However, it is not the kind of thing a person could reasonably be expected to do for 2,700. It would take too long, be the source of too many human errors, and not, in general, be a smart use of the available resource.

However, what if we encoded the possible combinations and inserted them in a relational table with additional attributes? These attributes would include whether the aggregate was available at all, whether it was current (time stamp), and other identifying characteristics. Note that this would not be a large relational table, under any interpretation, even if it were several thousand rows in size. Two additional degrees of automation would then be "enabled" as part of an "aggregate navigator."

Table 14.1: All Possible Combinations of Three Three-Place Hierarchies Resulting in Distinct Aggregates

What Hierarchy?
Category
Brand
Product

Who Hierarchy?
Area
Region
Customer

When Hierarchy?
Month
Week
Day

All Possible Combinations of Three Three-Place Hierarchical Elements Resulting in Aggregates

Category	Area	Month *
Category	Area	Week *
Category	Area	Day
Category	Region	Month *
Category	Region	Week *
Category	Region	Day
Category	Customer	Month
Category	Customer	Week
Category	Customer	Day
Brand	Area	Month *
Brand	Area	Week *
Brand	Area	Day
Brand	Region	Month *
Brand	Region	Week *

(Continued)

Table 14.1:   (Continued)

All Possible Combinations of Three Three-Place Hierarchical Elements Resulting in Aggregates

Brand	Region	Day
Brand	Customer	Month
Brand	Customer	Week
Brand	Customer	Day
Product	Area	Month
Product	Area	Week
Product	Area	Day
Product	Region	Month
Product	Region	Week
Product	Region	Day
Product	Customer	Month
Product	Customer	Week
Product	Customer	Day

First, when a piece of SQL was about to be submitted, a prior lookup in the aggregate master table would occur. If the aggregate were already available, it would be used immediately to return the result; otherwise, the SQL submission would proceed transparently, performing the calculation. This would require "discipline" in the design and development of the interface to the data warehouse. This would include a consistent, precise, and agreed-upon encoding of abbreviations of levels in hierarchies—things such as "PR" for "product," "BR" for "brand," "CA" for "category," "CU" for "customer," etc. This encoding would enable the aggregate calculation or lookup to become encapsulated functionality, which would perform transparently and seamlessly, regardless of whether a calculation or an aggregate lookup was occurring.

Second, when aggregates were built (prebuilt), the successful completion of the process would be "posted" to the aggregate master as "available" for downstream inquiry processes. In addition, if an aggregate were being built for the first time ever, a mechanism would be invoked to update or add an entry to the aggregate master that such-and-such a combination was now available as an aggregate. This is perhaps not a trivial exercise to get right the first time. However, it is the kind of thing at which software and computers are known to excel. As an idea, aggregate navigation does not need to be complicated. The above discussion has provided a narrative corresponding to a design.

It must be acknowledged that the approach outlined here and above is not the only possible approach. Other approaches are available. For example, a complete list of fact tables could be constructed, including aggregate fact tables, that line up with their corresponding detailed table as to data type, columns, and access column types. The submitted SQL is then parsed, and a lookup occurs against the list of fact tables, such as might already be stored in a relational catalog. If the tables are ordered from high level to more detailed aggregates, the first hit is the most general and efficient candidate. This has the advantage of requiring less of the above-cited "discipline" in checking an aggregate master structure. It also means that the SQL cannot be statically bound in advance and, indeed, will have to be rewritten on the fly.

Ultimately, aggregate navigator design mechanisms (and leading products that incorporate them) may be a footnote to a more general solution. It is a feature of the history of technology that specific "best of breed" products roll out such features as aggregate navigators, star join indexes, or parallel join options three to five years ahead of their incorporation into mainstream database vendor products.[3] This is likely to be the case with aggregate navigation, as well. Here, the general solution is an "aggregate aware" Optimizer. Here, the mechanism works something like using DDL to create a view corresponding to the aggregate. This act of issuing a Create, in effect, registers the summary or global table with the RDBMS catalog as a virtual but stable artifact. The Optimizer is then able automatically to apply the aggregate thus stored as it decides on the query access method. Like a view, the aggregate is materialized and cached at execution time and made available to the query. The query rewrite is handled by the Optimizer, not by the developer. This approach is then enhanced by aggregate "wizards" or "assistants," who offer recommendations on aggregates most likely to enhance ("optimize") processing.

INFORMATION DENSITY

Information density is based on the intuition that an aggregate—for example, of brand, region, and month—is more compact in terms of the information it summarizes than any individual detail included within the aggregate. It is the relation between the many details that enriches the aggregate's information density. It is the structure of the hierarchy itself that makes the difference in organizing the details into the aggregate. So, as used here, *density* is really a synonym for *organized* or *structured*.

Figure 14.1 shows different aspects of the information density hierarchy. Imagine that the figure in the diagram is a pyramid being viewed from above. Thus, at the pinnacle of the pyramid is a platform, on which are located such informationally dense features as connectedness, predictability, compactness, and structure. At the base of the pyramid—that is, at the bottom of the hierarchy—are the informationally diffuse features indicated as unpredictable (random), disconnected, or unstructured.

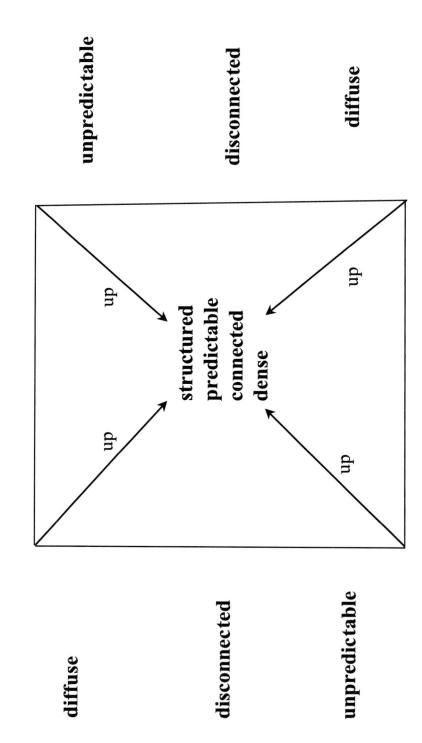

Figure 14:1:
Information Density Hierarchy

An example of connectedness providing information density includes the ability to navigate from aggregate to detail. The ability to drill down from aggregate into details is a kind of connection that makes for increased informational density. The ability to predict the behavior of a dependent variable from the state of an independent variable is yet another example of information density. If a person is a dog owner and we know that dog owners are more loyal than cat owners, we have a basis to predicate whether or not dog owners will continue to remain customers or jump to the competition. Compactness is exemplified by the instance of summarizing details into aggregates. Examples of unstructured information includes free-form text or images in the form of BLOBs. These require special-purpose functions (and extra computing resources) to surface the complex structures that really are present in them but hidden. It is not that there is no structure in unstructured data, but that it is not a structure that can be captured by such elementary data types as integer, character, or date. What seemed unintelligibly chaotic really turns out to be a structure, highly complex until the right pattern is overlaid to reveal that it is actually simple—not a BLOB (for example), but a picture of a face. Thus, in this particular case, the semantic distinction of complex/simple falls completely on the structured side of the structured/unstructured distinction. This is also true of several other indexes of information density.

The point to note is that all of these semantic distinctions—compact and diffuse, abstract and concrete, broad (extensive) and narrow—are on the organized and structured side of the elliptical boundary, as depicted in Figure 14.2: Information Density Semantics. How can this be? The answer is provided by the structure of hierarchy itself, as we will now see.

The Magic Number Seven

In a celebrated article, "The Magic Number Seven Plus or Minus Two," George Miller (1956) speculates that the number seven is considered lucky and occurs frequently in literature and folk tales because our short-term memory is able to retain about seven pieces of information. There is experimental evidence to support this hypothesis, but the really interesting thing is that we can return seven "chunks" of information, regardless of the level in the hierarchy of categories at which we find ourselves. So, for example, we could remember seven detail records at the customer-product-day level or we could equally easily remember seven aggregate records at the area-brand-month level in the hierarchy. However, the latter provides the individual with a far greater information density. This is not to imply a value judgment as to which is better, but it does imply that sheer quantity is orthogonal to information density. As the aggregates climb the dimensional hierarchy, the aggregates are indeed denser, even though the many details that they summarize are very sparse, when examined up close. This conclusion underscores the often made observation that the size of the data warehousing system is not the proper focus, although some companies seem to brag about the challenges of managing shear bulk. What makes the difference is not size, but rather information density. Anecdotal evidence is available that the same rule applies to the number of data warehousing dimensions that can be cached in the mind of the end-user. Of course, we build automated systems to be able to extend our capabilities.

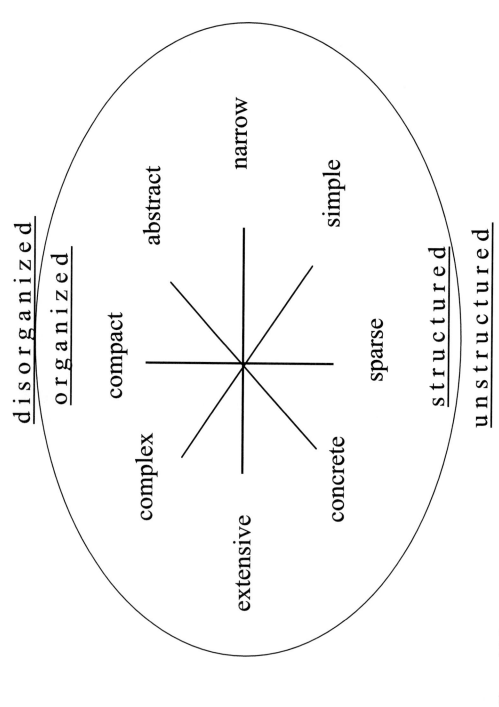

Figure 14:2:
Information Density Semantics

This common-sense intuition is independent of the mathematical formalism used to define information based on the naturally occurring logarithm. However, completeness at least requires mention of the formal way that a single distinction—yes or no—can be represented by the formula $\log^2(2) = 1$ (one bit). As indicated, the formula that measures the possible states of information or, more properly speaking, confusion, is the logarithm, which, in our example of yes or no, yields one bit. That is, one bit presents us with a two-way possibility as to its (the bit's) state. If we do not know what state it is in, a certain disorder or lack of organization is indicated. So what actually gets defined formally is not information but negative information. (The formal name for that is *entropy*.)

This leads us to the another famous example of information density along with aggregation—making a decision whether to go left or right down the fork in the path. When a constraint such as GO LEFT = YES is applied to that distinction of state so that it is determined, we have information in the positive sense. Knowing to go left is informationally richer than knowing to go either left or right. The latter requires a constraint such as GO LEFT = YES to get beyond triviality. However, to get back behind the formalism to a real decision requires an alignment with the environment. We know whether to take the left fork in the path rather than the right one *because* that is the direction to get to Grandma's house. Thus, this result and its representation, according to our simple supply chain model—in this case, to deliver a grocery basket to Grandma—is a part of information semantics, not mathematics. There is no room for dispute that the mathematics of information theory are important, but the semantics of how the system aligns with the world is important, too. This has some interesting consequences. The provider of the information pipeline (the logarithmic function, in our case) is driven down to being a commodity provider, relative to whoever knows what the customer is buying (or taking delivery of) and when (see also Penzias, 1998). The latter requires alignment, and that means the introduction of the semantic distinctions as sketched in Figure 14.2. Notice also that what emerges once again is a form of the one fundamental question that the data warehouse is designed to raise and answer.

CANONICAL AGGREGATES

These canonical aggregates are the ones that will govern the questions that get answered on a frequent basis and in a timely way. Naturally, some queries and their aggregates are more important than others. This example (Figure 14.3: Decide on Canonical Aggregates) suggests that national-brand, regional-category, and national-product combinations are the most critical for this company's purposes. Often, the aggregates will be what can usefully be built on-line in a 15-second, a 2-minute, or a 15-minute window. Other aggregates have to be taken into a big batch build process on an overnight basis to be prepared in advance.

How can management tell which aggregates are to be given the status and dignity of belonging to the canonical set of summaries to be added to the metadata repository and made subtext, supporting the governing SLA? An overlapping, interacting set of answers is available. First of all, listen to the business experts—what information do the so-called super-users require to get the knowledge they require to make decisions? Of one hundred or more possible aggregates—brand by region by week, customer by product by quarter, category by market by year—is there a select subset (for example, 20%) that comes up most of the time (for example, 80%)? If so, the solution is at hand. Use these to start. Likewise, ask the customer, and do so in a formal, documented way, perhaps as part of joint application development (JAD) sessions or other suitably ceremonial design session. In addition, if no one really knows what you've got or it turns out that the reports are questionable, sample the raw transactional data and find out what is available. Failing that, it is back to the college of hard knocks—trial and error. Offer to start by implementing what seem to be useful aggregates, according to the best available guess or estimate. The key word here is *useful*. Because meaning is often in the mind of the end-user, what seems useful to the information technology function may be more or less useful to the customer. Still, it is a place from which to start and iterate. Finally, the limits of technology imply what kinds of aggregates can be performed interactively and on the fly, and which ones have to be prepared in advance, calculated in batch, registered in metadata, and stored for later access.

Electing to promote and implement another aggregate as a predefined summary, rather than an on-the-fly calculation is rather like determining whether or not to add another index to a table. The trade-offs are similar. The extra work of building and maintaining it is rewarded with improved performance in accessing the data. Indeed, aggregates function similarly to indexes—even though they are separate structures that might have indexes of their own—because they summarize corresponding and underlying detail.

What is the definitive set of canonical aggregates is subject to development and change over time. Because the questions of significance to the business are likely to be the subject of evolution, a process is needed to add or remove aggregates from the canon. This might look like a formal request from the end-user to the information

	National	Area	Region	District	Zone	MicroZone
Category			X			
Group						
Brand	X			X		
SubBrand						
Product	X					

Figure 14:3:
Decide on Canonical Aggregates

technology function. More proactive, however, would be a process whereby IT becomes aware of a long-running query through the mechanism of ongoing monitoring and tuning. Having thus percolated into awareness, the offer might be forthcoming from IT to promote the query to the status of an aggregate registered in the metadata repository. The front-end tools with which the end-user directly works would be made aggregate aware and would pull down the now or subsequently available aggregate, rather than launching the accumulation process to sum the details interactively. The connection between aggregations and OLAP is a direct one. It is to that discussion that we turn in Chapter Fifteen: OLAP Technologies.

SUMMARY . . . .

The aggregation of detailed transactional data into summaries based on dimensional hierarchies is one of the best ways of improving data warehousing business results, operations, and performance across the board. However, how does one know what to aggregate and what to leave as detail? A useful rule of thumb is cited for determining what to aggregate and what to leave alone. Naturally, the operation and successful implementation of such a rule is determined by system capacity and performance. However, it is also determined by the Service Level Agreement (SLA), within which satisfactory performance is defined. How specific canonical aggregates can be identified and promoted as the result of an SLA is exemplified in the discussion. Aggregate navigation is defined, described, and an outline of one possible design of an aggregate navigator is provided. Next, information density is discussed. It is based on the intuition that an aggregate—say of brand, region, month—is more compact in terms of the information it summarizes than any individual detail included within the aggregate. It is the relations between the many details that enriches the aggregate's information density. It is the structure of the hierarchy itself that makes the difference in organizing the details into the aggregate. "Density" is really a synonym for "organized" or "structured." Finally, canonical aggregates are the ones that will govern the questions that get answered on a frequent basis and in a timely way. Naturally, some queries and their aggregates are more important than others. Often the aggregates that are candidates to be build on-line (interactively) will be partitioned into what can usefully be constructed in a 15-second window, a two-minute window, or a fifteen-minute window. Depending on the SLA, the latter may have to be taken into batch. Other aggregates longer than these certainly have to be taken into a big batch build process in a long-running overnight job in order to be prepared in advance.

[1] *Personal communication.*

[2] Further particulars on SLAs and the management of them are to be found in Loosley and Douglas (1998) and Inmon, Rudin, Buss, and Sousa (1999).

[3] Please let me express my appreciation to Murray Pratt, Kraft, Inc., Northfield, Illinois, for pointing out this trend to me *(personal communication).*

Part 4

Applications and Speculations

(Chapters 15 through 19)

The desktop application is where the results of the information supply chain show up and bear fruit. The distinctions between desktop OLAP, server OLAP, and relational OLAP applications are discussed. OLAP system structures include cubes, hypercubes, and multicubes, which are defined and discussed. The business case for the convergence of data warehousing and the Web lies in improved work flow, alignment of information sharing commitments, and management coordination. Several varieties of knowledge are made possible by the use of the applications built on data warehousing systems—superior knowledge of customer behavior, opportunities for brand development, etc. All of these are augmented by the Web in terms of rapid response, extent and depth of business relationship, and integration of heterogeneous sources of information. The Web as a delivery system makes the Internet itself, including intra- and extranets, into a killer application, one that redefines the limits of what is possible. Key Internet technologies are reviewed in detail. No matter what the front-end application—whether Java enhanced HTML, Active-X, components of Delphi, Power Builder, Visual Basic or one of their derivatives—*they are all chasing data*. Prediction is an uncertain undertaking. Still, it is a good bet that the grand paradigms and theories of today will become the special cases of tomorrow. The conclusion attempts to extrapolate current trends as well as get a glimpse of the sources of discontinuous changes. Speculative ideas are offered about agent technology, the Web, and the future of data warehousing.

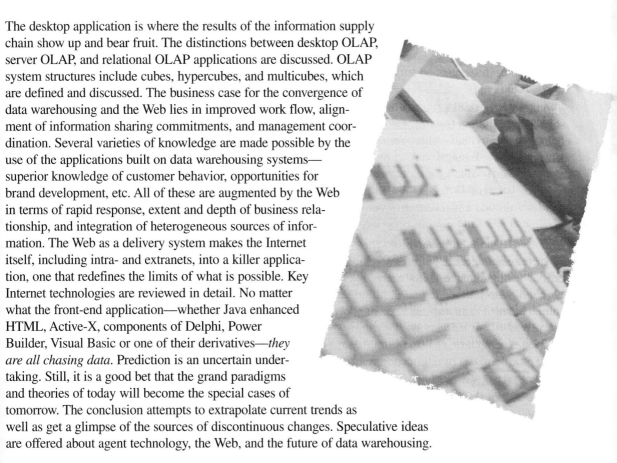

15 *OLAP Technologies*

In this chapter...

*"There is a lot of overlap between
typical descriptions of OLAP
and of data warehousing. . . .
However, there are some genuinely
complementary differences."*
Erik Thomsen[1]

OLAP ARCHITECTURE

On-line analytic processing shifts architectural accountability in the direction of the desktop, where a rich set of functions are applied to the data there. Often, before being sliced and diced by these analytic functions, the desktop data arrives by way of the information supply chain through a middle-tier OLAP server, having been aggregated or otherwise "cubed" there.[2]

A discussion of OLAP architecture encounters many principles, such as those applied in our discussions of data warehousing. The definitions of hierarchical dimensions, granularity of quantitative data, sparsity, aggregations, and cubes belong at the top of the list. Though a difference in emphasis is to be found, the principles worked out in the context of data warehousing are still valid in engaging OLAP technologies. The good work we have already completed on a model of technology enables us to better understand the dynamics of OLAP and data warehousing. Naturally, both OLAP and data warehousing fall on the decision support side of the distinction between transactional and decision support systems. Like most technologies, they are driving in the direction of open standards, interfaces, and accessibility through a commodity $99 front-end desktop product. In fact, these two complementary technologies are driving to embrace one another like converging streams flowing rapidly together under the mutual influence of one another.[3] This is because the principles that each brings to the table—in short, rigorous analysis of consistent data dimensions—are both required to generate enterprise knowledge in the full sense. How so? Let's take a step back to see.

One of logical sources of OLAP is dissatisfaction with the few built-in functions provided by relational SQL. Without enhancements, SQL cannot express many common-sense questions required by business analysts, including cross-category groupings: Compare this quarter's sales in the Midwest region to that in the Eastern region for the same period. Until recently, SQL did not even allow both a column summation, along with a running or cumulative total. What are weekly sales by product, along with weekly year-to-date figures (though that is now supported in the latest versions)? The idea of built-in functions is great, according to the proponents of OLAP. Now let's do it right. Now let's have real additional functionality—rank ordering, average by time period, category as a percentage of total. For example, show sales by product, along with the percentage of total sales by means of a ratio-to-total function. The way in which spreadsheet tools provide thirty or more built-in functions is a real inspiration to the OLAP end-users and vendors. However, let's dispense with the limitations of calculating in cells, as in spreadsheets. The basic principle motivating the expansion of OLAP is functionality.

Meanwhile, the name *OLAP* itself makes a performance promise—in plain English, *on-line* promises a prompt response time. Naturally, limitations of memory cache on the desktop and the combinatorial intensity of building intersecting data dimensions drives this vision in the direction of deploying a powerful server to provide predefined cubes as the target of subsequent analysis. Always close at hand is the problem of dealing with combinatorial explosion—the thousand customers by thousand products by thousand dates is a billion rows. So, of course, is the consideration that not every customer buys every product every day. The data is "sparse"—not all of these combinations are instantiated. OLAP needs to be clever about the ways in which data is stored and accessed, including managing sparsity. Specialized data structures using array technology and data compression are deployed and are able to optimize the storage of sparse data. Thus, the multidimensional database on the OLAP server was born. Combined with the commitment to desktop analysis, the outcome is the resulting principle so characteristic of OLAP—the tight coupling of data and presentation.

Multidimensional OLAP databases (MOLAP) are proprietary implementations of data cube array and manipulation technology on the server. Relational OLAP (ROLAP) makes use of standard databases from Oracle, IBM, Informix (and Red Brick), Sybase, Teradata, Tandem, MS SQL Server, etc. but provides a decisions support server from which multi-pass special SQL functions are launched and the results captured. Furthermore, on the MOLAP side of the fence, the distinction is usually made between desktop OLAP—minicubes on the desktop—and server OLAP using proprietary multi-dimensional databases (MDDB). The latter are usually reserved for power users whereas OLAP desktops are widely distributed to all end-users. Just for the sake of examples, desktop OLAP is represented by such vendors as Business Objects, Brio, and Cognos; whereas the best known OLAP servers include Hyperion's Essbase and Oracle's Express. Both are in the path of Microsoft's Open Information Model (OIM) initiatives.

Microsoft (MS) OLE/DB for OLAP Services (formerly code-named Plato) targets server side OLAP. Meanwhile, Microsoft's PivotTable Services will become a part of MS Excel in Window's 2000 and targets the desktop OLAP vendors. In a bold statement of the obvious, the impact of putting 60 million copies of PivotTable Services into the market is to make such terms as "decision support" and "data warehousing" into household words. It is worth noting that SQL Server is not a requirement for OLAP Services, which can use any ODBC (OLE/DB) database. However, precomputed aggregates can only be stored in proprietary (MOLAP) form in MS SQL Server. The gotcha is the requirement for PivotTable Services to execute on NT. However, it is unlikely that customers will be charging off to implement the initial release of MS OLAP Services into production. Security is available only at the cube, not at the cell or dimensional level. However, as is so often the case with Microsoft, the initial version of the product is a contender, and the follow on versions have the capacity to transform the market. In any case, systems larger than 20 -30 gigabytes will continue to require a significant system design and integration effort using mainstream relational databases such as Oracle, DB2, Sybase, or Informix at least for the duration of the first edition of this book. The impact of Microsoft's OLE/DB for OLAP Services will tend to make small and medium sized data warehousing initiatives into a commodity. Larger multi-system coordination will continue to require complex development efforts. Such efforts put a premium on project management competencies that cannot be encompassed in a cook book, staffing acquisition and development skills, and business leadership in a cross-functional context.

In their current implementations, ROLAP tools have been popularized by such companies as MicroStrategy, Information Advantage, and MetaCube. The latter has been acquired by Informix, and Information Advantage has incorporated its DecisionSuite product into its business intelligence portal (more about that in the next chapter in the section on business intelligence portals). As an example, let us consider MicroStrategy's approach. From a technical perspective, the SQL generated by their DSS Agent and Server is "multi-pass SQL." That is, the decision support server engine simulates such spreadsheetlike functions as rank ordering, roll up, and period average (etc.) by making multiple passes of the data and storing intermediate results in temporary tables created under the covers and on the fly. Naturally, this requires careful planning, prediction, monitoring, and management, since temporary tables can rapidly multiply and bring system performance to a dramatic halt. However, it is precisely the nature of the ad hoc query environment to undercut planning and prediction. That is the dilemma. And that is the reason vanilla database vendors such as Oracle and DB2 are providing more built-in SQL functions. (Note that the Web sites for the vendors mentioned in this section as well many more not mentioned can be found at Larry Greenfield's celebrated data warehousing Web site http://pwp.starnetinc/larryg/index.html. It seems the entire industry owes Larry a debt of gratitude for assembling an impressive product catalog and information repository.)

The imperative to deliver fast results from the OLAP-enabled desktop has led to compromises by the developers of products—it always does. However, not all of the compromises have resulted in the hoped-for engineering solutions. In particular, the trade-offs between efficiencies in data presentation and preparation has occasioned tough choices. The OLAP tool's mastery of the data preparation drill has suffered for a variety of reasons, most of which have nothing to do with the strengths and limitations of OLAP itself. The limitations get charged to OLAP, nonetheless. In many real-world situations, OLAP has flourished in splendid isolation because, for example, the enterprise data center has been engaged with other urgent priorities relating to transactional systems and operations. The data center has been engaged with other priorities relating to data warehousing. As usual, the urgent has driven out the important. A leadership vacuum has allowed technology enthusiasts at the department level to lead the way. However, just as often, the OLAP data preparation process is either abdicated or delegated in a haphazard, opportunistic way, dependent as it is on departmental (not enterprise) initiative. The results are no less powerful when they work, but visibility to the enterprise is missing. Of course, the proponents of OLAP would likely point out that waiting on conformed enterprise data is inconsistent with the speed of business at which we operate today. (They properly emphasize the part about the "on-line" promise.) However, that is no longer a valid excuse when consistent enterprise data is available, admittedly after too long a wait. The pioneers are the ones with the arrows in their backs, one of the arrows bearing the marking *rework* is about to be unleashed. Hence, the next trade-off: quick results versus scalable and durable ones. This requires a delicate balancing act, rather than quick answers.

Indeed, a noteworthy observation is that SQL vendors are providing more and more built-in functions with every new database product release. In addition, user-defined functions are a gesture in the direction of creating a cottage industry in providing such functionality by rallying third-party vendors to the task. This is happening under the marketing pressure and influence of both end-users and OLAP vendors. Meanwhile, OLAP vendors are providing additional features that provide "reach through" and "links" to underlying, back-end relational database systems. This has resulted in blurring the distinction between different classes of tools. Multidimensional OLAP databases (MOLAP) and relational OLAP (ROLAP) ones are both on the radar. The distinction between MOLAP and ROLAP is eroded, while bringing into focus the goal of product convergence in the interest of enterprise knowledge. [4] Although emphasizing different environments—the data center versus the information center—data warehousing and OLAP are mutually influencing one another in the direction of convergence. Consider the following.

There is much more to data warehousing than scrubbing and aggregating data, but the point is that data warehousing is serious about its data preparation. Likewise, there is much more to OLAP than clever desktop functionality in slicing and dicing data. However, under any interpretation, OLAP is serious about its data analysis. These are complementary core capabilities. They complete one another. The truth is that both are required to generate knowledge in the full sense. On the one hand, those who say, "Getting the data is an IT department issue," or, on the other hand, "Here's the data, what you do with it is your problem" are both short-sighted. Data preparation requires visibility to what questions are to be answered by means of it (the data), and the plan to formulate and answer questions is bound to reach back into the sources of the data and influence its capture and formation. Both are required to generate knowledge that is actionable in the service of realizing basic business imperatives. (See Figure 15.1: OLAP and Data Warehousing Mutual Influence.)

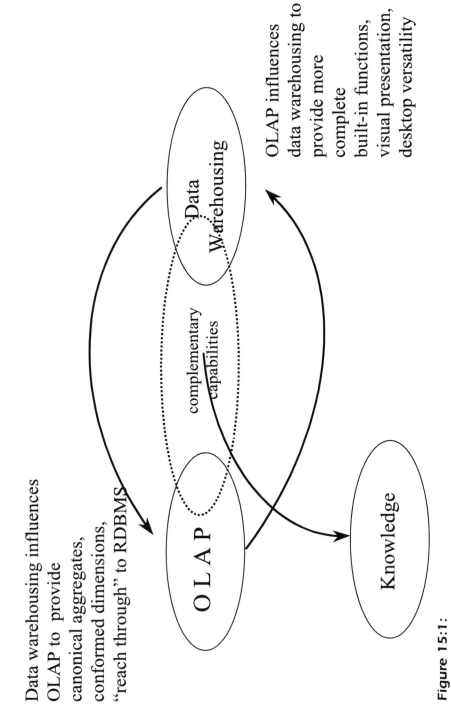

Data warehousing influences OLAP to provide canonical aggregates, conformed dimensions, "reach through" to RDBMS

complementary capabilities

Data Warehousing

OLAP influences data warehousing to provide more complete built-in functions, visual presentation, desktop versatility

O L A P

Knowledge

Figure 15:1:
OLAP and Data Warehousing Mutual Influence

CUBES, HYPERCUBES, AND MULTICUBES

Much ink has been spilt over our human ability to depict three dimensions visually. More will be spilt here. The issue is that many data cubes are the intersection of and combine four or more dimensions. (The reader may wish to review Figure 1.9: The Data Cube, and Figure 1.7: The Star Schema, at this point if he or she does not remember them or is not reading this text in sequential order.) Visual presentation is a powerful aid to understanding. However, we are up against a limitations hardwired into the human biocomputer. It's just that we relate to everyday things in three-dimensional space and in a time sequence "flowing" irreversibly (for business purposes) from future to past. Visual presentation of more than three dimensions as a spatial cube must employ a workaround. Multiple dimensions are assigned to the x-axis, and the other two dimensions, in one approach, are assigned to the y- and z-axis. This leads to the OLAP distinction between a cube and a hypercube, the latter being reserved for cubes of more than three dimensions. (A "multicube" is a cube or hypercube formed by joining two or more (hyper)cubes along a common, shared data element from one of their dimensional hierarchies.) A multidimensional database (MDDB) is the collection of aggregations as cubes, hypercubes, or multicubes, as constructed by the OLAP server in its (the database's) own vendor- or tool-specific data format and stored for subsequent OLAP processing. Without a doubt, visual presentation is an aid to understanding, but so is logic.

In fact, cubes of more than three dimensions are easily presented as a logical association in the form of a table. For example, Table 15.1 shows a table of four dimensions. Here, each of the basic dimensions—customer, product, date (time), and promotion are presented in skeletal form without their other data elements. All possible combinations are necessarily generated by a full Cartesian product (see Figure 8.8: Data Manipulation Language, for an example of Cartesian product). Also worthy of note is the way that the star schema itself is a "hypercube" of more than three dimensions (Figure 1.7). Of course, what is hard (impossible) to do is to put this into a three-dimensional picture.

Many OLAP aggregation engines are good at dealing with data sparsity, but so are relational databases, in which the fact structures are reasonably well normalized. Sparsity is the condition whereby not all possible customer-product-date combinations are instantiated. That is, most customers do not buy every product, every day. Normalized relational joins are a direct and powerful method of dealing with sparsity. The way that normalized relational joins work is simple and elegant from the point of view of handling sparsity. If a particular combination of dimensions is not exemplified, it does not occur in the table. For example, if customer 444555666 never buys product 999888777, the row *does not occur at all*. It simply isn't there, period. You can't get any more economical than that. There is not even any data to compress. All of the customer-product-date-promotion instances in Table 15.1 are examples of customers who have made purchases of those products on those dates while the indicated

Table 15.1:   Depicting More Than Three Dimensions

Customer Id
111222333
444555666
777888999

Product Id
333222111
666444555
999888777

Date Id
1999-01-31
1999-02-28
1999-03-31

Promotion Id
AAA
BBB
CCC

Customer Id	Product Id	Data Id	Promotion Id	Other Data
111222333	333222111	1999-01-31	AAA	. . .
111222333	333222111	1999-01-31	BBB	
111222333	333222111	1999-01-31	CCC	
111222333	333222111	1999-02-28	AAA	
111222333	333222111	1999-02-28	BBB	
111222333	333222111	1999-02-28	CCC	
111222333	333222111	1999-03-31	AAA	

(Continued)

Table 15.1: (Continued)

Customer Id	Product Id	Data Id	Promotion Id	Other Data
111222333	333222111	1999-03-31	BBB	...
111222333	333222111	1999-03-31	CCC	
111222333	666555444	1999-01-31	AAA	
111222333	666555444	1999-01-31	BBB	
111222333	666555444	1999-01-31	CCC	
111222333	666555444	1999-02-28	AAA	
111222333	666555444	1999-02-28	BBB	
111222333	666555444	1999-02-28	CCC	
• • •				
777888999	999888777	1999-03-31	AAA	
777888999	999888777	1999-03-31	BBB	
777888999	999888777	1999-03-31	CCC	

promotions were in effect. In the real world of consumer behavior, the data will be much sparser than that. Many of these combinations will not occur, nor will they be presented as rows in the table. If the OLAP engine is using a special proprietary data structure that necessarily represents all possible combinations, additional work will be incurred, compressing or performing "sparse data management," according to that proprietary algorithm. Finally, note that examples are available where relational data stores benefit from denormalizing and presenting all possible transaction time periods for a given product-customer transaction.

In either case—multidimensional or relational data—this is neither good nor bad, in itself. Rather, the point is to provide insight into the underlying mechanisms that sometimes result in claims and counter-claims getting so entangled. The trade-off is between the set of rich and powerful analytic functions and the underlying proprietary arrays or denormalized data that sometimes require a placeholder for otherwise sparse logical combinations.

OLAP FEATURES

Like data warehousing, OLAP has a long and distinguished history. At about the same time in 1993 that Bill Inmon was inventing and popularizing the very term *data warehouse*, E.F. Codd of relational database definition fame coined the term *OLAP* as part of work performed under contract for Essbase. Codd was aiming at doing for OLAP what he had done for relational technology. He proposed 12 principles, since expanded to 18 features, by which to define authentic OLAP. These principles were to be guiding rules at which the technology should aim and by which vendor products could be evaluated. In that regard, the aim has fallen somewhat short of the lofty mark. Even before Codd, the roots of OLAP can be found in a product called *Express*, developed in the 1970s at Management Decision Systems, ultimately acquired by Oracle, and rewritten multiple times.[5] The proprietary Metaphor computer, basically a server with relational-database-like capabilities plus hardware, was launched in 1983. Although mainly an approach to multidimensional relational data warehousing, the importance of the user interface was appreciated by its developers, as alumni of Xerox PARC, where the GUI was prototyped as part of the Star Workstation. In many ways, OLAP is still emerging from its cocoon of proprietary products, where many technical innovations first hit the market before finding the path of a science of open standards and interfaces.

The goal in reviewing Dr. Codd's 18 features is to deepen our understanding of what OLAP is, where it is going, and why it lies on the critical path of the essential guide to data warehousing. In fact, a careful reading of Codd's features indicates that the roots of and requirements to qualify as OLAP are grounded firmly in the relational perspective. As originally proposed, these rules were meant as defining characteristics against which to evaluate OLAP products (especially Essbase). In fact, some features end up describing essential minimal characteristics (EMCs) of any OLAP tool. Others end up describing EMCs from a relational perspective, rather than a desktop one. Others present EMC that has never been realized in any tool. Still others are "nice to have." Although Dr. Codd took some "heat" over how closely to his criteria the Essbase product fit, an even more interesting thing is to consider how close is the fit to a relational database, as such, and how close is the fit to the relational database when extenders of the kind provided by a so-called UDB are included. Although unlikely that the latter was explicitly visible to anyone outside a research lab in 1993, a case can be made that a technological convergence was operating, quite independently of who said what or when it was published. Finally, a couple are reasonably described as "grand challenge" goals. They would be a breakthrough, redefining what is possible but, realistically, they will not happen without a major combined industry research effort.

The first feature of a "multidimensional conceptual view" says, in effect, to line up the structure of the technology with that of the business. This is a recurring theme throughout this book (see, in particular, the discussion on building unified representations of the customer and product)—line up the structures of the technology with those of the business. The work of Ralph Kimball (and others, see Kimball, 1995; Hackney, 1997; Yazdani, 1998; Zagelow, 1998) demonstrates that the multidimensional and relational approaches are not only consistent but arguably substitutable for one another. If this is made an EMC, the initiatives that are at risk of not making it "over the bar" are the departmental ones. Everyone is likely to agree that this is nice to have. The trade-off—as usual—is between comprehensive, consistent results and timely ones.

The second feature of "intuitive data manipulation" calls for making use of the power of the GUI. Drilling down by double clicking on data, "drag and drop," and other pointing device (mouse) features are now taken for granted by both end-users and product vendors. However, recall this was a major breakthrough in 1993 when client-server had the "buzz." It is now an EMC and not just of OLAP tools.

The third feature of "accessibility" indicates that OLAP-like data warehousing and relational technology at large have the goal of presenting data every which way. This sounds like the useful requirement from Kimball of constructing "conforming dimensions" by analogy with a commonly shared enterprise "data bus," analogous to the computing bus connecting hardware components. The goal of presenting a single logical view of data from various sources is essential to enterprise computing. Again, however, if this is made an EMC, MOLAP seems at a disadvantage over ROLAP and HOLAP. As usual, departmental OLAP initiatives do not make it over the bar.

The fourth feature of "batch extract versus interpretative" is actually realized by those hybrid tools that allow storing multidimensional cubes on an OLAP engine or server, as well as "active reach-through" to underlying relational data. For a relational expert, this is an EMC.

The fifth feature of "OLAP analysis models" captures at a high level the kinds of analyses that OLAP supports. Codd has a field day with terminology, including: *categorical* as descriptive static reporting; *exegetical* as interpretive and, hence, explanatory; *contemplative* as entailing hypothetical, conditional "if" analysis; and *formulaic* as the navel into the unknown. Dr. Codd would regard this as an EMC, though it is an issue if anyone else really has a consistent interpretation of the distinctions here.

The sixth feature of "client-server" states that not only should OLAP be implemented by distinguishing client and server, but these two components should be "loosely coupled" so that different clients can hook up to different servers. This would be furthered by the OLAP Council's API if it succeeds in attaining widespread implementation by vendors.[6] This kind of call for standardization or "openness" might also be furthered by Web-based clients, because the Internet browser is a candidate for universal client.

The seventh feature of "transparency" is also a call for "openness." The OLAP server ends up acting like middleware navigating between heterogeneous data sources behind a generic front-end, such as a spreadsheet. This is rather like the metadata "grand challenge" discussed above. Interoperability is both a worthy and a tough goal to attain. Aiming at this is an EMC, but in another possible world. However, look for incremental progress, as well as redefining breakthroughs in context rather than a single solution.

The eighth feature of "multiuser" support looks toward that essential function of any database—to assure data integrity and security during concurrent update activities by multiple end-users. Update? See the above discussion (and throughout) about data warehousing "read mostly" really being "read and write." (EMC given the possibility for an update.)

The ninth feature of "treatment of nonnormalized data" requires OLAP data to be decoupled from legacy system data sources from which it was extracted. There is no automatic backward propagation of updates or calculations back to the data source. This seems like a good description of the design principle of "loose coupling, strong cohesion." It is a design requirement for any structured system, not just OLAP ones, but it is an EMC honored more in the breech than in actual implementation.

The tenth feature of "storing OLAP results" indicates that decision support and source data (including transactional systems) should be separated. Presumably, one should be able to perform calculations—"what if" analyses, without overwriting the source data (EMC, insofar as distinguishing decision support and transactional data; "nice to have," insofar as making the result of calculations persistent requires putting them somewhere, and that somewhere is *not* on top of the detailed data).

The eleventh feature of "extraction of missing values" indicates that missing values are to be distinguished from zero. This is another way of stating the requirement for the systematic treatment of null—unknown or missing—values. This is consistent with two-valued logic, where the unknown value is one of the two allowed values, but we just don't know which one. Here, one gets a strong sense of the degree to which the OLAP rules are an extension of the twelve principles of relational databases (EMC from a relational perspective).

The twelfth feature of "treatment of missing values" indicates that the OLAP engine should ignore them. At least some OLAP experts prefer tools that are able to specify default values, just in case *missing* does in fact mean "zero." (This is an EMC that is nice if you do *not* have it—that is, having a choice is nice: being able either to specify a default for missing values or to accept the rigorous ignoring of missing values.)

The thirteenth feature, "flexible reporting," is an adaptation of logical data independence in the relational model to the OLAP context. Decoupling the logical order of the data and its presentation is one of the things that relational systems do well. However, this seems to be a generalization of that requirement for the OLAP environment (EMC).

The fourteenth feature, "consistent reporting performance," is the "Holy Grail" of all on-line processing, not just an EMC requirement for OLAP. Through design effort, it is attainable, using the methods outlined above in Chapters Eleven and Fourteen, on performance and aggregation, respectively. The method of predefining and calculating cubes in advance is one of the most reliable for attaining uniform performance. In fact, performance is less a function of the sheer number of dimensions or hierarchies being combined than of whether or not resulting cube is precalculated. (Because it sets the bar too high, it ends up being a "nice to have.")

The fifteenth feature of "automatic adjustment of physical level" is an adaptation of physical data independence in the relational model to the OLAP context. The ability to ALTER the underlying physical structures without unloading the structure, deleting and redefining the schema, and putting the data back is one of the most powerful features of the relational model. However, there is nothing automatic about it. This may set the bar too high, regardless of the type of system. Nevertheless, visibility to such adjustments and tools to automate or make such actions easy are a "nice to have," in any context.

The sixteenth feature, "generic dimensionality," requires more than "conformed dimensions." It requires that dimensions be equivalent in both structure and operational capabilities. Perhaps what Dr. Codd was reaching for here was really robust metadata that allow generic comparisons and operations across differing dimensions. However, as stated, this feature seems either inaccurate or unrealistic. Even if an exception is made for the dimension of time, which is a notoriously specific dimension unlike anything else in our universe that is uniquely defined by time itself, it may turn out that almost every dimension has its peculiarities. *Viva la difference!* (EMC— except that no product has ever implemented it.)

The seventeenth feature of "unlimited dimensions and aggregation levels" is hard to assess because it sets the bar impossibly high. The general rule is that the data will expand or, within limits, contract to fill the available space; the computing requirements will do the same. This is also like a grand challenge. In any case, it would be nice to have.

The eighteenth feature of "unrestricted cross-dimensional operations" indicates that symbolic operations must be allowed across dimensions, not just calculations of measurable quantities. The term *operation* here goes proxy for many kinds of manipulations and comparisons of functions, such as allocations of costs to products in activity-based costing (ABC)—preference functions of consumers for certain kinds of products based on perceived benefits ("utility" in the economic sense). This is visionary material from the perspective of data warehousing. The user-defined functions of relational "universal" databases offer tools required to construct functionality of this kind. Once again, one gets a strong sense of the degree to which the OLAP rules are an extension of the twelve principles of relational databases. It is a nice to have in any context. OLAP is ahead of the curve here.

THE STRENGTHS OF OLAP

Specialization is the key to doing something well. The connection between aggregations and OLAP is a direct one. This entire class of tools exists to build or prebuild aggregations and cubes, then to apply specialized built-in functions to these aggregations and cubes. Whether summarized on the desktop or on a separate OLAP server, the results are impressive. These built-in functions provide the "analysis" in the OLAP. These built-in functions are significant extensions of the kinds of analyses that can be performed by standard SQL. These extensions include moving averages, moving sums, rankings, cumulative counts of all kinds, gross margin return on inventory, etc. For example, the standard SQL average divides the quantities in the column being averaged by the number of rows, not by the number of time periods. The customized functions employ the latter. This is an example of their power, advantage, and where they come into their own.

Just as important, many situations exist in which OLAP is well positioned to provide prompt performance in an interactive interface. This is the "on-line" in OLAP. As we saw in Chapter Eleven on performance, preformatting aggregations and caching data in buffers are two of the most powerful methods of delivering fast response to queries and questions. OLAP tools deploy and fine-tune these methods. A multidimensional database (MDDB) is a collection of cubes or aggregations as constructed by the OLAP server in its own vendor- or tool-specific data format and stored for subsequent desktop processing. Although we often imagine a large hypercube to be cached in buffer on a high, powerful client work station, there is no reason it cannot be managed in memory buffers on the OLAP server. Thus, if it were read only, it would be available to multiple authorized users without the requirement for global locking.

User friendly is one of those abused terms like *intuitive*, *performance*, or *transparent*, which should always be made relative to a specific purpose or agreement in context. Nevertheless, an OLAP point-and-click interface is, in general, much easier to master than (for example) the command line interface to a data administration tool. The intention of OLAP is to engineer the interface to benefit the end-user's information presentation capabilities and results. Usability studies are being productively applied to attaining the goal of getting the interface out of the way and satisfying the end of ease of use and productive activity on behalf of OLAP. This is a strength.

Along a similar line, SQL was supposed to be a high-level, English-like language, with which business analysts, planners, and knowledge workers of various types can launch their own queries against various corporate data stores. However, except for basic queries, SQL turns out to be more complex than one might wish. Learning it is just not a priority for many busy business analysts. A high-level interface to generate the (lower) high-level (SQL) interface is needed. Furthermore, its (SQL's) capabilities are a lot more limited, in comparison, for example, with the rich functions available in a spreadsheet. OLAP succeeds in bringing much of this richness to information analysis without the spreadsheets constraints.

OLAP is a dynamic and evolving solution to knowledge capture and creation. OLAP servers are increasingly open to linking backward and forward to data in relational data sources, thus blurring further the distinction between multidimensional and relational data sources. (This is by no means guaranteed, so, if you require such functionality, make sure the tool includes it.) The product development march in the direction of "openness, " publicly available specifications, and APIs is a positive thing. The cost, increasing complexity, and management of combinatorial explosion are discussed below under limitations.

LIMITATIONS

Although powerful and fundamental, every approach presents trade-offs and limitations. Those of the OLAP approach are considered here. OLAP tools have limited data preparation capabilities. Many would admit that they have none, suggesting that data preparation is an IT issue or upstream opportunity. OLAP engines generally leave data extraction and preparation to the end-user, the information technology department, or other special proprietary tools designed to work as a back-end to the OLAP engine. OLAP severs are not intended to be data extraction or data scrubbing tools—they require clean data and data in the right format, where *right* is defined as what they are expecting. At the risk of mixing the metaphor, let those among you who has clean data cast the first stone. Thus, we are back to the "system integration shuffle" of getting all of our tools and processes to work together because OLAP, by its own admission, is not the complete solution. Many OLAP vendors could do a better job of avoiding such a "knock" by admitting this limitation up front.

Other limitations on the OLAP engine extend from limited storage capabilities to proprietary data formats that are closed to interoperability with other tools. For example, if you have a 1-gigabyte cube and you want a presentation of the product-customer-period over 10 other time periods, all of a sudden, 10 gigabytes of data have to be stored. That is less of a problem for a back-end server, but it is definitely an issue for a proprietary MDDB. Given a high-powered work station, the 1-gigabyte example might be cached in memory, but a persisting data store is going to be required for the complete time series. That was why databases were invented.

Another limitation of OLAP, as implemented by MDDB products, is the difficulty and complexity of building the MDDB itself. The set of data available to be analyzed in an MDDB is small, compared with what can be analyzed by means of an OLAP tool executing against a regular relational database. To address these limitations, some MDDB tool vendors have moved to hybrid systems with "reach-through" to a relational database. In hybrid systems, the cubes—the high-level aggregates—are stored in the MDDB. The detailed data is stored in an underlying relational database. This results in further coordination and system integration requirements. Additional metadata are now needed. Metadata contain a mapping of summarized and derived information in the OLAP engine to detailed information in the RDBMS. When detail data is requested, the system drills through the MDDB to the relational database to retrieve it. Thus, the OLAP cube behaves more like an aggregation or index to the underlying relational (warehouse) data than like an independent system. As indicated above, despite specific limitations in this area, OLAP severs are increasingly open to linking backward to data in relational data sources.

The analysis and navigation requirements sometimes determine the details of the structure of the OLAP cubes. The cubes (and hypercubes) are structured around the way that the cube is to be analyzed and passed around. As the analysis or navigation requirements change, the data structures will also require physical reconfiguring or rebuilding of the cubes. This can be similar to legacy hierarchical and network DBMSs. There, a separate data schema was required for each application that used it.

Finally, if the end-user just wants to use the OLAP tool as an SQL generator, the better option is to learn SQL itself. On the other hand, if the standard deviation, moving averages by time, and other advanced spreadsheet functions are really needed, the better option is to stick with the OLAP tool. Given the complexity of OLAP active "reach-through" to the relational data warehouse, there is no way to make it happen without cross-functional staffing. Of course, expertise in the business comes first, but then one might wonder, whether, by the time the business analyst masters the complexity of building the semantic layer of tool X or the complexity of tool Y that enables the semantic layer to be eliminated, she or he could have mastered the complexities of SQL. This would give them a logically coherent, high-level, English-like application interface that corresponds to an open international standard. In truth, it is amazing to see one vendor boast about the flexibility of its semantic layer—the mapping from cubes on the desktop to the underlying data stores—and another boasting that it doesn't even have a semantic layer. What vendors do agree on is the importance of a usable, coherent interface to the data and that such an interface is of the essence.

OLAP Tool Evaluation Check List

Here is a check list of features for which to look in evaluating and acquiring OLAP tools:

- What are the basic representations of the tool—hierarchies, dimensions, structures, cubes—and how are they defined, manipulated, and stored?

- Do the data dimensions function independently from how they are combined into cubes, and what are the details (examples) of such combinations? Are cubes stored on the desktop or on the server? Are they stored in a MDDB or an RDBMS?

- How is data sourced? What is involved in mapping input into the tool? What kinds of input can or must be used to produce the intermediate results and output—RDBMS structure, flat file, ways of encoding character data, code page, etc.?

- Does the tool allow, enable, drill down, or drill through back into the detailed data from which the cubes (and other structures) were constructed?

- Must the drill path be defined in advance or is it supported dynamically and on the fly?

- Does the tool have preferences, "lock in," or special capabilities as to whether the source (or target) of the data is of a star schema or snow flake layout?

- What are the elementary data types and how do they line up with the data types of the candidate source data? Along similar lines, are foreign currency, time and date, or user-defined data types allowed?

- How is sparse data and null (not defined or meaningless) data handled? Is "under-the-covers" compression used, and does the mechanism optimize (enhance) storage without significantly setting back runtime performance?

- What are the available built-in, quasi-mathematical functions for computing derived data aggregations, moving averages, cumulative count, cumulative percentage, rankings, and percentages?

- Once defined, how are cubes and aggregations compared, stored, and versioned? Are versions even possible? Are cubes able to be compared, joined, or otherwise combined by hierarchies, dimensions, or must they be rebuilt from scratch?

- Is a single metadata repository provided, accessible, and useable by the OLAP desktop, OLAP server, or relational engine? If multiple repositories are required, what is the extent of the local metadata and how do the local meta data interoperate?

- Specifically, if the tool uses a proprietary data structure to store the cubes, hypercubes, or multicubes, does the underlying technology require that all possible combinations be represented? If so, what mechanisms—compression—are employed as part of sparse data management to limit combinatorial explosion?

- What are the physical limitations? What is the maximum size of a dimension or hierarchy in terms of levels, rows, cells, columns, and entries? What is the maximum logical storage limit on the server or on the desktop, given adequate available physical resources? (Same questions about cubes or other defined structures.)

- What are the built-in reports and report-building capabilities? What sorts of interfaces are available? Can an OLAP report be e-mailed to another end-user from within the OLAP tool?

- What is the sense of the quantity of time commitment from the IT department staff to set up the tool and administer it? What is the availability of (and necessity for) training courses in the tool?

- How does the tool interoperate with other tools in its own and related categories? What sorts of hooks or links are available? Can data warehouse metadata be made visible from within the tool? (Continued)

OLAP Tool Evaluation Check List (Continued)

- What are all the usual parameters about hardware requirements, operating system environment, and software compatibility, and are they covered? What are the defined constraints, limitations, and tuning parameters, and how do these compare with the target implementation environment?

- What are the security facilities of the tool? Is multiuser security envisioned and supported? Is group-level security available so that it can be administered, based on profiles to which individuals are assigned or disassociated? Is access logged so that an audit trail is left? What are the different levels of security authorization and administration?

- Does the tool distinguish between different levels of users—administrators, beginners, and expert end-users and what different capabilities are provided for?

- Is the tool Web-enabled? That is, is reporting over a WAN using Internet-friendly technologies a part of the tool? An add-on to the tool? A separately licensable product from the same vendor? Follow up with this line of questioning: What are the Web technologies used to deliver the cube or other OLAP structures—CGI gateways, Java applets, C++ DLLs, an object request broker?

- How does the tool describe itself, and where is it located in the general matrix of client-server architecture—desktop OLAP, server-side OLAP, relational LOLAP, etc.?

- What really is the user interface to the tool? Is it a separate spreadsheet application? Is the OLAP cube (or structure) closely coupled with a presentation layer, or is it a separate component?

- What is the quality of documentation, availability on alternate media (Web site and CD-ROM)? Availability and cost for support? Viability of the vendor as an ongoing business enterprise?

- What are the in-depth, "down-and-dirty" reports of two or three other customers (reference sites) who actually have the tool in production and have been using it for a while?

SUMMARY . . . .

OLAP architecture applies many of the same principles as data warehousing. These include definitions of hierarchical dimensions, granularity of quantitative data, sparsity, aggregations, and cubes. There is a difference in emphasis between data warehousing and OLAP, but the same principles are valid in each context. Naturally, both OLAP and data warehousing fall on the decision support side of the distinction between transactional and decision support systems. These two complementary technologies are converging under the mutual influence of one another. There is much more to data warehousing than scrubbing and aggregating data. But data warehousing is serious about its data preparation. Likewise, there is much more to OLAP than clever desktop functionality in slicing and dicing data. But, under any interpretation, OLAP is serious about its data analysis. These are complementary core capabilities. They complete one another. The distinctions between desktop OLAP, server OLAP, and relational OLAP are discussed. OLAP system structures include cubes, hypercubes, and multicubes, which are defined and discussed. The issue of data sparsity is engaged and the trade-offs it involves are sketched. A critical overview is presented of the defining features of OLAP as sketched in Codd's eighteen rules. The strengths and limitations of OLAP are discussed, and a OLAP tool evaluation check list is laid out.

[1] Thomsen, Erik, **OLAP Solutions**, New York, NY: John Wiley & Sons, 1997: 483.

[2] At this point, the reader may wish to review Figure 1.3: Alternate Client-Server Partitioning, from Chapter One.

3 This discussion follows Erik Thomsen's (1997) insight that OLAP and data warehousing are complementary technologies, as indicated by the aphorism with which the chapter begins.

[4] The terminology is rapidly reaching a point of diminishing returns; but the market always seems to require a label to make a product distinction: "Multidimensional on-line analytic processing"—the relatively more proprietary (and functionally relatively richer)—approach and "Relational on-line analytic processing"—the approach that enables explicit links with an underlying RDBMS. In that spirit, vendors that promise hybrid products able to work both angles have got "HOLAP"—hybrid on-line analytic processing. For example, IBM has licensed Hyperion Essbase technology and simulates a cube in DB2 OLAP server. Microsoft SQL Server OLAP services (PLATO) and HOLOS from Seagate are also in the HOLAP product space.

[5] See Chapter Two on a short history of data, especially the section on the very idea of decision support, for further details on history, including other product references, as well as a white paper by Nigel Pendse at www.olapreport. (See www.olapreport/origins.htm.)

[6] See www.olapcouncil.org where a free copy of the API specification can be downloaded.

16 *Data Warehousing and the Web*

In this chapter...

THE BUSINESS CASE

The business case for a convergence of data warehousing and the World Wide Web (hereafter "the Web") works at several levels. Much of the leverage lies in the areas of
improved work flow, coordination of information-sharing commitments, and management coordination. Several varieties of knowledge are made possible by the use of the
data warehouse—superior knowledge of customer behavior, opportunities for brand
development, and the time stamping of the moment of value when customer and product
interact. All of these are augmented by the Web in terms of rapid response, extent and
depth of business relationship, and integration of heterogeneous sources of information.

Legacy or ERP systems are not the most open computing configurations or platforms on the basis of which to coordinate work. In truth, these systems can be significant obstacles to the flow of information and work through a firm or between trading
partners. Intranets (and extranets) built on Web technology can remove these obstacles. They offer a pragmatic approach to the challenge of information sharing. In terms
of numbers of desktops installed and supportable, intranet technology scales more
robustly than the distribution and maintenance of bulky Windows executable software
components (instances of which have to be installed on every Windows desktop).

Web-based technologies imply lower total cost of ownership in terms of distributing and updating software from centralized servers, in contrast with installing and
updating software components on every client work station. They increase the number
of people in a firm who have access to crucial business information across what is literally a WAN by providing them with a simple "universal" client—the Web browser. In
business-to-business extranets, you can give a corporate customer of travel, credit card,
or cash management services a Web browser and the ability to analyze employee
spending behavior or patterns without having to bring the data in-house. Providing corporate customers with periodic summaries of their transactions or accounts, sliced and
diced in useful ways, poses many significant security, maintenance, and infrastructure
challenges. However, the business value also promises to be significant.

Truth be told, companies have done this for years—put a terminal in a customer
site to make visible internal vendor systems. However, they have had to use private

networks and what are now described as legacy technologies. Such placements of terminals have required specific agreements, the leasing of dedicated and expensive communication lines, and customized one-to-one designs. What Web-based technologies do is "lower the bar" to such an approach. What once required large-scale system integration—SNA networks, leased lines, and mainframes at the back-end—is now available to small- and medium-sized companies.

No one should imagine that such results can be obtained from the ridiculously low figures occasionally quoted in the trade press, however. For a realistic example, a midsized real estate firm with $2 billion in annual sales built a simple communication utility with no on-line transaction capability (EC) for about $2 million.[2] This is not to say that a company with $20 billion in sales in the same industry would require a $20 million intranet, but it might.

Economic value resides in reduced response time to market, changes based on effective information sharing, superior coordination of customer-sustaining activities among staff committed to shared values, and enhanced hand-offs and execution in supply chain management. Whenever business intelligence (e.g., knowledge of customer behavior) is a key element in ensuring customer satisfaction, the power of "action at a distance" makes a difference. An extranet built using Web-based technologies is an effective way to traverse both the physical and organizational distance in sharing and coordinating the flow of transactions and knowledge between trading partners, firms in the same value chain, or customers and vendors. In one example, building and operating the data warehousing functions of a fast-food firm is such a formidable undertaking that it has been outsourced to a separate firm. These two firms are ideally linked by an extranet for information delivery and coordination of work flow.

Information-intensive companies can be an example of themselves; the economic value they generate is a function of the knowledge they create and distribute. Likewise, their own internal agility and service is a function of their capabilities in the creation and dissemination of knowledge. In this instance, the shoemaker's children are not barefoot, but clad in high-end athletic wear.

Controlling costs, optimizing the supply chain, forecasting, and cross-selling do not have to be internally focused business initiatives. Using Web-enabling technologies, a firm can undertake initiatives that can make warehouse data visible to suppliers, customers, trading partners, or other stakeholders. For example, ShopKo Stores, Inc., a discount retailer and pharmacy, is providing its suppliers with access to their point of sale data over the Web. A package solution will enable its suppliers to get access to and analyze data on how their products are selling. This is a significant step in the direction of supplier-managed inventory with reduced out-of-stock sales losses, JIT replenishment of inventory, and an informed, knowledgeable convergence of product availability with customer demand and purchases (Klawikowski, 1997: 14). In this way, the knowledge embedded in the data warehouse will be more widely and readily distributed than ever before, through the convergence of two technology innovations—the Web and the data warehouse.

THE WEB AS A DELIVERY SYSTEM

The case for the convergence of data warehousing with Web-based mechanisms to manage and distribute information can be summarized succinctly. It is the availability of decision support information "any place, any time, on anyone's desktop."[3] This is not just a superior delivery system, though it may be that, too. New possibilities are opened through the basic principles of Web computing—action at a distance, access to information any place and any time, interfirm coordination, and cooperation at new levels. The vision is clear: that of data warehousing and the Web as providing an "information utility." What if information were as available, accessible, and as ubiquitous as electricity? These services are always there—like a commitment.[4] Just as we take for granted the reliability and availability of electric and telephone service, so too Web-related infrastructures are envisioned as being a source of information just as pervasive and powerful. The challenge and task at hand for the information technology function in the firm is to create a level of service on a par with that of the other utilities.

The truth is that things are never as simple or inexpensive as one might wish. The same is true of the Web-based distribution mechanisms—in particular, intranets and extranets—we shall be discussing. Like the bicycle the parents bought for their child for Christmas, "some assembly is required." Still, the power of action at a distance, open standards, and time-tested, "good-enough" technology is a compelling model on which to base the propagation of data warehousing throughout the enterprise. Even more, in comparison with the "hard-wired" work flows of legacy or ERP systems, never known for their flexibility, Internet-based Web technologies offer useful alternatives in integrating internal information resources. Let's take a step back in the remainder of this and the next section, and gain perspective and background on the situation, at the level proper to a managerial briefing on basic definitions and applications.

The Internet itself is arguably a killer application. The vehicle bringing this to the awareness of both the Main Street market and the information systems technology elite is the World Wide Web. A "killer application" is one that represents a "discontinuous change" in the way we work and do business. For example, famous killer applications of the past decade have included the PC and its ability to run a spreadsheet; the midrange server and its ability to support a relational database; and the GUI and the usability of the client-server architecture it empowers. In Chapter Two on data history one important conclusion was that, amid the flux of all the paradigm shifts, what stood fast was data and the imperative to manage data as a corporate resource. The Internet and Web delivery mechanisms in all their forms do *not* change that. What they change is the extent of platforms able to be navigated, the comprehensiveness of the information to be integrated, and the service requests to which response is possible.

The ramp up to this use of the Web as part of an information utility is the design and implementation of intranets. An intranet is a TCP/IP network, using Web technologies such as HTML, HTTP, and CGI unconnected to the global Internet proper. It is a network inside the firewall. A firewall is a special-purpose server, sometimes also loosely designated as a gateway, capable of filtering the data traffic (down to the packet level) between the private network and the publicly visible and accessible Internet. This is done by means of an alternate use of a special-purpose computer, the router, one of the basic building blocks of the Internet because of its ability to route packets of data to addresses by many alternate paths. The router's ability to define, tabulate, and look up allowed addresses and functionality makes it ideal to defining a boundary between the inside and outside of a corporate network. Hence, the significance of the term *firewall*. When combined with a communication link to a physically separate hardware platform, the firewall becomes a "proxy server," capable of running software on behalf of the internal client machine.

Thus, intranets are used to "boot-strap" deploying Web-based services and connections. This is a natural extension, because the underlying technologies are continuous with one another. The general idea is that a team with something to share with other teams can put it on a Web server and make the information available for retrieval and transformation within the organization. The traditional IT department now finds itself partnering with marketing, advertising, customer support, product design, product delivery, inventory management, and other roles critical to design and implement the delivery of data warehousing information on Web servers.

In contrast, an extranet is generally defined as a network using the same Web technologies to allow several trading partners to communicate in secret, using encryption technology, over the global Internet proper without the public having any visibility to the request and response messages. (See Figure 16.1: The Internet, Intranets, and Extranets, where the extranet is represented by dashed lines.) This is because the requests and responses between the supplier and client companies are sent out over the Internet in encrypted form, so the relationship is real but the connection is intermittent. Under the scenario depicted, the client also has a firewall and an intranet. However, strictly speaking, all the client really needs is a Web browser and authorization to access the resources behind the supplier's firewall. Such a network is labeled a *virtual private network*, *VPN*. A more expensive variation includes the option where the trading partners purchase telecommunication bandwidth for their own private use. This results in a dedicated private network (DPN). Here again, no part of the global Internet is traversed. Still, security is no less a priority in this case, though for different reasons. Casual eavesdropping is less of a problem here, but dedicated hacking is still a source of mischief, so vigilance is essential.

Within the relationship space of the Internet itself, the data warehousing emphasis is on intranets and extranets, rather than Web publishing or electronic commerce. Of course, EC systems are information suppliers and a source of input to data warehouses about how customers are using products and services, but that is not the approach or perspective here. Rather, the perspective is that of a data warehouse as an information supplier to the rest of the organization using Web-based technologies.

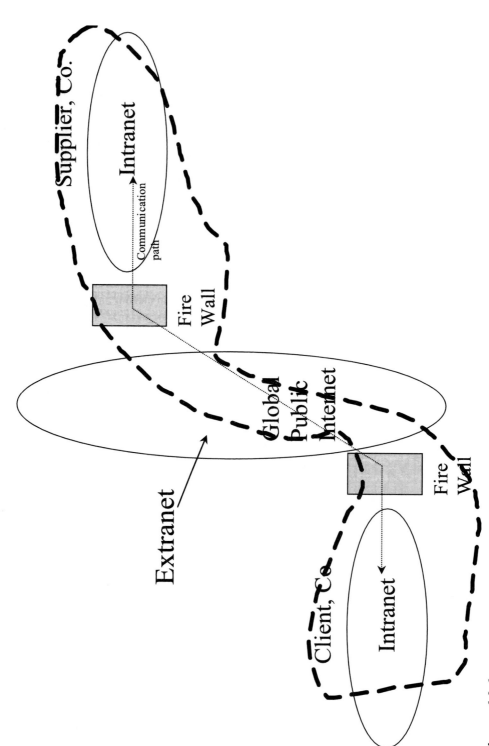

Figure 16:1:
The Internet, Intranets, and Extranets

KEY INTERNET TECHNOLOGIES

Naturally, issues of software infrastructure are central to the operation of the business applications and opportunities that "float on top" of the technical foundation. As an essential guide, this chapter will assume no previous background with the infrastructure. If the classic definition of client-server is accepted—that is, a computing architecture that distributes cycles between front-end presentation work stations, back-end data stores, and application functionality and connectivity—the Internet is truly the mother of all client-server computing. It represents a legacy of client-server computing without, however, the usual negative connotation of *legacy,* meaning "obsolete." As an analogy, think of the Web as doing for the Internet-based technologies what three-tier structure does for client-server architecture—bringing it to a new level of power and effectiveness.

Key Internet technologies map very nicely to the definition of client-server architecture. Because data warehousing systems do the same, that sets up a nice equation (or syllogism), based on what one might describe as "the transitive property of system architectures." If the Web maps to client-server systems and client-server systems are exemplified by data warehousing architectures, the Web maps to data warehousing architecture.[5] Let us consider the layers in turn.

The prime candidate for the universal client interface is the Web browser. It is a client-side presentation tool that interprets and presents the content stored on Web (HTTP) servers using HTML. It is capable of chasing ("navigating") links between widely dispersed servers based on the communication protocol called *Hypertext Transport Protocol* (HTTP). When combined with HTTP and URLs, HTML makes possible the "hot links" so characteristic of Web "surfing," whereby clicking on a location automatically transports the user to the next page on a different server across the planet. This is a major feature of the Web that gives it the characteristic "hypertext" quality—layers of text (pages) between which one can navigate, jumping to the next site by clicking on the "hot spot." The Web browser, of course, is the tool for interpreting the HTML tags. It is the now-famous "skinny client." It is worth noting that exploring a decision support report from a data warehousing system is a lot like surfing. The analyst may start out wanting to know about the performance of a special promotion in the Northeast; drill down on that category in comparing Northeast with Southwest; then aggregate up in the Southwest for a broader view of the overall performance in that area. So it is no accident that the two approaches have a sympathetic convergence.

From an IT perspective, this is a winning proposition. Instead of having to maintain Windows-related code on each of hundreds or thousands of desktops, the graphical controls presenting the data warehouse information in tabular or visual form can be built and maintained in a centralized library on a centralized server. When a new software release occurs, instead of having to troubleshoot (and possibly even physically visit) these many desktops, the code is updated in one centralized place. It is then used there or dynamically downloaded when the end-user invokes the application. This is nearly a silver bullet, reducing the total cost of ownership of the application.

At the front-end is a presentation layer coded in HTML. A "markup" language is different from a "what you see is what you get" approach, though the end result is still a GUI presentation. In HTML, the control structure is visible in the surface of the document, rather like turning on the option of a word processing package to make the invisible characters visible. In HTML, commands are associated with *tags*, to mark components of a document, including embedded images, links, and applets. Here, the ideas of hypertext links are crucial. These are hot spots, the clicking of which activates the underlying addressing mechanism to deliver the customer to a potentially different HTML page or even a different part of the Web in the time it takes to download content. This results in behavior similar to drill-down in a windowing point-and click context.

At the back-end is a data access layer often coded using a lowest common denominator approach. This approach is called a *common gateway interface* (CGI) program. This is designed to take the parameters delivered from the client to the server (for example, the parts of an SQL statement—operator, predicates, data source) and forward them to the database or application program (and vice versa). If this sounds like a "kludge," it is. Various initiatives are underway to circumvent or replace the need for such gateways. These include everything from proprietary APIs to Java database connectivity (JDBC), to transaction processors such as active server pages (ASP) or Java Beans components capable of establishing a conversation. Understanding these requires a grasp of what they are intended to circumvent and make obsolete. This will require further discussion. The lesson, however, is clear. No matter what the front-end—whether Java-enhanced HTML, Active-X components, Delphi, Power Builder, Visual Basic, or one of its derivatives—*they are all chasing data*. They all are required to deliver enterprise-relevant information, generally from a data model implemented in a relational database. Frequently, the relational databases include data warehousing.

Although an oversimplification, the technique basically is to load data retrieved from the database into controls embedded in the HTML document. As the data is retrieved from the database, it is handed off for possible further formatting and manipulation on an application server, then for subsequent insertion into presentation controls to be displayed by the client browser. Data warehousing is demanding enough procedurally, so that it generally requires a middle tier of custom components to mediate data retrieval, formatting, and display. Given the considerations of performance, bandwidth, and multisite coordination that were treated in Chapter Eleven on data warehouse performance, the use of aggregations and prior data formatting is a favored method of managing response time. In doing this, the data must run the gauntlet of the network protocol layer (to which we now turn).

In the middle is the protocol layer, HTTP. For purposes of this chapter, sufficient understanding of a "network protocol" is available in comparing it to "protocol" at a staff meeting. What gets defined (in this case, in software) is a set of rule-governed behaviors that determines who on a network talks first, what to do when a message arrives, and how to start and end an information exchange (not yet a conversation). HTTP is specially designed efficiently to make the hypertext jumps that characterize the hot spots on Web pages. This is the "magic" of hyptertext, which allows the Web surfer suddenly to be on a different server at a different level of abstraction in a different discussion. This involves trade-offs, including its being a "stateless" protocol. The underlying IP connection is held only for the duration of one operation. No conversation within an enduring circuit exists. This is very efficient when jumping from a server local to Chicago to one local to CERN, Switzerland. However, processing is complicated when a conversation is required. A conversation is a request and a response related to one another. When such a back-and-forth interaction is required, programming or a related method to store state variables as hidden values on a HTML page or a temporary file on the target server is needed. This is precisely the function of those curious items called *cookies*. They provide a small area of storage on the client work station to store "state information," such as session identifier and related data. (This harkens back to the days of IBM's teleprocessing monitor, CICS, before the invention of temporary storage, when variables were made invisible and cached on the so-called green screen [see 3270 dumb terminal in Glossary]).

As a matter of terminology, Web servers are often called HTTP servers, and the hypertext links are labels for URLs. These are the addresses on the Internet, toward which the client-side browsers are pointed and to which they navigate. For example, the domain name corresponding (and masking) the address of the Web home page of the Association for Computing Machinery, Inc. is http://www.acm.org.

Drilling down even further, the crucial thing about the underlying Internet network protocol, TCP/IP, is that it is *routable*. What does this mean? It means it can escape from the LAN and go forth into the WAN.

The router, arguably a less visible killer application, is a special-purpose computer interconnecting multiple network segments and forwarding packets of data. This is accomplished by matching data packet addresses with destination and path routes stored in software tables and cached in memory on the router itself for quick (but not instantaneous) lookup.

Because TCP/IP was developed using federal tax dollars and subsequently turned over to a not-for-profit society (the Internet Society) consisting of research and working groups (especially the Internet Engineering Task Force [IETF]), no one vendor can define or own it. The standard is maintained by a complex, but publicly defined, process of formal request documents, proposals, and standards decisions and publications. Like democracy itself, this can be slow and cumbersome. Imperfect, to be sure, but the alternatives of technology dictatorship or anarchy seem to be even less attractive.

The current 32-bit IP protocol defines a total address space of several billion addresses, not all of which are usable or groupable into convenient subnetworks, due to implementation and technical considerations. Although a couple of billion is indeed a large number, it is finite. Due to the explosive growth of the Internet, it will not be sufficient for the indefinite future. "Information appliances"—combination cellular phones, beepers, and personal digital assistants—are expected to be large consumers of the remaining addresses. The current debate is not about addresses being exhausted, though that is theoretically predicted to happen in about the year 2008. Rather, the debate is about how much inconvenience will be caused by implementing the solution, "IP the next generation" (IPng). This "solution" is nearly available, with its 128-bit address. Even if theoretically backward-compatible, the possibility exists that some organizations may still be required to renumber network node addresses, due to licensing or implementation considerations. Not good news for network administrations, but not necessarily a show stopper from the perspective of the Webification of the planet.

No discussion of the Web delivery mechanism would be complete without the discussion of security issues. The more valuable the information stored in the data warehouse, the more tempting a target it is to hackers, mischief makers, or even cyberterrorists, whose methods precisely consist in random attacks ("innocence" is no defense). If such things as credit card numbers or confidential health care diagnoses or even sensitive financial forecasts are associated with individuals, then stored in data warehouse customer dimensions, the risk and liability exposure both to individuals and to corporations may be significant. Hence, the requirement for security of access and secrecy in transmission. This involves encryption.

Simply defined, encryption is a method designed to make data secret, to encode and decode it, to keep it secure from unauthorized access. In general, encryption comes in two forms. The first is called *symmetrical*. This relies on the same single key to encode and decode the messages. This method is exemplified by the Data Encryption Standard (DES) endorsed by the U.S. government. An indication of the strength of the key is its length. The DES standard uses a 40-bit length, recently increased to 56 bits. A team at Bell Labs, using spare computing cycles on hundreds of Internet-connected machines, was able to unscramble a message in the enlarged key using brute force methods. In short, they "cracked" the code using substantial expertise and resources, but did so in a remarkably short amount of time. What had been predicted to require millennia of computing time was accomplished in an elapsed time of a few weeks. That probably does not threaten encrypted transactions or messages I might want to send to my mother, coded for privacy, because the cost of marshalling such resources for an attack is far vaster than any possible payoff. However, that is indeed a problem from the point of view of using such a key for national security traffic or Federal Reserve transfers. Stronger encryption must henceforth be employed. It is not the only problem from a commercial business point of view, where one is doing business with many people one does not know and will never meet. This is because the key of symmetrical codes is hard to distribute in a secure way. Because, in order to communicate with one another, we must both get the secret code, what do we do? Put it in an envelope, seal the envelope by licking it, and drop it in a mail box? Send a diskette? Send an e-mail? Send a courier? True, we could agree to meet in my office and perform the handoff, but what if hundreds of trading partners or people you are not likely to meet personally have to do business using such keys? The solution is not available using symmetric methods.

The solution is asymmetric or public key encryption This encryption method is based on the idea of a function that is easy to compute in one direction and hard to do so in reverse. For example, it is easier to multiply two numbers to get a product (25 x 4 = 100) than it is to figure out (factor out) which two numbers were used to generate that product, knowing only the final number (100/10 = 10, 100/5 = 20, 100/2 = 50, etc.). This is vastly oversimplified. However, the idea is to generate a mathematically related public and private key, where the relationship is one of the "hard-to-reverse" type. The public key is used to encode the message to me, but who keeps track of the public key? That public key is available from an authorized, trusted third party—a certification authority (CA)—such as the post office or a phone company or a credit card company. The whole point is to be able to publish it (the key) in a kind of white pages. By itself, the public key is incomplete. You don't have to worry about listing it publicly. It enables one to encrypt a message that can be decrypted by only the holder of the corresponding private key-pair. The holder of the private key is the only one who can decode the message. Likewise, the public key would enable one to decrypt a message—or a part of a message, such as a signature—from the holder of the private key, implying that only its owner really could have sent it. Note that the message encoding mechanism may be embedded in software or (as is more likely) proprietary firmware licensed from RSA Data Security, Inc. Where hundreds of anonymous persons or organizations (who will certainly never meet one another) must exchange information in a trusted way, public-key encryption is the method of choice.

Closely related to encryption is the idea of a digital signature. This is a special function applied to the message you want to send using your own private key that can be decoded using the corresponding public key. The fact that the message can be decoded using your public key proves rigorously that it must be from you.

The matter is even more tricky than it might seem. There is a performance penalty for all this public-private key encoding and decoding. DES remains a very efficient algorithm. This gives rise to clever combination solutions. The RSA method is used, in effect, as the envelope in which securely to distribute the more tractable 56-bit symmetrical DES code. Where practical, keeping the message short or using the code for only a minute (or so) also reduces the available sample of data on which to unleash a decryption attack.

It remains true that a 40-bit (or 56-bit) encryption key can be "hacked" (decoded) in a couple of weeks, using a million dollars worth of parallel processing computing power (and a bit of luck). Note, however, that this sets a threshold within which communication can operate securely, even using exportable encryption.[6] Also, although not a product exportable to other countries, doubling or tripling the bits in the encryption key in the software (as is also the case with the RSA patents) puts it beyond the reach of brute force decrypting computing power for at least the next decade. However, it causes the encrypting/decrypting process to execute more slowly.

Internet Munitions

The National Security Agency (NSA), which is charged with monitoring threats to the U.S. from terrorists, billion-dollar drug cartels, and foreign enemies (and make no mistake, there are many), along with the Department of Defense, have classified "strong" encryption, along with cruise missile technology, as munitions. Special permission, a license, from the State Department is required to export such software. The NSA wants to be sure that it is able to read everyone's messages if the national interest so dictates. In itself, that may be less of a problem than that of trying to have the legislative branch oversee such a secret agency. The computing power available to the NSA itself is classified. The assumption is they have enough technology (which includes mathematical expertise as well as hardware) to decrypt 56-bit messages— or they would not have recommended allowing their unrestricted export. When the limit is raised to 80 bits (say), one may assume technical advances have occurred, and so on. Unfortunately, the genie is out of the bottle. Strong encryption is available from foreign firms and from foreign subsidiaries and partners of domestic ones. Another part of the problem is the ease with which software can be copied and pirated. Obviously, the problem will not be solved in this textbox.

No discussion of Web-based data warehousing is complete without treating Java. The Java programming language has been described by James Gosling, one of its designers at Sun Microsystems, as "a blue collar language…not Ph.D. thesis material but a language for a job. " Given that 250,000 developers are working on Java components, even if it were not an eminently practical language (which it is), the available evidence is that it is a successful one, although perhaps not in the exact way expected by the conventional wisdom. The way in which a Java program is downloaded from a server to the client work station and executed results in it being described as "executable content." Executable content preserves the value of client-server within a Web environment. Computing cycles are distributed to and executed on the desktop when it makes sense to do so. Rich opportunities for interaction and functionality are delivered from a central point of management, maintenance, and control. Although Java is a fully endowed programming language, able to support both complete applications and server class libraries, the "applet" is what made Java famous. An applet is literally a "little application" written in Java, able to be downloaded as machine-independent bytecode from the server to the Web browser-enabled client, and distinct for its being connected to a Web HTML page by means of a tag <applet>. Applets are distinct from full-blown Java applications, in that they execute on the client in the so-called security sandbox without access to the client hard disk or operating system.

Now add to the equation Java's significant technical innovations: the generation and execution of hardware-independent bytecode by means of the Java virtual machine (JVM). This means that the client can remain both anonymous and secure as to the operating system and hardware being executed, provided that the Web browser understands the available applet tag and the JVM is available for the platform. These are solved problems. However, one outstanding issue is how to standardize on the request for data without introducing "plug-ins" or database binary code on the client.

Not surprising, the trade-off is between security and manageability, which leads to Java's other major innovation, the idea of the applet "sandbox." The way we talk about things tells us a lot about how we think. The benefits of manageability include the centralized distribution of business functionality ("executable content") to the desktop from the server; the regaining of control over the total cost of ownership and maintenance of the desktop; the write-once, execute-anywhere[7] features of the JVM; and the power of action at a distance on the WAN. For security reasons, the Java applet can communicate only with the Web server from which it was downloaded. As indicated, this is the Java sandbox. The sandbox provides a compelling security metaphor. It provides a security architecture both in language and in software. Do whatever you want in the sandbox. You can't hack your way out by means of pointers, because Java has none. You can't mess with the hard disk because, from the sandbox, it's invisible. You can't communicate with any server except that from which you were downloaded.

Although all the usual disclaimers apply and there are no absolute security guarantees, compare the sandbox approach to the deterrent of digital signatures. (For example, Active-X—a computing standard within the DCOM architecture [see Glossary]—employs digital signatures, and Java will eventually make them an option.) The sandbox provides a quarantine in advance. The digital signature does indeed indicate that the author of the code belongs to a firm that has registered successfully with a certification authority and that the author's certification has not been revoked. Realistically, however, that is not much of a guarantee of good character. Read the CA's disclaimers of responsibility in the fine print. The CA verifies that the check clears, but that does not mean it performs a background verification of good character. In the worst case, the digital signature makes possible an after-the-fact pursuit of the hacker through cyberspace, once the damage has occurred. In effect, the hacker is guaranteed to be identified, to the extent of being associated with a mathematically unique digital identifier. Significant deterrent or small comfort? One answer is to avoid the horns of the dilemma altogether by building castles, not indeed of sand, but of Java. If this sounds like enthusiasm, well, it is. The model exemplified by Java is a genuine technology innovation that has also elicited a response in the market.

Security is analogous to quality in an important way. Indeed, in a previous discussion, the point was made that data security is an important mark of its quality. In addition, the related idea was emphasized that data quality is not just the job of the quality assurance department. The idea that quality is the responsibility of those guys "over there" and that everyone is free of responsibility for the quality of the work in front of them invites a reduction to absurdity. A similar consideration applies to security. There is a legitimate coordination function on an organization-wide basis. Education, administration, upgrading, monitoring, and leading the response to exceptions, problems, or outright attacks properly belongs to a security department. However, everyone, without exception, has a role to play. First among this "everyone" is the manager of the data warehousing function. The formulation of policies as the data warehouse is made available to more and more staff using Web-based technologies is a key responsibility. The same applies to building and maintaining executive support, awareness, and a healthy skepticism that requires legitimate reasons for access, along with authorizing signatures from the thus empowered staff and superiors. After reviewing digital signatures and one-way functions, asking end-users of the data warehouse to sign a piece of paper may seem pedestrian and common. It may even seem "retro." It is, however, of the essence. Make no mistake about it—signing a piece of paper emphasizes the signer's commitment, responsibility, and accountability. It occasions a moment of reflection, especially when accompanied by a security policy in plain English and free of legalese. As my Tai Chi instructor used to say about security, there is no sense having doors of iron and walls of paper.[8] Consistency across the board and across the firm requires managerial leadership. Providing such a multi-faceted approach to security and including both the technical and managerial dimensions is an example of that.

WEB HARVESTING:
THE WEB AS THE ULTIMATE DATA STORE

The Web presents data warehousing opportunities in both form and content. So far, we have emphasized the form. The use of Web-centric technologies—TCP/IP, HTML, HTTP, CGI gateways, Web servers—to deliver data warehouse information to end-users across the WAN has been emphasized. Because data warehouse data will be proprietary, it is not the sort of data that one would expect to share with the anonymous pubic. So here we are talking about intranets or extranets, not the Internet at large. As indicated, this is not just a superior delivery system, though it may also be that. More importantly, new possibilities for inter- and intrafirm cooperation and coordination, the power of action at a distance, and access to information any time and any place are opened through the basic principles of Web computing.

Thus, the first Web opportunity is driven by the Web browser as the universal client. Because intranets and the Internet are everywhere and transforming business through the power of wide area communications, requirements to be able to access a data warehouse through Web browsers have already surfaced and are likely to intensify. However, more is required than slapping a Web browser on the front-end of a data warehouse presentation layer, obvious and powerful though that move may be.

The second opportunity is different. It regards the Web itself as content. It goes to the infrastructure of the Web itself as a distributed computing system. Think of the Web itself as a diverse, distributed, loosely structured data store. The defining database schema, however, is continuously being changed. A loosely connected network of servers—the Web infrastructure—is undergoing constant transformation as servers are added and drop off, constantly entering and exiting. Think of the Web itself as the ultimate database. A seemingly impossible task? Think again. At least one organization has commercialized research from Stanford University in a tool able to use specific metadata wrappers to make Web data sources appear to the search engine as a relational database able to be queried using SQL.[9] This potentially transforms the Web into a single virtual database that shows up in a relational form.

To be sure, innovations in technology can provide openings for business, and that is what we encounter here. Think of the Internet itself as a killer application and ultimate proof of the concept of distributed computing. But how does one get one's arms around it? As usual, tools will help, but it is unlikely that a single tool or even a suite of them will provide structure to this diverse, distributed, loosely structured data store. The discipline of an entire methodology is required.

Such a methodology is now available. The idea of using the Web as raw input to an organized system of information farming (see Hackathorn, 1998)[10] is the only proper response to our intuition that the marvelous resources of the Web are an abundance of riches that escape us like a mirage on the horizon. This is because it requires discipline and a commitment to defined, improvable business priorities to get beyond the hunter-gatherer ("surfing") model. Raw data, as well as information available in governmental and corporate databases, has exploded in recent years. Although constant vigilance (and skepticism) is the price of ensuring data quality, the risks are manageable when dealing with such high-end data providers as IBM, the U.S. Securities and Exchange Commission (SEC), and companies that are publicly traded and subject to public oversight. For example, the Electronic Data Gathering, Analysis, and Retrieval (EDGAR) database maintained by the SEC contains extensive reports on publicly traded companies and is updated daily. IBM operates and maintains a site off of which every patent issued by the U.S. government for the past 27 years is available for inspection (www.patents.ibm.com). Hard copy is available by overnight mail for a modest fee. It used to require hours or even days of library research work to get one's hands on material of this kind and quality.

These Web-based data stores are *not* data warehouses. They are more like unstructured dimensions. They are inputs to an information supply chain—input along with the operational systems that record raw transactions. The data warehouse is still the target at the end of this supply chain, out of which knowledge is presented. These inputs must be captured, extracted, evaluated according to quality criteria, cleansed as necessary, and transformed to match the structure of the target data warehouse. Discovery, capture, transformation (structuring), presentation, and delivery remain the essence of the information supply chain. For example, postal address and zip code data, customer demographic data, financial feeds of every imaginable kind about product performance—these are all low-hanging fruit from the perspective of data acquisition and availability. Prices of securities and currencies can be used to supplement time series data on actionable opportunities in managing a unified representation of the product. These raw inputs can be used to scrub data as operational name and address data is cleansed into the unified representation of the customer, product, and market. Thus is engaged what is operationally the most challenging phase of Web farming—the rendezvous of the data warehouse with the Web.

THE BUSINESS INTELLIGENCE PORTAL

The promise of the business intelligence (BI) portal is to put structure back into "decision support." What this means requires an examination of both business portal technology and decision making. The development of decision support systems shows a progressive advance from unstructured to structured decision making. For instance, inventory control, which used to require experience and special managerial skills, is now mostly automated, thanks to data warehousing systems. Now, forecasting methods based on extensive history of actual demand are extended and applied to structuring supply chain operations that had previously resisted structuring. Likewise, with customer relationship management—as a unified view of the customer across all accounts emerges, what used to require that marketing "sixth sense" becomes amenable to quantifiable trends, quadrants, and structured decision making. What was unstructured data becomes structured and semistructured. The boundaries of the unstructured and tacit are pushed back, step by step, in a raid on the inarticulate.

The BI portal is a part of this trend. The self-justifying, intuitive thing about the BI portal is that it provides identity of purpose amidst diversity of information sources. A firm's information supply chain or customer portfolio can be disclosed in depth in its unity of enterprise content while the particular role of the information consumer can be customized using profiles, filers, and security constraints. What is more, portals have become a point of business identity by furnishing an original synthesis of existing technologies. They put an new spin on several technologies, which, in isolation, were doomed to impotence or oblivion but, when joined, allow emergent properties—such as knowledge—to be delivered. This makes the result seem like more than the sum of the parts. The rehabilitated and reinforced technologies include so-called push technology, content aggregation, application servers, and search engines. As for emergent properties, customers don't want more data; they want more knowledge. The real hard to attain treasure here, knowledge, becomes the target in the relationship between the information source and the decision maker, as framed by the BI portal.

As discussed in detail in Chapter Seven on total data warehouse quality, conventional wisdom places data, information, and knowledge on the same continuum. This makes it seem like a miracle that dirty data is scrubbed and the result is knowledge. At one end of the line is raw data. The quality of the data is progressively improved by subjecting it to a defined, rigorous quality improvement process—also called the *information supply chain*—and the result is information. The quality of the information is further improved, and the result is knowledge. The defined process approach makes knowledge into a point on the horizon toward which information improvement is continuously driving. However, because there's always room for improvement, you can never quite get there. What is required to bridge the otherwise insurmountable gap between information and knowledge is the practice of making business decisions. Such a practice feeds back into information and adds the requirement of being able to ground a decision on it. This grounding requires the commitment that is the mark of knowledge. This is the one respect in which the older and less elegant term *decision support* is still perhaps superior to the caché of *business intelligence*. The echo of a commitment can still be heard in the "decision" of "decision support."

At this point, it will be useful to motivate an understanding of the inherent attraction that a BI portal holds over information consumers. Naturally, a "portal" is an entry point to a domain. In this case, *portal* has come to refer to an entry point to the Web. Recall the inscription over Dante's mythical account of the portal of hell—"Abandon all hope ye who enter here!" A portal expresses a lot about a place. In our case, the imperative inscribed over the BI portal would be, "Know the customer, know the business, and know the market!"

By now, most people are aware that the model being imitated by BI portals is that of Yahoo!'s MyYahoo! In effect, MyYahoo! provides the customer with a personal Web identity. An identity is what provides continuity amidst change. This differs from sameness or constancy, in that identity provides for overlapping features and resemblances that may gradually evolve and change. In simple consumer-oriented terms, an identity is whether a person is presented in electronic mail as a person@aol.com or -@ibm.net, or -@acm.org. This is rather like the sports team with which a person identifies. As a basic example, because MyYahoo! has collected consumer address information, it is able to present the current weather based on location automatically. Thus, the personal portal delivers information to the customer based on a profile of interests provided by the person, consisting of everything from stock market security ticker symbol, sports teams, current events, hit movies, and corporations in the news. Such profiling extends to collaborative filtering, based on communities of interest.

The number of entertainment options distinguishes it from a similar approach, for example, provided by ***The Wall Street Journal*** Interactive Edition. For a modest extra fee, subscribers to the ***Journal*** obtain five separately nameable portfolios that not only track the security price but gather articles in which the firm is named or even provide e-mail alerts of relevant new items in the news. Briefing books on publicly traded firms are available, reports required by and submitted to the SEC are available online—as an example of content aggregation—and a host of other content-based research tools is available.

This model of a business portal on the Internet for the individual business person is then abstracted, generalized, and transferred in the direction of commercial enterprise by BI portal vendors that provide products and development kits for the construction of a customized BI portal for a firm's intranet or extranet. Several features characterize the architecture and implementation of BI portals. As we examine these features in this section, relevant products and Web URLs will be mentioned. As indicated, innovations often show up embedded in proprietary architectures and products. That is likewise the case here. (Please note that these products have not been evaluated in a lab, and no endorsements are intended. All the usual disclaimers apply.)

Working from the front-end toward the back, the information consumer ("user") interface is the universal thin client, the Web browser, an important feature of which is the use of search engines to navigate through reports, briefing books, customer demographic content, product profiles, and business publications of all kinds and contents.

The ancient mathematician Archimedes is supposed to have shouted "Eureka!"—that is, "I have found it"—and run naked down the street (because he was just stepping into the bath) when he solved a problem posed by the King of Syracuse. Business analysts using a product named *MyEureka!*—as well as MineShare's Information Portal (in beta), Sqribe's ReportMart EIP, Viador's Sage, and VIT's Information Assistant—are to be cautioned about such over-enthusiasm. Clever naming aside, it is the search functionality—"I have found it"—that is the point here. Familiar Internet search technologies rely either on databases or repositories filled with content coded by human information sifters or automated searches against the text and tags of Web pages themselves. Search by keywords is indifferent to the manner of indexing. The search mechanism is only as good as the "setup," the work of encoding the content. Naturally, a mechanism is required to enable the end-user easily and effectively to search for content additions and updates. In one way or another, this is building an index, storing it, and using it to look up and retrieve the information. To have a fully "open solution," documents would have to be tagged and stored extensible markup language (XML) in preparation for interpretation by the search engine.

For instance, Microsoft's Channel Definition Format (CDF) is a candidate standard using XML to specify the location of content and the delivery protocol. A markup language—of which HTML is a hard-coded subset—is a technique for embedding format features in the surface structure of the text itself. Thus, tags such as <Header>, <body>, and <Applet> communicate how the text immediately following in sequence is to be interpreted by the browser. They represent structure scattered throughout the text itself. What XML (itself a limited but practical subset of SGML) adds to HTML is the ability dynamically to define new tags, rather than rely on the predefined, hard-coded set. Within practical limits, XML provides self-describing data structures of self-defining depth and complexity by means of a document type definition (DTD). This is a kind of metadata, informing us of the structure of the data, like a database descriptor (DBD) or schema.

Regardless of the under-lying mechanism, this is one of the significant deliverables of BI portal technology—to put the end-user in the driver's seat of rich information delivery without the intervention of the IT department service request process. This idea of information consumer self-service is a powerful one. The extent to which this promise is justified, given extensive behind-the-scenes IT provisioning to support delivery, remains to be seen. Still, the prospect is encouraging because this technology does continue building on the theme of making IT into a behind-the-scenes information utility serving the business needs of end-users who connect according to their own schedule and preferences.

Related to the idea of "self-service" at an information utility is that of so-called push technology. Listen before shouting "It's baaack!" BI portals are an enhancement, a repositioning, and a reuse in the best sense of the words *push technology*. Indeed, watch for vendors with expertise in push, publish, and subscribe, and related channel technologies to reposition themselves into the portal "space." As the reader may recall, *push* was the approach of the famous PointCast software, which literally pushed this technology onto the front pages—from where it fell almost as quickly, due to being indistinguishable, according to one pundit (Brian Walsh), from being hit over the head with a rolled-up copy of **USA Today**. Sometimes, the technology that makes something popular is completely different than the one that makes it useful to the business enterprise. That may, indeed, be the case with push technology, as so far defined. This is an idea too good and powerful to be relegated to the category of the eight-track tape of the 1990s; as a proof of concept, it had much to offer. (In addition, there were problems with the consumption of precious network bandwidth to get sports scores during working hours—a problem that presumably will not occur when the content relates to proper business imperatives.)

Naturally, *push* is a play on the metaphor of the TV channel as applied to the Web. Now, take this metaphor and extend it—a different metaphor, a different architecture for the technology. Let's see what's showing on the data warehousing channel. In the most general sense, a channel is a category of information offered by a content provider. Here, a content provider is a content accumulator, a content aggregator, who takes various sources of information—news, stock feeds, sports, entertainment, data warehousing aggregates—and makes them available from a content aggregation server to subscribers. The subscribers—information consumers—point their browsers at the server on a scheduled and periodic basis, determined by a profile on the client, to obtain the updated content. The channel maps to a URL on or through a Web server.[11]

For example, the broker Charles Schwab has built what used to be considered an extranet but is now a BI portal to publish mutual fund sales results to some 300 Schwab partner companies over a secure private network. This is still the "low-hanging fruit." Instead of receiving monthly paper sales reports, authorized partners use their Web browsers to view or dynamically generate reports on their company's sales results.

All of the solutions so far really entail client polling simulating push from the server rather than true publish and subscribe from and to the server. Polling can cause unnecessary message traffic as data consumers repeatedly check for updates that have not yet occurred; unnecessary traffic as the same updates are repeatedly sent many times, based on recipient polling; and the need for server power that scales linearly in proportion to clients.

Yet another innovation[12] attempts to overcome the objection that the network is flooded with point-to-point updates. Client network use is monitored. A "Polite Agent" protocol then transmits data in Infopacks from the server to the client in the background during periods of network inactivity. The transfer is interruptible. This means that the objection against using push on bandwidth-constrained environments—PointCast's Achilles heel and downfall—is overcome by transferring content in multiple sessions. Incremental downloading in multiple sessions is a simple and powerful method of avoiding straining network resources. As an instance, benefits accrue to sales personnel who are out where the rubber meets the road and need to compare actuals versus forecasts from the data warehouse. They can call in occasionally and get the latest reports on who is buying what and where. Naturally, they can also get product data, customer lists, presentations, and sales prospects in chunks.[13]

Right now, from the perspective of the channel metaphor, push technology occupies the children's hour—though it does so with style. When it grows up and is ready for prime time, then it does so as "multicast." What, then, is multicast?

When you have a lot of people who want the same information at the same, automated pull will not suffice. Intelligent polling and one-to-one data pumping will not scale. This is because they lack support of the network infrastructure—at the router level. Polling is doomed as a two-tier solution in a dynamic and challenging n-tier environment. Such dynamic environments exist on the financial trading floor, in pharmaceuticals, telecommunications, and certain dimensions of manufacturing.

What is the next level of functionality? Let's return to work flow and how push technology affects it. Understanding work flow as a coordination of commitments means information is published and subscribed to, then delivered only to those who subscribe, not broadcast potentially to the entire Internet. That requires something called *multicast*.[14] Multicast is intermediate between a true broadcast, which is one to all, and polling, which is one-to-one (over and over again). A broadcast sends information to all clients on the network, whether they are listening or not. As broadcasts cross subnetwork boundaries, they use precious bandwidth (and router CPU cycles to process the packets), even if only a fraction of the machines are interested in the information. This is an entire class of intra- or Internet traffic. (See the text box entitled Multicast Push Channels.)

Multicast Push Channels

Multicast uses class D Internet (IP) addresses, which are reserved for multicast traffic. Class D IP addresses begin with 1110, which reserves addresses 224.0.0.0 through 229.255.255.255. These addresses, in turn, end up defining a "channel." Today, most TCP/IP software on clients ("stacks") are multicast aware (including Windows 95 and NT, as well as leading UNIX implementations). In addition, routers must be configured to be aware of multicast traffic using the Internet group management protocol (IGMP, RFC 1112). That is where "some assembly is required" to bring multicast into being but also where the payoff in conserving bandwidth occurs. If no client machines have dynamically registered with the multicast-aware router, no traffic gets sent to that subnet, thereby preserving bandwidth. Thus, multicast achieves high message fan-out without consuming high bandwidth. This cannot be handled merely from the client work station. However, it is completely consistent with and supported by the current Internet infrastructure.

Here, the model is publish and subscribe, in the full sense. What is meant by publishing is transformed. Naturally, we are not talking about publishing a static web page. Rather, publishing becomes a matter of information and work coordination focusing on delivering data warehouse data or completing or coordinating a business task. Information flow is abstracted from point-to-point connections—no hardwired locations of physical IP addresses or Domain Name Services (DNS) names here. Here, the information flow process enabled by the multicast software infrastructure begins to evolve into a full-fledged ORB.

Data warehousing uses of this are on the horizon. In Chapter Thirteen on metadata, one of the roles of metadata was to track the timeliness of the data warehousing refresh cycle. The metadata repository was supposed to contain flags indicating the completion (or not) of the latest synchronization of aggregates and details, dimensional refreshes, and detail fact structure loads. Instead of requiring the end-user to check these completion flags, the status can be proactively "pushed" out to them.

The data warehouse information update is multicast one time instead of once for each client. This is also cleverly called *narrow casting* by some BI vendors. The update is transmitted only to those parts of the network in which there are clients who have registered an interest. Therefore, scalability is leveraged because a greater number of subscribers can be accommodated by the transmission ("broadcast") without having to add more servers. For example, how do actual historical sales, inventory, or deliveries compare with planned or estimated? Are inventory levels low, given the projected estimates out of the data warehouse? Is client business won or lost? Are product sales triggering critical thresholds? Are support calls for a product reaching a high level, requiring reinforcements or intervention? Inventory tracking, marketing, financial trading, accounting, help desk, and customer support applications each manage separate databases and are updated from an single, existing point of method invocation. The key is a metadata server where clients register their interests in data warehousing subjects (fact structures) and to which the data warehousing content provider makes reference in publishing its updates. Information flow—one can, indeed, say data warehousing workflow—now coordinates transactions occurring at one point and being reported to many recipients.

In bringing the data warehouse to life via the Web (and giving structured content to the Web via the data warehouse), we have indicated that action at a distance is the source of the power and attractiveness of Web computing. That is, the main action is interaction at a distance. Therefore, we must be sensitive to the strengths and weaknesses of the interactive model of computing. What is the most painful thing about sitting at a work station and interacting with the data warehouse via the Web server in real time? Downloading data. Clicking and waiting. And waiting. And waiting.

This suggests that any technology that reduces work station wait time will be irresistible. Irresistible the way a cash station is and waiting in line at a bank is not. Irresistible the way information finding you is intuitively more appealing than undertaking an extensive search. Web "push technology" is one such technology. Instead of clicking and waiting for a download, push technology makes possible scheduled background polling and fetching of data. This perception is the intuitively obvious, self-justifying feature of push technology. In an environment in which large amounts of data are stored in a data warehouse and potentially require delivery across the network, anything that enables data to be scheduled and pushed in asynchronous, off-peak times is an attractive value proposition.

As suggested, putting the information consumer in the driver's seat by means of a search function is as good as the content aggregation that supports it. If one drills down on a content aggregation server, one gets to gateways to diverse data sources, such as dimensional databases. At this point, we are constructing reports—somewhere—registering them in an information repository, delivery server, or content aggregator—and making them available for publish and subscribe distribution. This is a powerful and efficient approach, in that most of the heavy lifting is performed by the back-end relational databases, OLAP engines, or cube constructors. However, what if we want to construct business analyses dynamically? What if we require flexible representation at the browser level that maps directly to changes in states of the business, as represented in the back-end data stores? Is yet another server required?

The idea of an application server is undergoing a repositioning and transformation in two separate directions. In one instance, it is becoming an "analytic engine." In the other instance, it is becoming a repository for reports and structural glue required to promote interoperation and integration. This, in turn, becomes the basis for metadata. In both cases, this positioning is being used to locate business logic where it should be—on the middle tier. As it is being used in the literature right now, the difference between an application server and an analytic engine has to do with the abstractness of the approach and generality of the solution. If industry-specific business problems are being solved using component libraries of prefabricated business objects, you've got an "analytic engine." If you are just interested in scalability and joining many-to-many heterogeneous databases with a coherent LUW, you've still got an "application server." Of course, the analytic engine offers scalability and architectural benefits, too. Arguably most of the analytic power in the analytic engine comes from the component library, not from the server, as such. Naturally, as soon as an application is constructed, it has to be executed somewhere, and that should not be on the client! Several Java-based business component libraries are now available.

The claim is that these components are not raw class library widgets but drag-and-drop business artifacts that can be manipulated by business analysts with limited computing interests. Remember when PowerSoft's DataWindow made it the premier Rapid Application Development (RAD) tool in its day, so that the company even applied for a software patent on the technology? One small software development firm is trying to find a parallel to that success with data-aware components coded in Java. These integrate with nonvisual as well as presentation components to perform business analysis. When additional controls that incorporate time-series logic, standard deviation, and smoothing functions for forecasting applications, such as those offered by analytic engine vendors, the application is making pretensions to represent the dynamic state of the business. Indeed, at least one success story targets an application using Java business components that replaced a klunky PowerBuilder desktop "pibble" with data-aware Java applets. Naturally, these components require a sever from which to be distributed and, in some instances, on which to execute. That is yet another step in the direction of an analytic engine. Ready-to-use, high-level Java applets can be dragged and dropped onto an HTML page. It is a winning idea and well positioned with that of an analytic engine.[15]

The BI portals were supposed to help us manage and integrate the fire hose of information being directed at the enterprise. Now, we find that the portal itself requires assistance in integrating all of the components. This implicates it in the metadata grand challenge.

As discussed earlier, a "grand challenge" is a problem, the solution to which redefines what is possible, both with technology and with human behavior itself. It may seem a surprise to rank metadata as a grand challenge. However, if we look at the behavior of the market—recognition of the importance of metadata and frustration at the definition and redefinition of the problem(s)—it starts to dawn on us that we are dealing with a problem bigger than any of us might like to admit. Still, grand problems tend to evoke grand efforts by innovators and entrepreneurs. In that sense, the BI portal is like metadata itself. It is an architecture that encompasses many requirements, not a specific product. Like any really tough problem, the solution will require both step-by-step progress in increments, as well as breakthroughs, redefining the limits of the possible. Such incremental progress is visible in the coordinating functions provided by BI portal products. Products addressing the metadata grand challenge have names like "deliveryManager, "BI Repository," and "metaAnything." Also, truth be told, every vendor is required to have a narrative about the role of metadata, and many data stores are being "fortified" with the intelligence required to provide them with the dignity characteristic of metadata. Though there is no guarantee, reality does eventually tend to catch up with the rhetoric. (See Table 16.1 for a summary of products by requirements.)

Table 16.1:   Business Intelligence Portal Product Space

Requirement	AlphaBlox www.Alphablox.com	Information Advantage www.Infoadvan.com	MineShare www.MineShare.com
Thin client: Portal Interface		MyEureka! Information Portal	MineShare Information Portal
Business component library	The Blox—data blox, query blox, etc.		MineShare Architect
Application Server		Query Engines Report Server	
Analytic engine	AlphabBlox Analysis Server Envir (BASE)		MineShare Server
Content Aggregation server		Content Server	
Firewall			
"Push" (channel)		BI Report Caster	MineShare Publisher
Metadata Indexing			

SQRIBE www.Sqribe.com	Viador www.Viador.com	VIT www.Vit.com	WhiteLight www.WhiteLight.com
Report-Mart EIP	Sage	Information Assistant	
Visual Sqribe (not Java)	Low-Level Java SDK		ACE Basics CDK
SQR Server	Information Center	Delivery Manager	
			Analytic Server
		BI Directory	
	Senteniel		
Report Surfing; SmartCuts	Courier Channel	Delivery Services	
BI Repository		metaWarehouse	

Finally, a complete portal architecture also requires integrated, flexible security mechanisms. These include a firewall to restrict access to the data sources to authorized individuals and extensive security mechanisms to manage access to heterogeneous data sources. Group-level, role-based security makes it possible for some groups to view reports that are completely invisible to other, unauthorized groups, while both groups view reports to which shared access is required. (Also see Figure 16.2: Business Intelligence Portal Architecture.)

Two other trends require mentioning in the "product space." First, watch for the "big guys" to reposition work group software into the portal domain. In particular, IBM's Lotus Notes and Microsoft's Exchange will be retrofitted to accommodate the front-end functionality of the BI portal. Second, ERP firms, such as SAP and Oracle, can be expected to propose BI portal add-ons to the data warehousing aggregation server that they are providing for their transactional ERP systems. There's a model of technology development here. Often, the most dramatic innovations show up as parts of proprietary solutions, from small firms able to incubate the core ideas. This is a proper thing, precisely so that the innovators can reap the rewards of their ideas. Then the innovation is recast in terms of generally available de facto ("open") standards and APIs. Broader access is accompanied by making the idea into a commodity. Thus it is with the convergence of the Web and the data warehouse. This convergence has been predicted (and, indeed, has been ongoing) for some time now. The number of conferences and presentations in which the Web functions as the ultimate delivery system for data warehouses is reaching critical mass from a "buzz word" point of view.[16] Everyone agreed—it's a great idea. Yet everyone also seemed to believe that something was missing. That something was a unifying architecture such as a BI portal. In short, when the Web and the data warehousing system converge, what it looks like is a BI portal.[17]

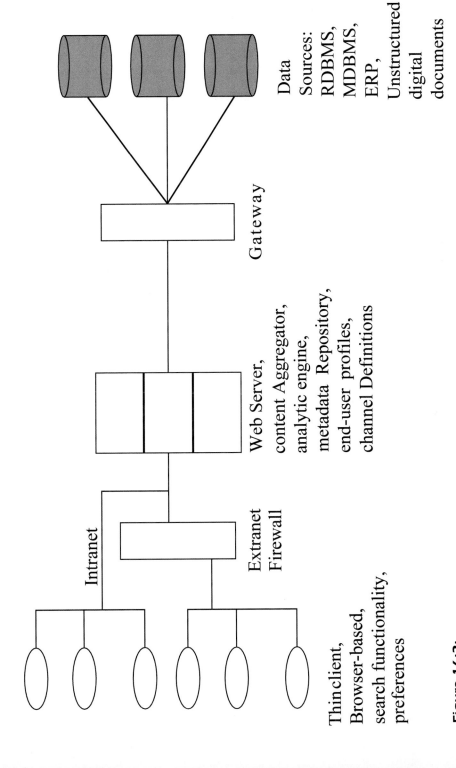

Figure 16:2:
Business Intelligence Portal Architecture

SUMMARY . . . .

The business case for the convergence of data warehousing and the Web lies in improved work flow, coordination of information sharing commitments, and management coordination. Several varieties of knowledge are made possible by the use of the data warehousing systems—superior knowledge of customer behavior, opportunities for brand development, the time stamping of the moment of value when customer and product interact. All of these are augmented by the Web in terms of rapid response, extent and depth of business relationship, and integration of heterogeneous sources of information. The Web as a delivery system makes the Internet itself, including intra- and extranets, into a killer application, one that redefines the limits of what is possible. Key Internet technologies are reviewed in detail. No matter what the front-end— whether Java enhanced HTML, Active-X, components of Delphi, Power Builder, Visual Basic or one of their derivatives—*they are all chasing data*. They all are required to deliver enterprise-relevant information from a data model implemented in a relational database. These relational databases include data warehouses. Now take the discussion to a higher level of abstraction and think of the Web itself as a diverse, distributed, loosely structured data store. The defining database schema, however, is continuously being changed. A loosely connected network of servers—the Web infrastructure—is undergoing constant transformation as servers are added and drop off, constantly entering and exiting. Think of the Web itself as the ultimate database. The discipline of an entire methodology is required to get one's arms around it. Such a methodology is identified in the literature and discussed. Meanwhile, when the Web and the data warehousing system converge, what it looks like is a business intelligence portal. What this is, its reality and potential, are presented.

---

[1] Hackathorn, Richard D. *Web Farming for the Data Warehouse*, San Francisco, CA: Morgan Kaufmann Publishers, 1999, p. 31.

[2] See Keen, Mougayar, and Torregrossa, 1998: p. 72-75 for this and other engaging examples.

[3] I still prefer the use of *decision support* to what is becoming its replacement *business intelligence*. Although I know I am swimming upstream here, I prefer to keep kicking. This is because *decision support* implies the commitment of making a choice. A decision is a commitment to one direction rather than another. This, in turn, fits nicely with the commitment implied in saying that a person "knows" something. True, they might be wrong, but they will be held accountable for what was asserted.

[4] It's a serious breakdown when they are not, usually accompanied by calling out the National Guard and other elements of disaster relief. This may lead one to speculate that, because of the commitment implied in knowledge, one should perhaps say *knowledge utility* rather than *information utility*. However, I will stick with the customary usage, because it is the customary usage and because so much progress remains to be made in raising the level of the quality and commitment of service.

[5] Actually, this is more a mnemonic device or piece of practical reasoning for action than an example of valid reasoning. The implied minor premise that "some client-server systems are exemplified by data warehousing architectures" does not sufficiently constrain or restrict (medieval logicians would have said *distribute*) the middle term, *client-server*. Still, both the conclusion and its converse are true.

[6] "Exportable" is a story in itself. See the text box entitled Internet Munitions.

[7] This "everywhere" has become "many places" under the pressure of proprietary hooks introduced by

the vendors of the various integrated development environments (IDEs). In fact, SUN has sued Microsoft, alleging violations of the Java licensing agreement. The gist of the matter is whether Java will remain portable across multiple platforms—UNIX (dozens of varieties), Windows, Mac—or whether the Java standard will become "balkanized," fragmented, and end up like UNIX—a standard in name only. That a company believes it has a "legal cause of action" instead of (or in addition to) an evolving product or market is never good news. If a research study were to track the amount of litigation against technology innovation, the prediction is that these two curves would move opposite one another. In my opinion, they may have crossed in about 1997. At this date, the jury—literally—is still out.

[8] The yellow sticky with a password written on it and posted on a terminal is a "wall of paper."

[9] See www.junglee.com.

[10] See especially http://www.webfarming.com for an overview. Much of what is said here is my own "spin" on what is surely the most original and disciplined applications of what everyone agrees is a wonderful source of knowledge. We were all wondering how to manage the lack of structure. Well, an answer is at hand. Finally, I could be wrong, but the farmer in the charming artwork accompanying this site looks more than a little bit like Dr. Hackathorn.

[11] Viador Courier makes use of the metaphor of an in-box, which suggests that alerts are e-mail-based. Sqribe has ReportSurfing and SmartCuts, which is channellike, URL-based navigation. MineShare is preparing a channel-based Publisher. MyEureka! explicitly makes use of the metaphor of the channel in its BI ReportCaster. MyEureka! calls hypertext support *Hot Objects,* and it is what makes its reports act like Web pages, with hot spot, drill-down capabilities. Sqribe (recently acquired by Brio) calls similar hot links *SmartCuts,* which make possible "ReportSurfing." URLs are documented in Table 16.1.

[12] See BackWeb at www.BackWeb.com.

[13] No discussion of push technology would be complete without mention of Marimba's Castanet. This is not a BI portal. However, it applies the channel metaphor to files that constitute a Java application, applet, HTML source directory, or content authored with Bongo (a tool similar to Shockwave). Basically, Castanet is different from all the other contenders, in that it is about software distribution (currently Java software), not content aggregation. Applications are delivered to end-users, updated, and maintained without their involvement. Although we might well disagree with they hype that push will replace client-server, considerations of scheduling, time management, distribution of content to knowledge workers, and its over-night success in capturing imaginations suggests that there is a place for push technology in the panoply of enterprise platforms. (See www.Marimba.com.)

[14] This may already have happened with an unsung company, Tibco (see www.tibco.com), whose technology is increasingly being licensed and embedded in products from Cisco, 3Com, Oracle, and Informix.

[15] Other vendors in the space along with Alphablox with what are, in effect, Java-based business class libraries include MineShare's Architect, Sqribe's Visual Sqribe (not Java-based), and WhiteLight's ACE Basics CDK (Component development kit). Viador offers a lower-level Java software development kit for those requiring more customization.

[16] It is to his credit that Rick Tanler foresaw this convergence, though not the specific category of the BI portal, in his 1996 book, *The Intranet Data Warehouse*. The esteemed author was recently sighted as the CEO of business portal product provider, Information Advantage.

Meanwhile, many people are excited by the BI portal because it is the first product in decades to provide a customizeable business context and framework different than that of Microsoft Windows.

[17] A version of this material on *business intelligence portals* was published in Intelligent Enterprise in August 1999. Let me thank Justin Kestelyn, Executive Editor, Eileen Berminghan, Senior Editor, and Dave Stodder, Editorial Director, for their support of this work.

17 *Data Mining*

In this chapter...

*The vein of research data
is almost always richer than
it appears to be on the surface,
but it can only be of value if mined."*
Morris Rosenberg[1]

DATA MINING AND DATA WAREHOUSING

The goals of data warehousing and data mining overlap. Both aim at understanding customer behavior, managing and building the brand, tracking product performance in the market, and marshalling methods of knowledge discovery, consolidation, and systemization in the interest of delivering business value. Both data warehousing and data mining can assist us in directed knowledge discovery. We have a question that guides, "directs" our inquiry. What answer does the data provide? Data mining definitely stretches the envelope as defined by data warehousing, and, ultimately the two approaches are different in both form and detail. They cannot be substituted for one another. From a business perspective, they employ different methods. They are positioned in different places in the technology hierarchy. Finally, they are at different stages of growth in the life cycle of technology innovation.

Data mining is the only one of the two approaches that is capable of undirected knowledge discovery—it can provide us with insight into what questions about the business we should be posing in the first place. It can help us to formulate the questions that we bring to the data warehouse. Up to this point, the discussion has remained diplomatically vague about how the questions addressed to the data warehouse data get formulated and invented. How do they percolate up in the first place? Even in the case of ad hoc queries against the data warehouse, the assumption was that the business analyst's understanding of the business was instrumental in enabling him or her to formulate the questions. The business insight needed to craft the questions to be answered by warehouse data remained hidden in that black box—the analyst's head. Data mining now gives us tools with which to engage in question formulation. In science, that is sometimes called *hypothesis formation*, where the *hypothesis* is treated as a question to be addressed, validated, refuted, or confirmed by the data. The confirmation or refutation of the hypothesis counts as knowledge in the strict sense. Indeed, we sometimes gain more knowledge from refuting a hypothesis than from confirming one. Refutation is absolute; whereas confirmation is always partial and tentative. Data mining uses methods of statistical analysis along with those of operations and optimization research. Whereas the data in the warehouse is a good target for such processes, due to technical reasons, a sequential file extract often has to be taken from the data warehouse and passed to the data mining application. As indicated, data mining stretches the envelope of possible data warehousing questions asked, issues engaged, and answers delivered. Predicting the behavior of securities on the stock market; fraud detection in insurance and credit cards; and financial portfolio optimization—these are not thought of as typical data warehousing tasks, but they are being attacked by data mining methods.

In the hierarchy of technologies, data warehousing is first and foremost an architecture, whereas data mining is best described as an application. Thus, while data mining is logically prior to the data warehouse in its role in formulating the very questions to be asked of the data warehouse, it is not physically prior. The scrubbed, consistent data in the data warehouse is a good target for data mining extraction and analysis. Without the quality data of the data warehouse, data mining is at risk of turning up "fool's gold." Without the penetrating analytic capabilities of data mining, the data warehouse is at risk of providing a convincing demonstration of the trivial. If that seems circular, it is. Alas, a better data warehouse could be built if we had the results of our data mining application of the warehouse in the first place. This cannot be allowed to stop us, however. As usual, system development is a boot-strap operation. Selecting the input variables to the data mining operation cannot be done without knowledge of the business problems and elements being addressed.[2] The solution is to conceptualize the relation between architecture and application. The services provided by the warehouse to the data mining client include clean, consistent data. The data mining application, in turn, will "feed back" to the data warehouse with requirements to prepare data flags indicating the accuracy and reasonableness of facts taken from legacy systems; the transformation of continuous values into categories as needed for mining; and status and details describing demographic behavior.

Meanwhile, the approaches of data mining and warehousing are at different stages in their life cycles. Data warehousing is a mature (though, of course, still evolving) technology. On the other hand, commercial data mining products—in the profile about to be described—were not even available prior to about 1995. True, the roots of data mining are to be found in statistics, including such software as the statistical package for the social sciences (SPSS) and statistical software function libraries from SAS. In 1968, Morris Rosenberg, a sociologist and early data miner, wrote (1968): "The vein of research data is almost always richer than it appears to be on the surface, but it can only be of value if *mined*." Now, data mining technology has hit its stride with the provisioning of tools with GUI front-ends, drag-and-drop association of variables, drill down from summary to detail data, fewer requirements that flat files always be used as input, and shrink-wrapped approaches to installation and use. Data mining is, thus, no longer the stuff of research theses and Ph.D. dissertations at MIT and Carnegie Mellon Universities. Still, it is true that, relative to such de facto data warehousing standards as relational databases and SQL, data mining is still at the early stage where the technical innovations are deeply embedded in proprietary tools being applied for the first time to commercial business applications. As indicated, data mining proper is an approach capable of performing undirected knowledge discovery.

For example, the goal of this method of open-ended ("undirected") knowledge discovery is to apply analytic methods to the items in the consumer's "market basket." A market basket is just that—what people pick up, put in their basket, and take to the checkout counter to purchase at the market. The answer to this question will tell us how we can position these items in valuable, limited shelf space and at end aisle displays. This, in turn, will increase the likelihood of positive purchasing decisions, provide enhanced convenience, and furnish meaningful product promotion combinations. We see immediately that many combinations are obvious. We don't require elaborate technology to tell us that associated purchases occur of paint and paint brushes, aspirin and cough syrup, wine and cheese, bacon and eggs. Many combinations have to be filtered out, given a low priority, or discarded in the search for nuggets or rich veins of data that can be exploited (thus, the "mining" metaphor). At this point, an example will help.

The example, humorous but true, that made data mining famous is from a retail business application of such a market basket analysis. Careful analysis of market baskets at stores disclosed an association or affinity in purchasing behavior of disposable diapers and beer. Beer and diapers showed up as getting bought together. This is a pattern, and it implies a model of behavior, albeit, a simple one. However, the meaning of this association is not obvious. It is far from clear that the pattern is a meaningful or useful one. The distance between a bizarre coincidence and meaningful, actionable behavior for competitive business advantage is—what? It is continuing the posing of questions until the questioner is rewarded with an interpretation that gives meaning to the behavior. This has the potential to provide new knowledge, on the basis of which action can be taken to benefit the business and the bottom line. Taken in isolation, this pattern is just a curious "factoid." How do we make sense out of it? We are immediately plunged into a data mining exercise.

What, then, about this affinity in certain market baskets between diapers and beer? Let's take a step back and use this as an example of how data miners work.

The first step after surfacing an association between two items is confirmation that it is statistically significant. Given the size of the sample, one can look up in a table in the back of any statistics textbook the probability that the association is due to chance. Let's say there's a 20% chance that the association is due to accident. Although far from certain, these are good odds that we are on the right track. Further sampling, research, or testing might reduce this probability to the 5% range. After validating the accuracy and significance of the data (yes, there is an association between purchasing beer and disposable diapers) the next step is to bring to bear an understanding of human behavior—in this case, the consumer. This is sometimes also called *knowledge of the business*. It would be useful to gather supplementary dimensional data, as well. Here is where the availability of further data warehousing intelligence will prove to be invaluable. What time were these purchases made? Were they made at supermarkets or at convenience stores? The interpretation really turns on these additional factors, which are derived from context, including understanding consumer behavior, and the shopping situation. It is part of the validation process. A moment comes when sense, common and otherwise, is satisfied. The new father goes out to the convenience store because the new baby has used up all of the disposable diapers and, on the way to the checkout counter, he grabs a six-pack of beer. *Voilá*! Strictly speaking, one could position beer at the end of the diaper aisle without understanding why. A lift in sales would be supported by this action, because what amounts to practical knowledge of a statistical correlation would have been provided by the data mining exercise. But when an understanding of consumer behavior is added—something not able to be provided by the data mining tool alone—causal understanding as to the reasons motivating people is added to correlation. Additional pragmatic knowledge might be crafted in which a cents-off promotion of baby snacks and grown-up snacks—for example, pretzels and sweet pureed carrots—is offered.

So far, all of this has been an exercise in data mining. Even after the tools are installed and functioning flawlessly, a successful outcome is still dependent on ruthless questioning of the meaning of the data. Where does the data warehouse come in? The data warehouse provides the cleansed, consistent, quality-conformed, accurate data for the mining tool. The warehouse provides additional dimensional data, in this case, about the time and place of purchase to make possible a meaningful interpretation. In short, the warehouse provides not only data preparation services but, just as importantly, context and background for a meaningful interpretation of the data to the data mining client.

DATA MINING ENABLING TECHNOLOGIES

Data mining has reached "take-off" speed as an emerging technology with the convergence of several areas of expertise, each of which, by itself, lacks critical mass. This is depicted in Figure 17.1: Data Mining Enabling Technologies.

An overview of the main "bubbles" in this picture will be instructive. In this case, the technology trend being pursued is that of providing what amounts to a "shrink-wrapped market research analyst" on the desktop. As data mining technology becomes progressively more practical and available on the desktops of average knowledge workers, rather than specialists, the vision of a final form as a $99 shrink-wrapped product comes into focus. Such a product does not now exist, and the prospect of actually succeeding in this task, however worthy the vision and goal, will require comment in what follows.

Proceeding through the elements in Figure 17.1, data mining, as we mentioned, began historically with statistics. In general, many-to-many comparisons of data elements—also called *variables*—result in computationally intense operations. Optimization research is concerned with developing satisfactory, "heuristic" solutions to complex computational problems where no effective algorithm is available. We shall see shortly why this is important. Understanding of consumer behavior, as devel-

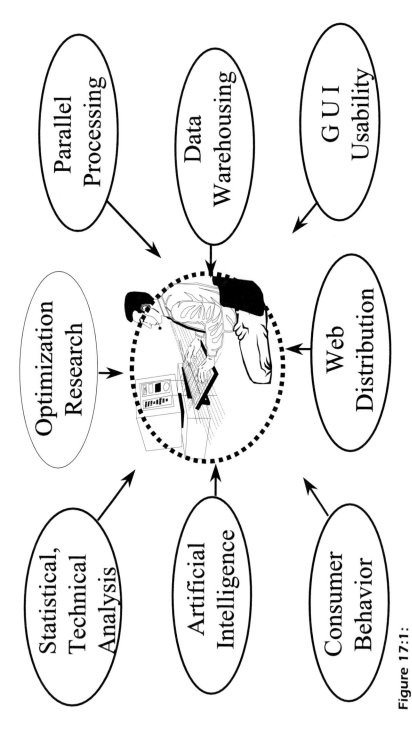

Figure 17:1:
Data Mining Enabling Technologies

oped in the advertising and consumer market research fields, is essential to data mining, because the efforts are to influence behavior in pragmatic ways. Artificial intelligence provides at least one important method—actually a complex of specialized hardware and software—the artificial neural network. Although highly specialized tools, artificial neural networks have made possible predicting outcomes of patterns of behavior that otherwise escape our understanding. Such widely diverging domains as the behavior of consumers, stocks and bonds, and fraud detection have been attacked with significant success. In this post-client-server age, usability is an important component of all systems, and the GUI provides entry-level usability to any data mining tool that wants to be a contender. Finally, clean, scrubbed, consistent data—from a data warehouse—is on the critical path to obtaining consistent and actionable data mining results. The data warehouse and certain of its closely related techniques, especially parallel processing, are enabling factors of data mining.

DATA MINING METHODS

As indicated, statistics have provided methods of classifying entities (called *populations* in statistics) into a smaller number of exclusive and exhaustive groups—clusters—based on similarities of attributes among them; it has provided methods of estimating the correlation between independent and dependent variables or the events they represent; and it has furnished methods of predicting an entity's likelihood of belonging to a particular dependent class or group, based on independent variables. Some of these methods have been a part of software programs since SPSS and SAS in the late 1970s; whereas more sophisticated implementations and functionality have appeared in the middle to late 1990s.

The one essential distinction provided by statistics is that between an independent and dependent variable. It is an oversimplification, but a useful one, to state that most data mining tools employ different methods to identify and relate independent and dependent variables. In short, the independent variable is "responsible for" the dependent one. The way in which the variables relate provides a pattern and a model for the behavior of the downstream variable.

The independent variable is the prior, antecedent, causal, or "upstream" variable; whereas the dependent variable is the subsequent, consequent, effect, "downstream" variable. For example, being a smoker and having an increased risk of lung cancer are the independent and dependent variables, respectively. In the case of smoking, evidence is available to support the interpretation that these two variables are related as cause and effect. Many other kinds of being related are possible. For example, having access to a personal computer (independent variable) is a necessary condition for engaging in on-line banking (dependent variable). (Other examples of these and many other relations between variables are summarized in Table 17.1: Relations Between Variables.)

Table 17.1:   Relations Between Variables

Term	Definition	Example(s)
Dependent variable	determined; downstream; logically after; consequent; effect	the probability that an insurance claim is fraudulent; the price of a stock; the direction of the DowJones average; whether a customer will 'attrit' (go to the competition).
Independent variable	that which is responsible for; upstream; logically prior; antecedent; cause	the diagnosis on an insurance claim; the beta (or risk level) of a security; interest rates; customer income
Symmetrical relation between variables	variables are alternate indicators of the same concept; effects of a common cause	hay fever and size of the corn crop—both corn and ragweed are promoted by favorable growing conditions
Functional interdependence between variables	(symmetrical) variables are mapped to one another by a defined operation or mechanism	beta (risk measure) and risk-reward premium; heart and lungs
Parts of a common system or complex	(symmetrical) variables are both parts of a larger whole; variable do not cause one another; but don't try to remove one of them	joining country club and attending the opera; mortality and morbidity; hot dogs available, so are hamburgers
Reciprocal relation between variables	(symmetrical)—hard to say which is cause and which effect; but the variables are closely connected	temperature and thermostat; live in a 5000 sq. ft. house and drive a luxury car
Accidental relation between variables	(symmetrical)— a correlation without meaning; unintelligible	storks' nests and births in the neighborhood
Necessary connection	(asymmetrical) logically connected by precondition	property owner and eligibility for an equity line of credit; being vice president and holding office
Stimulus and response	(asymmetrical) biological organism determines behavior	being exposed to the advertisement and making a buy decision

(Continued)

Table 17.1:   (Continued)

Term	Definition	Example(s)
Disposition and response	(asymmetrical) attitude influences behavior	politically conservative and attends weekly religious worship
Property and a disposition	(asymmetrical) descriptive category indicates emerging result	smoker and increased risk of cancer
Cause and effect	(asymmetrical) customary conjunction plus explanatory account	30 consecutive days of 100+ degree weather and corn crop withers and dies

Naturally, technology is limited by the business process, the context, and the enterprise environment in which it is implemented. We are accustomed to regarding things in this way. However, here, we are looking at specific technology limitations. Even without such particular considerations, technology also limits technology. What does this mean? See the text box title "The Traveling Salesman Problem Type."

The Traveling Salesman Problem Type

A common view of data mining is that it provides tools to "elaborate" or "specify" combinations of independent and dependent variables by exhaustively scanning all possible combinations of associations. Figure 17.2: Limits of Technology, provides a clear presentation that such an approach is not feasible. By the time a two-way comparison of 40 variables is undertaken on an above-average RISC chip in the late 1990s, the execution time is 12.7 days. If this goes to a three-way comparison, 3,855 centuries would be required to completed the process. Of course, this is longer than recorded history. The bottom right-hand process is longer than the history of the known universe. These types of problems are described as able to be completed in nonpolynomial (NP) time—so they are NP-complete. The solution space is expanding as a polynomial number—a number of the form n^2—whereas, the problem space is expanding exponentially–a number of the form 2^n. As 4, 5, 6, etc. are substituted for n, the NP number grows much faster. This class of problems is like the traveling salesman dilemma. By the time the number of cities to be visited by the absolute shortest route is more than 30, we are getting into the lower right-hand corner of Figure 17.2. In a problem of this kind, brute force methods will not yield results. Even if the power of the computing processor is dramatically improved, the result is a speeding up that reduces the time (for example) to three-quarters that of the history of the known universe. We can't catch up with a problem where adding another variable increases the execution time by an order of magnitude, whereas adding another computer provides only a fractional integral factor of improvement. Thus, the search for an exact, efficient algorithm should be given a lower priority than mechanisms that can be applied to attain local shortcuts, optimums on a case-by-case basis. If our optimization technique—whether decision tree, neural network, or genetic algorithm—degenerates into a brute force search, we are finished. A "heuristic" approach is needed. That is, a "clue" or other means of pruning back options, based on understanding of the business processes, context, human behavior, or other situational factor.

Time complexity function	n=10	20	30	40	50	60
n	.00001 second	.00002 second	.00003 second	.00004 second	.00005 second	.00006 second
n^2	.0001 second	.0004 second	.0009 second	.0016 second	.0025 second	.0036 second
n^3	.001 second	.008 second	.027 second	.064 second	.125 second	.216 second
n^5	.1 second	3.2 second	24.3 second	1.7 minutes	5.2 minutes	13.0 minutes
2^n	.001 second	1.0 second	17.9 minutes	12.7 days	35.7 years	366 centuries
3^n	.059 second	58 minutes	6.5 years	3855 centuries	2×10^8 centuries	2×10^{13} centuries

Figure 17:2:
Limits of Technology. Adapted from Garey and Johnson, *Computers and Intractability* (see References)

There are no easy answers here as to how to formulate questions. Rather, a diversity of interpretations are encountered. This is the basis of the slogan that "correlation is not the same as causation." *Correlation* is a juxtaposing of associated facts. *Causation* is an interpretation. Between variables, there are no spurious relationships, only spurious interpretations. The reason we say that data alone is not knowledge, but merely data, is its lack of structure, organization, direction, and coherence. The meaning is missing without an interpretation to bring the data to life and make it articulate. Just as an interpretation without supporting data would be said to be empty; likewise, data without a unifying interpretation is meaningless and leaves the collector of the data blind. The challenge for the data miner—and what distinguishes the data miner from the data hacker—is to discover and verify meaning amidst apparent disorder and, occasionally, chaos. The lesson is, don't ever stop asking questions; the advantage is to the one who has a data warehouse of which to ask them. The data warehouse can be an invaluable aid in providing depth to the data miner's efforts.

From a data mining perspective, additional assistance is available, in that variables are "block booked." That is, in the old days, when Hollywood licensed movies for presentation at the local movie theaters, it would "block book" one popular, highly profitable film with several other less popular or even unattractive films. Likewise, with variables—saying that a customer, patient, insured subscriber, or even a financial security has a certain profile implies a collection of variables. The challenge is to distinguish the many relationships that can hold between them. Being wealthy, well educated, living in a certain part of town, investing in certain ways are block booked. Securities that trade in the high-technology arena have a different profile than those of firms manufacturing durable consumer goods. To understand the relationship between independent and dependent variables, the data miner must take account of related variables and "stratify," "control," "decompose," and "associate" them with the independent and dependent variables, in turn.

As an illustration, an execution of undirected knowledge discovery showed that wealthy customers with children who had graduated from college were starting to draw on home equity lines of credit.[3] This is a surprising result. One might expect those with children in college to do so—but why those with children who had graduated? In this case, the independent variable turned out to be a hidden variable. The dependent variable was what the financial institution was interested in influencing—determining drawing on home equity credit. The alleged independent variables—a measure of wealth and children who had finally graduated college—were accurate but incomplete. What further candidate independent variables could be gathered, marshalled, and tested to provide a breakthrough in understanding? It could be as simple as calling up the customers and asking them what was going on—if you could get someone to talk to you. Alternatively, further research might have involved cross-referencing and checking other accounts, transactions, or activities laid down in the automated systems by these individuals. Note that someone had to decide to do this. Cross-referencing accounts of customers with such a profile (a measure of wealth, children out of college, drawing on home equity credit) might show that they had other accounts, accounts that represented home-based businesses. Bingo! The "Aha!" moment in which the interpretation comes together and indicates that they were starting home-based businesses. This conclusion has implications as to what further services these people might need. Many different kinds of promotions, customer care opportunities, and marketing opportunities can be directed at supporting home-based businesses.

Whatever the results of undirected knowledge discovery, they are all driving in the direction of directed knowledge engagement. Once a hypothesis is formulated, it must be further tested, explored, verified, or refuted. This is where the other methods of data mining—artificial neural networks, decision trees, and classification come in. We now turn to them.

Artificial intelligence research in the middle to late 1980s produced methods such as artificial neural networks, fuzzy logic, case-based reasoning, and rule-based expert systems. With the exception of artificial neural networks (hereafter referred to simply as *neural networks* unless they could be confused with biological ones), these methods have not enjoyed the success that was initially envisioned for them. In the case of neural networks, a method of improving the accuracy and reliability of the results they produce was discovered. It is called *back propagation,* and it provided a breakthrough in the ability to "train" the neural network.[4]

The neural network is an array of logic components that map an input to an output. These are the independent and dependent variables. Because these logic units function by combining inputs up to a threshold, at which point they "fire"—that is, produce an output—they resemble the operation of biological processes, such as perception and sensation. This results in a certain amount of "hype" about simulating the way that the human brain solves problems. Nevertheless, a genuine sense is available in which artificial neural networks learn—that is, encode and adjust to—patterns directly from data ("experience"). It is convenient to distinguish a "training" phase. Here, the input training data is presented and encoded ("stored") in the neural network. Next, training is distinguished from testing. Additional data from the same sample population (where the outcome is already known) is run through the network, and the results are judged in terms of the number of errors made. On this basis, the network is tuned. Finally, an evaluation phase occurs, in which the remaining input data (which was not used for training or testing), whose classification is still unknown, is processed by the neural network. The result is the classification of this data by the network into groups associated with a predicated outcome. If the input, independent variables, include having a selected measure of wealth, children done with college, and contemplating starting a home-based business, they are candidates for promotions advocating an easy line of equity credit. Finally, the success of such a promotion must be the target of follow-up data gathering to determine whether the results were influenced by the promotional efforts.

Consider another example. Let's say that we have a set of customers who we know for a fact bought into a promotion to use their credit cards more. The data elements and values profiling these customers are used as input to the neural network as a training sample determining the known outcome. After this, training is performed repeatedly; another set of customers is presented as input. The output from these former customers is the predication as to how these latter customers will behave. If presented with the promotion, will they buy it in sufficient proportion to make it worthwhile? If the economics are sensible, the promotion occurs. Naturally, the loop must be closed by gathering data as to whether the prediction is accurate. This becomes the basis for additional training of the neural network.

The neural network approach provides a "black box." The path between the input variables and the output variables is actually a predictive model. Given these inputs, the output is predicted to result. If the customer has a certain demographic profile, as described by these independent variables (income, family size, job title, etc.), they are likely to respond to our offer (and do so with a greater likelihood than those lacking such a profile). The trade-off is between improving on a roll of the dice and the amount of work required in data preparation. Given a neural network that is sufficiently complicated and has enough training and testing, the prospects of producing an accurate and actionable result are better than chance. On the other hand, the trade-off is that work needs to be done in finding the right training data, getting the input data into just the right format, testing the results of the training, and completing the training in a timely way, so that the remainder of the sample extract can be evaluated (that is, evaluated before something shifts in the market or business environment, requiring that the process of training the model be started over again). The reports from Wall Street indicate that a separate neural network is required for every separate security to be traded in the stock market.[5] This is a "high-end" solution, significant years away from the vision of the "shrink-wrapped" research analyst on the desktop. For those with the resources to invest up front, such methods can pay off. However, this implies an answer to the question posed in the first paragraph of this chapter— whether the data mining tool can succeed in shrink-wrapping the market research analyst and delivering him to the average worker's desktop. Because it hasn't happened yet doesn't mean that it won't. However, there are "buts." Can another method improve on neural networks?

From the logical perspective, the complaint about neural networks is that they remain "black boxes." The results are good, but the explanatory power is limited. If intelligibility is required, they really can't provide it. Decision trees provide methods of predication that are more transparent and surveyable, and, in that sense, more intelligible. The decision tree is a mesh of "if-then-else" paths linking independent and dependent variables. The decision trees themselves are derived from statistical algorithms, including one defined in the 1970s, now implemented in data mining software. (See the Glossary on "CART"—classification and regression trees—"CHAID," and "C4.5," a name apparently invented by a mathematician, not a marketing specialist.) Candidate variables and input data with these variables are specified to the decision tree tool, and it is unleashed. Tuning parameters are available, such as the number of levels to be attained in the tree; the numeric level of statistical significance at which nodes in the tree are split or merged; and other conditions under which "pruning" (elimination of branches) will occur; or even whether the branches will have two or more paths emanating from them. It is not obvious which independent variable provides the best—most information-constraining—initial splitting of the data into branching pathways. Making such a determination of a "splitter" can require many iterations. However, once built, the explanatory power of the decision tree is high. The tree shows what paths are taken and what forking paths in the mesh of "if- then" logic are pursued. So one can walk through exceptions, anomalies, or questionable results on a case-by-case basis as part of a problem-solving investigation. This is, of course, labor-intensive, but at least it can be done.

For example, in an industry where there are many choices—checking accounts, brokerage services, on-line grocery deliveries—one of the significant questions is, How does one know that a customer is about to jump to the competition? Because it is known to be less expensive to retain a current customer than to gain a new one, if one had sufficient advance notice, steps could be taken to retain the customer. This would support the business goal of reducing attrition. One would start with a sample of customers who have "attrited." The data would have to be prepared ("scrubbed") to remove those who were examples of attrition because they left the country, renounced worldly goods and joined a monastery, died, or otherwise stopped using any service of the kind in question. Many data mining tasks end here and cannot be completed, because the data is not available. If you need to know whether the customer is the owner of a dog or cat (because dog owners tend to be more "loyal," a relevant personality trait here) and the database lacks a field for pet type, you are at an impasse. There is no solution, other than additional data capture. Otherwise, undirected clustering prior to building the tree is required to surface useful independent variables. A short list of independent variables about the customer might include just changed jobs, earns between $65 K and $95 K a year, uses the account less than twice a month, has been a customer either less than one year or between three and six years, or lives in the same zip-plus-four postal code as others who have jumped (for example). Iterations of the splitting algorithms are applied to the data at this point to find out which split makes the most progress toward classifying the training records. Based on the occurrences of errors, a confidence level can be determined, and pruning the tree may be useful or necessary. At this point, a model is emerging that ties input variables—in this case, demographic ones—to the predicted dependent result, which would be that the customer is at risk of jumping to the competition (see Figure 17.3 for a visual summary of the decision tree). When additional customers are processed against this model, some of them are filtered into the "at risk of attrition" classification. This result has the dignity of knowledge—it has the status of a commitment—on which to base action. The action in question is something to improve on the predicted outcome—offer the customer a promotion, send a satisfaction survey and address the dissatisfaction, or undertake other suitable "customer care" activities. The expectation is that follow-up on the results of the customer care activities would show a reduction in the attrition rate. This entails measuring the result of the action to correct, improve, refine, or otherwise iterate the decision tree model on which it is based.

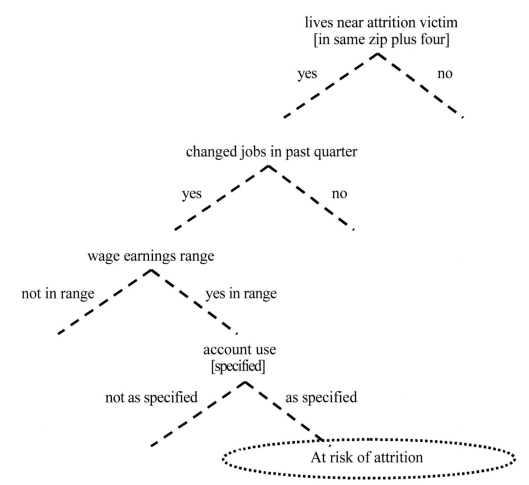

Figure 17:3:
Decision Tree

As indicated earlier, data mining is expanding the envelope of problems that can be engaged using automated data extraction and analysis methods. However, given the number of variables to be compared in applying data mining methods to the technical analysis of stock market securities, problems which are NP-complete (of the traveling salesman type) occur with frustrating frequency. The allocation of financial assets between stocks, bonds, and a definition of risk-free investment (U.S. Treasury notes) for a given risk level is such a problem. Brute force methods end up launching processes that never complete. Operation research types of linear function methods have their uses but are limited because the solutions are rarely linear functions. The results are discontinuous with linear progress occurring until a "cliff" or "discontinuity" is encountered. Progress has resulted from the application of "genetic algorithms" to such nonlinear or operationally complex problems. What are they?[6]

To appreciate genetic algorithms, you have to have an idea of what evolution is—you know, the transformation of a rich protein soup in an atmosphere dynamic with ozone and lightning into macromolecules, proteins, single-celled organisms, edible algae, plants, fish, animals, and, finally, human beings. Table 17.2 summarizes some principles of evolution. The insight of the inventor of the field of research (John Holland, 1992) was to realize evolution is not just a theory. It is a method of optimization; and one that can be effectively speeded up. Genetic algorithms are moving from a research context into that of the real world. Thanks to the work of Professor Holland, a powerful parallel has been found between the centuries-long process of evolution and the nanosecond ticks of a process of encoding. Rather than exhaustively trying all possible outcomes by a brute force search (see Figure 17.1 on the limits of technology), the genetic algorithm encodes part of the history of its interaction with the environment, the part that allowed it to survive and reproduce (or, for example in an economic context, to make a profit). This can lead to local optimums—niches, in ecological terms—that, nevertheless, can be quite satisfactory and productive.

One of Holland's innovations is the introduction of a quasi-logical formalism—a schema (or schemata, plural) that acts as a kind of "wild card," encoding multiple candidate adaptations. This approach speeds up the process of testing by knocking down multiple false leads all at once and converging on a local optimum over a relatively short number of generations (and period of time) as the successful generations pass on their schemata to the following one. This aspect of disqualifying multiple false leads all at once is "intrinsic parallelism." It is a function of the formal notation, not of the number of computers employed. It is activated by the encoding of a wild card—so that the search of a set of features can return all that qualify as a set level result, instead of qualifying (or disqualifying) the features one at a time by separate sequential scans of the search space. These methods have attracted the interest of the finance and investment communities in portfolio balancing and optimization of asset mix for various target levels of risk acceptance. Other problems that have been addressed include optimization problems in operations research, technical analysis in securities, the theory of hedging, risk analysis, and capital asset portfolio modeling. Genetic algorithms have been employed "upstream" from neural networks to determine the optimum mix of variables to be encoded in the neural network.

Table 17.2: Principles of Evolution and Genetic Algorithms

Evolutionary Principle	Definition	Genetic Algorithm Analogy
Environment	Context of adaptation	Problem space
Natural Selection	Behavior of organism in the environment and whether it solves the problem of organism's survival	Information about success of the adaptive plan; counter-example
Variations	Change in chromosome, resulting in change in the allele (or phenotype)	Changes in schemata
Genes	Encoding of traits internal to the organism	Schemata
Allele	A pair of alternative traits, properties, or characteristics of the organism	Structures
Survival	History of the organism is carried within itself, organism passes its genes to its offspring; because the genes encode traits that allowed organism to survive	Intrinsically parallel processing; outcome, utility, performance

DATA MINING: MANAGEMENT PERSPECTIVE

Knowledge discovery can be aided, supported, and enabled by technology. However, technology cannot replace managerial judgment, insight, or context. All of these are required to direct, assess, and provide the locus of responsibility for business results. The ultimate locus of responsibility is, of course, management. Many of these considerations might be generalized and applied to both data warehousing and data mining. The reason they are gathered here is because the concluding focus is on the introduction of new technology into the business environment. That is less the case with data warehousing than with data mining. However, not exclusively so. Therefore, a word of caution.

If neural networks and genetic algorithms can learn from experience (or at least from an encoding of experience), management had better do so as well. This cannot be emphasized enough. When management learns from experience and makes its experience available in a nondogmatic, supportive way to the information technology function, win-win results are produced.

If the organization already has relational technology, do the data mining tools being selected work with the existing data infrastructure or will heroic efforts be required to get them to fit? This is a very practical consideration. Several data warehousing vendors have purchased entire companies whose sole product is a data mining software package, approach, patent, or algorithm. They are in the process of retrofitting the data mining and warehousing tools to interoperate. However, in many cases, that is a work in progress, which will be tested and debugged in the next year or so. Therefore, a word of caution: Be diligent in investigating the interoperability of tools. In short, align the data mining tool with the company's production environment: if you have relational, does it work—reach through and interoperate with relational (*work* does *not* mean take a flat file extract from the one and forward it to the other)?

Some of the data mining distinctions and methods that we have discussed in this chapter have arisen in an academic context, where theory proceeds practice and, sometimes, never arrives at it. As always, the challenge in a business environment is to make research practical. There are large corporate and academic labs that are devoted to that endeavor (Bells Labs, Xerox PARC, IBM Thomas Watson Research Center). The amazing thing is this is also the challenge faced every day by the data miner. Guidance and perspective provided by management and the cross-functional team are indispensable to the success of the undertaking.

Even so, it is useful to remember that imperfect results are actionable; whereas analysis is just analysis. Likewise, remember Herbert Simon on "satisficing"—using a good enough technology, a satisfactory technology, rather than a globally optimal or perfect one to engage and solve the business problem. In the context of data mining, one of the key questions is how to guard against misinterpretation. The answer is easier said than accomplished. The defense against misinterpretation is the acquisition and development of deep experience and knowledge of human behavior—the customer, the business (products and services), and the market (intersection of the latter two). This is where data mining is distinguished from data hacking. The data miner has a depth of understanding, experience, and perspective; the data hacker has, well, data. As usual, you can't shrink-wrap knowledge of the business.

Discovering and determining meaning is a business task, not a statistical or data mining one. As indicated, the results of undirected affinity analysis are rich in "the useful, the trivial, and the unintelligible." The challenge is to distinguish between them. No easy and simple way exists to tell a data mining tool the difference between these three distinctions. A tool may very well be happy with producing the logical equivalent of the "insight" that paint and paint brushes are purchased at the same time. Other, more subtle examples abound. When wealthy people whose kids are done with college draw on equity lines of credit, the difference between the "unintelligible" and the "useful" is where the requirement is for managerial insight and the perseverance to stay the course in the face of doubt. Management is required to champion meaning amid apparent accident. It is management that makes the difference.

SUMMARY . . . .

Data warehousing is first and foremost an architecture whereas data mining is an application. However, the goals of data warehousing and data mining overlap. Both aim at understanding customer behavior, managing and building the brand, tracking product performance in the market, and marshaling methods of knowledge discovery, consolidation, and systemization in the interest of delivering business value. Both data warehousing and data mining can assist us in directed knowledge discovery. Data mining definitely stretches the envelope as defined by data warehousing, and, ultimately the two approaches are different in both form and detail. From a business perspective, they employ different methods. Data warehousing deploys databases, SQL, and open information technology components; data mining uses statistical methods embedded in proprietary software products to explore innovative contexts and problems. Data mining stretches the envelope of possible data warehousing questions asked, issues engaged, and answers delivered. Predicting the behavior of securities on the stock market; fraud detection in insurance and credit cards; and financial portfolio optimization—these are not thought of as typical data warehousing tasks. However, they are being engaged by data mining methods. The celebrated example of the market basket analysis that surfaced the combination of beer and diapers is examined to see how data miners work. Next the particulars of data mining enabling technologies and data mining methods are reviewed in detail. Finally, management is reminded that discovering and determining the meaning of facts is a business task, not a statistical or data mining one; and it is management that makes the difference.

[1] See Rosenberg, Morris, ***The Logic of Survey Analysis***, New York, NY: Basic Books, 1968, p. 207.

[2] This circular "boot-strap operation" is also referred to as a *hermeneutic circle*, because it requires interpreting the part (the data mining application) in terms of the whole (the data warehouse), and vice versa. In this context, the hermeneutic circle refers to selecting dependent and independent variables out of a large domain of candidate variables, distinguishing and understanding the part in relation to the whole, and vice versa. This method, which is as much art as science, is iterative, includes trial and error, and occurs elsewhere in the computing literature as the method of "round-trip gestalt design" methods (see Grady Booch, 1995, ***Object Solutions***); in short, it is somewhat more than another name for our ignorance and not to be confused with a vicious circle (see Berry and Linoff, 1997 on the "virtuous cycle in practice").

[3] Reported by Berry and Linoff (1997).

[4] Back propagation is a training method for improving the accuracy of artificial neural networks—it compares the output of a calculated and expected result from a network and adjusts the threshold at which the component "fires" by providing feedback to minimize the detected difference. See *back propagation* in the Glossary.

[5] See pp. 234–35, Dhar, Vasant and Stein, Roger, ***Seven Methods For Transforming Corporate Data into Business Intelligence***, Upper Saddle River, NJ: Prentice Hall, 1997. This is also a good place to note that data mining methods, algorithms, and heuristics—strengths and limitations—are substantially more complex and deep than can be treated in a one-chapter overview. The goal in this chapter is to provide accurate and useful oversimplifications without pretending to provide a complete account. For a more complete study, see Dhar and Stein.

[6] These methods are rigorous, based on provable theorems, and productive, yet, ultimately, they fall under "heuristics," because they are less comprehensive than a guaranteed effectively computable function, always guaranteed to give the "global optimum" answer and stop. This is because, like heuristics, genetic algorithms may converge on a "local optimum."

18 *Breakdowns: What Can Go Wrong*

In this chapter...

*"We have the potential
to respond to breakdown
with a shift of domains in which
we enter into new commitments."*
Terry Winograd and Fernando Flores[1]

THE SHORT LIST

The sorts of things that can go wrong are as measureless as the sands on the beach. Rather than rounding up the usual suspects—the wrong tool, the wrong vendor, the wrong tape mount, the wrong error report—the goal here is to highlight those things most similar to design defects, questionable methods, or wrong-headed approaches at a conceptual level.

Each of the things that can go wrong with data warehousing present a "breakdown." The smooth forward flow of progress, the effortless and elegant forward motion, the generation of results—the perception and reality of all of these are interrupted abruptly. An obstacle is presented, and we are thrown back on aspects of the data warehousing context that we had believed were working fine but are now seen to be problematic, broken, or unavailable. Strictly speaking, every breakdown is an opportunity to make explicit the assumptions and commitments that are already a part of our background of understanding of the data warehousing situation. Every *breakdown* is an opportunity to have a *breakthrough* in system design, customer service, brand management, or decisive marketing.

THE LEANING CUBE OF DATA

The leaning cube of data is a breakdown in the coordination of commitments of the data warehousing information supply chain. What does that mean? It is the breakdown to which data warehousing processes succumb when the information supply chain is short-circuited. For example, powdered soft drinks that are sold in late spring often are returned in early autumn. They weren't sold. Unless those returns are captured, the sales numbers are skewed. Likewise, prior to the widespread deployment of EDI, manufacturing organizations often experienced a 10–40% correction rate on invoices. The warehouse must capture this data as meaningful business events to uphold the mutual commitments between transactional and decision support systems and the results generated. In this case, the coordination required is applying the adjustments that represent returns by customers to inventory or corrections of invoices. They are part of an overall data warehousing process, not stand-alone transactions. The importance of "closing the loop" must be emphasized.

In broad terms, it is actually the occurrence and overcoming of breakdowns that give us visibility to how the data warehouse information supply chain is a coordination system. The leaning cube of data results when the elementary transactions of the data warehouse are taken in isolation. An isolated transaction is not a relationship with a customer, knowledge of customer expectations, on-time product delivery, or satisfying other similar commitments. It is not development of the brand or useful knowledge of features of the supply chain. It is not an appreciation of the moment of value when the customer decides that the product is the one that solves his or her problem– not an isolated transaction, but insight into how to build a relationship with the customer, whether product differentiation or being the low-cost provider is the key to straightening out the cube. The point of data warehousing is to cross-reference the transaction data by the hierarchical product distinctions and customer distinctions. Within this framework, the transactions become articulate. They speak volumes about the relationship between customer and the company's products. That can be used to build the relationship with and commitment to the customer in a context of trust, intimacy, and knowledge. They can be used to build commitment to the brand in the context of recognition, mind share, and knowledge. As a tool for coordinating these commitments, the data warehouse is like the dashboard used by management in driving the business.

Dancing Naked in the Net

This was the title of Chauncey Bell's presentation to an Electronic Commerce Conference in Toronto in November 1997 (see www.BDA.com). One of the central ideas was that any breakdowns in quality, the delivery of impeccable service, or commitment to delivering value will be magnified on a planetary basis by being on the Web. The antidote is to build relationships with customers using infrastructures for commitment and action in the new digital media, thus getting technology on your side. Although initially believed to be the Web, these media also require the support of data warehousing infrastructure. The take-away here is the challenge and opportunity does not just describe a new form of electronic commerce. It is also a valid description of data warehousing as a coordination commitment technology. Commerce is an information intensive form of life. Except for the production and delivery of physical goods, commerce consists of forms of information gathering, transformation, and distribution. The commitment to customer relationships, brand development, and market dynamics requires visibility to entities provided by data warehousing systems.

THE DATA WAREHOUSE GARAGE SALE

The data garage sale—in addition to being a generic name for a failed data warehouse—is an attempt to build a data warehouse by taking a straight copy of transaction data and operating on it. In general, trying to copy raw transactions directly to a data warehouse results in a data garage sale, not in an enterprise data warehouse. The kinds of breakdowns that are generated as a result of this approach look like poor system performance—response time outside of acceptable targets, batch windows extending into periods of committed on-line use, and even deterioration in the availability of the operational system if the two systems are coupled. In addition, data integrity breakdowns and semantic inconsistencies start to show up, due to issues of the operational synchronization of updating and loading data dimensions to accommodate required points in time. The updates do not arrive at the data warehouse copy at the same time that they arrive at the original instance of the data. When these breakdowns in data integrity show up, this is an especially grave result, because loss of credibility is likely to follow quickly. Unlike the leaning cube of data—where a narrowness in perspective masks a fundamentally sound design—the problem here is hard to fix and often fatal. A data garage sale is just that.

It is important to note that the data garage sale is not to be confused with a back office operation of assembling or staging data as it is forwarded from transactional systems to data warehousing ones. The processes of extracting, transforming, and rearranging data prior to actually loading it into the data warehouse can be messy. Data in such a "half-baked" form is not suitable for end-user inspection or access. Such necessary intermediate operations, including dumping to an operational data store, are not to be confused with a data garage sale. The latter occurs only when one tries to "sell" the customer on the intermediate result, instead of on the completed information product, the data warehouse.

Furthermore, the data garage sale is a proxy for all kinds of data quality problems. If data is incomplete, inconsistent, unreliable, stale (not timely or not synchronized), ambiguous, vague, or insecure, a worst-case scenario is in the offing. The commitment to data integrity is so fundamental, self-justifying, and of obvious value in data warehousing as to require almost no further discussion. Without data integrity, nothing else really counts. It is one of those commitments that requires renewal, effort, and attention every day. The establishment of an end-to-end data integrity coordination process is the required and sensible proactive planning approach. By the time that data quality symptoms are visible or generating side effects, it is too late to be proactive. Extra effort will be required to get things back on track.

WILL THE FUTURE BE LIKE THE PAST?

We rely on regularities in the behavior of persons, natural processes, social processes, and markets. The usual three years of data required as history in building a forecasting system is the systemization of regularities from the past. A breakdown occurs when the future course of events fails to live up to our expectations and, more importantly, to our commitments as defined by past events. How good a predictor of the future is the past? That is a function of many factors, many of which are themselves, subject to uncertainty. It is a function of industry segment, innovations in technology, business practices, governmental regulations, macroeconomic context, and discontinuous and external surprises. By definition, these are unpredictable. So, for example, powdered soft drinks are a mature product with predicable patterns—volume is up in the spring and summer, with returns occurring shortly thereafter. However, the weather is exceptionally warm or cold. Consumers are enamored with healthy living and start drinking athletic coolers after sporting activities. A product substitute emerges. With a new product or one with new uses, the future literally "ain't what it used to be." In the face of uncertainty, there is no substitute for management's steel nerves, judgment, determination, and commitment to stay the course. That said, it must be admitted that one's confidence can be shaken when predictable and regular patterns break down. This is a classic problem: our knowledge is limited.

A significant variation on the theme of the future (not) being like the past is called *post hoc, propter hoc*, meaning "after this, because of this." This breakdown is considered an informal fallacy in logic. The breakdown is to attribute causality to an event when no causality exists. The whistle blows, and the train leaves the station. The whistle did not *cause* the train to leave the station. To imagine that the whistle caused the train to depart is a wrong-headed analysis of the problem, a wrong attribution of a cause, and a wrong conclusion as to the causality. Both the train leaving and the whistle are an expression of one and the same underlying cause—the energy generated by the diesel turbine to power the electrical system in the locomotive. Because something happens *after* another event, does it thereby happen *because* of that event? To consider a more realistic example, what expresses the relation of causality between a product promotion and alleged lift in sales? This is an inference fraught with possible misinterpretations. Has the increase in sales just been shifted around, as seems to happen with automobile rebates, so that a subsequent dip will occur? Has the sales increase been attained by "stealing" sales from a substitutable product within the same brand? Does the plan call for ongoing monitoring to enable this distinction to be captured? Therefore, a word of caution here. Even when deploying statistical measures that express the likelihood that the outcome of a promotion is due to change, one is able to reduce uncertainty and risk, not to eliminate it. So if, for example, if there is a 5% chance that the outcome of the promotion is due to chance, that still weakens the connection between cause and effect in dramatic ways. This may be a good-enough result if selling newspapers, but would a person want one's last-minute tax return delivered to the IRS with that level of assurance, not to mention a similar level of assurance that all is well when stepping into an airplane?

Here, the breakdown is that of "false cause," identifying something as being causally effective when it is not. Simply stated, the opportunity in overcoming the breakdown is a more accurate commitment to logic. In a way, even when properly identified, causality is the complement of commitment. It is whatever is leftover after commitments are accounted for. Commitment is a function of a human conversation or design, in which agreement is reached. A promise is made. Things happen because systems are designed to reflect, support, and implement agreements—commitments—between departments and social organizations, such as business units. Causality is often regarded as a blind mechanism, which, when it works, does so unfailingly and regardless of what people say. The "take away" here is that, even when properly identified, causality is always already a reaction to a previous effect, which, in turn, was the result of a previous cause, and so on. It is a phenomenon in the realm of reaction. The temptation for management (as for most persons) is always to react. However, the rule is that reaction, no matter how successful, always causes at least one thing—more reaction. To break out of the breakdown implied in the cycle of reactions, understanding the context of action is vital. That means that both causal explanation and understanding of the context must be a part of a coordinated plan against which results can be checked, measured, and modified.

MODEL BECOMES OBSOLETE

We have spoken about the data warehouse model of the business. This book began with reflections on learning to live with uncertainty. Data warehousing was one way of doing so and of reducing the risk of surprises that uncertainty always implies by means of warehousing enabled knowledge of the customer, product, and market. We have also spoken about how the connection between independent and dependent variables is a model of the business. We have now come full circle. The data warehouse model of the business is the set of star schemas of intersecting data dimensions and, just as importantly, the relationship with the customer, thereby made possible. What is the shelf life of this model? What are the impacts of competitive, regulatory, or externally determined changes in the business environment?

The requirement becomes one of "recoding" the commitments underlying and driving the calculations made in the model. For example, if the operation of the financial data warehouse model is that T-bills move in the same direction as corporate bonds because they have done so since the end of the Gulf War in 1990, this is really a part of the background commitment—one might also say "assumption"—giving meaning to the behavior of these financial entities. Twenty-twenty hindsight is required to see that this direction of movement is really a commitment, not merely an assumption. When something happens to invalidate this part of the background of operations, it can cost us. If the consequences are mild, we say it's a harmless assumption, otherwise, it was a commitment.[2] When the future is different than the past would lead us to believe, it is often due to so-called exogenous factors that our background commitments call into question. An example of an exogenous factor in the financial area was provided in the summer of 1998. Although the markets were nervous about currency devaluations in Asia, no one expected a default in the European bond market. Of course, Russia is a European country. A Russian "moratorium" on bond payments, based on the convertibility of the Russian ruble and the dollar, had the effect of a default. This caused T-bills to move in the opposite direction from corporate bonds. People didn't want to hold any corporate bonds, which usually have a modest amount of risk, due to the domino effect of events rendering the Russian bonds unconvertible. T-bills are an entity defined as risk free in current financial models, a commitment that has not yet come into doubt. Thus, the model of the business implemented in the data warehouse system must be reworked, recoded, and retested.

MISSING VARIABLES

The point is not only about the future and the past—the always crucial dimensions of time. It is about the breakdown of our expectations. It is about the behavior of the target business dimension—whether the behavior of a consumer or a market security or a product. How do the data warehouse facts behave within a given range of values for any selected data dimension? As an illustration, consider the dimension of price. Here, price is the independent, "upstream" variable; purchasing behavior (the decision to buy the product) is the dependent, "downstream" variable recorded in the fact table. Price is a fundamental attribute often subordinated to product as part of a transaction. It accounts for many discontinuities and apparent inconsistencies in behaviors. People will buy when they perceive a correspondence between price and value. Raise the price and they may perceive more value. Raise the price even more and people will seek out substitute products or do without. Thus, when a threshold price is crossed, the demand for the product undergoes a discontinuous change. Increasing the price produces less overall revenue, because other products are available for substitution, people do without, or the product is regarded as not essential. We cannot provide a short course in economics here. However, one of the basic ideas is that of elasticity of demand. The definition of *elasticity* is that it is the ratio of the percent change in quantity sold to percent change in price. So, for example, when the elasticity becomes less than one, price increases result in an overall decreases in revenue because the number of units sold is less than proportional to the gain in revenue from the increased price. The "take away" here from this admittedly complex example is that behavior is not always a linear function. Discontinuities of all kinds occur. This means that the validity of a business model and its implementation in a data warehousing system must be made the target of periodic, even continuous, assessment.

What are the consequences of this discussion? In no way should it be taken to imply that "all is relative" and, therefore, we should abandon the project of finding meaning amid apparently random behavior or that the commitment to knowing the customer and building the brand should be taken any less seriously. When the future turns out to be significantly different than expected and when assumptions or models are invalidated by counter-examples, the only thing that does stand fast is the commitment made by management to fundamental business and economic imperatives of service, productivity, and value. That, too, is what is meant by learning to live with uncertainty.

OBSESSIVE WASHING

Data scrubbing is a resource-intensive operation. It is an important, at times critical, path or function. Common sense and experience demonstrate that accurate results of inquiries against the data warehouse are dependent on the marshalling and aggregation of consistent and complete input to the facts and data dimensions composing it. The breakdown here is to confuse the data scrubbing subtask with the data warehousing project itself.

If you put data scrubbing on the critical path to the data warehouse, make sure you get there. Data scrubbing is not an end in itself. It is a means to producing good-enough (accurate) information and intelligence (knowledge) out of the warehouse. Thus, a word of caution: *Avoid obsessive washing.*

The preparation of the consistent and complete inventory of products, customers, and other relevant dimensions can benefit from the 80/20 rule. For everyday commercial business applications, rather than trying to get all data perfect, work with totally scrubbing to perfection that 20% of customers who represent 80% of the business, and try to get the other 80% of customers within 20% of perfection. If the transactional operational system has data integrity problems, can they be fixed at the source, rather than at the target? What are the prospects of actually fixing the transactional system, rather than moving the problem downstream to data warehousing operations? Perhaps this is easier said than done. Data scrubbing is a required and useful exercise in building a data warehouse. It is not always a data warehouse project. Simply stated, the commitments that require coordination here are data quality and data availability. Both are essential design points. A breakdown in the former was considered above as the data garage sale. A breakdown in the latter can result in what is here described as obsessive washing.

Avoiding the fallacy of data scrubbing without end leads to an interesting enterprise strategy that data warehouse managers have deployed to get out of a jam: When product and customer data have to be cleaned up to feed and support the data warehouse, "the tail wags the dog." The data warehouse, which is at the back-end, causes the upstream data stores and processing to be improved to support the enterprise-wide warehouse effort. This, too, is a useful example of a coordination of commitments—in this case, commitments between the transactional and decision support systems. This is, in general, a desirable result. From the perspective of theoretic knowledge, the wonder is that quality data could not be acknowledged, pursued, and embraced as an end in itself. From the view of instrumental and pragmatic knowledge, that's just the way the world of business works—timely, good-enough results trump unattainable perfection.

COMBINATORIAL EXPLOSION

Managing large volumes of data takes planning, advanced methods and tools, and skillful implementation capabilities. Data warehousing breakdowns in this area also show up as complaints about system performance—slow interactive response time, batch windows that spill over into the on-line time of day, and work not completed on time. The number of combinations generated by multiple intersecting dimensions grows rapidly, despite data sparsity, because the operation is multiplication, not addition. It is true, a large relational database using read-ahead buffering, can qualify a thousand pages a second. That results in a million-row query taking about 15 minutes. No problem, right? What about a billion-row query? Remember, a billion is only 1,000 customers times 1,000 products times 1,000 time periods. 1,000 times 15 minutes is about 250 hours, and that *is* a problem. That is what is meant by *combinatorial explosion*. (The reader may wish, at this point, to review Figure 17.2: Limits of Technology.) It is true that not all possible combinations occur, but most firms have many more than these three basic dimensions, as well as more entries in each dimension.

Management of sparsity is one of the critical success factors in controlling and minimizing combinatorial explosion. If data is more than about 90% sparse—that is, 10% or less of customer-product-date combinations are actually instantiated—then, significantly enough, denormalization of the time dimension, as described in the discussion of design for performance (Chapter Seven: Data Warehousing Technical Design) can both save storage and deliver improved response time.

Parallel processing, data partitioning, and judicious use of data caching can all be useful in stemming the tide of combinatorial explosion. Ultimately, a truly NP-complete problem will outstrip all of the resources that can be thrown at it. These especially occur in the context of data mining, where arbitrary many-to-many comparisons can unleash a truly "explosive" process. Thus, technology limits technology itself. The commitment to technology must be coordinated with, and limited by an understanding of, truly complex problems. This is where heuristics, optimization, and business judgment must be marshalled to define the scope of the possible and the feasible.

TECHNOLOGY AND BUSINESS MISALIGNMENT

In one case, fraud went undetected for a while because, in spite of sophisticated automated systems, there was insufficient supervision, oversight, and diligence on the part of management. In this instance, no matter how elaborate the fraud detection network—basically driven off of permissible system overrides—it was defeated by account administrators who approved all items under $50 rather than checking them out, as required by the contract with the governmental regulatory agency. You can see how complicated the case becomes when you realize that management incentives for on-time payment of given numbers of items made it beneficial to management to process these small items quickly without diligent inspection. Here, the fraud was not the payment of an item itself (because, in themselves, the items were as accurate or inaccurate as the rest of the processed items). Rather, the contractual violations and lack of diligence in performing oversight were a problem that ultimately cost the company over $100 million in triple damages, significant negative front-page press about a respected and well-known brand and possible collateral material damage in the loss of price advantages and unrelated client business.

One might expect the lesson to be something like "technology is only a means to an end" or "as a tool, technology can be misused." However, in many cases like this, technology is an all-encompassing framework determining options and trade-offs. Technology is not only a tool; it is a framework for meaning, knowledge, and commitments. The breakdown occurs when the structure of the business is misaligned with that of the business system, as represented in the technology. Instead of being a system for coordinating commitments, the system became a source of delay. One solution? Override it! Naturally, in all such cases, matters are more complex and messy than can be fairly dealt with in a couple of short newspaper articles. However, this much is a matter of public record. Management was paid bonuses based on numbers of items processed, but the automated system required large numbers of small claims to be handled manually by staff in a labor-intensive assembly line. The rest is speculation. Not wishing to be perceived as "slave drivers" and apparently lacking the technical acumen or project capabilities to implement an automated approach to the drudge work, management abdicated its responsibility and was subsequently found negligent in doing so. Naturally, it was ultimately the electronic traces and digital audit trails that made the determination of what happened a "no brainer." This outcome was by no means inevitable or necessary. Although hindsight is always 20-20, the alignment of the business and the technology—the coordination of commitments of these two functions in the persons of the responsible managers—is an indispensable ingredient in the integrity and the accomplishments of the business.

BECOMING A COMMODITY

This is the equivalent of death and taxes for all successful technologies. All technologies tend to become commodities. When the data warehouse technology (or any technology, for that matter) becomes a commodity—open, available, accessible, and used by all—it ceases to be a competitive advantage to the owning firm, given a suitably high level of technical competence and ability to execute on the part of the competing firm. The strategic advantage to be conferred on the business by the technology "edge" has become a commodity. That counts as a breakdown. That means that the competition can, in effect, go down to the software market, purchase the product conferring the advantage, take it home, break open the shrink wrap, and compete in the market space once thought to be owned by you and you alone. It doesn't mean that the technology in question is irrelevant or can be junked. It means that anyone who does not have it is at a disadvantage, possibly a severe one, and at risk of losing market share or perspective on product innovations to the competition.

So-called proprietary solutions—for example, the Red Brick class library of functions—were 3–5 years ahead of de facto standard ("open") relational technology solutions. You paid extra for the additional functionality or performance, and the payback period had to be relatively short, because relational database vendors (IBM, Informix, Oracle, Sybase) were closing in fast on the proprietary functions of which the leading inventors were so rightly proud.[3]

What is not likely to be a commodity any time soon—and what is hard to make a commodity, given the multiplicity of sources of legacy data—is the data warehouse navigation layer and metadata repository. Knowing what you've got and being able to access, deploy, and leverage it is a kind of organizational self-knowledge. Here, management can make a difference. Alignment of the technology with the business is powerfully exemplified by how successful data warehouses represent the customer, product (brand), and interactive (time-significant) features of the business. The royal road to the data warehouse is to model it on the form of the business itself and to let basic business imperatives guide its design and deployment.

This is likely to become a source of marketing hype from those needing something to sell. However, it promises to remain a complex system integration, coordination, and customization task for years to come. An advantage in this area—due to skillful project management, intelligent application of object-oriented software methods, and understanding of business data semantics—can be expected to provide the owner with flexible economies of performance and agility.

The important idea to keep in mind is that, as technology, including data warehousing, slides inevitably toward becoming a commodity, management is more than ever what makes the critical difference. Management's knowledge of the business cannot be shrink-wrapped. Over a time horizon that stretches into several years, this knowledge can be made explicit, refined, captured, and built into the architecture, infrastructure, and applications of the information technology assets and resources of the firm. A data warehouse aligned with the business imperatives of customer, product, and market knowledge is one of the most powerful mechanisms for doing this, available to business leaders and managers at every level. It is a powerful formula for transforming a potential breakdown into a breakthrough in business insight and knowledge.

SUMMARY . . . .

Everything that goes wrong—every breakdown—is an opportunity to produce a breakthrough in design, service, management, or decision making. For example, the leaning cube of data results when elementary data warehousing transactions are taken in isolation. The point of data warehousing is to cross-reference the transaction data by the hierarchical product and customer distinctions. Within this framework the transactions become articulate. The data garage is an attempt to build a data warehouse by taking a straight copy of transaction data and operating on it. Trying to copy raw transaction directly to a data warehouse and operating on it without significant transformation results in symptoms that show up as poor performance. Next, a breakdown occurs when the future course of events fails to live up to our expectations and, more importantly, our commitments as defined by past events. How good a predictor of the future is the past? This is a classic problem, our knowledge is limited even after it has been extended by data warehousing systems. What is the shelf life of the model of the business embedded in the data warehouse? The antidote to this and the related issue of the model becoming obsolete is to monitor its validity and periodically update the commitments driving the calculations made in the model. In any correlation of independent and dependent variables the possibility surfaces of missing, distorted, or misinterpreted variables. Simply stated, the commitments that require coordination here are data quality and data availability. The hazards of combinatorial explosion, technology and business misalignment, and the slide towards becoming a commodity are reviewed and antidotes are suggested.

Winograd, Terry and Flores, Fernando, *Understanding Computers and Cognition: A New Foundation for Design*, Norwood, NJ: Ablex Publishing, 1986: 124. See also Bell, Chauncey, "Dancing Naked in the Net," presented at Electronic Commerce and On-line Profits, Toronto, November, 1997, which develops similar ideas (www.BDA.com).

2 Insert here the joke about "bacon and eggs." The hen was "involved," the pig was "committed." More seriously, what seems like an assumption from one perspective is actually a commitment on which we base our actions from another perspective. This is a feature of life—we are required to act with incomplete knowledge. We are regularly deciding in situations of uncertainty.

3 Special thanks to Murray Pratt of Kraft Foods for calling my attention to this technology trajectory *(personal communication)*. As this is being prepared in late 1998, Informix and Red Brick have announced the purchase of the latter by Informix. That is one method of bringing the advantage of advanced extensions to the more readily marketable "open" product.

19 *Future Prospects*

In this chapter...

*"Prediction is hard,
especially of the future."*
attributed to Niels Bohr

ENTERPRISE SERVER SKILLS TO BE IN HIGH DEMAND

As we attempt to get a glimpse of what lies across the visible horizon, we must say that all of the usual disclaimers apply. Current trends can be extended into the future by continuing along the way that things are currently going (that is, extrapolating on the basis of current tendencies). That is a valuable exercise, but it lacks visibility to innovations—whether technical, institutional, or otherwise—that are not a part of the current dominant designs of computing approaches, whether client-server, Web-enabled, or network-centric computing. Just as the manufacturers of impact typewriters were among the last to envision the computer-based word processor and mainframe proponents were late to embrace client-server as an enterprise computing solution, those innovations that produce discontinuous change always seem to come from out of left field. Although prediction is fraught with uncertainty, a good bet is that the grand paradigms and theories of today will become the special cases of tomorrow. This conclusion will attempt both to extrapolate current trends, as well as to get a glimpse of the sources of discontinuous changes that could be approaching.

In the tidal wave of data coming at corporations, one simple truth stands fast, the one fundamental question in a thousand and one forms and variations on the theme is: Who is buying our products and at which time and place are they doing so? This is the question that data warehousing systems are designed and built to answer. Insofar as the data requires database servers of all kinds to administer it, the server is the strategy. Another way of saying the same thing: The data, which holds the answer to the one fundamental question, *is* the business enterprise. Given the volumes of data in question, both proprietary and traditional solutions abound. The mainframe is born again as the "enterprise server." Competencies in the technologies required to manage, operate, and deliver value in data-centric environments are in high demand and are likely to remain that way.

The UDB is a technology trend that sits on the cusp of incremental progress and discontinuous change.[1] In many ways, it is completely continuous with relational database systems and presents step-by-step progress with them, based on "accessing data every which way" in a rule-governed form, according to Codd's twelve principles. This is an advantage from the perspective of compatibility with existing business systems and implementations. In an ongoing business enterprise, "we are like sailors in the open sea who have to rebuild their ship without being able to dismantle it in dry dock and reconstruct it from scratch."[2] On the other hand, the variety of data types that can be handled—text, image, web-based documents, video, etc.—promises new applications about which previously we could not even dream.

Thus, the name *universal*, itself, comes from extending the RDBMS with the addition of object-oriented features, not all of which are homogeneous with the original model or intention of the RDBMS. Specifically, at the top of the list are support of new complex data types, such as collections, hierarchies, and BLOBs—capable of holding images, sound bytes, and videos—and user-defined data types, useful for representing real-world business objects and components. Add to these user-definable functions, including those purchasable "off the shelf" from a growing cottage industry of vendors providing data widgets of all kinds (extenders, blades, cartridges, links to the Web, or, in short, custom components), and the merger of the object-oriented and relational models looks like a real success. Finally, the UDB is defined to include those features from traditional relational databases—triggers, SPs, and built-in functions—that simulate the encapsulation and subordination of data to methods characteristic of object-oriented technology's messagelike invoking of methods to access and manipulate data.

When new data types are introduced, class libraries take on new importance. Functions are needed to manipulate these data types and, unless a firm is prepared to undertake development from scratch, the purchase of such shrink-wrapped components makes good business sense. These include libraries handling time-series data, geographical coordinates, and text, image, video, and sound bytes. Links from within relational technology to external files and data stores deserve a complete discussion of their own, not possible here. This is not just because most of the data on the planet still resides in nonrelational formats, though that, too, is true. This is because of that ultimate proof of concept of distributed computing—the Web. The goal of making the Web appear as if it were a vast relational database requires a link to a URL from within the RDBMS. Likewise, externalization of the Web content requires links in the opposite direction. Although this part is still a work in progress, it is engaging to consider the direction of development as we have done briefly here.

Thus, the claim to "universality" is based on the way that user-defined data types and functions can be employed to extend the set of available objects and methods almost indefinitely. This will make possible first the warehousing, then the data mining of business data contained in unstructured documents, which, as indicated, still accounts for over 90% of the information in firms.

THE CROSS-FICTIONAL, OOPS, -FUNCTIONAL TEAM

The number of business and technology competencies converging on the data warehouse is substantial. From a technical perspective, all of the elements of client-server are included, and more. Back-end database administration skills are toward the top of the list of required functions. The GUI with which the slicing and dicing of data is presented requires advanced desktop integration talents. Understanding of connectivity, middleware, and networking protocol issues is essential, whether or not the data warehouse will end up in a distributed environment. If the data warehouse is to be Web-enabled and made available to end-users through an intranet or extranet, an additional set of skills relating to Web-based computing is required. In addition, a list of business process managers is likely to include advocates for the customers to be represented in and served by the warehouse and specialists in the product and services to be delivered, forecast, or managed by the warehouse. It is a useful oversimplification to require a business process role for each significant warehouse dimension—customer, product, channel, and financial cycle time. Depending on the complexity and allowing for multiple roles per person, each of the dimensions represented in the warehouse requires someone—whether manager, analyst, or both—to define and determine the knowledge to be captured and presented through the data warehouse. The project leader who undertakes the task of coordinating all of these experts is likely to require substantial negotiating skills, conflict resolution methods and organizational influence. Experience with stand-up comedy and improvisation would also be useful. Because these are unlikely to be combined in the person of an individual project leader, that person will require the hands-on involvement and support of an executive leader and sponsorship. These are indispensable and critical success factors.

The reason the title of this section contains an intentional slip of the pen, masquerading as an accidental one, is to signal that the cross-functional team is, itself, a kind of organizational challenge. Even when the difficulties of department interoperability are fully appreciated, the weight of tradition of the stovepipe organization is so great that, unfortunately, the cross-functional team often turns out to be a fiction. Without being able to review here the tradition of business organizations and the benefits and limits of hierarchical, stovepipe, and functional forms of the firm, it suffices to say that business and computing systems are now almost indistinguishable from one another. Without exception, software, databases, and networks are an essential part of "enabling" both basic and advanced business processes. Therefore, the coordination of commitments required to bring into being and operate such complex business systems are bound to be cross-functional.

Data warehousing is a direct descendent of the call to manage data across the enterprise that we discussed in Chapter Two on the history of data, calling it the jewel in the crown of enterprise systems. Bringing about such a result is bound to require a coordination of commitments that can be delivered only by the cross-functional teamwork of multiple departments. The cross-functional team ends up performing for the firm in a role analogous to metadata for the data warehouse proper (that is, mapping of the detailed elements of the business dimensions and facts from one business system to another—in short, providing interoperability).

Ultimately, the insertion of data warehousing itself into the firm is a discontinuous and disruptive event. That calls forth the cross-functional team. However, in a stovepipe organization, that is a work around, which admittedly is just fine if it does, indeed, work. Experience shows that the cross-functional team ends up succeeding best when it is part of a cross-functional organization. That can provide a Catch-22 or a productive insight. In either case, it points in the direction of governance.

GOVERNANCE

The truth is that the enterprise data warehouse project provides management with a completely independent and objective index as to the form of governance that prevails in a firm, regardless of what management otherwise reports or claims. This is because the data warehouse is a derivative structure whose form reflects that of the entire firm. However, the problem with this as an approach to data warehousing—it is, in fact, a classic Catch-22—is that, by the time the pretenses of the "feudal" firm are unmasked, it is too late to rescue the data warehouse project. In the final analysis, the data warehouse's coherence or lack of it mirrors that of the enterprise as a whole.

We have seen a demonstration of this in the way that the dimensions of the data warehouse represent the structure of the firm's customer and product (or service) structures. If the firm has a feudal structure, so will any prospective data warehouse. However, that usually means that the system is not the best example of a data warehouse. Indeed, a data warehouse with a feudal structure is not even a data mart. No self-respecting data mart has a stovepipe structure, though it may well represent a subset of enterprise data from which the inconsistencies have been driven out. Rather, what you get is a legacy system in the form of a data mart—what Doug Hackney has both wisely and cleverly designated a *legamart*. Other ways of describing it are a data garage sale, a data staging area, or a copy of transactional production data.

Governance refers to crafting, publishing, and using an information policy to operate the data warehousing system and subsystems of a firm according to plan. Here, policy functions rather like a constitution that defends society from the opportunistic actions of passing administrations (see Strassmann, 1995: 5). Checks and balances are instituted and enforced to prevent arbitrary and capricious behavior that is detrimental to the firm as a whole. Governance, when applied to a data warehouse system, means policies and procedures that enable specific agreements about what data belongs in the warehouse, the ownership of the resources, and access to the repository of knowledge that will be represented in the data warehouse. To be sure, as with any shared resources (networks, databases, and centralized enterprise servers), issues of chargeback, usage, and the point of view of the interests of the firm as a whole are at the top of the list. However, with the data warehouse, additional complications arise.

In the case of a data warehouse, the matter is particularly urgent. The relevant databases may contain customers that are targeted by multiple lines of business, brands that contain products manufactured at different locations by different business units, and marketing aggregates that contain numbers significant to different sales forces. Meanwhile, the enterprise data warehouse development team confronts the classic dilemma of stovepipe departments, applications, and business processes. Each claims ownership of data assets usefully shared with a centralized repository of warehouse business knowledge. Relational technology can actually help here, through the definition of Views that isolate and make visible virtual partitions of data to those and only those that require access to them without changing the underlying physical structures. However, technology alone is just a Band-Aid—although we are glad enough to have one if we skin a knee. For governance to balance these conflicting claims, interests, and agendas, high-level policy formulation and alignment are essential.

In one example of a successful data warehouse used to reduce inventory across the enterprise, the warehouse was prototyped and scaled up in one of three major lines of business. Because inventory reduction was an enterprise goal, the other divisions— actually separate companies that had been acquired by a corporate parent—were strongly "incented" to sign up for participation in the project. Here, "incentives" include compensation agreements detailing quantitative targets that were both aggressive and attainable. In fact, the inclusion of the other divisions required changes to the product structure, because at least one was continuous process, not category- or hierarchy-based. However, because the quantitative targets envisioned getting all of the divisions onto the data warehouse, the incentives were toward interdivisional cooperation, not competition. The perspective of enterprise governance implies this kind of "give and take." The lessons are clear. Not only is executive sponsorship required, but that sponsorship must translate into incentives that are aligned across the entire firm.

This discussion truly belongs under "prospects for the future," because the outcome requires aligning incentives, business imperatives, and technology, in ways neither trivial nor easy to accomplish. The federal model of checks and balances—as opposed to feudal vassals and jousts—is not really a new one but one that the importance of which is appreciated by governing boards and management teams anew. The construction and operation of data warehousing systems makes the adoption of federal forms of governance both useful and an increasingly critical path for integration of the business and technology functions in the data warehouse.

THE OPERATIONAL DATA WAREHOUSE

By *operational data warehouse,* what is meant is not a data warehouse that directly accesses or uses operational data. What is meant, rather, is a data warehouse that performs up to acceptable operational standards. Examples of this certainly exist, and, in far too many ways, it is still a prospect for the future.

The operational data warehouse conforms to the standards of predictability, availability, and accessibility that are expected of and characterized by an SLA. Without an SLA, the IT function and the management team are "in reaction." Condemned to react to the loudest complaints, business priorities receive second-place priority. That is trouble. With an SLA, performance problems are subordinated to business priorities. When they do occur, problems can be well defined, and that enables the marshalling and scheduling of the resources required to solve them. The existence of a data warehousing SLA is a sure sign that the data warehouse is on the sure path of enterprise operations—validity, accountability, and professional standing.

To be sure, long-running queries can be expected to be submitted. However, due to the availability of a robust metadata repository, those queries that represent high-level aggregations—all brands for all customers for the past year (for example)—are either sent off to a lengthy overnight batch process, directed by a navigation layer to the precalculated, prestored aggregate, or killed by a run-time governor before they can cause damage to other users of the system. This description is stated as if it is a present reality, but in how many firms is it a future prospect and a goal hard to attain? This implies a design and implementation effort over and above making a copy of the exiting operational data, giving the end-user a query tool, and inviting her or him to call the help desk with any exceptions.

As data warehousing grows in importance and function, and moves from the periphery toward the center of the knowledge-driven organization, operational requirements loom large. The development and maintenance of the data warehousing systems tends to slide toward being a cost of doing business.

REQUEST FOR UPDATE

As a general rule, data warehouses tend to be read-only or read-mostly structures. True, a day's or week's worth of data may be extracted, aggregated, and loaded in a single "big batch process." That is a kind of update, but it is a load of a complete file, not a tweaking of a single record. This is in contrast to transactional systems, which are designed to handle many brief updates to small amounts of information—adding a line item to an order, modifying the status of a work-in-progress folder on a claim, or correcting a name and address. Thus, the common place: The transactional system is made to get data in; the data warehouse, to get it back out again. Of course, this is an oversimplification, because all systems require both operations from time to time.

In many cases, the end-user's request for update to the data warehouse is misguided and likely to create mischief. For example, in data warehousing in banking, where rigorous auditing requirements exist, one doesn't really make a correction to a record. Rather, one adds an entirely new transaction that backs out, modifies, or otherwise adjusts the original record. If one or two records are changing, as when a customer changes their name due to a "life event," usually marriage or divorce, the addition of a version or sequence number that will represent both the continuity and the evolution of the customer is feasible. However, in the case of significant global changes to the customer or product hierarchy, as when two firms merge that have overlapping customer or product dimensions that must be combined, the side effects of changes are so significant that considerable up-front analysis is required to determine the impact. Often, the only practical choice is rebuilding the entire hierarchy and accepting that history has been revised in a consistent way. What is today one of the things that can go wrong is tomorrow's "special case," a new operational requirement to merge previously heterogeneous customer or product dimensions.

Thus, the request for update to the data warehouse is likely to be one of the prospects for the future. We must be careful not to overgeneralize. However, having issued this word of caution, the request for update actually makes sense in the context of forecasting applications. The system proposes to the planner a forecast for customer by product by date combinations based on a smoothing of three to five years of historical data as run through an aggregation model. Next the forecast is likely to require tweaking—micro-updates—based on local variations, product promotions, or BI about particular customers known to the planning analyst. The ability to make such an update and to store and track it along with the initially generated estimates or projections, is a powerful knowledge acquisition, retention, and learning tool. It is also an update to the data warehouse. Leading companies have had such systems in production for several years already, though the scale of the update is relatively modest—in the gigabyte, not terabyte, range. Insofar as the update capability enables the planner to know more, it presents an attractive scenario and is likely to call forth the invention of design and implementation effort to capture the value presented by this knowledge.

THE WEB OPPORTUNITY: AGENT TECHNOLOGY

Prospects for the future of data warehousing are an invitation to offer ideas on the kinds of discontinuous changes that may occur. In this section, we turn back to that cauldron of innovation and distraction, the Web, with avowedly speculative considerations.

So far, we have discussed the Web in two forms. The first is the use of Web-centric technologies—TCP/IP, HTML, HTTP, CGI gateways, Web servers—to deliver data warehouse information to end-users across the WAN. We have pointed out that because data warehouse data will be proprietary, it is not the sort of data that one would expect to share with anonymous people over the public Internet. We discussed applications deploying intranets or extranets, not the public Internet at large. We indicated that Web-based technologies are not just a superior delivery system—though that is what is most visible. Rather, the emphasis is on the new possibilities opened through the basic principles of Web computing—action at a distance, access to information any place, any time, and interfirm coordination and cooperation at new levels. The second opportunity goes to the content of the Web itself as a distributed computing system. The Web itself has become the ultimate data store, the proverbial mother of all databases. Cultivating this data store in a disciplined and organized way is an exciting prospect. The idea of using the Web as part of a system of information farming (see Hackathorn, 1998) requires an appreciation of business priorities beyond the hunter-gatherer ("surfing") model. The discovery of content, its acquisition, structuring dissemination, and rendezvous and integration with the data warehouse proper, internal to the firm, is a rigorous drill. The technology—and just as important, methodology—is now available. Building the business case is a work in progress.

In the context of the vast distributed computing landscape of the Internet, clients may not always be able to rely on the convenience of executable content or the preestablished harmony of push technology's publish and subscribe model. Especially in the discovery and acquisition phases of data warehousing Web farming, new models of computing are useful and, indeed, required to navigate, manage, and engage in meaningful work in such a loosely defined environment. These new models of computing include the capacity to take the initiative, be proactive within a defined context, and make decisions based on specified criteria. The prospect is the shift from decision support of business analysts and knowledge managers outside the boundary of the system to decision guidance by software assistants—agents internal to the system. When these features are built into software components, we are dealing with software agents. This has profound implications, because agents end up behaving like delegates, proxies, and the types of beings who represent others—that is, agents. As indicated, this is where the discussion becomes openly speculative, as is proper in a section on future prospects.

There is a progression from "executable content"—Java applets downloaded across a network—to customized push technology based on client profiling and collaborative filtering. The latter is the feature of on-line book stores that tell you that if you enjoyed this book by Agosta, you might also like books by Hackathron, Hackney,

Inmon, Kimball, Tanler, Thomsen, etc. The exploration of these loosely overlapping associations leads inexorably in the direction of increasing agency. Here, *agency* means "autonomy"—literally, being governed by internal rule or law, self-rule. Although *agents* is a dynamic word, capable of taking on many meanings, and likely soon to be hyped beyond measure, the meaning here is precise and limited. Features of agency that go over and above the necessary minimal level of autonomy—self-rule—include mobility, adaptability, and personal relevance. Many examples of software agents rely on personal profiling. Is shopping the killer application for which we need agents? So-called collaborative filtering has received favorable press by providing customers with recommendations of music, books, and movies, based on shared, overlapping interests.[3] This approach has also been criticized as a powerful method of delivering the insignificant when applied to personal shopping and profiling. However, what about knowledge management, data warehousing, metadata automation, inventory management, network monitoring, and related infrastructure automation? Remember, sometimes the application that makes a technology popular is not the one for which it is most needed by the enterprise. That is perhaps also the case here.

When the environment is complex enough, any coherent software with good, basic if-then-else logic can simulate some aspects of agency. This is done by bringing order and predictability to the behavior of a set of variables too large for any human being intelligently to survey or comprehend. Thus, a good scheduling tool that tracks the dependencies and execution of batch jobs in an enterprise server presents the possibilities of "lights-out" operations. Those are operations without human intervention after initial setup. This is also the mechanism of database triggers and agents, where a threshold is reached, for example, in an inventory bucket, a trigger is executed, and a messaging agent sends an alert, by e-mail or pager, that intervention is required. Full-blown agency in the sense of autonomy, however, is lacking.

Let's take a step back and consider what insight can be gained from a short, very short, history of agents. The 17th-century philosopher Gottfried Leibniz, best known as the inventor of integral calculus and the idea of symbolic logic, developed the concept of the agent to a deep level. Thus, there is nothing new under the sun. What is new is the implementation. Before silicon tools to automate computing methods existed, he found agents in nature and called them "monads." According to Leibniz, knowledge is brought into being by logical analysis, designed to bring clarity to the monad's internal state. Thus, Leibniz was the original knowledge manager. He was the last person on the planet to know everything there was to know in his time. Leibniz claimed that bringing a concept to experience and organizing experience into a structure as represented in symbols—what we might now call "data cubes" and "aggregates"—gave us knowledge. That definition remains as true today as it was then. Because we interact with people all the time, exchanging messages and tasks and agreements, most people find the metaphor of an agent to be friendly, comfortable, and intuitively understandable. We intuitively understand delegating tasks to agents and receiving knowledge back.

At this point, our short history is "fast forwarded" to today. Today, the idea of agency is being implemented in frameworks using Java.[4] As indicated, the network orientation of Java includes downloading executable code in a manner that is machine-independent. Executable content points in the direction of increasing agency. So it is no accident that leading agent frameworks—called *ontologies* because they bring agents into being—are all written in Java. However, agents require more than downloading code. They require the ability to move program STATE around the network. Program state implies that the program itself is jumping around, deciding where to go next, based on operations, inferences, or calculations made internally. That is bound to be a challenging thing in a Web environment based on a protocol (HTTP) proud of its statelessness. This section is not intended to be a product overview or comparison but a discussion of how agent software may affect our understanding of data management in the Web context of data warehousing.

What agents in all of the agent systems have in common is that they:

- require a mechanism capable of moving code from one server to another;
- include class libraries for communicating with remote agents as they migrate from one location to another on the network;
- provide a way of simulating the transportation of program state from one location to another;
- provide an agent server and the equivalent of an agent sandbox.

In general, agents replace "conversations." Instead of a long-distance conversation, an agent is sent at virtually the speed of electrons. The agent then, in effect, conducts negotiations on-site. That is, if the conversation is long and complex enough, then, from a performance point of view, it makes sense to incur the overhead of sending an intelligent messenger, the agent, who then makes up the overhead by conducting a high-performance conversation at the remote location and reports back the result. Further instructions are then issued to close or abort the deal. It is a kind of two-phase commit protocol, with the difference that the decision point does not require the continuous connection of all the parties. Business-to-business data warehousing systems, where one trading partner accesses the warehouse of another often require moving large amounts of data warehousing data between the trading partners. Rather than do that, send an agent to bring back the answer to a specific question. Thus, the agent acts rather like a shipping specialist—in this case, function shipping.

Most agent systems provides a context within which agents are created, executed, managed, transferred, and terminated. In general, the place is a gateway between agent's visiting a host and the host's resources. The sorts of things that agents might want to do are nicely abstracted in the Java class library supplied. As an illustration, General Magic's Odyssey includes tickets, specifying how and where an agent travels; petitions, specifying who an agents wants to communicate with; and process-related functionality. By default, Odyssey uses Java's remote method invocation

(RMI) as the transport mechanism to move an agent from one location to another. That means that Odyssey works with any browser that supports JDK 1.1, which at this date is only Sun's HotJava. Interestingly enough, General Magic has obtained a patent on Odyssey's "system and method for distributed computation based upon the movement, execution, and interaction of processes in a network."[5]

Because the function of the agent server will be to listen for requests coming off of the network from remote locations, a well-known socket number can be assigned to the host. The itineraries of roving agents can be registered with an associated lightweight database, where agents can be made persistent by being stored. For example, with the Voyager product when the moveTo() function is encountered, the re-motely enabled Java class, which is the agent (messenger), is loaded into the destination server by the Voyager network class loader automatically. A callback function is then executed to restore the code to the state in which it was executing at the point where it quiesced and moved. This is the mechanism used to simulate the direct transmission of internal program state. A virtual reference allows communication between address spaces. Because the universe is the total address space of the Internet, a 16-byte globally unique identifier (GUID) is assigned at the time of construction. (In this sense, the solution seems inspired by and related to Active-X.)

Now, we are ready to take the step from applets to Aglets.[6] The applet metaphor has been extended in the direction of agents by coining the term *Aglet*. The Aglet Work Bench provides many of these capabilities. The "atp daemon" is the server that listens for incoming Aglets over the network. Instead of virtual references, an agent transfer protocol (atp) is invoked to move code between contexts. The server context provides all Aglets with a uniform environment, within which initialization and execution of the code base occurs. Special functions that are invoked when the agent "wakes up" at the remote location are used to determine the initial and continuing state, based on the messaging and retrieval of auxiliary variables. The code base provides the base URL of the directory that contains the Aglet's compiled class code.

Notice that not all of the code specified in the Java's class path can move along with the Aglet when it is dispatched or migrated. For example, an Aglet may be using database connectivity code to access a local database. Transmitting that exact same code really does not make any sense, because that depends on the type of database accessed, which, at the remote location, may be a different database from a different vendor. Instead, the context will provide the version of database connectivity code appropriate to the remote location.

Most importantly, the context provides an agent sandbox. This is a transfer of the metaphor of the Java applet security metaphor in the direction of agency. When agents arrive, by definition, they are untrusted. To be sure, even untrusted agents can make offers and requests, subject to subsequent verification. Those agents that have previously registered with the Webmaster or administrator and provide their digital signature to prove it become eligible for additional access, services, and transactions.

In summary, agent systems provide a context in which agents are created, executed, managed, transferred, and terminated. Context is furnished by a gateway between agents visiting a host and host resources. Other agent technology metaphors extend to agent travel, ticketing, and requests. Most important, the context provides an agent sandbox. This applet security metaphor of the sandbox is, thus, shifted in the direction of agency. When agents arrive, by definition, they are untrusted and quarantined. Rather than moving large amounts of data warehousing data between trading partners, send an agent to bring back the answer to a specific question. The agent acts rather like a function-shipping specialist. The entire spectrum of knowledge acquisition, management, and distribution applications opens up here—collaborative design in data warehouse dimensions, engineering, and planning. Although popular examples of software agents in the trade press rely on personal profiling, the betting money is that shopping is more an intuitive and engaging example than a killer application of agents, the authentic domain of which lies in knowledge management, network monitoring, and data warehousing infrastructure automation.

Thus, the royal road to the data warehouse is to model it on the form of the business itself and to let basic business imperatives guide its design and deployment. As the Web enablement of business —and, indeed, of the entire planet—proceeds, every expectation is that the data warehouse and the Web will converge in fundamental ways. The way that comes to make a difference, not just from a technological, but from a business, point of view, is through the one fundamental question of data warehousing emphasized in this essential guide: Which customers are buying what products, and when and where are they doing so? The possibilities and power from a business perspective opened up by knowing the answer to this one elementary question in a timely and detailed way are great and transforming in a fundamental way. Risk is always a factor to be calculated and controlled by savvy and engaged management. The opportunity afforded by the availability of a data warehouse system aligned with business structures and imperatives is the reduction of uncertainty. Through the knowledge made available in the data warehouse, business leaders and managers acquire a formidable tool in their quest for value.

THE FUTURE OF DATA WAREHOUSING

As a technology, data warehousing is completely continuous with the mission envisioned by managing data as a corporate asset. As a business process, data warehousing is completely aligned with the imperatives expressed in fundamental decision support processes aimed at developing brand identities, attaining customer intimacy, and managing market dynamics. Now don't go and quote the following out of context. However, as a technology, the future of data warehousing is the same as the future of all other technologies—that is, to become obsolete, and to do so at an ever-accelerating rate. Still, as a method of knowing customers, developing brand identities, and understanding market dynamics, data warehousing promises to be increasingly identified with fundamental business processes indistinguishable from the direction and governance of the enterprise as a whole. Successfully managing the interaction and intersection of the sometimes conflicting trajectories of these technological and business imperatives will distinguish those firms that succeed in leveraging data warehousing systems for enhanced economic and business value from those that struggle to keep up and catch up.

The painful truth is that IT departments excel at building stove pipe systems because we've gotten so much practice at it in the course of developing three decades of transactional applications. Short term objectives that further long term interests are everyone's greatly desired Holy Grail. They represent sub-goals that are hard to identify, define, or promote. Transactional systems have been opportunistically thrown together to keep the ship of the enterprise afloat since long before the IBM 360 computer in 1964. Why should data warehousing systems be any different? Unfortunately, the continuing proliferation of tactical data warehousing solutions—products that don't interoperate, prototypes passed off as the final product that (naturally) don't scale or perform, and data mart silos that are inconsistent legacy systems when implemented—may actually accelerate over the short term. The jury is still out on the painful (and costly) systems integration effort constituted by the ERP movement. The only analogy to data warehousing here are those costly "big bang" enterprise resource planning projects distinguished by their cost overruns and disappointing results. A firm that is *satisfied*—please define that term carefully—with the result of its ERP implementation and operations may reasonably consider using the same vendor and consulting firm to build its data warehouse. However, except in terms of cost and time frame, this has many of the features of a tactical solution. The truth is a firm can't buy a strategy off the shelf. The constructions of unified representations of customers, brands, and markets requires a cross-functional coordination of commitments. The data warehouse, when properly aligned, designed and implemented, according to these representations, is a strategic asset. Thus, the critical path in managing risk and implementation effort is the design of the data warehouse according to consistent and unified representations of the customer, product, service, and related dimensions. In the final analysis, one must design the crucial customer, product, and service dimensions top down and implement the factual business processes bottom up, cross-referencing and synthesizing the whole and the parts. That's not all there is to it, but that's a good start. Several trends will help to make this cross-referencing a reality.

The role of metadata is crucial to the success of data warehousing. Without the structural knowledge represented by metadata, the interoperation of data warehousing and the underlying transactional systems degenerates into maintenance headaches. The dominance of IBM, Microsoft, and Oracle in the database market gives them the muscle to define a set of related metadata standards that is small enough to allow customers to "boot strap" themselves into satisfactory, if not always optimal, operational configurations with good enough tools. The take-away here: if the "big guys," under pressure from their big customers, decide metadata standards are a priority, then they will have products on the market with remarkable speed. Both the market and the industry will benefit.

Amid improvements in performance, scalability, and functionality of back-end databases, decision support functions of the desktop (so-called desktop OLAP) will become a commodity. That is according to the rule that every software technology ultimately ends up being presented as a $99 desktop product. Of course, in the case of data warehousing, access to large data stores through complex networking infrastructure is also a prerequisite. Anecdotal evidence is available that a significant event in this process occurred in the decision support market in the 4th quarter 1998 with Microsoft OLAP Services (Plato). As Microsoft looks forward to rolling out sixty million (or so) copies of PivotTable Services, bundled with Excel in Windows 2000, as the ultimate desktop OLAP decision support tool, data warehousing ends up at the impact point of a collision of dominant designs. On the one hand, desktop OLAP literally promises to make "data warehousing" a household word on the Windows 2000 (NT) workstation. On the other hand, the business intelligence portal delivers data warehousing and supporting aggregated content to the Web-enabled desktop over the Internet. No messy client-side executables, rather you get centralized distribution and maintenance, and the power of the Web's action at a distance. These remain very appealing attributes. Although the front-end technologies are fundamentally divergent—Windows client or Internet browser—the coexistence of both approaches is a probable result. This is not a cop out. It is a reflection of the reality of complex historical technology paths (which are hard to reverse once laid down), diverse business requirements, and existing infrastructure.

Faced with the challenges and costs of complex system integration projects, one might reasonably expect to hear more about the out sourcing of data warehousing by firms whose core competencies are sales and marketing, not technology integration. For example, companies such as A.C. Nielsen, IRI, and Harte-Hanks, which already sell commercial decision support market research information, are positioned to ramp up to perform such out sourced data warehouse functions. They probably don't have the capacity on-line today. However, they have (and can afford to augment) their competencies. Negotiating and substituting an out sourcing contract, a transaction in the market, for internal vertical coordination is an approach to determining the value of the required effort. This is an expensive exercise, but as a thought experiment, it is always useful to ball park just how much it would cost to out source data warehousing. Why should it cost less to do it in-house? And if it really does cost less, then that's a highly useful input to the decision process. One obvious limiting factor to an out sourcing approach is the sensitivity of the data warehousing information and the nearness of decision support processes to the heart of a firm's very reason for existing. Such out sourcing might resemble more of a strategic partnership and alliance rather than buying hardware cycles from a computing utility.

Tactical innovations in software and products will abound in the universe of data warehousing. Some will have strategic significance. The products from ROLAP and MOLAP vendors are converging, and these vendors will look to escape from the Oracle, Microsoft, and IBM marketing juggernauts by providing industry specific solutions in vertical market niches. There may also be a large scale adoption of Microsoft metadata standards as a good enough, de facto solution. However, watch out for Java-based analytic engines that enable drop-in data-aware components for distribution of decision support data over the Web. Meanwhile, at least for the duration of the first edition of this book, data warehousing systems larger than about 20 gigabytes will require complex design and development efforts that put a premium on project management competencies, staffing skills, and business leadership at the cross-functional level. Note that systems smaller than that (20 gigabytes) are not to be regarded as trivial; but they may more easily be accommodated without best-of-breed vendor integration. At the same time, the sale of data warehousing information over the Internet will continue apace, and any methodology for Web harvesting of this ultimate, unstructured data store will prove to be useful. The hunger for knowledge of the customer, one-on-one marketing, and such high performance applications as fraud detection and data encryption will consume the substantial strides made in delivering computing cycles by massive parallel processing computers and databases.

In addition, the feedback loop between data warehousing and transactional systems will be increasingly important as most firms complete initial data warehousing systems. Once most firms have data warehouses, those that succeed in using them to influence, direct, and optimize their transactional processes will gain economic and business benefits. Thus, applications that require the kind of consistent, scrubbed data provided by data warehouses will provide added value and become even more of a focus. In many ways, data warehousing systems are infrastructure. The economic and business benefits are delivered by the superstructure. In the product dimension, these include applications that provide enhanced supply chain management, forecasting, and just-in-time everything. On the customer side, these applications include cross-selling among different lines of business, improved customer intimacy, superior customer prospecting and retention through data mining, and managing the relationship with the customer across all channels. Finally, the identification of knowledge management as a separate discipline makes it sound like this is something one does after getting to know customers, building products, and developing IT systems to support all these business processes. That is misleading. If the staff are already writing down and sharing lessons learned with colleagues, then a knowledge management initiative may very well work as a bottom up way of making explicit what works and bringing along the stragglers. Otherwise, it is likely to be misperceived as the latest management fad. Nevertheless, data warehousing is an undertaking that goes to the heart of fundamental business imperatives such as *knowing* customers, product forecasts, and markets. Thus, the future of data warehousing lies in its use to leverage knowledge into action in the service of the organization's commitments to customers, brands, and fundamental business results.

SUMMARY . . . .

Prediction is an uncertain undertaking. Still, it is a good bet that the grand paradigms of today will become the special cases of tomorrow. The conclusion attempts to extrapolate current trends as well as get a glimpse of the sources of discontinuous changes that could be approaching. Amid the tidal wave of changes coming at firms, the one simple truth that stand fast is the data is the enterprise. As an example, the role of the universal database is considered as both an incremental and discontinuous technology. We are like sailors in the open sea who have to rebuild their ship without being able to dismantle it in dry dock. Building the cross-functional team is an organizational challenge and an imperative. Business systems and computing systems are almost indistinguishable from one another. Software, databases, and networks are an essential part of enabling business processes. The coordination of commitments required to build and operate such complex artifacts are bound to be cross-functional. Governance refers to crafting, publishing, and using an information policies to operate the data warehousing system and subsystems of a firm according to plan. Here policy functions rather like a constitution that defends society from the opportunistic actions of a single passing administration. In the case of a data warehouse the matter is particularly urgent. The relevant databases may contain customers that are targeted by multiple lines of business, brands that contain products manufactured at different locations by different business units, and marketing aggregates that contain numbers significant to different sales forces. Federal forms of governance require sophistication to design and implement, but provide rewarding results. Meanwhile, the operational data warehouse refers to the way warehousing systems inevitably slide in the direction of 7x24 operations similar to mission critical transactional systems. Although initially "read mostly" structures, the request for update, especially in the context of "as if" scenario or forecasting, is a prospect for the future that is actually at hand. Discussing prospects for the future of data warehousing is an invitation to offer ideas on the kinds of discontinuous changes that may occur. Avowedly speculative ideas are discussed about agent technology, data warehousing, the Web, and the future of data warehousing.

[1] For a thorough overview that succeeds in being fairly vendor-independent, see Saracco, Cynthia M. *Universal Database Management: A Guide to Object/Relational Technology*, San Francisco, CA: Morgan Kaufmann Publishers, 1998. See also my review of this text in *Computing Review*, October, 1998.

[2] This famous saying was originally said about the enterprise of scientific inquiry and the development of knowledge. However, it applies equally well to any ongoing enterprise that cannot cease functioning for two years while reengineering or rebuilding. To "keep the ship afloat," one piece at a time must be replaced, rather than a complete overhaul. See Neurath, 1932.

[3] See www.firefly.com.

[4] As of late 1997, the main agent frameworks written in pure Java include: IBM's Aglets (IBM calls its Java agents *Aglets* by analogy with Applets), General Magic's Odyssey, and ObjectSpace's Voyager (www.trl.ibm.co.jp/Aglets/index.html; www.genmagic.com/agents; www.objectspace.com/Voyager).

[5] This means their 293-page account of their software is a matter of public record, including detailed arguments, apparently persuasive to the patent authority, on how it subtly differs from about twenty other software and hardware agent solutions. Available at and through www.patents.ibm.com.

[6] By IBM's Tokyo Research Lab (see www.TRL.ibm.com).

Glossary

ABC: Activity-based costing

A system for making business decisions based on cost information traced on a case-by-case basis to such fundamental business activities as specific tasks related to product design, development, manufacturing and distribution, customer acquisition, service, and support. Usually contrasted with standard financial reports and arbitrary accounting methods, as mandated by taxing authorities or overhead estimation. ABC is sometimes considered a form of business process reengineering because it insists on surfacing a manageable number of cost drivers that can realistically be used to trace variable business costs to customer, products, and processes. It then turns out that, when viewed over a reasonably broad time horizon of month-to-month or quarter-to-quarter, many supposedly fixed costs are actually variable. Unless the firm is in a commodity-based industry where costs map directly to labor and simple materials, implementation of a form of ABC is usually required to build a profitability data warehouse, because an accurate estimation of costs is upstream from an accurate determination of profitability. (See Kaplan and Cooper, 1998.)

ADT: Abstract data type

A collection of data attributes combined with a set of functions for manipulating them. Sometimes considered an early version of object-oriented programming.

Active-X

Not a product, Active-X is a computing standard within the DCOM/COM architecture. Basically, Active-X is Microsoft's proposal for downloading (moving) executable content around the network and turning 1 million VB 5.0 programmers into Internet developers. Although this component model is not restricted to Visual Basic (VB) (and, for example, Java can be used to develop Active-X controls), it relies on a close coupling with the Windows NT operating system on the client. However, in 1996, Microsoft proposed to the Open Group that the latter become the holder of the Active-X as a publicly available, modifiable standard. (See DCOM, Java, Open Group.)

Agent

In the context of software, code that has sufficient minimal autonomy to perform personal profiling or collaborative filtering. In particular, a software component that satisfies the following: (1) able to move code from one server to another; (2) supported by a class library for enabling communications between agents as they move from one location to another on the network; (3) a way of simulating the transport of program state from one location to another; (4) an agent server and the equivalent of an agent sandbox. (See Aglet, Java, Ontology.)

Aggregate

A summation of detailed transaction records, usually along multiple intersecting dimensions of a hierarchy in a data warehouse; for example, if customer, product, date are elementary items, an aggregation along the same trajectory would be region, brand, quarter. (See Cube, Hypercube, MDDB, Multicube.)

Aglets

A Java-based agent model from IBM based on the idea of applets, implemented by means of Java classes. Promises the same machine independence, "write once, execute anywhere," and sandbox security mechanism as classical client-based Java applets. (See Applet, Java, Ontology.)

Applet

Literally, a "little application," written in Java, able to be downloaded as machine-independent bytecode from the server to the Web browser-enabled client, and distinguished for its being connected to a Web HTML page by means of a tag <applet>. Applets are distinct from full-blown Java applications, in that they execute on the client in the so-called security sandbox without access to the client hard disk or operating system. (See HTML, Java, WWW.)

Application server

The server that executes the business process logic and functionality—as opposed to the database server (stored procedures), the presentation layer, or network server. The application server is undergoing a repositioning and transformation in two separate directions. In one instance, it is becoming an "analytic engine." In the other instance, it is becoming a repository for reports and structural glue required to promote interoperation and integration. This, in turn, becomes the basis for metadata. In both cases, this positioning is being used to locate business logic where it should be—on the middle tier. This makes the application server the middle tier in three-tiered client-server. The difference between an application server and an analytic engine has to do with the abstractness of the approach and generality of the solution. If industry-specific business problems are being solved using component libraries of prefabricated business objects, an "analytic engine" is the requirement. If scalability is the issue or joining many-to-many heterogeneous databases within a coherent logical unit of work, then you've got an "application server." (See GUI, SQL, Three-tiered client-server.)

Architecture

First principles of coordinating commitments between different aspects, components, or dimensions of systems and subsystems. For example, client-server architecture distinguishes three functional layers—database, application, and presentation—by three implementation layers—desktop computers, middle-sized servers, and enterprise servers. Application servers, communication servers, and security servers are also required and round out the picture, so the actual number of layers is a useful oversimplification. The business commitments coordinated by these layers (in any combination) are data asset management and manipulation, business logic and communication, and usability. (See DCE, ORB, RDBMS, Two-tiered client-server, Three-tiered client-server.)

Artificial neural network

The neural network is an array of logic components that map an input to an output. These are the independent and dependent variables. Because these logic units function by combining inputs up to a threshold, at which point they "fire"—that is, produce an output—they resemble the operation of biological processes such as perception and sensation. A genuine sense is available in which artificial neural networks learn—that is, encode and adjust to—patterns directly from data. It is convenient to distinguish a "training" phase. Here, the input training data is presented and encoded ("stored") in the neural network. Next, training is distinguished from "testing." Here, additional data from the same sample population (where the outcome is already known) is run through the network and the results judged in terms of the number of errors made. On this basis, the network is tuned. Finally, an evaluation phase occurs, in which the remaining input data (which was not used for training or testing) whose classification is still unknown is processed by the neural network. The result is the classification of this data by the neural network into groups associated with a predicted outcome. This is then used as the basis for action in a business initiative designed to generate value. (See Back propagation.)

ATM: Asynchronous transfer mode

A high-speed packet switching standard implemented in telecommunication switches and software by dividing a message into small units (packets), allowing many different messages to be sent down the same high-bandwidth transmission link and reassembled at the destination. ATM is being used to build infrastructure for the networks of the future, though recently it has been eclipsed in the trade press by frame relay, which meshes better with current network infrastructure, standards compliance, and network interoperability. Nevertheless, ATM remains a contender, with superior quality of service, scalability, and fault tolerance, and can be used to connect the different nodes of such massively parallel computing platforms as IBM's SP processor (which is where it comes up in this text).

Back propagation

In 1982, John Hopfield invented back propagation, a way of training neural networks used in data mining that compares the output of a calculated and expected result from a network and adjusts the weights—the threshold determining when the neuron will "fire" and produce output—by providing feedback to minimize the detected difference (error). (See Artificial neural network.)

Bloatware

The reduction to absurdity of hundred-megabyte personal computing suites—including word processor, spreadsheet, e-mail, graphics package—where only a fraction of the functionality (say, 20%) is ever used. Bloatware causes the PC paradigm to "fall over" of its own weight and calls forth the approaches to client computing such as thin (skinny) client or network-centric alternatives. (See Fat client, Thin client, Two-tiered client-server.)

Business intelligence

Originally a term based in data mining but now being generalized to encompass all of decision support systems, *business intelligence* is intended to suggest the connotation of "intelligence" as driven by the CIA or KGB spying during the Cold War. That is, "intelligence" as secret information or knowledge that gives a strategic advantage to the one who possess it—only now, instead of secret codes to intercept missiles, it relates to consumer behavior as described by market research analysts. This book tends to stick with the classic term *decision support*. This is because decision support implies making a decision, and making a decision requires a commitment—take an action leading down path A rather than path B. That is the main action in business and, in a sense, what is missing from "business intelligence"—the sense of commitment to make a difference in an action-oriented way. Nevertheless, if one realizes and accepts that the "intelligence" gathering activities have to be consistent with what is on the front page of the business section of the newspaper and that "secret" data is really very rare, business intelligence may, after all, carry the day as the decisive term of art. (See Data mining, Data warehousing, EIS, OLAP.)

CART

The classification and regression tress (CART), published by L. Brieman, R.A. Friedman, R.A. Olshen and C.J. Stone in 1984 and implemented, among other places, by the Darwin StarTree data mining software package from Thinking Machines, adapts a measure of diversity from economics. (See CHAID, C4.5, Data mining.)

Causation

Defined in this text as a customary conjunction combined with an explanatory mechanism that can be confirmed or refuted, at least in theory. J. Cohen & P. Cohen, *Applied Multiple Regression/ Correlation Analysis for Behavioral Sciences*, 2nd Ed. (Hillsdale, NJ: Erlbaum, 1983, 80, suggest that we need three conditions to assert causality: (1) a convincing theoretical model, (2) statistically significant correlations, and (3) the causal event occurring earlier in time than the result described as the effect.

CDF: Channel Definition Format

A candidate standard from Microsoft, employing XML to specify the location of content and delivery protocol. (See Push technology, XML.)

Centeroids

Data mining terms. See K-means.

CGI: Common gateway interface

A standard for passing data from a client application through an HTTP server—that is, communicating through a Web server—whereby input is provided through environment variables and output is written to standard output. Generally used to communicate between a Web server and a database server or application server, specifically, the layer between the HTTP server and the back-end, and limited in scalability by the need to start a new process for every request. (See HTTP, WWW.)

CHAID

X^2 is a data mining term taken from statistics referring to the sum of the squares of the standardized differences between the expected and observed frequencies of some occurrence in each sample—a measure of the probability that an apparent association is due to chance. First published by J.A. Hartigan in 1975 and implemented by SPSS and SAS; independent variables that do not produce significant differences in the target field are merged. (See Data mining, CART, C4.5, SPSS.)

Channel

A wide-ranging metaphor for the implementation of so-called push technology, which can mean anything from the location of content on a Web server to a schedule for providing updates to clients based on their polling profile to a specific format for defining content to a publish-and-subscribe approach to client-server. (See CDF, Metaphor, Push technology, XML.)

CICS: Customer Information Control System

IBM's teleprocessing monitor, reportedly developed for a particular client in 1967, then generalized, it has undergone major extensions from macro to command level, rewrites of its internals using object-oriented methods, all the while maintaining (mostly) the same application program interface to the program; with IBM's acquisition of Encina's Transarc transaction monitor, IBM ported major CICS concepts and facilities off the mainframe platform and onto their versions of UNIX. CICS is a legendary—not necessarily legacy—example of "bullet proof" transaction processing across large distributed platforms (all from IBM, of course), driving the kinds of high transaction rates characteristic of airline reservation systems. (See Data center, MVS.)

CLI: Call-level interface

A call-level interface to a database, accomplishing what SQL does but using a function-like syntax similar to the C language; CLI is a generalization of the run-away successful de facto standard API, Microsoft's ODBC. CLI is a specification managed by the Open Group (of which X/Open is a part), which allows calls to be made to database access without knowing in advance which relational database will actually be storing and returning the data. (See ODBC, Open Group, RDBMS, SQL.)

Cookie

In the context of Web communications using the Netscape browser, a cookie is a piece of storage that is cached (stored) by the Web server on the client work station. It contains such data as session id—and possibly other client identifying characteristics—used by the Web server to simulate a give-and-take, multiphase conversational state, even though the processing protocol (HTTP) is stateless. (See HTTP, Internet, WWW.)

CORBA

See ORB.

Cube

An intersection of multiple dimensions, for example, customer-product-time, that determines the key of data warehouse facts; also used to refer to aggregates, which are cubes of nonelementary, nondetail levels in the dimensional hierarchy. When cubes come in more than three dimensions, they are sometimes referred to as *hypercubes*; when multiple cubes are joined along a common data element, they are referred to as *multicubes*. In general, cubes are contrasted with the star schema in comparing the methods and results of OLAP engines with relational databases. However, this is an inaccurate oversimplification, because cubes can be translated into star schemas and vice versa. The real issue is trade-offs involving performance and efficiency. High-level aggregations are more efficiently stored as cubes, having been precalculated; alternative rollups across changing dimensions are more efficiently and flexibly performed by star schemas based on available details. (See Aggregate, Hypercube, Multicube, OLAP, RDBMS, Star Schema.)

C4.5 algorithm, published by J.R. Quilan in 1992, is implemented by the commercial data mining product Clementine (Integral Solutions). It differs from CART, in that it produces only categorical output values, rather than continuous ones, and attempts to perform pruning of the branches prior to growing them rather than afterward. (See CART, CHAID, Data mining, SPSS.)

Data center

The location where centralized computing resources are physically managed, secured, and maintained; usually housing the mainframe computers or enterprise servers, acres of disk drives, row upon row of tape drives and mass storage tape robots, other auxiliary devices such as optical juke boxes, raised floor to accommodate all the cables, extra air conditioning to dissipate the enormous heat generated by all the hardware, Halon fire control system, security cameras, controlled entry and exit by means of digital swipe card. (See CICS, IMS, Mainframe, MVS.)

Data-centric

An approach to system architecture that emphasizes the primacy of data and data-driven logic; the function of the data-centric system architecture is to represent, store, transform, and manipulate, as opposed to computing-centric, network-centric, or client-centric designs, which, respectively, emphasize the primacy of number crunching, telecommunications, end-user interface usability. Naturally, most systems are a mixture of multiple features of this kind—and no system can exist without an essential minimal set of each of them. But the point remains—data warehousing systems are essentially data-centric. (See DB2, Oracle, RDBMS, SQL Server.)

Data mining

Methods of directed and undirected knowledge discovery, relying on statistical algorithms, neural networks, and optimization research, to discover, verify, and apply patterns in data to understanding and managing the behavior of customers, products, services, market dynamics, and other critical business transactions. Many data mining tools employ methods to identify and relate independent and dependent variables—the independent variable being "responsible for" the dependent one, and the way in which the variables "relate," providing a pattern and a model for the behavior of the downstream variable(s). Originally used in market research to surface business intelligence, data mining is receiving wider use in decision support and executive information systems. (See Business intelligence, CART, CHAID, C4.5, Decision support, SPSS.)

Data warehousing

An architecture that aims to align business imperatives, such as customer knowledge and brand development, with the system structures representing the business—usually such constructs as dimensions, facts, and aggregates—addressing decision support (now often called *business intelligence*) questions and issues about customers, products, services, and markets, and making possible applications that transform inarticulate, dumb data into useful business knowledge. (See Business intelligence, Data mining, Decision support, EIS, OLAP.)

DB2

IBM's relational database product, available on such operating systems as MVS, AIX (UNIX), OS/2, and NT. All these versions are converging on the idea of a "universal database" (UDB)—"universal" because of the variety of data types

and functions able to be accommodated, including the potential for indefinite extensions by means of user-defined data types and user-defined functions. Although DB2 was relatively slow to catch up with the requirement to support the database stored procedure (SP) and triggers, it has now done so (including Java and even COBOL SPs) and, at least in its mainframe version, is far-and-away ahead in supporting 7x24, around-the-clock operations with on-line data reorganization, concurrent copy, and many options for database locking. Although not the first commercial implementation of SQL—that honor belongs to Relational Software's Oracle (yes, the company later renamed itself after the product)—DB2 was the most successful product in the mainframe environment, which gained it major mind share. In 1973, the IBM Research Lab in San Jose, California developed a relational prototype called System R, the access to which was provided by a new database language called Structured English Query Language (SEQUEL). These two initiatives were eventually implemented as DB2. (See Chamberlin, 1998.) (See RDBMS, SQL, UDB.)

DCE: Distributed Computing Environment

A software system from the Open Software Foundation, since 1996 with X/Open, Ltd. under the umbrella of the Open Group, dedicated to the principles of providing interoperability across the distributed network between computers from different vendors by means of a uniform application programming interface to the underlying distributed network. DCE services are based on a remote procedure call (RPC) model and provide such services as directory management, file, security, thread, time synchronization. (See Open Group, RPC.)

DCOM

Microsoft's solution for distributed object management and handling, based on the Open

Software Foundation's Distributed Computing environment (DCE) remote procedure call (RPC) protocol. Components are registered on the local machine through a globally unique identifier (GUID), which makes them visible across separate address spaces and servers. Software AG is the junior partner with Microsoft to port DCOM to Sun Solaris and IBM's OS/390, an effort skeptically addressed by the Gartner Group as extend and assimilate. DCOM is an important part of any end-to-end Microsoft solution. (See DCE, Open Group, RPC.)

Decision support system

A system designed to assist business professionals—brand managers, marketing specialists, customer care experts, general managers, and knowledge workers of all kinds—in making choices about the allocation of resources in promotions, advertising, pricing, and planning. In the late 1970s, DSS was coined to distinguish these systems from MIS (management information systems), the latter referring more to operations and less to analysis. The consensus is that DSS is the original matrix out of which executive information systems (EIS), data mining, data warehousing, and on-line analytic processing (OLAP) first emerged. Although emptied of much of its meaning, from the point of view of terminology, "decision support" has one advantage. It implies the commitment and engagement of making a decision. (See Business intelligence, Data warehousing, Data mining, EIS, OLAP.)

Desktop

In the context of client-server, perhaps the most famous metaphor in computing for describing the electronic workspace as a configuration of iconic folders, opened by clicking on them, scheduling tool, e-mail, and related applications such as spreadsheets, graphics, and groupware. The desktop provides the GUI, which represents the presentation layer of the client-server system. (See Architecture, GUI, X Windows.)

DHTML: Dynamic HTML (Hypertext Markup Language)

A collection of technologies to turn HTML pages into application-like components, including cascading style sheets, HTML-based scripting, built-in data-aware objects, positioning, and proprietary tags. Any "markup" language is distinguished by having format definitions embedded in the surface of the text itself. For example, tags—<header, <bold>, <italics>—are such features in an arbitrary markup language. The distinguishing feature of vanilla HTML is its ability to embed hyperlinks—in effect, "hot spots"—that connect to other remote Web sites via the characteristic URL (e.g., http://www.acm.org). DHTML provides many additional tools for building Web pages. These tools make Web page authoring more like programming. (See HTML, SGML, XML.)

Digital signature

A cryptographic technology, based on hard-to-factor prime numbers, culminating in the 1977 patent of Diffie-Hellmann key exchange, whereby the authentication and identification of the author of a message can be validated. David Chaum (1985), the founder of DigiCash, Inc., invented the blind digital signature and holds several patents on this encryption technology, which makes possible authentication without identification (and is the basis of anonymous digital cash). See X509.

Dimension

A data modeling structure exemplified by such entities as customer, product, time period, channel, etc. In the context of data modeling, one of the entities constituting the periphery of the star schema; those entities that intersect to define the logical position of a fact table—for example, the composite key (index) customer, product, place, and time defines a variety of quantitative, additive, continuous fact level transactions such as sale, delivery, and return by the customer of a product at a store on a given data. (See Fact, RDBMS, Star schema.)

Dimensional data modeling

Defined here as a subset of entity-relationship diagramming, dimensional data modeling emphasizes denormalizing the dimensions (those entities such as products, customers, promotions, time, location) and brings the fact structures to proper third-normal form. It is a matter of some controversy whether this is a separate discipline—it is *not* a matter of controversy that dimensions and facts are essential constituents of designing and building a data warehouse. (See Dimension, E-R diagram, Fact, Snowflake.)

DLL: Dynamic Link Library

A major component of Windows-based software, the DLL is like a subroutine to mainline processing, an executable section dynamically invoked. (See Fat client, GUI.)

Dominant design

A configuration of hardware and software computing assets (including brand image, market channel, switching costs, and client practices) to which both competitors and leaders must conform in practice if they are to win market share and customers. For example, Windows, the Intel x86 chip, MVS, RDBMS, TCP/IP, are arguably dominant designs in their respective domains. See Utterback, 1995, and Christensen, 1997, for details on dominant design and disruptive technology innovations. (See MVS, RDBMS, TCP/IP, Windows.)

DRDA: Distributed relational database architecture

A set of principles that defines a standard for communicating, accessing, and updating local and remote databases from requesters and servers. Although originally formulated by IBM, DRDA was handed off to an open standards committee, the X-Open Group, for subsequent administration and evolution. IBM's implemen-

tation of the standard is called Distributed Database Connectivity Services (DDCS), and it is a gateway enabling cross-platform connectivity and remote and distributed units of work for those databases that provide such support. Many other vendors support defined levels of DRDA compliance. Basically, database-to-database interoperability is defined by distinguishing client requests from an application requester (AR) to an application server (AS). The four levels of database transaction are distinguished: (1) single access of a client of a database, (2) multiple accesses, including update of a single database, (3) distributed update of multiple sites, and (4) distributed access, including multisite join. The work involved, including any updates, occurs within the discipline of the two-phased commit protocol. (See Architecture, Open Group, RDBMS.)

EDI

Electronic data interchange: The computer-to-computer exchange of requests and responses according to a standard format as defined by the American National Standard Institute (ANSI) that is the basis for how businesses can electronically send documents, inquiries, and transactions to and from one another. Usually an entire industry—automotive, trucking, health insurance, retail—will adapt a subset of the ANSI standard to their intracompany transactions. Originally, EDI was exclusively the domain of value added network (VAN) providers, and since the advent of the Internet, some implementations of EDI messaging have shifted in that direction. (See Internet, VPN, Workflow.)

EIS: Executive information system

When business managers with enough rank and clout realized they had the influence needed to command an intuitive, easy-to-use interface, decision support systems were transformed into executive information systems (EIS). The emphasis is on a simplified executive interface suitable for mouse or touch screen. In one example, an executive requested 30 buttons on a graphic interface, each of which would present an answer to a question that executive considered critical to guiding, controlling, or making plans for his business unit. Naturally, behind this simplicity and surface transparency lay an enormously complex infrastructure of databases and networks designed to present the answers he craved to the critical questions at hand. Of course, it was this infrastructure, which had taken many dozens of staff years to build, that provided the competitive advantages. The presentation was a last essential link in the chain that included capturing hand-held computer data as well as purchased information from market research companies. However, it was the presentation layer that received the designation "EIS," not the underlying infrastructure. (See Business intelligence, Data warehousing, Decision support, OLAP.)

ER diagram: Entity-relationship diagram

An approach to data modeling that relies on applying rules to "normalize" the data, i.e., reduce redundancy and avoid update inconsistencies. These rules are called the "normal forms" of representing data—"normal" because they, in effect, reduce the data to a lowest common denominator, rather like factoring a fraction, eliminating redundancies, exceptions, and allowing comparison between different structures using the same data elements. Chapter Seven: Data Warehousing Technical Design, in particular Tables 7.1, Basic Entity Relationship and 7.3, Forms of Normalization, may usefully be consulted on this approach. (See Dimension, Fact, RDBMS, Snowflake, Star schema.)

ERP: Enterprise resource planning

Software packages designed to run the enterprise from end to end. Originally a big hit in manufacturing and personnel applications, ERP seemed to command the front page of every trade journal in 1998. These are transaction, not data warehousing, systems, whose data structures are highly snow-flaked, normalized, and optimized for high-volume update activity. The "sweet spot" for the implementation of ERP systems are those firms that are fragmented ("diversified") in form but that would benefit from centralization. Benefits include better integration and related processing efficiencies with trading partners, all of whom may choose as an industry to align on a particular vendor's package. This tends to improve vertical communications, both within a firm and between firms in the same industry up and down the supply chain. Note that business processes have to be changed to accommodate the ERP system, not vice versa. (See RDBMS, Snow-flaked, SQL.)

Extranet

Like the Internet proper and intranets, an extranet is a wide area network using Internet technologies—TCP/IP, HTML, Web servers, etc.—but restricted to authorized users in multiple companies or organizations by prior agreement. The emphasis is on business-to-business communications between trading partners. An extranet, like an intranet, is a network "invisible" to the public on the larger Internet, but communications between extranet partners travel over the public Internet in an encrypted, secure form out beyond the firewall. (See also Firewall, Internet, Intranet.)

Fact

In the context of data warehousing, a continuous, additive quantity as defined by the intersection of data dimensions. The main body—as opposed to the points—of the star in the star schema. The logical place of intersection of the dimensions—for example, the composite key (index) customer, product, place, and time defines a variety of possible fact structures (consisting of transactions) such as amount of sale, delivery quantity, or return by the customer of a product to a store on a given date. (See Dimension, Star schema.)

Fat client

A client work station executing software (typically Windows) off of the hard drive, requiring the distribution of software upgrades and maintenance one work station at a time, including modifications to the software registry or startup procedures; generally contrasted with thin (skinny) client or network computers that lack a hard drive or insertable disk drive. "Fat client" is generally considered a mild term of abuse; but see "bloatware." (See Bloatware, Desktop, Thin client.)

FEP: Front-end processor

A special-purpose computer designed to be a communications front-end to a mainframe computer so that distributed networks with IBM's System Network Architecture (SNA) could be built to include mainframes at the distributed nodes. The proprietary FEP has been rearchitected so that it is now, in effect, a router. (See Mainframe, Router, SNA.)

Firewall

A server and related software used to separate in a secure way the local intranet of a firm from the larger, insecure, public Internet. The "fire"— dangerous hackers, information terrorists, or mischief makers—are understood to be outside the wall. The idea is to make sure that is where they stay. Firewalls function either by packet filtering or by means of what amounts to a proxy server that keeps the external and mirrored internal processes completely separate. The problem with the proxy sever approach is that the processes to be "mirrored" must be basic ones— such as FTP (file transfer protocol) or Telnet— and not the more interesting and complex ones required for business, because supporting the latter requires substantial customization.

Function shipping

In the context of distributed processing, transferring from local to remote location and executing at the remote location a piece of SQL, file access, or function, rather than moving the data.

Originally popularized by IBM's CICS in the context of accessing remote files as if they are part of the local system, function shipping is now relevant in massive parallel processing, where a piece of SQL is shipped to remote nodes rather than the data being moved from these nodes to the local one. (See CICS, SQL.)

GUI: Graphical user interface

A way of presenting information to and receiving responses from the end-user of a personal computing work station that relies on iconic widgets like text boxes, drop-down list boxes, various kinds of push buttons, radio buttons, and scroll bars, usually employing a pointing device, such as mouse and other windowing (visual) metaphors, such as drop and drag, point and click, and drill down. (See Architecture, Three-tiered client-server, Two-tiered client-server, X Windows.)

Hermeneutic circle

Refers to selecting dependent and independent variables out of a large domain of candidate variables, distinguishing and understanding the part in relation to the whole, and vice versa, and iterative (sometimes trial and error) heuristic means of "round trip gestalt design" methods (see Grady Booch on *Object Solutions*); in short, somewhat more than another name for our ignorance; not to be confused with a vicious circle (see Berry and Linoff (1997) on the "virtuous cycle in practice"). (See Knowledge, Ontology, Pragmatics, Semantics.)

Heuristic

A method that promotes a satisfactory, not necessarily the optimal or complete, solution to a problem; generally contrasted with effective algorithm, which is a step-by-step method for attaining a result; a *satisfactory solution* is sometimes also called a *local optimum*. In contrast to an algorithm that employs a brute force search of all possible combinations of a search space, a heuristic aims to provide a "clue" or useful means of pruning back options, based on understanding of context or situation.

HOLAP: Hybrid on-line analytic processing

An approach to OLAP which attempts to combine a multidimensional database (MDDB) to build aggregates for desktop "slicing and dicing" with a back-end standard, "open" relational database; the benefit is additional insight as "drill down" on the desktop results in "reach-through" from the MDDB to the RDBMS; the disadvantages are increased complexity, resources, and software integration challenges. The mechanism underlying HOLAP sometimes consists in simulating cubes using relational technology by storing the cube like arrays in a proprietary format within the RDBMS, (See Cube, MDDB, MOLAP, OLAP, ROLAP, RDBMS.)

HSM: Hierarchical Storage Management

A concept, as well as a product from various storage technology vendors, that represents storage as a continuum of cost and capabilities arranged in a hierarchical way. For example, the most expensive and fastest storage is main memory, a little less performance and less costly is disk access, followed, in turn, by near-line storage in such mass storage media as optical data servers, robot tape libraries, and, finally, storing media on the shelf. The breakthrough capability is to automate, migrating between these different media by means of System Managed Storage software governed by storage management polices and procedures. (See MVS, SMS.)

HTML: Hypertext Markup Language

The coding language in which pages for the World Wide Web (the Web) are written and characterized by explicit tags, containing formatting and structure information, and supporting the ability to "jump" to other document addresses from embedded hot spots. HTML is regarded as a "manageable"—that is, small—subset of SGML. Efforts are underway—for purposes of knowledge management—to extend HTML and render its information content dynamic and flexible by means of XML. When combined with HTTP and URLs, HTML makes possible "hot links," whereby clicking on a location automatically transports the user to the next page on the same or even a different server across the planet. This is a major feature of the Web that gives it the characteristic "hypertext" quality—layers of text (pages) between which one navigates by clicking. (See HTTP, SGML, URL, XML.)

HTTP: Hypertext Transfer Protocol

The TCP/IP-based communication protocol used by the Web. A server capable of understanding this protocol is an HTTP server—that is, a Web server, which spends its time listening for a TCP/IP communication over a so-called socket, usually on port 80. Most significant, this is a "connectionless" protocol (not conversational), so state information must be hidden in a special piece of client storage called a *cookie* or in a temporary file on the HTTP server. When combined with URLs, HTTP makes possible "hot links," whereby clicking on a location automatically transports the user to the next page on the same or even a different server across the planet. (See Cookie, HTML, TCP/IP, URL, WWW.)

HTTP Server

See HTTP above.

Hypercube

An OLAP term referring to a cube of more than three intersecting dimensions. The latter are impossible to represent in three-dimensional space in a pictorial form; however, they can be represented accurately and completely by means of many-to-many relational associations (see Table 15.1 for an example). (See Cube, Multicube, OLAP, RDBMS.)

Hypertext

See HTML.

IDL: Interface definition language

A mapping of data elements from one language to another—for example, from C to COBOL, as required in order for applications written in one language to interact with those written in another language. (See ORB/CORBA, RPC.)

IDMS: Integrated Database Management System

Originally a product of Cullinet Software, purchased by Computer Associates (CA), IDMS implements the so-called network model of database management systems. In contrast with a hierarchic structure, where a child record has only one parent, in a network mode, the child record can have any number of parents, including zero. (See IMS, Legacy systems, MVS.)

IETF: Internet Engineering Task Force

The development agency of working groups of computing professionals, researchers, and academics working on developing and evolving standards for Internet infrastructure technologies such as TCP/IP, HTML, HTTP, etc. See www.ietf.org where the agency is described as "an open international community of network designers, service providers, vendors, and researchers" dedicated to the "evolution of the Internet architecture and the smooth operation of the Internet."

IGMP: Internet Group Management Protocol

The protocol by which host computers communicate with routers supporting multicast IP group addresses (and vice versa). The hosts are functionally visible to the router as being members in a multicast group. IP traffic relevant to the group is forwarded; what is not registered as being relevant to the host in question, because no hosts are registered as qualified or interested, is simply not sent. In contrast with a broadcast approach, this results in conserving significant bandwidth. (See Channel, Push technology.)

IIOP: Internet Inter ORB Protocol

An ORB for the Internet. See ORB.

IMS

IBM's hierarchical database management system, IMS was (and still is) a high-performance database for organizing enterprise data whose structure is stable, unlikely to change, and is able to support parent-child navigation between segments. Navigation by means of pointers is fast but inflexible. For example, a bill of material application where parts contain other parts is a natural fit in an IMS database. Nevertheless, IMS requires advanced data processing skills to administer and use—records, called "segments," are defined by means of macrolike, assembler-level data elements. Changing a database schema, regardless of how small the change is, can be a major headache, requiring advanced database administration expertise. IMS is regarded as a "legacy system" database, for which no new applications are being developed. (See IDMS, Legacy system, MVS.)

Internet

The global network of networks, the Internet almost defies definition. Originally conceived as a way to provide the government and national defense industry with overlapping, redundant, alternate routes for communicating in the event that several large American cities were destroyed by an enemy surprise nuclear attack, the Internet took off and received much use in the research and university communities as NSFnet (National Science Foundation) to support data exchange between supercomputing centers. In about 1993, two new technologies—the first Web browser, Mosaic, developed by a team at the University of Illinois and HTML (Hypertext Markup Language) made possible the World Wide Web (WWW). This breakthrough in usability made the Internet accessible to the ordinary person. Internet e-mail, Web publishing, and electronic commerce began in earnest shortly thereafter, and the momentum has continued to build. Much of the Internet's success is based on its use of open technologies, based on standards administered by committees independent of individual vendors. In addition to the Web browser and HTML, key technologies include the network protocol, TCP/IP, the router, UNIX, and Java. In general, the Internet is evolving in the direction of being a public information utility—like dial-tone, the electric power grid, or the interstate highway system. Another fact worth mentioning is that every affluent nine-year-old child regards a PC as an appliance for accessing Yahooligans, the Barbie Web page (depending on gender), or movie reviews—under parental supervision. A nonnetworked PC is like a PC without a printer—incomplete. (See Active-X, HTML, HTTP, Intranet, Java, TCP/IP, UNIX, WWW.)

Intranet

A network using Internet technologies—TCP/IP, HTML, Web servers, etc.—but restricted to authorized users in a single company or organization. An intranet is a network "invisible" to the larger Internet or, if a communication link exists, it is restricted by being behind a firewall, a computer used to filter out unauthorized messages or users. (See Extranet, Firewall, HTML, Internet, WWW.)

IPng: Internet protocol, the next generation

An IP protocol that expands the word size from 32 to 128 bits, thus significantly increasing the address space, the number of definable nodes (users) on the Internet. The danger of running out of addresses is thus transformed into the challenge of migrating from IP to IPng. (See Internet, TCP/IP.)

Java

A programming language originally defined and published by SUN, providing a set of functions and libraries that work like a simplified version of C++; a programming language—but much more, because Java was designed with the Internet in mind and includes such Internet-friendly, network-centric technical innovations as being downloaded as an applet for execution at the client from the server across the Internet, having special security features designed for the Internet, including lack of pointers, so it's hard to "hack" and (relatively) easy to debug. (See Applet, JDBC, JVM, Sand box.)

JDBC: Java database connectivity

An application programming interface (API) consisting of Java class libraries and components, by which a variety of databases from different vendors can be accessed through one uniform interface. As with the ODBC approach, it is no matter if the underlying database engine changes, the application database interface and application does not change. (See Java, JVM, ODBC.)

JVM: Java Virtual Machine

The software that executes Java bytecode on a given hardware/operating system platform. The JVM represents the overhead or cost of providing cross-platform independence. JVM is an interpreter of Java code previously compiled to bytecode, an intermediate low-level representation of instructions, one step above operating-system-dependent calls. (See Applet, Internet, Java, JDBC.)

K-means

A data mining term referring to a method of cluster detection (see Michael Anderberg, *Cluster Analysis for Applications*, 1973 or Mark Aldenderfer and Rogert Blashfield, *Cluster Analysis*, 1984). K data points are selected to function as seeds, around which other records are grouped, according to distance measures and weights. These "seeds" are also called *centeroids*. (See CART, CHAID, C4.5, Data mining.)

Knowledge

The formal bringing of a concept to experience and the organizing of experience (as represented in a data warehouse dimension, fact, or other related document) into a structure in which the experience validates (or invalidates) the candidate knowledge. The determining difference between knowledge and information is that knowledge entails (or implies) a commitment. If someone says "I know," that implies accountability, responsibility, and commitment to a decision. If it turns out that the person is wrong, others are allowed to demand an explanation and to hold the person accountable for error. Excuses are always possible, of course, but if the person says "I believe" or "the best available intelligence indicates," no excuses are needed if one is wrong; whereas in the case of "I know," the excuses will indeed be required. (See Metaphor, Pragmatics, Ontology, Semantics.)

Knowledge engineering
Also referred to as knowledge management, is a methodology for identifying, indexing, storing, and retrieving information, content, and knowledge, not only in the context of leveraging resources for the competitive advantage of commercial enterprises, but also to the development and maintenance of databases enabling breakthrough values redefining the limits of the possible and even transcending commercial gain such as the human genome project, global navigation and positioning, or the eradication of diseases such as small pox (for example). Commercial applications and benefits of a rigorous approach to the cultivation and systemization of quality information remain an exciting area of growth whose potential has not been fully tested. (See Business intelligence, Decision support, Knowledge, Ontology, Semantics.)

Legacy system
The joke is that a legacy system is defined as "any system that is in production." In 1993, legacy systems were COBOL, mainframe-based accounting, billing, inventory, payroll, etc. applications; in 1997, legacy systems included Power

Builder, SQL Server client-server applications performing many of the same functions; in 2001, who knows—the ERP applications being installed this season, Web publishing initiatives using CGI? Really "legacy" is best defined in terms of strengths and limitations of architecture, components, documentation, management, and maintenance. The surprising thing about legacy systems has been their durability. People building systems in the 1980s never expected them to still be around fifteen years later, but many of them are. It turns out that, if designed properly—a big "if"—software is basically immortal. Once the curve of discovered bugs levels off, the legacy system is more stable and robust than recent alternatives that have not proven themselves in such a variety of different situations. That is also the case with many legacy systems that are the bread-and-butter systems for day-to-day transactions and business operations. Really *legacy* is best defined in terms of strengths and limitations of architecture, components, documentation, management, and maintenance. (See CICS, MVS, IMS, OS/2.)

Mainframe
Originally, a large centralized computer employing a proprietary computing chip—emitted coupler logic—so hot and powerful that it required coolant; resulting in data center humor, "Hey, the mainframe is down—call da plumber!" In terms of millions of instructions per second (MIPS), a measure of raw computing power, the mainframe is still the top end of the market, whether built by IBM, Amdahl, Fujitsu, or Hitachi, and still required to run IBM's flagship enterprise software such as CICS, DB2, HSM, IMS, MVS, and SMS. The power and capacity of the mainframe to handle large-scale computing challenges remains awe-inspiring to those who know the details. Indeed, as a result of the client-server and Internet revolutions, the mainframe has been reborn as the "enterprise server" or "super-server." However, in terms of price/performance

benchmarks, the mainframe has never been the same since the client-server revolution. The declines in mainframe sales experienced in the mid-1990s have leveled off. However, organizations continue to grope for alternatives to large centrally managed data centers, including parallel processing solutions constructed of commodity RISC or INTEL components or, as indicated, even "solid-state" mainframes born again as enterprise servers. (See CICS, DB2, FEP, HSM, IMS, MVS, SMS, SNA.)

MDDB: Multidimensional database

A database specializing in the aggregating, caching, manipulating, and presenting of data cubes to and for OLAP "slicing and dicing" desktop functions; the collection of aggregations as cubes, hypercubes, or multicubes as constructed by the aggregation engine, the OLAP or MDDB server, in its (the database's) own proprietary vendor- or tool-specific data format and stored for subsequent OLAP processing. (See Aggregate, Cube, Hypercube, Multicube.)

Metadata

The short working definition of metadata is that it is an architecture—principles coordinating of commitments—for the *interoperability* between (otherwise isolated) systems and subsystems. These systems will typically be transactional legacy systems that feed the decision support data warehouse and vice versa. Metadata encompass so many different kinds and varieties of knowledge of system interoperability and for so many purposes that it is, indeed, a challenge of unappreciated proportions to get one's arms around them. What is required is a measure of library science. This is usually understood as the science of indexing knowledge, storing it, and retrieving it back efficiently and easily. That is why the architecture of metadata is said to be the architecture of knowledge. Traditionally the containers for this knowledge have been books. In our case, the data have included such matters as

data structures, specific aggregations, systems interconnections and components, and even job schedules. Insofar as system interoperability is a grand challenge resisting simple solution, the same is true of metadata. As used in this text, *metadata* is a completely generic term, spelled in lowercase, and independent of any specific metadata vendor product. (See Architecture, Knowledge, Metaphor, ORB, Semantics.)

Metaphor

Literally means a "carrying across"—in this case, a transfer of meaning from one context to another. Metaphor is an equating—really, a mapping one to another—of two things, meanings, or situations that are apparently different. When these two things have been compared—the desktop and electronic windowing software—our understanding and perceptions of them are altered. Technology is filled with metaphor. A new technology usually introduces a new metaphor. The electronic *desktop*, data *mining*, the information *assembly line*, the PointCast *channel*, text and h*y*pertext in the Web, the *firewall*, the *sandbox*, the *warehouse* itself—all of these are metaphors. By equating the meanings of words that seemed to be different in scope or context, metaphors change our way of looking at things. As if this required further justification or reinforcing, Metaphor was the name of a corporation that produced an early version of a data warehousing product emphasizing OLAP in the early 1990s prior to being absorbed by another large corporate entity. There is a nice short history of this at www.OLAPREPORT.com. (See also Channel, Desktop, Firewall, HTML, Metadata, OLAP, Sandbox, Windows.)

MIME: Multipurpose Internet Mail Extensions

Extensions to SMTP to allow multiple and mixed document types (including mixed media) to be included in e-mail. The Web uses MIME data types to specify content being sent from an

HTTP server to a client. (See Internet, SMTP, TCP/IP.)

MOLAP: Multidimensional on-line analytic processing

An approach to OLAP that employs a proprietary database, a multidimensional database (see MDDB above); MOLAP is considered to be the relatively more proprietary (and functionally relatively richer) approach than ROLAP (see ROLAP below). (See also HOLAP, MDDB, OLAP, ROLAP.)

MOM: Message-oriented middleware

A means of controlling data integrity as changes are distributed to databases using an asynchronous, intermittent connection. This is usually contrasted with a synchronous, two-phased commit protocol. Here, each stage in the process of storing and forwarding changes is protected as a recoverable step, but the overall process is asynchronous. This requires breaking down the synchronous logical unit of work (LUW) into several parts, each of which has guaranteed data integrity in its own right. A "message" now gets defined as the transmission of all the related records (events) in a transaction from one site to another. The message, as the transaction is now called, is then written from the source queue to the target queue. This is a recoverable transaction. If something goes wrong, the incomplete message can be backed out, requeued and tried again. If the server is temporarily unavailable, the message can be allowed to await the resumption of service. The job is incomplete, to be sure, but if the outage is short, the client can continue the process of pumping transactions into the top of the queue process without "hanging," waiting for a response from the server. (See RPC, Two-phased commit protocol.)

Multicast

A defined type of Internet traffic using class D IP addresses. Class D IP addresses begin with 1110, with each address ending up being a channel. Multicast requires that routers be configured to recognize which client work stations are interested in receiving which multicast information packets. Network bandwidth (a limited resource) is saved by forwarding packets only to those that are interested. This is considered the "way to do push technology right" by isolating subnetworks not interested in the broadcast being "pushed" from the broadcast and, thus, saving bandwidth. (See Channel, Push technology, XML.)

Multicube

An OLAP term designating a cube or hypercube formed by joining two or more cubes or hypercubes along a common, shared data element from one of their dimensional hierarchies. (See Cube, Hypercube, OLAP.)

MVS

IBM's flagship mainframe operating system, Multiple Virtual Storage, is the center of an enormous number of large-scale data center software products to which it is responsible for distributing work, allocating resources, and coordinating results and exceptions. Toward the top of the list are disk access methods, telecommunication access methods, System Managed Storage (SMS), Hierarchical Storage Management (HSM), relational database management systems (RDBMS), teleprocessing monitors, hierarchical databases management systems, job scheduling, and automated work load balancing. One reason MVS is a "contender" in the data warehousing arena is its capabilities to manage vast quantities of disk storage (and, hence, data) through such operational subsystems as CICS, IMS, HSM, SMS, and DB2, as well as its capabilities to schedule large numbers of concurrent, overlapping batch and interactive processes (jobs). Who would have thought that MVS job control language (JCL) would, after all, turn out to be a competitive technology advantage? (See Data Center, HSM, Operating system, RDBMS, SMS.)

Network computer

Also called *network appliance*, *Java station*, or *thin client*, an approach to client-server computing that aims at dispensing with Microsoft Windows and relies on downloading applets written in Java to provide the graphical presentation through a graphical browser. The network computer lacks a hard drive or insertable diskette port, which enhances security and relies on centralized (network-centric) distribution and maintenance. (See Thin client, Web browser.)

Neural network

See Artificial neural network.

NT

Microsoft's flagship 32-bit preemptive multitasking operating system; a competitor with the UNIX operating system at the entry level of the UNIX market. Frequently loved and praised by administrators for ease of installation, use, and readiness providing out-of-the-box network connectivity through TCP/IP and, despite early lack of global network directory, criticized for information center versus data center focus, proprietary orientation (i.e., a Microsoft product), and limited scalability (e.g., large Oracle databases still perform better on UNIX). (See MVS, Operating system, OS/2, Unix.)

ODBC: Open Database Connectivity

A Microsoft application programming interface (API) providing a uniform method (semantics) for accessing databases from different vendors. The API is uniform and "under the covers." Different "drivers" are provided for each different database product. ODBC itself has the status of a de facto standard. It rules. Drivers—the code that connects uniform client CALLs to the potentially different databases—are available from a variety of (non-Microsoft) vendors. This enables a software developer to write an application without knowing in advance what underlying databases (DB2, Informix, Oracle, SQL Server) to which connection will be made.

Although ODBC remains a Microsoft API (and, thus, product [see www.microsoft.com/data/odbc/]), ODBC is now based on the SQL Call Level Interface (CLI), which is a specification maintained by the X/Open Group, Ltd. (See Open Group, CLI, RDBMS, SQL.)

OLAP

On-line analytic processing is primarily distinguished from on-line transactions processing (OLTP) as decision support from transactional systems. OLAP applications are responsible for the elaborate development of "slice and dice" functions for data analysis on the desktop. These functions are distinct from both spreadsheet functions and built-in functions of SQL. In terms of variety and depth, they most closely approach the model of spreadsheet functions, though not burdened by the spreadsheet limitations of calculating on cells. Desktop OLAP refers to microcubes that are manipulated on the client, and server OLAP refers to cubes that are manipulated as part of an MDDB on the server. (See HOLAP, MDDB, MOLAP, ROLAP, SQL.)

Ontology

The study of what makes an entity what it is; closely related to data modeling of entities and attributes; today, also oriented toward knowledge management, how we come to *know* what something is from the framework in which it is represented; knowledge frameworks are available as Web-based research projects in ontology; see such initiatives as Simple HTML Ontology Extensions (www.cs.umd.edu/projects/plus/-SHOE/ and Ontolingua, a tool for the construction of collaborative ontologies (www.cs.umbc.edu/-agents/kse/ontology). (See Knowledge, Metaphor, Pragmatics, Semantics.)

OMG: Object Management Group

A 760+ member consortium whose mission is to promote and develop a Common Object Request Broker Architecture (CORBA) to provide interoperability between systems. See www.omg.org. (See IDL, ORB.)

Open Group

Created in 1996 as the holding company for the Open Software Foundation and X/Open, Ltd., it is a consortium of some 200+ corporations dedicated to the development of open standards. See www.opengroup.org. The Open Group currently manages the specifications for such industry standards as DCE, DRDA, and X Windows. In addition, although ODBC remains a Microsoft application programming interface, it is now based on the Call Level Interface (CLI) for databases, which is an X/Open specification. So things can get complicated with who owns what and what is a product versus a specification for which there may be competing implementations. Meanwhile, the Open Group is promoting a UNIX-98 brand, for which UNIX vendors can qualify as having attained a specified level of certification and interoperability, as a way of managing the fragmentation of the UNIX domain. (See DCE, DRDA, ODBC, UNIX, X Windows.)

Open systems

Computing systems built and operated according to vendor-independent specifications and standards, often, "open systems" means those based on such technologies as UNIX, the C programming language, and communication protocols such as TCP/IP. Strictly speaking, an open system is one that uses products implementing specifications that are the result of a public process of subscription, negotiation, and publication by a committee such as the International Standard Organization (ISO) or the American National Standards Committee (ANSI)—whose domains on the Internet use URLs ending in ".org" rather than ".com". However, standards have been a disappointment to many, in that there are so many of them, thus defeating the purpose of openness in the first place, interoperability.

Among the most successful outcomes are those instances where, due to overwhelming customer demand for an originally proprietary product, the vendor actually "spins off" the defining interface, API, or specification to an independent rule-making committee, which is henceforth responsible for the development, publication, and licensing of the standard. (See CLI, RDBMS, TCP/IP, UNIX.)

Operating system

The software that coordinates and manages all the subsystems, components, and applications on a computer, providing a variety of services, including managing input-output devices such as disk drives, network access, display terminals, pointing devices, and, of course, the distribution of computing cycles between applications. (See MVS, NT, OS/2, UNIX.)

Oracle

The name of a company and a relational database product. Oracle was the first commercial implementation of SQL in 1979 by a company called Relational Software, Inc. The company later named itself after the product. First implemented under UNIX on the Digital PDP-11 machine, the product was later migrated to other platforms, including the mainframe. With the success of Enterprise Resource Planning (ERP) software in the middle and late 1990s, the Oracle database (as well as the company) has enjoyed significant success, since many of these ERP packages targeted the UNIX- and NT-based platforms on which the Oracle relational database has market dominance. Like other relational databases aspiring to "universality," Oracle emphasizes that it makes a good back-end for Internet applications. It is also supporting the coding of stored procedures using Java instead of its proprietary PL/SQL language. (For further details of a fascinating history, see Chamberlin, 1998: 27.) (See RDBMS, Stored Procedure, Trigger.)

ORB/CORBA

The Common Object Request Broker Architecture from the Object Management Group Consortium (see www.omg.org). A specification for a software framework—as implemented (for example) by such companies and products, respectively, as Iona's Orbix or Visigenic's ObjectBroker, the central components of which are an interface definition language (IDL) capable of translating between and providing stubs for the different data types of diverse computing platforms and languages, and a messaging mechanism—not necessarily remote procedure calls (RPCs)—between them, thus facilitating the interoperability between different applications on operating systems, hardware, and servers. (See IDL, OMG, RPC.)

OS/2

IBM's first preemptive multitasking system for the PC, originally developed in cooperation with Microsoft, OS/2, and NT shared kernel code for a while until the "divorce" occurred in the early 1990s as Microsoft targeted IBM's core customer base—the enterprise data center. Although eclipsed by the success of NT and the resources of thousands of developers in Redmond, Washington, OS/2 still rules many thousands of desktops in the insurance industry, which was an early adopter of what, in its day, was the best available technology. It is sometimes said to be how you can tell the pioneers—they are the ones with the arrows in their backs. That might be said about IBM and OS/2—they were pioneers and have the arrows to prove it. (See MVS, Operating System, NT, UNIX.)

OSF: Open Software Foundation

See Open Group.

Plug In

A piece of code on the Web client, permanently installed as part of the client operating system base, which enables the client to perform an auxiliary service such as play a video, interpret a special image format, or other multimedia trick. The disadvantage of "plug ins" is that they eliminate cross-platform independence of the server content. Every client must install this code. (See HTML, Internet, Java, WWW.)

Pragmatics

The study of meaning in context; how language is used as a tool; how to do things with words; and how language and symbol systems create commitments. (See Knowledge, Metaphor, Ontology, Semantics.)

Push technology

Push is a play on the metaphor of the TV channel as applied to the Web. We all have an appreciation of the TV as an appliance, as a pipeline, as a media, and for the delivery of news, data, information, and entertainment. Now, take this metaphor and apply it to the Web. In the most general sense, a channel is a category of information offered by a content provider. Here, a content provider is a content accumulator, a content aggregator, who takes various sources of information—news, stock feeds, sports, entertainment, data warehousing aggregates—and makes them available from a Web server to subscribers. The subscribers point their browsers at the server on a scheduled and periodic basis, determined by a profile on the client, to obtain the updated content. Thus, this version of "push" is really "polling." This is the approach of the famous PointCast software, which literally pushed this technology onto the front pages—from where it fell almost as quickly, due to being indistinguishable, according to one pundit (Brian Walsh), from being hit over the head with a copy of *USA Today*. However, as a proof of concept, it had much to offer. (See Multicast, Router, WWW, XML.)

RAID: Redundant arrays of independent disks

A storage technology solution that uses data striping—writing data to different extents at different places on the disks (RAID 0)—with duplicating the data on a mirrored disk (RAID 1) to provide redundancy and fault tolerance against a "crash" of a single disk; or, alternately, duplicating the data by means of parity (RAID 5), an encoding of data on other disks, from which the data can be recreated in the event that one of the disks in the array crashes. (See HSM, SMS.)

RDBMS: Relational database management system

The presentation of data as mappings of rows and columns in tables, able to be accessed and manipulated by a small set of functions or operations. The power of the relational model stems from its simplicity, its theoretic underpinnings (it is an implementation of the mathematics of set theory), and its ability to capture and connect a wide variety of representations of distinctions in business and technology. The fundamental concept of a "relation" is a mapping or associating of attributes to one another, based on a distinguishing feature or property. It is arguably a dominant design at the back-end of the client-server system or wherever data requires flexible storage and retrieval. E.F. Codd proposed twelve principles that define a relational database (Codd, 1972 and Chapter Eight, Section "Twelve Principles.") (See DB2, Dominant design, Oracle, SQL, SQL Server, UDB.)

RISC: Reduced instruction set computing

An approach to computing chips optimized for raw computational speed rather than complex data manipulation, RISC chips were the basis for the first high-powered UNIX work stations; usually contrasted with INTEL's Pentium CISC (complex instruction set computing) chip. (See Operating system, UNIX.)

RPC: Remote procedure call

Considered the essence of DCE, the RPC is designed to make a complex communication across a distributed network appear to be a sim-

ple one with local resources. In short, the RPC mediates and manages the relation between client and server by means of an interface definition language (IDL), which maps data types to data between heterogeneous systems, generates stub code to make them look similar to one another, and provides for the marshalling of resources "under the covers" to provide a uniform fit between them. The RPC was designed as a synchronous model of communication, requiring resources to be available and interact in real time. (See DCE, IDL, Open Group, Two-phased commit.)

RMI: Remote method invocation

A network communication interface providing network transparency and avoiding explicit socket coding, using an RPC-like mechanism for Java processes. Intended as a pure Java competitor to Interface Definition Language (IDL) coding in an object request broker making use of a centralized registry (rmiregister) function to broker interoperability requests between remote Java address spaces. (Part of the Java Development Kit (JDK) 1.1 release.) Ends up being an alternative to Microsoft's DCOM and OMG's CORBA. (See IDL, Java, OMG, ORB, RPC.)

ROLAP: Relational on-line analytic processing

An approach to OLAP that emphasizes "reach-through" to standard "open" relational databases (not an MDDB [see above]) from the desktop on which analytic "slicing and dicing" is occurring. ROLAP simulates slicing and dicing functions such as rollup, rank ordering, and average over time by using multipass SQL that stores intermediate results in temporary tables. (See HOLAP, MDDB, OLAP, RDBMS.)

Router

A special-purpose computer interconnecting multiple network segments and forwarding packets of data to destinations. This is accomplished by matching data packet addresses with destination and path routes stored in software tables and cached in memory on the router itself for quick (but not instantaneous) look-up. The software tables containing the routing information are part of a domain name server (DNS) hierarchy—a kind of name and TCP/IP address database—that is propagated to and stored on the other routers in the vast Internet network of networks. Reportedly as recently as 1998, the alpha server, a kind of server of servers, for the entire Internet was located in or near the late Jim Postal's closet in Berkeley, California. Even if not true, this story will provide a sense in which the Internet "boot-strapped" itself out of the research community, whose roots it is still gradually shedding. (See Internet, Socket, TCP/IP, WWW.)

RSA

The initials of Drs. Rivest, Shamir, and Adleman, who, in 1978, introduced and patented the first full-fledged public-key encryption function. (See Digital Signature, Sand box.)

Sandbox

A security metaphor fundamental to Java programming. Initially, the sandbox referred to the way Java applets downloaded across the network to a client were restricted ("quarantined") in their access to the client computing resources. Untrusted applets cannot access the operating system, cannot use pointers (which do not exist in Java), or access the hard drive (which is invisible to them). The sandbox metaphor is being extended to an area to quarantine any untrusted Java code on any server, including the Web server or any implementation of an agent server. (See Agent, Aglet, Applet, Internet, Java, Metaphor.)

SCS

System Controlled Storage. See SMS.

Semantics

The study of meaning; the relation of representing between the world (of business, for example) and the system that simulates the behavior of the entities (of business) in the world. Semantics include whatever else is leftover after everything that can be explained by syntax, structure, and logical forms has been thus accounted for and explained. (See Knowledge, Metaphor, Ontology, Pragmatics.)

Servlets

A Java-based model from SUN for server processes, based on the idea of applets, implemented by means of an API (application programming interface) of methods in Java classes. Just as applets promise and provide platform independence ("write once, execute anywhere") on the client side, servlets provide the same independence on the server side. However, servlets do not support a user interface ("faceless"). (See Applet, Java, Sand box.)

SGML: Standard Generalized Markup Language

An International Standards Organization (ISO) document standard (8879) formally published in 1986. It is a complex, elaborate, exhaustive 500-page specification for the extensibility, validation, and structuring of documents. Many consider it too complicated to be practical. However, SGML is considered significant because HTML (Hypertext Markup Language) was originally designed by Tim Berniers-Lee as a hard-coded subset of tags from SGML. SGML is also the basis of XML. (See HTML, TCP/IP, WWW, XML.)

SMS: System Managed Storage

The name of IBM's automated storage control product, SMS is a major operational subsystem, managing potentially vast farms of disk storage for the operating system, by means of automated storage management criteria, storage policy procedures, and storage performance criteria implemented by automated class selection routines (basically, a proprietary scripting language) which are checked upon storage allocation, access, and manipulation. (See DB2, HSM, MVS.)

SMTP: Simple Mail Transfer Protocol

UNIX operating system-based e-mail application riding atop TCP/IP. Character-based. Requires "add on," such as MIME and NOTIFY, to attain the strength needed to support mission-critical applications featuring multiple document types and registered mail. (See Internet, MIME, TCP/IP, UNIX.)

SNA: System Network Architecture

Originally IBM's proprietary vision for building distributed communications networks, now rearchitected and significantly "opened" to support encapsulating TCP/IP in the SNA communications protocol while the legacy front-end processor (FEP)—"fronting" the mainframe—has been rebuilt as a router. (See Mainframe, MVS, Router, TCP/IP.)

Snow-flaked

In the context of data warehousing, a data model that is highly normalized with many small entities, taken to fourth- or fifth-normal form, such that, when laid out visually, the model looks like a snowflake. (See Fact, Dimension, Star schema.)

Sockets

The basic components of communication in the Berkeley Software Distribution (BSD) release of UNIX, enabling a program to communicate through TCP/IP, using a method that makes interacting with the target of the message seem like performing I/O to a file ("file-like semantics"); providing a termination point of communication to which a name can be linked and furnishing an interface that provides abstraction from the underlying transport mechanism. (See Internet, TCP/IP, UNIX.)

SPSS: Statistical Package for the Social Sciences

A set of software methods implementing statistical algorithms, first used in research in sociology, then consumer market research in the late 1970s; now regarded as an early data mining tool. (See CART, CHAID, C4.5, Data mining.)

SQL: Structured Query Language

The standard for accessing and updating data on relational databases. SQL consists of a data definition language (DDL) to define tables, indexes, and other structures; data manipulation language (DML) to apply relational operations to data (select, update, delete, join, project); and a data control language (DCL) to manage security. (See DB2, Oracle, RDBMS, SQL Server, Stored Procedure, Trigger.)

SQL Server

The name for specific relational database products, as well as a generic relational database. SQL Server was originally shared between Microsoft and Sybase, with the former supporting the OS/2 version (yes—OS/2—now, of course, the NT version) and the latter the UNIX version, until 1992, when the two versions of the product "divorced" with each going their own way. In its various forms, SQL Server was one of the crucial "enablers" of the client-server revolution, bringing stored procedures, triggers, replication, and, above all, the relational database model to the back-end of the client-server system. (See RDBMS, Stored procedure, SQL, Trigger.)

Star schema

A data model particularly applicable to data warehousing, whereby a central fact table is surrounded by and joined to multiple data dimensions representing such abstract entities as time and location, as well as more concrete entities such as customer, product, promotion, etc. When laid out visually, the model looks like a star, hence, star schema. (See Dimension, Fact, Snow-flaked.)

Stored procedure (SP)

A database application component, including SQL and "if-then" procedural logic registered with the database engine, executing on the database, and returning the results of database access or update to the front-end or application components as a results set. SPs were one of the "enabling" technologies of the client-server revolution, which, when combined with the GUI, made possible the central development and maintenance of database access. SPs used to require coding of their application looping logic in a proprietary language such as Transact SQL or PL/SQL. Recently, vendors have moved in the direction of "openness" by allowing SPs to be coded in COBOL, C, or even Java, thus leveraging a large body of knowledge of these development tools. (See GUI, RDBMS, SQL, SQL Server.)

Surfing

Jumping from one Web "hot link" to another, based on associative, not categorical, logic. "Surfing" implies a random exploration without explicit or rigorous logic. Not quite like changing channels at random on a TV, because a loose, associative connection is implied. Possibly also a reference to "Cerfing" after the technology leadership and name of Vinton Cerf, definer of the Ethernet communications protocol, early Internet proponent, and now Chief Scientist at MCI/Worldcom, Inc. (See HTTP, Internet, TCP/IP, WWW.)

TCP/IP: Transmission control protocol / Internet protocol

A set of network protocols, at the transport and network layers of the network model, providing reliable (TCP) as well as "send-and-pray" (IP) communications between nodes in a communication network. The Internet is built on IP, a decision partly based on the needs of wide area communication sites to be only occasionally and remotely connected. (See Internet, IPng, WWW.)

Thin client

Generally contrasted with fat client, thin client represents a client work station presentation layer that executes the graphical windowing software from a server, using the PC merely as a display station, often without a functioning hard drive of its own or insertable disk drive. However, it also includes the Citrix Win Server, which executes Windows off the server, and X

Windows implementations executed off the windowing server, as well as network appliances in the narrow sense. The latter designate a network computer ("appliance"), driven by downloading apps from a centralized Web server across an intra- or Internet, using Web technologies. (See Applet, Fat client, HTTP server, Network Computer, X Windows.)

Three-tiered client-server

Generally considered the "industrial-strength" version of client-server, defined by distinguishing presentation, application (business logic), and database access services distributed in various ways across the three platforms of the individual work station, mid-sized server(s), and enterprise server(s). The number of tiers in a client-server system is limited only by the number of separable functions, communication infrastructures, and architectural gyrations that can be envisioned, hence, "n-tier" client-server. (See Application server, Architecture, Two-tiered client-server.)

Trigger

In the context of database management, an active mechanism whereby a piece of SQL is associated with a column in a table and executed when a condition represented by an action against the table is satisfied. So, for example, upon an insertion into an order detail table, the order header is checked for a valid parent record by executing the associated piece of SQL (the triggered SQL) and upon the validation of which the insertion is allowed to complete. In this way, referential integrity can be procedurally checked by logic active at execution time. (See RDBMS, SQL, Stored procedure.)

Two-phase commit protocol

A bullet-proof method of synchronizing updates to multiple database and teleprocessing logs, such that either all or none of the changes are committed. Basically, a coordinating node asks all the participants to acknowledge their readiness to commit, then gives the green light to complete the commit or, if a node is not responding, issues a rollback. Although "bullet-proof," a short "in doubt" phase exists, during which loss of the coordinating node requires manual intervention upon resumption of processing. This "in doubt" phase is brief in comparison with the amount of time that resources (databases) are left in an unsynchronized state by the alternative approach, asynchronous message queuing processes. Nevertheless, the two-phase commit protocol is very rigorous, and some question its practicality in large distributed networks, where the potential exists for one of the nodes to "block" or render the synchronization process incomplete. (See MOM.)

Two-tiered client-server

A version of client-server architecture in which the presentation layer connects directly to the database server, often using ODBC, without an intermediate application server; generally distinguished by having the business logic distributed between processing logic on the client work station and database stored procedure. (See Architecture, ODBC, Three-tiered client-server.)

UDB: Universal database

Relational databases which include extenders to accommodate such non-traditional data types as images, BLOBS (binary large objects), text, video, sound, including user-defined data types and user-defined functions to manipulate them. In many ways, the UDB is completely continuous with relational database systems and presents step-by-step progress with them based on "accessing data every which way" in a rule-governed form according to Codd's twelve principles. In other ways, the variety of data types that can be handled—text, image, Web-based documents, video, etc.—promises new applications about which previously we could not even dream. This promises to be a source of discontinuous change. The claim to "universality" is based on the way user-defined data types and functions can be employed to extend the set of available objects and methods almost indefinitely. (See DB2, Oracle, RDBMS, SQL, SQL Server.)

UNIX

In 1975, the ACM (Association for Computing Machinery) published Thompson and Ritchie's essay on UNIX; the Bell System began to make extensive use of UNIX and licensed UNIX to various universities. Fast forward to 1989, when AT&T announced plans to "spin off" UNIX support as a separate organization that received stock in 1990 and became UNIX Systems Labs (USL), which was acquired by Novell in 1991 and maintained as a separate open operating system standard. UNIX is an operating system standard implemented with variations by dozens of vendors—SUN's Solaris, Hewlett Packards's HP-UX, IBM's AIX, USL's Berkeley Software Development (BSD), Santa Cruz Operation's SCO-UNIX, and even, under one interpretation, Open Software Foundation's DCE. UNIX is considered a robust multitasking operating system for medium to large systems. Its strengths are its "industrial strength," battle-hardened tradition, scalability, and open standards process. Its weaknesses include its "bit head" orientation, fragmentation of the standard by dozens of versions, and relative complexity of installation and use. (See MVS, NT, Operating system, OS/2.)

URL: Uniform Resource Locator

The symbolic label used to address resources on the Web, containing the protocol and domain name (or IP address). In short, an address on the Web. For example: HTTP://www.acm.org. When combined with HTTP, URLs make possible "hot links," whereby clicking on a location automatically transports the user to the next page on the same or even a different server across the planet. This is a major feature of the Web that gives it the characteristic "hypertext" quality—layers of text (pages), between which one navigates by clicking. (See HTML, HTTP, Internet, WWW.)

VPN: Virtual private network

Generally defined as a network using the same Web technologies as the Internet to allow several trading partners to communicate in secret, using encryption technology, over the global public Internet proper without the public having any visibility to the request and response messages. Because public wires are traversed but no one can comprehend the content, the network is "virtually private." (See Extranet, Intranet, Internet.)

Web browser

The "skinny (thin) client" capable of navigating to, downloading, and interpreting HTML pages from HTTP servers. The first Web browser, Mosaic, was developed by a team at the University of Illinois Super Computing Center at Champaign/Urbana, Illinois. (See HTML, HTTP, Thin client, URL, WWW.)

Web server

See HTTP server.

Windows

The dominant GUI design for the desktop and product from Microsoft, representing a "point-and-click," "drag-and-drop" work space on the electronic desktop, through which the knowledge worker accesses the resources of the enterprise in graphical form. (See Desktop, GUI, Operating system, X Windows.)

Work flow

Originally defined as a step-by-step information assembly line, work flow is more completely understood as a coordination of commitments between requesters and performers. This operates similar to a system interface in being understood to be a "contract" between an end-user (person or application) and an underlying implementation between a client and a server. Work flow is conceptualized as a set of interrelating commitments to request a service and provide

one. Each request and response can, indeed, be regarded as one of the steps in an information assembly line. But the output is a consequence of the commitments, which may, in point of fact, be either in series or concurrent, not the steps as isolated transactions in an assembly line. (See Knowledge, Ontology, Pragmatics, Semantics.)

WWW: The World Wide Web: The Web

"The World Wide Web (W3) was developed to be a pool of human knowledge, which would allow collaborators in remote sites to share their ideas and all aspects of a common project." (quoted from Tim Berners-Lee *et al.*, "The World Wide Web," *Communications of the ACM*, August 1994, Vol. 37, No. 8, p. 76.) Tim Berners-Lee is credited with originating the Web in 1990 at CERN, the European Particle Physics Laboratory in Geneva, Switzerland. One of the special features of the Web is the ability to click on "hot links" and be transported to another page on a remote server. (See HTML, HTTP, Internet.)

X Windows

A windowing specification similar in usability to Microsoft's Windows. However, X Windows is profoundly different in implementation. Whereas MS Windows is client-based presentation logic, X Windows includes the distinction between client and server in a networked implementation. X Windows is a windowing server with the capacity to service many windowing applications on diverse and remote computers. X Windows is really an open standard developed at MIT (Massachusetts Institute of Technology) in 1984. It was developed as part of a project named Athena in conjunction with DEC. In 1988, the leading work station manufacturers (Apple, AT&T, Digital, HP, IBM, SUN) formed a consortium, the X Consortium, to lobby ANSI on making X Windows a standard. The X Window System reverses traditional client-server logic; the graphic display is multitasking and executes on the server. The client is not the end-user but rather where the windowing application executes, the X Windows server. For example, Motif is a popular implementation of the X Windows standard on UNIX. (See Desktop, GUI, UNIX, Windows.)

X/Open, Ltd
See Open Group.

XML: Extensible markup language
A practical subset of the SGML standard by which a text provides self-defining data structures through a document type definition (DTD). XML allows extending the hard-coded set of hypertext markup language (HTML) as a kind of metadata, information about the structure of data, like a database schema only for Web documents. This makes Web pages extensible in terms of coding, indexing, and retrieving the kinds of information they contain. Industry groups can define and implement "tags" that uniquely encode the information important to their particular vertical segments of the economy—health insurance, trucking, food retailing, etc. This has the potential to bring library science and knowledge management to the Web, such that the data can be sufficiently structured, validated, and organized to give it the dignity belonging to "knowledge" in the full sense of the term. (See Channel, Knowledge, Push technology, Multicast, SMGL.)

X509
The international trade organization standard corresponding to Digital Signature (see Digital Signature).

3270 terminal
A "dumb terminal" without processing capability connected to an IBM mainframe system. One might call this display station the ultimate thin client, except for its being a proprietary approach to displaying data and executing the protocol of a particular vendor, not a public standard. All the computing cycles are on the central server, the mainframe. (See Mainframe, MVS, SNA, Thin Client.)

References

Agerwala, T., et al. "SP2 System Architecture," *IBM Systems Journal*, Vol. 34, No. 2, 1995, pp. 152ff.

Agosta, L. "Advances in Web Computing: Agent Technology," *Data Management Review*, Vol. 8, No. 6, June 1998.

Agosta, L. *Empathy and Interpretation*, Ph.D. Dissertation, Department of Philosophy, University of Chicago, 1977.

Agosta, L. "The Executive's Guide to the Data Warehouse," *Proceedings of Information Technology Forum*, San Francisco, May 1998, CD-ROM format.

Agosta, L. "Review of *The Data Warehouse Toolkit* by Ralph Kimball," *Computing Reviews*, November 1996, p. 559 [9611-0868].

Agosta, L. "Review of *DB2 Design and Development Guide* by Gabrielle Wiorkowski (2nd Edition)" *Computing Reviews*, December 1990, [9012-0928].

Agosta, L. "Review of *Every Manager's Guide to Business Processes* by Peter G. W. Keen," *Computing Reviews*, December 1996, p. 637 [9612-0982].

Agosta, L. "Review of *Harmony: Business, Technology and Life After Paperwork* by Arno Penzias," *Computing Reviews*, August 1996 [9608-0569].

Agosta, L. "Review of *The Innovator's Dilemma: When New Technologies Cause Great Firms to Fail* by Clayton Christensen," *Computing Reviews*, February 1998, Vol. 39, No. 2, p. 106 [9802-0061].

Agosta, L. "Review of *Mastering the Dynamics of Innovation* by James M. Utterback," *Computing Reviews*, November 1997, Vol. 38, No.11, p. 564 [9711-0904].

Agosta, L. "Review of *Object-Oriented Methods* by Ian Graham (2nd Edition)," *Computing Reviews*, March 1995, p. 145 [9503-0143].

Agosta, L. "Technical Tip: So Much For the Conventional Wisdom," *IDUG Solutions Journal*, March 1998, Vol. 5, No. 1, pp. 34ff.

Agosta, L. "20 Questions (and Answers) To Attain Data Warehouse Performance," *Proceedings of the International DB2 Users' Group: 9th North American Conference*, Vol. 4, May 1997, pp. 501–526.

Agosta, L. "Web Computing: Extending the Client-Server Revolution," *Data Management Review*, January, 1997, pp. 34ff.

Agosta, L. "Workflow Systems: Extending the Client-Server Revolution: Part I," *Data Management Review*, September 1995, pp. 16ff.

Agosta, L. "Workflow Systems: Extending the Client-Server Revolution: Part II," *Data Management Review*, October 1995, pp. 12ff.

Barquin, R. and Edelstein, H., Editors, *Building, Using and Managing the Data Warehouse*, Upper Saddle River, NJ: Prentice Hall, 1997.

Baru, C.K., et al. "DB2 Parallel Edition," *IBM Systems Journal*, Vol. 34, No. 2, 1995, pp. 292ff.

Bell, C. "Dancing Naked in the Net," paper presented at Electronic Commerce and On-line Profits, Toronto, CA, November 1997.

Berners-Lee, T., et al. "The World Wide Web," *Communications of the ACM*, August 1994, Vol. 37, No. 8, p. 76.

Berry, M.J.A. and Linoff, G. *Data Mining Techniques: For Marketing, Sales, and Customer Support*, New York: John Wiley & Sons, 1997.

Boehm, B.W. *Software Engineering Economics*, Englewood Cliffs, NJ: Prentice-Hall, 1981.

Booch, G. *Object Solutions: Managing the Object-Oriented Project*, Reading, MA: Addison-Wesley, 1996.

Borges, J.L. "The Library of Babel," *Labyrinths: Selected Stories & Other Writings*, New York: New Directions Publishing, 1964.

Brown, G.S. *The Laws of Form*, New York: The Julian Press, Inc. 1972.

Card, D.N. with Glass, R.L. *Measuring Software Design Quality*, Englewood Cliffs, NJ: Prentice Hall, 1990.

Chamberlin, D. *A Complete Guide to DB2 Universal Database*, San Francisco: Morgan Kaufmann Publishers, 1998.

Chaum, D. "Security Without Identification: Transaction Systems to Make Big Brother Obsolete," *Communications of the ACM*, October, 1985, Vol. 28, No. 10.

Chen, P. *The Entity-Relationship Approach to Logical Database Design*, Wellesley, MA: QED Science, 1977.

Christensen, C. *The Innovator's Dilemma: When New Technologies Cause Great Firms to Fail*, Boston, MA: Harvard Business School Press, 1997.

Codd, E.F. "Relational Completeness of Data Base Sublanguages," *Data Base Systems*, Courant Computer Science Symposia Series, Vol. 6. Englewood Cliffs, NJ: Prentice-Hall, 1972.

Date, C.J. *An Introduction to Database Systems*, Reading, MA: Addison-Wesley, 1986.

Davenport, T.H. *Information Ecology: Mastering the Information and Knowledge Environment*, New York: Oxford University Press, 1997.

Deming, E.W. *Out of Crisis*, Cambridge, MA: MIT Press, 1986.

Dhar, V. and Stein, R. *Seven Methods For Transforming Corporate Data into Business Intelligence*, Upper Saddle River, NJ: Prentice Hall, 1997.

Drucker, P.F. *Management: Tasks, Responsibilities, Practices*, New York: Harper and Row, 1974.

Dupuis, V. "Mastering Metadata," *Proceedings of the International DB2 Users' Group: 9th North American Conference*, May 1997, Chicago: International DB2 User's Group (IDUG).

Edelstein, H. "Knowledge Discovery and Data Mining," *Proceedings of Information Technology Forum*, San Francisco, May 1998, CD-ROM format.

Garvey, M.R. and Johnson, D.S. *Computers and Intractability: A Guide to the Theory of NP-Completeness*, New York: W.H. Freeman, 1979.

Graham, I. *Object-Oriented Methods*, 2nd edition, Reading, MA: Addison-Wesley, 1991.

Hackathorn, R.D. "Reaping the Web for Your Data Warehouse," *DBMS*, August 1998, Vol. 11, No. 9, pp. 36–40.

Hackathorn, R.D. *Web Farming For the Data Warehouse*, San Francisco: Morgan Kaufmann Publishers, 1998.

Hackney, D. *Understanding and Implementing Successful Data Marts*, Reading, MA: Addison-Wesley, 1997.

Hagel, J. and Armstrong, A. *Net Gain: Expanding Markets Through Virtual Communities*, Boston, MA: Harvard Business School Press, 1998.

Harré, R. *The Principles of Scientific Thinking*, Chicago: University of Chicago Press, 1970.

Holland, J.H. *Adaptation in Natural and Artificial Systems*, Cambridge, MA: MIT Press, 1992.

Huang, K.-T., Lee, Y.W., and Wang, R.Y. *Quality Information and Knowledge*, Upper Saddle River, NJ: Prentice Hall, 1999.

IBM. *Formal Register of Existing Differences in SQL*, SC26-3316-00, 1993.

Inmon, W.H. *Building the Data Warehouse*, Wellesley, MA: QED Publishing Group, 1993.

Inmon, W.H. "The Data Warehouse and Data Mining," *Communications of the ACM*, November 1996, Vol. 39, No. 11, pp. 49ff.

Jacobson, I., Christerson, M., Jonsson, P. and Oevergaard, G. *Object-Oriented Software Engineering: A Use Case Driven Approach*, Reading, MA: ACM Press, 1992.

Johnson, H.T. and Kaplan, R.S. *Relevance Lost: The Rise and Fall of Management Accounting*, Boston: Harvard Business School Press, 1988.

Kant, I. *Critique of Pure Reason*, translated by Norman Kemp Smith, New York: Macmillan Publishing, 1927. Originally published in 1781.

Kaplan, R.S. and Cooper, R. *Cost and Effect: Using Integrated Costs Systems to Drive Profitability and Performance*, Boston: Harvard Business School Press, 1998.

Kaufman, A. "Case Study: Decision Support on the Web: Lessons Learned," paper presented at The Data Warehouse Institute, August 1998.

Keen, P.G.W. *Every Manager's Guide to Information Technology: A Glossary of Key Terms and Concepts for Today's Business Leader*, 2nd edition, Boston: Harvard Business School Press, 1995.

Keen, P.G.W. *The Process Edge: Creating Value Where It Counts*, Boston, Massachusetts: Harvard Business School Press, 1997.

Keen, P.G.W., *Shaping the Future: Business Design through Information Technology*, Boston: Harvard Business School Press, 1991.

Keen, P.G.W. and Knapp, E.M. *Every Manager's Guide to Business Processes: A Glossary of Key Terms and Concepts for Today's Business Leader*, Boston: Harvard Business School Press, 1996.

Keen, P.G.W. and Morton, M.S.S. *Decision Support Systems: An Organizational Perspective*, Reading, MA: Addison-Wesley, 1978.

Keen, P.G.W., Mougayar, W., Torregrossa, T. *The Business Internet and Intranets: A Manager's Guide to Key Terms and Concepts*, Boston, Massachusetts: Harvard Business School Press, 1998.

Kimball, R. *The Data Warehouse Toolkit: Practical Techniques for Building Dimensional Data Warehouses*, New York: John Wiley & Sons, 1995.

Kimball, R. "Meta Meta Data Data," *DBMS Magazine*, March 1998, pp. 18ff.

Kimball, R., Reeves, L., Ross, M., Thornthwaite, W., *The Data Warehouse Lifecycle Toolkit*, New York: John Wiley & Sons, 1998.

Klawikowski, G. "ShopKo Initiative Overhauls System for Data Analysis," *Data Warehousing: What Works*, the Data Warehousing Institute, 1997.

Kodami, F. *Analyzing Japanese High Technologies*, London: Pinter, 1991.

Liddle, D. "Design of the Conceptual Model," *Bringing Design to Software*, Terry Winograd, ed. New York: Addison-Wesley Publishing (ACM Press), 1996, pp. 17–31.

Liskov, B. and Guttag, J. *Abstraction and Specification in Program Development*, New York: McGraw Hill, 1986.

Loosley, C. and Douglas, F. *High Performance Client/Server: A Guide to Building and Managing Robust Distributed Systems*, New York: John Wiley & Sons, 1998.

McMillan, H. "How DB2 OS/390 Handles REORG in a High Availability Environment," *Proceedings of the International DB2 User's Group: 10th North American Conference*, May 1998, Chicago: International DB2 User's Group (IDUG).

Miller, G. "The Magic Number Seven, Plus or Minus Two," *Psychological Review*, Vol. 63, 1956, pp. 81–97.

Mimno, P. Selecting the Right Data Warehouse Products & Tools, presented at *DCI's Data Warehouse World Conference*, Chicago, May 1999.

Negroponte, N. *Being Digital*, New York: Vintage Books, 1995.

Neurath, O. "Protocolsätze," *Erkenntnis,* Vol. 3, 1932, pp. 204–214.

Olle, W.T., Hagelstein, J., Macdonald, I.G., Roland, C., Sol, H.G., VanAssche, F.J.M., and Verrijn-Stuart, A.A. *Information Systems Methodologies: A Framework For Understanding*, 2nd edition, Reading, MA: Addison-Wesley, 1991.

Parnas, D. and Clements, P. "A Rational Design Process: How and Why to Fake It," *IEEE Transactions on Software Engineering*, Vol. SE-12(2), 1986.

Penzias, A. *Harmony: Business, Technology, and Life After Paperwork*, New York: HarperCollins: 1995.

Penzias, A. "Talking Networks, Disease, and Yes, Dry Cleaning With Arno Penzias, Nobel Laureate," *Fortune*, Vol. 137, No. 11 (June 8, 1998), pp. 258–262.

Paulk, M.C., Weber, C.V., Curtis, B. and Chrissis, M.B., eds. *The Capability Maturity Model: Guidelines for Improving the Software Process*, Reading, MA: Addison-Wesley, 1994.

Raiffa, H. and Schlaifer, R.S. *Applied Statistical Decision Theory*, Cambridge, MA, MIT Press, 1968.

Rolland, F.D. *The Essence of Databases*, London: Prentice Hall Europe, 1998.

Rosenberg, M. *The Logic of Survey Analysis*, New York: Basic Books, 1968.

Saracco, C.M. *Universal Database Management: A Guide to Object/Relational Technology*, San Francisco: Morgan Kaufmann Publishers, 1998.

Simon, H. *The Sciences of the Artificial*, Cambridge, MA: MIT Press, 1969.

Spewak, S.H. and Hill, S.C. *Enterprise Architecture Planning: Developing a Blueprint for Data, Applications, and Technology*, Wellesley, MA: Q.E.D. Information Sciences, Inc., 1993.

Stewart, G.B. III. *The Quest for Value*, New York: Harper Business, 1991.

Strassmann, P. and Hespos, R. "Stochastic Decision Trees," *Management Technology*, 1957.

Strassmann, P.A. *The Politics of Information Management: Policy Guidelines*, New Canaan, CT: The Information Economics Press, 1995.

Strassmann, P.A. *The Squandered Computer: Evaluating the Business Alignment of Information Technologies*, New Canaan, CT: The Information Economics Press, 1997.

Tanler, R. *The Intranet Data Warehouse*, New York: John Wiley & Sons, 1997.

Taylor, D. *Object-Oriented Technology: A Manager's Guide*, Reading, MA: Addison-Wesley, 1990.

Thomsen, E. *OLAP Solutions: Building Multidimensional Information Systems*, New York: John Wiley & Sons, 1997.

Utterback, J.M. *Mastering the Dynamics of Innovation*, Boston: Harvard Business School Press, 1995.

Wand, Y. and Wang, R.Y. "Anchoring Data Quality Dimensions in Ontological Foundations," *Communications of the ACM*, November 1996, Vol. 39, No. 11, pp. 86-95.

Wang, R.Y., "A Product Perspective on Total Data Quality Management," *Communications of the ACM*, February 1998, vol. 41, No. 2, p. 58ff.

Watson, H.J. and Haley, B.J., "Managerial Considerations," *Communications of the ACM*, September 1998, Vol. 41, No. 9, pp. 32–37. (This entire edition is dedicated to data warehousing.)

Wayland, R.E. and Cole, P.M. *Customer Connections: New Strategies for Growth*, Boston: Harvard Business School Press, 1997.

Winograd, T. and Flores, F. *Understanding Computers and Cognition: A New Foundation for Design*, Reading, MA: Addison-Wesley, 1986.

Wiorkowski, G. *DB2: Design and Development Guide*, 2nd edition, Reading, MA: Addison-Wesley, 1990.

Wiorkowski, G. *DB2 OS/390: Development for Performance*, Rockwall, TX: www.GabrielleDB2.com, 1998. Available as CD-ROM or download from Web.

Yazdani, S. and Wong, S.S. *Data Warehousing with Oracle: An Administrator's Handbook*, Upper Saddle River, NJ: Prentice Hall, 1998.

Zachman, J. "Framewok for Information Systems Architecture," *IBM Systems Journal,* 1987, Vol. 26, No. 3, pp. 276–292.

Zagelow, G. and Bontempo, C. "The IBM Data Warehouse Architecture," *Communications of the ACM*, September 1998, Vol. 41, No.9, pp. 38ff.

Index